ENVIRONMENTAL POLICY

ENVIRONMENTAL POLICY

NEW DIRECTIONS FOR THE TWENTY-FIRST CENTURY

Seventh Edition

Edited by

Norman J. Vig
Carleton College

Michael E. Kraft
University of Wisconsin–Green Bay

CQ PRESS

A Division of SAGE
Washington, D.C.

CQ Press
2300 N Street, NW, Suite 800
Washington, DC 20037

Phone: 202-729-1900; toll-free, 1-866-4CQ-PRESS (1-866-427-7737)

Web: www.cqpress.com

Cover design: Auburn Associates, Inc.
Typesetting: C&M Digitals (P) Ltd.

♾ The paper used in this publication exceeds the requirements of the American National Standard
for Information Sciences—Permanence of Paper for Printed Library Materials, ANSI Z39.48-1992.

Printed and bound in the United States of America

13   12   11   10   2   3   4   5

Library of Congress Cataloging-in-Publication Data

Environmental policy : new directions for the twenty-first century / edited by
Norman J. Vig, Michael E. Kraft. — 7th ed.
    p. cm.
  Includes bibliographical references and index.
  ISBN 978-0-87289-973-5 (pbk. : alk. paper) 1. Environmental policy—United States.
  I. Vig, Norman J. II. Kraft, Michael E. III. Title.

GE180.E546 2009
363.7'0560973—dc22

                                                                    2009010111

To Carol and Sandy,
for their love and support

Contents

Part IV. Global and Domestic Issues and Controversies

Part V. Conclusion

Appendixes

Tables, Figures, and Boxes

Tables

Figures

Boxes

Preface

At the end of the first decade of the twenty-first century, environmental policy is being challenged as never before. New demands worldwide for dealing with the risks of climate change, threats to biological diversity, and similar issues will force governments everywhere to rethink policy strategies and find new ways to reconcile environmental and economic goals. In the United States the new century began on an ominous note when President George W. Bush announced that the U.S. government would abandon the Kyoto Protocol (1997), which for the first time established binding national limits on greenhouse gas emissions. Conservative Republican members of Congress, as well as the Bush White House, voiced strong concerns about environmental policies and programs, and they pushed for new approaches that favored economic development and imposed fewer restrictions on business activities. Democrats in Congress (the majority party again after the 2006 and 2008 elections) fought back and tended to favor environmental protection over economic development, but a worsening economy added new pressures to old commitments and priorities, such as prohibitions on offshore drilling for oil and gas at a time of high gasoline prices.

The election of President Barack Obama in November 2008 brought a dramatic change in policy positions and priorities after eight years of the Bush administration, and environmentalists are likely to push for major changes in national energy policy and action on climate change, among other initiatives. They also hope to reverse many of the administrative rules and regulations adopted during the Bush years that gave scant consideration to the environmental effects of economic development. When Obama's appointments to key environmental and energy positions were announced in late 2008, environmentalists applauded the selections, particularly Lisa P. Jackson as administrator of the Environmental Protection Agency, Steven Chu as secretary of energy, John Holdren as the White House science adviser, and Carol Browner, President Clinton's EPA administrator, as the White House coordinator of energy and climate policy.

One consequence of the ongoing debate over the direction of environmental policy is that too little consensus has existed in Congress to revise the nation's major environmental laws, which most scholars and specialists in the field believe must be changed to address contemporary challenges. Even with the Democratic majorities that President Obama will have in the 111th Congress (2009–2011), that task remains a formidable challenge. Yet one conclusion is clear enough. As much as the debate over the environment shifted in important ways during the 1990s and early 2000s, there is no doubt that government and politics will continue to play a central role in shaping our environmental future.

When the first environmental decade was launched in the early 1970s, protecting our air, water, and other natural resources seemed a relatively simple proposition. The polluters and exploiters of nature would be brought to heel by tough laws requiring them to clean up or get out of business within five or ten years. But preserving the life support systems of the planet now appears a more daunting task than anyone imagined back then. Not only are problems such as global climate change more complex than controlling earlier sources of pollution, but also the success of U.S. policies is tied, now more than ever, to the actions of other nations.

This book seeks to explain the most important developments in environmental policy and politics since the 1960s and to analyze the central issues that· face us today. Like the previous editions, it focuses on the underlying trends, institutional strengths and shortcomings, and policy dilemmas that all policy actors face in attempting to resolve environmental controversies. Chapters have been thoroughly revised and updated, and several are brand new to this edition. We have also attempted to place George W. Bush's administration and the congressional agenda in the context of the ongoing debate over the cost and effectiveness of past environmental policies, as well as the search for ways to reconcile and integrate economic, environmental, and social goals through sustainable development. As such, the book has broad relevance for the environmental community and for all concerned with the difficulties and complexities of finding solutions to environmental problems.

Part I provides a retrospective view of policy development as well as a framework for analyzing policy change in the United States. Chapter 1 serves as an introduction to the book by outlining the basic issues in U.S. environmental policy since the early 1970s, the development of institutional capabilities for addressing them, and the successes and failures in implementing policies and achieving results. In chapter 2 Barry G. Rabe considers the evolving role of the states in environmental policy at a time when the recent devolution of responsibilities may face scrutiny from new federal leaders. He focuses on innovative policy approaches used by the states and the promise of—as well as the constraints on—state action on the environment. Part I ends with a chapter by Deborah Lynn Guber and Christopher J. Bosso that analyzes trends in public opinion and the changing strategies of the environmental movement. They find that public support for environmental policies is not as strong or reliable as often assumed and that environmental groups continue to suffer from persistent conflicts over the most suitable political strategies to embrace.

Part II analyzes the role of federal institutions in environmental policymaking. Chapter 4, by Norman J. Vig, discusses the role of recent presidents as environmental actors, evaluating their leadership on the basis of several common criteria. In chapter 5 Michael E. Kraft examines the role of Congress in environmental policy, with special attention to partisan conflicts over the environment and policy gridlock. The chapter focuses on recent debates and actions on national energy policy and climate change, over which Congress has struggled for much of the past decade. In chapter 6 Rosemary O'Leary uses several in-depth case studies of judicial action to explore how the courts shape environmental policy.

Some of the broader dilemmas in environmental policy formulation and implementation are examined in Part III. In chapter 7 Walter A. Rosenbaum takes a hard and critical look at the Environmental Protection Agency, the nation's chief environmental institution. In particular, he examines controversies over the agency's use of science in regulatory standard setting and the role the White House plays in agency decision making. Chapter 8, by Mark Lubell and Brian Segee, examines comparable tensions and actions in the natural resource agencies, primarily within the Interior Department; they give special consideration to the promises and limitations of collaborative ecosystem management as one way to deal with ongoing controversies. In chapter 9, Sheila M. Olmstead introduces economic perspectives on environmental policy, including the use of benefit-cost analysis, and she assesses the potential of market forces as an alternative or supplement to conventional regulation. Chapter 10 moves the spotlight to evolving business practices. In this chapter, Daniel Press and Daniel A. Mazmanian examine the "greening of industry," particularly the increasing use of market-based initiatives such as voluntary pollution prevention, information disclosure, and environmental management systems. They find that a creative combination of voluntary actions and government regulation offers the best promise of success. Finally, in chapter 11, Robert C. Paehlke examines the intriguing efforts by communities throughout the nation to integrate environmental sustainability into policy decisions in areas as diverse as energy use, housing, transportation, land use, and urban social life, considerations made even more important today in an era of sharply higher energy costs.

Part IV shifts attention to selected issues and controversies, both global and domestic. In chapter 12 Henrik Selin and Stacy D. VanDeveer survey the key scientific evidence and major disputes over climate change, as well as the evolution of the issue, especially since the late 1980s. They also assess government responses to the problem of climate change and the outlook for public policy actions. In chapter 13 Richard J. Tobin examines the plight of developing nations that are struggling with a formidable array of threats brought about by rapid population growth and resource exploitation. He surveys the pertinent evidence, recounts cases of policy success and failure, and indicates the remaining barriers (including insufficient commitment by rich countries) to achieving sustainable development in these nations. In chapter 14 Elizabeth C. Economy analyzes the shortcomings of environmental policy in China in light of that nation's worsening environmental conditions and, in the process, speaks to risks of globalization as developing nations seek rapid economic growth, often without much realization of the ecological and public health consequences or an ability to control them. The last chapter in Part IV, by Richard A. Matthew, reviews the way environmental challenges such as climate change, water scarcity, and access to energy resources increasingly are seen as national security issues. He describes the major initiatives of the Clinton and Bush administrations and looks ahead to the environmental security challenges facing the Obama administration and how they might be addressed in 2009 and beyond.

In the final chapter we summarize the arguments for integrating the concept of sustainable development more fully into policymaking at all levels of government. Moreover, we review the agenda of outstanding environmental problems facing the nation and the world, and we discuss a series of innovative policy instruments that might help us to better address these issues in the future.

We thank the contributing authors for their generosity, cooperative spirit, and patience in response to our seemingly ruthless editorial requests. It is a pleasure to work with such a conscientious and punctual group of scholars. Special thanks are also due to the staff of CQ Press, including Brenda Carter, Charisse Kiino, Allie McKay, Gwenda Larsen, Paul Pressau, and Steve Pazdan, and to freelance copy editor Amy Marks, for their customarily splendid editorial work. We also gratefully acknowledge support from the Department of Public and Environmental Affairs at the University of Wisconsin–Green Bay. Finally, we thank our students at Carleton College and UW–Green Bay for forcing us to rethink our assumptions about what really matters. As always, any remaining errors and omissions are our own responsibility.

Norman J. Vig
Michael E. Kraft

Contributors

About the Editors

Michael E. Kraft is professor of political science and public affairs and Herbert Fisk Johnson Professor of Environmental Studies at the University of Wisconsin–Green Bay. He is the author of, among other works, *Environmental Policy and Politics*, 5th ed. (2010) and coauthor of *Public Policy: Politics, Analysis, and Alternatives*, 3d ed. (2010). In addition, he is coeditor of *Business and Environmental Policy* (2007), with Sheldon Kamieniecki; and *Toward Sustainable Communities: Transition and Transformations in Environmental Policy*, 2d ed. (2009), with Daniel A. Mazmanian.

Norman J. Vig is Winifred and Atherton Bean Professor of Science, Technology and Society, Emeritus, at Carleton College. He has written extensively on environmental policy, science and technology policy, and comparative politics and is coeditor, with Michael G. Faure, of *Green Giants? Environmental Policies of the United States and the European Union* (2004) and, with Regina S. Axelrod and David Leonard Downie, of *The Global Environment: Institutions, Law, and Policy*, 2d ed. (2005).

About the Contributors

Christopher J. Bosso is Associate Dean of Arts and Sciences and professor of political science at Northeastern University. He writes about environmental groups, on environmental politics more generally, and the regulatory impacts of emerging technologies. His most recent book, *Environment, Inc.: From Grassroots to Beltway* (2005), is co-winner of the American Political Science Association's Lynton Caldwell Award for the best book in environmental politics and policy.

Elizabeth C. Economy is C. V. Starr Senior Fellow and Director for Asia Studies at the Council on Foreign Relations. Her most recent book, *The River Runs Black*, won the 2005 International Convention on Asia Scholars award for best social sciences book. Her writings appear often in publications such as *Foreign Affairs*, the *New York Times*, the *Washington Post*, and the *International Herald Tribune*, and she is a frequent radio and television commentator on U.S.-China relations. She regularly testifies before Congress and consults for the U.S. government and companies on Chinese environmental issues. She is currently working on a new book focusing on the implications of China's global quest for natural resources.

Deborah Lynn Guber is associate professor of political science at the University of Vermont, where she specializes in public opinion, U.S. electoral politics, and environmental policy. Her work has appeared in journals such as *Social Science Quarterly, Society and Natural Resources,* and *State and Local Government Review.* She is the author of *The Grassroots of a Green Revolution: Polling America on the Environment* (2003).

Mark Lubell is an associate professor in the Department of Environmental Science and Policy at the University of California, Davis, where he teaches courses in environmental politics and policy, public policy, public land management, water policy and politics, and political science research methods. He is the coauthor of *Swimming Upstream: Collaborative Approaches to Watershed Management* (2005), and he has published articles in leading journals in political science and public policy, including *Political Research Quarterly,* the *Journal of Policy Analysis and Management,* the *Journal of Politics,* the *Policy Studies Journal,* and the *American Journal of Political Science.*

Richard A. Matthew is the founding director of the Center for Unconventional Security Affairs and an associate professor of international and environmental politics in the Schools of Social Ecology and Social Science at the University of California, Irvine. He is the author or coeditor of several publications: *Contested Grounds: Security and Conflict in the New Environmental Politics* (1999), *Dichotomy of Power: Nation versus State in World Politics* (2002), *Conserving the Peace: Resources, Livelihoods, and Security* (2002), *Reframing the Agenda: The Impact of NGO and Middle Power Cooperation in International Security Policy* (2003), *Landmines and Human Security: International Relations and War's Hidden Legacy* (2004), and *Global Environmental Politics and Human Security* (2009).

Daniel A. Mazmanian is the Bedrosian Chair of Governance, and director of the Judith and John Bedrosian Center on Governance and the Public Enterprise, in the School of Policy, Planning, and Development (SPPD) at the University of Southern California. From 2000 to 2005 he served as C. Erwin and Ione Piper Dean and Professor of SPPD and prior to that as dean of the School of Natural Resources and Environment at the University of Michigan. Among his several books are *Can Organizations Change? Environmental Protection, Citizen Participation, and the Corps of Engineers* (1979), *Implementation and Public Policy* (1989), *Beyond Superfailure: America's Toxics Policy for the 1990s* (1992), and *Toward Sustainable Communities,* 2d ed. (2009).

Rosemary O'Leary is an environmental lawyer, Phanstiel Chair, and a distinguished professor of public administration, with additional appointments in political science and law, at the Maxwell School of Syracuse University. She has written extensively on the courts and environmental policy. She is the winner of ten national research awards, including two "best book" awards for *Managing for the Environment,* written with Robert Durant, Daniel Fiorino, and Paul Weiland (1999). Her book *The Promise and Performance of Environmental Conflict Resolution,* coedited with Lisa Bingham, won the 2005 award for "Best Book in Environmental and Natural Resources Administration," given by the American Society for Public Administration. She has served as a consultant to federal and state environmental agencies and is the director of the Collaborative Governance Initiative.

Sheila M. Olmstead is an associate professor of environmental economics at Yale University's School of Forestry and Environmental Studies. She is the coauthor, with Nathaniel O. Keohane, of *Markets and the Environment* (2007), and she has published articles in a number of leading journals, including *Environment, Land Economics,* the *Journal of Environmental Economics and Management,* and the *Harvard Environmental Law Review.* Her research interests focus on environmental and natural resource economics and policy, including both natural resource management and pollution control.

Robert C. Paehlke is a professor in the Environmental and Resource Studies Program at Trent University, Peterborough, Ontario. He is the author of *Environmentalism and the Future of Progressive Politics* (1989), *Democracy's Dilemma: Environment, Social Equity, and the Global Economy* (2003), and *Some Like It Cold: The Politics of Climate Change in Canada* (2008); coeditor of *Managing Leviathan: Environmental Politics and the Administrative State,* 2d ed. (2005); and editor of *Conservation and Environmentalism: An Encyclopedia* (1995). He is a founding editor of the Canadian journal *Alternatives: Perspectives on Society, Technology, and Environment.*

Daniel Press is professor and chair of environmental studies at the University of California, Santa Cruz, where he teaches environmental politics and policy. He is the author of *Democratic Dilemmas in the Age of Ecology* (1994) and *Saving Open Space: The Politics of Local Preservation in California* (2002).

Barry G. Rabe is a professor at the Gerald Ford School of Public Policy at the University of Michigan, where he also holds appointments in the School of Natural Resources and Environment and the Program in the Environment. He is also a nonresident senior fellow at the Brookings Institution. He is the author of four books, including *Statehouse and Greenhouse: The Emerging Politics of American Climate Change Policy,* which won the 2005 Caldwell Award for the best book published on environmental politics and policy in the past three years. In 2006 he became the first social scientist to win a Climate Protection Award from the U.S. Environmental Protection Agency. In 2008, he was a visiting professor at the University of Virginia, where he helped organize the National Conference on Climate Governance and edited *Greenhouse Governance: Addressing Climate Change in America* (2010).

Walter A. Rosenbaum is professor of political science emeritus at the University of Florida in Gainesville and visiting professor, Program in the Environment, at the University of Michigan, where he specializes in environmental and energy policy. He also served as a senior consultant to the Assistant Administrator for Policy, Planning, and Evaluation at the U.S.

Environmental Protection Agency and is currently a consultant to the Federal Emergency Management Agency. Among his many published works is *Environmental Politics and Policy*, 7th ed. (2008).

Brian Segee is a staff attorney with the Environmental Defense Center in Santa Barbara, California, a nonprofit law firm representing environmental and community groups in central and southern coastal California. He formerly was staff attorney with the national wildlife conservation organization Defenders of Wildlife in Washington, D.C., where his work encompassed a broad range of conservation issues, including species protection, federal lands, water and wetlands, transportation, borderlands conservation, and global warming.

Henrik Selin is an assistant professor in the Department of International Relations at Boston University, where he teaches classes and conducts research on global and regional politics of the environment and sustainable development. He is the author or coauthor of more than two dozen journal articles and book chapters as well as the coeditor of *Changing Climates in North American Politics: Institutions, Policymaking, and Multilevel Governance* (2009) and *Transatlantic Environment and Energy Politics: Comparative and International Perspectives* (2009).

Richard J. Tobin recently retired from the World Bank in Washington, D.C. He formerly provided technical assistance to governments in developing countries through the U.S. Agency for International Development. His book *The Expendable Future: U.S. Politics and the Protection of Biological Diversity* received the Policy Studies Organization's Outstanding Book Award.

Stacy D. VanDeveer is associate professor of political science at the University of New Hampshire. His research interests include international environmental policymaking and its domestic impacts, the connections between environmental and security issues, and the role of expertise in policymaking. He has received research funding from the U.S. National Science Foundation, the European Union, and the Swedish Foundation for Strategic Environmental Research (MISTRA), among others. In addition to authoring and coauthoring numerous articles, book chapters, working papers, and reports, he is the coeditor of *Saving the Seas* (1997), *EU Enlargement and the Environment* (2005), *Changing Climates in North American Politics* (2009), *Transatlantic Environment and Energy Politics* (2009), and *Comparative Environmental Politics* (forthcoming).

1

Environmental Policy over Four Decades
Achievements and New Directions
Michael E. Kraft and Norman J. Vig

E nvironmental issues soared to a prominent place on the political agenda in the United States and other industrial nations in the early 1970s. The new visibility was accompanied by abundant evidence domestically and internationally of heightened public concern over environmental threats.[1] By the 1990s policymakers around the world had pledged to deal with a range of important environmental challenges, from protection of biological diversity to air and water pollution control. Such commitments were particularly manifest at the 1992 UN Conference on Environment and Development (the Earth Summit) held in Rio de Janeiro, Brazil, where an ambitious agenda for redirecting the world's economies toward sustainable development was approved, and at the December 1997 Conference of the Parties in Kyoto, Japan, where delegates agreed to a landmark treaty on global warming. Although it received far less media coverage, the World Summit on Sustainable Development, held in Johannesburg, South Africa, in September 2002, reaffirmed the commitments made a decade earlier at the Earth Summit, with particular attention to the challenge of alleviating global poverty.

Despite these notable pledges and actions, rising criticism of environmental programs also was evident throughout the 1990s and the first decade of the twenty-first century both domestically and internationally. So too were a multiplicity of efforts to chart new policy directions. For instance, intense opposition to environmental and natural resource policies arose in the 104th Congress (1995–1997), when the Republican Party took control of both the House and Senate for the first time in forty years. Ultimately, much like the earlier effort in Ronald Reagan's administration, the anti-regulatory campaign on Capitol Hill failed to gain much public support.[2] Nonetheless, pitched battles over environmental and energy policy continued in every Congress through the 110th (2007–2009), and they were equally evident in the executive branch as the Bush White House sought to rewrite environmental rules and regulations to favor industry and to dramatically increase development of U.S. oil and natural gas supplies on public lands.[3] Yet growing dissatisfaction with the effectiveness, efficiency, and equity of environmental policies was by no means confined to congressional conservatives and the Bush administration. It could be found among a broad array of interests, including the business community, environmental policy analysts, environmental justice groups, and state and local government officials.[4]

Since 1992, governments at all levels have struggled to redesign environmental policy for the twenty-first century. Under Presidents Bill Clinton and George W. Bush, the U.S. Environmental Protection Agency (EPA) tried to "reinvent" environmental regulation through the use of collaborative decision making involving multiple stakeholders, public-private partnerships, market-based incentives, information disclosure, and enhanced flexibility in rulemaking and enforcement (see chapters 7, 9, and 10).[5] Particularly during the Clinton administration, new emphases within the EPA and other federal agencies and departments on ecosystem management and sustainable development sought to foster comprehensive, integrated, and long-term strategies for environmental protection and natural resource management (see chapter 8).[6] Many state and local governments have pursued similar goals, with adoption of a wide range of innovative policies that promise to address some of the most important criticisms directed at contemporary environmental policy (see chapters 2 and 11). The election of President Barack Obama in 2008 signaled the likelihood of even greater attention to innovative policy ideas in the years ahead as the nation demonstrated a new sense of urgency about climate change and a determination to address a range of environmental, energy, and resource challenges despite a poor economy.

The precise way in which Congress, the states, and local governments will change environmental policies remains unclear. The partisan gridlock of the past decade may give way to greater consensus on the need to act. Yet policy change rarely comes easily in the U.S. political system. Its success will likely depend on several key conditions: public support for change, how the various policy actors stake out and defend their positions on the issues, the way the media cover these disputes, the relative influence of opposing interests, and the state of the economy. Political leadership, as always, will play a role, especially in reconciling deep divisions between the major political parties on environmental protection and natural resource issues. Political conflict over the environment is not going to vanish any time soon. Indeed, it will likely increase as the United States and other nations struggle to define how they will respond to the latest generation of environmental problems.

In this chapter we examine the continuities and changes in environmental politics and policy since 1970 and discuss their implications for the early twenty-first century. We review the policymaking process in the United States, and we assess the performance of government institutions and political leadership. We give special attention to the major programs adopted in the 1970s, their achievements to date, and the need for policy redesign and priority setting for the years ahead. The chapters that follow address in greater detail many of the questions explored in this introduction.

The Role of Government and Politics

The high level of political conflict over environmental protection efforts during recent years underscores the important role government plays in devising solutions to the nation's and the world's mounting environmental ills.

Global climate change, population growth, the spread of toxic and hazardous chemicals, loss of biological diversity, and air and water pollution all require diverse actions by individuals and institutions at all levels of society and in both the public and private sectors. These actions range from scientific research and technological innovation to improved environmental education and significant changes in corporate and consumer behavior. As political scientists we believe government has an indispensable role to play in environmental protection and improvement. The chapters in this volume thus focus on environmental policies and the government institutions and political processes that affect them. Our goal is to illuminate that role and to suggest needed changes and strategies.

The government plays a preeminent role in this policy arena primarily because environmental threats represent public or collective goods problems. They cannot be resolved through purely private actions. There is no question that individuals and nongovernmental organizations, such as environmental groups and research institutes, can do much to protect environmental quality and promote public health. The potential for such action is demonstrated by the impressive growth of sustainable community efforts during the 1990s and early 2000s and the diversified efforts by business and industry to prevent pollution and improve energy efficiency through development of greener products and services (see chapters 10 and 11).

Yet such actions are often insufficient without the backing of public policy, for example, laws mandating control of toxic chemicals that are supported by the authority of government. The justification for government intervention lies partly in the inherent limitations of the market system and the nature of human behavior. Self-interested individuals and a relatively unfettered economic marketplace guided mainly by a concern for short-term profits tend to create spillover effects, or externalities; pollution and other kinds of environmental degradation are examples. Collective action is needed to correct such market failures. In addition, the scope and urgency of environmental problems typically exceed the capacity of private markets and individual efforts to deal with them effectively. For these reasons, among others, the United States and other nations have relied on government policies—at local, state, national, and international levels—to address environmental and resource challenges.

Adopting public policies does not imply that voluntary and cooperative actions by citizens in their communities or various environmental initiatives by businesses cannot be the primary vehicle of change in many instances. Nor does it suggest that governments should not consider a full range of policy approaches—including market-based incentives, new forms of collaborative decision making, and information provision strategies—to supplement conventional regulatory policies where needed. The guiding principle should be to use the approaches that work best—those that bring about the desired improvements in environmental quality, minimize health and ecological risks, and help to integrate and balance environmental and economic goals.

Political Institutions and Public Policy

Public policy is a course of government action or inaction in response to social problems. It is expressed in goals articulated by political leaders; in formal statutes, rules, and regulations; and in the practices of administrative agencies and courts charged with implementing or overseeing programs. Policy states an intent to achieve certain goals and objectives through a conscious choice of means, usually within a specified period of time. In a constitutional democracy like the United States, policymaking is distinctive in several respects: It must take place through constitutional processes, it requires the sanction of law, and it is binding on all members of society.

The constitutional requirements for policymaking were established well over two hundred years ago, and they remain much the same today. The U.S. political system is based on a division of authority among three branches of government and between the federal government and the states. Originally intended to limit government power and to protect individual liberty, today this division of power may impede the ability of government to adopt timely and coherent environmental policy. Dedication to principles of federalism means that environmental policy responsibilities are distributed among the federal government, the fifty states, and thousands of local governments (see chapter 2).

Responsibility for the environment is divided within the branches of the federal government as well, most notably in the U.S. Congress, with power shared between the House and Senate, and jurisdiction over environmental policies scattered among dozens of committees and subcommittees (Table 1-1). For example, some twenty Senate and 28 House committees have some jurisdiction over EPA activities.[7] The executive branch is also institutionally fragmented, with at least some responsibility for the environment and natural resources located in twelve cabinet departments and in the EPA, the Nuclear Regulatory Commission, and other agencies (Figure 1-1). Although most environmental policies are concentrated in the EPA and in the Interior and Agriculture Departments, the Departments of Energy, Defense, Transportation, and State are increasingly important actors as well. Finally, the more than 100 federal trial and appellate courts play key roles in interpreting environmental legislation and adjudicating disputes over administrative and regulatory actions (see chapter 6).

The implications of this constitutional arrangement for policymaking were evident in the early 1980s as Congress and the courts checked and balanced the Reagan administration's efforts to reverse environmental policies of the previous decade. They were equally clear during the 1990s when the Clinton administration vigorously opposed actions in Congress to weaken environmental programs. They could be seen again in the presidency of George W. Bush, when Congress challenged the president's proposed national energy policy and many other environmental initiatives, particularly when the Democrats regained both houses of Congress following the 2006 election.

Table 1-1 Major Congressional Committees with Environmental Responsibilities[a]

Committee	Environmental Policy Jurisdiction
HOUSE	
Agriculture	Agriculture generally; forestry in general and private forest reserves; agricultural and industrial chemistry; pesticides; soil conservation; food safety and human nutrition; rural development; water conservation related to activities of the Department of Agriculture
Appropriations[b]	Appropriations for all programs
Energy and Commerce	Measures related to the exploration, production, storage, marketing, pricing, and regulation of energy sources, including all fossil fuels, solar, and renewable energy; energy conservation and information; measures related to general management of the Department of Energy and the Federal Energy Regulatory Commission; regulation of the domestic nuclear energy industry; research and development of nuclear power and nuclear waste; air pollution; safe drinking water; pesticide control; Superfund and hazardous waste disposal; toxic substances control; health and the environment
Natural Resources	Public lands and natural resources in general; irrigation and reclamation; water and power; mineral resources on public lands and mining; grazing; national parks, forests, and wilderness areas; fisheries and wildlife, including research, restoration, refuges, and conservation; oceanography, international fishing agreements, and coastal zone management; Geological Survey
Science and Technology	Environmental research and development; marine research; energy research and development in all federally owned nonmilitary energy laboratories; research in national laboratories; NASA, National Weather Service, and National Science Foundation
Transportation and Infrastructure	Transportation, including civil aviation, railroads, water transportation, and transportation infrastructure; Coast Guard and marine transportation; federal management of emergencies and natural disasters; flood control and improvement of waterways; water resources and the environment; pollution of navigable waters; bridges and dams
SENATE	
Agriculture, Nutrition and Forestry	Agriculture in general; food from fresh waters; soil conservation and groundwater; forestry in general; human nutrition; rural development and watersheds; pests and pesticides; food inspection and safety

(continued on next page)

Table 1-1   Major Congressional Committees with Environmental
Responsibilities *(Continued)*

Committee	Environmental Policy Jurisdiction
Appropriations[b]	Appropriations for all programs
Commerce, Science and Transportation	Interstate commerce and transportation generally; coastal zone management; inland waterways; marine fisheries; oceans, weather, and atmospheric activities; transportation and commerce aspects of outer continental shelf lands; science, engineering, and technology research and development; surface transportation
Energy and Natural Resources	Energy policy, regulation, conservation, research and development; coal; oil, and gas production and distribution; civilian nuclear energy; solar energy systems; mines, mining, and minerals; irrigation and reclamation; water and power; national parks and recreation areas; wilderness areas; wild and scenic rivers; public lands and forests; historic sites
Environment and Public Works	Environmental policy, research, and development; air, water, and noise pollution; climate change; construction and maintenance of highways; safe drinking water; environmental aspects of outer continental shelf lands and ocean dumping; environmental effects of toxic substances other than pesticides; fisheries and wildlife; Superfund and hazardous wastes; solid waste disposal and recycling; nonmilitary environmental regulation and control of nuclear energy; water resources, flood control, and improvements of rivers and harbors; public works, bridges, and dams

Sources: Compiled from descriptions of committee jurisdictions reported in Rebecca Kimitch, "CQ Guide to the Committees: Democrats Opt to Spread the Power," *CQ Weekly Online* (April 16, 2007): 1080–1083, http://library.cqpress.com/cqweekly/weeklyreport110-000002489956, and from House and Senate committee Web sites.

a. In addition to the standing committees listed here, select or special committees may be created for a limited time. For example, in early 2007, House Speaker Nancy Pelosi, D-Calif., established a fifteen-member Select Energy Independence and Global Warming committee, chaired by Rep. Edward Markey, D-Mass. Each committee also operates with subcommittees (generally five or six) to permit further specialization. Committee Web pages offer extensive information about jurisdiction, issues, membership, and pending actions, and include both majority and minority views on the issues.

b. Both the House and Senate appropriations committees have interior and environment subcommittees that handle all Interior Department agencies as well as the Forest Service. As of 2005, EPA appropriations were added to their jurisdictions. The Energy Department, Army Corps of Engineers, and Nuclear Regulatory Commission fall under the jurisdiction of the subcommittees on Energy and Water Development. Tax policy affects many environmental, energy, and natural resource policies and is governed by the Senate Finance Committee and the House Ways and Means Committee.

Conflict between the two major parties on environmental issues during the 1990s and early 2000s had one striking effect. It shifted attention to the role of the states in environmental policy. As Barry Rabe discusses in chapter 2, the states often have been at the center of the most innovative actions on environmental and energy policy, including climate change, when the federal government remained mired in partisan disputes. By 2008, for example,

Figure 1-1 Executive Branch Agencies with Environmental Responsibilities

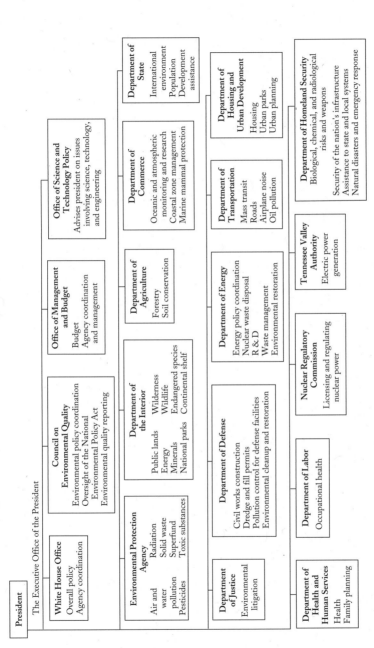

Sources: Council on Environmental Quality, *Environmental Quality: Sixteenth Annual Report of the Council on Environmental Quality* (Washington, D.C.: U.S. Government Printing Office, 1987); *United States Government Manual 2008/09* (Washington, D.C.: U.S. Government Printing Office, 2008), available at www.gpoaccess.gov/gmanual), and authors.

over half of the states had adopted some form of climate change policy, particularly to favor use of renewable energy sources, when Congress and the White House could reach no agreement on what to do.[8]

More generally, divided authority produces slow and incremental alterations in public policy, typically after broad consultation and agreement among diverse interests both within and outside of government. Such political interaction and accommodation of interests enhance the overall legitimacy of the resulting public policies. Over time, however, the cumulative effect often has been disjointed policies that fall short of the ecological or holistic principles of policy design so often touted by environmental scientists, planners, and activists.

Nonetheless, when issues are highly visible, the public is supportive, and political leaders act cohesively, the U.S. political system has proved flexible enough to permit substantial policy innovation.[9] As we shall see, this was the case in the early to mid-1970s, when Congress enacted major changes in U.S. environmental policy, and in the mid-1980s, when Congress overrode objections of the Reagan administration and greatly strengthened policies on hazardous waste and water quality, among others. Passage of the monumental Clean Air Act Amendments of 1990 is an example of the same alignment of forces. With bipartisan support, Congress adopted the act by a margin of 401 to 25 in the House and 89 to 10 in the Senate. Comparable bipartisanship during the mid-1990s produced major changes in the Safe Drinking Water Act and in regulation of pesticide residues in food, and in 2005 and 2007 it led Congress to approve new national energy policies (see chapter 5).

Policy Processes: Agendas, Streams, and Cycles

Students of public policy have proposed several models for analyzing how issues get on the political agenda and move through the policy processes of government. These theoretical frameworks help us to understand both long-term policy trends and short-term cycles of progressive action and political reaction. One set of essential questions concerns *agenda setting*: How do new problems emerge as political issues that demand the government's attention, if they do achieve such recognition? For example, why did the federal government initiate controls on industrial pollution in the 1960s and early 1970s but do little about national energy issues until well into the 1970s, and even then only to a limited extent? Why was it so difficult for climate change to gain the attention of policymakers over the years? Its rise on the political agenda was quite slow, although it finally became a significant issue by the 2008 presidential election campaign (see chapter 3).

As the case of climate change illustrates, in an issue's rise to prominence, hurdles almost always must be overcome. The issue must first gain societal recognition as a problem, often in response to demographic, technological, or other social changes. Then it must get on the docket of government institutions, usually through the exercise of organized interest group pressure. Finally it must receive enough attention by government policymakers to reach the stage of decisional or policy action. An issue is not likely to reach this latter stage unless conditions are ripe—for example, a triggering event that focuses public opinion sharply, as occurred with the Exxon *Valdez* oil spill in 1989.[10] One model by political scientist John Kingdon analyzes agenda setting according to the convergence of three streams that can be said to flow through the political system at any time: (1) evidence of the existence of problems, (2) available policies to deal with them, and (3) the political climate or willingness to act. Although largely independent of one another, these problem, policy, and political streams can be brought together at critical times when policy entrepreneurs (key activists and policymakers) are able to take advantage of the moment and make the case for policy action.[11]

Once an issue is on the agenda, it must pass through several more stages in the policy process. These stages are often referred to as the *policy cycle*. Although terminology varies, most students of public policy delineate at least five stages of policy development beyond agenda setting. These are (1) *policy formulation* (designing and drafting policy goals and strategies for achieving them, which may involve extensive use of environmental science, economics, and policy analysis), (2) *policy legitimation* (mobilizing political support and formal enactment by law or other means), (3) *policy implementation* (putting programs into effect through provision of institutional resources and administrative decisions), (4) *policy evaluation* (measuring results in relation to goals and costs), and (5) *policy change* (modifying goals or means, including termination of programs).[12]

The policy cycle model is useful because it emphasizes all phases of policymaking. For example, how well a law is implemented is as important as the goals and motivations of those who designed and enacted the legislation. The model also suggests the continuous nature of the policy process. No policy decision or solution is final because changing conditions, new information, and shifting opinions will require policy reevaluation and revision. Other short-term forces and events, such as presidential or congressional elections or environmental accidents, can profoundly affect the course of policy over its life cycle. Thus policy at any given time is shaped by the interaction of long-term social, economic, technological, and political forces and short-term fluctuations in the political climate. All of these factors are manifest in the development of environmental policy.

The Development of Environmental Policy from the 1970s to the Twenty-First Century

As implied in the policy cycle model, the history of environmental policy in the United States is not one of steady improvement in human relations with the natural environment. Rather, it has been highly uneven, with significant discontinuities, particularly since the late 1960s. The pace and nature of policy change, as is true for most areas of public policy, reflect the dominant social values at any given time, the saliency of the issues, and the prevailing economic and political conditions.

Sometimes, as was the case in the 1970s, the combination facilitates major advances in environmental policy, and at other times, such as the early 1980s and early 2000s, we have periods of reaction and retrenchment. Despite these variations, over the past four decades there has been substantial public support for environmental protection and expanding government authority to act.[13] We focus here on the major changes from 1970 to the early twenty-first century, and we discuss the future agenda for environmental politics and policy in the concluding chapter of the book.

Policy Actions Prior to 1970

Until about 1970 the federal government played a sharply limited role in environmental policymaking—public land management being a major exception. For nearly a century, Congress had set aside portions of the public domain for preservation as national parks, forests, grazing lands, recreation areas, and wildlife refuges. The multiple use and sustained yield doctrines that grew out of the conservation movement at the beginning of the twentieth century, strongly supported by President Theodore Roosevelt, ensured that this national trust would contribute to economic growth under the stewardship of the Interior and Agriculture Departments. Steady progress was also made, however, in managing the lands in the public interest and protecting them from development.[14] After several years of debate, Congress passed the Wilderness Act of 1964 to preserve some of the remaining forest lands in pristine condition, "untrammeled by man's presence." At the same time, it approved the Land and Water Conservation Fund Act of 1964 to fund federal purchases of land for conservation purposes, and the Wild and Scenic Rivers Act of 1968 to protect selected rivers with "outstandingly remarkable features," including biological, scenic, and cultural value.[15]

During the mid-1960s the United States also began a major effort to reduce world population growth in developing nations through financial aid for foreign population programs, chiefly family planning and population research. President Lyndon B. Johnson and congressional sponsors of the programs tied them explicitly to a concern for "growing scarcity in world resources."[16]

Despite this longtime concern for resource conservation and land management, and the new interest in population issues, federal environmental policy was only slowly extended to control of industrial pollution and human waste. Air and water pollution were long considered to be strictly local or state matters, and they were not high on the national agenda until around 1970. In a very early federal action, the Refuse Act of 1899 required individuals who wanted to dump refuse into navigable waters to obtain a permit from the Army Corps of Engineers; however, the agency largely ignored the pollution aspects of the act.[17] After World War II, policies to control the most obvious forms of pollution were gradually developed at the local, state, and federal levels. For example, the federal government began assisting local authorities in building sewage treatment plants and initiated a limited program for air pollution research. Following the Clean Air Act of 1963 and amendments to the Water Pollution Control Act of 1948, Washington began prodding the states to set pollution abatement standards and to formulate implementation plans based on federal guidelines.[18]

Agenda Setting for the 1970s

The first Earth Day was April 22, 1970. Nationwide "teach-ins" about environmental problems demonstrated the environment's new place on the nation's social and political agendas. With an increasingly affluent and well-educated society placing new emphasis on the quality of life, concern for environmental protection grew apace and was evident across the population, if not necessarily to the same degree among all groups.[19] The effect was a broadly based public demand for more vigorous and comprehensive federal action to prevent environmental degradation. In an almost unprecedented fashion, a new environmental policy agenda rapidly emerged. Policymakers viewed the newly visible environmental issues as politically attractive, and they eagerly supported tough new measures, even when the full impacts and costs of these measures were unknown. As a result, laws were quickly enacted and implemented throughout the 1970s but with a growing concern over their costs and effects on the economy and an increasing realization that administrative agencies at all levels of government often lacked the capacity to assume their new responsibilities.

Congress set the stage for the spurt in policy innovation at the end of 1969 when it passed the National Environmental Policy Act (NEPA). The act declared that

> it is the continuing policy of the Federal Government, in cooperation with State and local governments, and other concerned public and private organizations, to use all practicable means and measures, including financial and technical assistance, in a manner calculated to foster and promote the general welfare, to create and maintain conditions under which man and nature can exist in productive harmony, and fulfill the social, economic, and other requirements of present and future generations of Americans.[20]

The law required detailed environmental impact statements for nearly all major federal actions and established the Council on Environmental Quality to advise the president and Congress on environmental issues. President Richard Nixon then seized the initiative by signing NEPA as his first official act of 1970 and proclaiming the 1970s as the "environmental decade." In February 1970 he sent a special message to Congress calling for a new law to control air pollution. The race was on as the White House and congressional leaders vied for environmentalists' support.

Policy Escalation in the 1970s

By the spring of 1970, rising public concern about the environment galvanized the Ninety-first Congress to action. Sen. Edmund Muskie, D-Maine, then the leading Democratic hopeful for the presidential nomination in 1972, emerged as the dominant policy entrepreneur for environmental protection issues. As chair of what is now the Senate Environment and Public Works Committee, he formulated proposals that went well beyond those favored by the president. Following a process of policy escalation, both houses of Congress approved the stronger measures and set the tone for environmental policymaking for much of the 1970s. Congress had frequently played a more dominant role than the president in initiating environmental policies, and that pattern continued in the 1970s. This was particularly so when the Democratic Party controlled Congress during the Nixon and Ford presidencies. Although support for environmental protection was bipartisan during this era, Democrats provided more leadership on the issue in Congress and were more likely to vote for strong environmental policy provisions than were Republicans.[21]

The increase in new federal legislation in the next decade was truly remarkable, especially since, as we noted earlier, policymaking in U.S. politics is usually incremental. Appendix 1 lists the major environmental protection and natural resource policies enacted from 1969 to early 2009. They are arranged by presidential administration primarily to show a pattern of significant policy development throughout the period, not to attribute chief responsibility for the various laws to the particular presidents. These landmark measures covered air and water pollution control (the latter enacted in 1972 over a presidential veto), pesticide regulation, endangered species protection, control of hazardous and toxic chemicals, ocean and coastline protection, better stewardship of public lands, requirements for restoration of strip-mined lands, the setting aside of more than 100 million acres of Alaskan wilderness for varying degrees of protection, and the creation of a "Superfund" (in the Comprehensive Environmental Response, Compensation, and Liability Act, or CERCLA) for cleaning up toxic waste sites. Nearly all of these policies reflected a conviction that the federal government must have sufficient authority to compel polluters and resource users to adhere to demanding national pollution control standards and new decision-making procedures that ensure responsible use of natural resources.

There were other signs of commitment to environmental policy goals as Congress and a succession of presidential administrations through Jimmy Carter's cooperated on conservation issues. For example, the area designated as national wilderness (excluding Alaska) more than doubled, from 10 million acres in 1970 to more than 23 million acres in 1980. Seventy-five units, totaling some 2.5 million acres, were added to the national park system in the same period. The national wildlife refuge system grew similarly. Throughout the 1970s the Land and Water Conservation Fund, financed primarily through royalties from offshore oil and gas leasing, was used to purchase additional private land for park development, wildlife refuges, and national forests.

The government's enthusiasm for environmental and conservation policy did not extend to all issues on the environmentalists' agenda. Two noteworthy cases are population policy and energy policy. The Commission on Population Growth and the American Future recommended in 1972 that the nation should "welcome and plan for a stabilized population," but its advice was ignored. Birth rates in the United States were declining, and population issues were politically controversial. Despite occasional reports that highlighted the effect of population growth on the environment, such as the *Global 2000 Report to the President* in 1980, the issue remained largely dormant over the next two decades.[22]

For energy issues the dominant pattern was not neglect but policy gridlock. Here the connection to environmental policy was clearer to policymakers than it had been on population growth. Indeed, opposition to pollution control programs as well as land preservation came primarily from conflicting demands for energy production in the aftermath of the Arab oil embargo in 1973. The Nixon, Ford, and Carter administrations all attempted to formulate national policies for achieving energy independence by increasing energy supplies, with Carter's efforts by far the most sustained and comprehensive. Carter also emphasized conservation and environmental safeguards. For the most part, however, these efforts were unsuccessful. No consensus on national energy policy emerged among the public or in Congress, and presidential leadership was insufficient to overcome these political constraints.[23]

Congress maintained its strong commitment to environmental policy throughout the 1970s, even as the salience of these issues for the public seemed to wane. For example, it revised the Clean Air Act of 1970 and the Clean Water Act of 1972 through amendments approved in 1977. Yet concerns over the impact of environmental regulation on the economy and specific objections to implementation of the new laws, particularly the Clean Air Act, began creating a backlash by the end of the Carter administration.

Political Reaction in the 1980s

The Reagan presidency brought to the federal government a markedly different environmental policy agenda (see chapter 4). Virtually all environmental protection and resource policies enacted during the 1970s were reevaluated in light of the president's desire to reduce the scope of government regulation, shift responsibilities to the states, and rely more on the private sector. Whatever the merits of Reagan's new policy agenda, it was put into effect through a risky strategy that relied on ideologically committed presidential appointees to the EPA and the Agriculture, Interior, and Energy Departments and on sharp cutbacks in budgets for environmental programs.[24]

Congress initially cooperated with Reagan, particularly in approving budget cuts, but it soon reverted to its accustomed defense of existing environmental policy, frequently criticizing the president's management of the EPA and the Interior Department under Anne Gorsuch (later Burford) and James Watt, respectively; both Burford and Watt were forced to resign by the end of 1983. Among Congress's most notable achievements of the 1980s were its strengthening of the Resource Conservation and Recovery Act (1984) and enactment of the Superfund Amendments and Reauthorization Act (1986), the Safe Drinking Water Act (1986), and the Clean Water Act (1987) (see appendix 1).

As we discuss later in this chapter, budget cuts and loss of capacity in environmental institutions took a serious toll during the 1980s. Yet even the determined efforts of a popular president could not halt the advance of environmental policy. Public support for environmental improvement, the driving force for policy development in the 1970s, increased markedly during Reagan's presidency and represented the public's stunning rejection of the president's agenda.[25]

Paradoxically, Reagan actually strengthened environmental forces in the nation. Through his lax enforcement of pollution laws and pro-development resource policies, he created political issues around which national and grassroots environmental groups could organize. These groups appealed successfully to a public that was increasingly disturbed by the health and environmental risks of industrial society and by threats to ecological stability. As a result, membership in national environmental groups soared and new grassroots organizations developed, creating further political incentives for environmental activism at all levels of government (see chapter 3).[26]

By the fall of 1989 there was little mistaking congressional receptivity to continuing the advance of environmental policy into the 1990s. Especially in his first two years as president, George H. W. Bush was eager to adopt a more positive environmental policy agenda than his predecessor, particularly evident in his support for the demanding Clean Air Act Amendments of 1990. Bush's White House, however, was deeply divided on environmental issues for both ideological and economic reasons.

Seeking New Policy Directions: From the 1990s to the Twenty-First Century

Environmental issues received considerable attention during the 1992 presidential election campaign. Bush, running for reelection, criticized environmentalists as extremists who were putting Americans out of work. The Democratic candidate, Bill Clinton, took a far more supportive stance on the environment, symbolized by his selection of Sen. Al Gore, D-Tenn., as his running mate. Gore was the author of a best-selling book, *Earth in the Balance,* and had one of the strongest environmental records in Congress.

Much to the disappointment of environmentalists, Clinton exerted only sporadic leadership on the environment throughout his two terms in office. However, he and Gore quietly pushed an extensive agenda of environmental policy reform as part of their broader effort to "reinvent government," making it more efficient and responsive to public concerns. Clinton was also generally praised for his environmental appointments and for his administration's support for initiatives such as restoration of the Florida Everglades and other actions based on new approaches to ecosystem management. Clinton reversed many of the Reagan- and Bush-era executive actions that were widely criticized by environmentalists, and he favored increased spending on environmental programs, alternative energy and conservation research, and international population policy.

Clinton also earned praise from environmental groups when he began speaking out forcefully against anti-environmental policy decisions of Republican Congresses (see chapters 4 and 5), for his efforts through the President's Council on Sustainable Development to encourage new ways to reconcile environmental protection and economic development, and for his "lands legacy" initiatives.[27] Still, Clinton displeased environmentalists as often as he gratified them.

The environmental policy agenda of George W. Bush's presidency is addressed in chapter 4 and throughout the rest of the book. As widely expected from statements Bush made on the campaign trail and from his record as governor of Texas, he and his cabinet departed significantly from the positions of the Clinton administration. The economic impact of environmental policy emerged as a major concern, and the president gave far more emphasis to economic development than he did to environmental protection or resource conservation.

Like his father, Bush recognized the political reality of popular support for environmental protection and resource conservation. Yet as a conservative Republican he was also inclined to represent the views of the party's core constituencies, particularly industrial corporations and timber, mining, agriculture, and oil interests. He drew heavily from those constituencies, as well as conservative ideological groups, to staff the EPA and the Interior, Agriculture, and Energy Departments, filling positions with what the press termed industry insiders.[28] In addition, he sought to further reduce the burden of environmental protection through the use of voluntary, flexible, and cooperative programs and to transfer to the states more responsibility for enforcement of federal laws.

Perhaps the most remarkable decision was the administration's unilateral withdrawal of the United States from the Kyoto Protocol on global climate change. The administration's tendency to minimize environmental concerns was equally clear in its proposed national energy policy of 2001 (which concentrated on increased production of fossil fuels) and in many decisions throughout Bush's two terms on clean air rules, water quality standards, mining regulations, and protection of national forests and parks that were widely denounced by environmentalists.[29]

Many of these decisions received considerably less media coverage than might have been expected. In part, this appeared to reflect the administration's strategy of keeping a low profile on potentially unpopular environmental policy actions. But the president benefited further from the sharply altered political agenda after the terrorist attacks of September 11, 2001, as well as the decision in 2003 to invade Iraq.[30]

Budgets and Policy Implementation

In this review of environmental policy development since 1970, we have highlighted the adoption of landmark policies and the political conflicts that shaped them. Another part of this story is the changes over time in budgetary support for the agencies responsible for implementing the policies.

Agency budgets are an important part of institutional capacity, which in turn affects the degree to which public policies might help to improve environmental quality. Although spending more money hardly guarantees policy success, substantial budget cuts can significantly undermine established programs. For example, the massive reductions in environmental funding during the 1980s had long-term adverse effects on the government's ability to implement environmental policies. Equally sharp budget cuts proposed by Congress in the mid- to late- 1990s and by the Bush administration in the 2000s raised the same prospect, although generally they failed to win approval until after 2004, when concern about rising federal budget deficits grew. Changes in budgetary support for environmental protection since the 1980s merit brief comment here. More detail is provided in the appendices.

In constant dollars (that is, adjusting for inflation), the total spending authorized by the federal government for all natural resource and environmental programs was the same in 2008 as it was in 1980 (see appendix 4). However, in some program areas, such as pollution control and abatement, reflecting the work of the EPA, spending declined substantially (about 35 percent) from 1980 to 2008. In contrast, spending on conservation and land management rose appreciably between 1980 and 2008, by about 150 percent. For most budget categories, spending decreased during the 1980s before recovering under the administrations of George H. W. Bush and Bill Clinton, and to some extent under George W. Bush. A notable exception, other than the case of pollution control, is spending on water resources, where the phase-out of federal grant programs resulted in a sharp decline in expenditures between 1980 and 2008 (35 percent). Even when the budget picture was improving, most agencies faced important fiscal challenges. Their responsibilities rose under environmental policies approved during the 1970s, 1980s, and 1990s, and they often found themselves with insufficient resources to implement those new policies fully and to achieve the environmental quality goals they embodied.

These constraints can be seen in the budgets and staffs of selected environmental and natural resource agencies. For example, in constant dollars, the EPA's operating budget as we calculate it (the EPA determines it somewhat differently) was no higher in 2008 than it was in 1980, despite the many new duties Congress gave the agency during this period (see appendix 2). The EPA's staff grew by a greater percentage than its budget, rising from slightly fewer than 13,000 in 1980, the last year of the Carter administration, to just short of 17,300 by 2008. Most other agencies saw a decrease in staff over the same period, some remained at about the same level, and a few, like the EPA, enjoyed an increase (see appendix 3).

For the near term, the reality is that budgets are likely to be sharply constrained, and they will be an important factor in the performance of environmental and resource agencies. Even before the economic downturn of 2008, the Bush administration fiscal 2009 budget projections showed steady or decreasing funding for environmental programs out to 2013. If President Obama and Congress want to shift priorities and resources to favor these programs, their ability to do so will be affected by the bleak economic and fiscal conditions the nation faces.

Improvements in Environmental Quality

It is difficult, both conceptually and empirically, to measure the success or failure of environmental policies.[31] Yet one of the most important tests of any public policy is whether it achieves its stated objectives. For environmental policies, we should ask if air and water quality are improving, hazardous waste sites are being cleaned up, and biological diversity is protected adequately. Almost always, we also want to know what these improvements cost, not just to government but for society as a whole. There is no simple way to answer those questions, and it is important to understand why that is so even if some limited responses are possible.[32]

Measuring Environmental Conditions and Trends

Environmental policies entail long-term commitments to broad social values and goals that are not easily quantified. Short-term and highly visible costs are easier to measure than long-term, diffuse, and intangible benefits, and these differences often lead to intense debates over the value of environmental programs. For example, should the EPA toughen air quality standards to reduce adverse health effects or hold off out of concern for the economic impacts? The answer often seems to depend on which president sits in the White House and how sensitive the EPA is to public concerns over the relative benefits and costs.

Variable and often unreliable monitoring of environmental conditions and inconsistent collection of data over time also make it difficult to assess environmental trends. The time period selected for a given analysis can affect the results, and many scholars discount some data collected prior to the mid-1970s as unreliable. One thing is certain, however. Evaluation of environmental policies depends on significant improvements in monitoring and data collection at both state and federal levels. With better and more appropriate data, we should be able to speak more confidently of policy successes and failures in the future.

In the meantime, scientists and pundits continue to debate whether particular environmental conditions are deteriorating or improving, and for what reasons. Many state-of-the-environment reports that address such conditions and trends are issued by government agencies and environmental research institutes.[33] For the United States, EPA and other agency reports,

growing population and strong economic growth could be considered an important achievement. At the same time, water quality clearly falls short of the goals of federal clean water acts.

Further evidence can be seen in the data on wetlands loss. The EPA estimates that in the period 1986 to 1997 the nation experienced an average net loss each year of about 58,000 acres of marshes, swamps, and other ecologically important wetlands to commercial and residential development, agriculture, road construction, and modification of hydrologic conditions. The agency in 2008 reported that for 1998 to 2004, there has been a net *gain* of wetland acreage of 32,000 acres a year; it is counting acres that have been improved, restored, or created. However, it also noted that "these data do not evaluate wetland quality or condition. Wetland condition is difficult to characterize fully, and there is no national indicator to measure it directly." Environmental groups argue that the nation continues to lose thousands of acres of wetlands each year. Contributing to the uncertainty about the status of wetlands, the EPA reports that for the most recent period, the states and tribes assessed only 2 percent of remaining wetlands, providing scant data on their quality.[41]

To date, little progress has been made in halting groundwater contamination despite passage of the Safe Drinking Water Act of 1974 and the Resource Conservation and Recovery Act of 1976 and their later amendments. In its 2000 Water Quality Inventory, the EPA reported that groundwater quality can be adversely affected by human actions that introduce contaminants and that "problems caused by elevated levels of petroleum hydrocarbon compounds, volatile organic compounds, nitrate, pesticides, and metals have been detected in ground water across the nation." The agency also noted that measuring groundwater quality is a complex task and data collection "is still too immature to provide comprehensive national assessments." Heading the list of contaminant sources are leaking underground storage tanks, septic systems, landfills, spills, fertilizer applications, and large industrial facilities. With some 46 percent of the nation's population relying on groundwater for drinking water (99 percent in rural areas), far more remains to be done.[42]

Toxic and Hazardous Wastes. Progress in dealing with hazardous wastes and other toxic chemicals has been the least satisfactory of all pollution control programs. Implementation of the major laws has been extraordinarily slow due to the extent and complexity of the problems, scientific uncertainty, litigation by industry, public fear of siting treatment and storage facilities nearby, budgetary limitations, and poor management and lax enforcement by the EPA. As a result, gains have been modest when judged by the most common measures.

One of the most carefully watched measures of government actions to reduce the risk of toxic and hazardous chemicals pertains to the federal Superfund program. For years it made painfully slow progress in cleaning up the nation's worst hazardous waste sites. By the late 1990s, however, the pace of action improved. The EPA reported that, as of September 2000, 757

Superfund sites had been fully cleaned up and construction (remediation or removal of material) was taking place at another 417 sites. By the end of fiscal year 2008, the agency said it continued to make "significant progress in cleaning up America's most contaminated hazardous waste sites and making them ready for productive use." Construction was completed at 30 sites during 2008, for a cumulative total of 1,060 sites of those on the National Priorities List.[43] These achievements often come at a high price, with much dispute over the costs and benefits.

Historically the EPA has set a sluggish pace in the related area of testing toxic chemicals, including pesticides. For example, under a 1972 law mandating control of pesticides and herbicides, only a handful of chemicals used to manufacture the 50,000 pesticides in use in the United States had been fully tested or retested. The Food Quality Protection Act of 1996 required the EPA to undertake extensive assessment of the risks posed by new and existing pesticides. Following a lawsuit, the EPA apparently is moving more quickly toward meeting the act's goal of protecting human health and the environment from these risks.[44]

Natural Resources. Comparable indicators of environmental progress can be cited for natural resource use. As is the case with pollution control, however, interpretation of the data is problematic. We have few good measures of ecosystem health or ways to value ecosystem services, and much of the usual information in government reports concerns land set aside for recreational and aesthetic purposes rather than for protection of ecosystem functions.[45] Nonetheless, the trends in land conservation and wilderness protection suggest important progress over more than three decades of modern environmental and natural resource policies.

For example, the national park system grew from about 26 million acres in 1960 to over 84 million acres by 2008, and the number of units in the system doubled. Since adoption of the 1964 Wilderness Act, Congress has set aside 108 million acres of wilderness through the national wilderness preservation system. Since 1968 it has designated over 165 wild and scenic rivers with more than 11,000 protected miles. The Fish and Wildlife Service manages more than 93 million acres in about 540 units of the national wildlife refuge system—triple the land area managed in 1970.[46]

Protection of biological diversity through the Endangered Species Act has produced some success as well, although far less than its supporters believe essential. By late 2008, thirty-five years after passage of the act, more than 1,300 U.S. plant and animal species had been listed as either endangered or threatened. Over 520 critical habitats have been designated, nearly 950 habitat conservation plans have been approved, and more than 1,100 recovery plans have been put into effect. Yet only a few endangered species have recovered fully. The Fish and Wildlife Service reported in 2006 that 33 percent of all listed species were stable, 8 percent were improving, and 34 percent were declining. The status of 23 percent of listed species was uncertain, and the other 2 percent was presumed to be extinct or living only in captivity.[47]

Assessing Environmental Progress

As the data reviewed in the preceding sections suggest, the nation made impressive gains between 1970 and 2008 in controlling many conventional pollutants and in expanding parks, wilderness areas, and other protected public lands. Despite some setbacks, progress on environmental quality continues, even if it is highly uneven from one period to the next. In the future, however, further advances will be more difficult, costly, and controversial. This is largely because the easy problems have already been addressed. At this point, marginal gains—for example, in air and water quality—will cost more per unit of improvement than in the past. Moreover, second-generation environmental threats such as toxic chemicals, hazardous wastes, and nuclear wastes are proving even more difficult to regulate than the "bulk" air and water pollutants that were the main targets in the 1970s. In these cases, substantial progress may not be evident for years to come, and it will be expensive.

The same is true for the third generation of environmental problems, such as global climate change and protection of biodiversity. Solutions require an unprecedented degree of cooperation among nations and substantial improvement in institutional capacity for research, data collection, and analysis as well as policy development and implementation. Hence, success is likely to come slowly as national and international commitments to environmental protection grow and capabilities improve.

Some long-standing problems, such as population growth, will continue to be addressed primarily within nation-states, even though the staggering effects on natural resources and environmental quality are felt worldwide. By early 2009 the Earth's population of 6.8 billion people was increasing at an estimated 1.2 percent (or about 82 million people) each year, with continued growth expected for perhaps another 100 years. The U.S. population was growing at only a slightly slower rate of 1 percent a year, and analysts from the Pew Research Center in 2008 projected a rise to 438 million people by 2050, up from 306 million in 2009 (see chapter 13).

Conclusion

Since the 1970s public concern and support for environmental protection have risen significantly, spurring the development of an expansive array of policies that substantially increased the government's responsibilities for the environment and natural resources, both domestically and internationally. The implementation of these policies, however, has been far more difficult and controversial than their supporters ever imagined. Moreover, the policies have not been entirely successful, particularly when measured by tangible improvements in environmental quality. Further progress will likely require the United States to search for more efficient and effective ways to achieve these goals, including the use of alternatives to conventional command-and-control regulation.[48] Despite these qualifications, the record since the 1970s demonstrates convincingly that the U.S. government is able to produce significant environmental gains through public policies. Unquestionably the environment would be worse today if the policies enacted during the 1970s and 1980s had not been in place.

Emerging environmental threats on the national and international agenda are even more formidable than the first generation of problems addressed by government in the 1970s and the second generation that dominated political debate in the 1980s. Responding to these threats will require creative new efforts to improve the performance of government and other social institutions, and effective leadership to design appropriate strategies both within government and in society itself. This new policy agenda is addressed in Part IV of the book and in the concluding chapter.

Government obviously is an important player in the environmental arena, and the federal government will continue to have unique responsibilities. In late 2008, then president-elect Obama assembled an experienced and talented environmental policy team to address these challenges. At that time he vowed to make energy and environmental issues "a leading priority of my presidency and a defining test of our time. We cannot accept complacency nor accept any more broken promises."[49] It is equally clear that government rarely can pursue forceful initiatives without broad public support. Ultimately, society's values and priorities will shape the government's response to a rapidly changing world environment that, in all probability, will involve major economic and social dislocations over the coming decades.

Notes

1. See survey data reviewed in chap. 3; Riley E. Dunlap, "Public Opinion and Environmental Policy," in *Environmental Politics and Policy: Theories and Evidence*, 2d ed., ed. James P. Lester (Durham: Duke University Press, 1995); Riley E. Dunlap, George H. Gallup Jr., and Alec M. Gallup, "Of Global Concern: Results of the Health of the Planet Survey," *Environment* 35(9) (1993): 7–15, 33–40.
2. Norman J. Vig and Michael E. Kraft, eds., *Environmental Policy in the 1980s: Reagan's New Agenda* (Washington, D.C.: CQ Press, 1984).
3. See, for example, Natural Resources Defense Council, *Rewriting the Rules (2005 Special Edition): The Bush Administration's First Term Environmental Record*, January 19, 2005, www.nrdc.org/legislation/rollbacks/rollbacksinx.asp. The effort continued to the end of the Bush presidency. See, for example, R. Jeffrey Smith, "Unfinished Business: The White House Is Rushing to Weaken Rules That Protect the Environment and Consumers," *Washington Post National Weekly Edition*, November 10–16, 2008, 33.
4. Robert Durant, Rosemary O'Leary, and Daniel Fiorino, eds., *Environmental Governance Reconsidered: Challenges, Choices, and Opportunities* (Cambridge: MIT Press, 2004); Daniel Fiorino, *The New Environmental Regulation* (Cambridge: MIT Press, 2006); Marc Allen Eisner, *Governing the Environment: The Transformation of Environmental Regulation* (Boulder, Colo.: Lynne Rienner, 2007); and Christopher McGrory Klyza and David Sousa, *American Environmental Policy, 1990–2006: Beyond Gridlock* (Cambridge: MIT Press, 2008).
5. Daniel A. Mazmanian and Michael E. Kraft, eds., *Toward Sustainable Communities: Transition and Transformations in Environmental Policy*, 2d ed. (Cambridge: MIT Press, 2009); Durant, O'Leary, and Fiorino, *Environmental Governance Reconsidered*; and Klyza and Sousa, *American Environmental Policy*.

6. Judith A. Layzer, *Natural Experiments: Ecosystem-Based Management and the Environment* (Cambridge: MIT Press, 2008); Hanna J. Cortner and Margaret A. Moote, *The Politics of Ecosystem Management* (Washington, D.C.: Island Press, 1998); Marian R. Chertow and Daniel C. Esty, eds., *Thinking Ecologically: The Next Generation of Environmental Policy* (New Haven: Yale University Press, 1997); President's Council on Sustainable Development, *Sustainable America: A New Consensus for Prosperity, Opportunity, and a Healthy Environment* (Washington, D.C.: President's Council on Sustainable Development, 1996).

7. See chap. 7. See also National Academy of Public Administration (NAPA), *Setting Priorities, Getting Results: A New Direction for EPA* (Washington, D.C.: NAPA, 1995), 124–125.

8. See also Klyza and Sousa, *American Environmental Policy,* chap. 7.

9. John W. Kingdon, *Agendas, Alternatives, and Public Policies,* 2d ed. (New York: HarperCollins, 1995); Frank R. Baumgartner and Bryan D. Jones, *Agendas and Instability in American Politics* (Chicago: University of Chicago Press, 1993).

10. Roger W. Cobb and Charles D. Elder, *Participation in American Politics: The Dynamics of Agenda-Building* (Boston: Allyn & Bacon, 1972). See also Thomas A. Birkland, *After Disaster: Agenda Setting, Public Policy, and Focusing Events* (Washington, D.C.: Georgetown University Press, 1997).

11. Kingdon, *Agendas.*

12. For a more thorough discussion of how the policy cycle model applies to environmental issues, see Michael E. Kraft, *Environmental Policy and Politics,* 4th ed. (New York: Pearson Longman, 2007), chap. 3. The general model is discussed at length in James E. Anderson, *Public Policymaking: An Introduction,* 6th ed. (Boston: Houghton Mifflin, 2006).

13. Dunlap, "Public Opinion and Environmental Policy"; and Deborah Lynn Guber, *The Grassroots of a Green Revolution: Polling America on the Environment* (Cambridge: MIT Press, 2003).

14. Paul J. Culhane, *Public Lands Politics: Interest Group Influence on the Forest Service and the Bureau of Land Management* (Baltimore: Johns Hopkins University Press, 1981), esp. chap. 1. See also Richard N. L. Andrews, *Managing the Environment, Managing Ourselves: A History of American Environmental Policy,* 2d ed. (New Haven: Yale University Press, 2006); and Sally K. Fairfax, Lauren Gwin, Mary Ann King, Leigh Raymond, and Laura A. Watt, *Buying Nature: The Limits of Land Acquisition as a Conservation Strategy: 1780–2004* (Cambridge: MIT Press, 2005).

15. Andrews, *Managing the Environment*; Kraft, *Environmental Policy and Politics,* chap. 4.

16. Michael E. Kraft, "Population Policy," in *Encyclopedia of Policy Studies,* 2d ed., ed. Stuart S. Nagel (New York: Marcel Dekker, 1994).

17. J. Clarence Davies III and Barbara S. Davies, *The Politics of Pollution,* 2d ed. (Indianapolis, Ind.: Bobbs-Merrill, 1975).

18. Evan J. Ringquist, *Environmental Protection at the State Level: Politics and Progress in Controlling Pollution* (Armonk, N.Y.: M. E. Sharpe, 1993), chap. 2; Davies and Davies, *Politics of Pollution,* chap. 2. A much fuller history of the origins and development of modern environmental policy than is provided here can be found in Andrews, *Managing the Environment,* and Michael J. Lacey, ed., *Government and Environmental Politics: Essays on Historical Developments since World War Two* (Baltimore: Johns Hopkins University Press, 1989).

19. Hays, *Beauty, Health, and Permanence.* See also Dunlap, "Public Opinion and Environmental Policy," and Robert Cameron Mitchell, "Public Opinion and Environmental Politics in the 1970s and 1980s," in *Environmental Policy in the 1980s,* ed. Vig and Kraft.

20. Public Law 91-90 (42 USC 4321–4347), sec. 101. See Lynton Keith Caldwell, *The National Environmental Policy Act: An Agenda for the Future* (Bloomington: Indiana University Press, 1998).

21. Michael E. Kraft, "Congress and Environmental Policy"; Sheldon Kamieniecki, "Political Parties and Environmental Policy," in *Environmental Politics and Policy,* ed.

Lester; Charles R. Shipan and William R. Lowry, "Environmental Policy and Party Divergence in Congress," *Political Research Quarterly* 54 (June 2001): 245–263.

22. Kraft, "Population Policy"; Council on Environmental Quality and Department of State, *The Global 2000 Report to the President* (Washington, D.C.: U.S. Government Printing Office, 1980).

23. James Everett Katz, *Congress and National Energy Policy* (New Brunswick, N.J.: Transaction, 1984).

24. Vig and Kraft, *Environmental Policy in the 1980s*.

25. See Riley E. Dunlap, "Public Opinion on the Environment in the Reagan Era," *Environment* 29 (July–August 1987): 6–11, 32–37; Mitchell, "Public Opinion and Environmental Politics."

26. The changing membership numbers can be found in Kraft, *Environmental Policy and Politics*, chap. 4. See also Christopher J. Bosso, *Environment, Inc.: From Grassroots to Beltway* (Lawrence: University Press of Kansas, 2005).

27. President's Council on Sustainable Development, *Sustainable America*.

28. Katharine Q. Seelye, "Bush Picks Industry Insiders to Fill Environmental Posts," *New York Times,* May 12, 2001, 1.

29. See Natural Resources Defense Council, "Rewriting the Rules"; Bruce Barcott, "Changing All the Rules," *New York Times Magazine,* April 4, 2004, 39–44, 66, 73, 76–77; and Margaret Kriz, "Vanishing Act," *National Journal,* April 12, 2008, 18–23.

30. Eric Pianin, "War Is Hell: The Environmental Agenda Takes a Back Seat to Fighting Terrorism," *Washington Post National Weekly Edition,* October 29–November 4, 2001, 12–13. See also Barcott, "Changing All the Rules"; and Joel Brinkley, "Out of the Spotlight, Bush Overhauls U.S. Regulations," *New York Times,* August 14, 2004, 1, A10.

31. Robert V. Bartlett, "Evaluating Environmental Policy," in *Environmental Policy in the 1990s,* 2d ed., ed. Vig and Kraft; Evan J. Ringquist, "Evaluating Environmental Policy Outcomes," in *Environmental Politics and Policy,* ed. Lester; Gerrit J. Knaap and Tschangho John Kim, eds., *Environmental Program Evaluation: A Primer* (Champaign: University of Illinois Press, 1998).

32. One of the most thorough evaluations of environmental protection policies of this kind can be found in J. Clarence Davies and Jan Mazurek, *Pollution Control in the United States: Evaluating the System* (Washington, D.C.: NAPA, 1995).

33. See, for example, UN Development Programme, UN Environment Programme, World Bank, and World Resources Institute, *World Resources 2008: Roots of Resilience—Growing the Wealth of the Poor* (Washington, D.C.: World Resources Institute, 2008), available at www.wri.org.

34. In previous years, the annual report of the Council on Environmental Quality consolidated data on environmental conditions and trends reported from the executive agencies. However, current information can now be found at specific agency Web sites. For a guide to online state-of-the-environment reports for all levels of government, see *Environment* 42 (April 2000): 3–4. A new consolidated EPA *Report on the Environment: Highlights of National Trends* brings together the kind of information we review here. The 2008 report is available at www.epa.gov/roehd/pdf/roe_hd_layout_508.pdf. However, it contains much less detail than is available from specific EPA and other agency reports discussed in this chapter.

35. For a fuller account, see Kraft, *Environmental Policy and Politics*, chap. 2. Another useful source comes from the H. John Heinz III Center for Science, Economics, and the Environment, *The State of the Nation's Ecosystems 2008: Measuring the Land, Water, and Living Resources of the United States* (Washington, D.C.: Island Press, 2008). The Heinz Center report is one of the most comprehensive reports and is updated periodically. Summaries of the report are available at the center's Web site (www.heinzctr.org/ecosystems).

36. U.S. Environmental Protection Agency (EPA), "Air Emissions Trends—Continued Progress through 2003," January 2005, www.epa.gov/airtrends/econ-emissions.html.

37. EPA, "National Air Quality—Status and Trends through 2007," November 2008, www.epa.gov/air/airtrends/2008.
38. Ibid.
39. EPA, "2006 TRI Public Data Release," February 21, 2008, www.epa.gov/tri/tridata/tri06/index.htm. The volume of releases refers only to TRI facilities that reported to the EPA that year. Facilities falling below a threshold level are not required to report, nor are many smaller facilities. Environmental Defense Fund makes TRI data available in many different formats, including as maps of polluting facilities in cities and neighborhoods; see www.scorecard.org.
40. EPA, "Watershed Assessment, Tracking, and Environmental Reports: National Summary of State Information," http://iaspub.epa.gov/waters10/attains_nation_cy.control#total_assessed_waters.
41. Ibid. The quotation is from the 2008 EPA *Report on the Environment,* cited above, p. 13.
42. *National Water Quality Inventory: 2000 Report to Congress* (Washington, D.C.: Office of Water, EPA). The U.S. Geological Survey has an extensive program of monitoring and assessing groundwater. See its Web site (www.usgs.gov).
43. EPA, "Superfund Cleanup Figures," November 17, 2003, www.epa.gov/superfund/action/process/mgmtrpt.htm; "Superfund National Accomplishments Summary Fiscal Year 2004," November 22, 2004, www.epa.gov/superfund/action/process/numbers04.htm; and "Progress Continues in Cleaning Up Hazardous Waste Sites," news release, EPA, November 17, 2008.
44. The pertinent documents can be found at the EPA's Web site for pesticide programs, www.epa.gov/pesticides/index.htm.
45. Hallett J. Harris and Denise Scheberle, "Ode to the Miner's Canary: The Search for Environmental Indicators," in *Environmental Program Evaluation,* ed. Knaap and Kim. See also Gretchen C. Daily, ed., *Nature's Services: Societal Dependence on Natural Ecosystems* (Washington, D.C.: Island Press, 1997); and Water Science and Technology Board, *Valuing Ecosystem Services: Toward Better Environmental Decision-Making* (Washington, D.C.: National Academies Press, 2004).
46. The numbers come from the various agency Web sites and from Kraft, *Environmental Policy and Politics,* chaps. 6 and 7.
47. The Fish and Wildlife Service Web site (www.fws.gov) provides extensive data on threatened and endangered species and habitat recovery plans. The figures on improving and declining species come from the U.S. Fish and Wildlife Service, *2005–2006 Recovery Report to Congress,* April 2008, www.fws.gov/Endangered/recovery/reports_to_congress/2005-6/summary_2005-6Recovery.pdf.
48. See Mazmanian and Kraft, *Toward Sustainable Communities;* Fiorino, *The New Environmental Regulation;* and Eisner, *Governing the Environment.*
49. The quotation is from John M. Broder and Andrew C. Revkin, "Hard Task for New Team on Energy and Climate," *New York Times,* December 16, 2008, 1, A22. See also David A. Fahrenthold, "Ready for Challenges: Obama's Environmental Team: No Radicals," *Washington Post National Weekly Edition,* December 22, 2008–January 4, 2009, 34.

2

Racing to the Top, the Bottom, or the Middle of the Pack?

The Evolving State Government Role in Environmental Protection

Barry G. Rabe

> *The problem which all federalized nations have to solve is how to secure an efficient central government and preserve national unity, while allowing free scope for the diversities, and free play to the ... members of the federation. It is ... to keep the centrifugal and centripetal forces in equilibrium, so that neither the planet States shall fly off into space, nor the sun of the Central government draw them into its consuming fires.*
>
> Lord James Bryce,
> *The American Commonwealth*

Before the 1970s the conventional wisdom on federalism viewed "the planet States" as sufficiently lethargic to require a powerful "Central government" in many areas of environmental policy. States were widely derided as mired in corruption, hostile to innovation, and unable to take a serious role in environmental policy out of fear of alienating key economic constituencies. If anything, they were seen as "racing to the bottom" among their neighbors, attempting to impose as few regulatory burdens as possible.[1] In more recent times the tables have turned—so much so that the conventional wisdom now berates an overheated federal government that squelches state creativity and capability to tailor environmental policies to local realities. The majority of recent U.S. Environmental Protection Agency (EPA) administrators assumed their Washington duties after extensive stints in state government and have routinely proclaimed states as central players in environmental policy. The decentralization mantra of recent decades called for the extended transfer of environmental policy resources and regulatory authority from Washington, D.C., to states and localities. Governors-turned-presidents, such as Ronald Reagan, Bill Clinton, and George W. Bush, extolled the wisdom of such a strategy, at least in their rhetoric. Of course, such a transfer would pose a potentially formidable test of the thesis that more localized units know best.

What accounts for this sea change in our understanding of the role of states in environmental policy? How have states evolved in recent decades and what sorts of functions do they assume most comfortably and effectively? Despite state resurgence, are there areas in which states fall short? Looking ahead, should regulatory authority devolve to the states, or are there better ways to sort out federal and state responsibilities? Furthermore, will the Barack Obama presidency and the possibility of renewed federal government involvement in environmental issues change our understanding of the proper distribution of federal and state authority?

This chapter addresses these questions, relying heavily on evidence of state performance in environmental policy. The chapter provides both an overview of state evolution and a set of brief case studies that explore state strengths and limitations. These state-specific accounts are interwoven with assessments of the federal government's role, for good or ill, in the development of state environmental policy.

The States as "New Heroes" of American Federalism

Policy analysts are generally most adept at analyzing institutional foibles and policy failures. Indeed, much of the literature on environmental policy follows this pattern, with criticism particularly voluminous and potent when directed toward federal efforts in this area. By contrast, states have received much more favorable treatment. Many influential books and reports on state government and federalism portray states as highly dynamic and effective. Environmental policy is often depicted as a prime example of this general pattern of state effectiveness. Some analysts routinely characterize states as the "new heroes" of American federalism, having long since eclipsed a doddering federal government. According to this line of argument, states are consistently at the cutting edge of policy innovation, eager to find creative solutions to environmental problems, and "racing to the top" with a goal of national preeminence in the field. When the states fall short, an overzealous federal partner is often said to be at fault.

Such commentary has considerable empirical support. The vast majority of state governments have undergone fundamental changes since the first Earth Day, in 1970. Many states have drafted new constitutions and gained access to unprecedented revenues through expanded taxing powers. Substantial amounts of federal transfer dollars have further swelled state coffers, allowing them to pursue policy commitments that previously would have been unthinkable. In turn, state bureaucracies have expanded and become more professionalized, as have the staffs serving governors and legislatures. This activity has been stimulated by increasingly competitive two-party systems in many regions, intensifying pressure on elected officials to deliver desired services. Expanded use of direct democracy provisions, such as the initiative and referendum, and increasing activism by state courts and elected state attorneys general have further contributed to this new era. Studies of this resurgent "statehouse democracy" show that policymaking at the state level has proven highly responsive to dominant public opinion within each state.[2] On the whole, public opinion data consistently find that citizens have a considerably higher degree of "trust and confidence" in the package of public services and regulations dispensed from their state capitals than in those from Washington.[3]

This transformed state role is evident in virtually every area of environmental policy. States directly regulate approximately 20 percent of the total U.S. economy, including many areas in which environmental concerns come into play.[4] The Environmental Council of the States has estimated that states operate approximately three-quarters of all federal environmental programs that can be delegated to them. Collectively, states issue more than 90 percent of all environmental permits, complete more than 90 percent of all environmental enforcement actions, and collect nearly 95 percent of the data used by the federal government. Despite this expanded role, federal financial support to states in the form of grants to support environmental protection efforts "actually dwindled" between 1981 and 2005.[5] Many areas of environmental policy are clearly dominated by states, including most aspects of waste management, groundwater protection, land use management, transportation, and electricity regulation. Even in policy areas that bear a firm federal imprint, such as air pollution control and pesticides regulation, states have considerable opportunity to oversee implementation and move beyond federal standards if they so choose. In air quality alone, "at least 15 state agencies have adopted stringent ... laws or regulations to fill a gap in federal standards, and at least 29 local air agencies are authorized to adopt more stringent air quality controls," according to a 2008 report of the Woodrow Wilson International Center for Scholars.[6] Political scientist DeWitt John speaks for a wide range of policy analysts in noting that "states are willing to spend their own dollars and enact their own policies, without being forced by the federal government to do so. Virtually all states have taken some steps to go beyond federally imposed requirements, and some have taken the lead in several areas."[7] A study completed by Resources for the Future, an environmental think tank, confirms that a "basic tenet of correct thinking about current environmental policy is the desirability of decentralization" from the federal government to the states and that "hundreds of other reports over the past decade" have reached this conclusion.[8] And political scientists Christopher McGrory Klyza and David Sousa confirm in an award-winning 2008 book that "the greater flexibility of state government can yield policy innovation, opening the way to the next generation of environmental policy."[9]

That growing commitment is further reflected in the institutional arrangements established by states to address environmental problems. Many states have long since moved beyond their traditional placement of environmental programs in public health departments in favor of comprehensive agencies that gather most environmental responsibilities under a single organizational umbrella. These agencies have sweeping, cross-programmatic responsibilities and have grown steadily in staff and complexity in recent decades. Ironically many of these agencies mirror the organizational framework of the much-maligned EPA, dividing regulatory activity by environmental media of air, land, and water and thereby increasing the likelihood of shifting environmental contamination back and forth across medium boundaries. Despite this fragmentation, such institutions provide states with a firm institutional foundation for addressing a variety of environmental concerns. In turn, many states have continued to experiment with new organizational arrangements to meet evolving challenges, including the use of networks to facilitate cooperation among various departments and agencies.[10]

This expanded state commitment to environmental policy may be accelerated not only by the broader factors introduced above but also by features somewhat unique to this policy area. First, a growing number of scholars contend that broad public support for environmental protection provides considerable impetus for bottom-up policy development. Such "civic environmentalism" stimulates numerous state and local stakeholders to take creative collective action independent of federal intervention.[11] In turn, game-theoretic analyses of efforts to protect so-called common-pool resources such as river basins side decisively with local or regional approaches to resource protection as opposed to top-down controls. Many such analyses go so far as to argue that any central government intervention in such settings is often unnecessary at best and downright destructive at worst.[12]

Second, the proliferation of environmental policy professionals, representing industry, advocacy groups, foundations, and particularly state agencies, has created a sizable base of talent and ideas for policy innovation. Contrary to conventional depictions of agency officials as shackled by elected "principals," an alternative view finds considerable policy entrepreneurship—or "bureaucratic autonomy"—in state and local policymaking circles.[13] This pattern is especially evident in environmental policy, where numerous areas of specialization place a premium on expert ideas and allow for considerable innovation within agencies.[14] Networks of professionals, working in similar capacities but in different states, have become increasingly influential in recent years. These networks facilitate information exchange, foster the diffusion of innovation, and pool resources to pursue joint initiatives. Specialized groups, such as the Environmental Council of the States and the National Association of State Energy Officials, also band together to influence federal policy. Other entities, such as the Northeast States for Coordinated Air Use Management, the Great Lakes Commission, and the Western Governors' Association, represent the interests of states in certain regions.

Third, environmental policy in many states is stimulated by direct democracy, facilitating initiatives, referendums, and recall of elected officials not allowed at the federal level. In every state except Delaware, state constitutional amendments must be approved by voters via referendum. Thirty-one states and Washington, D.C., also have some form of direct democracy for approving legislation, representing well over half the U.S. population. Use of this policy tool has grown at an exponential rate to consider a wide array of state environmental policy options, including nuclear plant closure, mandatory disclosure of commercial product toxicity, and public land acquisition. In November 2008, for example, Missouri voters decided by a margin of nearly two to one that all electric utilities operating in the state must steadily increase the amount of energy they provide from renewable sources, reaching a level of at least 20 percent by 2020. At the same time, twenty-three state and local initiatives were approved, raising more than $75 billion from sales tax increases and bond issuance to support new mass transit initiatives.[15]

The Cutting Edge of Policy: Cases of State Innovation

The convergence of these various political forces has unleashed substantial new environmental policy at the state level. A variety of scholars have attempted to analyze some of this activity through ranking schemes that determine which states are most active and innovative. They consistently conclude that certain states tend to take the lead in most areas of policy innovation, followed by an often uneven pattern of innovation diffusion across state and regional boundaries.[16] For example, 2008 data provided by the Pew Center on Global Climate Change provide insight on state receptivity to a range of policies that could reduce greenhouse gases and, in many instances, offer other environmental benefits such as lower rates of conventional air pollution or greater energy efficiency. From a total of twenty possible state policy options, the fifty states plus the District of Columbia are ranked in Table 2-1 by the total number of these options that they have adopted, ranging from California with a perfect score of twenty to Mississippi at the bottom with three. This ranking suggests considerable variation among states, producing a pattern very consistent with previous analyses of this type. Of course, any such ranking system has many limitations, particularly in moving beyond measures of activity toward evaluation of actual pollution reduction and environmental quality.

Somewhat related studies attempt to examine which economic and political factors are most likely to influence the rigor of state policy or the level of resources devoted to it.[17] An important but less examined question concerns recent developments in state environmental policy and whether these developments constitute a marked improvement over conventional approaches in terms of environmental performance. Evidence from select states suggests that a number of state innovations offer worthy alternatives to prevailing approaches. Indeed, many of these innovations constituted direct responses to shortcomings in existing regulatory design. The brief case studies that follow indicate the breadth and potential effectiveness of state innovation.

Table 2-1   Receptiveness of States to Environmental Policies

State	Total Number of Programs	State	Total Number of Programs
California	20	Florida	11
Connecticut	19	North Carolina	11
Oregon	18	Idaho	10
Rhode Island	18	Michigan	10
Massachusetts	17	Ohio	10
New Jersey	17	Virginia	10
New York	17	Indiana	8
Vermont	17	Kansas	8
Washington	17	Kentucky	8
Illinois	16	Oklahoma	8
Maryland	16	South Carolina	8
New Mexico	16	Arkansas	7
Arizona	15	District of Columbia	7
Hawaii	15	Georgia	7
Maine	15	Missouri	7
Minnesota	15	Louisiana	6
Pennsylvania	15	North Dakota	6
Wisconsin	15	Tennessee	6
Iowa	14	West Virginia	6
Nevada	14	Wyoming	6
Montana	13	Alaska	5
New Hampshire	13	Alabama	5
Texas	13	Nebraska	4
Utah	13	South Dakota	4
Colorado	12	Mississippi	3
Delaware	12		

Source: Pew Center on Global Climate Change.

Anticipating Environmental Challenges

One of the greatest challenges facing U.S. environmental policy is the need to shift from a pollution control mode that reacts after damage has occurred to one that anticipates potential problems and attempts to prevent them. Growing evidence suggests that some states have launched serious planning processes and are attempting to pursue preventative strategies in an increasingly systematic and effective way. All fifty states have at least one pollution prevention program, thirty-six of which are backed by state legislation. The oldest and most common of these involve technical assistance to industries and networking services that link potential collaborators. A smaller but growing set of state programs is redefining pollution prevention in larger terms, cutting across conventional programmatic boundaries with a series of mandates and incentives to pursue prevention opportunities.

Among the more active states, Minnesota has one of the most comprehensive programs. The 1990 Minnesota Toxic Pollution Prevention Act requires approximately 350 Minnesota firms to submit annual toxic pollution prevention plans. These plans must outline each firm's current use and release of a long list of toxic pollutants and establish formal goals for their reduction or elimination over a specified period of time. Firms have considerable latitude in determining how to attain these goals, contrary to the technology-forcing character of much federal regulation. But they must meet state-established reduction timetables and pay fees on releases. Overall releases of these substances have dropped markedly and consistently since the early 1990s.

From these earlier efforts, Minnesota and other states have established multidisciplinary teams that attempt to forecast potential environmental threats from "emerging contaminants" and respond accordingly. A small but growing number of states have used these teams to begin to chart ways to address possible environmental threats from expanded use of nanotechnology. On the one hand, "nano" constitutes an exciting technological breakthrough, via use of staggeringly small particles that may improve the quality of a wide range of manufactured goods. Some of these products may even have environmental benefits, such as improved emissions reduction technology. At the same time, possible human exposure to such tiny particles could pose a range of health risks whether through inhalation or contact via touch. Thus far, federal policies have focused primarily on funding to promote expanded use of nanomaterials, leading some states to begin to weigh possible threats and policy responses.

Economic Incentives

Economists have long lamented the penchant for command-and-control rules and regulations in U.S. environmental policy. They would prefer to see a more economically sensitive set of policies, such as fees on emissions and incentives to reward good environmental performance. Neither federal nor state governments have escaped such critical scrutiny, although a number of states have attempted to respond in recent years. In all, the states have enacted more than 400 measures that can be characterized as "green taxes," including environmentally related charges and tax incentives. Many states have become increasingly reliant on emissions or waste fees to provide both an economic disincentive to environmental degradation and a source of funds for program management.

A growing number of states are also revising their tax policies for environmental purposes. For example, Iowa exempts from taxation all pollution-control equipment purchased for use in the state, whereas Maryland and other states offer major tax incentives to purchasers of low-emission vehicles such as hybrids. Numerous states provide a series of tax credits or low-interest loans for the purchase of recycling equipment or capital investments necessary to facilitate recycling or reuse of a particular product. Many states and localities have also developed some form of tax on solid waste, usually involving a direct fee for garbage pickup while offering free collection of recyclables.

Perhaps the most visible economic incentive programs involve refundable taxes on beverage containers. Ten states—covering 30 percent of the population—have such programs in place. Provisions of these programs vary somewhat, although most operate with limited direct involvement by state officials. Deposits pass along through a system that includes consumers, container redemption facilities such as grocery stores, and firms that reuse or recycle the containers. Michigan's program is widely regarded as among the most successful of these state efforts and, like a number of others, is a product of direct democracy. Michigan's program stands alone in placing a dime deposit on containers—double the more conventional nickel—which may contribute to its unusually high compliance rate.

This type of policy has diffused to other products, including tires, for which the federal government has no current policy involvement. A few states began to experiment in the mid-1980s with fees on new tire purchases that could be used to launch a recycling market for old tires. More than forty states now have some version of this policy, which has increased the national recycling rate for scrap tires significantly. In turn, a growing number of states have applied this same approach to other items such as lead-acid batteries, motor oil, pesticide containers, appliances with ozone-depleting substances, and electronic waste materials such as used computers.

States also have authority to tax all forms of energy, which many policy analysts contend may constitute one of the most effective ways to deter environmental degradation, as energy use contributes to so many environmental problems. However, most states have been cautious to move beyond their relatively modest levels of taxation for transportation fuels such as gasoline, which averaged 21.9 cents per gallon in 2008, especially during 2007 and 2008 when the costs for these fuels soared. One possible model in this area involves so-called public benefit funds or social benefit charges, a mechanism used in twenty-two states to tax electricity by both residential and household consumers and channel most of the proceeds to clean-energy alternatives.

Yet another area for state innovation based on economic incentives may be the literal use of state fiscal clout to attempt to leverage environmental change. States preside over substantial funds set aside for investment to support the future retirement of their employees and have increasingly experimented with ways to direct these investments toward socially productive ends while honoring their fiduciary responsibilities. In 2004, for example, California established the Green Wave Environmental Investment Initiative. This effort required the state's two largest public pension funds, with an estimated combined value of over $250 billion, to direct their investments toward "cutting-edge clean technologies and environmentally responsible companies." Many other states are moving in similar directions, frequently guided by elected state treasurers.

Filling the Federal Void: Reducing Greenhouse Gases

Global climate change and the challenge of reducing the release of greenhouse gases such as carbon dioxide and methane have been characterized almost exclusively as the responsibility of national governments and international regimes. The United States has commonly been perceived as disengaged regarding climate policy. This is reflected in the country's 2001 withdrawal from the Kyoto Protocol and failure during the Clinton and Bush administrations to enact policies to reduce these emissions, although this perception may begin to change under the Obama administration (see chapters 12 and 16). In the meantime, states have steadily begun to fill the "policy gap" created by federal inaction, with an increasingly diverse set of policies that address every sector of activity that generates greenhouse gases.

Many states are responsible for substantial amounts of greenhouse gas emissions, even by global standards. If all states were to secede and become independent nations, eighteen of them would rank among the top fifty nations in the world in terms of releases. Texas, for example, exceeds the United Kingdom in emissions, just as Ohio surpasses Turkey. In response, all states have enacted some policy with the effect of reducing greenhouse gases and many have proven extremely active in this area (see Table 2-1). Twenty-eight states representing nearly 60 percent of the U.S. population have enacted "renewable portfolio standards," which mandate that a certain level of state electricity must come from renewable sources such as wind and solar. Under such a policy, Pennsylvania, for example, is required to move from 1.5 percent renewable energy in 2007 to 18 percent by 2020, with significant potential for reducing carbon and other emissions in this transition. In turn, twenty-three states are developing some form of a carbon cap-and-trade system, building on earlier emissions trading experience for other contaminants. For example, ten northeastern states have formed an agreement known as the Regional Greenhouse Gas Initiative, which launched in 2009 a flexible plan to gradually reduce carbon emissions from coal-burning power plants based in the region, using a model similar to that in place in the European Union.[18]

California has been particularly active in this arena, including 2002 legislation that established the first carbon dioxide emissions standards for motor vehicles in North America or Europe. Although this pioneering legislation has been embraced formally by fourteen other states, its implementation is contingent on federal ascent, discussed later in this chapter. But California meanwhile has forged ahead with additional legislation, including the 2006 Global Warming Solutions Act. This legislation imposes a statutory target to reduce statewide emissions to 1990 levels by 2020 and steadily reduce them to a point 80 percent below 1990 levels by 2050. It proposes to attain those goals through an all-out policy assault on virtually every sector that generates greenhouse gases, including industry, electricity, transportation, commercial, and residential activity. A number of states have begun to follow this more comprehensive approach with their own legislation, making them among the most ambitious polities on climate change in the world.

Taking It to the Federal Government

At the same time that states have eclipsed the federal government through new policies, they have also made increasingly aggressive use of litigation to attempt to force the federal government to take new steps or reconsider previous ones. This approach is largely attributable to strong reactions in many state capitals to actions of the Bush administration; how it might evolve under the Obama administration is unclear. But it has been further triggered by an increasingly active set of state attorneys general who have begun to develop joint litigation strategies to influence federal policy. Unlike their federal counterpart, most state attorneys general are elected officials and their powers have expanded significantly since the mid-1970s. They frequently represent a political party different from that of the sitting governor and often use their powers as a base from which to seek higher office. Forty percent of state attorneys general ultimately seek the governorship of their state, and it is no coincidence that prominent national officials such as former president Bill Clinton, Sen. Joseph Lieberman (I-Conn.), and former Bush administration interior secretary Gale Norton were all attorneys general of their respective home states.[19]

Collectively these officials have increasingly become a force to be reckoned with, not only in their home states but also as they expand their engagement through challenges brought into the federal courts. Indeed, one of the most common tactics in recent years has been for coalitions of respective attorneys general to join forces against the federal government and challenge some federal policy or interpretation. In some instances, state organizations such as the Environmental Council of the States or the National Conference of State Legislatures have joined formally in support of these challenges. During the Bush years, for example, different clusters of attorneys general successfully challenged a variety of administration decisions. These challenges included efforts to thwart Bush plans to weaken energy efficiency standards for air conditioners, give far more latitude to electric power plants in making facility upgrades without incorporating new pollution controls, and allow weaker controls on mercury emissions. States also began to explore litigable challenges to federal inaction on climate change, including a multistate suit against the Bush administration for failure to regulate carbon dioxide under the Clean Air Act. In 2007 the U.S. Supreme Court endorsed the state position in *Massachusetts, et al. v. U.S. Environmental Protection Agency*, although the Bush administration resisted the decision and additional litigation ensued.

State Limits

Such a promising set of innovations would seem to augur well for the states' involvement in environmental policy. Any such enthusiasm must be tempered, however, by a continuing concern over how evenly that innovative vigor extends over the entire nation. One enduring rationale for giving the federal government so much authority in environmental policy is that states face inherent limitations in environmental policy. Rather than a consistent, across-the-board pattern of dynamism, we see a more uneven pattern of performance than conventional wisdom might anticipate. Just as some states consistently strive for national leadership, others move in the opposite direction, seemingly doing as little as possible and rarely taking innovative steps. This imbalance becomes particularly evident when environmental problems are not confined to a specific state's boundaries. Many environmental issues are by definition transboundary, raising important questions of interstate and interregional equity in allocating responsibility for the burden of environmental protection.

Uneven State Performance

Many efforts to rank states according to their environmental regulatory rigor, institutional capacity, or general innovativeness find the same subset of states at the top of the list year after year. By contrast, a significant number of states consistently tend to fall much farther down the list, somewhat consistent with their placement in Table 2-1, raising questions as to their overall regulatory capacity and commitment. As political scientist William Lowry notes, "Not all states are responding appropriately to policy needs within their borders.... If matching between need and response were always high and weak programs existed only where pollution was low, this would not be a problem. However, this is not the case."[20] Given all the hoopla surrounding the newfound dynamism of states in environmental policy, and public policy more generally, there has been remarkably little analysis of the performance of states that not only fail to crack top-ten rankings but also consistently lag below the median.

What we do know about such states should surely give one pause over the extent to which state dynamism is truly cross-cutting. Despite considerable economic growth in formerly poor regions, such as the Southeast, substantial variation endures among state governments in their rates of public expenditure, including their total and per-capita expenditures on environmental protection. Such disparities are consistent with studies of state political culture and social capital, which indicate vast differences in likely state receptivity to governmental efforts to foster environmental improvement.[21]

Although many states are unveiling exciting new programs, there is growing reason to worry about how effectively states in general handle core functions either delegated to them under federal programs or left exclusively to their oversight. Studies of water quality program implementation during the 1990s found enormous variation in the methods used by states to determine water quality and in the willingness of states to take enforcement actions when violations were discovered.[22] States also use highly variable water quality standards in areas such as sewage contamination, groundwater protection, nonpoint water pollution, wetland preservation, fish advisories, and beach closures. Inconsistencies abound in reporting accuracy, suggesting that national assessments of water quality trends that rely on data from state reports may be highly suspect.

More recent studies that examine federal policies designed to encourage states to address the burgeoning problem of nonpoint source policy confirm that this variability endures. As one particularly thorough study has concluded, "it appears that Congress's admonitions about achieving high levels of water quality through active state (non-point source) programs have been vigorously pursued in some cases and not in others."[23] Even in high-saliency cases, such as the protection of the Everglades, the state has preferred a federal rescue rather than unilateral action. As political scientist Sheldon Kamieniecki notes, Florida's "state government, which has been continuously pressured from all sides, has waffled in its intentions to improve the wetlands ecosystem in South Florida."[24]

Comparable problems have emerged in state enforcement of air quality and waste management programs, where officially reported numbers on regulatory actions, emissions levels, waste disposal capacity, and waste reduction levels are of similarly questionable utility.[25] Despite efforts in some states to integrate and streamline permitting, many states have extensive backlogs in the permit programs they operate and thereby have no real indication of facility compliance with various regulatory standards. Indeed, states appear divided over whether they would even utilize expanded authority in the air quality arena. Under Section 116 of the Clean Air Act Amendments, for example, states have the option of securing greater stringency than under federal standards. But only twenty-four states allow their lead agencies to consider adopting more stringent standards, whereas twenty-four others preclude such steps "except under certain limited conditions" and the remaining two preclude such action entirely.[26]

A number of studies since the early 1990s have raised serious questions about basic program implementation in a number of states, including a scathing 1998 assessment by the EPA inspector general.[27] These analyses concluded that, in many states, major violations of federal environmental laws often go unreported, permit deadlines are routinely ignored, and mandatory emissions tests frequently are not conducted. These problems appear particularly extensive in certain states, many with significant concentrations of large industry. In 2004, for example, twenty-nine states were found to have created "legal loopholes" that allow major air emissions "spikes" from facility malfunctions and start-ups to be ignored and thereby keep regulated firms in compliance with federal law.[28]

Measurement of the impact of state programs on environmental outcomes remains imprecise in many areas. Existing indicators confirm the enormous variation among states, although less is known about such variation than in the 1990s, given that federal agencies such as the EPA have simply stopped collecting state-by-state data in many areas of environmental policy. State governments—alongside their local counterparts—have understandably claimed much of the credit for increasing solid waste recycling rates from a national average of 10 percent in 1990 to 32 percent in 2005. At the same time, state recycling performance varies markedly, as do per-capita rates of toxic waste generation and greenhouse gas release.

Enduring Federal Dependency

More sweeping assertions of state resurgence are undermined further by the penchant of many states to cling to organizational designs and program priorities set in Washington, D.C. Although some states have demonstrated that far-reaching agency reorganization and other integrative policies can be pursued without significant opposition—or grant reduction—from the federal government, the vast majority of states continue to adhere to a medium-based pollution control framework for agency organization that contributes to enduring programmatic fragmentation. Although a growing number of state officials speak favorably about shifting toward integrative approaches, many remain hard pressed to demonstrate how their states have begun to move in that direction. Many Clinton-era federal initiatives to give states more freedom to innovate were used to streamline operations rather than foster prevention or integration. The Bush administration weakened many of these initiatives and, more generally, proved extremely reluctant to give states expanded authority or encouragement to innovate.[29]

In fact, a good deal of the most innovative state-level activity has been at least partially stimulated—and underwritten—through federal grants. Indeed, in Canada, where central government grant assistance—and regulatory presence—is extremely limited, provinces have proven far less innovative than their American state counterparts.[30] Although a number of states have developed fee systems to cover a growing portion of their costs, many continue to rely heavily on federal grants to fund some core environmental protection activities. States have continued to receive other important types of federal support, including grants and technical assistance to complete "state-of-the-state" environment reports, undertake comparative risk assessment projects, launch inventories and action plans for greenhouse gas reductions, and implement some voluntary federal programs. On the whole, states have received between one-quarter and one-third of their total environmental and natural resource program funding from federal grants in recent decades, although a few states rely on the federal government for as much as 40 to 50 percent of their total funding.[31]

Furthermore, for all the opprobrium heaped on the federal government in environmental policy, it has provided states with at least four other forms of valuable assistance, some of which has contributed directly to the resurgence and innovation of state environmental policy. First, federal development in 1986 of a Toxics Release Inventory, modeled after programs initially attempted in Maryland and New Jersey, has emerged as a vital component of many of the most promising state policy initiatives. This program has generated unprecedented information concerning toxic releases and has provided states with an essential data source for exploring alternative regulatory approaches.[32] Many state pollution prevention programs would be unthinkable without such an annual information source. This program has also provided a model for other disclosure and emissions efforts, such as the thirty-nine-state Climate Registry, a bottom-up attempt to establish a unified database for carbon emissions. Second, states remain almost totally dependent on the federal government for essential insights gained through research and development. Each year the federal government outspends the states in environmental research and development by substantial amounts, and states have shown little inclination to assume this burden by funding research programs tailored to their particular technological and informational needs.

Third, many successful efforts to coordinate environmental protection on a multistate, regional basis have received considerable federal input and support. A series of initiatives in the Chesapeake Bay, the Great Lakes Basin, and New England have received much acclaim for tackling difficult issues and forging regional partnerships; federal participation—through grants, technical assistance, coordination, and efforts to unify regional standards—has proven useful in these cases.[33] By contrast, other major bioregions, including Puget Sound, the Gulf of Mexico, the Columbia River system, and the Mississippi River Basin, have lacked comparable federal participation and have generally not experienced creative interstate partnerships.[34] Their experience contradicts the popular thesis that regional coordination only improves when central authority is minimal or nonexistent, although recent regional initiatives to reduce greenhouse gases in the northeast and the west or to prevent large-scale water diversions in the Great Lakes have in fact moved ahead without active federal engagement or support.[35]

Fourth, the EPA's ham-handedness is legendary, but its role in overseeing state-level program implementation looks far more constructive when examining the role played by the agency's ten regional offices. Most state-level interaction with the EPA involves such regional offices, which employ approximately two-thirds of the total EPA workforce. Relations between state and regional officials are generally more cordial and constructive than those between state and central EPA officials, and such relations may even be, in some instances, characterized by high levels of mutual involvement and trust.[36] Regional offices have played a central role in many of the most promising state-level innovations, including those in Minnesota and New Jersey. Their involvement may include formal advocacy on behalf of the state with central headquarters, direct collaboration on meshing state initiatives with federal requirements, and special grant support or technical assistance. This appears to be particularly common when regional office heads have prior state experience, as was evident in a number of instances in both the Clinton and Bush administrations.

The Interstate Environmental Balance of Trade

States may be structurally ill-equipped to handle a large range of environmental concerns. In particular, they may be reluctant to invest significant energies to tackle problems that might literally migrate to another state in the absence of intervention. The days of state agencies being captured securely in the hip pockets of major industries are probably long gone, reflecting fundamental changes in state government.[37] Nonetheless, state regulatory dynamism does appear to diminish in the face of such cross-boundary issues.

The state imperative of economic development clearly contributes to this phenomenon. As states increasingly devise development strategies that resemble the industrial policies of European Union nations, a range of scholars have concluded they are far more deeply committed to strategies that promote investment or development than to those that involve social service provision or public health promotion.[38] A number of states now offer incentives in excess of $50,000 per new job to prospective developers and have intensified efforts to retain jobs in the struggling manufacturing sector. Environmental protection can be eminently compatible with economic development goals, promoting overall quality of life and general environmental attractiveness that entices private investment. In many states, the tourism industry has played an active role in seeking strong environmental programs designed to maintain natural assets. In some instances, states may be keen to take action that may produce internal environmental benefits while not having much internal economic impact. California and other states that have formally endorsed setting strict carbon emissions standards from vehicles, for example, have very few jobs in the vehicle manufacturing sector.

But much of what a state might undertake in environmental policy may largely benefit other states or regions, thereby reducing an individual state's incentive to take meaningful action. In fact, in many instances, states continue to pursue a "we make it, you take it" strategy. As political scientist William Gormley Jr. notes, sometimes "states can readily export their problems to other states," resulting in potentially serious environmental "balance of trade" problems.[39] In such situations, states may be inclined to export environmental contaminants to other states while enjoying any economic benefits to be derived from the activity that generated the contamination.

Such cross-boundary transfer takes many forms and may be particularly prevalent in environmental policy areas in which long-distance migration of pollutants is most likely. Air quality policy has long fit this pattern. States such as Ohio and Pennsylvania, for example, have depended heavily on burning massive quantities of high-sulfur coal to meet energy demands. Prevailing winds invariably transfer pollutants from this activity to other regions, particularly New England, leading to serious concern about acid deposition and related contamination threats. In turn, states throughout the nation have relied heavily on so-called dispersion enhancement to improve local air quality. Average industrial stack height in the United States soared from 243 feet in 1960 to 730 feet in 1980.[40] Although this increase resulted in significant air quality improvement in many areas near elevated stacks, it generally served to disperse air pollution problems elsewhere. It has also contributed to the growing problem of airborne toxics that ultimately pollute water or land in other regions. Between 80 and 90 percent of many of the most dangerous toxic substances found in Lake Superior, for example, stem from air deposition, much of which is generated outside of the Great Lakes Basin.

Growing interstate conflicts, often becoming protracted battles in the federal courts, have emerged in recent decades as states allege they are recipients of such unwanted "imports." Midwestern and eastern states continue to be mired in a number of these disputes. Even a multiyear effort funded by the EPA to encourage all thirty-seven states east of the Rocky Mountains to find a collective solution to the transport of ground-level ozone failed to produce agreements on core recommendations. But no region of the nation appears immune from this kind of conflict. In 2008 a battle of nearly two decades among Alabama, Florida, and Georgia over access to waters from Lake Lanier and six rivers that cross their borders reached new intensity. Given growing water scarcity in these high-growth states, federal mediation by then–Interior secretary Dirk Kempthorne failed to establish a new water-sharing agreement by an established March 1 deadline. This failure triggered a flurry of additional litigation, leaving the fate of this common resource uncertain.[41]

Perhaps nowhere is the problem of interstate transfer more evident than in the disposal of solid, hazardous, and nuclear wastes. In many respects states have been given enormous latitude to devise their own systems of waste management and facility siting, working either independently or in concert with other states. Many states, including a number of those usually deemed among the most innovative and committed environmentally, continue to generate massive quantities of waste and have been hugely unsuccessful in siting modern treatment, storage, and disposal facilities. Instead, out-of-state (and region) export has been an increasingly common pattern, with wastes often shipped to facilities opened before concern over waste and facility siting became widespread. At its worst, the system resembles a shell game in which waste is ultimately deposited in the least resistant state or facility at a given moment. In Michigan, a proactive effort to develop long-term capacity for solid waste management in previous decades has backfired, with the state serving as a magnet of sorts for waste from several other states as well as the Canadian province of Ontario. However, no area of waste management is as contentious as high-level nuclear waste, which requires between 10,000 and 100,000 years of isolation. A quarter-century intergovernmental battle to ship all of these wastes, most of which are generated east of the Mississippi River, to a site in Nevada, which generates no such wastes, illustrates the intense distributional politics involved in such matters.

Rethinking Environmental Federalism

The presidency of George W. Bush raised a new set of questions concerning the future of state and federal government roles in environmental policy. Bush's record as Texas governor and his 2000 campaign rhetoric suggested considerable sympathy for decentralization strategies in environmental protection and other areas. During the 2000 campaign, Bush called for increased transfer of environmental program enforcement to state governments. He also relied heavily on former state officials to assume leadership roles in federal regulatory agencies with environmental jurisdiction. This was perhaps most notable at the EPA, where Bush tapped New Jersey governor Christine Todd Whitman to serve as administrator and suggested possible intergovernmental bargaining whereby some federal grant cuts might be accompanied by greater delegation of authority to states.

Any possibility of a devolutionary approach disappeared quickly, reflected in Whitman's short tenure and a series of policies designed to expand the federal role over states. Some of these shifts may have been accelerated by the administration's focus on consolidating power after the September 11, 2001, terrorist attacks, but more generally they appeared to reflect a strategy to concentrate power within the executive branch of the federal government. Whether taking the form of a legislative amendment or an administrative reinterpretation of existing statute, many efforts were made to constrain state power, including reduced authority in dam licensure cases, siting of controversial facilities such as energy import terminals, or input into permitting decisions for select industries.[42]

Perhaps the clearest indicator of the Bush administration's approach toward the states occurred in 2008, when the EPA rejected California's request for a waiver from federal legislation to implement a carbon emissions reduction program for vehicles (see chapter 7). This step was the first such rejection of a waiver from Sacramento in the nearly four decades since this provision was established in response to early California action on air quality. This conflict is reflective of the widespread hostility between state and federal authorities in many areas of environmental protection that expanded dramatically during the 2000s. As one veteran state environmental agency head noted in 2006, after a gradual and extended effort to foster intergovernmental collaboration, "now it's just blown to hell."[43] In his 2008 presidential campaign, Barack Obama expressed support for granting California its waiver request and his administration's response to this issue may be a useful barometer to its approach to environmental federalism.

A Failed Attempt at Accountable Decentralization

It has been difficult for any recent administration to achieve major shifts in federal and state authority in environmental policy, leaving many uncertainties facing President Obama and his successors. The Clinton administration learned this lesson through the limited impact of its National Environmental Performance Partnership System (NEPPS), launched in May 1995. NEPPS was linked to Clinton efforts to reinvent government and was heralded as a way to give states substantially greater flexibility in the management of many federal environmental programs if they could demonstrate innovation and actual performance in improving environmental quality. NEPPS also offered Performance Partnership Grants that would allow participating states to concentrate resources on innovative projects that promised environmental performance improvements.

More than forty states elected to participate in the NEPPS program, which required extensive negotiations between state and federal agency counterparts. Although a few promising examples of innovation can be noted, this initiative failed to approach its ambitious goals and, in the words of two recent analysts, "there have been few real gains."[44] NEPPS stemmed from an administrative action and thereby lacked the clout of legislation. In response, federal authorities at the EPA often resisted altering established practices and thereby did not demonstrate the creativity or flexibility anticipated by

NEPPS proponents. In turn, states proved far less amenable to innovation than expected. They tended to balk at any possibility that the federal government would establish—and publicize—serious performance measures that would evaluate their effectiveness and determine their ability to deviate from federal controls.

Ultimately many NEPPS agreements were signed, especially in the waning years of the Clinton administration, and remain in place. But the Bush administration never pursued NEPPS with enthusiasm or as a precedent for an expanded method to reallocate federal and state authority. It thereby remains a very limited test of the viability of accountable decentralization, whereby state autonomy is increased formally in exchange for demonstrable performance.

Challenges to State Routines

The future role of states in environmental policy may be further shaped by three additional developments. First, it remains increasingly unclear whether states will have sufficient fiscal resources to maintain core environmental protection functions and continue to consider new initiatives. Most states enjoyed generally robust fiscal health during the middle years of the 2000s, with overall tax revenues growing and swelling both annual surpluses and rainy-day funds. However, state fiscal conditions became increasingly gloomy in subsequent years, as the economic decline in many regions and crises in the housing and banking sectors served to shrink state coffers and prompt serious consideration of major program cuts in many statehouses. A 2008 assessment by the National Association of State Budget Officers found that eighteen states were planning to reduce their overall budgets below current levels for fiscal year 2010 and overall projected spending increases were among the lowest in more than three decades. In turn, pressures for expanded spending in certain domains, such as medical care, further threatened state fiscal support for environmental protection. A number of states with long-standing records of active engagement in environmental policy innovation, including California and New York, were beginning to contemplate potentially large reductions of state personnel.

Second, the 2008 election reversed somewhat a pattern of divided, joint-party control of state government. Although most attention was focused on the presidential and congressional elections, Democrats also experienced considerable success in state races, taking majorities in both legislative chambers in Delaware, Nevada, New York, and Wisconsin and picking up one governorship (in Missouri). As a result, Democrats began 2009 with unified control of legislative and executive branches in twenty-seven states, whereas Republicans maintained comparative control in only fourteen. This reflected a continuing shift from recent decades in which the majority of states had some form of divided party control. Environmental and energy issues were significant concerns in a number of state races, raising questions of whether growing Democratic control in state and federal governments will translate into new environmental policy steps.

Third, the 2008 election opened up the possibility of new federal environmental legislation, with substantial ramifications for state and federal relations. As discussed elsewhere in this volume, many pieces of federal environmental law could be candidates for revision. But climate change is quite likely to be a dominant issue for President Obama and the 111th Congress, with deliberations most likely to focus on some version of a carbon cap-and-trade program. To date, much of the discussion over a federal carbon trading regime has advanced as if the United States were a unitary system of government. Indeed, the first 420 congressional hearings on climate change, between 1975 and 2008, gave scant attention to state and intergovernmental concerns, much less consideration of any lessons that might be derived from state experience in fashioning a federal strategy.

But intergovernmental issues are bound to arise in the 111th Congress and beyond. No two states (or their federal representatives) are likely to have similar reactions to prospective federal legislation. Even before the new president and Congress were sworn into office in 2009, ten northeastern states launched their own version of a carbon cap-and-trade program, and work was continuing toward implementing somewhat similar policies among clusters of western and midwestern states. In contrast, the remaining states had made no such commitment. So it remains unclear how the federal government might enter into a policy playing field in which nearly one-half of the states are already engaged whereas the remainder are not.[45]

The possible complexities became evident in June 2008, when Sen. Barbara Boxer, D-Calif., indicated that a federal cap-and-trade program would produce substantial revenue, some of which would be returned to states. She estimated that one federal proposal then under review would shift some $565 billion back to states over its lifetime but gave no formula for allocation. Almost immediately, different positions on this issue emerged from various states. For states such as California, with substantial investment in climate change policy, the argument was advanced that they should be rewarded for taking early action. In contrast, others such as many in the Southeast, argued that they lacked experience in this arena and that funds should come their way to compensate them for major disruptions likely to accompany implementation. States with extended coastal areas, such as Alaska, contended that they deserved a substantial share of the bounty to begin to prepare for adaptation to rising sea levels. The possible counterarguments are endless but underscore the inherent intergovernmental and state government issues even in an area that has generally been portrayed as one that will be dominated by Washington.

Looking Ahead

Amid the continued squabbling over the proper role of the federal government vis-à-vis the states in environmental policy, remarkably little effort has been made to sort out which functions might best be concentrated in Washington and which transferred to state capitals. Some current and retired federal legislators of both parties offered useful proposals during the 1990s that might allocate such responsibilities more reasonably than at present. These proposals have been supplemented by thoughtful scholarly works by think tanks, political scientists, economists, and other policy analysts. Interestingly, many of these experts concur that environmental protection policy defies easy designation as warranting extreme centralization or decentralization. Instead, many observers endorse a process of selective decentralization, one leading to an appropriately balanced set of responsibilities across governmental levels. It might be particularly useful to revisit these options before taking major new environmental policy steps, including any far-reaching federal effort to address climate change.

In moving toward a more functional environmental federalism, certain broad design principles might be useful to consider. The Clinton administration experiment with NEPPS was billed as a major attempt at such reallocation, but a more serious effort would require establishment of state environmental performance measures that were publicized and utilized to determine a more appropriate allocation of functions. This would, in all likelihood, require legislation rather than managerial experimentation that can be erased as political leadership changes. It would also demand new flexibility from the EPA as well as a newfound willingness of states to be held accountable for their performance and treated accordingly.

A more discerning environmental federalism might also begin by concentrating federal regulatory energies on problems that are clearly national in character. Many air and water pollution problems, for example, are by definition cross-boundary concerns unlikely to be resolved by a series of unilateral state actions. In contrast, problems such as protecting indoor air quality and cleanup of abandoned hazardous waste dumps may present more geographically confinable challenges; they are perhaps best handled through substantial delegation of authority to states. As policy analyst John Donahue notes, "most waste sites are situated within a single state, and stay there," yet are governed by highly centralized Superfund legislation, in direct contrast to more decentralized programs in environmental areas in which cross-boundary transfers are prevalent.[46] Under a more rational system, the federal regulatory presence might intensify as the likelihood of cross-boundary contaminant transfer escalates.

Such an initial attempt to sort out functions might be reinforced by federal policy efforts to encourage states or regions to take responsibility for internally generated environmental problems rather than tacitly allow exportation to occur. In the area of waste management, for example, federal per-mile fees on waste shipment might provide a disincentive for long-distance transfer, instead encouraging states, regions, and waste generators to either develop their own capacity or pursue waste reduction options more aggressively. In the rapidly evolving area of climate change, the federal government might assess fees for each ton of released greenhouse gases from various fossil fuels such as coal and natural gas. The creation of such a federal "carbon tax" would provide an incentive to reduce emissions nationwide and a pool of funds that might be used for mitigation, adaptation, and other strategies. This would also create incentives for states to continue to innovate and to develop locally tailored strategies to reduce their emissions, thereby reducing their carbon tax burden and simultaneously pursuing other goals, such as expanded development of local sources of renewable energy, land use reforms to reduce vehicle use, or capture of methane from solid waste landfills.

In many areas, some shared federal and state role remains appropriate, reflecting the inherent complexity of many environmental problems. Effective intergovernmental partnerships may already be well established in certain areas. Even a 1995 National Academy of Public Administration study that excoriated many aspects of federal environmental policy conceded that the existing partnership between federal and state governments "is basically sound, and major structural changes are not warranted. The system has worked."[47] But even if essentially sound, the partnership could clearly benefit from further maturation, especially after a period of strained relations that emerged during the George W. Bush presidency. Alongside the sorting-out activities discussed earlier in this section, both federal and state governments could do much more to promote creative sharing of policy ideas and environmental data. Such information has received remarkably limited dissemination across state and regional boundaries, and potentially considerable advantage is to be gained from an active process of intergovernmental policy learning. More broadly, the federal government might explore other ways to encourage states to work cooperatively, especially on common-boundary problems. State capacity to find creative solutions to pressing environmental problems is on the ascendance, as we have seen. But as Lord Bryce concluded many decades ago, cooperation among states does not arise automatically.

Suggested Web Sites

Environmental Council of the States (www.ecos.org) The Environmental Council of the States represents the lead environmental protection agencies of all fifty states. The site contains access to state environmental data as well as the organization's monthly publication, *Green Reports.*

Initiative and Referendum Institute (www.iandrinstitute.org) The Initiative and Referendum Institute is affiliated with the Law School of the University of Southern California and provides detailed analysis of state-based direct democracy activities, including a special focus on environmental ballot propositions.

National Conference of State Legislatures (www.ncsl.org) The National Conference of State Legislatures conducts extensive research on a wide range of environmental, energy, and natural resource issues for its primary constituency, state legislators, as well as the general citizenry. The organization offers an extensive set of publications, including specialized reports and books.

National Governors Association (www.nga.org) The National Governors Association maintains an active research program concerning state environmental protection, natural resource, and energy concerns. It has placed special emphasis on maintaining a database on state "best practices," which it uses to promote diffusion of promising innovations and to demonstrate state government capacity in federal policy deliberations.

Stateline (www.stateline.org) The Pew Center on the States sponsors this site, which provides a number of useful vantage points for examining state politics and policy. There are special sections for environmental and energy policy. This site is particularly strong in providing information on state election results and offering links to articles about state issues published in periodicals across the nation.

Notes

1. Mark Carl Rom, "Policy Races in the American States," in *Racing to the Bottom?* ed. Kathryn Harrison (Vancouver: University of British Columbia Press, 2006), 229–256.
2. Robert S. Erikson, Gerald C. Wright, and John P. McIver, *Statehouse Democracy: Public Opinion and Policy in the American States* (New York: Cambridge University Press, 1993).
3. John Kincaid and Richard L. Cole, "Public Opinion on Issues of Federalism in 2007: A Bush Plus?" *Publius: The Journal of Federalism* 38 (summer 2008): 469–487.
4. Paul Teske, *Regulation in the States* (Washington, D.C.: Brookings Institution Press, 2004), 9.
5. William T. Gormley Jr., "Money and Mandates: The Politics of Intergovernmental Conflict," *Publius: The Journal of Federalism* 36 (fall 2006): 523–540; R. Daniel Keleman, *The Rules of Federalism* (Cambridge: Harvard University Press, 2004), 63.
6. Suellen Keiner, *Room at the Bottom? Potential State Strategies for Managing the Risk and Benefits of Nanotechnology* (Washington, D.C.: Woodrow Wilson International Center for Scholars, 2008), 7–8.
7. DeWitt John, *Civic Environmentalism: Alternatives to Regulation in States and Communities* (Washington, D.C.: CQ Press, 1994), 80; John and Marian Mlay, "Community-Based Environmental Protection: Encouraging Civic Environmentalism," in *Better Environmental Decisions: Strategies for Governments, Businesses, and Communities,* ed. Ken Sexton et al. (Washington, D.C.: Island Press, 1999), 353–376.
8. J. Clarence Davies et al., *Reforming Permitting* (Washington, D.C.: Resources for the Future, 2001), 58.
9. Christopher McGrory Klyza and David Sousa, *American Environmental Policy, 1990–2006: Beyond Gridlock* (Cambridge: MIT Press, 2008), 247.
10. Barry G. Rabe, "Governing the Climate from Sacramento," in *Unlocking the Power of Networks,* ed. Stephen Goldsmith and Donald F. Kettl (Washington, D.C.: Brookings Institution Press, 2009), 34–61.
11. John, *Civic Environmentalism.*
12. Elinor Ostrom, *Governing the Commons: The Evolution of Institutions for Collective Action* (New York: Cambridge University Press, 1990); Elinor Ostrom, Roy Gardner, and James Walker, *Rules, Games, and Common-Pool Resources* (Ann Arbor: University of Michigan Press, 1994). For a contrary view, see Edward P. Schwartz and Michael R. Tomz, "The Long-Run Advantages of Centralization for Collective Action," *American Political Science Review* 91 (September 1997): 685–694.
13. Daniel P. Carpenter, *The Forging of Bureaucratic Autonomy* (Princeton: Princeton University Press, 2001); Michael Mintrom, *Policy Entrepreneurs and School Choice* (Washington, D.C.: Georgetown University Press, 2000).
14. Barry G. Rabe, *Statehouse and Greenhouse: The Emerging Politics of American Climate Change Policy* (Washington, D.C.: Brookings Institution Press, 2004).
15. Christopher Conney and Paul Glader, "Mass-Transit Projects Fared Surprisingly Well as Voters Preferred New Taxes to High Gas Prices," *Wall Street Journal,* November 12, 2008, A6.

16. Andrew Karch, *Democratic Laboratories: Policy Diffusion among the American States* (Ann Arbor: University of Michigan Press, 2007).
17. Evan J. Ringquist, *Environmental Protection at the State Level: Politics and Progress in Controlling Pollution* (Armonk, N.Y.: M. E. Sharpe, 1993); James P. Lester, "A New Federalism? Environmental Policy in the States," in *Environmental Policy in the 1990s*, ed. Norman J. Vig and Michael E. Kraft (Washington, D.C.: CQ Press, 1994), 51–68.
18. Barry G. Rabe, "Regionalism and Global Climate Change Policy: Revisiting Multistate Collaboration as an Intergovernmental Management Tool," in *Intergovernmental Management in the 21st Century*, ed. Timothy J. Conlan and Paul L. Posner (Washington, D.C.: Brookings Institution Press, 2008), 176–208; Tom Arrandale, "Carbon Goes to Market," *Governing* (September 2008): 26–30.
19. Colin Provost, "State Attorneys General, Entrepreneurship, and Consumer Protection in the New Federalism," *Publius: The Journal of Federalism* 33 (spring 2003): 37–53.
20. William R. Lowry, *The Dimensions of Federalism: State Governments and Pollution Control Policies* (Durham: Duke University Press, 1992), 125.
21. Robert D. Putnam, *Bowling Alone: The Collapse and Revival of American Community* (New York: Simon and Schuster, 2000), sect. 4; Tom W. Rice and Alexander F. Sumberg, "Civic Culture and Government Performance in the American States," *Publius: The Journal of Federalism* 27 (winter 1997): 99–114.
22. U.S. General Accounting Office (GAO, renamed the Government Accountability Office), "Water Pollution: Differences among the States in Issuing Permits Limiting the Discharge of Pollutants" (Washington, D.C.: GAO, 1996); Robert W. Adler, Jessica C. Landman, and Diane M. Cameron, *The Clean Water Act 20 Years Later* (Washington, D.C.: Island Press, 1993).
23. John A. Hoornbeek, "The Promise and Pitfalls of Devolution: Water Pollution Policies in the American States," *Publius: The Journal of Federalism* 35 (winter 2005): 87–114.
24. Sheldon Kamieniecki, *Corporate America and Environmental Policy* (Palo Alto: Stanford University Press, 2006), 253.
25. Ringquist, *Environmental Protection at the State Level*; Daniel A. Mazmanian and David Morell, *Beyond Superfailure: America's Toxics Policy for the 1990s* (Boulder: Westview Press, 1992), 107–110.
26. Keiner, *Room at the Bottom?* 21–23.
27. U.S. Environmental Protection Agency (EPA), *Office of Inspector General Semiannual Report to Congress* (Washington, D.C.: EPA, May 1998); John H. Cushman Jr., "E.P.A. and States Found to Be Lax on Pollution Law," *New York Times*, June 7, 1998, 1.
28. Kelly Haragan, *Gaming the System* (Washington, D.C.: Environmental Integrity Project, 2004).
29. Barry G. Rabe, "Environmental Policy and the Bush Era: The Collision between the Administrative Presidency and State Experimentation," *Publius: The Journal of Federalism* 37 (summer 2007): 413–431.
30. David R. Boyd, *Unnatural Law: Rethinking Canadian Environmental Law and Policy* (Vancouver: University of British Columbia Press, 2003).
31. R. Steven Brown and Michael J. Kiefer, "Budgets Are Bruised, But Still Strong," *ECOStates* (summer 2003): 10–15.
32. James T. Hamilton, *Regulation through Revelation* (Cambridge: Cambridge University Press, 2005).
33. Tom Horton and William M. Eichbaum, *Turning the Tide: Saving the Chesapeake Bay* (Washington, D.C.: Island Press, 1991); Barry G. Rabe and Marc Gaden, "Sustainability in a Regional Context: The Case of the Great Lakes Basin," in *Toward Sustainable Communities: Transition and Transformations in Environmental Policy*, ed. Daniel A Mazmanian and Michael E. Kraft, 2d ed. (Cambridge: MIT Press, 2009), 266–269.
34. Adler, Landman, and Cameron, *The Clean Water Act 20 Years Later*, 221–224, 251.
35. Rabe, "Regionalism and Global Climate Change Policy"; Peter Annin, *The Great Lakes Water Wars* (Washington, D.C.: Island Press, 2006).

36. Denise Scheberle, *Federalism and Environmental Policy: Trust and the Politics of Implementation,* revised ed. (Washington, D.C.: Georgetown University Press, 2004), chap. 7.
37. Teske, *Regulation in the States.*
38. John D. Donahue, *Disunited States: What's at Stake as Washington Fades and the States Take the Lead* (New York: Basic Books, 1997); Paul E. Peterson, *The Price of Federalism* (Washington, D.C.: Brookings Institution Press), chap. 4; Frank R. Baumgartner and Bryan D. Jones, *Agendas and Instability in American Politics* (Chicago: University of Chicago Press, 1993), chap. 11.
39. William T. Gormley Jr., "Intergovernmental Conflict on Environmental Policy: The Attitudinal Connection," *Western Political Quarterly* 40 (1987): 298–299.
40. Lowry, *The Dimensions of Federalism,* 45.
41. John Dinan, "The State of American Federalism 2007–2008," *Publius: The Journal of Federalism* 38 (summer 2008): 400–401; Alan Greenblatt, "Southern Water Torture," *Governing* (February 2008): 15–16.
42. Barry G. Rabe, "Environmental Policy and the Bush Era," 417–420.
43. Tom Arrandale, "Tigers No More," *Governing* (April 2006): 68.
44. Klyza and Sousa, *American Environmental Policy, 1990–2006,* 253.
45. Barry G. Rabe, "States on Steroids: The Intergovernmental Odyssey of American Climate Change Policy," *Review of Policy Research* 25 (March 2008): 105–128.
46. Donahue, *Disunited States,* 65.
47. National Academy of Public Administration (NAPA), *Setting Priorities, Getting Results: A New Direction for EPA* (Washington, D.C.: NAPA, 1995), 71.

3

Past the Tipping Point?
Public Discourse and the Role of the Environmental Movement in a Post-Bush Era

Deborah Lynn Guber and Christopher J. Bosso

It was, some might say, a year of improbable events. In 2007, after languishing for decades on the back burner of American politics, the issue of global warming was thrust into the mainstream at last by a low-budget documentary that in cinematic terms amounted to little more than "a man, a message, and a scary slide show."[1] Within months, those associated with the film *An Inconvenient Truth,* including its narrator—former presidential candidate Al Gore—had earned, in some combination or another, a Grammy nomination, an Emmy award, and two Oscars.[2] When it was announced later that year that Gore would share a Nobel Peace Prize for his efforts, alongside the experts who had labored long on the U.N. Intergovernmental Panel on Climate Change (IPCC), the environmental movement, its chief scientists, and its most prominent champion suddenly found themselves elevated to the ranks of Mother Theresa, Nelson Mandela, and the Dalai Lama.

If Gore's transition from "presidential loser into Saint Al, the earnest, impassioned, pointer-wielding Cassandra of the environmental movement" was a surprise to some, the public conversion of his political nemesis, George W. Bush, was no less dramatic.[3] Ever since Bush's inauguration in 2001, the League of Conservation Voters had branded him "the most anti-environmental president in our nation's history" for his efforts to weaken the Clean Air Act and the Clean Water Act and his persistent demands to drill for oil in the Arctic National Wildlife Refuge (ANWR).[4] The Bush administration had long been reticent on the subject of global warming, but when the IPCC's work was finalized in early 2007, its rhetoric—if not its policies—abruptly changed course.[5] The White House heralded the study as a "landmark" report that reflected a "sizeable and robust body of knowledge regarding the physical science of climate change," including the finding that "the Earth is warming" and that human activities are "very likely" the dominant cause.[6] In a speech on energy security delivered at the State Department in early autumn, even Bush had to concede that our understanding of the issue had "come a long way."[7]

When the president caught up with his former rival at a White House reception for Nobel laureates shortly after Thanksgiving 2007, and the two fell into a private conversation about global warming that was described afterward as "very nice" and "very cordial," the peculiar event further underscored the obvious.[8] It may have been a bad year for the environment and for melting polar ice caps in particular, but for activists who had spent the better part of twenty years pressing the issue onto the public stage, 2007 was a very good year, indeed.[9]

Scientists use the term *tipping point* to refer to the threshold at which a system's state is irretrievably altered. Regarding global warming, some observers believe that moment will come with the destruction of the Amazon rainforests, the collapse of monsoon season, or the loss of sea ice in summer.[10] For scholars who study the politics of problem definition, the concept seems to work equally well.[11] In fact, since the publication in 2000 of Malcolm Gladwell's book of the same name, the term has become part of the vernacular of politics, applied not just to the environment, but to situations as diverse as the war in Iraq, genocide in Darfur, consumer confidence in the economy, and candidate momentum during presidential campaigns.[12] Based on that collection of experiences, the phrase can be taken to mean any (or all) of the following:

- The point at which awareness and understanding of an issue reaches critical mass[13]
- The point at which an issue's opponents "throw in the towel" and accept the inevitable[14]
- The point at which urgency forces lawmakers to take decisive action[15]

With those standards in mind, the year 2007—with its unlikely fusion of science, politics, and old-fashioned Hollywood glamour—may well have marked a long-awaited tipping point for climate change. The IPCC report confirming that evidence of warming was "unequivocal" forced all but the most diehard skeptics to acknowledge scientific consensus on the nature of the problem, if not its precise solution.[16] For some observers, that gave reason to hope that two major and related barriers to action would likewise be relieved, at least over time: the media's stubborn professional commitment to a narrowly construed "norm of balance" in their coverage of global warming, on the one hand, and the public's persistent belief that the science remains unsettled, on the other.[17]

In the meantime, however, the shift from science to politics brought an even more advantageous and unexpected twist. In January 2007, on the eve of the annual State of the Union address, the CEOs of ten major corporations urged President Bush to set a mandatory ceiling on greenhouse gas emissions.[18] By November, in what one columnist called "an unprecedented show of solidarity," the leaders of 150 global companies, including Coca-Cola, General Electric, Nike, and Shell, were calling for a "legally binding framework" in which they could invest wisely in low-carbon technologies, without the fear of placing themselves and their stockholders at a competitive disadvantage in the marketplace.[19] Corporate America, its fingers firmly on the public's pulse, apparently wanted government to take the lead.[20] At least on the surface, some of global warming's most powerful adversaries seemed poised to become its allies.

Finally, in perhaps the most significant development of 2007, environmentalists had reason to celebrate policy success at last—not in Washington, perhaps, but in a multitude of initiatives passed at regional, state, and local levels (see chapters 2 and 12).[21] In 2007, thirty-six states had "climate action plans" in place or under development, led by California and its Republican governor, Arnold Schwarzenegger, while the mayors of 522 cities had agreed to abide by the standards of the Kyoto Protocol despite the reluctance of national lawmakers to do to the same.[22]

By the end of the year, American environmentalism seemed at a crossroads. According to the Pulitzer Prize–winning columnist Thomas L. Friedman, it could no longer be dismissed as entirely "liberal," "tree-hugging," "unpatriotic," or "vaguely French." For citizens, corporations, and governments alike, Friedman insisted that being green was now "the most patriotic, capitalistic, geopolitical, healthy and competitive thing they could do."[23] But for the foot soldiers of the movement—those made cautious by decades of disappointment, resistance, and delay—the contours of this new terrain were less obvious and the challenge of deciding what to do next loomed large.[24]

In this chapter we explore the politics of climate change as emblematic of a new age of environmentalism in the United States, and the opportunities and constraints it imposes on political actors and the institutions they inhabit. In doing so, we look to the vagaries of public opinion on environmental issues, the difficulty of translating broad public support into substantive policy outcomes, and the role of the environmental movement in linking mass attitudes to government action. For everyone involved, much—but certainly not all—of the political opportunity structure shaping environmental policymaking was reconfigured dramatically with the election of President Barack Obama and the enlargement of Democratic majorities in both chambers of Congress. Taken as a whole, the events of 2007 and the results of the 2008 election solidified a momentous shift from the previous eight years. Even so, and even as we argue that the debate over the science of global warming is indeed at an end, a wider and more significant ground war over public opinion, the range of policy options, and the framing of political discourse has just begun.

Motivating the Public on Global Warming

In October 2004, two young activists published a blistering indictment of the mainstream environmental community, under the provocative title "The Death of Environmentalism." In it, they criticized the movement's continued reliance on the same strategic framework it had used with some success since 1970. The first challenge was to define the problem publicly, usually in terms that were narrow and easily recognized as "environmental"; the second was to craft a technical remedy; and the third was to sell the plan to lawmakers through conventional means, such as letter-writing campaigns and direct lobbying. On the subject of global warming, that strategy might involve forging coalitions with business leaders, encouraging Congress to adopt cap-and-trade programs, or pushing consumers to embrace fluorescent light bulbs and hybrid cars. But first and foremost, it meant communicating the urgency of the problem to a public ill-equipped to understand the weight of scientific evidence. To the authors of the essay, Michael Shellenberger and Ted Nordhaus, that essential link had become one of the movement's great failures. In their view, tactics that had once worked to address even second-generation problems such as air pollution or acid rain would not mobilize meaningful public support in the fight against global warming.[25]

While many saw "The Death of Environmentalism" as overly dramatic and needlessly divisive, there was widespread agreement on at least one major point: the environmental movement had become seemingly complacent in harnessing the power of public opinion. As Carl Pope, executive director of the Sierra Club, admitted, "We have inadequately mobilized public concerns and values to create political pressure. As a result decision makers have not been forced to confront the need for fundamental changes in the way our society uses carbon (and other greenhouse gasses)."[26] Often overly confident in polls that showed widespread popular support for their proposals, environmentalists were "winning on the issues" but losing politically to more savvy opponents who understood better how to frame those issues to their tactical advantage.[27]

Within the next three years, much would change—enough, at least, to prompt a writer for *The American Prospect* to say that it was "a world away" from where the country had been when Nordhaus and Shellenberger first penned their critique.[28] But the breakthrough of 2007 was started largely from the top down by people like Gore, by those considered "influentials," "legitimizers," or "opinion leaders."[29] In writing *The Tipping Point* (2000), Gladwell expressed faith in these agents of change, in "people with a particular and rare set of social skills," and in their power to connect, inform, and persuade others.[30] Much of this task seems to have been achieved, yet as scholars of public opinion have long known and environmentalists repeatedly discovered to their frustration, convincing ordinary citizens to *act* on their beliefs is far more difficult than Gladwell imagined.[31]

An Improving Climate for Change?

Few Americans had heard or read anything about *global warming* or *the greenhouse effect* before these terms emerged from the pages of scientific journals and congressional hearing rooms during the famously hot summer of 1988. By 2006, when most major polling organizations had stopped asking the question altogether, 91 percent of those interviewed by the Pew Research Center said that they had.[32] Other key indicators also show signs of progress over time. In 1992, when asked how well they understood global warming, 22 percent of those interviewed by the Gallup Organization said "not at all."[33] By the spring of 2008, that number had fallen to just 2 percent. After decades of political debate, public relations campaigns, and media attention, most felt that they knew the issue either "fairly well" (59 percent) or "very well" (21 percent).[34]

Today a majority of Americans believe that climate change is real and that its consequences will be serious—a position adopted, not coincidentally, by both major-party candidates for president in 2008, Democrat Barack Obama and Republican John McCain. While roughly 10 percent of those interviewed at any given time insist that global warming "will never happen," those who acknowledge the problem are inclined to believe that its effects will be felt sooner rather than later. In a March 2008 survey, 61 percent of respondents thought that warming trends had "already begun," a result that was 13 percentage points higher than when Gallup first posed the question back in 1997.

For environmental advocates, however, the lack of movement on other measures of public opinion is disappointing. Even with an increase in general awareness about climate change and the immediacy of its effects, relatively few Americans feel a heightened sense of anxiety or alarm, despite the concerted efforts of Gore and others in "making climate hot."[35] When asked by Gallup in early 2008 how much they personally worried about each of a dozen different environmental problems, respondents—as usual—placed "the greenhouse effect" second to last, well below various forms of air and water pollution, soil contamination, and habitat loss for wildlife.[36] It is a result that has changed little in the past twenty years. In fact, the Pew Research Center found that disinterest in global warming sets the United States apart from other countries. Among the fifteen nations they surveyed worldwide in 2006, concern was lowest in the United States. In a sample that included citizens from Western Europe, as well as India, Russia, Nigeria, and Pakistan, the only other country with an equally low score was China.[37]

Knowing More, Caring Less

Why do Americans not feel a greater sense of urgency about global warming, especially given their belief that it is a real phenomenon with serious environmental consequences? Experts on public opinion point to several explanations. For one thing, "creeping" threats that occur gradually over time are usually less visible to the untrained eye.[38] Also, since voters and taxpayers tend to give priority to immediate problems over long-term uncertainties, climate change may be too far removed from personal experience in both time and space to motivate action.[39] For instance, although many of those polled by Gallup believed that warming trends had "already begun," a majority of respondents (58 percent) thought it would not pose a "serious threat" to their way of life within their own lifetimes.[40] For similar reasons, another recent study found that those who live far away from seacoasts and flood plains were less likely to associate global warming—and the rising tides it will bring—with an acute sense of physical vulnerability.[41]

Still others argue that the magnitude of the issue and its technical complexity are to blame. As John Immerwahr notes, what the public is most skeptical about is not the existence of global warming *per se*, but rather their ability to address the problem effectively as citizens and consumers.[42] This may help to explain why scholars at Texas A&M University found that the more respondents knew about global warming, the *less* concern they seemed to feel, in part because awareness of the gravity of the problem diminished their own sense of efficacy and personal responsibility. "Global warming is an extreme collective action dilemma," wrote the authors, "with the actions of one person having a negligible effect in the aggregate. Informed persons appear to realize this objective fact."[43]

Finally, even though Americans express confidence in their knowledge about global warming, evidence suggests that misunderstandings abound. In an update to its annual "report card" published in 2005, the National Environmental Education Foundation in Washington, D.C. found that only one-third of U.S. adults were capable of passing a "relatively simple knowledge quiz" that focused on a range of environmental concepts, including biodiversity, renewable energy, and solid waste.[44] When challenged specifically on the science of climate change, the results are often far worse. In an innovative experiment at the Massachusetts Institute of Technology (MIT), one team of researchers found that even highly educated graduate students had a poor grasp of global warming, and that the intuitive or common sense approaches they took in selecting trajectories were frequently wrong.[45]

Major polling organizations have struggled with the issue for years. In 1997, when the Pew Research Center wisely asked its respondents how they would describe the "greenhouse effect," based on what they had heard or read, if anything, more than a third of those polled (38 percent) could not define the concept even in the vaguest of terms, identifying it instead, when presented with a close-ended list of options, as either a "new advance in agriculture" or a "new architectural style," rather than as an "environmental danger."[46] A similar and equally discouraging result was found in the 2000 General Social Survey (GSS), when more than half of those polled (54 percent) believed—incorrectly—that the greenhouse effect was caused by a hole in the earth's atmosphere.[47]

For environmental activists and climate scientists, correcting such errors is no easy task. Those in the professional environmental advocacy community, in particular, seem to have a deep faith in the kind of rational decision-making that motivates both Gore and the IPCC. As Bryan Walsh, a journalist for *Time* magazine, explains: "It's the idea that if we simply marshal enough facts, enough data, enough PowerPoint slides, and present them to the world, the will to solve the problem will follow as simple as 2 + 2 = 4."[48] Instead, surveys and other experiments routinely show the opposite, which has led some observers to suspect that knowledge about global warming does not translate automatically—or even easily—into popular concern or increased salience, let alone policy preferences.[49]

To be sure, Americans place genuine value on environmental quality. Yet they also support lower crime rates, better public schools, and a strong economy—among a host of other goals—many of which surpass the environment as national priorities, at least in the public's perception. Climate change faces competition for room on a crowded political agenda. As a result, its prominence and relative importance have remained low in the minds of average citizens, not yet generating the power needed to push into the top tier of the nation's "most important problems," to borrow a phrase from one of the common measures of issue salience used by pollsters. If that continues to be the case, well-intentioned efforts to raise awareness and to convey information, in and of themselves, will likely fall short in creating a tangible sense of urgency, particularly if other issues—such as the economic crisis that hit in September 2008—seem more immediate.[50]

In the end, however, beliefs about global warming are shaped less by factual knowledge than by a variety of other factors: by elite opinion leaders, media narratives, and political rhetoric, but also by personal experience and assorted "real-world cues," each of which provides a frame of reference with the power to filter and mislead.[51] For instance, a persistent problem is that people tend to conflate global warming with natural weather cycles, a specious connection that is often encouraged in poorly constructed polls.[52] In July 2008, 43 percent of those interviewed by ABC News said that weather patterns in their area had been "more unstable" over the past three years, while 58 percent thought that "average temperatures around the world" had inched higher.[53] They were also asked about a number of specific incidents, including "flooding in the Midwest" and "severe storms in Southeast Asia." Roughly half of those surveyed believed that these, too, were a consequence of climate change.[54]

If average citizens are likely to estimate the dangers of global warming by reference to anecdotal changes in the weather, it becomes easy to dismiss the issue as nonurgent, or at least intractable. Based on intuition alone, people tend to accept that weather events—even extreme ones, such as Hurricane Katrina—are uncontrollable.[55] They are considered natural disasters, or even acts of God. For the issue to generate public concern, and for that concern to move onto the policy agenda, a different "causal story" is required. As Deborah Stone argues, a bad condition does not become a problem until it can be seen, not as accident or fate, but as something "caused by human actions and amenable to human intervention."[56]

Shooting the Messenger

Unfortunately for the U.S. environmental movement and the growing cadre of scientists that has attempted to define global warming in precisely those terms, the process of problem definition is one easily manipulated, not only by actors with competing political arguments but also by the news media itself. As scholars increasingly point out, journalists no longer pursue the difficult goal of objectivity but instead settle for a "norm of balance," whereby both sides of an issue are presented without respect to the quality and weight of the evidence.[57]

The effects of such media coverage are instructive. A team of researchers led by Jon Krosnick used President Clinton's campaign to build support for the Kyoto Protocol in 1997 as a natural experiment on opinion formation by administering two national surveys, one before the fall debate and one immediately after. They found that while the salience of the issue rose temporarily, the distribution of opinions did not change, nor did respondents feel more knowledgeable on the subject in the end, in part because of the confusing array of viewpoints expressed in the press.[58] The mainstream media's commitment to this norm of balanced coverage had encouraged people to see climate change as an unsettled area of conflict and confusion rather than as scientific consensus.[59]

A decade later, a majority of Americans continue to believe that substantial disagreement exists among scientists on the subject, despite the unambiguous language of the IPCC report. The National Opinion Research Center at the University of Chicago found in its GSS that respondents were far more likely to believe that scientists understood the causes of global warming well, at least compared to elected officials and business leaders. Within the same comparative context, they also thought—by a wide margin—that scientists should have the most influence in deciding what to do about global warming, perhaps because they were the group most likely "to support what is best for the country as a whole versus what serves their own narrow self-interests." Still, GSS participants sensed a lack of consensus. On a scale from 1 to 5, where 1 meant "near complete agreement" and 5 meant "no agreement at all," the mean response to a question about the extent to which environmental scientists "agree among themselves about the existence and causes of global warming" fell precisely to the center of the scale.[60]

As Naomi Oreskes points out in *Science* magazine, that view was undoubtedly at odds with the facts. She examined nearly one thousand abstracts published in peer-reviewed journals between 1993 and 2003 and found none that disagreed with the consensus position on climate change.[61] Nevertheless, the perception has remained. In discussing the issue with focus groups, Immerwahr may have been convinced that people were waiting for "credible signals from the scientific community." Yet the inertia of attitudes on the subject suggests that the public's understanding of global warming is not just a function of science but also of the credibility of the participants and of how the issue is framed by opponents and presented in the press.[62] To put it another way, in politics the messenger always matters.

A Growing Partisan Divide

In following the debate over the Kyoto Protocol in 1997, Krosnick and his colleagues found that opinions changed little overall, but that "beneath this apparently calm surface" there was the hint of a partisan divide, caused by citizens who took their cues largely from the elites they trusted most—an effect that was most pronounced among those who had little knowledge of global warming to begin with.[63] At the time, this was an important observation and a relatively new one at that. Roll call votes in Congress on environmental issues had always split strongly along party lines, but the divide among average Americans was generally more subtle and was connected as much to ideological considerations as to the issue itself.[64]

Figure 3-1 A Widening Partisan Divide on Global Warming

Gallup poll question: "Which of the following statements reflects your view of when the effects of global warming will begin to happen—they have already begun to happen, they will start happening within a few years, they will start happening within your lifetime, they will not happen within your lifetime, but they will affect future generations, or they will never happen?"

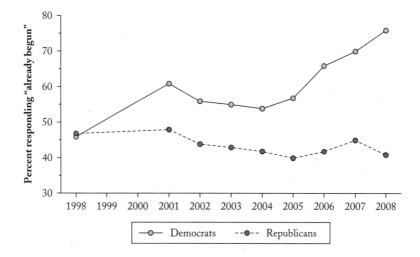

Source: Riley E. Dunlap. "Climate-Change Views: Republican-Democratic Gaps Expand," The Gallup Organization, 2008. Retrieved from www.gallup.com/poll/107569/ClimateChange-Views-Republican Democratic-Gaps-Expand.aspx.

In recent years, however, party polarization has deepened at every level. Between 1997 and 2008, the percentage of Democrats who told Gallup that global warming had "already begun" increased dramatically from 46 to 76 percent. Meanwhile, the number of Republicans who thought the same *fell* by six percentage points, from 47 to 41 (see Figure 3-1). Over time, Republicans were also increasingly inclined to believe that the seriousness of global warming was "exaggerated" by the media, and that warming trends were the result of natural causes rather than human activity.[65] In fact, the Pew Research Center found that since the release of *An Inconvenient Truth* in 2007, the number of Americans who believed that there was "solid evidence" of global warming actually declined from 77 to 71 percent overall, due mainly to increased skepticism among Republicans.[66]

For environmentalists, such fundamental differences pose vexing problems for their capacity to connect across the mass public and, by extension, build bipartisan support for policy initiatives. As Riley Dunlap and Aaron McCright point out in a careful study of Gallup data, "partisan polarization is more pronounced among those individuals reporting greater understanding of global warming."[67] Indeed, among respondents who said they understood the issue either "fairly well" or "very well," the correlations between party affiliation and five different beliefs about global warming increased steadily by year between 1997 and 2008. Those same measures were weaker and more stable across the board for those who said they knew little about climate change.

Not only does information about global warming influence partisans in different ways, so too does a more general education. In April 2008 the Pew Research Center found that Democrats with college degrees were far more likely to believe that global warming was the result of human activity (75 percent), relative to Democrats who did not graduate from college (52 percent). On the other hand, Republicans who attended college were *less* likely than their counterparts to think the same, by a margin of 19 to 31 percent.[68] While those divisions may well reflect divergence in both media consumption and the effects of people taking cues from the leaders they trust most, it might also be the direct result of elite discourse. In short, it is possible that messengers like Gore have politicized the issue of climate change in unintended and truly unhelpful ways.[69]

What Now? Mobilizing Concern into Action

So far, we have argued that, on the issue of climate change at least, the U.S. environmental movement has reached a tipping point. It is an achievement filled with great opportunity, but one that also poses new challenges for the advocacy organizations that work to translate public concern into political action. First, despite an increase in the number of Americans who acknowledge global warming and its perils, the salience of the issue remains low. For environmentalists, it is a nagging problem that is unlikely to be rectified by ad campaigns alone, despite the well-intentioned efforts of Gore and others on projects like WeCanSolveIt.org.[70] Second, public perceptions of scientific uncertainty remain despite objective evidence substantiating the reality of climate change. Such beliefs are no longer a function of science itself, but of how the issue is framed—consciously by opponents and perhaps subconsciously by the mainstream media. Finally, global warming has become an intensely partisan issue, a tendency that will have to be overcome if sustainable behavioral responses and policy solutions are to occur over the long haul.

In this regard, and recalling the "Death of Environmentalism" debate discussed earlier, the challenges of framing issues and promoting sustainable solutions fall squarely on the shoulders of the advocacy organizations that comprise the U.S. environmental "movement," a term of holistic unity that masks diverse values, priorities, and strategic visions.[71] Indeed, environmentalists seem united mostly with regard to a common political enemy. In looking at the history of contemporary environmentalism, one is often struck by the fact that its eras seem marked largely by its ideological foes—Ronald Reagan in the 1980s, Newt Gingrich and the Republican House of Representatives in the 1990s, and, of course, George W. Bush and Dick Cheney in the 2000s. It is no wonder that the authors of "Death of Environmentalism" hit such a nerve: by this reckoning and whatever its other successes, the mainstream environmental movement has consistently failed to translate generalized public support for environmental goals into actual votes for president or Congress.

Whatever the merits of this broader debate—and interest groups as independent actors may have less clout in swaying elections or in lobbying for policy outcomes than any care to admit—the election of Barack Obama and the enlargement of Democratic majorities in both chambers of Congress creates an ostensibly more favorable political context for environmental gains that nevertheless forces activists to rethink their strategies and tactics. As organizations they spent the 2000s fighting and surviving the Bush administration, and through their concerted efforts played no small role in staving off even worse harms than could have occurred. But these were by necessity defensive strategies. The coming of the Obama administration, ushered into power on a seemingly thorough public repudiation of unfettered global free markets and the deregulatory ethos of late twentieth century conservatism, presents environmentalists with their greatest political opportunity in over a generation, a window for major policy change not seen since the early 1970s. For environmentalists the challenge is to capitalize on this window of opportunity and make *politically* sustainable progress on climate change and other major problems on their respective agendas.

To think about these specific challenges, we point to two broad functions that U.S. interest groups theoretically provide: (1) they aggregate and mobilize like-minded citizens, and (2) they represent aggregated interests in government. We then ask how environmental groups generally fare in both instances and, more important, what prospects they have for taking advantage of the political opportunities now before them.

Building a Sustainable Green Coalition?

As any basic government text reminds us, the topography of American politics is shaped by constitutional rules that purposefully fragment political power and by an electoral system that creates a bias toward two-party dominance. As a result, compared to their European cousins, for example, organized interest groups in the United States play disproportionately central roles in educating, organizing, and mobilizing into action relevant sectors of the mass public. Indeed, one can argue that in the American context, interest groups are quasi-parties, providing all but those last elemental functions of parties in parliamentary systems—organizing and running government.

The ability of organized interests to fulfill these functions varies with the sector and the issue, of course. In general, groups aligned with geographically defined and economically based constituencies, such as wheat growers and coal miners, are able to speak to, aggregate, and mobilize their adherents in a more sustained and targeted fashion than are groups whose supporters are more dispersed or whose causes are more diffuse. Moreover, the topography of representation of farmers, unionized industrial workers, and employees in extractive industries like coal, oil, or timber aligns with the geographically based system of electoral representation, notably in the two chambers of Congress.

For all their capacity to educate citizens and maintain a watchful eye on policymakers, environmental groups still struggle to build and sustain the kinds of geographically situated coalitions that can match the potency of extractive industries. For one thing, environmental goods often are perceived as diffuse, long-term, and intangible even as jobs are not. By default, those defending the economic and lifestyle status quo have the easier task, particularly when the costs of policy change are proximate, tangible, and seem to sit disproportionately on those whose livelihoods are at stake.

Moreover, remarkably few of the nation's major environmental groups maintain local or state chapters—old-line groups like Sierra Club, National Audubon, and the National Wildlife Federation being notable exceptions—so they have been too easily caricatured by foes (and even some friends) as outsiders with few local connections and little legitimacy. Compounding this outsider image is the reality that many environmental groups find it hard to look beyond the educated (and white) middle class that historically contributes the bulk of their political, ideological, and financial support. Battles over issues such as automobile mileage (CAFE) standards, timber cutting in old growth forests, and oil exploration in ANWR too easily feed into an overarching narrative that environmentalism is anti-jobs, if not anti-worker, an imagery of elitism and class warfare adroitly manipulated by self-interested corporations and free-market ideologues.[72] It was no surprise, for example, that the Bush administration could count among its allies in the fights over the Kyoto Treaty, ANWR, and CAFE standards several of the nation's major industrial unions, an irony given the administration's otherwise spotty record on labor issues.

In many ways the problem of climate change offers environmentalists an unparalleled opportunity to reframe that overarching narrative and, in doing so, forge new and more politically effective coalitions with previously unlikely potential allies, labor unions in particular. For decades, environmentalists and organized labor confronted one another over the stringency of environmental regulation and energy conservation. The wrenching economic changes wrought by global competition, wildly fluctuating energy prices, and dramatic economic dislocation have pushed shrinking industrial unions to seek new allies even as environmentalists look to make inroads among working-class voters in areas where they might share common goals, including an antipathy toward conservatives on issues such as free trade and labor relations.

Such recognition of shared goals—and common enemies—has led to the formation of several so-called blue-green coalitions in recent years. The Apollo Alliance, founded in 2003, brings together old-line environmental groups such as the Sierra Club and National Wildlife Federation and major industrial unions such as the UAW (representing auto workers, among others), United Mine Workers, and United Steelworkers. The Apollo Alliance's goal is to promote a national effort to create more "green" American manufacturing jobs—in "clean coal" technologies, hybrid automobiles, and transportation infrastructure, in particular—and to form a united effort to promote global "fair trade."[73] Another coalition is the Blue Green Alliance, between the Sierra Club and Natural Resources Defense Council, on one side, and United Steelworkers and Communications Workers of

America, on the other, which together represent some four million people in a partnership designed to promote job-creating solutions to global warming. This coalition, formed in 2006, has focused its attention to date on building grassroots alliances in key union states such as Michigan, Minnesota, Ohio, Pennsylvania, Washington, and Wisconsin.

From a strategic sense, it is notable that the groups involved in these efforts range from the ideologically center-right (National Wildlife Federation) to center-left (Sierra Club)—as opposed to critics of free-market capitalism such as Friends of the Earth—and that they shy away from debates over consumer culture and materialism that tend to alienate working-class Americans. They instead focus on promoting "progressive" trade policies and investing in new generations of "green jobs," themes likelier to appeal to their labor union partners.[74] In doing so, they seek to reframe the broader issue of climate change away from a problem demanding individual sacrifice and raising the specter of lowered living standards into an *opportunity* for a national investment in science and technology, new jobs, and the promise of a prosperous and more environmentally sustainable future. That the 2008 Obama campaign framed its entire environment and energy platform under the rubric of a "New Energy for America" agenda—or that Obama announced this agenda in Lansing, Michigan—was no surprise to anyone paying close attention to the political and policy opportunities to be created in a blue-green coalition.[75]

Other coalitions are less geographic than philosophical, but no less important to framing the issue of climate change for policymakers. In February 2006 over eighty evangelical Christian leaders, a group historically hostile to what many considered the pagan underpinnings of contemporary environmentalism, announced an "Evangelical Climate Initiative" to fight global warming.[76] The initiative, opposed by religious conservatives aligned with the Bush administration, expressed support for market-based incentives to reduce greenhouse gases and plans for an educational campaign designed to convince fellow believers that combating global warming was a moral question sanctioned in the biblical injunction for Christians to be good stewards of the Earth. Funds for this campaign came from individuals and, more notably, major foundations like the Pew Charitable Trusts, the Hewlett Foundation, and the Rockefeller Brothers Foundation, philanthropies not historically known to support religious causes but that saw an opportunity to create new alliances in a common effort to combat global warming. A related effort by the Evangelical Environmental Network promotes "Creation Care," an overarching theology of "stopping and preventing activities that are harmful (e.g., air and water pollution, species extinction), and participating in activities that further Christ's reconciliation of all of creation to God."[77] The political importance of evangelical demands for action on climate change are considerable, particularly if they soften conservative opposition to environmental efforts in Congress and in the states. An array of Catholic, Jewish, Muslim, and other religious leaders have also called for action on global warming within their respective communities (for example, the U.S.

Conference of Bishops, the Coalition on Environment and Jewish Life, and the Islamic Society of North America) as well as through broader interfaith organizations such as the National Council of Churches and the National Religious Partnership for the Environment, cumulatively expanding a supportive if not necessarily unified coalition for policy change.[78] Mainstream environmental groups, long skittish about partnerships with any particular religious community, may see opportunities in the shifting attitudes of believers as a whole, given President Obama's expressed views about faith and environmental stewardship.[79]

Such alliances are hardly the only story, of course. Confronted with federal inaction, environmental groups worked closely with state governors—and notably with less doctrinaire Republicans like California governor Arnold Schwarzenegger—to foster innovations in energy conservation and transportation, in effect creating a national climate change policy one state at a time.[80] These initiatives are also leading to the creation of new state-focused organizations and reformulation of some older ones. Of note is Environment America, a Boston-based federation of state advocacy organizations formed in 2007 by two dozen now-renamed "public interest research groups" (PIRGs) with origins in Ralph Nader's Public Citizen of the early 1970s.[81] Knitting the PIRGs into a more tightly integrated federation focused on state-level efforts to promote clean energy and address climate change made a virtue out of necessity, given their search for a renewed mission and sounder finances. In the long run, however, it also must be seen as part of an overall effort by environmentalists to broaden their coalition of support for more assertive efforts to address climate change when the opportunity to do so presents itself.

Representing Interests in Government—Regaining Access?

Another major function of interest groups is to represent their constituencies in government. This role is particularly important for environmentalists, given the political dominance of the two major mass-based parties and the parallel absence of an effective green party. Environmental groups have developed a wide range of organizational capacities—lobbyists to lawyers, as it were—to cover the breadth of available access points at whatever level of government was involved. However, the opportunity to gain access is neither spread equally nor consistently. Moreover, changes in the political opportunity structure, the broader structural and societal contexts of the moment, have potent impacts on who gets access, under what conditions, and to what effect.[82]

In the previous edition of this book we observed that in the mid-2000s environmentalists confronted a particularly challenging political opportunity structure: an ideologically hostile presidency whose overall policy agenda ran contrary to almost everything promoted by mainstream American environmentalism; an enfeebled Environmental Protection Agency (EPA) with little political clout; a Congress dominated by a Republican Party that itself had become defined by its most conservative, anti-environmentalist wing; and, as a result of a judicial appointment process dominated by Republican presidents going back to Reagan, a federal judiciary that increasingly came to elevate property rights over environmental goods and backed executive branch discretion over public access or, even, its right to know. In sum, we concluded, environmentalists in the Bush era were once again outsiders looking in, a status affecting their capacity to represent their interests in government and requiring of them a range of strategies aimed at reframing issues, providing new solutions, and building new coalitions, all in the hope of repositioning themselves and their values within the broader discourse.[83]

What do we make of the dramatically reshaped opportunity structure in 2009? The election of Barack Obama is the most significant element in the new equation, in particular because the president defines the agenda. But a nontrivial part of the equation is that Congress is more solidly in the hands of Democrats than it has been in years. Congressional committees with jurisdiction over environmental and energy issues are in friendlier hands, greatly improving the likelihood of agenda-influencing congressional hearings on environmental issues and, for environmental group lobbyists, greater access to the legislative process.[84] With Obama's election also comes a more accessible federal establishment beyond the White House itself—the EPA and the Office of Management and Budget, in particular—and, finally, one surmises, the appointment of federal judges with views less overtly hostile to environmentalist claims. Even with the lagged effects of the past eight years, including a weakened executive establishment and dozens of Bush administration executive orders that critics fear the new administration will have a tough time rescinding or altering, environmentalists have not encountered such favorable political conditions in over three decades.[85]

Resources. But the new terrain poses its own set of challenges. First is the question of having adequate resources to take advantage of these opportunities. The irony of 2008 is that the same economic conditions that helped to usher in a new political opportunity structure also potentially undermines the capacity of many environmental organizations to take advantage of it. For most groups the immediate concern is the overall effect of the fall 2008 economic meltdown on their finances. Without doubt, most environmental groups will suffer financially from the sudden and dramatic drop in individual wealth at all levels of the philanthropic scale. Groups that depend disproportionately on larger donations will see the most immediate and sharpest declines, while those that had long cultivated a broader base of supporters will have to work that much harder to stay in place. Depending on the overall length and severity of the current financial crisis, some smaller and more narrowly configured groups may not survive.

The still as yet unknown impacts of the current economic crisis follow a period of steady if not spectacular or equally shared growth in environmental group revenues during the 2000s (see Table 3-1), particularly compared to the last half of the 1990s. The groups that generally fared best financially during the 2000s were those that purchase and conserve land (for example, Ducks Unlimited, Nature Conservancy, Conservation Fund, Conservation International), followed by the major multipurpose organizations such as the

Table 3-1   Revenues for Selected National Environmental
Organizations, FY 2001–2007[a]

Organization (by year of founding)	Web Site	Revenue (in millions)			
		2001	2003	2005	2007
Sierra Club	sierraclub.org	$52.2	$83.7	$85.2	$91.0
National Audubon Society	audubon.org	$98.2	$78.6	$78.3	$116.3
National Parks Conservation Association	npca.org	$22.8	$20.9	$31.8	$33.2
Izaak Walton League	iwla.org	$5.2	$4.3	$3.9	$4.3
The Wilderness Society	tws.org	$24.1	$18.8	$29.5	$32.2
National Wildlife Federation	nwf.org	$112.0	$102.1	$112.8	$83.6
Ducks Unlimited	ducks.org	$123.8	$125.1	$133.0	$213.1
Defenders of Wildlife	defenders.org	$24.1	$21.8	$26.1	$35.2
The Nature Conservancy	nature.org	$546.6	$972.4	$800.4	$1,017.1
World Wildlife Fund—U.S.	worldwildlife.org	$118.4	$93.3	$116.7	$160.8
Environmental Defense Fund	environmentaldefense.org	$42.9	$43.8	$48.8	$94.2
Friends of the Earth	foe.org	$3.8	$3.8	$3.6	$3.5
Natural Resources Defense Council	nrdc.org	$55.7	$46.4	$76.5	$75.1
League of Conservation Voters	lcv.org	$6.2	$7.0	$8.4	$6.6
Earthjustice	earthjustice.org	$21.5	$17.9	$19.4	$26.1
Clean Water Action	cleanwateraction.org	$4.4	$10.7	$11.6	$9.7
Greenpeace USA	greenpeaceusa.org	$14.5	$25.9	$12.2	$15.8
Trust for Public Land	tpl.org	$154.5	$126.5	$121.0	$220.2
Ocean Conservancy	oceanconservancy.org	$9.5	$8.9	$12.8	$16.5
American Rivers	amrivers.org	$5.6	$5.5	$8.6	$7.5
Sea Shepherd Conservation Society	seashepherd.org	$1.0	$1.0	$1.1	$2.5
Center for Health, Environment and Justice	chej.org	$1.6	$1.0	$0.9	$1.1
Earth Island Institute	earthisland.org	$4.5	$4.9	$3.9	$6.6
National Park Trust	parktrust.org	$3.6	$1.2	$2.1	$1.5
Conservation Fund	conservationfund.org	$64.2	$60.1	$65.5	$104.7
Rainforest Action Network	ran.org	$2.4	$2.2	$2.6	$3.6
Conservation International	conservation.org	$68.9	$222.7	$117.3	$108.2
Environmental Working Group	ewg.org	$2.2	$1.8	$3.5	$4.3

Sources: Annual reports and IRS Form 990.
a. Gross revenues for fiscal or tax years, the use of which varies among organizations.

Sierra Club, Environmental Defense Fund, and Natural Resources Defense Council. By contrast, more clearly ideological advocacy groups like Friends of the Earth and Greenpeace continued to struggle financially, suggesting a narrower appeal within the overall fund-raising universe.

Even assuming an eventual economic upturn, a possibly longer-term problem is more strategic, and gets at the heart of so many criticisms of mainstream environmentalism. The Bush administration may have been the movement's ideological and policy *bête noire*, but it was an easy target against which to mobilize supporters and raise funds. It will be much more difficult for mainstream environmentalists to mobilize supporters against an Obama administration *and* a Democratic Congress. Against whom will environmentalists rail in making their pitches?

Another problem for many environmental groups is competition from Web-based groups like MoveOn. In recent years such groups have raised staggering amounts of money from small donations and mobilized supporters without needing an extensive (and expensive) organizational structure.[86] Given MoveOn's general advocacy orientation, an immediate question is how its capacity to shape issue agendas complements or competes with professional staff organizations like the Natural Resources Defense Council, on the one hand, and generalized protest groups like Greenpeace and Friends of the Earth, on the other. Longer term, the great unknown is the degree to which these new types of groups can mobilize supporters.

Partisan Dependency. Finally, while an Obama presidency and a Democratic Congress is fortuitous for environmental groups in the short term, coming as it does at the very moment when many will be struggling to stay afloat financially, in the long run they will need to find a way to support the new administration without being perceived as being in the lap of the Democratic Party. To cite an earlier example, the Clinton era debate over ratification of the North American Free Trade Agreement divided the major national environmental groups, with critics charging that many of the groups that supported Senate ratification of the treaty did so only to maintain access to the Clinton administration, in which many of their own people had recently obtained positions of influence. By doing so, these groups were alleged to have succumbed to what the writer Kirkpatrick Sale called "the inherently conservatizing pressure to play by the 'rules of the game' in the compromise world of Washington, D.C."[87] Environmental group leaders might respond that, after years of hard fighting against the Bush administration, they welcome the dilemma of dealing with friends on the inside. But they also know that being seen as too close to those in power might affect their capacity to speak their minds, with consequences for their relations with their own supporters.[88]

The Twenty-first Century Movement?

If the theme of a tipping point that runs through this chapter makes sense, then the 2008 election may mark the end of late-twentieth-century ideological and partisan arrangements. After all, contemporary environmentalism has been defined as much as anything by the overarching ideological and partisan debate over the role of government. If the libertarian, deregulatory strain of conservatism has lost its hold as the dominant narrative, as conservative *New York Times* columnist David Brooks, for one, suggests, its role as contemporary environmentalism's dominant ideological foe also may be in the past.[89] Perhaps 2008 also marks the transition between the environmentalism that began in 1969 and something new.

If so, a more fundamental question remains: What will a twenty-first-century environmental movement look like? Will it be essentially a variation on the environmental community that emerged in the last decades of the twentieth century, with its wide array of advocacy groups, or will it be very different, dominated by MoveOn-type mass organizations, its adherents mobilized by an online call to arms? This is not a trivial concern, if only because groups like MoveOn seem to be able to reach younger supporters in ways that many older environmental groups have yet to figure out. The baby boomers who drove contemporary environmentalism for nearly four decades, first through their volunteer activism and later through their wallets, will recede in dominance in the future, and all advocacy groups need to decide how to connect with the generations that follow. Environmental groups have shown remarkable capacity to change with the times and technology, but it is not yet clear how the professional staff organizations that came to dominate the national environmental advocacy community will compete with or accommodate the leaner, more agile organizations supported by Web-generated micro-donations.

American environmentalism may well be at the tipping point, with the convergence of mass acceptance of climate change and the game-changing arrival of the Obama administration. It may be the most important moment for environmentalism in a generation. For the organizations that profess to speak for environmental values, where they head from here is the great unknown.

Suggested Web Sites

Apollo Alliance (www.apolloalliance.org) A national coalition of labor unions, environmental organizations, businesses, and community leaders "working to catalyze a clean energy revolution in America to reduce our nation's dependence on foreign oil, cut the carbon emissions that are destabilizing our climate, and expand opportunities for American businesses and workers."

Blue Green Alliance (www.bluegreenalliance.org) A coalition of labor unions and environmental groups, led by the United Steel Workers and the Sierra Club, that works at the grassroots in the midwestern industrial states on issues of global warming and clean energy, fair trade, and reducing toxic chemical exposure to workers and residents.

Environment America (www.environmentamerica.org) A federation of state-based environmental advocacy organizations founded in 2007, with origins in the Ralph Nader–inspired "public interest research group" movement begun in the 1970s.

The Gallup Organization (www.gallup.com) A leading provider of polling data on energy and the environment, as well as a host of other economic, social, and political issues.

National Religious Partnership for the Environment (www.nrpe.org) A coalition founded in 1993 by four major religious organizations and alliances that together serve tens of millions of Americans:

U.S. Conference of Catholic Bishops (www.usccb.org/sdwp/ejp)

National Council of Churches of Christ (www.nccecojustice.org)

Coalition on the Environment and Jewish Life (www.coejl.org)

Evangelical Environmental Network (www.creationcare.org)

Notes

1. Paul Farhi, "The Little Film That Became a Hot Property: Millions Warmed to Gore's Environmental Message," *Washington Post,* October 13, 2007, C1.
2. The producers of *An Inconvenient Truth*—but not Gore—won a 2007 Academy Award for best documentary, and Melissa Etheridge won best original song for the film's anthem, "I Need to Wake Up." Gore later won an Emmy in the category of "interactive television services" for unrelated work on Current TV; see Farhi, "The Little Film That Became a Hot Property."
3. Farhi, "The Little Film That Became a Hot Property."
4. Erin Kelly, "Environmentalists Hope for Progress with New President," *USA Today,* April 19, 2008.
5. Intergovernmental Panel on Climate Change (IPCC), *Climate Change 2007: Impacts, Adaptation and Vulnerability, Contribution of Working Group II to the Fourth Assessment Report of the Intergovernmental Panel on Climate Change,* ed. M. L. Parry, O. F. Canziani, J. P. Palutikof, P. J. van der Linden, and C. E. Hanson (Cambridge: Cambridge University Press, 2007).
6. Office of Science and Technology Policy, "Intergovernmental Panel on Climate Change Finalizes Report," February 2, 2007, www.whitehouse.gov/news/releases/2007/02/print/20070202.html; see also IPCC, *Climate Change 2007.*
7. John Heilprin, "Bush Seeks New Image on Global Warming," *Associated Press Online,* September 28, 2007; Office of the Press Secretary, "President Bush Participates in Major Economies Meeting on Energy Security and Climate Change," September 28, 2007, www.whitehouse.gov/news/releases/2007/09/20070928-2.html. For more on the "evolution" of Bush's views on the environment, see Peter Baker, "In Bush's Final Year, the Agenda Gets Greener," *Washington Post,* December 29, 2007, A1.
8. Sheryl Gay Stolberg, "Gore Makes It Back to Oval Office, if Only for a Chat," *New York Times,* November 27, 2007, A26.
9. Al Gore, "Moving beyond Kyoto," *New York Times,* July 1, 2007, A13; Elizabeth Pennisi, Jesse Smith, and Richard Stone, "Momentous Changes at the Poles," *Science* (March 16, 2007): 1513; Stefan Rahmstorf, "A Semi-Empirical Approach to Projecting Future Sea-Level Rise," *Science* (January 19, 2007): 368–370.
10. Timothy M. Lenton, Hermann Held, Elmar Kriegler, Jim W. Hall, Wolfgang Lucht, Stefan Rahmstorf, and Hans Joachim Schellnhuber, "Tipping Elements in the Earth's Climate System," *Proceedings of the National Academy of Sciences of the United States* 105 (February 12, 2008): 1786–1793. For a more accessible discussion, see Paul Eccleston, "Climate Change 'Tipping Point' Within 100 Years," *The Telegraph [UK],* February 5, 2008.
11. See B. Dan Wood and Alesha Doan, "The Politics of Problem Definition: Applying and Testing Threshold Models," *American Journal of Political Science* 47 (2003): 640–653.
12. Malcolm Gladwell, *The Tipping Point: How Little Things Can Make a Big Difference* (Boston: Little, Brown, 2000); Daniel Yankelovich, "The Tipping Points," *Foreign Affairs* (May/June 2006); Thomas L. Friedman, "Iraq at the Tipping Point," *New York*

Times, November 18, 2004, 31; Tania Valdemoro, "Darfur Activists Speak at Holocaust Memorial," *Miami Herald*, April 24, 2008; Reuters, "Consumer Confidence Plunges to 13-Year Low," *New York Times*, September 17, 2005, 6; Joan Vennochi, "Tuesday's Tipping Point," *Boston Globe*, February 3, 2008, C9.

13. Bryan Walsh, "A Green Tipping Point," *Time*, October 12, 2007, www.time.com/time/world/article/0,8599,1670871,00.html.

14. Peter Brown, Fareed Zakaria, Andrew Klavan, and Brian Loughnane, "As the Mercury Rises, Global Warming Will Lose Its Salience," *The Australian*, January 30, 2007, 13.

15. Susanne C. Moser and Lisa Dilling, "Making Climate Hot: Communicating the Urgency and Challenge of Global Climate Change," *Environment* 46 (December 2004): 32–46.

16. Elisabeth Rosenthal and Andrew C. Revkin, "Science Panel Says Global Warming Is 'Unequivocal'," *New York Times*, February 3, 2007, A1. Ironically, noted skeptic Sen. James Inhofe, R-Okla., argued that the "man-made global warming fear machine crossed the 'tipping point' in 2007. I am convinced that future climate historians will look back at 2007 as the year the global warming fears began crumbling," http://epw.senate.gov/public/index.cfm?FuseAction=Minority.PressReleases&ContentRecord_id=dcc7c65f-802a-23ad-4668-0aec926c60c8.

17. Maxwell T. Boykoff and Jules M. Boykoff, "Balance as Bias: Global Warming and the U.S. Prestige Press," *Global Environmental Change* 15 (July 2004): 125–136; Jon A. Krosnick, Allyson L. Holbrook, Laura Lowe, and Penny S. Visser, "The Origins and Consequences of Democratic Citizens' Policy Agendas: A Study of Popular Concern about Global Warming," *Climatic Change*, 77 (2006): 7–43; Maxwell T. Boykoff and Jules M. Boykoff, "Climate Change and Journalistic Norms: A Case Study of U.S. Mass-Media Coverage," *Geoforum* 38 (November 2007): 1190–1204; Maxwell T. Boykoff, "From Convergence to Contention: United States Mass Media Representations of Anthropogenic Climate Science," *Transactions of the Institute of British Geographers* 32 (2007): 477–489; Maxwell T. Boykoff, "Flogging a Dead Norm? Media Coverage of Anthropogenic Climate Change in United States and United Kingdom, 2003–2006," *Area* 39 (2007): 470–481; and Paul M. Kellstedt, Sammy Zahran, and Arnold Vedlitz, "Personal Efficacy, the Information Environment, and Attitudes toward Global Warming and Climate Change in the United States," *Risk Analysis*, 28 (2008): 113–126.

18. Steven Mufson, "CEOs Urge Bush to Limit Greenhouse Gas Emissions," *Washington Post*, January 6, 2007, A6.

19. Juliet Eilperin, "150 Global Firms Seek Mandatory Cuts in Greenhouse Gas Emissions," *Washington Post*, November 30, 2007, A3.

20. Eric Lipton and Gardiner Harris, "In Turnaround, Industries Seek U.S. Regulations," *New York Times*, September 16, 2007, A1; Laura Steele, "Global Warming: A New Twist on an Old Fight," *Kiplinger Business Forecasts*, February 16, 2007, www.kiplinger.com/businessresource/forecast/archive/global_warming__a_new_twist_on_an_old_fight.html.

21. Barry G. Rabe, *Statehouse and Greenhouse* (Washington, D.C.: Brookings Institution Press, 2004); see also Pew Center on Climate Change, "What's Being Done ... in the States," www.pewclimate.org/what_s_being_done/in_the_states.

22. Pew Center on Climate Change, "Learning from State Action on Climate Change," December 2007, www.pewclimate.org/docUploads/States%20Brief%20Template%20_November%202007_.pdf; Anthony Faiola and Robin Shulman, "Cities Take Lead on Environment as Debate Drags at Federal Level: 522 Mayors Have Agreed to Meet Kyoto Standards," *Washington Post*, June 9, 2007, A1.

23. Thomas L. Friedman, "The Power of Green," *New York Times Magazine*, April 15, 2007; and Thomas L. Friedman, "And the Color of the Year Is . . . ," *New York Times*, December 22, 2006.

24. Christine Russell, "Climate Change: Now What? Scientists Agree It's Real, but There's no Consensus on Solutions. Readers Need a Guide to the Options," *Columbia Journalism Review* 47 (July–August 2008): 45–49. See also Michael Shellenberger and

Ted Nordhaus, "The Death of Environmentalism: Global Warming Politics in a Post Environmental World," October 2004, www.thebreakthrough.org/PDF/Death_of_Environmentalism.pdf.

25. Shellenberger and Nordhaus, "The Death of Environmentalism."

26. Carl Pope, "And Now for Something Completely Different," January 13, 2005, www.grist.org/news/maindish/2005/01/13/pope-reprint/index.html. See also Moser and Dilling, "Making Climate Hot," 32.

27. Shellenberger and Nordhaus, "The Death of Environmentalism," 11–12, 32.

28. Kate Sheppard, "Life after the Death of Environmentalism," *The American Prospect*, October 11, 2007, www.prospect.org/cs/articles?article=life_after_the_death_of_environmentalism.

29. Elihu Katz and Paul Lazarsfeld, *Personal Influence: The Part Played by People in the Flow of Mass Communications* (Glencoe, Ill.: Free Press, 1955); Charles J. Stewart, Craig Allen Smith, and Robert E. Denton Jr., *Persuasion and Social Movements*, 3d ed. (Prospect Heights, Ill.: Waveland, 1994).

30. Gladwell (2000: 33) labels them "connectors," "mavens," and "salesmen." For a similar approach, see Charles T. Rubin, *The Green Crusade: Rethinking the Roots of Environmentalism* (New York: Free Press, 1994).

31. As every president knows, using the "bully pulpit" to shape public opinion is difficult, even for those in the highest positions of power and prestige. See Lawrence R. Jacobs and Robert Y. Shapiro, *Politicians Don't Pander: Political Manipulation and the Loss of Democratic Responsiveness* (Chicago: University of Chicago Press, 2000); George C. Edwards, *On Deaf Ears: The Limits of the Bully Pulpit* (New Haven: Yale University Press, 2006); Brandon Rottinghaus, "The Provisional Pulpit: Presidential Leadership of Public Opinion, 1953–2001," paper prepared for delivery at the 2005 annual meeting of the American Political Science Association, September 1–4, 2005.

32. The question wording used by Pew was as follows: "Now I will read a list of some things that have happened in the world recently. For each one, please tell me if you've heard of it or not." When asked, 91 percent had heard of "the environmental problem of global warming," 9 percent had not. Pew Global Attitudes Project and Princeton Survey Research Associates International, May 2–14, 2006. Retrieved August 27, 2008, from the iPOLL Databank, Roper Center for Public Opinion Research, University of Connecticut, www.ropercenter.uconn.edu.ezproxy.uvm.edu/ipoll.html. For more on trends related to global warming, see Matthew C. Nisbet and Teresa Myers, "The Polls—Trends: Twenty Years of Public Opinion about Global Warming," *Public Opinion Quarterly* 71 (fall 2007): 444–470.

33. Nisbet and Myers, "The Polls," 448, table 4.

34. Gallup Organization, March 6–9, 2008, retrieved August 27, 2008, www.rope center.uconn.edu.ezproxy.uvm.edu/ipoll.html. The 2006 General Social Survey records a similar result. See National Opinion Research Center, University of Chicago, March 10–August 7, 2006, retrieved September 11, 2008, www.ropercenter.uconn.edu.ezproxy.uvm.edu/ipoll.html.

35. Moser and Dilling, "Making Climate Hot."

36. Gallup Organization, March 6–9, 2008, retrieved August 27, 2008, www.ropercenter.uconn.edu.ezproxy.uvm.edu/ipoll.html. See also Frank Newport, "Little Increase in Americans' Global Warming Worries," Gallup Organization, April 21, 2008, www.gallup.com/poll/106660/Little-Increase-Americans-Global-Warming-Worries.aspx.

37. Both countries are leading producers of greenhouse gases. Pew Global Attitudes Project, "America's Image Slips, but Allies Share U.S. Concerns over Iran, Hamas: No Global Warming Alarm in the U.S., China," June 13, 2006, http://pewglobal.org/reports/display.php?ReportID=252.

38. Moser and Dilling, "Making Climate Hot."

39. Scholars have long recognized that attitudes are more accessible in memory when they are personally—as opposed to nationally, or even globally—important. See Jon A.

Krosnick and Joanne M. Miller, "The Origins of Policy Issue Salience: Sociotropic Importance for the Nation or Personal Importance to the Citizen?" Paper presented at the annual meeting of the American Political Science Association, Philadelphia, August 27–31, 2003; Howard Lavine, John L. Sullivan, Eugene Borgida, and Cynthia J. Thomsen, "The Relationship of National and Personal Issue Salience to Attitude Accessibility on Foreign and Domestic Policy Issues," *Political Psychology* 17 (1996): 293–316.

40. Gallup Organization, March 6–9, 2008, retrieved August 27, 2008, www.ropercenter .uconn.edu.ezproxy.uvm.edu/ipoll.html.

41. Samuel D. Brody, Sammy Zahran, Arnold Vedlitz, and Himanshu Grover, "Examining the Relationship between Physical Vulnerability and Public Perceptions of Global Climate Change in the United States," *Environment and Behavior* 40 (January 2008): 72–95.

42. John Immerwahr, *Waiting for a Signal: Public Attitudes toward Global Warming, the Environment and Geophysical Research,* American Geophysical Union, 1999, www.agu.org/sci_soc/attitude_study.html.

43. Kellstedt, Zahran, and Vedlitz, "Personal Efficacy, the Information Environment, and Attitudes toward Global Warming and Climate Change in the United States," 120.

44. Kevin Coyle, *Environmental Literacy in America* (Washington, D.C.: National Environmental Education and Training Foundation, 2005).

45. John D. Sterman and Linda Booth Sweeney, "Cloudy Skies: Assessing Public Understanding of Global Warming," *System Dynamics Review* 18 (2002): 207–240.

46. Pew Research Center for the People and the Press, November 1997 News Interest Index [datafile], November 12–16, 1997 (n = 1,200): Q7.

47. The percentage of respondents combines the responses "definitely true" and "probably true." Nisbet and Myers, "The Polls," 449, table 7.

48. Bryan Walsh, "A Green Tipping Point," *Time,* October 12, 2007.

49. Penny S. Visser, George Y. Bizer, and Jon A. Krosnick, "Exploring the Latent Structure of Strength-Related Attitude Attributes," *Advances in Experimental Social Psychology* 38 (2006): 1–67; Richard J. Bord, Ann Fisher, and Robert E. O'Connor, "Is Accurate Understanding of Global Warming Necessary to Promote Willingness to Sacrifice?" *Risk: Health, Safety and the Environment* 8 (fall 1997): 339–349.

50. Immerwahr, *Waiting for a Signal*; see also Krosnick et al., "The Origins and Consequences of Democratic Citizens' Policy Agendas"; Julia B. Corbett, *Communicating Nature: How We Create and Understand Environmental Messages* (Washington, D.C.: Island Press, 2006), 67; Bord, Fisher, and O'Connor, "Is Accurate Understanding of Global Warming Necessary to Promote Willingness to Sacrifice?"

51. Krosnick et al., "The Origins and Consequences of Democratic Citizens' Policy Agendas"; Christopher Borick and Barry Rabe, "A Reason to Believe: Examining the Factors That Determine Individual Views on Global Warming," *Issues in Governance Studies* 16 (July 2008): 1–14.

52. Ann Bostrom and Daniel Lashof, "Weather or Climate Change?" in *Creating a Climate for Change: Communicating Climate Change and Facilitating Social Change,* ed. Susanne C. Moser and Lisa Dilling (Cambridge: Cambridge University Press, 2007), 32.

53. Survey by Planet Green, the Woods Institute for the Environment at Stanford University, and ABC News, July 23–28, 2008, retrieved August 27, 2008, www.rope center.uconn.edu.ezproxy.uvm.edu/ipoll.html.

54. Forty-five percent thought that "the flooding in the Midwest in the last twelve months" was related to global warming, while 50 percent thought it was connected to "the severe storms in Southeast Asia." Survey by Planet Green, July 23–28, 2008.

55. Moser and Dilling, "Making Climate Hot," 36; Bostrom and Lashof, "Weather or Climate Change?" 40.

56. Deborah A. Stone, "Causal Stories and the Formation of Policy Agendas," *Political Science Quarterly* 104 (summer 1999): 281.

57. This is sometimes called "balance as bias." See Boykoff and Boykoff, "Balance as Bias"; Krosnick et al., "The Origins and Consequences of Democratic Citizens' Policy Agendas."

58. Jon A. Krosnick, Allyson L. Holbrook, and Penny S. Visser, "The Impact of the Fall 1997 Debate about Global Warming on American Public Opinion," *Public Understanding of Science* 9 (2000): 239–260; Penny S. Visser, George Y. Bizer, and Jon A. Krosnick, "Exploring the Latent Structure of Strength-Related Attitude Attributes," *Advances in Experimental Social Psychology* 38 (2006): 1–67.

59. Boykoff, "From Convergence to Contention"; Boykoff and Boykoff, "Balance as Bias"; Krosnick et al., "The Origins and Consequences of Democratic Citizens' Policy Agendas"; Michael Hanlon, "Apocalypse When? Careless and Exaggerated Stories about Global Warming Play into the Hands of Those Who Wish to Deny That It Is Happening at All," *New Scientist,* November 17, 2007, 20.

60. Survey by National Opinion Research Center, University of Chicago, March 10–August 7, 2006, retrieved September 27, 2008, www.ropercenter.uconn.edu. ezproxy.uvm.edu/ipoll.html.

61. Naomi Oreskes, "The Scientific Consensus on Climate Change," *Science,* December 3, 2004, 1686.

62. Immerwahr, *Waiting for a Signal,* 25.

63. Krosnick, Holbrook, and Visser, "The Impact of the Fall 1997 Debate about Global Warming on American Public Opinion," 239, 254.

64. See Sheldon Kamieniecki, "Political Parties and Environmental Policy," in *Environmental Politics and Policy: Theories and Evidence,* 2d ed., ed. James P. Lester (Durham: Duke University Press, 1995), 146–167; Charles R. Shipan and William R. Lowry, "Environmental Policy and Party Divergence in Congress," *Political Research Quarterly* 54 (2001): 245–263; Deborah Lynn Guber, *The Grassroots of a Green Revolution: Polling America on the Environment* (Boston: MIT Press, 2003), chap. 5.

65. Riley E. Dunlap and Aaron M. McCright, "A Widening Gap: Republican and Democratic Views on Climate Change," *Environment* (September/October 2008): 26–35.

66. Pew Research Center for the People and the Press, "A Deeper Partisan Divide over Global Warming," May 8, 2008, http://people-press.org/report/417/a-deeper-partisan-divide-over-global-warming.

67. Dunlap and McCright, A Widening Gap," 33.

68. Pew Research Center, "A Deeper Partisan Divide."

69. Borick and Rabe, "A Reason to Believe"; Newport, "Little Increase in Americans' Global Warming Worries"; Lydia Saad, "Did Hollywood's Glare Heat Up Public Concern about Global Warming?" Gallup Organization, March 21, 2007, www.gallup.com/poll/26932/Did-Hollywoods-Glare-Heat-Public-Concern-About-Global-Warming.aspx.

70. Andrew C. Revkin, "Gore Alliance Starts Ad Campaign on Global Warming," *New York Times,* April 1, 2008, 8.

71. For a fuller analysis, see Christopher Bosso, *Environment, Inc.: From Grassroots to Beltway* (Lawrence: University Press of Kansas, 2005).

72. See Deborah L. Guber and Christopher Bosso "Framing ANWR: Citizens, Consumers, and the Privileged Position of Business," in *Business and Environmental Policy,* ed. Michael E. Kraft and Sheldon Kamieniecki (Cambridge: MIT Press, 2006), 35–59.

73. See www.apolloalliance.org.

74. Press release, "Blue Green Alliance Grows to More Than Four Million," October 9, 2008, *PR Newswire,* via Lexis-Nexis. See www.bluegreenalliance.org.

75. "New Energy for America," my.barackobama.com/page/content/newenergy.

76. Laura Goodstein, "Evangelical Leaders Join Global Warming Initiative," *New York Times,* February 28, 2006, www.nytimes.com/2006/02/08/national/08warm.html. See also http://christiansandclimate.org.

77. For more, see the Evangelical Environmental Network, www.creationcare.org.

78. Pew Forum on Religion and Public Life, "Polls Show Strong Backing for Environmental Protection across Religious Groups," pewforum.org/docs/?DocID=121, U.S.

Conference of Catholic Bishops, www.usccb.org; Coalition on Environment and Jewish Life, www.coejl.org/index.php; Islamic Society of North America, www.isna.net; National Council of Churches, www.nccecojustice.org; National Religious Partnership for the Environment, www.nrpe.org.

79. See, for example, an interchange between Obama and Richard Cizik of the National Association of Evangelicals during as a CNN-sponsored "Democratic Candidates Compassion Forum," April 13, 2008, http://transcripts.cnn.com/TRANSCRIPTS/0804/13/se.01.html.

80. See Rabe, *Statehouse and Greenhouse.*

81. See www.environmentamerica.org.

82. See David S. Meyer and Douglas R. Imig, "Political Opportunity and the Rise and Decline of Interest Group Sectors," *Social Science Journal* 30 (1993): 253–270.

83. See also Christopher McGrory Klyza and David Sousa, *American Environmental Policy, 1990–2006* (Cambridge: MIT Press, 2008).

84. See Bosso, *Environment, Inc.,* chap. 5 and figure 5-1; Jeffrey Berry and Clyde Wilcox, *The Interest Group Society,* 5th ed. (New York: Pearson Longman, 2009), 166–168 and figure 9-1.

85. Ceci Connolly and R. Jeffrey Smith, "Obama Positioned to Quickly Reverse Bush Actions: Stem Cell, Climate Rules among Targets of President-Elect's Team," *Washington Post,* November 9, 2008, A1.

86. An observation made by David Karpf in a draft, "MoveOn.Org and the Second Interest Group Realignment," July 2008.

87. Kirkpatrick Sale, "The U.S. Green Movement Today," *The Nation,* July 19, 1993, 94; Michelle Ruess and Tom Diemer, "Environmentalists Split on Trade Policy," *Cleveland Plain Dealer,* July 18, 1993, 4A; see also Christopher Bosso, "Seizing Back the Day: The Challenge to Environmental Activism in the 1990s," *Environmental Policy in the 1990s,* 3d ed., ed. Norman J. Vig and Michael E. Kraft (Washington, D.C.: CQ Press), 53–74.

88. On these dilemmas, see Ronald G. Shaiko, *Voices and Echoes for the Environment* (New York: Columbia University Press, 1999).

89. David Brooks, "Big Government Ahead," *New York Times,* October 13, 2008, www.nytimes.com/2008/10/14/opinion/14brooks.html.

4

Presidential Powers and Environmental Policy

Norman J. Vig

We cannot afford more of the same timid politics when the future of our planet is at stake. Global warming is not a someday problem, it is now.

Barack Obama speaking at Portsmouth,
New Hampshire, October 8, 2007

Drill, Baby, Drill!

Chant at Republican National Convention,
September 3, 2008

The presidential election of 2008 may go down in history as the first global election. Not only were people around the world keenly interested in the outcome, but both major candidates espoused far-reaching policies for developing alternative energy sources and preventing catastrophic global climate change.[1] Although high domestic gasoline prices and a deepening financial crisis led to counter-pressures by the fall—especially from conservative Republicans—it appeared that the nation may finally have reached a tipping point on these issues after decades of gridlock (see chapter 3).[2]

Shortly after the election, Barack Obama called for a vast new public works program that would simultaneously address economic, national security, and environmental issues: "We'll put people back to work rebuilding our crumbling roads and bridges, modernizing schools that are failing our children, and building wind farms and solar panels, fuel-efficient cars and the alternative energy technologies that can free us from our dependence on foreign oil and keep our economy competitive in the years ahead."[3] In December he met with former vice president Al Gore to discuss climate change and declared that "We all believe what the scientists have been telling us for years now, that this is a matter of urgency and national security, and it has to be dealt with in a serious way."[4] He vowed to create millions of "green jobs" and "repower" America.

Whether President Obama can deliver on these promises remains to be seen. What is certain is that all presidents since the beginning of the modern environmental movement in the 1960s have had a significant, if not always salutary, impact on the course of national environmental policy. Nevertheless, they operate within a system of constitutional and political constraints that limit their power. Many other actors also influence policy development, and presidents often fail to get their way. I discuss Obama's proposals in more detail later in this chapter, but first it is important to examine the powers of the presidency to effect environmental change.

Presidential Powers and Constraints

The formal roles of the president have been summarized as commander in chief of the armed forces, chief diplomat, chief executive, legislative leader, and opinion/party leader.[5] If we look only at environmental policy, the president's role as chief executive has probably been most important.[6] The president's powers to make cabinet and subcabinet appointments, to propose agency and program budgets, to issue executive orders, and to oversee the regulatory process are especially important prerogatives as chief executive. Some presidents have also played a leading role in enacting environmental legislation and in rallying public opinion behind new environmental policies. The role of chief diplomat has also become more important as many environmental problems have required international solutions. Military activities also have major impacts on the environment (chapter 15).

Presidential powers can also be analyzed from a policy cycle perspective such as that introduced in chapter 1. First, presidents have a major role in *agenda setting*. They can bring issues to the public's attention, define the terms of public debate, and rally public opinion and constituency support through speeches, press conferences, and other media events. Second, they can take the lead in *policy formulation* by devoting presidential staff and other resources to particular issues, by mobilizing expertise inside and outside government, and by consulting interest groups and members of Congress in designing and proposing legislation. Third, they can *legitimate policy* by supporting legislation in Congress and brokering compromises. Conversely, they can block unwanted legislation through the use of the veto power.[7] Fourth, presidents use their powers to oversee the bureaucracy in myriad ways to influence *policy implementation*. Finally, they constantly *assess and evaluate* existing policies and propose reforms.

Presidents have different governing styles, and some exercise their powers more aggressively and secretly than others. Presidents Richard Nixon and George W. Bush pushed their executive powers to the limit—and many would argue beyond constitutional limits.[8] Others attempt to govern in a more open and collaborative manner, as Barack Obama has pledged to do.

In the end, however, presidents cannot govern alone; they are all part of a government of "separated powers."[9] They must rely on Congress to enact legislation and provide the funding to carry out all activities of the federal government. When Congress and the presidency are controlled by different parties, the president may have little control over the policy agenda. But even when the president's own party has a majority in one or both houses, majority coalitions on particular issues may be difficult if not impossible to build. It has become increasingly difficult to enact legislation since most major bills are now subject to filibusters in the Senate, which require sixty votes to overcome. Nearly all major rules and regulations are also challenged in the courts by affected parties, often tying up administrative actions in litigation that goes on for years (see chapter 6). Finally, of course, events beyond the president's control—such as the terrorist attacks of September 11, 2001, and the financial meltdown of late 2008—can profoundly alter the president's agenda and prospects for success.

Presidential success thus rests in large part on circumstances, and some moments in history are more conducive to radical policy change than others.[10] There have been two periods in recent times when the mood of the public has demanded strong presidential leadership on the environment. The first was 1970–1972 when the modern environmental movement that gathered force in the 1960s reached a crescendo. President Nixon understood the strength of this movement and decided to lead rather than follow its momentum. He declared the 1970s "the environmental decade"; signed the National Environmental Policy Act, the Clean Air Act, the Endangered Species Act, and other landmark legislation; and created the U.S. Environmental Protection Agency (EPA) by executive order.[11] The second recent wave of pro-environmental opinion gathered force in the 1980s during the presidency of Ronald Reagan and peaked during 1988–1990. After serving as Reagan's vice president and then being elected president in 1988, George H. W. Bush declared himself "the environmental president" and supported passage of a major Clean Air Act in 1990, much as Nixon had in 1970. Shifts in public opinion in 2007–2008 may provide President Obama with the opportunity to launch a third wave of environmental activism (chapter 3).

Classifying Environmental Presidencies

A president's influence on environmental policy can be evaluated by examining a few basic indicators: (1) the president's environmental *agenda* as expressed in campaign statements, policy documents, and major speeches such as inaugural and state of the union addresses, (2) presidential *appointments* to key positions in government departments and agencies and to the White House staff, (3) the relative priority given to environmental programs in the president's proposed *budgets*, (4) presidential *legislative initiatives* or vetoes, (5) *executive orders* issued by the president, (6) White House *oversight* of environmental regulation, and (7) presidential support for or opposition to *international environmental agreements*. By these criteria some presidents can be seen as much more pro-environmental than others.

Measuring actual performance outcomes is more difficult. For example, President Bill Clinton achieved few of the policy changes he espoused during his 1992 campaign yet ended his presidency with a strong contribution to public lands conservation. Incumbents should be judged in terms of not only how much of their initial agenda they achieve but also how successful they are relative to the circumstances and constraints they face. Ultimately, of course, the success of policy changes should be gauged in terms of their effects on the environment. Do they, for example, result in more or less pollution? But given the multitude of factors that affect the environment and the difficulties of monitoring and measuring environmental quality, it is rarely possible to make definitive statements about specific policy outcomes (see chapter 1).

We can, however, classify presidents generally in terms of their attitudes toward the seriousness of environmental problems, the relative priority they give to environmental protection compared with other policy problems, and whether they attempt to strengthen or weaken existing environmental policies and institutions. In this broad perspective, recent presidents seem to fall into three main categories: opportunistic leaders, frustrated underachievers, and rollback advocates.[12]

Opportunistic Leaders

Two presidents, Richard Nixon and the elder George Bush, held office at the peak of public opinion surges demanding action to strengthen environmental protection. Although both had served as vice president in conservative Republican administrations and neither had a strong record on environmental policy, both adopted the conservationist mantel of Theodore Roosevelt and supported major advances in national environmental protection early in their presidencies. As opposition to further policy changes mounted from traditional Republican constituencies, however, both reverted to more conservative policies later in their terms. Nixon, for example, vetoed the Federal Water Pollution Control Act Amendments of 1972 (which passed over his veto), and Bush declared a moratorium on all new environmental regulation and refused to endorse binding international agreements to deal with climate change and biodiversity at the 1992 Earth Summit in Rio de Janeiro, Brazil.

Frustrated Underachievers

Two Democratic presidents, Jimmy Carter and Bill Clinton, came to office with large environmental agendas and strong support from environmental constituencies but accomplished less than expected. Carter had little success in dealing with the energy crisis of the late 1970s, whereas Clinton had only minor legislative achievements in the field of environmental policy. Both presidents were forced by competing priorities and lack of public and congressional support to compromise their environmental agendas. Yet both achieved belated success in protecting public lands and tightening environmental regulations before leaving office. Carter preserved millions of acres of Alaskan wilderness and helped pass the Superfund bill to clean up toxic waste sites after losing the 1980 election, and Clinton issued executive orders creating or enlarging twenty-two national monuments and protecting millions of acres of forest lands during his waning days in office.

Rollback Advocates

Two presidents have entered office with negative environmental agendas: Ronald Reagan and George W. Bush. Both represented antiregulatory forces in the Republican Party that sought to roll back or weaken existing environmental legislation. Reagan launched a crusade against what he considered unnecessary social regulation that he believed impeded economic growth. His stance on the environment aroused enormous controversy, and he was forced to moderate his policies by 1984. Bush also stressed the importance of economic growth over environmental protection. He launched a wide range of initiatives to soften environmental regulation during his first term but ultimately failed to alter basic environmental legislation.

In the following sections I first review the presidencies of Ronald Reagan, George H. W. Bush, and Bill Clinton as examples of these three categories. In each case I examine their use of presidential powers and evaluate their presidencies using the criteria mentioned in this introduction. I then offer a fuller assessment of George W. Bush's record and Barack Obama's prospects.

The Reagan Revolution: Challenge to Environmentalism

The "environmental decade" of the 1970s came to an abrupt halt with Reagan's victory in 1980. Although the environment was not a major issue in the election, Reagan was the first president to come to office with an avowedly anti-environmental agenda. Reflecting the Sagebrush Rebellion— an attempt by several western states to claim ownership of federal lands—as well as long years of public relations work for corporate and conservative causes, Reagan viewed environmental conservation as fundamentally at odds with economic growth and prosperity. He saw environmental regulation as a barrier to "supply side" economics and sought to reverse or weaken many of the policies of the previous decade.[13] Although only partially successful, Reagan's radical agenda laid the groundwork for a renewed attack on environmental policy a decade later.

After a period of economic decline, Reagan's landslide victory appeared to reflect a strong mandate for policy change. And with a new Republican majority in the Senate, he was able to gain congressional support for the Economic Recovery Act of 1981, which embodied much of his program. The law reduced income taxes by nearly 25 percent and deeply cut spending for environmental and social programs. Despite this initial victory, however, Reagan faced a Congress that was divided on most issues and did not support his broader environmental goals. On the contrary, the bipartisan majority that had enacted most of the environmental legislation of the 1970s remained largely intact.

Faced with this situation, Reagan turned to what has been termed an "administrative presidency."[14] Essentially this involved an attempt to change federal policies by maximizing control of policy implementation within the executive branch. That is, rather than trying to rewrite legislation, Reagan used his powers as chief executive to alter the direction of policy.

The administrative strategy initially had four major components: (1) careful screening of all appointees to environmental and other agencies to ensure compliance with Reagan's ideological goals, (2) tight policy coordination through cabinet councils and White House staff, (3) deep cuts in the budgets of environmental agencies and programs, and (4) an enhanced form of regulatory oversight to eliminate or revise regulations considered burdensome by industry.

Reagan's appointment of officials who were overtly hostile to the mission of their agencies aroused strong opposition from the environmental community. In particular, his selection of Anne Gorsuch (later Burford) to head the EPA and James Watt as secretary of the interior provoked controversy from the beginning because both were attorneys who had spent long years litigating against environmental regulation. Both made it clear that they intended to rewrite the rules and procedures of their agencies to accommodate industries such as mining, logging, and oil and gas.

In the White House, Reagan lost no time in changing the policy machinery to accomplish the same goal. He attempted to abolish the Council on Environmental Quality (CEQ), and when that effort failed because it would require congressional legislation, he drastically cut its staff and ignored its members' advice. In its place he appointed Vice President George Bush to head a new Task Force on Regulatory Relief to review and propose revisions or rescissions of regulations in response to complaints from business. All regulations were analyzed by a staff agency, the Office of Information and Regulatory Affairs (OIRA) in the Office of Management and Budget. OIRA held up, reviewed, and revised hundreds of EPA and other regulations to reduce their effect on industry. Although regulatory oversight is an accepted and necessary function of the modern presidency, the Reagan White House's effort to shape and control all regulatory activity in the interests of political clients raised serious questions of improper administrative procedure and violation of statutory intent.[15]

Finally, Reagan's budget cuts had major effects on the capacity of environmental agencies to implement their growing policy mandates. The EPA lost approximately one-third of its operating budget and one-fifth of its personnel in the early 1980s. The CEQ lost most of its staff and barely continued to function. In the Interior Department and elsewhere, funds were shifted from environmental to development programs.[16]

Not surprisingly, Congress responded by investigating OIRA procedures and other activities of Reagan appointees, especially Burford and Watt. Burford came under heavy attack for confidential dealings with business and political interests that allegedly led to sweetheart deals on matters such as Superfund cleanups. After refusing to disclose documents, she was found in contempt of Congress and forced to resign (along with twenty other high-level EPA officials) in March 1983. Watt was pilloried in Congress for his efforts to open virtually all public lands (including wilderness areas) and offshore coastal areas to mining and oil and gas development. He resigned later in 1983 after making some thoughtless remarks about the ethnic composition of a commission appointed to investigate his coal-leasing policies. By that time he had alienated almost everyone in Congress.[17]

Because of these embarrassments and widespread public and congressional opposition to weakening environmental protection, Reagan's deregulatory campaign was largely spent by the end of his first term. Recognizing that his policies had backfired, the president took few new initiatives during his second term. His appointees to the EPA and Interior after 1983 diffused some of the political conflict generated by Watt and Burford. EPA administrators (William Ruckelshaus and Lee Thomas) were able to restore some funding and credibility to their agency.

Reagan clearly lost the battle of public opinion on the environment. His policies had the unintended effect of revitalizing environmental organizations. Membership in such groups increased dramatically, and polls indicated a steady growth in the public's concern for the environment that peaked in the late 1980s. It is not surprising that Bush decided to distance himself from Reagan's environmental record in the 1988 election.

The Bush Transition

The elder Bush's presidency returned to a more moderate tradition of Republican leadership, particularly in the first two years. While promising to "stay the course" on Reagan's economic policies, Bush also pledged a "kinder and gentler" America. Although his domestic policy agenda was the most limited of any recent president, it included action on the environment. Indeed, during the campaign Bush declared himself a "conservationist" in the tradition of Teddy Roosevelt and promised to be an "environmental president."[18]

If Bush surprised almost everyone by seizing the initiative on what most assumed was a strong issue for the Democrats, he impressed environmentalists even more by soliciting their advice and by appointing a number of environmental leaders to his administration. William Reilly, the highly respected president of the World Wildlife Fund and the Conservation Foundation, became EPA administrator; and Michael Deland, formerly New England director of the EPA, became chairman of the CEQ. Bush promised to restore the CEQ to an influential role and made it clear that he intended to work closely with the Democratic Congress to pass a new Clean Air Act early in his administration.

Yet Bush's nominees to head the public lands and natural resource agencies were not much different from those of the Reagan administration. In particular, his choice of Manuel Lujan Jr., a ten-term retired representative from New Mexico, to serve as secretary of the interior indicated that no major departures would be made in western land policies. The president's top White House advisers were also much more conservative on environmental matters than were Reilly and Deland. This was especially true of his chief of staff, John Sununu.

Bush pursued a bipartisan strategy in passing the Clean Air Act Amendments of 1990, arguably the single most important legislative achievement of his presidency. His draft bill, sent to Congress on July 21, 1989, had three major goals: to control acid rain by reducing sulfur dioxide emissions from coal-burning power plants by nearly half by 2000, to reduce air pollution in eighty urban areas that still had not met 1977 air quality standards, and to lower emissions of nearly 200 airborne toxic chemicals by 75 to 90 percent by 2000. To reach the acid precipitation goals—to which the White House devoted most of its attention—Bush proposed a cap-and-trade system rather than command-and-control regulation to achieve emissions reductions more efficiently (see chapter 9).

But it was probably Bush's role as chief diplomat that most defined his environmental image. The president threatened to boycott the UN Conference on Environment and Development (the Earth Summit) in June 1992 until he had ensured that the climate change convention to be signed would contain no binding targets for carbon dioxide reduction. He further alienated much of the world as well as the U.S. environmental community by refusing to sign the Convention on Biological Diversity despite efforts by his delegation chief, William Reilly, to seek a last-minute compromise.[19] Thus, despite Bush's other accomplishments in foreign policy, the United States was isolated and embarrassed in international environmental diplomacy.

The Clinton Presidency: Frustrated Ambitions

President Bill Clinton entered office with high expectations from environmentalists. His campaign promises included many environmental pledges: to raise the corporate average fuel economy (CAFE) standard for automobiles, encourage mass transit programs, support renewable energy research and development, limit U.S. carbon dioxide emissions to 1990 levels by 2000, create a new solid waste reduction program and provide other incentives for recycling, pass a new Clean Water Act with standards for non-point sources, reform the Superfund program and tighten enforcement of toxic waste laws, protect ancient forests and wetlands, preserve the Arctic National Wildlife Refuge, sign the biodiversity convention, and restore funding to UN population programs.[20]

Beyond this impressive list of commitments, Clinton and Vice President Gore departed from traditional rhetoric about the relationship between environmental protection and economic growth. They argued that the jobs-versus-environment debate presented a false choice because environmental cleanup creates jobs and the future competitiveness of the U.S. economy will depend on developing environmentally clean, energy-efficient technologies. They proposed a variety of investment incentives and infrastructure projects to promote such green technologies. (President Obama has adopted much the same philosophy.)

Clinton's early actions indicated that he intended to deliver on his environmental agenda. The environmental community largely applauded his appointments to key environmental positions. Perhaps most important, Gore was given the lead responsibility for formulating and coordinating environmental policy. His influence was quickly seen in the reorganization of the White House and in Clinton's budget proposals, which contained elements of the new thinking that he and Gore had espoused during the campaign.

One of the administration's first acts was to establish a new Office of Environmental Policy (OEP). The new office was to coordinate departmental policies on environmental issues and to ensure integration of environmental considerations into the work of all departments.[21] OEP director Kathleen McGinty and EPA administrator Carol Browner were former Senate environmental aides to Gore. There was also a considerable strengthening of the president's staff for international environmental affairs. Finally, a new President's Council on Sustainable Development was appointed in June 1993.

Other appointments to the cabinet and executive office staffs were largely pro-environmental. The most notable environmental leader was Bruce Babbitt, a former Arizona governor and president of the League of Conservation Voters, who became secretary of the interior. In contrast to his predecessors in the Reagan and Bush administrations, Babbitt came to office with a strong reform agenda for western public lands management.[22]

Although Clinton entered office with an expansive agenda and Democratic majorities in both houses of Congress, his environmental agenda quickly got bogged down. Two events early in the term gave the administration an appearance of environmental policy failure. Babbitt promptly launched a campaign to "revolutionize" western land use policies, including a proposal in Clinton's first budget to raise grazing fees on public lands closer to private market levels (something natural resource economists had advocated for many years). The predictable result was a furious outcry from cattle ranchers and their representatives in Congress. After meeting with several western Democratic senators, Clinton backed down and removed the proposal from the bill. Much the same thing happened on the so-called BTU tax. This was a proposal to levy a broad-based tax on the energy content of fuels as a means of promoting energy conservation and addressing climate change. Originally included in the president's budget package at Gore's request, it was eventually dropped in favor of a much smaller gasoline tax (4.3 cents per gallon) in the face of fierce opposition from members of both parties in Congress.

Clinton failed to satisfy environmentalists on other issues as well. Many opposed his support for the North American Free Trade Agreement (NAFTA) and the World Trade Organization. And although Clinton signed the biodiversity convention rejected by President Bush and announced his intention to stabilize carbon dioxide emissions by 2000, his administration failed to implement either policy. The biodiversity treaty was not submitted for ratification by the Senate, and the administration's climate change action plan announced in October 1993 called only for weak voluntary measures.

The 1994 elections gave Republicans control of both houses of Congress and thirty-one governorships. Claiming a mandate for the "Contract with America," the new House Speaker, Newt Gingrich, R-Ga., vowed "to begin decisively changing the shape of the government."[23] With the help of industry lobbyists, the new congressional leaders unleashed a massive effort to rewrite the environmental legislation of the past quarter-century.[24] Although Clinton derailed most of these initiatives, he was unable to pursue many of his own programs.

Like Reagan, Clinton was forced by congressional opposition to rely primarily on his powers as chief executive to pursue his environmental agenda. A "reinventing environmental regulation" program launched in 1995 produced some fifty new programs. EPA administrator Browner also strengthened existing regulations and enforcement. For example, in 1997 she issued tighter ambient air quality standards for ozone and small particulate matter. In the final year of the Clinton administration, the EPA proposed a series of new regulations tightening standards on other forms of pollution, including diesel emissions from trucks and buses and arsenic in drinking water.

In addition to strengthening the EPA, the Clinton administration took numerous measures to protect public lands and endangered species. For example, it helped to broker agreements to protect the Florida Everglades, Yellowstone National Park, and ancient redwood groves in California. The White House actively promoted voluntary agreements to establish habitat conservation plans to protect endangered species and other wildlife throughout the country.[25] More dramatically, Clinton used his executive authority under the Antiquities Act of 1906 to issue proclamations establishing nineteen new national monuments and enlarging three others, the total covering 6.1 million acres.[26] Finally, in January 2001, just prior to leaving office, Clinton issued a long-awaited executive order protecting nearly 60 million acres of roadless areas in national forests from future road construction and hence from logging and development.[27] He could thus claim to have protected more public land in the contiguous U.S. than any president since Theodore Roosevelt.[28]

Even so, the Clinton administration largely failed to develop an effective response to perhaps the greatest challenge of the new century, climate change. Although the administration agreed to support an international protocol setting binding targets and timetables for greenhouse gas reductions, it refused to commit the United States to meaningful reductions prior to the Kyoto treaty negotiations in December 1997. By then the president was severely constrained by congressional opposition to any agreement limiting U.S. emissions.[29] Ultimately Clinton authorized Vice President Gore to break the deadlock at Kyoto with an offer to reduce U.S. greenhouse gas emissions to 7 percent below 1990 levels by 2008–2012, and the United States signed the treaty in 1998. However, Congress made it clear that it would not ratify the agreement and prohibited all efforts to implement it.

President George W. Bush: Regulatory Retreat

George W. Bush took office in 2001 with a weak mandate to govern. He had lost the popular vote to Al Gore and had been declared the Electoral College winner only after several weeks of wrangling over contested Florida ballots, culminating with intervention by the Supreme Court. The Republicans also barely controlled the House of Representatives and lost control of the Senate when Sen. James Jeffords, R-Vt., declared himself an independent in May 2001. Not until the midterm elections of 2002 did Bush secure a majority in both houses of Congress.

By then President Bush had an entirely new leadership mandate as a result of the September 11, 2001, terrorist attacks on New York City and Washington, D.C. As the self-declared "war president," Bush was able to dominate the domestic as well as international scene as few American presidents have done. He launched wars in Afghanistan and Iraq and repeatedly cited the "war on terror" to justify expanded presidential powers in virtually every area of policy. Despite greatly increased military spending, Bush achieved a series of major tax cuts and passed new legislation regarding education and health care, which contributed to his reelection in 2004. However, as public support for the war in Iraq waned, the Democrats regained control of both houses of Congress in the 2006 midterm elections. By the end of Bush's second term the administration was in full retreat as the economy fell into deep recession and the financial system suffered the worst crisis since the Great Depression. Against the opposition of many of his erstwhile Republican allies, Bush supported massive government intervention in the economy to prevent the collapse of the banking, insurance, housing, and auto industries in the waning days of his administration.

Given these dire crises and failures, it is difficult to compare the Bush presidency to any other recent administration. Nevertheless, if we focus only on environmental policies, we can discern some familiar patterns. Like Ronald Reagan, Bush used the executive powers of the presidency to advance an antiregulatory, pro-business agenda throughout most of his tenure. He exercised the powers of appointment, budget, regulatory oversight, and rulemaking to weaken environmental policies.[30] Vice President Dick Cheney played a leading role in selecting cabinet appointees and implementing Bush's energy and environmental policies.[31]

Many of Bush's policy decisions are discussed in subsequent chapters (see especially chapters 7 and 8). The following section offers a brief summary of his administrative style.

Bush's Administrative Style

George W. Bush practiced what one political scientist has called a "pure executive style."[32] By this he meant that Bush relied on the powers of his office rather than on cooperation with other parts of government or on compromise with contending forces. In the process he extended presidential powers to the maximum and demanded a "unitary executive," that is, full control of the executive branch regardless of any restrictions established by Congress. He attempted to carry out his agenda with a minimum of collaboration and transparency, often invoking presidential prerogatives to keep information and advice secret from Congress and the public.

Appointments. With the exception of Christine Todd Whitman, the former governor of New Jersey who was appointed to head the EPA, Bush's initial appointments to environmental and natural resource agencies were largely drawn from business corporations or from conservative interest groups, law firms, and think tanks. Among the more controversial of these appointees were Secretary of Interior Gale Norton, a protégée of James Watt and a strong advocate of resource development; J. Steven Griles, her deputy secretary and a longtime coal and oil industry lobbyist; Julie MacDonald, deputy assistant secretary of interior for fish and wildlife (responsible for the Endangered Species Act); and Mark Rey, a timber industry lobbyist, as undersecretary of agriculture for natural resources and environment (including the U.S. Forest Service). All of these officials left office under a cloud of investigation after ignoring numerous environmental roadblocks to resource exploitation. (Griles later went to prison for obstruction of justice in the Jack Abramoff case.)

Bush's White House and Executive Office staffs were also filled with business advocates, including chief of staff Andrew H. Card Jr.; CEQ chairman James Connaughton and his chief of staff, Philip Cooney (who edited scientific reports on global warming); and OIRA heads John D. Graham and his successor, Susan E. Dudley (the latter from the staunchly antiregulatory Mercatus Center at George Mason University).[33]

Some of Bush's other environmental appointees were less controversial, if not less partisan. When Whitman resigned in 2003 after being undercut on climate change and clean air standards by the vice president and other cabinet members, Bush appointed Michael Leavitt, the conservative governor of Utah, as EPA administrator. Leavitt moved on to become secretary of health and human services in 2005, and Stephen L. Johnson was named EPA administrator. Although a career scientist at the EPA, Johnson repeatedly bowed to White House pressures on key decisions and failed to restore the reputation of the agency.[34] The former governor and senator from Idaho, Dirk Kempthorne, succeeded Norton as secretary of interior in 2006 and largely continued her policies.

Overall, a comparative study of all presidential environmental and natural resource (ENR) appointees since 1976 concluded that although the Bush appointees were no less qualified by education and experience than those of other presidents, the Bush administration stood out for its "resumption of Reagan-era strategies of tight control over ENR appointee selection, high expectations for political loyalty among appointees, and appointees' elevated demands for agency responsiveness."[35]

Political Control. Much of this "responsiveness" was enforced by aggressive political control from the White House and Executive Office of the

President. Although Bush did not establish a formal mechanism such as Reagan's cabinet councils, his staff and the Office of the Vice President kept close watch over agency decision making. OIRA carried out extensive regulatory review of proposed regulations, demanding that agencies justify all new rules on the basis of strict benefit-cost analysis. Existing rules were also reviewed at the behest of business groups in order to reduce the burden of regulation wherever possible.[36] The president issued a new executive order requiring that each agency must have a regulatory policy office run by a political appointee to manage the regulatory review process.[37] In addition to these formal procedures, which often had the effect of slowing down or reversing regulation ("paralysis by analysis"), the vice president and White House operatives often intervened directly in the details of agency decision making.[38]

The result was a highly politicized form of administration in which the political interests of the president and his supporters frequently overrode scientific and technical considerations in the bureaucracy. Indeed, the Bush-Cheney administration was repeatedly shown to have ignored the advice of scientific experts or distorted scientific information to justify policy decisions (see chapters 7 and 8 for examples). There is a large literature on this subject, much of it generated by whistle-blowers.[39] A report by the Union of Concerned Scientists released in April 2008 found that 889 of nearly 1,600 staff scientists at the EPA reported that they had experienced political interference in their work in the previous five years.[40] The House Oversight and Government Reform Committee held hearings and collected 27,000 pages of documents on climate change science, concluding that there had been a systematic effort by the Bush administration to "manipulate climate science and mislead policymakers and the public about the dangers of global warming."[41] And in December 2008 the inspector general of the Interior Department issued a report finding that Julie MacDonald and other department officials had altered scientific evidence regarding protection of endangered species in at least fifteen cases.[42] It is doubtful that any previous administration had misused science to this extent.

Budget Priorities. President Bush's first budget proposal, for fiscal year 2002, called for a modest 4 percent increase in overall domestic discretionary spending but an 8 percent reduction in funding for natural resource and environmental programs (the largest cut for any sector). The EPA's budget was to be slashed by nearly $500 million, or 6.4 percent, and the Interior Department budget was slated for a 3.5 percent cut.[43] Congress, however, did not approve these budget cuts; in fact, the EPA's budget was *increased* to $7.9 billion, $600 million more than the president had requested. The overall budget (including grant programs) peaked at almost $8.4 billion in FY 2004, but declined thereafter to $7.4 billion in FY 2008.[44] In real terms (adjusted for inflation) the EPA's operating budget, which covers all of its regulatory activities, remained flat during 2000–2008 (see appendix 2). Although overall support for natural resource and environmental programs rose during 2000–2008, funding for pollution control and abatement fell sharply in real terms (see appendix 4). Nevertheless, Bush continued to push for cuts. He proposed only $7.1 billion for the EPA in his FY 2009 budget, and current funding was projected to decline to $6.8 billion through 2013.[45] These actual and proposed cuts made it difficult for the EPA to fill positions and, along with constant political interference, contributed to low staff morale in the agency.

Executive Actions. President Bush's energy and environmental agenda was quickly shaped after he took office. A national energy plan, entitled *Reliable, Affordable, and Environmentally Sound Energy for America's Future,* was drafted in secrecy during spring 2001 by a task force appointed by Vice President Cheney.[46] By all accounts, virtually all of the outside experts consulted were from energy producers and related industries, and many of the report's 106 recommendations directly reflected these interests.[47] The plan called for major increases in future energy supplies, including domestic oil, gas, nuclear, and "clean coal" development, and for streamlining environmental regulations to accelerate new energy production. A bill incorporating these and other aspects of the Bush-Cheney plan, together with additional tax breaks for the energy industries (some $32 billion in all), quickly passed the House of Representatives in 2001 but later stalled in the Senate when authorization to drill in the Arctic National Wildlife Refuge was defeated.[48] Eventually, an energy bill passed in 2005 providing massive subsidies to energy producers (see chapter 5), but by then many of the original plan's recommendations had already been implemented by administrative actions. For example, coal, oil, and gas leasing had already been greatly expanded in the West (see chapter 8). President Bush also set aside or rewrote many of the Clinton administration's last-minute resource conservation rules, including the Roadless Area Rule.

Energy policy provided a template for many of Bush's other executive actions. After meeting (usually secretly) with business representatives, legislation and possible regulatory changes were drawn up. In some cases legislation was then proposed—for example, the "Clear Skies" bill introduced in Congress in 2002 incorporated many of industries' suggestions for scaling back pollution control requirements of the Clean Air Act.[49] When this legislation went nowhere, Bush proceeded to issue executive orders that, in effect, implemented similar rules by fiat. For example, one of the more controversial rules reduced requirements for installation of new pollution equipment when power plants and oil refineries expanded or increased production (the "new source review" provision of the Clean Air Act). A broader Clean Air Interstate Rule issued in 2005 set standards for conventional air pollutants such as sulfur dioxide and ozone in twenty-eight eastern states, while another rule regulated mercury emissions from coal-fired power plants. These rules raised current standards but were lower than those recommended by EPA scientists (see chapter 7). However, they were all eventually struck down by the courts, although the Interstate Rule was reinstated in December 2008 as "better than having no rule at all"[50] by the D.C. Court of Appeals (for other examples, see chapter 6).

Perhaps Bush's most notorious executive action was his rejection of the Kyoto Protocol on climate change early in his term. Calling the treaty "fatally flawed," the president unilaterally withdrew United States participation in the international regime for regulating greenhouse gases. This was part of a larger shift away from international treaty obligations in the Bush White House, but it presaged an eight-year effort to block any mandatory requirements for controlling carbon dioxide and other greenhouse gases. Bush attempted to shift negotiations away from the Kyoto framework by proposing new voluntary commitments by major emitting nations, including large developing countries such as China (which surpassed the United States as the leading source of greenhouse gases in 2008). However, little came of these efforts, as the rest of the world continued negotiations toward a post-Kyoto treaty (see chapter 12).

Like previous presidents, Bush attempted to institutionalize many of his administration's policies by issuing last-minute rules and regulations to bind his successor. These included regulations making it easier to dispose of wastes from mountain-top coal mining under the Clean Water Act, rules opening more public lands for oil and gas drilling, and new rules freeing federal agencies from the obligation to consult independent scientists under the Endangered Species Act before approving projects that might harm endangered wildlife.[51] The latter also excluded Endangered Species Act protection of the polar bear from being used to justify action on global warming (as polar ice sheets melt, the bears are increasingly threatened).

On the positive side, Bush used his powers under the Antiquities Act to create four national monuments in the Pacific Ocean. In 2006 he established the world's largest marine reserve covering 140,000 square miles in the Northwest Hawaiian Islands. Then, just before leaving office in January 2009, he designated three more monuments over huge tracts of ocean in the western Pacific near American Samoa. These sparsely inhabited areas of reefs, atolls, and undersea mountains will be protected from commercial fishing, drilling, and mineral extraction, thereby preserving their unique ecological features. Thus, despite his record of encouraging exploitation of public lands within the continental United States, Bush could claim to have done more to protect unique areas of the ocean than any other president.[52]

Policy Consequences

The Bush-Cheney administration's reliance on executive means to implement its agenda has had serious consequences for environmental policy. For the most part, executive rulemaking bypassed Congress and opened decisions to immediate legal challenge. In fact, most of the administration's proposed rule changes were rejected or remanded for revision by the courts, or are likely to be reversed by the Obama administration. The effects were thus primarily to delay implementation of existing laws and to prevent adoption of new requirements such as regulation of mercury pollution from coal-burning power plants. Other laws, such as the Endangered Species Act and the Clean Water Act, were poorly enforced and weakened by regulatory changes. Some regulations were revised under court orders to comply with requirements of the law. For example, new standards for ozone and lead emissions were issued under the Clean Air Act.[53] However, policy driven by the courts is an expensive, time-consuming, and inefficient process. On the other side of the coin, the Bush administration brought many fewer prosecutions against polluters than previous administrations.[54]

George W. Bush's principal environmental policy legacy, like his father's, is likely to be his refusal to address climate change. During his first term, Bush refused to acknowledge the growing scientific consensus on global warming and opposed all efforts to limit greenhouse gas emissions. Instead, he supported continuing research programs on climate science and technological development, including new efforts to develop hydrogen energy and other alternative fuels. However, as dependence on foreign oil and rising fuel prices became a more important national security issue, Bush began to revise his stance. In his 2006 State of the Union address, Bush decried the United States' "addiction to oil" and called for a 75 percent reduction of oil imports by 2025. This was largely to be achieved by massive expansion in production of ethanol and other biofuels.[55] Energy bills signed in 2005 and 2007 provided increased subsidies for alternative (as well as conventional) energy production and raised fuel-efficiency standards for cars to 35 miles per gallon by 2020 (see chapter 5).[56] But despite a landmark U.S. Supreme Court decision in April 2007 holding that the EPA could regulate greenhouse gases under the Clean Air Act, the White House refused to allow the agency to develop a regulatory strategy for climate change or to grant California a waiver to regulate carbon dioxide emissions from vehicles (see chapter 7). In April 2008 Bush belatedly called for the United States to halt the *growth* of greenhouse gas emissions by 2025.[57] As environmentalists were quick to point out, this would allow U.S. emissions to *rise* for another 17 years.

It is not possible to give a definitive quantitative assessment of the impacts of Bush administration policies on environmental quality. However, it appears that trends toward air quality improvement since the 1970s continued after 2000 (see chapter 1). This seems to be due primarily to an ongoing reduction in mobile source pollution from cars, trucks, and buses. However, emissions from the nation's electricity-generating plants and oil refiners have continued to grow, contributing to higher carbon dioxide and mercury levels. The Bush administration's effort to limit the regulation of coal-fired power plants is likely to be seen as one of its most significant environmental failures.

Barack Obama: A New Environmental Era?

During the election campaign Barack Obama made it clear that he would depart radically from his predecessor's environmental and energy policies. To cite his campaign Web site: "As president, Barack Obama will make combating global warming a top priority. He will reinvigorate the Environmental Protection Agency (EPA), respecting its professionalism and scientific integrity. And he will protect our children from toxins like lead, be a responsible steward of our natural treasures and reverse the Bush administration's attempts to chip away at our nation's clean air and water standards."[58] In short, Obama promised to change virtually all of the Bush-Cheney policies outlined in the preceding section and to adopt a more transparent and collaborative approach to decision making. Among Obama's policy proposals were the following:[59]

- To establish a market-based cap-and-trade program for reducing U.S. carbon emissions to 1990 levels by 2020 and by 80 percent below 1990 levels by 2050
- To invest $150 billion over ten years in advanced energy technologies and to help to create millions of new jobs in clean energy
- To require 10 percent of electricity to come from renewable sources by 2012, and 25 percent by 2025
- To set national building efficiency goals toward making all new buildings carbon neutral (zero emissions) by 2030
- To channel major investments into improving our national electricity grid to enable new forms of generation to efficiently go online
- To double automobile fuel economy within eighteen years and to put one million plug-in hybrid cars on the road by 2015
- To tighten standards for power plant emissions of mercury
- To restore full funding to the Clean Water State Revolving Fund for wastewater treatment and pollution cleanup
- To uphold the Roadless Area Rule and to increase funding for national parks and forest management and for the Land and Water Conservation Fund
- To restore American leadership on climate change by reengaging the United States in the UN negotiations on climate change and to create a new Global Energy Forum comprised of the largest emitting nations

President Obama's choices for cabinet and top White House staff positions indicated that he intended to carry out his agenda. His appointments included Carol Browner, EPA head in the Clinton administration, as White House coordinator of energy and climate policy ("climate czar"); Lisa Jackson, a chemical engineer who had served in the EPA and as commissioner of the New Jersey Department of Environmental Protection, as EPA administrator; Steven Chu, a Nobel prize–winning physicist who directed the Lawrence Berkeley National Laboratory, as energy secretary; Sen. Ken Salazar, D-Colo., as interior secretary; and Nancy Sutley, deputy mayor of Los Angeles for energy and environment, as chair of the CEQ.[60] The League of Conservation Voters hailed this group as "a Green Dream Team."[61] It appeared to be the strongest environmental administration ever appointed by a president.

Obama pledged to give science a more important role in environmental policymaking. In addition to Chu, he appointed John Holdren as White House science adviser, director of the Office of Science and Technology Policy, and chair of the President's Council of Advisers on Science and Technology. Holdren, a physics professor at Harvard, is a leading expert on energy and advocate for action on climate change. Obama also appointed Jane Lubchenco, a marine biologist from Oregon State University, to head the National Oceanic and Atmospheric Administration, which plays a key role in monitoring the effects of global warming.[62] In his inaugural address, the new president stated that he would "restore science to its rightful place" in the administration.[63] How this plays out remains to be seen. One area to watch is how the regulatory review process changes. Obama appointed Cass Sunstein, a law professor from Harvard, to head the OIRA. Sunstein's views on risk assessment and cost-benefit analysis do not appear to be very different from those of his predecessors, but he is more attuned to this president's priorities.[64]

In making his appointments, Obama indicated that he intended to govern in a very different style than his predecessor. Often citing Abraham Lincoln's "team of rivals," he spoke of welcoming debate and disagreement within his cabinet and administration before making critical policy decisions.[65] He denounced the Bush administration's secrecy and constitutional abuses of power, and promised to restore a proper balance between the executive and other branches of government. His chief of staff, Rahm Emanuel, is a former party leader in the House of Representatives, and Obama and other former senators in the cabinet, as well as Vice President Joe Biden, have strong ties to the Democratic Senate leadership. Given the new Democratic majorities in both houses of Congress, the administration is well placed to pursue legislative strategies.

Obama enjoyed a remarkable early victory in February 2009 when his $787 billion stimulus package was passed by Congress. The American Recovery and Reinvestment Act provided some $80 billion in direct spending, tax incentives, and loan guarantees for clean energy projects (see appendix 1). Obama provided further evidence of the priority his administration intends to give to the environment in his first budget, for fiscal year 2010. The budget requested $10.5 billion for the EPA (48 percent more than requested by President Bush in his final budget), including $3.9 billion for the EPA's core operating budget and $3.9 billion for its clean water and drinking water funds. The Departments of Energy and the Interior also received increases for climate change, renewable energy and other environmental programs.[66]

President Obama wasted no time in utilizing his executive powers as well. During his first week in office he issued executive orders reversing George W. Bush's ban on aid to international family planning agencies and requiring the EPA to reconsider its 2007 refusal to grant California and thirteen other states a waiver to set higher fuel economy standards for cars than required by federal law (this issue is discussed in chapter 7).[67] However, it is unlikely that President Obama will follow the "administrative presidency" model of Ronald Reagan, George W. Bush, or Bill Clinton, at least in his first term. He will place more emphasis on his powers as opinion leader (using the "bully pulpit") and party and legislative leader. But if this approach fails, he is likely to fall back on administrative strategies similar to those of other presidents.

Conclusion

The record of recent presidents demonstrates that the White House has had a significant but hardly singular or consistent role in shaping national environmental policy. Presidents Richard Nixon, Jimmy Carter, and George H. W. Bush had their greatest successes in supporting environmental legislation. Facing more hostile Congresses, Presidents Ronald Reagan, Bill Clinton, and George W. Bush had the most influence (for better or worse) as chief executives who used administrative strategies to shape the direction of environmental policies. Nixon and the elder Bush responded to public pressures to become opportunistic, but largely constructive, environmental presidents. Carter and Clinton had positive environmental agendas but failed to achieve many of their primary goals. Reagan and the younger Bush attempted to block or weaken environmental protections as part of deregulatory strategies, but failed to permanently alter the structure of environmental legislation adopted in the 1970s. Both provoked counter-reactions in politics and public opinion in favor of stronger environmental action.

Whether Barack Obama can take advantage of the apparently large policy window opened by the Bush-Cheney administration's failures and become a more successful environmental president than his predecessors remains to be seen. His task will not be easy. The deep economic crisis facing him as he took office will force him to focus on reviving the economy as his first task. But the economic crisis also provided opportunities to use large government expenditures to stimulate the development of renewable sources of energy and other forms of technology that will benefit the environment. As the *New York Times* put it, Obama could fabricate "a climate policy wrapped inside an energy policy wrapped inside an economic policy."[68]

At the same time, truly global problems such as climate change, loss of biodiversity, ocean degradation, hazardous and toxic waste pollution, the spread of human and animal diseases, and nuclear proliferation require international collaboration. President Obama and Secretary of State Hillary Rodham Clinton have indicated that the United States will again become a leader on climate change and other issues.[69] The president thus has a vital hand to play in future environmental policymaking on the global as well as the domestic stage.

Suggested Web Sites

Council on Environmental Quality (www.whitehouse.gov/ceq) Provides analysis of environmental conditions and links to other useful sources throughout the federal government.

Department of the Interior (www.interior.gov) Official Web site for the department and bureaus within it.

Environmental Protection Agency (www.epa.gov) Official Web site for the EPA.

The Heritage Foundation (www.heritage.org) Offers research and analysis on energy and environmental issues from a conservative perspective.

Natural Resources Defense Council (www.nrdc.org) Provides analysis and criticism by a leading environmental organization.

OMB Watch (www.ombwatch.org) Follows budgets and regulatory policies.

Pew Center on Global Climate Change (www.pewclimate.org) Provides information from the leading think tank on climate change issues.

President's official Web site (www.whitehouse.gov).

REP America (www.repamerica.org) Represents moderate Republicans for environmental protection.

Notes

1. The candidates' positions were set out in considerable detail on their campaign Web sites, www.barackobama.com and www.johnmccain.com. See also Elisabeth Bumiller and John M. Broder, "Greenhouse Gas Must be Capped, McCain Asserts," *New York Times,* May 13, 2008; and Margaret Kriz, "Shades of Green: John McCain's Decision to Actively Compete with Barack Obama on Environmental Issues Is Quite Different from the Approach of Recent GOP Nominees," *National Journal,* June 21, 2008.
2. "McCain and Obama Supporters Largely Agree on Approaches to Energy, Climate Change," September 23, 2008, www.worldpublicopinion.org/pipa/articles/home_page/542.php?nid=&id=&pnt=542.
3. John M. Broder, "Proposal Ties Economic Stimulus to Energy Savings," *New York Times,* December 4, 2008.
4. John M. Broder, "Obama Meets with Gore," *New York Times,* December 9, 2008.
5. Dennis L. Soden, ed., *The Environmental Presidency* (Albany: State University of New York Press, 1999), 3.
6. Ibid., 346.
7. The veto power was further enhanced during the Bush-Cheney administration by frequent use of signing statements, through which the White House unilaterally interpreted newly enacted laws and declared that it would not enforce provisions that it considered unconstitutional or that violated presidential prerogatives. See, e.g., Charlie Savage, *Takeover: The Return of the Imperial Presidency and the Subversion of American Democracy* (New York: Little, Brown, 2007), chap. 10. The extent to which this power is itself constitutional is debatable.
8. See Savage, *Takeover;* and Charles O. Jones, "Governing Executively: Bush's Paradoxical Style," in John C. Fortier and Norman J. Ornstein, eds., *Second-Term Blues: How George W. Bush Has Governed* (Washington, D.C.: Brookings Institution/American Enterprise Institute, 2007).
9. Charles O. Jones, *The Presidency in a Separated System* (Washington, D.C.: Brookings Institution Press, 1994); *Separate but Equal Branches: Congress and the Presidency* (Chatham, N.J.: Chatham House, 1995).
10. See Frank R. Baumgartner and Bryan D. Jones, *Agendas and Instability in American Politics* (Chicago: University of Chicago Press, 1993).
11. On Nixon's environmental legacy, see John C. Whitaker, *Striking a Balance: Environment and Natural Resources Policy in the Nixon-Ford Years* (Washington, D.C.: American Enterprise Institute, 1976); Charles O. Jones, *Clean Air* (Pittsburgh: University of

Pittsburgh Press, 1975); Jonathan Aitken, *Nixon: A Life* (Washington, D.C.: Regnery, 1993).

12. The presidency of Gerald R. Ford is not considered here because he essentially continued Richard Nixon's policies and did not leave a distinctive environmental legacy.

13. For a more detailed analysis of Reagan's environmental record, see Michael E. Kraft and Norman J. Vig, "Environmental Policy in the Reagan Presidency," *Political Science Quarterly* 99 (fall 1984): 414–439; Vig and Kraft, eds., *Environmental Policy in the 1980s: Reagan's New Agenda* (Washington, D.C.: CQ Press, 1984).

14. Richard P. Nathan, *The Administrative Presidency* (New York: Wiley, 1983).

15. See Barry D. Freedman, *Regulation in the Reagan-Bush Era: The Eruption of Presidential Influence* (Pittsburgh: University of Pittsburgh Press, 1995); V. Kerry Smith, *Environmental Policy under Reagan's Executive Order: The Role of Cost-Benefit Analysis* (Chapel Hill: University of North Carolina Press, 1984).

16. On the impact of the Reagan budget cuts, see especially Robert V. Bartlett, "The Budgetary Process and Environmental Policy," and J. Clarence Davies, "Environmental Institutions and the Reagan Administration," in *Environmental Policy in the 1980s*, ed. Vig and Kraft.

17. For a more detailed summary of Watt's policies, see Paul J. Culhane, "Sagebrush Rebels in Office: Jim Watt's Land and Water Policies," in *Environmental Policy in the 1980s*, ed. Vig and Kraft, 293–318; C. Brant Short, *Ronald Reagan and the Public Lands: America's Conservation Debate* (College Station: Texas A&M University Press, 1989). Burford tells her side of the story in Anne M. Burford (with John Greenya), *Are You Tough Enough?* (New York: McGraw-Hill, 1986).

18. John Holusha, "Bush Pledges Aid for Environment," *New York Times*, September 1, 1988; Bill Peterson, "Bush Vows to Fight Pollution, Install 'Conservation Ethic,'" *Washington Post*, September 1, 1988.

19. Keith Schneider, "White House Snubs U.S. Envoy's Plea to Sign Rio Treaty," *New York Times*, June 5, 1992.

20. Bill Clinton and Al Gore, *Putting People First* (New York: Times Books, 1992), 89–99.

21. Ann Devroy, "Clinton Announces Plan to Replace Environmental Council," *Washington Post*, February 9, 1993. At the end of 1994 the OEP was folded into the CEQ, which continued to play an active role in the White House.

22. Timothy Egan, "Sweeping Reversal of U.S. Land Policy Sought by Clinton," *New York Times*, February 24, 1993.

23. "Taking Speaker's Mantle, Gingrich Vows 'Profound Transformation,'" *Congressional Quarterly Weekly Report*, December 10, 1994, 3522.

24. For a summary of the Republican agenda and responses to it, see "GOP Sets the 104th Congress on New Regulatory Course," *Congressional Quarterly Weekly Report*, June 17, 1995, 1693–1701.

25. As an alternative way of implementing the Endangered Species Act, the Clinton administration supported completion of more than 250 habitat conservation plans protecting some 170 endangered plant and animal species while allowing controlled development on 20 million acres of private land. William Booth, "A Slow Start Built to an Environmental End-run," *Washington Post*, January 13, 2001.

26. For a description of these monuments, see Reed McManus, "Six Million Sweet Acres," *Sierra*, September–October 2001, 40–53.

27. Douglas Jehl, "Road Ban Set for One-Third of U.S. Forests," *New York Times*, January 5, 2001; Eric Pianin, "Ban Protects 58.5 Million Forest Acres," *Washington Post*, January 5, 2001.

28. Bill Clinton, *My Life* (New York: Knopf, 2004), 948.

29. In particular, the Byrd-Hagel resolution (passed 95–0 on June 12, 1997) opposed any agreement that would harm the U.S. economy or that did not require control of greenhouse gas emissions by developing countries.

30. Douglas Jehl, "On Rules for Environment, Bush Sees a Balance, Critics a Threat," *New York Times*, February 23, 2003; Jonathan Weisman, "In 2003, It's Reagan

Revolution Redux," *Washington Post,* February 4, 2003; Bill Keller, "Reagan's Son," *New York Times Magazine,* January 26, 2003.

31. On Cheney's unprecedented role, see Jo Becker and Barton Gellman, "Leaving No Tracks," *Washington Post,* June 27, 2007; and Barton Gellman, *Angler: The Cheney Vice Presidency* (New York: Penguin, 2008).

32. Jones, "Governing Executively," 116.

33. On Cooney's role, see, e.g., Andrew C. Revkin, "With White House Approval, E.P.A. Pollution Report Omits Global Warming Section," *New York Times,* September 15, 2002; Revkin and Katharine Q. Seelye, "Report by the E.P.A. Leaves Out Data on Climate Change," *New York Times,* June 19, 2003; on Graham, see "New Regulatory Czar Takes Charge," *Science,* October 5, 2001, 32–33; and Rebecca Adams, "Regulating the Rule-Makers: John Graham at OIRA," *CQ Weekly,* February 23, 2002, 520–526. For Dudley's views, see Susan Dudley, "The Bush Administration's Regulatory Record," *Regulation,* 27, 4 (winter 2004).

34. See chap. 7 and Margaret Kriz, "Vanishing Act," *National Journal,* April 12, 2008. On Christine Whitman's resignation, see Whitman, *It's My Party, Too* (New York: Penguin, 2005).

35. Matthew R. Auer, "Presidential Environmental Appointees in Comparative Perspective," *Public Administration Review* (January/February 2008), 77. Bush's appointments to the Supreme Court and other federal courts were also solidly conservative and will influence regulatory policies for decades to come. See Charlie Savage, "Appeals Courts Pushed to Right by Bush Choices," *New York Times,* October 29, 2008.

36. Joel Brinkley, "Out of Spotlight, Bush Overhauls U.S. Regulations," *New York Times,* August 16, 2004; Bruce Barcott, "Changing All the Rules," *New York Times Magazine,* April 4, 2004.

37. Robert Pear, "Bush Directive Increases Sway on Regulation," *New York Times,* January 30, 2007.

38. See, for example, Becker and Gellman, "Leaving No Tracks."

39. See especially Chris Mooney, *The Republican War on Science* (New York: Basic Books, 2005).

40. Union of Concerned Scientists, "Hundreds of EPA Scientists Report Political Interference Over Last Five Years," April 23, 2008. At www.ucsusa.org.

41. House of Representatives, Oversight and Government Reform Committee, "Report Describes Systematic White House Effort to Manipulate Climate Change Science," press release, Washington, D.C., December 10, 2007.

42. Charlie Savage, "Report Finds Manipulation of Interior Dept. Actions," *New York Times,* December 16, 2008.

43. "Bush's Budget: The Losers," *Washington Post,* April 10, 2001; "Who Gets What Slice of the President's First Federal Budget Pie," *New York Times,* April 10, 2001.

44. Budgets for the EPA and other agencies since 1976 can be found at www.gpoaccess .gov/usbudget/fy09/hist.html.

45. Kriz, "Vanishing Act"; "Proposals for Domestic Spending in 2009," *Washington Post,* February 5, 2008. Budget projections can be found at the Web site given in note 44.

46. See also David E. Sanger and Joseph Kahn, "Bush, Pushing Energy Plan, Offers Scores of Proposals to Find New Power Sources," *New York Times,* May 18, 2001; "Energy Report Highlights," *Washington Post,* May 18, 2001; Joseph Kahn, "Cheney Promotes Increasing Supply as Energy Policy," *New York Times,* May 1, 2001.

47. Katharine Q. Seelye, "Bush Task Force on Energy Worked in Mysterious Ways," *New York Times,* May 16, 2001; Joseph Kahn, "Bush Advisers on Energy Report Ties to Industry," *New York Times,* June 3, 2001; Kahn, "Cheney Refuses to Release Energy Task Force Records," *New York Times,* August 4, 2001; Dan Van Natta Jr. and Neela Banerjee, "Documents Show Energy Official Met Only with Industry Leaders," *New York Times,* March 26, 2002.

48. Eric Pianin and Glenn Kessler, "In the End, Energy Bill Fulfilled Most Industry Wishes," *Washington Post,* August 3, 2001.

49. White House, "Fact Sheet: President Bush Announces Clear Skies & Global Climate Change Initiatives," February 14, 2002. See also Katharine Q. Seelye, "White House Rejected a Stricter Alternative to Clear Skies Plan," *New York Times*, April 28, 2002.

50. Felicity Barringer, "In Reversal, Court Allows a Bush Plan on Pollution," *New York Times*, December 24, 2008; "E.P.A.'s Doctor No," editorial, *New York Times*, December 25, 2008. The Interstate Rule was reinstated after the Bush administration dropped efforts to issue new last-minute regulations easing pollution control requirements for coal-fired power plants; see "Effort to Relax Pollution Limits Is Dropped," *New York Times*, December 11, 2008.

51. Robert Pear and Felicity Barringer, "Coal Mining Debris Rule Is Approved," *New York Times*, December 3, 2008; Felicity Barringer, "U.S. to Open Public Land for Drilling," *New York Times*, November 8, 2008; Juliet Eilperin, "Endangered Species Act Changes Give Agencies More Say," *Washington Post*, August 12, 2008; and Felicity Barringer, "Rule Eases a Mandate under a Law on Wildlife," *New York Times*, December 12, 2008.

52. John M. Broder, "Bush to Protect Vast New Pacific Tracts," *New York Times*, January 6, 2009; and editorial, "Mr. Bush's Monument," *New York Times*, January 7, 2009.

53. Matthew L. Wald, "Environmental Agency Tightens Smog Standard," *New York Times*, March 13, 2008; Felicity Barringer, "E.P.A. Toughens Standard on Lead Emissions," *New York Times*, October 17, 2008.

54. For example, in 2006 the EPA employed only 172 investigators in its Criminal Investigation Division, well below the minimum of 200 agents required by law. The number of criminal prosecutions, investigations, and convictions dropped by one-third, and civil lawsuits by nearly 70 percent, during the period 2002–2006. The administration claimed that it preferred to seek settlements through plea bargains and voluntary compliance programs. John Solomon and Juliet Eilperin, "EPA Lags in Enforcing Pollution Law, Data Reveal," Minneapolis *Star Tribune*, September 30, 2007.

55. In his 2007 State of the Union address, Bush called for mandatory standards requiring that 35 million gallons of renewable and alternative fuels be produced by 2017, nearly a fivefold increase.

56. See John M. Broder, "Bush Signs Broad Energy Bill," *New York Times*, December 19, 2007; Steven Mufson, "President Bush Signs Energy Bill," *Washington Post*, December 19, 2007.

57. Sheryl Gay Stolberg, "Bush Calls for U.S. to Halt Rise in Gas Emissions by 2025," *New York Times*, April 17, 2008; editorial, "Empty Promises on Warming," *New York Times*, April 22, 2008.

58. "Barack Obama and Joe Biden: Promoting a Healthy Environment," www.barackobama .com.

59. Ibid., and "Barack Obama and Joe Biden: New Energy for America," www.barackobama .com.

60. John M. Broder, "Obama Team Set on Environment," *New York Times*, December 11, 2008; "Title, but Unclear Power, for a New Climate Czar," *New York Times*, December 12, 2008; "Praise and Criticism for Proposed Interior Secretary," *New York Times*, December 18, 2008.

61. Editorial, "Mr. Obama's Green Team," *New York Times*, December 13, 2008.

62. Gardiner Harris, "4 Top Science Advisers Are Named by Obama," *New York Times*, December 21, 2008; editorial, "A New Respect for Science," *New York Times*, December 22, 2008.

63. See Gardiner Harris and William J. Broad, "Scientists Welcome the New Administration with Joy and Hope," *New York Times*, January 22, 2009.

64. See Cass Sunstein, *Laws of Fear: Beyond the Precautionary Principle* (Cambridge: Cambridge University Press, 2005).

65. See Doris Kearns Goodwin, *Team of Rivals: The Political Genius of Abraham Lincoln* (New York: Simon & Schuster, 2005).

66. Editorial, "An $80 Billion Start," *New York Times,* February 18, 2009; Jackie Calmes and Robert Pear, "Obama Plans Major Shifts in Spending," *New York Times,* February 27, 2009.
67. Peter Baker, "Obama Reverses Rule on U.S. Abortion Aid," *New York Times,* January 24, 2009; John M. Broder and Peter Baker, "Obama's Order Likely to Tighten Auto Standards," *New York Times,* January 26, 2009.
68. Editorial, "Save the Economy, and the Planet," *New York Times,* November 27, 2008.
69. Elisabeth Rosenthal, "Obama's Backing Increases Hopes for Climate Pact," *New York Times,* March 1, 2009.

5

Environmental Policy in Congress
Michael E. Kraft

They are now being forced to look at this. What is the United States going to do on the most important issue facing the planet? ... You have to have something concrete to get people's attention. This did it.

Frances Beinecke, president of the
Natural Resources Defense Council, June 6, 2008

The majority says climate change is the most important issue facing the planet. Yet they've rushed the debate on that topic and brought the bill to a premature end.

Sen. Mitch McConnell, R-Ky.,
Senate minority leader, June 6, 2008[1]

In June 2008 the U.S. Senate held its first real floor debate on climate change policy, widely considered to be the dominant environmental issue of the twenty-first century. As the two statements that open this chapter suggest, the process and its outcome were not what the measure's sponsors hoped to see, other than to force senators to think about the issue for a limited time. The debate took all of three and a half days and consisted mostly of partisan bickering and procedural delaying tactics.

The bill itself, S. 3036, the Lieberman-Warner Climate Security Act of 2008, was impressive. It sought to reduce U.S. emissions of carbon dioxide and other greenhouse gases by 70 percent by 2050, less than what most climate scientists believe to be necessary but nonetheless a credible first step toward long-term goals. It would have done so by establishing a market-based cap-and-trade program for greenhouse gas emissions, both giving away and selling through auctions emission credits to industry (such as coal-fired power plants, refineries, and manufacturers), and redistributing the money to industries, states, and consumers over the next four decades. The funds from sales were intended to defray higher energy costs and to invest in clean energy technologies for wind and solar generation; to spur energy efficiency, use of cellulosic biofuels, and development of carbon sequestration techniques; and to foster the manufacture and use of hybrid vehicles and mass transit projects.[2]

Democrats knew their chances for approving the bill in 2008 were slim, but they wanted to get the Senate on record on several key issues that would be important for shaping climate legislation in the next Congress, when they hoped to control the White House and thus would be more likely to gain approval of a bill. Republicans had many objections to the bill and how it was handled. They complained that the bill's manager, Sen. Barbara Boxer, D-Calif., chair of the Senate's pivotal Environment and Public Works Committee, did not hold the extensive hearings that are routinely expected for such a complex and far-reaching measure, for example, to document the bill's impact on the economy, and that she made last-minute changes in the bill that confused matters. Republicans also wanted consideration of the bill to be deferred until after a scheduled congressional recess in July, and they demanded that more time be allowed to debate dozens of their proposed amendments. In addition, they were not inclined to go along with the Democratic majority because they were peeved about the Democrats' refusal to act on President George W. Bush's nominations for appellate courts.

As a key sign of Republican frustration with the Democratic leadership, Minority Leader McConnell objected to a routine motion to dispense with reading a major substitute amendment (essentially a new bill) offered by Senator Boxer, and demanded that Senate clerks read aloud the entire 492-page bill. It took eight hours to do so, prompting Senate majority leader Harry Reid, D-Nev., to complain about Republican obstructionism and to demand a rare live quorum call that would force all senators to come to the chamber to vote; Reid's motion failed 27–28. In the end, Senator Reid pulled the climate change bill from the Senate floor after falling twelve votes short of the sixty needed to end a threatened Republican filibuster.

Climate change legislation fared no better in the House. Rep. Rick Boucher, D-Va., chair of the House subcommittee charged with developing a climate bill, said he was unable to draft one because he and the full Energy and Commerce Committee chair, John D. Dingell, D-Mich., wanted a bipartisan bill. Yet they could not succeed because the panel's top Republican, Joe Barton of Texas, did not believe that human activity was responsible for climate change and therefore opposed legislation. Taken together, these developments brought an end to the advancement of climate change policy in the 110th Congress (2007–2009).[3]

Paul Bledsoe, a spokesman for the National Commission on Energy Policy, captured the tone and implications of the congressional actions well: "I don't think either side came off well, politically. Dysfunction doesn't serve either party's interest." He might have added that mid-2008 was one of the worst possible times to consider climate change legislation that would dramatically raise energy prices when the cost of gasoline had just soared to new highs. As Sen. James M. Inhofe, R-Okla., a longtime skeptic on climate change, put it in speaking of the Senate cloture vote to end the filibuster, "Now Democrats are on record as supporting legislation that would significantly increase prices at the pump and in our homes." Democrats drew a different conclusion. They noted that fifty-four senators, including six who did not attend the day of the vote but who favored the bill (among them Barack Obama, D-Ill., and John McCain, R-Ariz., who were on the campaign trail), represented a substantial gain over earlier and less demanding legislation in 2005.[4] In that vein, Sen. Byron L. Dorgan, D-N.D., called the 2008 debate a "dress rehearsal" for what he hoped would be final action in 2009. Such action may indeed come in light of President Obama's strong commitment to climate change policy. Yet as was evident in early 2009, not all of the fifty-four senators who backed the bill would be comfortable with a climate change policy that did not provide substantial help to industries and home-owners heavily dependent on fossil fuels, particularly in the industrial Midwest and Plains states.[5]

Environmental Challenges and Political Constraints

The abbreviated climate change debate in 2008 says much about the way Congress deals with environmental issues today, and the many obstacles it will face in trying to make headway in the future on climate change and other environmental and natural resource issues. The capacity of the 110th Congress to act, like many congressional sessions before it, was deeply affected by what analysts have called an "era of partisan warfare" on Capitol Hill. Increasingly each party had appealed to its core constituency through a continuous political campaign that emphasized an ideological "message politics." In this context, policy compromise between the parties was never easy, as each often sought to deny the other any semblance of victory, even at the cost of stalemate in dealing with pressing national problems such as energy use and climate change.[6] These dynamics are certain to change to some extent during the presidency of Barack Obama, especially with the twenty-one additional seats that Democrats gained in the House and the eight in the Senate in the 2008 elections. Those gains moved the party close to the much-sought sixty-vote margin in the Senate that could protect them against Republican filibusters.[7]

Beyond the numbers themselves, there are other indications that the Senate will be more receptive to environmental issues in the 111th Congress (2009–2011). As noted in several other chapters in this volume, the nation also may be at a critical "tipping point" in its capacity to address environmental and energy issues as credible scientific evidence mounts and support for action grows. There is little question that the political climate in 2009 is significantly different from what it was in June 2008, when the events summarized above took place. At the same time, experience suggests that it is almost never easy to gain broad bipartisan support in the contemporary Congress, as demonstrated in late 2008 and early 2009, when it acted on economic recovery measures that most Republicans could not support. In February 2009, for example, not a single Republican in the House voted in favor of President Obama's $787 billion economic stimulus package, and only three moderate Republican senators backed the legislation. The bill contained about $80 billion in spending, tax incentives, and loan guarantees for energy efficiency, renewable energy sources, mass transit, and technologies for capture and storage of greenhouse gases produced by coal-fired power plants.[8]

It was not always so. For nearly three decades, from the late 1960s to the mid-1990s, Congress enacted—and over time strengthened—an extraordinary range of environmental policies (see chapter 1 and appendix 1). In doing so, members within both political parties recognized and responded to rising public concern about environmental degradation. For the same reasons, they stoutly defended and even expanded those policies during the 1980s when they were assailed by Ronald Reagan's White House.[9]

This pattern changed with the election of the 104th Congress in 1994, as the new Republican majority brought to the Hill a very different position on the environment. It was far more critical of regulatory bureaucracies, such as the U.S. Environmental Protection Agency (EPA), and the policies they are charged with implementing.[10] On energy and natural resource issues, such as drilling for oil in the Arctic National Wildlife Refuge (ANWR), Republicans have tended to lean heavily toward increasing resource use and economic development rather than conservation. As party leaders pursued these goals from 1995 to 2006, they invariably faced intense opposition from Democrats who were just as determined to block what they characterized as ill-advised attempts to roll back years of progress in protecting public health and the environment.[11]

The 2006 election put Democrats in control of Congress once again, giving them substantial opportunities to challenge President George W. Bush on environmental and energy issues, and they did so frequently. But the short-term effect of political conflict over many of President Bush's proposals, from drilling for oil in ANWR and in offshore lands to his Clear Skies initiative, has been partisan polarization and policy stalemate. Building consensus on the issues has proved to be difficult, and Congress has been unable to approve either the sweeping changes sought by Republicans or the moderate reforms preferred by most Democrats. Thus existing policies—with their many acknowledged flaws—have largely continued in force.[12] The longer-term impacts under President Obama are less clear, although, as recounted in chapters 4 and 16, there are many reasons to be hopeful that cooperation across party lines will improve as the nation seeks to define and realize a new generation of environmental policy that is capable of meeting today's challenges.

Whatever the future holds, it is clear that only Congress can redesign environmental policy for the twenty-first century. It is important to understand how Congress makes decisions on environmental issues and why members adopt the positions and take the actions they do. In the sections below I examine efforts at policy change on Capitol Hill and compare them with the way Congress dealt with environmental issues previously. This assessment highlights the many distinctive roles that Congress plays in the policymaking process. I give special consideration to the phenomenon of policy stalemate or gridlock, which at times has been a defining characteristic of congressional involvement with environmental policy, even if it is likely to diminish somewhat in the future.

Congressional Authority and Environmental Policy

Under the Constitution, Congress shares authority with the president for federal policymaking on the environment. Every year members of Congress make critical decisions on hundreds of measures, from funding the operations of the EPA and other agencies to supporting highways, mass transit, forestry, farming, oil and gas exploration, energy research and development, creation of new wilderness areas, and international population and development assistance. All of these decisions can have significant impacts on environmental protection and sustainable development in the United States and around the world. Most of these actions are rarely front page news, and the public may hear little about them, which does not, however, diminish their importance.[13]

As discussed in chapter 1, we can distinguish congressional actions in several different stages of the policy process: agenda setting, formulation and adoption of policies, and implementation of them in executive agencies. Presidents have greater opportunities than does Congress to set the political agenda, that is, to call attention to specific problems and define the terms of debate. Still, members of Congress can have a major impact on the agenda through legislative and oversight hearings as well as through the abundant opportunities they have for introducing legislation, requesting and publicizing studies and reports, making speeches, taking positions, and voting. All of these actions can assist them in framing issues in a way that can promote their preferred solutions. The climate change bill debated in the Senate in 2008 is one example of this.

Because of their extensive executive powers, presidents also can dominate the process of policy implementation in the agencies (see chapter 4). Here too, however, Congress can substantially affect agency actions, especially through its budgetary decisions. These powers translate into an influential and continuing role of overseeing, and often criticizing, actions in executive agencies such as the EPA, Department of Energy, U.S. Geological Survey, Fish and Wildlife Service, Bureau of Land Management, and Forest Service. For example, in late 2008 and early 2009 congressional Democrats closely followed a series of regulatory changes affecting environmental and natural resource policies that were proposed in the last few months of the Bush administration, seeking ways to overturn them in the 111th Congress when they could expect support from President Obama.[14]

Moreover, through its constitutional power to advise and consent on presidential nominations to the agencies and the courts, the Senate has a role in choosing who is selected to fill critical positions. The Senate almost always approves presidential nominees when the same party controls both institutions. As one article in early 2009 put it in a headline, "Obama's Choice for EPA Chief Meets Little Criticism on Capitol Hill." In contrast, the Democratic Congress in 2007 and 2008 had been sharply critical of Stephen Johnson, EPA administrator under President Bush.[15] The Senate also challenged many of President Bush's nominations to federal appeals courts, in part because of their likely vote on environmental issues.[16]

Even if it cannot compete on an equal footing with the president in some of these policymaking activities, historically, Congress has been more influential than the White House in the formulation and adoption of environmental policies. For much of the modern environmental era, as noted earlier, it also has operated with broad bipartisan agreement on the issues.[17] Yet the way in which Congress exercises its formidable policymaking powers is shaped by several key variables, such as public opinion on the environment, whether the president's party also controls Congress—and by what margins, and members' willingness to defer to the president's recommendations.

Congress's actions on the environment also invariably reflect its dualistic nature as a political institution. In addition to serving as a national lawmaking body, it is an assembly of elected officials who represent politically disparate districts and states. Thus members seek to represent local and regional concerns and interests, and this sometimes puts them at odds with the president or their own party leaders. Indeed, powerful electoral incentives continually induce members of Congress to think as much about local and regional impacts of environmental policies as they do about the larger national interest.[18] Such political pressures led members in the early 2000s to drive up the cost of the president's energy proposals with what one journalist called an "abundance of pet projects, subsidies and tax breaks" to specific industries.[19] Much the same happened with the Energy Policy Act of 2005, discussed later in the chapter. It was widely criticized for what one journalist called its "spectacular giveaways" in tax credits and other subsidies to energy producers such as the oil and gas industry.[20]

Another distinctive institutional characteristic is the system of House and Senate standing committees, where most significant policy decisions take place. Dozens of committees and subcommittees have jurisdiction over environmental policy (see Table 1-1 in chapter 1), and the outcomes of specific legislative battles often turn on which members sit on and control those committees. The example at the beginning of the chapter highlighted Senator Boxer's role in 2008 as chair of the Senate Environment and Public Works Committee and her influence over climate change legislation. In the House, in late 2008 Rep. Henry Waxman, D-Calif., mounted a successful challenge to the long-standing Democratic leader of the Energy and Commerce Committee, John Dingell, and assumed control of the committee in the 111th Congress that began in 2009. Waxman had promised his colleagues he would work closely with the Obama administration to speed passage of energy, climate change, and health legislation.[21] Representative Dingell, 82 years old and the most senior member of the House of Representatives, had been the top Democrat on the committee for twenty-eight years, but he also had strong ties to the auto industry and had suffered from several health problems. Even before Dingell lost the chairmanship of the committee, House Speaker Nancy Pelosi tried to work around him in 2007 by establishing a new House Select Committee on Energy Independence and Global Warming and appointing

Edward J. Markey, D-Mass., to chair it. The committee was given authority to hold hearings as part of the agenda-setting process, but not to draft legislation, a compromise she worked out with Dingell.[22]

Taken together, these congressional characteristics have important implications for environmental policy. First, building policy consensus in Congress is rarely easy because of the diversity of members and interests whose concerns need to be met and the conflicts that can arise among committees and leaders. Second, policy compromises invariably reflect members' preoccupation with local and regional impacts of environmental decisions, such as how climate change policy will affect industries and homeowners in the Midwest. Third, the White House matters a great deal in how the issues are defined and whether policy decisions can be made acceptable to all concerned, but the president's influence is nevertheless limited by independent political calculations made on Capitol Hill.

Given these constraints, Congress frequently finds itself unable to make crucial decisions on environmental policy. The U.S. public may see a "do-nothing Congress," yet the reality is that all too often members can find no way to reconcile the conflicting views of multiple interests and constituencies. It remains to be seen if this pattern will be changed in 2009 and beyond.

There are, however, some striking exceptions to this common pattern of policy deadlock. In 1990 Congress approved a far-reaching extension of the Clean Air Act, the nation's most demanding environmental statute.[23] In 1996 it ended a long stalemate on pesticide policy through adoption of the Food Quality Protection Act, and in the same year it approved a major revision of the Safe Drinking Water Act. An intriguing question is how Congress can achieve a remarkable consensus on some environmental policies while remaining mired in gridlock on others. A brief examination of the way Congress has dealt with environmental issues since the early 1970s helps to explain this seeming anomaly. Such a review also provides a useful context in which to examine and assess the actions of recent Congresses and the outlook for environmental policymaking for the early twenty-first century.

Causes and Consequences of Environmental Gridlock

Policy gridlock refers to an inability to resolve conflicts in a policymaking body such as Congress, which results in government inaction in the face of important public problems. There is no consensus on *what* to do and therefore no movement occurs in any direction. Present policies, or slight revisions of them, continue until agreement is reached on the direction and magnitude of change. Sometimes environmental or other programs officially expire but continue to be funded by Congress through a waiver of the rules governing the annual appropriations process. The failure to renew the programs, however, contributes to administrative drift, ineffectual congressional oversight, and a propensity, as discussed later in the chapter, for members to use the appropriations process to achieve what cannot be gained through statutory change.[24] It should be said, however, that policy gridlock in

Congress has had some positive effects. It often has stimulated innovative environmental policy change at the state and local levels, in executive agencies, and in the courts.[25]

Political pundits and public officials bemoan policy gridlock in Congress. They are less likely to ask why it occurs or what might be done to overcome the prevailing tendency toward institutional stalemate.[26] There are no simple answers to those questions, but among the major reasons for gridlock are the complexity of environmental problems, the influence of organized interest groups, a lack of public consensus on the issues, the divergent policy views of Democrats and Republicans, the constitutionally mandated separation of powers between the presidency and Congress, and ineffectual political leadership. Different factors may be important at various times and for different kinds of disputes.

Most of these reasons are easy to understand, and in any given conflict—such as the disagreement over climate change policy recounted at the beginning of the chapter—they can be seen simply as the usual constraints that affect Congress's ability to formulate and adopt environmental policies. When the problems are complex and the scientific community is divided, action is more difficult. When diverse and opposing interests (such as oil companies, the auto industry, labor unions, and environmentalists) are deeply involved on an issue, compromise may be elusive. Business groups in particular are often influential in shaping environmental policy, although they do not always succeed in getting what they want, particularly when the policy disputes are highly visible.[27] When business groups are successful, often it is because the issues are not salient to ordinary people, they are not well informed on them, or they are divided over what to do (see chapter 3). Under these conditions, elected officials may not find it easy to agree on a course of action.[28] In short, absent a clear and forceful public voice, members of Congress cannot always respond to their constituents' generally favorable opinions for action on the environment.[29]

One of the most important reasons for policy stalemate is sharp ideological differences among the two major parties on environmental issues. Based on rankings by the League of Conservation Voters (LCV), the parties showed increasing divergence from the early 1970s through the early 2000s. On average they have differed by nearly 25 points on a 100-point scale, and those differences grew wider during the last two decades.[30] In recent years, Senate Democrats averaged about 85-percent support for the positions endorsed by the LCV and the environmental community. Senate Republicans averaged about 8 percent. In the House, Democrats averaged about 86 percent and Republicans 10 percent.[31] Sometimes political leadership can help to resolve environmental policy conflicts, whether it comes from the White House or Capitol Hill, but such leadership may or may not be sufficient. In light of the widespread hope that the Obama administration will be able to forge appropriate environmental and energy policies over the next several years, it will be interesting to see whether Congress is able to overcome these constraints.

From Consensus in the Environmental Decade to Deadlock in the 1990s

As chapter 1 makes clear, the 1970s offer examples of both successful and unsuccessful environmental policymaking. The record for this environmental decade is nevertheless remarkable, particularly in comparison with actions taken since then. The National Environmental Policy Act, Clean Air Act, Clean Water Act, Endangered Species Act, and Resource Conservation and Recovery Act, among others, were all signed into law in the 1970s, mostly between 1970 and 1976. We can debate the merits of these early statutes with the clarity of hindsight and in light of contemporary criticism of them. Yet their enactment demonstrates vividly that the U.S. political system is capable of developing major environmental policies in fairly short order under the right conditions. Consensus on environmental policy could prevail in the 1970s in part because the issues were new and politically popular, and attention was focused on broadly supported program goals, such as cleaning up the nation's air and water, rather than on the means used to achieve them (command-and-control regulation) or the costs of doing so. At that time there was also little overt and sustained opposition to these measures.

Environmental Gridlock Emerges

The pattern of the 1970s did not last. Congress's enthusiasm for environmental policy gradually gave way to apprehension about its impacts on the economy, and policy stalemate became the norm in the early 1980s. Ronald Reagan's election as president in 1980 also altered the political climate and threw Congress into a defensive posture. It was forced to react to the Reagan administration's aggressive policy actions. Rather than proposing new programs or expanding old ones, Congress focused its resources on oversight and criticism of the administration's policies, and bipartisan agreement became more difficult. Members were increasingly cross-pressured by environmental and industry groups, partisanship on these issues increased, and Congress and President Reagan battled repeatedly over budget and program priorities.[32] The cumulative effect of these developments in the early 1980s was that Congress was unable to agree on new environmental policy directions.

Gridlock Eases: 1984–1990

The legislative logjam began breaking up in late 1983, as the U.S. public and Congress repudiated Reagan's anti-environmental agenda (see chapter 4). The new pattern was evident by 1984 when, after several years of deliberation, Congress approved major amendments to the 1976 Resource Conservation and Recovery Act that strengthened the program and set tight new deadlines for EPA rulemaking on control of hazardous chemical wastes.

Although the Republicans still controlled the Senate, the 99th Congress (1985–1987) compiled a record dramatically at odds with the deferral politics of the 97th and 98th Congresses (1981–1985). In 1986 the Safe

Drinking Water Act was strengthened and expanded, and Congress approved the Superfund Amendments and Reauthorization Act, adding a separate Title III, the Emergency Planning and Community Right-to-Know Act (EPCRA). EPCRA was an entirely new program mandating nationwide reporting for toxic and hazardous chemicals produced, used, or stored in communities (resulting in the now well-known Toxics Release Inventory), as well as state and local emergency planning for accidental chemical releases. Democrats regained control of the Senate following the 1986 election, and Congress reauthorized the Clean Water Act over a presidential veto.

Still, Congress was unable to renew the Clean Air Act and the Federal Insecticide, Fungicide, and Rodenticide Act—the nation's key pesticide control act—as well as new legislation to control acid rain. The disappointment in this limited progress was captured in one analyst's assessment: "Congress stayed largely stalemated on a range of old environmental and energy problems in 1988, even while a generation of new ones clamored for attention."[33] Much the same could be said for the 101st and 102nd Congresses (1989–1993) during George H. W. Bush's administration.

Yet with the election of the elder Bush in 1988, Congress and the White House were able to agree on enactment of the innovative and stringent Clean Air Act Amendments of 1990 and the Energy Policy Act of 1992. The latter was an important if modest advancement in promoting energy conservation and a restructuring of the electric utility industry to promote greater competition and efficiency. Success on the Clean Air Act was particularly important because for years it was a stark symbol of Congress's inability to reauthorize controversial environmental programs. Passage was possible in 1990 because of improved scientific research that clarified the risks of dirty air, reports of worsening ozone in urban areas, and a realization that the U.S. public would tolerate no further delays in acting. President Bush had vowed to "break the gridlock" and support renewal of the Clean Air Act, and Sen. George Mitchell, D-Maine, newly elected as Senate majority leader, was equally determined to enact a bill.[34]

Policy Stalemate Returns

Unfortunately, approval of the 1990 Clean Air Act Amendments was no signal that a new era of cooperative and bipartisan policymaking on the environment was about to begin. Nor was the election of Bill Clinton and Al Gore in 1992, even as Democrats regained control of both houses of Congress. Most of the major environmental laws were once again up for renewal. Yet despite an emerging consensus on many of the laws, in the end the 103rd Congress (1993–1995) remained far too divided to act. Coalitions of environmental groups and business interests clashed regularly on all of these initiatives, and congressional leaders and the Clinton White House were unsuccessful in resolving the disputes.

The search for consensus on environmental policy became more difficult as the 1994 election neared. Republicans increasingly believed they would do well in November, and partisan politics helped to scuttle whatever hopes remained for action in 1994. Like the environmentalists, the Republicans, their conservative Democratic allies in these battles, and business leaders thought they could strike a more favorable compromise in the next Congress.

The 104th Congress: Revolutionary Fervor Meets Political Reality

Few analysts had predicted the astonishing outcomes of the 1994 midterm elections, even after one of the most expensive, negative, and anti-Washington campaigns in modern times. Republicans captured both houses of Congress, picking up an additional fifty-two seats in the House and eight in the Senate. They also did well in other elections throughout the country, contributing to their belief that voters had endorsed the Contract with America, which symbolized the new Republican agenda.[35]

The contract had promised a rolling back of government regulations and a shrinking of the federal government's role. There was no specific mention of environmental policy, however, and the document's language was carefully constructed for broad appeal to a disgruntled electorate. The contract drew heavily from the work of conservative and pro-business think tanks that for years had waged a multifaceted campaign to discredit environmentalist thinking and policies. Those efforts merged with a carefully developed GOP plan to gain control of Congress to further a conservative political agenda.[36]

The preponderance of evidence suggests that the Republican victory in November conveyed no public mandate to roll back environmental protection.[37] Yet the political result was clear enough. It put Republicans in charge of the House for the first time in four decades and set the stage for an extraordinary period of legislative action on environmental policy characterized by bitter relations between the two parties.

The resulting environmental policy deadlock should have come as no surprise. With several notable exceptions, consensus on the issues simply could not be built, and the revolution failed for the most part. The lesson seemed to be that a direct attack on popular environmental programs could not work because it would provoke a political backlash. Those who supported a new policy agenda turned instead to a strategy of evolutionary or incremental environmental policy change through a more subtle and less visible exercise of Congress's appropriations and oversight powers. Here they were more successful.[38] Moreover, as chapters 4, 7, and 8 make clear, the George W. Bush administration relied on a similar strategy of quiet pursuit of a deregulatory agenda from 2001 to early 2009.

Environmental Policy Actions in Recent Congresses

As discussed earlier, Congress influences nearly every environmental and resource policy though exercise of its powers to legislate, oversee executive agencies, advise and consent on nominations, and appropriate funds.

Sometimes these activities take place largely within the specialized committees and subcommittees and sometimes they reach the floor of the House and Senate, where they may attract greater media attention. Some of the decisions are made routinely and are relatively free of controversy (for example, appropriations for the national parks) whereas others stimulate more political conflict, as was the case with George W. Bush's Clear Skies bill, the long-running dispute over drilling for oil in ANWR, national energy legislation, and the recent climate change bill reviewed at the chapter's beginning. In this section I briefly review some of the most notable congressional actions from 1995 to early 2009 within three broad categories: regulatory reform initiatives (directed at the way agencies make decisions), appropriations (funding levels and use of budgetary riders), and proposals for changing the substance of environmental policy. For those who wish to follow ongoing debate over how Congress acts on environmental policy issues, a number of key Web sites are listed at the end of the chapter.

Regulatory Reform: Changing Agency Procedures

Regulatory reform has long been a central theme in U.S. environmental policy (see chapters 1 and 4). There is no real dispute about the need to reform agency rulemaking that has been widely faulted for being too inflexible, intrusive, cumbersome, and adversarial and sometimes based on insufficient consideration of science and economics.[39] However, considerable disagreement exists over precisely what elements of the regulatory process need to be reformed and how best to do so to ensure the changes are both fair and effective.

Beginning in 1995 and continuing for several Congresses, the Republican Party and conservative Democrats favored omnibus regulatory reform legislation that would affect all environmental policies by imposing broad and stringent mandates on bureaucratic agencies. Those mandates were directed particularly at the use of cost-benefit analysis and risk assessment in proposing new regulations. Proponents of such legislation also sought to open agency technical studies and rulemaking to additional legal challenges to help protect the business community against what they viewed as unjustifiable regulatory action. Opponents of both kinds of measures argued that such impositions and opportunities for lawsuits would wreak havoc within agencies, such as the EPA, that already faced daunting procedural hurdles and frequent legal disputes as they developed regulations. Thus they preferred more limited changes that would be considered as each environmental statute came up for renewal. They also sought to give agency professionals more discretion in considering how to weigh pertinent evidence and set program priorities.

Debate over regulatory reform measures in Congress has provided ample opportunity for the kind of message politics described earlier. Members have recounted colorful anecdotes of alleged regulatory abuses and pleas for relief for the business community. Opponents just as often challenged these arguments as only weakly linked to scientific or economic reality.[40] In the end, the House favored broad regulatory reform bills during the mid-1990s as part of the Contract with America, but the Senate failed to go along. GOP leaders were more successful, however, in gaining approval of several less ambitious, but nonetheless important, reform measures.

One of these bills was the Unfunded Mandates Reform Act, which Congress approved and the president signed in early 1995. The act erected new procedural barriers to keep Congress from approving statutes likely to impose federal requirements on state and local governments without providing funding to cover the costs. Another was the Small Business Regulatory Enforcement Fairness Act of 1996, which was attached to an unrelated but "must-pass" bill raising the public debt limit. It required agencies to assist small business in complying with regulations and forced agencies to submit proposed rules to Congress for review and possible rejection. A third was the Data Quality Act of 2000, enacted as a budgetary rider (see below) and designed to ensure the accuracy of data on which agencies base their regulations.

With the election of George W. Bush in 2000, the regulatory reform agenda shifted from imposing these kinds of congressional mandates on Clinton administration agencies to direct intervention by the White House. Bush appointed conservative and pro-business officials to nearly all environmental and natural resource agencies, and rulemaking shifted decisively toward the interests of the business community (see chapters 4, 7, and 8).[41] Barack Obama's election coincided with another shift in regulatory philosophy. In light of the financial meltdown on Wall Street in 2008 and reports of ineffective federal regulation of banking institutions and of food, drug, consumer safety, and the environment, public sentiment has shifted dramatically back in favor of strong or at least "smart" regulation that achieves its purposes without imposing unreasonable burdens.[42]

Appropriations Politics: Budgets and Riders

The implementation of environmental policies depends heavily on the funds that Congress appropriates each year. Thus if certain policy goals cannot be achieved through changing the governing statutes, or altering the rulemaking process, attention may turn instead to appropriations. This was the case during the Reagan administration in the 1980s, which severely cut environmental budgets, and it was a major element of the Republican strategy in Congress from 1995 to 2006 and in the George W. Bush administration (see chapter 4). One of the most avid revolutionaries in the GOP freshman class of 1995, Rep. David McIntosh, of Indiana, explained the logic of this approach: "The laws would remain on the books, but there would be no money to carry them out. It's a signal to the agencies to stop wasting time on these regulations."[43] With Democrats taking control of Congress once again after the 2006 elections, with stronger majorities after the 2008 election, and with a Democratic president, the focus changed considerably. The greatest constraint looking forward is less ideological opposition to funding environmental agencies than the massive federal budget deficit that will affect federal spending for years to come.

Regardless of which party controls Congress, the appropriations process has been used in two distinct ways to achieve policy change. One is through riders. These are legislative stipulations attached to appropriations bills to achieve policy goals such as restricting, remaking, or even eliminating federal programs. The other is through changes in the level of funding, either a cut in spending for programs that are not favored or an increase for those that are seen positively.

Appropriations Riders. Use of appropriations riders became a common strategy following the 1994 election. In the 104th Congress, for example, more than fifty anti-environmental riders were included in seven different budget bills, largely with the purpose of slowing or halting enforcement of laws by the EPA, the Interior Department, and other agencies until Congress could revise them. In one of the most controversial cases, seventeen riders were appended to the EPA appropriations bill in 1995 in an attempt to prohibit the agency from enforcing certain drinking-water and water quality standards and to keep it from regulating toxic air emissions from oil and gas refineries, among many other provisions. The EPA was told flatly that it could not spend any money on these activities.[44] President Clinton vetoed the bill.

The use of riders has continued in subsequent years, as has opposition to the strategy by environmental groups. In late 2004, for example, as Congress rolled a number of budget measures together in an omnibus package in a final effort to complete work on the fiscal year 2005 budget, a number of environmental riders were attached. These included exclusion of grazing permit renewals from environmental review and limitations on judicial review and public participation in logging projects in the Tongass National Forest. Some other riders were defeated, including several that would have weakened protection under the Endangered Species Act.

Why use these kinds of riders to achieve policy change? Such a strategy is attractive to its proponents because appropriations bills, unlike authorizing legislation, typically move quickly and Congress must enact them each year to keep the government operating. Many Republicans and business lobbyists also argue that use of riders is one of the few ways they have to rope in a bureaucracy that they believe needs additional constraints. They feel they are unable to address their concerns through changing the authorizing statutes themselves, a far more controversial and uncertain path to follow.[45]

Yet relying on riders is widely considered to be an inappropriate way to institute policy changes. The process provides little opportunity to debate the issues openly, and there are no public hearings or public votes. For example, provisions of the Data Quality Act of 2000, noted earlier, were written largely by an industry lobbyist and were enacted quietly as twenty-seven lines of text buried in a massive budget bill that President Clinton had to sign.[46] In a retrospective review in 2001, NRDC counted hundreds of anti-environmental riders attached to appropriations bills since 1995. Clinton blocked more than seventy-five of them, but many became law, including the Data Quality Act.[47]

Cutting Environmental Budgets. The history of congressional funding for environmental programs was discussed in chapter 1, and it is set out in appendix 2 for selected agencies and in appendix 4 for overall federal spending on natural resources and the environment. These budgets have been the focus of continuing conflict within Congress since the 1980s. For example, in the 104th Congress, GOP leaders enacted deep cuts in environmental spending only to face President Clinton's veto of the budget bill. Those conflicts led eventually to a temporary shutdown of the federal government, with the Republicans receiving the brunt of the public's wrath for the budget wars. Most of the environmental cuts were reversed. Disagreements over program priorities continued throughout the 1990s and 2000s.[48]

As noted in chapter 4, George W. Bush regularly sought to cut the EPA's budget but was rebuffed by Congress until 2004, after which it tended to go along with the president. Since then overall appropriations for the environment and natural resources have increased, although only slightly in real terms, while spending on pollution control (by the EPA, for example) has declined markedly, leaving the agency without the resources needed to implement the laws. The 111th Congress and the Obama administration may well try to reverse these trends in funding for environmental programs, but they also will be constrained by the enormous federal budget deficits they are likely to face over the next few years and a public that, while very supportive of the new president, is more skeptical and mistrustful of the federal government than at any time since modern polls have asked the question.[49]

Legislating Policy Change

As discussed earlier, in any given year Congress makes decisions on hundreds of environmental or resource programs. In this section I highlight selective actions in recent Congresses that demonstrate both the ability of members to reach across party lines to find common ground and the continuing ideological and partisan fights that often prevent action.

Pesticides, Drinking Water, and Transportation. Among the most notable achievements of the otherwise anti-environmental 104th and 105th Congresses are three conspicuous success stories involving control of pesticides and other agricultural chemicals, drinking water, and transportation. Especially for the first two of these actions, years of legislative gridlock were overcome as Republicans and Democrats uncharacteristically reached agreement on new policy directions.

The Food Quality Protection Act of 1996 was a major revision of the nation's pesticide law, which for decades had been a poster child for policy gridlock as environmentalists battled with the agricultural chemical and food industries. The act required the EPA to use a new, uniform, reasonable-risk approach to regulating pesticides used on food, fiber, and other crops, and it required that special attention be given to the diverse ways in which both children and adults are exposed to such chemicals. The act sped through

Congress in record time without a single dissenting vote because the food industry was desperate to get the new law enacted after court rulings that would have adversely affected it without the legislation. In addition, after the bruising battles of 1995, GOP lawmakers were eager to adopt an election-year environmental measure.[50]

The 1996 rewrite and reauthorization of the Safe Drinking Water Act sought to address many long-standing problems with the nation's drinking water program. It dealt more realistically with regulating contaminants based on their risk to public health and authorized $7 billion for state-administered loan and grant funds to help localities with compliance costs. It also created a new right-to-know provision that requires large water systems to provide their customers with annual reports on the safety of local water supplies. Bipartisan cooperation on the bill was made easier because it aided financially pressed state and local governments and, like the pesticide bill, allowed Republicans to score some election-year points with environmentalists.[51]

Another important legislative enactment took place in the 105th Congress. After prolonged debate over renewal of the nation's major highway act, in 1998 the House and Senate overwhelmingly approved the Transportation Equity Act for the 21st Century. It was a sweeping six-year, $218 billion measure that provided a 40-percent increase in spending to improve the nation's aging highways and included $5.4 billion for mass transit systems.[52] For reasons discussed early in the chapter, members of Congress find it easier to reach agreement when federal dollars are distributed among the states and congressional districts.

Brownfields, Healthy Forests, Agriculture, and Wilderness. Congress also completed action on a number of somewhat less visible issues that demonstrated its potential to fashion bipartisan compromises. In 2001 President Bush gained congressional approval of important legislation to reclaim so-called urban brownfields. The measure represented an unusual compromise between House Republicans who sought to reduce liability for small businesses under Superfund and Democrats who wanted to see contaminated and abandoned industrial sites in urban areas cleaned up.[53] The final bill authorized $250 million a year for five years to help states clean up and redevelop contaminated industrial sites. The compromise ended a long-standing dispute over liability provisions of the Superfund law that left abandoned more than 450,000 brownfield sites around the nation.

In a somewhat similar action, the 108th Congress in 2003 approved one of the Bush administration's environmental priorities, the Healthy Forests initiative. The measure was designed to permit increased logging in national forests to lessen the risk of wildfires. It reduced the number of environmental reviews that would be required for such logging projects and sped up judicial reviews of legal challenges to these projects. Environmental groups opposed the legislation, but bipartisan concern over communities at risk from wildfires was sufficient for enactment. Wildfires struck Southern California only days before the Senate voted 80–14 to approve the bill.[54]

The nation's farm bills always have important environmental components. In 2007 Congress approved a new farm bill, which authorized nearly $8 billion over 10 years for environmental protection, such as soil conservation and incentives to grow grasses that can be converted into cellulosic ethanol rather than to rely on corn-based ethanol. However, the measure also left largely intact much criticized agricultural subsidies.

Finally, throughout 2007 and 2008, Congress considered a dozen proposals for setting aside large parcels of federal land for wilderness protection, totaling about two million acres in eight states, largely without much media coverage. The measures were broadly supported within both parties, in part because environmentalists helped to build public support by working with opposing interests at the local level. Progress like this was also possible because of Democratic victories in the 2006 election that switched control of the House Natural Resources Committee from Republican Richard Pombo of California to Democrat Nick J. Rahall of West Virginia. Pombo was a fierce opponent of such wilderness protection and Rahall strongly favors it. Congress couldn't approve the wilderness bills in 2008, but by early 2009, in more favorable political climate, they passed the Senate as part of an Omnibus Public Lands Act on a vote of 73-21. The Wilderness Society described the action as the "greatest expansion of the National Wilderness Preservation System in 15 years." The House approved and President Obama signed the act in March 2009.[55]

National Energy Policy. In 2005 Congress finally enacted one of the Bush administration's priorities that the president had sought since 2001: the Energy Policy Act of 2005. It was the first major overhaul of U.S. energy policy since 1992. The original Bush energy plan was formulated in 2001 under closely guarded conditions by a task force headed by Vice President Dick Cheney in the aftermath of a short-term energy crisis in California and rising gasoline prices. The president's recommendations to Congress called for an increase in the production and use of fossil fuels and nuclear energy, gave modest attention to the role of energy conservation, and sparked intense debate on Capitol Hill with its emphasis on oil and gas drilling in ANWR. The Republican House quickly approved the measure in 2001, after what the press called "aggressive lobbying by the Bush administration, labor unions and the oil, gas and coal industries."[56] The vote largely followed party lines. The bill provided generous tax and research benefits to the oil, natural gas, coal, and nuclear power industries; and it rejected provisions that would have forced the auto industry to improve fuel efficiency for sport utility vehicles. The Senate was far more skeptical about the legislation and remained so over the next four years. To no one's surprise, ANWR became symbolic of the party split on energy issues: "I don't see any way around ANWR," said former senator J. Bennett Johnston, D-La. "It's a theological issue."[57]

Competing energy bills were debated on the Hill through mid-2005 without resolution and served as another example of legislative gridlock. Senate Democrats favored measures that balanced energy production and environmental concerns, including increases in auto and truck fuel-efficiency standards; they drew strong support from environmentalists and denunciation by industry and Republicans. Neither side was prepared to compromise as lobbying by car manufacturers, labor unions, the oil and gas industry, and environmentalists continued. Regional splits over whether to approve a liability waiver for the gasoline additive and groundwater contaminant MTBE also undercut consensus-building efforts. As one writer put it in 2002, the "debate between energy and the environment is important to core constituencies of both parties, the kind of loyal followers vital in a congressional election year."[58] Ironically the two sides were in agreement on most of the issues, such as tax incentives for energy production and conservation and new energy research programs.[59] A corporate tax cut bill enacted in 2004 incorporated some of those elements, such as oil and gas drilling tax breaks, renewable energy tax credits, and accelerated depreciation for an Alaskan natural gas pipeline.

Finally, the House and Senate reached agreement on an energy package and the president signed the 1,700 page bill on August 8, 2005.[60] In the end, the ANWR provisions were dropped from the bill, as were stipulations for improved fuel-efficiency standards. The bill included no mandate for reduction in greenhouse gas emissions, and it imposed no requirement that utilities rely on renewable power sources. The thrust of the legislation remained largely what Bush and Cheney sought in 2001, with substantial federal subsidies for expanding supplies of energy, particularly fossil fuels and nuclear power. However, the final measure included significant funding for energy research and development (including work on renewable energy sources), some new energy-efficiency standards for federal office buildings, and short-term tax credits for purchase of hybrid vehicles and renewable power systems for homes—and similar provisions for commercial buildings.[61] Even President Bush realized that the act didn't go far enough. In his State of the Union message in January 2006, the president noted that the nation was "addicted to oil, which is often imported from unstable parts of the world." Yet he remained opposed to raising federal fuel-efficiency standards or increasing the federal gasoline tax.[62]

One other important change in energy policy took place in December 2007, when Congress finally agreed to the first significant change in the Corporate Average Fuel Economy (CAFE) standards since 1975. The Energy Independence and Security Act of 2007 set a national automobile fuel economy standard of 35 miles per gallon by 2020. The act also sought to increase the supply of alternative fuel sources, particularly biofuels other than corn-based ethanol. In one of his first actions in office, President Obama in January 2009 ordered the Department of Transportation to move ahead on issuing regulations to put the new fuel economy standards into effect for cars sold in 2011.

Throughout 2008 lawmakers remained at an impasse over two other energy issues. One was to extend the tax credits and other incentives to encourage production of energy from renewable sources such as solar and wind, and to promote green technology and innovation, including biofuels, plug-in vehicles, and energy-efficient buildings and appliances. The tax credits were set to expire at the end of the year, and even though broad supported existed in both the House and Senate, those changes were linked to other, far more controversial tax breaks for businesses and individuals, particularly those for the domestic oil industry. By October, the $17 billion package was approved in a procedural move to help attract support in the Senate for President Bush's financial rescue bill; the measure was to be paid for by reducing current tax incentives that benefit the oil and gas industry.[63] The other development concerned a long-standing ban on off-shore drilling for oil and gas, which became a contentious issue in the 2008 election campaigns and eventually forced Democrats to concede some ground and favor drilling, although with significant restrictions.[64]

Beyond these two issues, other energy policy goals were advanced by President Obama's economic stimulus measure, which Congress approved in February 2009. As noted early in the chapter, the massive bill included some $80 billion in energy-related spending, tax credits, and loan guarantees intended to promote energy efficiency, use of renewable energy sources, and mass transit, among other goals. Had the energy components been a stand-alone measure, the *New York Times* observed, they would have amounted to "the biggest energy bill in history." Yet bipartisan cooperation was largely absent. In the end, only three Republicans in Congress, all in the Senate, voted for the bill.[65]

Continuing Partisan Conflict and Stalemate. The examples discussed here, and many more that could be cited, such as approval of an historic Great Lakes Compact in 2008 to prevent water diversion from the lakes and a new Higher Education Sustainability Act in 2008, show that Congress has been able to move ahead on a wide range of environmental and natural resource policies in the past several years.[66] Yet a number of other examples, much like President Obama's economic stimulus bill, illustrate the continuing partisan conflict that in recent years has blocked action on key federal laws such as the Superfund program, Endangered Species Act, Clean Water Act (for example, the Clean Water Restoration Act to reaffirm broad federal protection undercut by Supreme Court decisions), Clean Air Act, climate change, and reform of the notorious Mining Law of 1872, a poster child for what some have called legislative lost causes.[67]

The Superfund program, for example, has not been reauthorized for over two decades, and except for the brownfields measure discussed earlier, congressional agreement has not been forthcoming. In 1995 Congress let the special industry tax that funds the program expire, although President Obama has proposed reinstating it after 2011. The inaction has shifted the program from one for which "polluters pay" to one for which general tax revenues must be used instead. The result is that the program's cleanup fund is no longer adequate for cleanup of contaminated sites across the nation.[68]

The Endangered Species Act presents a similar level of conflict and lack of resolution. In 2001, then–House Resources Committee chair James V. Hansen, R-Utah, captured the dilemma well: "We haven't reauthorized it because no one could agree on how to reform and modernize the law. Everyone agrees there are problems with the Act, but no one can agree on how to fix them."[69] By late 2004, most Republican-backed proposals sought to require greater consideration of the rights of property owners and to force the Fish and Wildlife Service to rely more on peer-reviewed science in its species decisions. Opponents have argued that such bills would gut the act to appease small landowners and corporate developers, and that requirements for such "sound science" are mere ploys to prevent the service from acting.[70]

The Bush administration's Clear Skies initiative, proposed in 2002, was to make the first major changes to the Clean Air Act since the amendments of 1990. It was offered initially as an improvement to the act that would incorporate market incentives and create greater certainty over requirements on industry. Supporters of the Bush bill said it would significantly cut emissions at some 1,300 power plants across the country and help to bring most of the nation into compliance with federal clean air standards.

Opponents asserted that the legislation was far too weak and did not cut emissions as fast as would be required under the existing Clean Air Act. They also objected to the bill's omission of any regulation of carbon dioxide even as nearly all other industrialized nations sought to rein in the greenhouse gas.[71] In response to that omission, Senators John McCain, R-Ariz., and Joseph Lieberman, then D-Conn., cosponsored the Climate Stewardship Act of 2003, the forerunner of the measure discussed at the chapter's opening. It was designed to cap greenhouse gas emissions by power plants, refineries, and other industries and relied on tradable allowances to do so. The bill gained forty-three votes in the Senate in 2003 but ultimately was blocked, in McCain's words, by "the power and influence of the special interest lobby, especially public utilities and automobile manufacturers."[72] The bill has been reintroduced in succeeding congresses. The Clear Skies bill itself was defeated in the Senate in March 2005, and the Bush administration chose to pursue its goals through administrative rules instead (see chapter 4).

Conclusions

The political struggles on Capitol Hill summarized in this chapter reveal sharply contrasting visions for environmental policy although considerable progress has been made in the past decade. The revolutionary rhetoric of the 104th Congress had dissipated by the 2000s, and Congress has been able to revise several major statutes in an uncommon display of bipartisan cooperation. Nonetheless, for many other environmental programs, policy gridlock continued to frustrate all participants, and partisan differences prevented emerging issues such as climate change from being seriously addressed. Certainly, many hope that the widely voiced good will toward the Obama presidency will lead to broad changes in these patterns.

The constitutional divisions between the House and Senate guarantee that newly emergent political forces such as those represented in the House in the 1990s and in the Obama administration and Congress in 2009 cannot easily push their legislative agendas. Will the new alignment of forces in 2009 prove to be a tipping point, especially on climate change legislation? It could be, and opportunities for advancement are evident already. By mid-January 2009, the Senate Foreign Relations Committee arranged for former vice president Al Gore to testify on the need for the United States to exert international leadership on climate change. And by April new climate change legislation coauthored by Henry Waxman and Edward Markey had been introduced in the House.[73] Even so, working out the details will not be easy even when a broad consensus seems to be emerging on the imperative of acting on climate change, energy use, and environmental protection, and integrating such measures with sustainable economic development (see chapter 16). In the U.S. political system, effective policymaking will always require cooperation between the two branches and leadership within both to advance sensible policies and secure public approval for them. The public also has a role to play in these deliberations, and the history of congressional policymaking on the environment strongly suggests the power of public beliefs and action.

Suggested Web Sites

Competitive Enterprise Institute (www.cei.org) This conservative, pro-business group has been active on regulatory reform and many environmental issues. The site offers analyses and positions on a range of topics.

Environmental Protection Agency (www.epa.gov/epahome/rules.html) The EPA site for laws, rules, and regulations includes the full text of the dozen key laws administered by the EPA. It also has a link to current legislation before Congress.

Heritage Foundation (www.heritage.org) This leading conservative research institute offers news and studies on a range of environmental and energy issues.

League of Conservation Voters (www.lcv.org) The LCV compiles environmental voting records for all members of Congress.

Library of Congress Thomas search engine (http://thomas.loc.gov) This search engine for locating key congressional documents is one of the most comprehensive public sites available for legislative searches. See also www.house.gov and www.senate.gov for portals to the House and Senate, and the committee and individual member Web sites.

National Association of Manufacturers (www.nam.org) This leading business organization offers policy news, studies, and position statements on environmental issues as well as extensive resources for public action on the issues.

National Federation of Independent Business (www.nfib.com) NFIB is the nation's largest advocacy group for small business and has been especially active on regulatory reform issues.

Natural Resources Defense Council (www.nrdc.org) Perhaps the most active and influential of national environmental groups that lobby Congress, NRDC also provides detailed news coverage of congressional legislative developments.

Pew Center on Global Climate Change (www.pewclimate.org) The Pew Center follows climate change policy developments, including those in Congress, in great detail.

Sierra Club (www.sierraclub.org) The Sierra Club is one of the leading national environmental groups that tracks congressional legislative battles.

Notes

1. Frances Beinecke is quoted in Steven Mufson and Juliet Eilperin, "Senate Democrats May Pull Climate Bill," *Washington Post,* June 6, 2008, A2. Senator McConnell's statement is cited in Avery Palmer, "Climate Change Bill Stalls at the Start," *CQ Weekly,* June 9, 2008, online edition.
2. For a summary of the bill's content, which will be incorporated in revised form into new climate legislation in the 111th Congress, see the Pew Center on Global Climate Change reports, www.pewclimate.org/analysis/1-w. The Pew Center regularly compares the key feature of climate change bills introduced in Congress, as it did with some ten different cap-and-trade bills in the 110th Congress.
3. Mufson and Eilperin, "Senate Democrats May Pull Climate Bill."
4. For a summary account of the climate change debate, see Palmer, "Climate Change Bill Stalls at the Start"; Mufson and Eilperin, "Senate Democrats May Pull Climate Bill"; and David M. Herszenhorn, "More Talking Than Listening in the Senate Debate about Climate Change," *New York Times,* June 5, 2008, A19. The Bledsoe statement is from the Palmer article, and Inhofe remarks are cited in Mufson and Eilperin.
5. John M. Broder, "Geography Is Dividing Democrats over Energy," *New York Times,* January 27, 2009, 1, A21; "In Obama's Team, 2 Camps on Climate," *New York Times,* January 3, 2009, A10. Dorgan's statement is noted in Frances Beinecke, "The Once and Future Climate Bill," *OnEarth,* fall 2008, 11.
6. See Eric Schickler and Kathryn Pearson, "The House Leadership in an Era of Partisan Warfare," in *Congress Reconsidered,* 8th ed., ed. Lawrence C. Dodd and Bruce I. Oppenheimer (Washington, D.C.: CQ Press, 2005). For a similar perspective on the contemporary Senate, including the pattern of "message politics," where position taking displaces legislative deliberation, and the rising frequency of filibusters, see C. Lawrence Evans and Daniel Lipinski, "Obstruction and Leadership in the U.S. Senate," in the same volume. See also Thomas E. Mann and Norman J. Ornstein, *The Broken Branch: How Congress Is Failing America and How to Get It Back on Track* (New York: Oxford University Press, 2006).
7. The eight-seat gain in the Senate includes Al Franken's apparent victory in Minnesota, which was being contested in court in April 2009. On demographic and other changes that might make the Senate more receptive to environmental and energy issues, see Carl Hulse, "An Age Shift Brings a Youthful Feel to the Senate," *New York Times,* January 31, 2009. The additional seats in the House gave the Democrats a 257–178 margin in that body.
8. Sheryl Gay Stolberg and Adam Nagourney, "Partisan Fight Endures as Stimulus Bill Signed," *New York Times,* February 17, 2009, online edition.
9. See chapter 1 in this volume; and Michael E. Kraft, "Congress and Environmental Policy," in *Environmental Politics and Policy: Theories and Evidence,* 2d ed., ed. James P. Lester (Durham, N.C.: Duke University Press, 1995).
10. Ed Gillespie and Bob Schellhas, eds., *Contract with America* (New York: Times Books/Random House, 1994); Bob Benenson, "GOP Sets the 104th Congress on

New Regulatory Course," *Congressional Quarterly Weekly Report*, June 17, 1995, 1693–1705.

11. For a general review of this period, see Lawrence C. Dodd and Bruce I. Oppenheimer, "A Decade of Republican Control: The House of Representatives, 1995–2005," in *Congress Reconsidered*, 8th ed., ed. Dodd and Oppenheimer.

12. See Daniel A. Mazmanian and Michael E. Kraft, eds., *Toward Sustainable Communities: Transition and Transformations in Environmental Policy*, 2d ed. (Cambridge: MIT Press, 2009); Marc Allen Eisner, *Governing the Environment: The Transformation of Environmental Regulation* (Boulder, Colo.: Lynne Rienner, 2007); and Robert F. Durant, Daniel J. Fiorino, and Rosemary O'Leary, eds., *Environmental Governance Reconsidered: Challenges, Choices, and Opportunities* (Cambridge: MIT Press, 2004).

13. For a general analysis of roles that Congress plays in the U.S. political system, see Roger H. Davidson, Walter J. Oleszek, and Frances E. Lee, *Congress and Its Members*, 12th ed. (Washington, D.C.: CQ Press, 2009).

14. See Charlie Savage, "Democrats Look for Ways to Undo Late Bush-Era Rules by Agencies," *New York Times*, January 2, 2009.

15. Avery Palmer, "Obama's Choice for EPA Chief Meets Little Criticism on Capitol Hill," *CQ Weekly*, January 19, 2009, online edition.

16. For example, see Neil A. Lewis, "Democrats on Senate Panel Pummel Judicial Nominee," *New York Times*, March 2, 2005, A18.

17. Kraft, "Congress and Environmental Policy."

18. Davidson, Oleszek, and Lee, *Congress and Its Members*. See also Gary C. Jacobson, *The Politics of Congressional Elections*, 7th ed. (New York: Pearson Longman, 2009).

19. Carl Hulse, "Consensus on Energy Bill Arose One Project at a Time," *New York Times*, November 19, 2003, A14.

20. For a summary of the Energy Policy Act of 2005 and assessment of the political process that produced it, see Michael E. Kraft, *Environmental Policy and Politics*, 4th ed. (New York: Pearson Longman, 2007).

21. John M. Broder, "Democrats Oust Longtime Leader of House Panel: Waxman In, Dingell Out," *New York Times*, November 21, 2008, 1, A23.

22. Some commentators noted that Californians will be key players on climate change in the 111th Congress: committee chairs Henry Waxman and Barbara Boxer, and Speaker Nancy Pelosi all hail from the state. In addition, President Obama's secretary of energy is Steven Chu, formerly director of the Lawrence Berkeley National Laboratory in the state. The governor of California, Arnold Schwarzenegger, has long been a prominent advocate for action on climate change, and the state has some of the strongest climate policies in the nation. See Lyndsey Layton, "California Scheming," *Washington Post National Weekly Edition*, January 5–11, 2009, 18; and Felicity Barringer, "California Adopts a Plan on Emissions," *New York Times*, December 12, 2008, A25.

23. Richard E. Cohen, *Washington at Work: Back Rooms and Clean Air*, 2d ed. (New York: Macmillan, 1995); Gary C. Bryner, *Blue Skies, Green Politics: The Clean Air Act of 1990*, 2d ed. (Washington, D.C.: CQ Press, 1996).

24. For a general discussion of the effects of programs that continue without formal reauthorization, see David Baumann, "Government on Autopilot," *National Journal*, March 13, 1999, 688–692.

25. See Barry Rabe's chapter in this volume on state and local actions (chap. 2) and Christopher McGrory Klyza and David Sousa, *American Environmental Policy, 1990–2006: Beyond Gridlock* (Cambridge: MIT Press 2008) on how congressional gridlock has shifted policy experimentation to other venues.

26. For example, see Alex Wayne and Bill Swindell, "Capitol Hill Gridlock Leaves Programs in Limbo," *CQ Weekly*, December 4, 2004, 2834–2860. The phenomenon, of course, affects many other policy areas, not just the environment. One of the few scholarly analyses of the subject is Sarah A. Binder, *Stalemate: Causes and Consequences of Legislative Gridlock* (Washington, D.C.: Brookings Institution Press, 2003).

27. On the influence of business groups on the environment, see Sheldon Kamieniecki, *Corporate America and Environmental Policy: How Much Does Business Get Its Way?* (Palo Alto, Calif.: Stanford University Press, 2005); and Michael E. Kraft and Sheldon Kamieniecki, eds., *Business and Environmental Policy: Corporate Interests in the American Political System* (Cambridge: MIT Press, 2007).

28. This may help to explain the results of a recent study showing that members of Congress do tend to vote in a way that is consistent with their campaign promises on environmental issues, but that Republicans are "far more likely to break their campaign promises," and that pro-environmental campaign promises are more likely to be broken than are others. See Evan J. Ringquist and Carl Dasse, "Lies, Damned Lies, and Campaign Promises? Environmental Legislation in the 105th Congress," *Social Science Quarterly* 85 (June 2004): 400–419. The quotation is from p. 417.

29. In January 2009, a new poll by the Pew Research Center pointed to a decline in the saliency of environmental issues, and especially climate change, as Americans worried more about the state of the economy. The trick for members of Congress and the Obama administration is to effectively link action on energy and climate change to an improved economy, for example, through creation of "green jobs" in renewable energy production, energy efficiency, mass transit, and similar programs, which the administration touted and incorporated into a massive economic stimulus package Congress acted on in early 2009. See Andrew C. Revkin, "Environment Issues Slide in Poll of Public Concerns," *New York Times,* January 23, 2009, A13.

30. See Charles R. Shipan and William R. Lowry, "Environmental Policy and Party Divergence in Congress," *Political Research Quarterly* 54 (June 2001): 245–263.

31. League of Conservation Voters (LCV), "National Environmental Scorecard" (Washington, D.C.: LCV, November 2004, and later years). The scorecards are available at the league's Web site (www.lcv.org). The league used to report party averages in its annual scorecard, but it has stopped doing so. The sharp difference between the parties remains evident, however, within most state delegations, between the two parties' leadership on the key environmental committees, and between the House and Senate leaders of each party. The group's report on the 110th Congress, second session (2008), showed the same party divisions that have existed for years.

32. Mary Etta Cook and Roger H. Davidson, "Deferral Politics: Congressional Decision Making on Environmental Issues in the 1980s," in *Public Policy and the Natural Environment,* ed. Helen M. Ingram and R. Kenneth Godwin (Greenwich, Conn.: JAI, 1985). See also Norman J. Vig and Michael E. Kraft, eds., *Environmental Policy in the 1980s: Reagan's New Agenda* (Washington, D.C.: CQ Press, 1984).

33. Joseph A. Davis, "Environment/Energy," *1988 Congressional Quarterly Almanac* (Washington, D.C.: Congressional Quarterly, 1989), 137.

34. For a fuller discussion of the gridlock over clean air legislation, see Bryner, *Blue Skies, Green Politics.*

35. Rhodes Cook, "Rare Combination of Forces May Make History of '94," *Congressional Quarterly Weekly Report,* April 15, 1995, 1076–1081.

36. Katharine Q. Seelye, "Files Show How Gingrich Laid a Grand G.O.P. Plan," *New York Times,* December 3, 1995, 1, 16. See also John B. Bader, "The Contract with America: Origins and Assessments," in *Congress Reconsidered,* 6th ed., ed. Lawrence C. Dodd and Bruce I. Oppenheimer (Washington, D.C.: CQ Press, 1997).

37. Everett Carll Ladd, "The 1994 Congressional Elections: The Postindustrial Realignment Continues," *Political Science Quarterly* 110 (spring 1995): 1–23; Alfred J. Tuchfarber et al., "The Republican Tidal Wave of 1994: Testing Hypotheses about Realignment, Restructuring, and Rebellion," *PS: Political Science and Politics* 28 (December 1995): 689–696.

38. Allan Freedman, "GOP's Secret Weapon against Regulations: Finesse," *CQ Weekly,* September 5, 1998, 2314–2320; Charles Pope, "Environmental Bills Hitch a Ride through the Legislative Gantlet," *CQ Weekly,* April 4, 1998, 872–875.

39. See Durant, Fiorino, and O'Leary, *Environmental Governance Reconsidered*; Dan Fiorino, *The New Environmental Regulation* (Cambridge: MIT Press, 2006); and Eisner, *Governing the Environment*.
40. John H. Cushman Jr., "House Passes Bill That Would Limit Many Regulations," *New York Times*, March 4, 1995, 1, 8; Tom Kenworthy, "Letting the Truth Fall Where It May," *Washington Post National Weekly Edition*, March 27–April 2, 1995, 31.
41. See Kraft and Kamieniecki, *Business and Environmental Policy*; and Kamieniecki, *Corporate America and Environmental Policy*.
42. See Jackie Calmes, "Both Sides of the Aisle Say More Regulation, and Not Just of Banks," *New York Times*, October 14, 2008, A15.
43. Quoted in Bob Herbert, "Health and Safety Wars," *New York Times*, July 10, 1995, A11.
44. John H. Cushman Jr., "G.O.P.'s Plan for Environment Is Facing a Big Test in Congress," *New York Times*, July 17, 1995, 1, A9.
45. Pope, "Environmental Bills Hitch a Ride."
46. Andrew Revkin, "Law Revises Standards for Scientific Study," *New York Times*, March 21, 2002, A24.
47. Susan Zakin, "Riders from Hell," *Amicus Journal* (spring 2001): 20–22.
48. Carroll J. Doherty and the staff of *CQ Weekly*, "Congress Compiles a Modest Record in a Session Sidetracked by Scandal: Appropriations," *CQ Weekly*, November 14, 1998, 3086–3087 and 3090–3091.
49. Details of the budgetary battles can be followed through coverage by *CQ Weekly*. The president's budget proposals can be found at the Web site for the Office of Management and Budget (www.omb.gov), and commentary on it by environmental groups can be seen in reports by NRDC (www.nrdc.org), among others. The polls on mistrust are from the American National Election Study, the *New York Times*/CBS, and Third Way surveys and are reported in Will Englund, "10 Keys to a Successful Presidency," *National Journal*, January 17, 2009, 21.
50. David Hosansky, "Rewrite of Laws on Pesticides on Way to President's Desk," *Congressional Quarterly Weekly Report*, July 27, 1996, 2101–2103; Hosansky, "Provisions: Pesticide, Food Safety Law," *Congressional Quarterly Weekly Report*, September 7, 1996, 2546–2550.
51. David Hosansky, "Drinking Water Bill Clears; Clinton Expected to Sign," *Congressional Quarterly Weekly Report*, August 3, 1996, 2179–2180; Allan Freedman, "Provisions: Safe Drinking Water Act Amendments," *Congressional Quarterly Weekly Report*, September 14, 1996, 2622–2627.
52. Alan K. Ota, "What the Highway Bill Does," *CQ Weekly*, July 11, 1998, 1892–1898.
53. Rebecca Adams, "Pressure from White House and Hastert Pries Brownfields Bill from Committee," *CQ Weekly*, September 8, 2001, 2065–2066.
54. Mary Clare Jalonick, "Healthy Forests Initiative Provisions," *CQ Weekly*, January 24, 2004, 246–247.
55. Juliet Eilperin, "Keeping the Wilderness Untamed: Bills in Congress Could Add as Much as Two Million Acres of Unspoiled Land to Federal Control," *Washington Post National Edition*, June 23–July 6, 2008, 35; and Avery Palmer, "Long-Stalled Lands Bill Get Nod from Senate," *CQ Weekly*, January 19, 2009, 128.
56. Chuck McCutcheon, "House Passage of Bush Energy Plan Sets Up Clash with Senate," *CQ Weekly*, August 4, 2001, 1915–1917.
57. Rebecca Adams, "Politics Stokes Energy Debate," *CQ Weekly*, January 12, 2002, 109.
58. Ibid., 108.
59. For example, see Mary Clare Jalonick, "Encouraged by GOP Election Sweep, Energy Industry Likes Odds in 109th," *CQ Weekly*, November 13, 2004, 2696–2697.
60. Carl Hulse, "House Votes to Approve Broad Energy Legislation," *New York Times*, April 22, 2005.
61. See Ben Evans and Joseph J. Schatz, "Details of Energy Policy Law," *CQ Weekly*, September 5, 2005, 2337–2345.

62. Elizabeth Bumiller, "Bush's Goals on Energy Quickly Find Obstacles," *New York Times,* February 2, 2006, 1, A18.

63. Robert Pear, "Lawmakers at Impasse on Incentives for Renewable Energy," *New York Times,* September 30, 2008, C3.

64. Carl Hulse, "House Moves Toward New Offshore Oil Drilling," *New York Times,* September 17, 2008, online edition; and Avery Palmer, "Democrats' Drilling Bill Passes," *CQ Weekly,* September 22, 2008, online edition.

65. Editorial, "An $80 Billion Start," *New York Times,* February 18, 2009, A22.

66. The education act was part of the Higher Education Opportunity Act of 2008. It authorized competitive grants to institutions and associations in higher education to promote development of sustainability curricula, programs, and practices. It was the first new federal environmental education program in eighteen years.

67. The House has favored reform of the mining law, but the Senate has not. In 2007 the House voted 244–166 for an act that for the first time set a royalty payment to the government for mining on public lands, and established a clear and enforceable set of environmental protections for mining. The Senate has not gone along so far, and one of the key opponents has been Senate majority leader Harry Reid, who represents a state heavily dependent on mining. New mining legislation is pending in the 111th Congress.

68. Michael Janofsky, "Changes May Be Needed in Superfund, Chief Says," *New York Times,* December 5, 2004, A24. On the drop in program revenues, see Jennifer 8. Lee, "Drop in Budget Slows Superfund Program," *New York Times,* March 9, 2004, A23.

69. Cited in *Science and Environmental Policy Update,* the Ecological Society of America online newsletter, April 20, 2001.

70. Mary Clare Jalonick, "Environmental Panels' Chairmen Chip Away at Endangered Species Act, Refocusing Resources and Definitions," *CQ Weekly,* March 27, 2004, 756; Jalonick, "House Panel OKs Softening of Species Act," *CQ Weekly,* July 24, 2004, 1811.

71. Michael Janofsky, "Climate Debate Threatens Republican Clean-Air Bill," *New York Times,* January 27, 2005; Janofsky, "Vote Nearing, Clean Air Bill Prompts Rush of Lobbying," *New York Times,* February 15, 2005, A14.

72. Cited in Juliet Eilperin, "Standoff in Congress Blocks Action on Environmental Bills," *Washington Post,* October 18, 2004, A02.

73. Margaret Kriz, "Hot Opportunities," *National Journal,* July 7, 2007, 14–18; and Kate Phillips, "Gore Will Appear before Senate Panel on Climate Change," *New York Times,* Politics Blog, January 22, 2009. In 2008 Gore receive much media coverage on his call for the United States to boldly shift U.S. energy consumption to carbon-free fuel sources within a decade. The new climate change bill is described in John M. Broder, "Democrats Unveil Climate Bill," *New York Times,* March 31, 2009.

6

Environmental Policy in the Courts

Rosemary O'Leary

In 1966, on one of her frequent trips to a family cabin in rural upstate New York, Carol Yannacone was shocked to find hundreds of dead fish floating on the surface of Yaphank Lake, where she had spent her summers as a child. After discovering that the county had sprayed the foliage surrounding the lake with DDT to kill mosquitoes immediately prior to the fish kill, Yannacone persuaded her lawyer husband to file suit on her behalf against the county mosquito control commission. The suit requested an injunction to halt the spraying of pesticides containing DDT around the lake.

Although the Yannacones initially were able to win only a one-year injunction, they set into motion a chain of events that would permanently change environmental policy in the courts. It was through this lawsuit that a group of environmentalists and scientists formed the Environmental Defense Fund (EDF), a nonprofit group dedicated to promoting change in environmental policy through legal action. After eight years of protracted litigation, EDF won a court battle against the U.S. Environmental Protection Agency (EPA) that Judge David Bazelon heralded as the beginning of "a new era in the . . . long and fruitful collaboration of administrative agencies and reviewing courts."[1] That judicial decision triggered a permanent suspension of the registration of pesticides containing DDT in the United States.

Fast forward to 2008. By the end of his second term as president, George W. Bush was fully immersed in the concept of environmental policymaking in the courts. Environmental advocates were waging an all-out attack in the courts in an effort to challenge the president's attempted change of environmental policies.

In February 2008, for example, a three-judge federal court of appeals panel in Washington, D.C., issued a blow to President Bush as it unanimously struck down one of the administration's most significant attempts to change environmental policy in the form of EPA limits on mercury emissions from coal-fired power plants. The Bush administration had substituted weaker regulations for the "plain text" of the Clean Air Act without following the process set out in the law, the court said. The appellate court called this "the logic of the Queen of Hearts," referring to the character from Lewis Carroll's book *Alice's Adventures in Wonderland.* In the book, the foul-tempered queen has only one way of settling all difficulties, great or small, yelling, "Off with his head!" and severing the heads of anyone who dared to disagree with her.

This is just one of several significant judicial reversals of Bush administration policies on coal-burning power plants, and it is just one current example of the role of courts in environmental policymaking. The courts were perhaps the toughest on the Bush administration in conflicts over the Endangered Species Act. The Center for Biological Diversity examined seventy-eight federal court rulings and settlements concerning endangered species from January 2001 through April 2008 and found that the Bush administration won just one case. An interesting aspect of these reversals is the extent to which the courts have "scolded" the Bush administration for ignoring environmental law and science.[2] In both legal analyses and in "dicta" (remarks or observations made by a judge in a decision), courts are an integral part of the environmental policymaking process.

An important aspect of environmental conflicts, however, is that multiple forums exist for decision making. Litigation is by no means the only way to resolve environmental disputes. Most environmental conflicts never reach a court, and an estimated 50 to 90 percent of those that do are settled out of court. Discussion and debate are informal ways of resolving environmental conflict. Enacting legislation is another way to deal with such conflict. Environmental conflict resolution approaches, ranging from collaborative problem solving to mediation, are becoming more common in environmental policy.

The focus of this chapter, however, is environmental policy in the courts. First, a profile of the U.S. court system and a primer on judicial review of agency actions are offered. Next, the focus changes to how courts shape environmental policy, with several in-depth case analyses provided. The chapter concludes with a view to the future.

The Organization and Operation of the U.S. Court System

To understand environmental policy in the courts, a brief profile of the U.S. court system is essential. The United States has a dual court system, with different cases starting either in federal court or in state or county court. Keeping in mind that most legal disputes never go to court (they are resolved through one of the informal methods mentioned in the introduction to this chapter), this section describes the organization of the U.S. court system (Figure 6-1).

When legal disputes do go to court, most are resolved in state courts. Many of these disputes are criminal or domestic controversies. They usually start in trial courts and are heard by a judge and sometimes a jury. If the case is lost at the trial court level, appeal to an intermediate court of appeals is possible. At this level, the appeals court usually reviews only questions of law, not fact. If a party to a case is not satisfied with the outcome at the intermediate level, then the party may appeal to the state supreme court. In cases involving federal questions, final appeal to the U.S. Supreme Court is possible, but the Court has wide discretion as to which cases it will review.

Figure 6-1   The Dual Court System

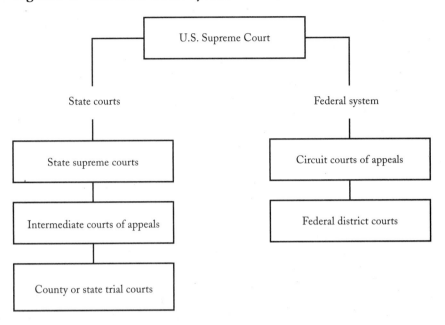

Most of the environmental cases discussed in this chapter began in the federal court system because they concerned interpretations of federal statutes or the Constitution. Cases that begin in the federal court system usually begin in the federal district courts. There are eighty-nine federal district courts staffed by approximately 649 active judges. (There are also so-called specialty courts such as the U.S. bankruptcy courts, the U.S. court of appeals for the armed forces, and the U.S. court of federal claims.)

Some statutes, however, provide for appeal of decisions of federal regulatory agencies directly to the federal courts of appeals, rather than through district courts. These cases, coupled with appeals from federal district courts, make for a full docket for the federal courts of appeals. There are thirteen federal circuit courts of appeals with about 165 active judges in total. Here, judges sit in groups of three when deciding cases. When there are conflicting opinions among the lower federal district courts within a circuit, all the judges of the circuit will sit together and hear a case. An unsatisfactory outcome in a circuit court can be appealed to the U.S. Supreme Court. Less than 10 percent of the requests for Supreme Court review usually are granted.

Sources of Law

The decisions of appellate courts are considered precedent. Precedent is judge-made law that guides and informs subsequent court decisions involving similar or analogous situations. But precedent is only one of several

sources of environmental law. The major sources of environmental law are as
follows:

- Constitutions (federal and state)
- Statutes (federal, state, and local)
- Administrative regulations (promulgated by administrative agencies)
- Treaties (signed by the president and ratified by the Senate)
- Executive orders (proclamations issued by presidents or governors)
- Appellate court decisions

Judicial Review of Agency Actions

One of the pivotal issues in environmental law today is the scope of
judicial review of an agency's action. The purpose of judicial review of
administrative decision making generally is to assure at least minimum levels
of fairness. It has been said that the scope of review for a specific administrative decision may range from 0 to 100 percent, meaning that depending
on the issue in question, a reviewing court may have broad or narrow powers
to decide a case—or somewhere in between.

When an agency makes a decision, it usually does three things. First, it
interprets the law in question. Second, it collects facts concerning a particular situation. Third, it uses its discretionary power to apply the law to the
facts. A court's review of an agency's actions in each of these three steps is
very different. (At the same time, it must be acknowledged that separating
an agency's actions into three categories can be difficult, as in instances when
there are mixed questions of law and fact.)

An agency's *interpretation of the law* usually demands a strong look by a
reviewing court. When constitutional issues are of concern, judges will rarely
defer to administrative interpretations. However, when an agency's interpretation of its own regulation is at issue, it is said that deference is "even more
clearly in order."[3] The general practice is that a court will give less deference
to an agency's legal conclusions than to its factual or discretionary decisions.

At the same time, courts have shown deference to administrative interpretations of the law. The signature case that illustrates this point is *Chevron
v. NRDC* [Natural Resources Defense Council],[4] which concerned the EPA's
"bubble concept" pursuant to the Clean Air Act. Under the bubble concept,
the EPA allows states to adopt a plant-wide definition of the term *stationary
source*. Under this definition, an existing plant that contained several pollu-
tion-emitting devices could install or modify one piece of equipment without meeting the permit conditions, if the alteration did not increase the total
emissions from the plant. This allowed a state to treat all of the pollution-
emitting sources within the same industrial group as if they were encased in
a single bubble.

Environmentalists sued the EPA, asserting that this definition of stationary source violated the Clean Air Act. In a unanimous decision, the
Supreme Court held that the EPA's plant-wide definition was permissible.

The Supreme Court's opinion is now referred to as the *Chevron* doctrine. It holds that when Congress has spoken clearly to the precise question at issue the rule of law demands agency adherence to its intent. However, if Congress has not addressed the matter precisely, then an agency may adopt any reasonable interpretation—regardless of whether a reviewing court may consider some other interpretation more reasonable or sensible. As such, the *Chevron* doctrine is often thought of as making it more difficult for courts to overrule agency interpretations.

An agency's *fact finding* usually demands less scrutiny by reviewing courts than do legal issues. Although an agency's decision may be reversed if it is unwarranted by the facts, courts generally acknowledge that agencies are in a better position to ascertain facts than is a reviewing court.

Judicial review of an agency's *discretionary powers* is usually deferential to a point, while maintaining an important oversight role for the courts. A court usually will make sure the agency has done a careful job of collecting and analyzing information, taking a hard look at the important issues and facts.

Even if a reviewing court decides that the agency correctly understood the law involved and concludes that the agency's view of the facts was reasonable, it may still negate the decision if the agency's activity is found to be "arbitrary, capricious, an abuse of discretion, or otherwise not in accordance with the law."[5] This can involve legal, factual, or discretionary issues. This type of review has been called several things: a rational basis review, an arbitrariness review, and an abuse of discretion review.

How Courts Shape Environmental Policy

As they decide environmental cases to assure minimum levels of fairness, courts shape environmental policy in many ways. First, the courts determine who does or does not have standing, or the right, to sue. Although many environmental statutes give citizens, broadly defined, the right to sue polluters or regulators,[6] procedural hurdles must still be cleared in order to gain access to the courts. Plaintiffs usually must demonstrate injury in fact, which is often not clear-cut and is subject to interpretation by judges. By controlling who may sue, courts affect the environmental policy agenda.

Second, and related to the first power, courts shape environmental policy by deciding which cases are ripe, or ready for review. For a case to be justiciable, an actual controversy must exist. The alleged wrong must be more than merely anticipated. To decide whether an issue is ripe for judicial review, courts will examine both the fitness of the issue for judicial decision and the hardship on the parties if a court withholds consideration. Deciding which cases are ripe and which are not makes the courts powerful gatekeepers.

A third way in which courts shape environmental policy is by their choice of standard of review. Will the court, for example, take a hard look at the actions of public environmental officials in this particular case, or will it defer to the administrative expertise of the agency? Under what conditions will government environmental experts be deemed to have exceeded their legislative or constitutional authority? To what standards will polluters be held?

A fourth way in which courts shape environmental policy is by interpreting environmental laws. Courts interpret statutes, administrative rules and regulations, executive orders, treaties, constitutions, and prior court decisions. Often these laws are ambiguous and vague. Situations may arise that the laws' drafters did not anticipate. Hence, judicial interpretation becomes of paramount importance. And given the precedent-setting nature of court orders, a judicial interpretation made today may determine not only current environmental policy but also that of the future.

A final major way in which courts shape environmental policy is through the remedies they choose. Will the court, for example, order a punitive fine for polluters, or probation? Judges generally have great discretion in their choice of remedy, thus affecting environmental policy.

The Supreme Court, the final arbiter of many precedent-setting environmental cases, shapes environmental policy primarily through the selection of cases it chooses to hear, the limits it places on other branches of government, and the limits it places on the states. Justices' values, ideological backgrounds, and policy preferences at times influence the outcome of environmental court decisions.

A study examining the impact of over two thousand federal court decisions on the EPA's policies and administration found that from an agency-wide perspective, compliance with court orders has become one of the EPA's top priorities, at times overtaking congressional mandates.[7] In an atmosphere of limited resources, coupled with unrealistic and numerous statutory mandates, the EPA has been forced to make decisions among competing priorities. With few exceptions, court orders have been the winners in this competition. The courts have dictated which issues get attention at the EPA. Thus the implications of courts shaping environmental policy are formidable and one may easily see why environmental advocates, concerned citizens, and big businesses often use lawsuits as tools to force policy changes in public environment and natural resource agencies. The cases discussed in the sections that follow paint a vivid portrait of environmental policymaking in the courts.

Standing to Sue: The Case of Global Warming

On October 12, 2007, Al Gore was awarded the Nobel Peace Prize for his campaign to curb global climate change. Gore shared the prize with the UN Intergovernmental Panel on Climate Change, whose head, Rajendra Pachauri, told leaders at a climate conference in Indonesia that a well-documented rise in global temperatures has coincided with a significant increase in the concentration of carbon dioxide in the atmosphere. "Heed the wisdom of science," Pachauri told conference participants on behalf of the UN, as scientists believe the two trends are related. When carbon dioxide is released into the atmosphere, it acts like the ceiling of a greenhouse, trapping solar energy and retarding the escape of reflected heat.

In 1999, eight years before Gore received the Nobel Peace Prize, the International Center for Technology Assessment joined other parties in petitioning the U.S. Environmental Protection Agency (EPA) to set standards for four greenhouse gases emitted by new motor vehicles: carbon dioxide, methane, nitrous oxide, and hydrofluorocarbons. The petition argued that these greenhouse gases are air pollutants and that scientists had concluded that global warming will endanger public health and the environment. Hence, they argued, the EPA is obligated to regulate greenhouse gas emissions from new mobile sources.

The EPA refused to regulate greenhouse gases, citing several reasons: First, the EPA said that the Clean Air Act "does not authorize regulation to address global climate change."[8] Tied in with this, the agency maintained that air pollutants associated with climate change "are not air pollutants under the [act's] regulatory provisions."[9] Moreover, the EPA stated that it disagreed with the regulatory approach urged by the petitioners and that it would not be "effective or appropriate for EPA to establish [greenhouse gas] standards for motor vehicles" at this time.[10] Instead, the EPA chose to encourage voluntary actions to curb emissions through incentives for more technological development.

The agency noted that "the science of climate change is extraordinarily complex and still evolving."[11] The agency also said that since many sources of air pollutants were associated with global climate change, to regulate only pollutants emitted by new motor vehicles would "result in an inefficient, piecemeal approach to addressing the climate change issue."[12] The agency concluded that it is the president's prerogative to address global climate change as an important foreign policy issue.

The petitioners appealed the EPA's decision to the Court of Appeals for the D.C. Circuit. That court split three different ways, with the majority ruling in favor of the EPA.[13] In 2006 the Supreme Court agreed to review the case, *Massachusetts v. Environmental Protection Agency*,[14] focusing on whether the EPA had authority to regulate greenhouse gases under the Clean Air Act and whether it could decline to exercise that authority based on policy considerations not mentioned in the statute.[15]

One of the pivotal issues the Supreme Court had to grapple with in the case was whether the plaintiffs—the state of Massachusetts as well as other states, local governments, and nonprofit environmental advocacy groups—had standing to sue. The Supreme Court has ruled consistently that, to have standing to sue, a party must demonstrate injury in fact, "a concrete and particularized, actual or imminent invasion of a legally protected interest."[16] In federal cases this requirement arises out of the U.S. Constitution's "case or controversy" requirement.[17]

In response, the EPA, supported by another group of states paired with six trade associations, countered that the plaintiffs did not have standing to sue. The EPA and its supporters maintained that because greenhouse gas emissions inflict widespread harm, the doctrine of standing presents an insurmountable obstacle. They argued that those who filed the lawsuit did not have a personal stake in the outcome of the controversy; specifically they could not demonstrate a particularized injury, actual or imminent, traceable to the defendant, as precedent requires. They also argued that the EPA's decision not to regulate greenhouse gas emissions from new motor vehicles contributed so insignificantly to any alleged injuries that the agency could not be made to answer for them.

On April 2, 2007, the Supreme Court disagreed with the EPA, siding with the state of Massachusetts, its partner states and local governments, and environmental advocates. Only one plaintiff needs to show standing, the Court said, and the state of Massachusetts clearly demonstrated a stake in the outcome of the controversy, given the projected rise in sea levels predicted to come from global warming. Calling the harms associated with climate change serious and well recognized, the Court found the risk of catastrophic harm, though remote, to be real. That risk would be reduced to some extent if the plaintiffs received the relief they requested in their lawsuit. Therefore, the Court found that the plaintiffs had standing to challenge the EPA.

After affirming the standing of the plaintiffs, the Supreme Court went on to issue a remarkable decision in which five of the nine justices chastised the Bush administration for its inaction on global warming. The Court declared that carbon dioxide and other greenhouse gases are air pollutants and must be regulated by the EPA under the Clean Air Act. The Court rebuked the administration's argument that, even if it did have authority to act, it would be unwise to regulate those pollutants at the current time. Rejecting rulemaking based on these impermissible considerations was arbitrary, capricious, and otherwise not in accordance with law, the Court said. The Court ordered the EPA to decide, pursuant to the mandates of the Clean Air Act, whether greenhouse gases may reasonably be anticipated to endanger public health or welfare.

Calling the decision "a watershed moment in the fight against global warming," a spokesperson for the Sierra Club environmental group said, "This is a total repudiation of the refusal of the Bush administration to use the authority he has to meet the challenge of global warming."[18] Legal scholars pointed out that the EPA will no longer have any excuse to refuse to regulate pollutants from other sources, such as power plants, that are governed by the same Clean Air Act sections. They also surmised that the EPA will have a harder time denying the state of California's proposal to tighten greenhouse gas emissions from automobiles in that state.

This landmark case illustrates how courts shape environmental policy by determining who has standing. Without a finding by the Supreme Court that the state of Massachusetts had standing, they would not have had the legal authority to sue. Without the legal authority to sue, this case never would have come to court.

Ripeness and Standard of Review:
The Case of Timber Cutting

The U.S. national forest system is vast. It includes 155 national forests, 20 national grasslands, eight land utilization projects, and other lands that together occupy nearly 300,000 square miles of land located in forty-four states, Puerto Rico, and the Virgin Islands. To manage those lands the National Forest Service, housed in the U.S. Department of Agriculture, develops land and resource management plans, as mandated by the National Forest Management Act of 1976. In developing the plans the Forest Service must take into account both environmental and commercial goals.

In the late 1980s the Forest Service developed a plan for the Wayne National Forest located in southern Ohio. When the plan was proposed, several environmental groups, including the Sierra Club and the Citizens Council on Conservation and Environmental Control, protested in administrative hearings that the plan was unlawful in part because it allowed below-cost timber sales and so encouraged clear-cutting. Opposing the environmental groups was the Ohio Forestry Association.

When the plan was not changed, the Sierra Club brought suit in federal court against the Forest Service and the secretary of agriculture. Among its requests to the district court, the Sierra Club asked for a declaration that the plan was unlawful because it authorized below-cost timber cutting. The Sierra Club also asked for an injunction to halt below-cost timber harvesting.

In a case full of twists and turns[19] the Supreme Court eventually ruled in favor of the Ohio Forestry Association in the 1998 case *Ohio Forestry Association, Inc. v. Sierra Club.*[20] Among the many arguments cited in its rationale, the Court said that the case was not ripe for review because it concerned abstract disagreements over administrative policies. Immediate judicial intervention would require the Court to second-guess thousands of technical decisions made by scientists and other forestry experts and might hinder the Forest Service's efforts to refine its policies, the Court said. Further, delayed judicial review would not cause significant hardship for the parties. (The forest plan for the Wayne National Forest, at issue in *Ohio Forestry*, was again challenged unsuccessfully by environmental advocates in 2005, in *Buckeye Forest Council v. U.S. Forest Service,*[21] which concerned the Endangered Species Act.)

The *Ohio Forestry* case is an example of how courts shape environmental policy by applying the concepts of standard of review and ripeness. Notable is the Court's reluctance to second-guess the judgments of government scientists and other technical analysts. In a case in which there is no showing of arbitrary or capricious government action, the Court will give great deference to experts in its review. Also notable is the Court's reluctance to review a plan that had not yet been implemented. Because no clear-cutting or timber sales had occurred, there was not yet a case or controversy, and so the case was not ripe for review. Regrettably, however, this means that concrete damage to the environment is needed before the Court will act.

Though wise from a legal perspective, this approach is short-sighted from an environmental perspective. Two legal scholars recently called for Congress to respond to this case by changing the law.[22] The scholars concluded that the case, coupled with other cases, created significant roadblocks in the path of those wishing to challenge federal government planning decisions. In addition, these cases have encouraged land management agencies to change their uses of land management plans from vehicles for determining which lands are suitable for various activities to "paperwork that makes no commitments about land suitability and sets few, if any, standards for governing future activities."[23]

Standard of Review: The Case of Air Quality

The Clean Air Act mandates that the EPA administrator promulgate National Ambient Air Quality Standards for each air pollutant for which air quality criteria have been issued. Once a standard has been promulgated, the administrator must review the standard and the criteria on which it is based every five years and revise the standard if necessary. On July 18, 1997, the EPA administrator revised the standards for particulate matter and ozone. Because ozone and particulate matter are both nonthreshold pollutants—that is, any amount harms the public health—the EPA set stringent standards that would cost hundreds of millions of dollars to implement nationwide.

The American Trucking Association, as well as other business groups and the states of Michigan, Ohio, and West Virginia, challenged the new standards in the U.S. Court of Appeals for the District of Columbia Circuit and then in the U.S. Supreme Court. Among other things, the plaintiffs argued that the statute that delegated the authority to the EPA to set the standards was unconstitutionally vague. They also argued that the EPA should perform a cost-benefit analysis when setting national air quality standards in order to keep costs in check.

In a unanimous decision in 2001, in the case of *Whitman v. American Trucking Association,*[24] the Supreme Court mostly upheld the EPA and its new regulations. The statute, while ambiguous, was not overly vague, wrote the Court, reversing the court of appeals. Furthermore, no cost-benefit analysis was needed. The EPA, based on the information about health effects contained in the technical documents it compiled, is to identify the maximum airborne concentration of a pollutant that the public health can tolerate, decrease the concentration to provide an adequate margin of safety, and set the standard at that level. Nowhere are the costs of achieving such a standard made part of that initial calculation, according to the Court.

Concerning the appropriate standard of review, the Court invoked the rule that if a statute is silent or ambiguous with respect to an issue, then a court must defer to a reasonable interpretation made by the agency administrator. The key words for understanding the concept of standard of review are *ambiguous, reasonable,* and *defer.* The statute must be silent or ambiguous, the agency's actions must be judged by the court to be reasonable, and the court will then defer to the agency.

The key word for understanding the essence of this specific case is *reasonable*, for in one ambiguous instance in this case the Court found the EPA's actions reasonable, whereas in another ambiguous instance in the same case the Court found the EPA's actions unreasonable. Specifically the EPA's actions concerning cost-benefit analysis were found to be reasonable. Contrasted to this, the EPA's interpretation concerning the implementation of the act in another ambiguous section was found to be unreasonable. In the second instance, the EPA read the statute in a way that completely nullified text meant to limit the agency's discretion. This, the Court said, was unlawful.

Once again we have a case that is a clear example of how courts shape environmental policy—here by choosing and applying a standard of review. An appropriate standard of review can, and should, change from case to case. In addition, reasonable judges can differ as to their view of what constitutes an appropriate standard of review. Further, once a standard of review is selected, the application of that standard becomes important. Crucial in this case were judgments concerning whether the EPA administrator acted reasonably. Hence, when judges are selected, an examination of their judicial philosophies and predispositions becomes important.

Interpretation of Environmental Laws

Judges shape environmental policy in how they interpret laws. Environmental laws are often broad and vague. Circumstances arise that the drafters of the laws did not foresee. Environmental statutes sometimes conflict with each other. Different stakeholders interpret mandates contrarily. The cases analyzed in this section exemplify how courts shape environmental policy through judicial interpretation of laws.

Interpreting Statutes: Two Cases Concerning the Endangered Species Act

The Endangered Species Act of 1973 contains a variety of protections designed to save from extinction species that the secretary of the interior designates as endangered or threatened.[25] Section 9 of the act makes it unlawful for any person to "take" any endangered or threatened species. *Take* is defined by the law as "harassing, harming, pursuing, hunting, shooting, wounding, killing, trapping, capturing or collecting any of the protected wildlife."[26] In the early 1990s the secretary promulgated a regulation that defined the statute's prohibition on takings to include "significant habitat modification or degradation where it actually kills or injures wildlife."[27]

A group calling itself Sweet Home Chapter of Communities for a Great Oregon filed suit alleging that the secretary of the interior exceeded his authority under the Endangered Species Act by promulgating that regulation. The plaintiff group comprised small landowners, logging companies, and families dependent on the forest products industries of the Pacific Northwest. They argued that the legislative history of the act demonstrated that Congress considered, and rejected, such a broad definition. Further, they argued that the regulation as applied to the habitat of the northern spotted owl and the red-cockaded woodpecker had injured them economically, because there were now vast areas of land that could not be logged. If the secretary wanted to protect the habitat of these endangered species, they maintained, the secretary would have to buy their land.

The district court entered summary judgment for the secretary of the interior, finding that the regulation was a reasonable interpretation of congressional intent.[28] In the U.S. Court of Appeals for the District of Columbia, a divided panel first affirmed the judgment of the lower court. After granting a rehearing, however, the panel reversed the lower court's ruling. The confusion, and final decision, centered on how to interpret the word *harm* in the Endangered Species Act, looking at the totality of the act.

The secretary of the interior appealed to the U.S. Supreme Court. In a 6–3 decision, in the case of *Babbitt v. Sweet Home Chapter of Communities for a Great Oregon* (1995),[29] the Supreme Court reversed the decision of the court of appeals and upheld the Department of the Interior's regulation. Examining the legislative history of the Endangered Species Act, and applying rules of statutory construction, the majority of the Court concluded that the secretary's definition of *harm* was reasonable. Further, the Court concluded that the writing of this technical and science-based regulation involved a complex policy choice. Congress entrusted the secretary with broad discretion in these matters, and the Court expressed a reluctance to substitute its views of wise policy for those of the secretary.

This path-breaking endangered species case demonstrates how courts shape environmental policy by the way they interpret statutes. Different judges at different stages of review in this case interpreted the statutory word *harm* differently. The protection of endangered species hinged on these interpretations. Tied in with this is the important notion of which rules of statutory construction courts choose to apply and how they apply them. Further, this case is another example of how courts are hesitant to substitute their view for the views of experts in scientific and technical matters, absent a showing of arbitrary or capricious action, or obvious error. The final Supreme Court decision set a precedent that strengthened endangered species policy throughout the United States.

Twelve years later, in 2007, the Supreme Court decided a case that concerned "dueling statutes," resulting in a *weakening* of the Endangered Species Act. In its interesting rationale, the Court juxtaposed the reasoning of the *Babbitt* decision with the reasoning of the *Chevron* decision.

Under the Clean Water Act, the EPA initially administers each state's National Pollution Discharge Elimination System (NPDES) permitting program. Once a state meets nine criteria, the EPA must transfer authority for the NPDES program to the state.

At the same time, the Endangered Species Act requires federal agencies to consult with agencies designated by the secretaries of commerce and the interior to ensure that a proposed agency action is unlikely to jeopardize an endangered or a threatened species. The Fish and Wildlife Service and the National Marine Fisheries Service administer the Endangered Species Act. Once a consultation process is complete, a written biological opinion is issued, which may suggest alternative actions to protect a jeopardized species or its critical habitat.

When Arizona officials sought EPA authorization to administer the state's NPDES program, the EPA initiated consultation with the Fish and Wildlife Service to determine whether the transfer would adversely affect any listed species. The Fish and Wildlife Service regional office wanted potential impacts taken into account, but the EPA disagreed, finding that the Clean Water Act's mandatory language stripped the EPA of authority to disapprove a transfer based on any other considerations. The dispute was referred to the agencies' national offices for resolution.

The Fish and Wildlife Service's biological opinion concluded that the requested transfer would not jeopardize listed species. The EPA concluded that Arizona had met each of the Clean Water Act's nine criteria and approved the transfer, noting that the biological opinion had fulfilled the ESA consultation mandate.

Defenders of Wildlife, an environmental advocacy group, filed a lawsuit against the EPA in the Ninth Circuit Court of Appeals. The National Association of Home Builders intervened to support the EPA. The Court of Appeals held in favor of Defenders of Wildlife, stating that the EPA's transfer to the state of Arizona of the authority to run its own NPDES program was arbitrary and capricious. It did not dispute that Arizona had met the Clean Water Act's nine criteria, but instead concluded that the Endangered Species Act required the EPA to determine whether its transfer decision would jeopardize listed endangered species.

The National Association of Homebuilders appealed the court of appeals decision to the U.S. Supreme Court. On June 25, 2007, in a 5–4 decision, *National Association of Home Builders v. Defenders of Wildlife*,[30] the Supreme Court reversed the decision of the court of appeals, noting that this case entailed a conflict of statutes.

Among its conclusions, the Supreme Court found that the Ninth Circuit's determination that the EPA's action was arbitrary and capricious was not supported by the record. The EPA is mandated by the Clean Water Act to turn over the operation of an NPDES program to a state if that state meets all nine criteria enumerated in the statute. The state of Arizona met all nine criteria; therefore, the EPA had no choice but to turn over the program to the state, the majority of the Court said.

As to the Endangered Species Act, the Court said that the statute's mandate applies only to discretionary agency actions. It does not apply to actions like the NPDES permitting transfer authorization that an agency is *required* by statute to undertake once certain specified triggering events have occurred. To decide otherwise would be to add a tenth criterion to the Clean Water Act.

The Court emphasized that while a later-enacted statute such as the Endangered Species Act can sometimes operate to amend or even repeal an earlier statutory provision such as that of the Clean Water Act, Congress did not expressly override the Clean Water Act in this case. The Supreme Court acknowledged that it owes "some degree of deference" to the secretary of the interior's reasonable interpretation of the Endangered Species Act under the *Babbitt* decision. At the same time, the Supreme Court, citing the *Chevron* case, said that deference is not due if Congress has made its intent clear in a statute but "if the statute is silent or ambiguous . . . the question . . . is whether the agency's answer is based on a permissible construction of the statute."[31] In this case, the EPA's interpretation was a reasonable construction of the Clean Water Act, and so the EPA was entitled to "*Chevron* deference."

Justice John Paul Stevens, joined by Justices David Hackett Souter, Ruth Bader Ginsburg, and Stephen Breyer, wrote a twenty-seven-page dissenting opinion, in which they argued that when faced with competing statutory mandates, the U.S. Supreme Court should balance both laws instead of choosing one over the other. In the dissenting justices' view, the EPA acted arbitrarily and capriciously by choosing the Clean Water Act over the Endangered Species Act. Citing the famous 1978 snail darter case, in which the discovery of the endangered snail darter halted the construction of a dam, the justices proclaimed that Congress had already given endangered species priority over the primary missions of federal agencies.

This fascinating case demonstrates how courts shape environmental policy by the way judges interpret "dueling" statutes and "dueling" precedents governing "dueling" federal agencies. The majority of justices chose the rationale of *Chevron* over the rationale of *Babbitt*. In addition, different judges interpreted the mandate of the Endangered Species Act differently, with the result being a general weakening of the act.

Interpreting Statutes and the Constitution: Regulatory Takings and Land Use

In 1986, David H. Lucas purchased two vacant oceanfront lots on the Isle of Palms in Charleston County, South Carolina, for $975,000. He intended to build single-family residences on the lots, but in 1988 the South Carolina Legislature enacted the Beachfront Management Act.[32] In Lucas's case this act prohibited him from constructing any permanent structure (including a dwelling) except for a small deck or walkway on the property. Lucas filed suit in the court of common pleas, asserting that the restrictions on the use of his lots amounted to government taking his property without justly compensating him, a so-called *regulatory taking*. The lower court agreed with Lucas, maintaining that the act rendered the land valueless, and awarded him over $1.2 million for the regulatory taking. Upon appeal the Supreme Court of South Carolina reversed the lower court's decision. The judges maintained that the regulation under attack prevented a use seriously harming the public. Consequently, they argued, no regulatory taking occurred.[33]

On June 29, 1992, however, the U.S. Supreme Court, in a 6–3 decision, reversed the holding of the highest court in South Carolina and remanded the case to it for further action.[34] In its decision, the Court articulated several pivotal principles that constitute a test for regulatory takings. First, the justices emphasized that regulations denying a property owner all "economically viable use of his land" require compensation, regardless of the public interest advanced in support of the restraint. As such, even when a regulation addresses or prevents a "harmful or noxious use," government must compensate owners when their property is rendered economically useless to them.

At the same time, however, the Court threw back to the South Carolina courts the issue of whether a taking occurred in Lucas's case. The lower courts had to examine the context of the state's power over the "bundle of rights" Lucas acquired when he took title to his property. Put differently, the pivotal question for all state regulators today is this: Do state environmental regulations merely make explicit what already was implicit in any property title (that is, the right to regulate its use), or are they decisions that come after a person acquires title that were not originally implied? In the latter case, they are takings that governments must compensate.

Equally important in *Lucas* was what the Court did *not* discuss in its narrowly worded opinion. First, the Court did not say that Lucas was entitled to compensation. Rather, it implied that the South Carolina Supreme Court was hasty in concluding that Lucas was not entitled to recompense. Second, the Court did not address the issue of property that is merely diminished in value—a far more common occurrence. Instead, it addressed only the issue of property that was rendered totally valueless. Finally, in pushing the regulatory takings issue back onto the state, the Court did not say that state laws may never change. Indeed, the majority held that "changed circumstances or new knowledge may make what was previously permissible no longer so." Hence, the Court left the door open for some regulation of newly discovered environmental harms after title to a property changes hands. Still, Lucas did prevail. Upon remand the South Carolina Supreme Court reversed its earlier decision and awarded Lucas over $1.5 million.

A few years later, the Supreme Court continued to develop the area of regulatory takings in a local government planning and zoning case that also is having profound effects on environmental policy. In *Dolan v. Tigard* (1994),[35] the owner of a plumbing and electrical supply store applied to the city of Tigard, Oregon, for a permit to redevelop a site. The plaintiff wanted to expand the size of her store and to pave the parking lot.

The city, pursuant to a state-required land use program, had adopted a comprehensive plan, a plan for pedestrian-and-bicycle pathways, and a master drainage plan. As such, the city's planning commission conditioned Dolan's permit on her doing two things. First, she had to dedicate (that is, convey title) to the city the portion of her property lying within a 100-year floodplain so that the city could improve a storm drainage system for the area. Second, she had to dedicate an additional fifteen-foot strip of land adjacent to the floodplain as a pedestrian-and-bicycle pathway. The planning commission argued that its conditions regarding the floodplain were "reasonably related" to the owner's request to intensify use of the site, given its impervious surface. Likewise, the commission claimed that creating the pedestrian-and-bicycle pathway system could lessen or offset the increased traffic congestion that the permit would cause.

In a previous case, *Nollan v. California Coastal Commission* (1987),[36] the Court had ruled that an agency needs to show that an "essential nexus" exists between the "end advanced" (that is, the enunciated purpose of the regulation) and the "condition imposed" by applying the regulation. The "essential nexus" requirement is still good law today. The *Nollan* court also held that a government must be prepared to prove in court that a "legitimate state interest" is "substantially advanced" by any regulation affecting property rights. In 2005 the Supreme Court removed the "substantially advanced" requirement as improper in a non-environmental case, *Lingle v. Chevron*,[37] because it did not address the effect of a regulation on property but rather was concerned solely with whether the underlying regulation itself was valid.

After reviewing various doctrines that state courts had used to guide such analyses, the Court in *Dolan* enunciated its own test of "rough proportionality" that is still valid today. It stated that "no precise mathematical calculation is required, but the city must make some sort of individualized determination that the required dedication is related both in nature and extent to the impact of the proposed development." If there is rough proportionality, then there is no taking. In this instance, the Court decided that the city had not made any such determination and concluded that the city's findings did not show a relationship between the floodplain easement and the owner's proposed new building. Furthermore, the city had failed to quantify precisely how much the pedestrian-and-bicycle pathway would proportionately offset some of the demand generated.

The implications of the Court's doctrine in this case are profound. The facts are hardly unique and represent the types of zoning decisions that local governments make daily. What is more, its logic potentially extends to all local government regulatory activities. Finally, the decision means that the courts can become even more involved than they are already in reviewing and judging the adequacy—the dissent in *Dolan* called this "micromanaging"—of local regulatory decisions.

These and other cases together indicate that with the burden of proof in takings cases falling on the government, considerable litigation is inevitable. As such, local governments will have to do more individualized analysis of the expected impacts of land use changes and the conditions they impose on them. Not only will this be more costly but it will likely have a chilling effect on regulatory activity at that level. Finally, because no clear guidance exists concerning how to operationalize concepts such as *rough proportionality*, local regulators should expect continuing litigation in different regulatory contexts. Lower and appellate courts will have to begin clarifying this test for them, a decidedly time-, labor-, and uncertainty-intensive exercise.

Consider, for example, what has happened to date in this regard. At any one time, more than two hundred takings cases have been pending in the U.S. court of federal claims. The majority of these cases on any given day are likely to concern environmental and natural resource regulations. Statutes most affected to date are the Clean Water Act, the Endangered Species Act, and the Wilderness Act. Nor are the stakes miniscule. Environmental advocates charge that if takings suits are successful, the trend will destroy years of hard-fought incremental progress in protecting the environment. Government regulators agree, adding that the trend could devastate already ailing government budgets. This will be true especially if proposed federal legislation is enacted that would take compensation payments from the coffers of the agency that issued such regulations.

In December 2003, for example, the U.S. court of federal claims ordered the federal government to pay California irrigators $26 million for water diverted to protect fish listed under the Endangered Species Act. The case, *Tulare Lake Basin Water Storage District v. United States*,[38] represents the first time the government had been ordered to pay a monetary award for a takings claim filed under the act. Since then, the federal claims court has been flooded with similar lawsuits. Thus regulatory takings cases are being watched closely by all stakeholders. Indeed, several new cases have already been appealed to the Supreme Court. These are excellent examples of how courts help shape environmental policy.

Choice of Remedy

A final way in which courts affect environmental policy is through their choice of remedies. When a recalcitrant polluter is taken to court, the two most common actions ordered by a court are mandatory compliance with environmental law and punitive monetary penalties to deter future violations. For example, in a Clean Water Act case, *Friends of the Earth, Inc. v. Laidlaw Environmental Services*,[39] which concerned a company that repeatedly violated the conditions of its permit, discharging pollutants such as mercury numerous times into a river, the settlement decree ordered Laidlaw to comply with the Clean Water Act, and the district court assessed punitive monetary penalties. In a case involving criminal violations of environmental law, the penalty might involve jail time or probation. In each of these scenarios, considerable judicial discretion is involved.

The Clean Air Act, the Clean Water Act, the Resource Conservation and Recovery Act, and the Emergency Planning and Community Right-to-Know-Act also allow those who win citizen suits to seek monetary penalties, which go to the U.S. Treasury rather than to the plaintiff. In these circumstances, again, a judge has immense discretion. Most often the only curbs on judges in these circumstances are statutorily set maximum amounts as well as lists of factors that judges must weigh.

A relatively new remedy being used more often in both judicial decrees and administrative orders is a supplemental environmental project (SEP).

SEPs are alternative payments in the form of projects or activities. Examples include environmental restoration, environmental education, and the establishment of green space such as parks. The Clean Air Act, for example, contains the following language concerning SEPs:

> The court in any action under this subsection ... shall have discretion to order that such civil penalties, in lieu of being deposited in the [U.S. Treasury Fund], be used in beneficial mitigation projects which are consistent with this chapter and enhance the public health or the environment.[40]

To award SEPs, judges must have the statutory authority to do so or at least be assured that the statute does not forbid them to do so. The vague language of the Clean Water Act, for example, has prompted some judges to be hesitant about awarding SEPs under that statute. Still, judges retain considerable discretion in setting up SEPs.

Although the EPA has included SEPs in its orders in various forms and under various names since the late 1970s, they became more widely accepted in the 1990s. In February 1994, President Clinton issued Executive Order 12898, which directed federal agencies to integrate environmental justice issues into agency policy. The EPA seized this opportunity by incorporating into many consent decrees SEPs that address environmental challenges in minority and low-income neighborhoods. The EPA's policy on SEPs was finalized in 1998.

An example SEP is the case in which the EPA's Region 1 received an anonymous tip to check out properties of the Massachusetts Highway Department (MHD). There they found nearly 200 barrels of illegally stored hazardous wastes in 149 MHD facilities. The resulting settlement, negotiated in less than a year and approved by a court, included over $20 million in cleanup costs and $5 million in SEPs.[41] A relatively small penalty of $100,000 also was ordered to be paid to federal government coffers. The SEPs undertaken by the MHD made a concrete difference in a way that traditional penalties often do not. They ranged from the development of an environmental education program for MHD personnel and for the public to the cleanup of environmentally contaminated minority neighborhoods throughout Massachusetts.

Recent SEPs have branched into other areas. In October 2008 the Texas Commission on Environmental Quality fined Houston Refining LP $481,105 for twenty-seven air and water violations documented from 2006 to 2008. The company contributed $192,442 of its fine to a SEP at the Houston-Galveston Area Emission Reduction Credit Organization's Clean Cities/Clean Vehicles Program in Harris County.

When the EPA found that the Southeastern Pennsylvania Transportation Authority (SEPTA) had violated hazardous waste and underground storage tank regulations at nine SEPTA facilities, SEPTA paid a civil penalty of $169,527 and agreed to spend no less than $1.1 million on a wind energy SEP between March 2009 and March 2011.

In April 2008, in one of New Mexico's largest environmental settlements, the state Environment Department fined DCP Midstream LP $60.8 million for violating air quality laws. DCP agreed to pay a $1.4 million civil penalty and to complete SEPs and facilities upgrades totaling $59 million to reduce emissions of nitrogen oxides, sulfur dioxide, carbon monoxide, and volatile organic compounds. The $1.4 million civil penalty was divided between $800,000 in a cash payment to the state general fund and $600,000 for various SEPs involving the Western Governors' Association and The Climate Registry.

These are just a few examples from the hundreds of SEPs ordered annually. Although mandatory compliance with environmental laws and monetary penalties remain the most often court-ordered remedies, one legal scholar sees real promise in the future use of SEPs.[42] The EPA has a special Web site on SEPs[43] and maintains a list of ideas for potential SEPs. The choice of remedy is yet another way in which courts shape environmental policy.

Conclusion: A View to the Future

Judge Bazelon was right: Since 1971, administrative agencies and reviewing courts have collaborated fruitfully, especially in the area of environmental policy. The courts in the United States have become permanent players in environmental policymaking. Supporting this conclusion are dozens of Web sites concerning environmental policy in the courts. The most useful of these sites are listed at the end of this chapter. Although the extent of judicial involvement in environmental cases will ebb and flow over the years, the courts will always be involved in environmental policy to some degree.

As this chapter has demonstrated, courts have a major influence in how environmental laws work in practice. Courts shape environmental policy in many ways. The most significant ways are by determining who has standing to sue, by deciding which cases are ripe for review, by the court's choice of standard of review, by interpreting statutes and the Constitution, by the remedies judges choose, and simply by resolving environmental conflicts.

Environmental court decisions are influenced by the state of the law, such as precedent and rules for interpreting statutes. They are also influenced by the courts' environment, such as mass public opinion, litigants and interest groups, congressional expansion or perhaps narrowing of jurisdiction, and presidential appointments. Environmental court decisions are influenced as well by justices' values: liberal, moderate, conservative, or somewhere in between. In addition, environmental court decisions are affected by group interaction on the bench, with individual justices at times influencing others.

The importance of judicial appointments cannot be overemphasized. Federal judges are appointed for life, barring illegal or unethical behavior. A young, zealous judicial appointee may advance an anti-environmental agenda for decades. While the Obama administration will have many opportunities to appoint judges with balanced views concerning environmental protection, it inherits a judicial system that critics have called anti-environmental.[44]

Making predictions concerning environmental policy in the courts during the next decade is risky business, but three trends seem to be emerging. First, a major change in the courts has been the growth of anti-environmental activism in the Supreme Court. This has manifested itself in the Court's agreeing to hear a much larger number of cases than in the past. Although two of these cases, *Massachusetts v. Environmental Protection Agency* and *Whitman v. American Trucking Associations,* both discussed in this chapter, produced pro-environmental results, on close questions the Court has been reliably anti-environmental. Many observers attribute this trend to "states' rights" justices. Should President Obama have the opportunity to appoint Supreme Court justices, the Court may become more balanced.

A second trend concerns the added obstacles that environmental justice attorneys face in getting into court. At the state level, standing requirements have tightened. At the federal level, enforcement of federal laws (and their implementing regulations) that do not come with their own citizen-suit provisions has become increasingly difficult. Courts have rejected implied private rights of action and tightened access under the Civil Rights Act.

A third possible future trend concerns the increased use of environmental conflict resolution, which is effectively group problem-solving. Advocates of this approach produce two primary criticisms of litigation as a dispute resolution process for environmental conflicts. First, litigation does not allow for adequate public participation in important environmental decisions. The costs of litigation are often prohibitive to interest groups, especially groups that are small or that represent local interests. The process of litigation is also extremely time consuming, often taking months for cases to come to trial. After accounting for appeals time, the entire litigation process can take years. The time delays inherent in litigation are costly to all of the parties involved. Second, advocates of environmental conflict resolution charge that litigation is ineffective for resolving the issues at stake in environmental disputes. Court decisions frequently fail to resolve the basic issues in dispute between the parties. The courts are often limited in their ability to address the substantive dimensions of environmental conflicts and thus render decisions only on procedural grounds.[45] Many of the underlying controversies remain unresolved; hence, more lawsuits often emerge in the future.

Despite these criticisms, the environmental policies that are developed, expanded, narrowed, and clarified in our courts will continue to affect the air we breathe, the water we drink, and the food we eat. The United States is the most litigious country in the world. Clearly environmental policy in the courts—at least in the United States—is here to stay.

Suggested Web Sites

Council on Environmental Quality (www.whitehouse.gov/ceq) Provides links to important environmental and natural resource agencies, as well as to reports. Especially helpful is the CEQ National Environmental Policy Act (NEPA) link (www.nepa.gov/nepa/nepanet.htm).

Environmental Law Institute (www.eli.org) Provides objective, non-partisan analysis of current environmental law issues.

Lexis and Westlaw (www.lexis.com; www.westlaw.com) Excellent commercial Web sites for basic materials concerning domestic environmental law.

Natural Resources Defense Council (www.nrdc.org) Provides expert analyses of issues and reports that are relevant to ongoing legal decisions.

U.S. Department of Interior (www.doi.gov/non-profit/lawx) Lists laws and regulations for the major agencies within the department.

U.S. Environmental Protection Agency (www.epa.gov/epahome/lawregs.htm) Offers links to laws, regulations, the U.S. Code, and pending legislation in Congress concerning the EPA.

U.S. Forest Service (www.fs.fed.us/publications) Gives access to laws, regulations, and publications concerning federal forests.

U.S. Institute for Environmental Conflict Resolution (www.ecr.gov) Provides a primer on environmental conflict resolution with an emphasis on evaluating its effectiveness.

Notes

1. *Environmental Defense Fund v. Ruckelshaus*, 439 F.2d 584 (1971).
2. Chris Bowman, "Analysis: Bush Team Battered by Courts on Environment," *The Sacramento Bee*, May 19, 2008.
3. *Udall v. Tallman*, 308 U.S. 1 (1965).
4. *Chevron v. NRDC*, 467 U.S. 837 (1984).
5. Administrative Procedure Act, Section 706[2][A].
6. Six of the EPA's seven major environmental statutes have citizen suit provisions.
7. Rosemary O'Leary, *Environmental Change: Federal Courts and the EPA* (Philadelphia: Temple University Press, 1993).
8. "Control of Emissions from New Highway Vehicles and Engines," 68 Fed. Reg. at 52,925 (September 8, 2003).
9. Ibid. at 52,928
10. Ibid. at 52,929.
11. Ibid. at 52,930.
12. Ibid. at 52,931.
13. *Massachusetts v. Environmental Protection Agency*, 415 F.3d 50 (D.C. Cir. 2005).
14. *Massachusetts v. Environmental Protection Agency*, 127 S.Ct. 1438 (2007).
15. *Massachusetts v. Environmental Protection Agency*, 126 S.Ct. 2960 (2006).
16. For a good discussion of this requirement, see *Lujan, Secretary of the Interior v. Defenders of Wildlife et al.*, 504 U.S. 555 (1992).
17. See U.S. Constitution, Article III, Section 2.
18. Fanny Carrier, "Environmentalists Hail 'Watershed' US Supreme Court Ruling," *Agence France Presse*, April 3, 2007.
19. *Sierra Club v. Thomas*, 105 F.3d 248 (1997).
20. *Ohio Forestry Association, Inc. v. Sierra Club*, 523 U.S. 726 (1998).
21. *Buckeye Forest Council v. U.S. Forest Service*, 378 F.Supp. 2d 844 (2005).
22. Michael C. Blumm and Sherry L. Bosse, "*Norton v. SUWA* and the Unraveling of Federal Public Land Planning," *Duke Environmental Law and Policy Forum* 18 (fall 2007): 105–161.
23. Ibid. at 111.
24. *Whitman v. American Trucking Association*, 531 U.S. 457 (2001).
25. 16 U.S.C. Section 1531.
26. 16 U.S.C. Section 1538 (a)(1).

27. 50 C.F.R. Section 17.3 (1994).
28. *Sweet Home Chapter of Communities for a Great Oregon v. Lujan*, 806 F.Supp. 279 (1992); 1 F.3d 1 (1993); 17 F.3d 1463 (1994).
29. *Babbitt v. Sweet Home Chapter of Communities for a Great Oregon*, 515 U.S. 687 (1995).
30. *National Association of Home Builders v. Defenders of Wildlife*, 551 U.S. 644 (2007).
31. 467 U.S. 837.
32. S.C. Code Ann. (1989) Sections 48-39-10 et seq.
33. *Lucas v. South Carolina Coastal Council*, 304 S.C. 376 (1991).
34. *Lucas v. South Carolina Coastal Council*, 505 U.S. 1003 (1992).
35. *Dolan v. Tigard*, 512 U.S. 374 (1994).
36. *Nollan v. California Coastal Commission*, 483 U.S. 825 (1987).
37. *Lingle v. Chevron*, 125 S.Ct. 2074 (2005).
38. Fed Cl. No. 98-101 (2003).
39. *Friends of the Earth, Inc. v. Laidlaw Environmental Services*, 528 U.S. 167 (2000).
40. Clean Air Act, Section 113.
41. *In the Matter of: The Commonwealth of Massachusetts, Massachusetts Highway Department*, EPA Docket No. RCRA-I-94-1071, Consent Agreement and Order, October 3, 1994.
42. Kenneth T. Kristl, "Making a Good Idea Even Better: Rethinking the Limits on Supplemental Environmental Projects," *Vermont Law Review* 31 (winter 2007): 217.
43. U.S. Environmental Protection Agency, "Supplemental Environmental Projects," February 10, 2004, www.epa.gov/compliance/civil/seps, October 1, 2008.
44. Glenn Scherer, "Appeals Courts Pushed to Right by Bush Choices," *New York Times*, October 29, 2008.
45. See Rosemary O'Leary and Lisa Bingham, eds., *The Promise and Performance of Environmental Conflict Resolution* (Washington D.C.: Resources for the Future, 2003).

7

Science, Politics, and Policy at the EPA

Walter A. Rosenbaum

I'm encouraged that at a time when there are so many challenging and indeed controversial environmental decisions and problems facing us that the President has nominated a respected scientist and career employee to the next Administrator of EPA. This is genuinely refreshing and encouraging.

Sen. Joe Lieberman (I-Conn.) on the nomination
of Stephen L. Johnson to be EPA administrator

Sen. Sheldon Whitehouse, D-R.I., formally announced the request for a Department of Justice investigation into the potential criminal conduct of EPA Administrator Stephen Johnson. Whitehouse listed five charges of "putting the interests of corporate polluters before science and the law" in ozone, lead, soot, tailpipe emissions, and global warming pollution. . . .

U.S. Senate Committee on Environment
and Public Works Press Release, July 29, 2008

In March 2005, Stephen Johnson, newly nominated administrator of the Environmental Protection Agency (EPA), could anticipate an edgy, probably contentious appearance before the U.S. Senate Committee on Environment and Public Works that must approve his appointment. By then, the entrance to the EPA administrator's office had become a revolving door. Through that door now came Johnson, President George W. Bush's third administrator in five years, headed into a vortex of political and scientific controversy that had been building about the agency since Bush's inauguration in 2001.

Johnson seemed a new kind of administrator, awakening expectations that he just might restore badly needed political stability and scientific credibility to the embattled agency. Unlike all previous EPA administrators, he was a professional scientist and career EPA employee, progressing through twenty-five years to increasingly important administrative positions and awards, becoming the acting administrator in January 2005. President Bush would soon commend him as "a talented scientist and skilled manager with a lifelong commitment to environmental stewardship," adding, "I've come to know Steve as an innovative problem-solver with good judgment and complete integrity."[1] Johnson needed all that good judgment and integrity in light of unrelenting controversy plaguing the agency from the inception of the Bush administration as its administrators struggled to reconcile "sound science," Bush administration policy, and Washington's combative politics while accomplishing the EPA's mission.

Prelude: "I Certainly Hope You'll Stick around a While"

By the time Stephen Johnson faced the Senate committee, conflict over "sound science" at the EPA had become a defining issue in the agency's turbulent relationship with George W. Bush's administration. The EPA and its administrators had been embroiled in a succession of high-profile controversies over the integrity of the EPA's scientific decision making and its alleged subversion by White House political pressure. The events preceding Johnson's appearance included the following:

- Accusations by EPA scientists and others in early 2003 that the White House had demanded, and gotten, extensive changes in the content of a major EPA climate change report that made climate warming seem less scientifically plausible.
- An EPA decision—despite the opposition of public health authorities, environmentalists, and the recommendation of the National Academy of Sciences—to review Clinton administration regulations that had tightened community drinking water standards for arsenic.
- The resignation in June 2003 of Christine Todd Whitman, Bush's first EPA administrator, in the wake of the criticism among scientists, environmentalists, and members of Congress that she had capitulated to White House pressure in writing the EPA's climate warming reports, and in setting regulatory standards.
- The resignation in early 2005 of Michael Leavitt, Whitman's successor at the EPA, whose brief tenure was accelerated by evidence that EPA recommendations on mercury emissions standards for power plants were based substantially on documents provided by the White House to support its preferences.

The committee—especially its Democratic members—was quick to remind Johnson that as a scientist he inherited a special responsibility to improve the agency's embattled scientific reputation and political independence. Sen. James Jeffords (I-Vt.) hoped that Johnson had "the fortitude to stand up against powerful interests to protect our air, water, and our lands. The EPA Administrator should not be a rubber-stamp for White House polices. . . ."[2] Sen. Joseph Lieberman, then D-Conn., complained that "science has not only been neglected or ignored, but even worse, has been selectively applied to support pre-determined conclusions."[3] To all such concern, Johnson's response was an emphatic reassurance. He would "make sure that when we are required to make regulatory or policy decisions, we are using the best available scientific information, and at the same time we should continue to pursue and encourage rigorous scientific inquiry" and he would follow "as open and transparent a decision making process as possible."[4]

Although the hearing went well enough to ensure Johnson's appointment, one remark lingered like a bleak omen. "I had great respect for your predecessors, both former Governors," remarked Sen. Max Baucus, D-Mont. "I asked both of them why they wanted the job and whether or not they thought they could stand up to defend the interests of their Agency to the Administration. Unfortunately, neither one of them stayed in the Agency for very long. Perhaps as a career EPA official, you have a better idea of what you're getting yourself into and I certainly hope, if confirmed, you'll stick around a while."[5]

Three years later, Johnson was in serious trouble, and Senator Baucus sounded like a prophet. Johnson's tenure was accompanied by unrelenting criticism concerning the administrator's scientific integrity and the EPA's political independence. Among the most provocative incidents were these:

- Johnson's decision in September 2006 to reject a staff recommendation to raise the regulatory standard for lethal particles of airborne soot despite a rare public plea by the EPA's own Clean Air Scientific Advisory Committee.[6]
- Sharp criticism in January 2007 by the National Academy of Sciences that a proposed new EPA method of risk analysis was "fundamentally flawed."[7]
- Johnson's decision to reject his technical staff's recommendation and to deny California the authority to create state emissions standards for climate warming emissions.[8]
- A survey reporting that 889 EPA scientists had personally experienced at least one incident of "inappropriate [political] interference" in their work during the previous five years.[9]
- The May 2008 dismissal of Mary Gade, EPA's Region 5 administrator, following her decision to support new requirements for Dow Chemical to remove dioxin from its contaminated Midland, Michigan, facility.

The controversies culminated with a scalding indictment by Democratic members of the same Senate committee that earlier approved his nomination. Now, they demanded that the Department of Justice launch a criminal investigation to determine whether Johnson "gave false and misleading statements, whether he lied to Congress, whether he committed perjury, and whether he obstructed Congress's investigation."[10]

Despite his administrative and scientific credentials, Johnson was now ensnared by a trinity of conflicting forces—science, politics, and policy—familiar to all EPA administrators, however diverse their talent for understanding and resolving the challenge. Resolving these conflicts is an especially formidable task because this collision of forces arises from dissonances deeply embedded in the EPA's organization and mission and, therefore, fundamental in shaping the EPA's character, its history, and its administrator's responsibilities.

The narrative begins with a brief consideration of the EPA's organization and mission to illuminate the often inconsistent, frequently contradictory forces shaping its institutional character. This provides a setting for understanding how policy, politics, and science intermingled to fashion two issues responsible for much of Johnson's mounting troubles as the Bush administration waned. One issue, a conflict concerning whether the EPA was using "sound science" in creating new regulatory standards for mercury air emissions, was carried over from an early Bush administration decision. The second issue was Johnson's creation: a decision to deny California's request, as permitted by the Clean Air Act, to receive a waiver allowing the state to create its own standards for regulating climate warming gases.

A Collision of Responsibilities: Presidential Leadership, Congressional Accountability, and "Sound Science"

The EPA and its administrator serve many masters. As part of the executive branch of the federal government, the EPA and its administrator are expected to be responsive to presidential policy initiatives and White House political leadership. The White House, for instance, had very definite, outspoken opinions about both the mercury emissions and California waiver issues. At the same time, Congress expects the EPA to be alert to congressional interests while interpreting environmental legislation as Congress intended and assuring that scientific judgments inform EPA policymaking. The scientific community, environmentalists, and science advocacy groups expect "sound science" to be the bedrock for the EPA's regulatory decisions. The federal courts exercise legal oversight to ensure that the EPA implements the law correctly. Amid such frequently competing expectations and responsibilities, political trouble is usually the administrator's daily bread. Even William Ruckelshaus, one of the EPA's most popular and successful administrators, could complain that "an EPA administrator gets two days in the sun, the day he's announced and the day he leaves, and everything in between is rain."[11]

An Essential and Arduous Mission

Measured by the size of its budget and workforce, the EPA is the federal government's largest regulatory agency. Created by presidential order in 1970, the EPA at the end of George W. Bush's presidency employed about 17,200 staff with an annual budget in fiscal year 2008 of approximately $7.5 billion. By any measure, the scope of its responsibilities and the resulting workload are enormous.

A Very Mixed Performance

As demonstrated in chapter 1, the nation's environmental quality has undoubtedly improved, in some cases dramatically, as a consequence of the

EPA's regulatory programs. The quality of this achievement is often obscured by impatience with the pace of environmental improvement, or by dissatisfaction with the regulatory costs involved, or by lack of appreciation for the scientific and technical difficulties regulation may entail. Still, the luster dims when the agency's entire regulatory performance is considered. Few EPA programs dependably produce attractive headlines, and unwelcome news is only an official report away. For example,

- In 2006 the EPA estimated that water quality in two-thirds of U.S. stream miles varied from "fair" to "poor," and approximately 25 to 30 percent of the nation's streams had high pollution levels.[12]
- In 2008 the congressional Government Accountability Office (GAO) reported that the EPA's Integrated Risk Information System (IRIS), a crucial database for measuring chronic human exposure to potentially harmful chemicals, was "at serious risk of becoming obsolete because EPA has not been able to routinely complete timely, credible assessments or decrease its backlog of 70 ongoing assessments" that had been in progress for five years.[13]
- In 2007, despite air quality improvement, more than 150 million Americans lived in counties where ambient air concentrations of two important EPA regulated pollutants, ground-level ozone and fine-particle pollution ($PM_{2.5}$), exceeded national air quality standards.[14]
- In 2007 the GAO reported that the EPA "faces significant challenges in seeking to hold businesses responsible for their environmental cleanup obligations.... For example, EPA has not implemented a 1980 statutory mandate under Superfund to require businesses handling hazardous substances to demonstrate their ability to pay for potential environmental cleanups...."[15]

Additionally, EPA programs are increasingly expensive. Many factors account for the sharply rising regulatory costs, and many programs are not grossly over budget. But the EPA's program costs seem to rise relentlessly, and, in politics, appearance often matters as much as reality.

The EPA's Job: A Dozen Different Directions

Almost every environmental problem seems to end in some manner at the EPA's doorstep. The EPA is wholly or largely responsible for the implementation of thirteen major environmental statutes and portions of several dozen more (Table 7-1). The major laws embrace an extraordinarily large and technically complex set of programs across the whole domain of environmental management. This staggering range of responsibility is one major reason the EPA has been chronically over-worked and repeatedly targeted for sweeping organizational reform since the late 1980s.

Over the years since the EPA's creation, Congress has loaded the agency with an enlarging agenda of ambitious regulatory programs without much guidance about how to establish priorities among major programs or within

Table 7-1 Major Environmental Laws Administered by the EPA

Statute	Provisions
Toxic Substances Control Act	Requires that the EPA be notified of any new chemical prior to its manufacture and authorizes the EPA to regulate production, use, or disposal of a chemical.
Federal Insecticide, Fungicide, and Rodenticide Act	Authorizes the EPA to register all pesticides and specify the terms and conditions of their use, and to remove unreasonably hazardous pesticides from the marketplace.
Federal Food, Drug, and Cosmetic Act	Authorizes the EPA in cooperation with the FDA to establish tolerance levels for pesticide residues on food and food products.
Resource Conservation and Recovery Act	Authorizes the EPA to identify hazardous wastes and regulate their generation, transportation, treatment, storage, and disposal.
Superfund (Comprehensive Environmental Response, Compensation, and Liability Act)	Requires the EPA to designate hazardous substances that can present substantial danger and authorizes the cleanup of sites contaminated with such substances.
Clean Air Act	Authorizes the EPA to set emissions standards to limit the release of hazardous air pollutants.
Clean Water Act	Requires the EPA to establish a list of toxic water pollutants and set standards.
Safe Drinking Water Act	Requires the EPA to set drinking water standards to protect public health from hazardous substances.
Marine Protection, Research, and Sanctuaries Act	Regulates ocean dumping of toxic contaminants.
Asbestos School Hazard Act	Authorizes the EPA to provide loans and grants to schools with financial need for abatement of severe asbestos hazards.
Asbestos Hazard Emergency Response Act	Requires the EPA to establish a comprehensive regulatory framework for controlling asbestos hazards in schools.
Emergency Planning and Community Right-to-Know Act	Requires states to develop programs for responding to hazardous chemical releases and requires industries to report on the presence and release of certain hazardous substances.
Food Quality Protection Act	Creates health-based safety standards for pesticide residues in food and adds special safety standard for children and infants. Requires the EPA to create a program for endocrine testing of new chemicals. Requires consumer right-to-know information about pesticide residues on food.

Sources: Environmental Protection Agency, *Environmental Progress and Challenges: EPA Update* (Washington, D.C.: Environmental Protection Agency, 1988), 113; and author.

them when they compete for scarce resources or administrative attention. The result is an incoherent regulatory agenda, comprising a massive pile of legislative mandates for different regulatory actions, many armed with unachievable deadlines, and leaving the agency without any firm and consistent sense of direction. After a searching study of the EPA's organization and performance in the mid-1990s, the National Academy of Public Administration put the blame largely on Congress:

> The EPA lacks focus, in part, because Congress has passed more than a dozen environmental statutes that drive the agency in a dozen directions, discouraging rational priority-setting or a coherent approach to environmental management. The EPA is sometimes ineffective because, in part, Congress has set impossible deadlines and unrealistic expectations, given the Agency's budget.[16]

In the absence of a clear mission statement, the EPA must create priorities according to whatever programs have the largest budgets, have the most demanding deadlines, attract the most politically potent constituencies, or excite the greatest congressional attention. A case in point is the Food Quality Protection Act (FQPA), passed by Congress in 1996. A significant portion of the FQPA was a hasty legislative reaction to a surge of national publicity concerning the possible existence of chemicals called "endocrine disruptors."[17] Some scientists and environmental organizations asserted that these chemicals, widely distributed in pesticide residues and food products, could be potent human carcinogens or might dangerously damage human and animal reproductive systems. Little is known about these substances, but Congress felt compelled to act. The FQPA ordered the EPA—while continuing its other regulatory responsibilities—to review immediately the relevant scientific literature, identify the chemical compounds that should be examined, create the appropriate testing protocols, and report the results to Congress in two years. Because these tasks required a review of scientific literature involving more than 600,000 chemicals and chemical compounds even before the testing protocols could be developed, the EPA's two-year mandate was a predestined failure. Equally unachievable EPA mandates can be found in most other major environmental measures passed by Congress. The continual appearance of imperious deadlines and other kinds of disruptive micromanagement in legislation entrusted to the EPA exemplifies a chronic tension between Congress and the EPA that severely complicates the agency's mission.

A Media-Based Organization

From its beginning, the most important organizational units in the EPA have been its program offices—usually called "media offices." These offices are committed to controlling pollution in a specific medium such as air or water, or to dealing with a specific form of pollution such as pesticides or toxics (Figure 7-1). Each office lives with its own statutory support

Figure 7-1   EPA Organizational Structure

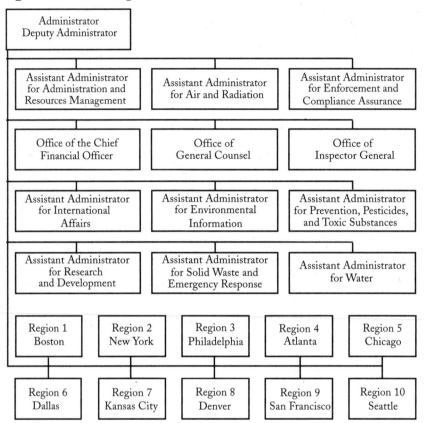

Source: Environmental Protection Agency, "EPA Organizational Structure," www.epa.gov/epahome/ organization.htm, February 10, 2008.

system: legislatively mandated programs, deadlines, criteria for decisions, and usually a steel grip on large portions of its office budget, to which it is entitled by the laws it enforces. Thus the Office of Toxic Substances administers the massive Superfund program, follows the mandated statutory procedures and deadlines in the law, and, in fiscal year 2007, claimed $1.3 billion of the EPA budget earmarked for toxic waste site cleanup.

Each of the offices is populated by a variety of professionals: engineers, scientists, statisticians, economists, professional planners, managers, lawyers, and mathematicians. "Along with this expertise," observes Thomas McGarity, "comes an entire professional [worldview] that incorporates attitudes and biases ranging far beyond specialized knowledge and particular facts"—viewpoints shaped by the specific mission of the program office and focused on that mission's tasks.[18] This tenacious media-based design appeals to Congress, environmentalists, pollution control professionals, and many other influential interests, albeit for different reasons. Each of the media offices, in effect, has its own political and professional constituency. Most important, any proposal to change the EPA's organizational design will incite apprehension about the possible damage to existing programs and raises the specter of a bitter political battle over the alternatives.

Creating Regulations: Interpreting the Law

Most of the statutes for which the EPA is responsible require the agency to create regulations—administrative rules having the force of law, as if written by Congress—that define details or procedures for implementing pollution control laws. This delegated authority is the grounding of all the regulation writing through which the EPA translates federal environmental laws into specific and detailed statements defining how the laws will be interpreted and applied to control specific pollutants or polluting activities. Most often, this means creating environmental standards for various hazardous or toxic pollutants and prescribing what technologies or procedures must be used to control or eliminate them.[19]

For example, the Clean Air Act (1970), the foundation of national air quality standards, directs the EPA to set permissible levels of air quality for numerous hazardous and toxic substances—major pollutants such as nitrogen oxides, sulfur oxides, and carbon monoxide—at levels that protect public health and create "an adequate margin of safety for the most sensitive populations" such as infants, the elderly, or those with asthma.[20]

The EPA's professional staff is expected to determine the specific ambient air quality standard for each of these pollutants, to set the permissible emissions levels for these pollutants from each source, and to design an enforcement procedure to ensure compliance with these standards from each source emitting a regulated pollutant. Congress routinely grants the EPA this delegated authority with each major environmental law assigned to the agency because Congress itself lacks the scientific expertise and resources required to make these complex technical decisions. In the case of the Clean Air Act, for instance, the EPA was largely responsible not only for setting air quality standards for each regulated pollutant but also for identifying which populations should be considered "most sensitive" to specific air pollutants and what "an adequate margin of safety" should be in setting standards.

Writing regulations to implement any environmental legislation is likely to be arduous, prolonged, and often contentious. This is particularly true for environmental regulations based on scientific information and judgment. As both the mercury emissions and California waiver issues demonstrate, needed scientific data may be insufficient, contradictory, or subject to different interpretation.[21] Interests affected by the regulations, such as environmental groups, scientists, corporations, local governments, states, and even other federal agencies, may battle over what scientific evidence is valid or where environmental standards should be set and how they should be enforced. Congress and the White House almost certainly will get involved. All this makes regulation writing difficult enough without the additional problems created because crucial portions of the laws the EPA is expected to administer may be vague, contradictory, or silent on important matters of interpretation. Thus the EPA's staff may have to navigate the complexities of legislative language with meager interpretive guidance, sure only of certain contention among stakeholders who stand to gain or lose from the agency's eventual interpretation.

Judicial Oversight

Like other executive agencies, the EPA is bound by the constitutional mandate that the laws be "faithfully executed." The agency's interpretation and implementation of environmental legislation is continually subject to judicial oversight intended to ensure that faithful execution. As the third essential branch of the federal government the judiciary is expected to act as a "check and balance" within the federal system, exercising impartial vigilance over the EPA's conduct while rising above the partisan passions and institutional rivalries common to Washington political life. It is axiomatic of Washington politics that federal judges are drawn into almost all major controversies over environmental legislation as different stakeholders attempt to turn the judicial venue to their advantage, which often means using the courts to challenge an administrator's interpretation of the law.

The federal judiciary has frequently been a watchdog, and often the final arbiter, in controversies over the EPA's authority (see chapter 6 for a comprehensive discussion about the role of the courts in environmental policymaking). By the time Stephen Johnson became administrator, the federal courts had already had a potent influence on the Bush administration's environmental policies. For example, the courts were considering whether the Clean Air Act gave the EPA the authority to regulate climate warming emissions (the Bush White House had contended otherwise), sustained the EPA's emissions standards for heavy-duty diesel engines (over trucking industry objections), and rejected an EPA rule creating a category of "low risk" facilities that would be exempt from especially strict control of toxic air pollutants.

An Edgy Congressional Partnership

Congress must necessarily delegate authority to the EPA, but it still treats the agency with almost schizophrenic inconsistency. Congress firmly advocates aggressive environmental protection in all its guises and expects the EPA to enforce vigorously the legislation it creates for that purpose. Legislators also have been quick to protect the agency's basic structure and programs from emasculation. Yet congressional frustration with the frequent delay in enforcing environmental laws leads to the habitual reliance on extravagant, extraordinarily detailed, and inflexible language in environmental law; to the constant mandating of precise deadlines for completing various programs; and to prescribing in exquisite detail how administrators are to carry out program activities.

In another perspective, the EPA often seems to Congress to be an unending source of unwelcome political controversy. With the possible exception of the Internal Revenue Service, few other federal agencies have a more legislatively troublesome regulatory mission. Thus, from the EPA's inception, the agency's work has been a matter of intense, unrelenting legislative scrutiny, concern, and criticism. And there are plenty of congressional committees available for the work. The EPA's programs currently fall within the jurisdiction of twenty Senate committees and twenty-eight committees in the House of Representatives. In short, Congress may be admirably supportive of the EPA, but in many respects Congress is the most disruptive presence in the EPA's work life.[22]

Data Deficiencies and Ambiguities

The nature of environmental science guarantees technical and political controversy over some of the EPA's scientific determinations. In particular, when the agency is compelled to make a regulatory decision, the relevant scientific data may be inconclusive and contentious. For example, data on the extent of human exposure to more than 1,400 chemicals considered to pose a threat to human health—and thus potentially subject to EPA regulation—is available for less than 8 percent of the chemicals.[23] State water quality reports are commonly haphazard; consequently, only about one-third of all U.S. surface waters have been surveyed for environmental quality.[24] Sometimes the data are conflicting, as often happens with estimates of the cancer risk from indoor exposure to numerous chemicals.

Moreover, a continually rising tide of ecological research often produces new data indicating that prior policy decisions may have been based on inadequate information and must be revised. For instance, twenty-five years after the EPA set its original air pollution standards for airborne particulates, a recognized health problem, the agency had to revise the standards, making them more stringent and compliance much more expensive because ongoing scientific research demonstrated that the earlier standards were based on insufficient data, though they were the best available at the time.

Another abundant source of scientific difficulty is that the effects of many suspected health hazards may not become clearly apparent until decades after their risks are first suspected and frequently long after the EPA may be compelled to make decisions about how they should be regulated. For instance, more than 25 percent of workers with significant workplace exposure to asbestos have died of lung cancer, but the effects of exposure often did not appear for twenty years or more. The human health risk from many newer industrial or commercial substances also may be latent and slow to appear, yet the EPA may have to decide whether they require regulation long before these consequences are manifest. Given these realities, scientific experts themselves can reach conflicting interpretations about the accuracy and policy implications of scientific data involved in regulatory decisions. "Very high quality, peer reviewed, scientific research articles and reports by highly respected research teams can, and often do, reach differing conclusions and results on substantially the same research," observes Bruce Alberts, past president of the National Research Council. "This is not a weakness of science, of the scientists performing the research.... It is simply characteristic of the initial difficulties often encountered in charting the unknown."[25]

Regulatory Federalism

Chapter 2 illustrated that the essential partnership between the EPA and the state governments, while generally cooperative, is also controversial. States are quick to complain that the EPA is often the intrusive "federal nanny," interfering excessively and inappropriately when states attempt to adjust federal regulations in response to uniquely local conditions. At the same time, states sometimes complain that the EPA is not aggressive enough in enforcing federal environmental regulations when the states are adversely affected by pollution. Most of these complaints are generic, inevitable in an environmental regulatory system grounded on federalism yet continually requiring attention and remediation from the EPA and Congress.

There has also been a fundamental transformation in the competence of the states as environmental regulators over the past several decades—a political sea-change to which both the EPA and Congress have been slow to adjust. As state regulatory experience and competence grows, state pressure has increased on Congress and the EPA to promote more collaboration and less command-and-control in working with the states, to demonstrate greater confidence in state regulatory skill, and in general to give the states a more assertive voice in the EPA's management. (See chapter 2 for a discussion of growing state regulatory competence.)

A Tale of Two Decisions: The Battle over Mercury Emissions and the California Waiver

The EPA's experience with setting environmental standards for mercury air emissions and responding to California's request for a regulatory waiver illustrate how contending political forces, differing and complex legislative mandates, competing data interpretations, and delegated authority converge during the EPA's routine responsibilities—in this case, using scientific data to formulate mercury pollution regulations and to interpret the Clean Air Act. Moreover, the narrative raises an important question often involved in this regulatory work: when is White House involvement in the EPA's scientific decision making appropriate?

Regulating with "Sound Science"

To regulate mercury emissions, or other substances, the EPA is customarily expected to use a complex array of scientific strategies.[26] It must create the relevant database; identify when and where human exposures to the potentially hazardous pollutant may occur; and then determine the appropriate environmental standards, control procedures, and enforcement measures to be adopted.

The EPA has evolved over considerable time a comprehensive organizational structure to promote sound scientific research and its appropriate integration into regulatory policymaking. This structure includes (1) a high-level Science Advisory Board composed of respected, independent scientific experts drawn from the professions, science, and industry who set standards, periodically review scientific research, and advise the EPA administrative leaders on science issues, (2) a Science Policy Council composed of high-level EPA scientific staff who directly advise the administrator, (3) a carefully developed "peer review policy" to ensure that all outside scientific evaluators of research used in the EPA's regulatory work (commonly called peer reviewers) are competent and independent in their judgments, and (4) staff specifically trained to monitor and report on the scientific quality of detailed program research in all of the EPA's program offices such as those regulating air pollution, water pollution, and toxics. In addition to these internal quality controls, the EPA continually receives oversight of its scientific fact finding from numerous committees in both congressional chambers and scrutiny from a multitude of scientific and technical organizations concerned with the professional quality of its work. In reality, most of the EPA's scientific decision making customarily provokes little public scientific or political controversy—no small matter considering that the agency in a typical year may produce more than eight hundred scientific documents reviewed, or scheduled for review, by external and internal experts.

What Standard for Mercury Emissions?

Small amounts of mercury are created naturally in the environment, but most hazardous exposures come from anthropogenic sources, that is, from human activities.[27] The federal government now regulates mercury emissions from medical and municipal waste incinerators, some electric power plants, chlorine chemical manufacturing, and iron and steel plants recycling automobile parts as the remaining sources of human exposure to mercury. The major unregulated source is the nation's 1,100 coal-fired electric-generating facilities, which discharge 40 percent of the mercury air emissions in the United States—approximately forty-eight tons yearly. Deposited on the ground, often with rain, mercury commonly migrates to water bodies. It has contaminated an estimated 12 million acres of lakes, estuaries, and wetlands, as well as 437,000 miles of streams, rivers, and coastlines, where it may also cause death or developmental disorders in fish and other wildlife. Forty-four states have issued warnings about consumption of mercury-contaminated fish.

All sides of the mercury issue agree on little more than the imperative to regulate mercury air emissions. Mercury is a potent neurotoxin that is especially dangerous to fetuses and growing children, in whom it can create severe developmental and neurological problems. Americans are exposed to high concentrations of mercury by consuming fish, particularly the tissue of large predators including shark, swordfish, and tuna, where it appears as methyl mercury.

Conflicting Proposals. In December 2003, then–EPA administrator Michael Leavitt released for the first time publicly the EPA's proposal for the first federal regulations controlling mercury emissions from electric power plants. The proposed new standard represented a Bush administration initiative and departed substantially from an earlier Clinton administration plan, which had never been formally proposed.[28] The Bush initiative provoked a critical reaction among environmentalists and their allies, who argued that the new EPA standard was based on a flawed interpretation of the relevant scientific data, which many critics said was deliberate.

Until the late 1990s the EPA considered mercury emissions from electric power plants to be adequately controlled as a "health hazard" under Section 112 of the Clean Air Act. In early 2000 the Clinton administration first considered new regulations that the EPA estimated could reduce power plant mercury emissions by as much as 90 percent if, as it hoped, the best available (but most expensive) technological controls were used. These controls could cost the electric power industry between $2 billion and $6 billion annually.[29] With Bush's presidential victory in 2000 this initiative was abandoned.

However, in early 2001 the environmental advocacy group Earthjustice initiated a lawsuit compelling the EPA to reclassify mercury as a neurotoxin and, thus, a "hazardous air pollutant" to be regulated by a different provision of the Clean Air Act, Section 111. After a prolonged series of further Earthjustice lawsuits on the mercury emissions issue, in 2003 the EPA imposed more stringent, and much costlier, controls on mercury emissions from electric power plants than would have been required if the emissions had still been classified as a health hazard.

A critical EPA decision following Bush's inauguration was to cite scientific data that, it asserted, demonstrated airborne mercury was *not* a "hazardous air pollutant," thereby significantly weakening and delaying the Clinton administration's earlier regulatory plan. By treating mercury again as a health hazard under the Clean Air Act, the Bush proposal relieved power plants of the requirement to achieve maximum possible mercury control by 2008, which would have been required if the emissions were considered a hazardous air pollutant. Instead, by treating the emissions as simply a health hazard, the Bush plan would not fully implement mercury controls until 2050 and would achieve only an estimated 29-percent reduction in mercury emissions by 2010, although it planned to achieve a 70-percent reduction by 2018. The reclassification also enabled electric power plants to trade mercury emissions rights for several decades (much like sulfur dioxide emissions were already traded to control acid rain under the Clean Air Act) and, in other ways, slowed the implementation of stringent mercury emissions controls throughout the electric power industry.[30]

Spokespersons for the Bush administration asserted their proposal would enable electric utilities to implement mercury emissions controls less expensively and more cost-effectively than the Clinton plan while reducing the total air pollution emissions from all coal-burning electric utilities. Additionally, they cited more than a decade's experience with acid rain emissions trading to demonstrate that utilities would have strong incentives to exceed the minimum pollution control standards required for mercury regulation.[31]

The Conflict Evolves. By December 2003 the EPA's proposal was a major public controversy. The agency had already logged more than 540,000 public comments during its review of mercury emissions controls, and 60,000 more would arrive the next year—the greatest volume of public response to an air pollution regulation ever recorded. The contention involved a multitude of inherently complex matters—economic, engineering, and technological issues as well as partisan political disputes, regional economic rivalries, and interstate conflicts—all of which drew into the fray associated advocacy groups of national and international importance, as well as partisans of both major political parties. No issue, however, provoked more contention than the reliability of the scientific data cited by the EPA to justify its decision to rewrite the Clinton administration proposals.

A Campaign to Suppress Science? Environmentalists asserted that the White House had flagrantly subverted the EPA's scientific research by creating a scientific justification for the EPA proposal that misstated and misrepresented the relevant scientific information. To support these indictments, critics cited newspaper articles reporting that "EPA veterans say they cannot recall another instance where the agency's technical experts were cut out of developing a major regulatory proposal."[32] The mercury regulations, claimed the critics, confirmed the Bush administration's pervasive intervention in scientific research throughout the federal government. "Mercury is just a particularly vivid example of what's going on in environmental protection and public policy in general," claimed a *New York Times* editorial.[33]

Copied Memos and Flyspecking. Evidence of the Bush administration's influence in shaping the scientific justification for the EPA's proposal was abundant. Several paragraphs of the proposed regulations were nearly identical to those in a memorandum to the White House from a Washington law firm where several former EPA air pollution officials were employed. Additionally, environmental spokespersons pointed to numerous instances in which White House advisors and agencies had "flyspecked" the EPA's scientific report—that is, meticulously edited numerous important and often subtle details—so that the toxic risks associated with mercury exposure appeared less certain. For example,

- An Office of Management and Budget economist apparently altered all references to the confirmed health risks of mercury by eliminating the word *confirmed.*
- The EPA's original statement that "recent published studies have shown an association between methyl mercury exposure and an increased

risk of heart attacks and coronary disease in adult men" had been changed to read "It has been hypothesized that there is an association between methyl-mercury exposure and an increased risk of coronary disease; however, this warrants further study as the new studies currently available present conflicting results."

- A staff member of the president's Council on Environmental Quality deleted EPA statements that children born to women with elevated mercury levels were at increased risk of "adverse health effects."[34]

A Matter of Interpretation? Undoubtedly, White House editing of the EPA's original scientific analysis created a much greater element of uncertainty for conclusions about the health effects of mercury exposure. EPA administrator Leavitt and his EPA spokespersons were unapologetic. The scientific data relevant to the mercury exposure, they argued, was subject to differing interpretations even among scientific experts, and the Bush EPA had chosen an interpretation with different policy implications that would ultimately produce more economically efficient and timely pollution control than the Clinton EPA's approach. In short, the science allowed for different regulatory options and the EPA was exercising its inherent authority to interpret the data and to recommend a policy response.

Moreover, although scientific critics of the Bush administration's mercury regulations attracted most of the media attention, other scientists found the EPA's interpretation of the mercury data appropriate: six of ten members on the National Academy of Sciences panel that prepared the report from which the EPA's own data were taken asserted that the EPA's changes "did not introduce inaccuracies" and that "many of the revisions sharpened scientific points being made and that justification could be made for or against other changes."[35] At the same time, many panel members expressed concern because the White House consistently minimized health risks when there would be disagreement. "What they're saying is not scientifically invalid on its face," observed one panel member. "Partially, they edited for clarity and relevance from a scientific viewpoint. But there appears to be an emphasis on wordsmithing that is not necessarily dictated by the science."[36] In brief, for many experts the controversy appeared to involve different *shadings* and *emphasis* in the way scientific information was translated into policy proposals, rather than sharply conflicting sets of data.

From the perspective of most environmentalists and many scientific spokespersons, however, the EPA had failed to protect its scientific decision making from "political interference." These criticisms were reinforced a few months later, when the respected science advocacy group, Union of Concerned Scientists, issued a widely publicized report, signed by sixty well-known scientists, including twenty Nobel laureates and a former EPA administrator, severely indicting the Bush administration for undermining the integrity of scientific research throughout federal agencies. "There is significant evidence that the scope and scale of the manipulation, suppression and misrepresentation of science by the Bush administration is unprecedented," concluded the group.[37] Bush's critics received further encouragement in February 2005, when the GAO issued a report concluding that the EPA's economic analysis of the Bush proposal was seriously flawed and unreliable.

New Administrator, Same Controversy. Mike Leavitt's replacement by Stephen Johnson in April 2005 did little to alter the EPA's commitment to the Bush emissions standards, despite conjecture that the new administrator might delay and revise them. Moreover, regulatory federalism and the federal courts now compounded the dispute.

The presence of state regulators in the controversy was predictable since, as observed earlier, the states ultimately implement most environmental laws and, consequently, the responsible state regulatory officials have an enduring and vocal interest in how the EPA interprets the law the states administer. Eight months after the EPA issued its contested mercury standards, two national associations of state air pollution control officials proposed to the EPA competing standards, based on alternative technological controls, which they asserted would eliminate more emissions, and do it faster, than the Bush plan.[38] Thus the contention between competing scientific claims, so common to environmental policy, again emerged.

The dispute lingered inconclusively through 2006 and 2007. Senate Democrats, once again the chamber majority, attempted unsuccessfully to block the Bush emissions plan by congressional action while, on a different front, other Bush opponents initiated an attack through the federal courts. In February 2008 the Circuit Court for the District of Columbia rejected the EPA plan in unusually acid language, asserting that the EPA had "ignored the law" through "a twisted logic" more appropriate to Alice in Wonderland.[39] The EPA had now to rewrite its proposed standards on terms acceptable to the court and certain to delay any mercury emissions controls well into the next decade. In the meantime, the court's ruling left no federal regulations in place to control mercury emissions. Instead, the Clean Air Act now compelled the states to regulate power plant emissions, to decide on a case-by-case basis what controls would be required for individual power plants, and to select the "maximum achievable control technology" if new controls were prescribed. However, the incoming Obama administration was widely expected to propose new federal emissions regulations much stricter than the judicially rejected Bush plan.

California and Climate Warming: The Waiver Controversy

By December 2007, Johnson was drawn deeper into the already volatile controversy over the EPA's role in implementing White House climate warming policy. Like the mercury emissions controversy, the new dispute involved a combustible mixture of politics, policy, and science. The issue was the administrator's interpretation of the Clean Air Act, resulting in a decision to deny California the authority—technically, to deny California a "waiver"—to create a statewide plan to regulate climate warming emissions.

Should the EPA Grant California a Waiver? The federal Clean Air Act entitles California to set its own vehicle emissions standards, provided these exceed federal rules and the EPA administrator grants California a waiver to set the standards. If this waiver exists, other states may adopt similar standards. Late in 2005, California applied for a waiver to set limits on vehicle emissions of heat-trapping gases such as carbon dioxide.

The EPA Denies the Waiver. For many decades the EPA had granted California waivers to create a multitude of other air emissions laws. Fourteen other states had adopted identical regulations in anticipation of California's waiver approval. But on December 21, over vehement objections from California and its fourteen state collaborators, Johnson denied California's request.[40] While the administrator's interpretation of the Clean Air Act incited the waiver controversy, it soon entailed additional criticism of the administrator's scientific justification for the rejection and of the White House role in the affair. The waiver was strongly supported by environmentalists, many public health officials, scientists, and the EPA's own staff, in addition to California and its state allies. The waiver's most vigorous opposition included automobile manufacturers; congressional representatives of major auto manufacturing states; and the White House, which favored a single national approach to regulating climate warming emissions.

The EPA administrator defended his interpretation of the Clean Air Act. California, he contended, did not qualify for a waiver because it was not *uniquely* affected by global warming and therefore lacked the "compelling and extraordinary" conditions the act required for a waiver. Moreover, asserted Johnson, a more beneficial policy approach already existed in the Bush administration's recently enacted energy legislation, which mandated higher national automobile fuel-economy standards and encouraged greater renewable energy consumption. These, concluded Johnson, would reduce national climate warming emissions through "a national approach to a national problem," setting uniform regulations for all fifty states rather than allowing a patchwork of regulations by other states. Additionally—and here the inevitable scientific and technical contention appeared—the Bush energy plans were more technically and economically effective.[41] (The Bush energy proposal and other important energy issues related to the California waiver are discussed in chapter 5, concerning congressional policymaking.)

No Legal or Technical Justification? The backlash to the waiver denial was swift and angry. Within days, California governor Arnold Schwarzenegger declared that California would join fourteen state partners in suing the administrator to compel the waiver grant. "It is unconscionable," he charged, "that the federal government is keeping California from adopting new standards." Sen. Barbara Boxer, D-Calif., a longtime Johnson critic and chair of the Senate Committee on Environment and Public Works, promptly arranged hearings in late January 2008 to investigate Johnson's decision.[42]

The high-profile hearings, spiced with political theatre, were combative. Boxer rebuked Johnson for ignoring his own legal and technical staff recommendations, then stonewalling the committee request for relevant documents. After flourishing a blank document provided by the EPA, Boxer dramatically produced a handful of tangled tape that had been peeled away from other documents the EPA provided Boxer's staff after insisting that the documents not be photocopied (the staff did it anyway). Committee Democrats assailed the waiver decision as "irresponsible" and "unconscionable," lacking scientific and legal justification. "Your agency's decision . . . just defies logic to me," complained Sen. Amy Klobuchar, D-Minn., "it's clearly a decision, I believe, that's based on politics and not on fact."[43] Nonetheless, Johnson firmly defended his decision. "While many urged me to approve or deny the California waiver request," he contended, "I am bound by the criteria in the Clean Air Act, not people's opinions. My job is to make the right decision, not the easy decision."[44]

Dueling Data. Both sides of the waiver controversy were armed with competing technical information. California officials, for example, calculated that by 2016 the state's proposed emissions standards would reduce carbon dioxide by 17.2 million metric tons, more than double the emissions eliminated by the new Bush energy bill, according to its proponents.[45] On the other hand, Johnson cited EPA studies estimating that the California emissions standards would produce a fuel average of only 33.8 miles per gallon (mpg) by 2016 whereas the new federal standards would result in an average of 35 mpg by 2020. California regulators asserted that the EPA had miscalculated: the California standards would actually achieve an average of 36 mpg at least.[46] In mid-2007, the Alliance of Automobile Manufacturers, an early waiver opponent, asserted that there would be effectively no difference between California and federal emissions standards in their impact on major air pollutants, and the health benefits of the greenhouse gas regulations would be "zero."[47] By the time the waiver battle reached the federal courts in mid-2008, there had yet to appear a technical database upon which the contending sides could agree.

"I Was Not Directed by Anyone." The House Committee on Oversight and Government Reform initiated a second congressional hearing in May, which Johnson ignored, at which his personal integrity, as well as his scientific and administrative judgment, were at issue. The most inflammatory testimony came from Jason Burnett, until recently an associate deputy EPA administrator working closely with Johnson, who testified that Johnson was prepared to approve the California waiver until he checked with the White House. "The response was that the president had a policy preference for a single standard," claimed Burnett, and Johnson then rejected his staff recommendation to grant the waiver.[48]

EPA spokesmen denied that Johnson had reversed himself as a result of presidential influence. "Administrator Johnson was presented with and reviewed a wide range of options and made his decisions based on the facts and the law," stated an EPA official, accusing Johnson's critics of "distraction-oriented political tactics."[49] Johnson affirmed again his independence from White House pressure concerning the waiver and emphasized his earlier response to the same criticism. "I was not directed by anyone. This was solely my decision based upon the law, based upon the facts."[50] Johnson again defended his decision in the aftermath of the May hearings:

One of the things that I've learned in my 27 years at EPA and being in a variety of decision-making capacities is that it's not a popularity contest. I need to understand what the law directs me to do, and understand what the science also directs me to do, and then, ultimately, what is the appropriate public policy, given those. These are not easy decisions. I completely reject the fact that I don't listen to my staff.[51]

Regardless of which side prevailed in the waning days of the Bush administration, the enormous media attention and political turmoil generated throughout Johnson's tenure ensured all the embedded issues would survive well into the next presidential administration. Additionally, Johnson's opponents were almost certain to keep the federal courts deeply involved in the fray. Even should the courts be uncharacteristically absent, congressional critics and their advocacy group allies would surely sustain the highly mobilized opposition to Johnson's controversial decisions.

The Obama administration's selection, in December 2008, of Lisa P. Jackson to succeed Johnson as EPA administrator was greeted enthusiastically by environmentalists, who considered Jackson's selection a certain sign of major changes in EPA policy. Jackson, the director of the New Jersey Department of Environmental Protection, a former EPA executive, and an African American, had already declared her support for new, tough national mercury emissions standards, aggressive federal action on climate change, and other policies rejected by the departing Bush administration. As a former high-level EPA employee, moreover, she inherited considerable goodwill from the EPA staff. She also inherited a multitude of policy challenges and soaring expectations for her performance that would be daunting for any EPA administrator.

Different Issues, a Continuing Challenge

To his critics, Stephen Johnson was flagrantly derelict in his administrative mission. He was allegedly a scientist who willfully distorted scientific evidence to serve his political agenda and failed to protect the EPA from invasive political influence. Moreover, he had also allegedly misinterpreted the Clean Air Act by rejecting the California waiver and sustaining the Bush mercury emissions standards. From the perspective of the administrator and his proponents, however, he made difficult decisions in the face of conflicting scientific and technical data, exercising the administrator's prerogative to interpret the law when the law permitted such discretion. And, as he insisted vehemently, he resisted political pressure and made the important decisions without direction from anyone.

Whatever the ultimate verdict concerning Johnson's contentious tenure, every future administrator can expect to face the same dissonant forces entangling Johnson because they are implicit in the EPA's mission. And when it comes to inciting intense political controversy—however different the issues—every new administrator is a potential Stephen Johnson because the EPA's mission is inherently political.

In light of the insistent political pressures inseparable from the EPA's mission, and despite the high-profile disputes described previously, EPA professional staff have maintained a credible level of integrity in their acquisition and interpretation of scientific information. Indeed, the waiver and mercury emissions cases illustrate that important controversies relating to the integrity of the EPA's science frequently involve how the agency's political leadership chooses to interpret the data, or how it revises scientific documents prepared by the professional staff, rather than the quality of the EPA's fundamental science gathering and analysis itself.

Competent scientific decision making depends, however, on continuing the circumstances that sustain it and creating tripwires that warn when the integrity of the process may be threatened. These circumstances include the following:

- Ongoing improvement in the EPA's existing organizational structure for acquisition, review, and critical interpretation of scientific data, including, especially, adequate funding.
- Opportunities for the EPA's professional staff to provide publicly available interpretations of scientific findings associated with regulatory proposals free of editing by White House officials or appointees at the EPA.
- Aggressive, independent monitoring of scientific activities by advocacy groups and regulatory stakeholders.
- Oversight by respected scientific societies and research institutions.
- Transparency of scientific procedures to meet expectations of the public and the media.

These are not conclusions for those who like their politics neat, the issues cleanly resolved, the ambiguities banished. Politics and science have a troublesome and durable affinity in government policymaking. This attraction can never be eliminated, but at best it can be constrained so that political values taint scientific determinations as little as possible. Regardless of party, other presidents will undoubtedly be tempted to intervene in EPA regulatory science as well and for reasons that may seem to the White House quite defensible. There is always a point at which scientific evidence alone cannot resolve regulatory decisions and political determinations have to be made. Thus the EPA's scientific mission will always be arduous and controversial, grounded in that edgy relationship with the White House and other political interests, including Congress. The EPA's critics themselves may not agree on the correct boundary between science and politics in EPA policymaking or know precisely when the agency's overall performance is balanced properly.

Suggested Web Sites

National Academy of Sciences (www.nas.edu) Links to many environmental topics, from which detailed reports and publications of the Academy are available. Especially useful links are to the "Environment" and "Policy" sections.

Natural Resources Defense Council (www.nrdc.org) Among the oldest and most influential national environmental advocacy organizations, NRDC offers valuable analysis of national environmental policy issues from an environmentalist perspective.

Office of Management and Budget (www.whitehouse.gov/omb) The OMB is the most important White House agency providing administrative staff and management for the president and is a major actor on environmental policy issues. An important source of information and analysis of presidential policy initiatives.

Union of Concerned Scientists (www.ucsusa.org) A nationally important, highly respected policy analysis and advocacy organization representing numerous scientific disciplines. A major source for nonpartisan, science-based analysis.

U.S. Environmental Protection Agency (www.epa.gov) Numerous links exist from this site to all major activities and issues of concern to the EPA, including a useful document library. Best place to start: "Site Map."

Notes

1. Felicity Barringer, "EPA Scientist Is Bush's Pick as New Chief," *New York Times*, March 5, 2005, 1A.
2. Hearing Before the Committee on Environment and Public Works, U.S. Senate, 109th Congress, First Session, April 6, 2005, p. 4.
3. Ibid., p. 19
4. Ibid., p. 22
5. Ibid., p. 12
6. Felicity Barringer, "EPA Chief Rejects Recommendations on Soot," *New York Times*, September 22, 2006, 1A.
7. Cornelia Dean, "Risk Assessment Plan Is Withdrawn," *New York Times*, January 12, 2007, A13.
8. Micheline Maynard, "E.P.A. Denies California Emissions Waiver," *New York Times*, December 19, 2007, 1A.
9. Union of Concerned Scientists, *Interference at the EPA: Science and Politics at the U.S. Environmental Protection Agency* (Cambridge, Mass.: Union of Concerned Scientists, 2008), chap. 4.
10. U.S. Senate Committee on Environment and Public Works, "Boxer, Whitehouse Release Justice Depart Investigation Letter on Testimony by EPA Administrator Stephen Johnson," October 10, 2008, http://epw.senate.gov/public/index.cfm? Fuse Action=Majority.PressReleases&ContentRecord_id=dcbb57d7-802a-23ad-4a11-8677e054234e&Region_id=&Issue_id=.
11. Janet Wilson, "Decisions under a Microscope," *Los Angeles Times*, January 25, 2008, A13.
12. U.S. Environmental Protection Agency (EPA), *National Streams Assessment: A Collaborative Survey of the Nation's Streams*, EPA 841-B-06-002 (Washington, D.C.: U.S. EPA, 2006).
13. Government Accountability Office (GAO), "Chemical Assessments: Low Probability and New Interagency Review Process Limit Usefulness and Credibility of EPA's Integrated Risk Information System," GAO-08-444 (March 2008), "Results in Brief."
14. U.S. EPA, *EPA's Report on the Environment* (Washington, D.C.: U.S. EPA, May 2008), 2-60, 2-61.
15. GAO, "Environmental Liabilities: EPA Should Do More to Ensure That Liable Parties Meet Their Cleanup Obligations," GAO-05-628 (August 12, 2005), "Highlights."

16. National Academy of Public Administration (NAPA), *Setting Priorities, Getting Results: A New Direction for the Environmental Protection Agency* (Washington, D.C.: NAPA, 1995), 8.

17. On endocrine disruptors, see Center for Bioenvironmental Research, Tulane and Xavier Universities, *Environmental Estrogens: What Does the Evidence Mean?* (New Orleans: Center for Bioenvironmental Research, 1996); Center for the Study of Environmental Endocrine Disruptors, *Significant Government Policy Developments* (Washington, D.C.: Center for the Study of Environmental Endocrine Disruptors, 1996); Center for the Study of Environmental Endocrine Disruptors, *Effects: State of Science Paper* (Washington, D.C.: Center for the Study of Environmental Endocrine Disruptors, 1995); U.S. EPA, "Endocrine Disruptor Screening Program Overview," February 6, 2004, www.epa.gov/scipoly/oscpendo/edspoverview.

18. Thomas O. McGarity, "The Internal Structure of EPA Rulemaking," *Law and Contemporary Problems* 54 (autumn 1991): 59.

19. This process, most often in the form of risk analysis, is informatively described in National Research Council, Commission on Life Sciences, Committee on the Institutional Means for Assessment of Risks to Public Health, *Risk Assessment in the Federal Government: Managing the Process* (Washington, D.C.: National Academies Press, 1983), chap. 1.

20. A useful summary of the Clean Air Act and its important subsequent amendments is found in Gary C. Bryner, *Blue Skies, Green Politics: The Clean Air Act of 1990 and Its Implementation,* 2d ed. (Washington, D.C.: CQ Press, 1995).

21. On problems associated with data interpretation, see National Research Council, *Risk Assessment in the Federal Government,* esp. chap. 1; Walter A. Rosenbaum, "Regulation at Risk: The Controversial Politics and Science of Comparative Risk Assessment," in *Flashpoints in Environmental Policymaking: Controversies in Achieving Sustainability,* ed. Sheldon Kamieniecki, George A. Gonzalez, and Robert O. Vos (Albany: State University of New York Press, 1997), 31–62.

22. U.S. EPA, Congressional and Intergovernmental Home, "Major Congressional Committees with Jurisdiction over EPA Issues," www.epa.gov/ocir/leglibrary/commit. htm. The turbulent history of congressional oversight of the EPA since the mid-1980s is discussed in Richard J. Lazarus, "The Tragedy of Distrust in the Implementation of Federal Environmental Law," *Law and Contemporary Problems* 311 (1991): 315–317; Richard A. Harris and Sidney M. Milkis, *The Politics of Regulatory Change* (New York: Oxford University Press, 1989); Mark J. Landy, Marc J. Roberts, and Stephen R. Thomas, *The Environmental Protection Agency,* chap. 8; Walter A. Rosenbaum, "The EPA at Risk"; Gary Bryner, "Congressional Decisions about Regulatory Reform: The 104th and 105th Congresses," in *Better Environmental Decisions,* ed. Ken Sexton, Alfred A. Marcus, K. William Easter, and Timothy D. Burkhardt (Washington, D.C.: Island Press, 1999), 91–112; Rogelio Garcia, "Federal Regulatory Reform Overview," *CRS Issue Brief for Congress,* No. IB95035 (May 22, 2001).

23. GAO, "EPA: Major Challenges and Program Risks," GAO/OGC 99-17 (January 1999).

24. GAO, "Water Quality: Identification and Remediation of Polluted Waters Impeded by Data Gaps," GAO/T-RCED 00-88 (February 2000), 5.

25. Letter of Bruce Alberts to the Executive Office of the President on OMB's Proposed Bulletin on Peer Review and Information Quality, www.whitehouse.gov/omb/inforeg/2003iq/115.pdf, December 4, 2004.

26. A useful review of scientific decision making at the EPA is found in Mark P. Powell, *Science at EPA: Information in the Regulatory Process* (Washington, D.C.: Resources for the Future, 1999).

27. For a comprehensive review of scientific and technical issues associated with mercury emissions, see U.S. EPA, "Controlling Power Plant Emissions: Overview," www.epa.gov/mercury/control_emissions/; see also Mark Clayton, "Mercury Rising," *Christian Science Monitor,* April 29, 2004, 1.

28. For the complete Clinton proposal and its related documents, see U.S. EPA, "Electric Utility Steam Generating Units Section 112 Rule Making," June 14, 2004, www. epa.gov/ttn/atw/combust/utiltox/utoxpg.html.

29. U.S. Department of Energy, Office of Fossil Energy, "Mercury Emission Control R&D," www.fossil.energy.gov/programs/powersystems/pollutioncontrols/overview_ mercurycontrols.html, September 19, 2004; Thomas Brown, William O'Dowd, Robert Reuther, and Dennis Smith, *Control of Mercury Emissions from Coal-Fired Power Plants: A Preliminary Cost Assessment* (Washington, D.C.: U.S. Department of Energy; Federal Technology Center, undated), www.netl.doe.gov/publications/proceedings/98/98ps/ps3b-6.pdf.

30. For a comprehensive analysis of the Bush proposal, see U.S. EPA, "National Emission Standards for Hazardous Air Pollutants for Industrial/Commercial/Industrial Boilers and Process Heaters," *Federal Register* 68 (January 13, 2003): 1659–1763; U.S. Energy Information, "Executive Summary," in *Reducing Emission of Sulfur Dioxide, Nitrogen Oxides and Mercury from Electric Power Plants,* October 17, 2001, www.eia.doe.gov/oiaf/servicerpt/mepp.

31. Rachael L. Swarns, "Bush Defends New Environmental Rules," *New York Times,* September 16, 2003, A22; see also Union of Concerned Scientists, "Executive Summary," in *Scientific Integrity in Policymaking: An Investigation into the Bush Administration's Misuse of Science* (Cambridge, Mass.: Union of Concerned Scientists, 2004).

32. Tom Hamburger and Alan C. Miller, "EPA Let Industry Dictate Policy on Mercury, Some Staffers Say," *Los Angeles Times,* March 3, 2004, 1.

33. Paul Krugman, "Editorial Desk: The Mercury Scandal," *New York Times,* April 6, 2004, A23.

34. Lisa Heinzerling and Rena Steinzor, "Political Intervention: The White House Doctors Mercury Conclusions," April 16, 2004, www.americanprogress.org/site/pp. asp?c=biJRJ8OVF&b=45899.

35. Jennifer 8. Lee, "White House Minimized the Risks of Mercury in Proposed Rules, Scientists Say," *New York Times,* April 7, 2004, A16.

36. Ibid.

37. Union of Concerned Scientists, *Scientific Integrity in Policymaking,* 2.

38. Michael Jasofsky, "Groups Propose Alternatives to EPA Rules on Mercury," *New York Times,* November 14, 2005, A1.

39. David A. Fahrenthold and Stephen Mufson, "Court Rejects Emission 'Trades,'" *Washington Post,* February 9, 2008, A03.

40. Juliet Eilperin, "EPA Chief Denies Calif. Limit on Auto Emissions," *Washington Post,* December 20, 2007, A01.

41. For a full text of the EPA's denial, see "California State Motor Vehicle Pollution Control Standards; Notice of Decision Denying a Waiver of Clean Air Act Preemption for California's 2009 and Subsequent Model Year Greenhouse Gas Emission Standards for New Motor Vehicles," www.epa.gov/otaq/url-fr/fr-waiver.pdf.

42. Felicity Barringer, "California Sues E.P.A. over Denial of Waiver," *New York Times,* January 3, 2008, A1.

43. Richard Simon, "EPA Chief Grilled over California Rejection of Emissions Waiver," *Los Angeles Times,* January 25, 2008, 1.

44. Ibid.

45. Felicity Barringer, "California Sues E.P.A."

46. Ibid.

47. Ibid.

48. Committee on Oversight and Governmental Reform, U.S. House of Representatives, *Deposition of Jason Burnett,* Washington, D.C., May 15, 2008, http://oversight.house.gov/documents/20080519143232.pdf.

49. Associated Press, "Report Charges Interference on Emissions," *New York Times,* May 20, 2008, A20.

50. Richard Simon, "EPA Chief Grilled."

51. Margaret Kriz, "The President's Man," *National Journal,* April 11, 2008.

8

Conflict and Cooperation in Natural Resource Management

Mark Lubell and Brian Segee

Jutting up 4,000 vertical feet from the Colorado River valley in western Colorado, the Roan Plateau (see Figure 8-1) is a treasured place. Environmentalists treasure the Roan as a biodiversity hotspot that provides habitat for rare species and large tracts of wilderness-quality land. Hunters and anglers (the so-called hook-and-bullet crowd) treasure it because it contains one of the largest mule deer populations in Colorado, elk calving grounds, large carnivore habitat, and genetically pure strains of Colorado River cutthroat trout. Energy companies treasure the Roan because the Bureau of Land Management (BLM) expects it to produce 1.79 trillion cubic feet (TCF) of natural gas in a twenty-year period (U.S. annual demand of natural gas is 23 TCF).[1] That is, if the numbers are right—environmental groups claim the BLM has overstated the amount of natural gas contained in the planning area and understated the pace of development. The Roan exemplifies a central dilemma of natural resource management—the conflict among competing and multiple uses of public lands.

At the center of the Roan conflict is how much development should occur on the top of the plateau. A large amount of energy development has already taken place on the private and public lands below the cliffs. On September 7, 2006, the BLM released a proposed Roan Plateau Resource Management Plan that allows the development of 210 new oil and gas wells on top of the plateau, designates 21,034 acres as "areas of critical environmental concern" (ACEC), and includes a variety of other environmental protections.

The plan was widely criticized by environmentalists, hunters, and anglers, and by Colorado governor Bill Ritter, who claimed that drilling on top of the plateau was unnecessary, the ACEC acreage was too small, and the environmental protections were insufficient. With a Democratic majority in the 110th Congress, Sen. Ken Salazar, D-Colo., put a procedural hold on the nomination process for the new BLM director, forcing the BLM to hear Ritter's demands for increasing the size of the ACEC and more stringent environmental protections. BLM officials duly noted Colorado's concerns but did not incorporate them into the final plan released in March 2008, which was nearly identical to the original proposal. In response, Colorado's congressional delegation began work on the Roan Plateau Oil and Gas Leasing Improvement Act to legislatively mandate more environmental protection,

Figure 8-1   Roan Plateau, Colorado

Photo courtesy of Jane Pargiter/EcoFlight.

and environmental groups filed lawsuits to overturn the plan. Despite these efforts, in September 2008 the BLM auctioned off 54,631 acres of land in the Roan planning area, taking in a record-breaking $113.9 million.[2]

The Roan's future hangs in the balance, and the way in which administrative, legislative, and judicial decisions combined to manage these competing priorities is a microcosm of natural resource politics under the George W. Bush administration. Largely unable to secure passage of legislation that would amend or repeal major environmental laws, the Bush administration instead turned to the powers of the "administrative presidency" to quietly rewrite the rules governing natural resources in the United States. The administrative presidency strategy relies on powers of the executive branch such as rulemaking, political appointments, executive orders, and budgetary allocations to control the behavior of public agencies and influence natural resource planning.[3] The Natural Resources Defense Council (NRDC) claims that, in 2004 alone, the Bush administration made 150 administrative changes that weakened environmental laws.[4] Even if these numbers are influenced by NRDC's environmental viewpoint, there is no doubt the Bush administration created a great deal of conflict by systematically changing natural resource management to favor economic development.[5] However, the political preferences of the observer heavily influence whether these policies are considered good or bad for public policy.

Perhaps paradoxically, at the same time that natural resource conflicts were festering, the concept of collaborative ecosystem management continued to grow. The goal of collaborative ecosystem management is fostering cooperation among multiple stakeholders in order to achieve a sustainable balance between ecosystem processes and human uses. Ecosystem management emerged in the late 1980s as the cutting-edge method of natural resource management. Many policy stakeholders were disillusioned by the ongoing conflict associated with more traditional natural resource policies, as well as the inability of those policies to solve fundamental environmental problems or integrate ecological concepts into policymaking. The broader political context has also encouraged collaboration because neither economic nor environmental interests have been able to form a large enough national coalition to dominate the political agenda, in contrast to the case of environmentalism in the 1970s. Regardless of its origins, ecosystem management is now a permanent fixture on the policy landscape and promises to remain so in the immediate future.[6] Even so, hot debate continues about the effectiveness of ecosystem management or other collaborative policies. In this chapter we examine this debate in the context of several of the most important ecosystem management programs in the country.

In the next section we describe how conflict is rooted in natural resource dilemmas, and the hallmarks of Bush administration politics in managing those conflicts. The dynamics of conflict are illustrated with four broad case studies: energy development on public lands, healthy forests, anadromous fish (for example, salmon and steelhead trout), and endangered species policy. We then describe the concept of collaborative ecosystem management in more detail and analyze the challenges faced in several important examples. In the conclusion we discuss the future of conflict and cooperation in natural resource management, with an eye toward predicting the changes in natural resource management likely to occur in the Barack Obama administration.

Resource Dilemmas and the Politics of the Bush Administration

Resource dilemmas occur when individual incentives lead to environmental behaviors that have negative effects on society. For example, rangeland is degraded when ranchers ignore the effects of their grazing practices on the quality of rangeland habitat and the economic welfare of other users. When all ranchers ignore these "social costs," rangeland resources are overexploited, leading to Garret Hardin's famous "tragedy of the commons."[7] The tragedy exists because the costs of resource use are spread to all users, while only individuals enjoy the benefits. Rational individuals have an incentive to use resources as long as individual benefits are greater than individual costs, and thus the combined decisions of all resource users lead to overconsumption. Similar problems occur with water, when people take more water than is available, exhaust the capacity of water to absorb pollution, or overexploit fisheries populations. Another source of conflict occurs when actors have different preferences over the best use of the resources, as is common in multiple-use lands where wilderness, energy extraction, and other values are in competition.

The outcomes of resource dilemmas are influenced by the public policies that govern how people make resource-use decisions. Public policy creates rules that define individual rights with respect to resource use—what actions people are allowed, required, or forbidden to take.[8] These rights are usually defined by land management plans, water rights, permits, and other government decisions. Public policy also creates processes by which stakeholders make collective choices about those on-the-ground rules. For example, the National Environmental Policy Act (NEPA) mandates the preparation of an environmental impact statement for federal government decisions deemed to have a significant environmental impact. Any change in legislative or administrative processes will affect how collective choices are made and the resource policies that result. Hence, the courts, president, Congress, and government agencies all combine to influence the outcomes of resource dilemmas. At the same time, interest groups and concerned citizens have different preferences regarding resource outcomes and thus will engage in political strategies throughout the government system. Because so many venues exist for changing the rules, the resulting policies can be vague and contradictory, leading to litigation and unintended consequences.

The outcomes of resource dilemmas should be evaluated in terms of both efficiency and equity. Regarding efficiency, policies should aim to minimize the social costs associated with resource use. In the tragedy of the commons case, this means keeping resource use at a sustainable level that is not beyond the natural replenishment rate for renewable resources like fisheries, water, and forests. For multiple-use issues, policies should aim to allocate those uses in ways that reflect their relative values to society (which can change over time), minimize the costs of conflict that are incurred when making those allocations, and ensure that resources and uses are shared in an equitable manner for current and future generations. These goals are admittedly abstract and difficult to define in real-world contexts, especially when different interests have different preferences over how resources should be used. For example, many environmentalists adopt a stronger eco-centric perspective that recognizes the intrinsic value of the biophysical system and seeks to minimize human impacts.

The Role of Government Agencies

Government agencies are perhaps the most important but least understood actors involved with resource dilemmas. Agency decisions are where the rubber meets the road with respect to how public policy influences resource outcomes; they are the heart of policy implementation. These decisions include adopting regulations to implement decisions made by other political actors (for example, legislation approved by Congress), allocating budget and personnel resources within the agency, constructing environmental projects, writing resource management plans, drafting environmental impact statements, and engaging in myriad other implementation activities. These decisions ultimately combine to define the required, permitted, and prohibited uses of natural resources.

In the case of public lands, most agencies are required to produce an overall management plan for the land under their jurisdiction. For example, every National Forest must have a management plan that designates what multiple uses are appropriate for different pieces of land, among many other issues. According to 2000 data, the federal government owns about 652.6 million acres of land. Four federal agencies are the primary managers of this land: the BLM (264.4 million acres), the U.S. Forest Service (192.4 million), the U.S. Fish and Wildlife Service (USFWS; 95.0 million), and the National Park Service (83.6 million).[9] The remaining 17.2 million acres are managed by a variety of federal agencies, including the Department of Defense and the Bureau of Reclamation. Each of these agencies has its own procedures for land management planning, which may come into conflict when agencies are required to work together at the level of ecosystems or landscapes.

Water resources are more complicated because policy outcomes are the result of the combined decisions of myriad local, state, and federal agencies. For example, the 1972 Clean Water Act requires most states to develop water quality plans for specific watersheds that influence how water discharge permits are issued to point sources of pollution like sewage treatment plants. At the same time, federal agencies like the Bureau of Reclamation or Army Corp of Engineers are making annual decisions about how to operate dams, such as how much water to release to meet irrigation, hydropower, and environmental goals and requirements. States play a central role in determining the water rights regarding withdrawals for water supply. Irrigation districts, local water utilities, individual landowners, and many other organizations are also usually making important decisions within a given watershed. There are approximately 3.7 million stream-miles, 40.6 million acres of lakes excluding the Great Lakes, and 87,300 square miles of estuaries and bays in the United States, and these waters face a variety of environmental problems.

Given the central role of government agencies, political actors spend a great deal of effort trying to control agency behavior. One way to control agency behavior is to access and influence the political "principals" that have authority over agencies: the president, Congress, and the courts. The president has several powers to shape agency decisions, including using the bully pulpit to influence public opinion, writing executive orders, endorsing budget proposals, appointing agency executives, seeking coordination between levels of government, and generally controlling how government agencies make regulations. These powers are the heart of the administrative strategy.

But the administrative strategy must take into account the other political actors in the system, who may work at different times for or against the president's agenda. Congressional legislation can directly change how agencies implement policy, and congressional oversight can make agencies more accountable to public or congressional preferences. Some legislation describes fairly vague guidelines that provide a great deal of discretion to agencies, while other legislation is more detailed and prescriptive. Courts review administrative decisions for compliance with legislative language and intent as set out in broad environmental laws like the National Forest Management Act of 1976 (NFMA), the Endangered Species Act of 1973 (ESA), or NEPA (1969), among others. The total set of rules governing resource use is thus a combination of authoritative decisions made by all of these political actors.

Hallmarks of the Bush Administration's Natural Resource Policy

A major hallmark of the Bush administration was to use the powers of the administrative presidency to rewrite many policies governing natural resource use on public lands and watersheds (summarized in Box 8-1; see also chapter 4). The strategy began with appointments of conservative Republicans to key executive positions. For example, Bush's first secretary of the interior was Gale Norton, a protégée of the famously conservative Reagan administration interior secretary James Watt. In the Department of Agriculture, former timber industry lobbyist Mark Rey was appointed as undersecretary for natural resources and the environment, giving him direct oversight of the U.S. Forest Service. Similar appointments were made throughout the bureaucracy.[10]

Bush also replaced several Clinton-era decisions with new policies emphasizing greater economic uses of natural resources. Some of the best-known examples are the rewriting of the National Forest System Roadless Area Conservation Rule, the winter use management plan in Yellowstone National Park, and the Sierra Nevada Framework governing management in many of California's national forests. These and many other policy changes throughout natural resource management were facilitated with administrative tools such as rulemaking, executive orders, memoranda to bureaucratic officials, and intergovernmental coordinating committees.

Officials of the Bush administration were also widely accused of manipulating scientific information to downplay the environmental consequences of development. Research by the Union of Concerned Scientists documented widespread political interference in scientific decision-making.[11] Some of the cases have been spectacular, such as when Julie MacDonald (deputy assistant secretary of fish, wildlife, and parks within the Department of the Interior) directly interfered with scientific decisions involving critical habitat designations for endangered species.[12] Other evidence suggests a more pervasive influence. A Department of the Interior Inspector General Report found that MacDonald influenced thirteen of twenty ESA decisions they reviewed, and was "aided and abetted" by a variety of USFWS political appointees and career employees.[13] Underscoring this finding, a survey of USFWS employees found that 56 percent knew of cases in which "commercial interests have inappropriately induced the reversal or withdrawal of scientific conclusions or decisions through political intervention"; and 70

Box 8-1   Hallmarks of the Bush Administration's Natural
Resource Policy

- Administrative powers of the president used to rewrite resource management policies
- Scientific information manipulated to support policy agenda
- Public attention deflected by complexity of administrative process and "greenwashed" names for policy initiatives
- Congressional support for administrative initiatives during Republican-controlled Congress (107th–109th), with more oversight during the Democratic-controlled 110th Congress
- Conflict driven by environmental interest groups defending status quo through administrative appeals and courts

---

percent agreed that "U.S. Department of the Interior political appointees have injected themselves into Ecological Services [the branch of USFWS responsible for administering the ESA] determinations."[14] The accuracy of these claims was a source of heated conflict between the Bush administration and its critics.[15]

Much of this activity occurred without widespread public attention. The administrative strategy occurs in the context of a complex and technical set of bureaucratic procedures and scientific issues that are the domain of specialists and not average citizens. The true purposes of many of the larger initiatives were "greenwashed" with positive language such as the Healthy Forests Initiative and the Clear Skies Initiative. The Bush administration insisted that such titles were sincere and that the policies did improve the environment. At the same time, public lands issues are usually not salient outside of some key constituencies, so the media largely ignored the administrative changes, with the exception of dramatic issues such as the Arctic National Wildlife Refuge and western wildfires. Some observers have even accused the Bush administration of using a "Friday folly" strategy of releasing important environmental decisions on Friday afternoons, when most media outlets are not paying attention.[16]

The congressional response to the administrative strategy followed partisan lines. Congress had a Republican majority for most of Bush's first term and half of his second (107th–109th Congresses). The Republican Congresses conducted very little oversight of agency decisions or personnel in the form of congressional hearings and investigations, although they did hold hearings criticizing the ESA and the science of climate change. In addition, the Republican Congresses were able to pass some new legislation to support Bush's policy initiatives. Among the most important of these were the Healthy Forests Restoration Act of 2002 and the Energy Policy Act of 2005. This pattern of deference changed significantly when the Democrats took control of Congress after the 2006 elections (110th Congress). Oversight increased greatly, and legislative proposals supportive of the administration ceased to make headway.

Environmental groups used a range of strategies to fight the administration's policy changes. Among the most important of these were administrative appeals of development projects such as timber sales, energy leases, and drilling permits. But these appeals were frequently denied because Bush administration appointees had instructions to expedite resource extraction. Hence, environmental groups used litigation strategies that generally accused agencies of violating existing laws like NEPA, the ESA, and the NFMA. Environmental groups also pursued political strategies such as public information campaigns designed to bring attention to behind-the-scenes administrative issues and electoral campaigns, such as the one spearheaded by Defenders of Wildlife Action Fund that helped defeat Republican representative Richard Pombo of California, who had led legislative efforts to rewrite and weaken the ESA.

Given the central role of litigation, the Bush administration pursued strategies to increase the win rate for development interests (see chapter 6). One method was the tried-and-true strategy of appointing conservative judges to lower levels of the federal court system, which promotes conservative preferences over a variety of issues including the environment.[17] Another strategy was the "sweetheart settlement," by which the Bush administration settled lawsuits brought by industry against Clinton-era policies, or even invited economic interests to sue the government with the expectation of a settlement.[18] For example, in 2003 the Department of the Interior settled a lawsuit brought by the state of Utah, agreeing with the state's argument that the BLM was prohibited from adding wilderness study areas in Utah beyond those in the original inventory submitted by the bureau in 1993 (ironically, under Bush's father, George H. W. Bush). The Clinton administration had ordered the new inventory, which had identified 2.6 million new acres of potential wilderness. This is just one of several important cases in which the Bush administration decided not to defend the government's interests, because settlements were more favorable to economic development.

In the next sections, we discuss how these hallmarks of Bush administration politics played out in several prominent conflicts. These cases, however, are only the tip of the iceberg. Bush's administrative strategy touched nearly every facet of natural resource management; however, there is space here to mention only some of the biggest decisions and events involved in each case. The outcomes of these cases were influenced by myriad smaller, less visible, and informal decisions. The citations in each case study provide more in-depth reviews, but even they cannot capture every instance of important decision making.

Energy Development on Public Lands

Increasing domestic energy production on federal public lands, marketed as increasing energy independence, was a primary goal of the Bush administration. These energy priorities were addressed early in the administration by the National Energy Policy Development Group chaired by Vice President Dick Cheney. This so-called energy task force produced the "National Energy Plan," which included a variety of recommendations designed to increase the pace of domestic energy production on public lands, such as streamlining permitting processes and releasing wilderness-quality lands for energy leasing.[19] Notably, the task force was dominated by large corporate energy interests and met in secretive meetings that were closed to the public. The Bush administration later won a hard-fought court battle in which, under the Freedom of Information Act, it refused to release documents relating to the task force's deliberations.

Many of the task force's recommendations were implemented through administrative mechanisms. For example, Executive Order 13212 instructed agencies to "expedite their review of permits or take other actions as necessary to accelerate" energy production.[20] These policy changes were supported by increasing the number of energy-related personnel in BLM field offices, revising BLM and U.S. Forest Service land management plans to increase the supply of lands to be leased, and giving direct instructions to agency personnel to accelerate energy production. The BLM also developed a National Energy Policy Implementation Plan outlining fifty-four actions for facilitating energy production. At the same time, increases in oil and natural gas prices fueled one of the largest energy booms in the history of the United States. As a result, there was a major increase in the number of acres leased and drilling permits approved—the annual number of permits approved more than tripled from 1999 (1,803 approved) to 2004 (6,399 approved).[21] The number of permits issued in Colorado alone was higher than ever.[22] These increases were accompanied by a decrease in the rate of environmental inspections, as more resources were shifted toward permit approvals. These strategies continued until the end of the Bush administration, when the BLM pushed through six resource management plans in Utah that opened up more land for energy development in what environmentalists called "the great giveaway."[23]

Congress followed suit with the Energy Policy Act of 2005, which authorized a variety of financial incentives for fossil-fuel energy production, ordered the BLM to create a federal permit streamlining pilot project, imposed only minimum environmental standards on resource development activities, and accelerated the processing of resource management plans, leasing activities, and permits. The BLM was also required to conduct an inventory of public lands to see what percentage of energy resources are "locked up" by land management restrictions. The vague language of the Energy Policy Act provided a great deal of discretion to agencies for energy development activities.

The conflict over energy development has focused on some specific hotspots. The Roan Plateau case described in the introduction is one of them. Another is the Powder River Basin in Wyoming and Montana, which has large reserves of natural gas being developed with the controversial technology of coalbed-methane mining. Of course, the most famous hotspot is the Arctic National Wildlife Refuge (Arctic Refuge), which has long been a prominent battleground between environmentalists and energy development interests. Interestingly, the Energy Policy Act of 2005 did not authorize opening up the Arctic Refuge for oil drilling, although the original version of the bill contained a provision to allow leasing. However, resource development proponents could not muster enough political support to overcome the strong public opinion in favor of prohibiting energy development in the Arctic Refuge.

In addition to extensive legislative efforts to prevent energy development in the Arctic Refuge and other protected areas, environmental groups fought back by appealing and litigating leasing and drilling permit decisions. For example, environmental groups protested 2.5 million of 7.3 million acres of land offered for lease in Colorado, Montana, and New Mexico from 2001 to 2007.[24] When these appeals largely failed (for example, 20 percent of appeals succeeded in Utah; less than 1 percent succeeded in Wyoming), environmental groups turned to the courts. In 2006 the district court in Utah agreed with environmental groups that the BLM had failed to adequately analyze the environmental effects of oil and gas leases on sixteen parcels of land that were classified as wilderness study areas or areas of critical environmental concern.[25] In 2007 the Theodore Roosevelt Conservation Partnership, an advocate for hunters and fishers, challenged the environmental impact statement associated with the development of two thousand coalbed-methane wells in the Atlantic Rim Project Area in Wyoming.[26] A central theme of both environmental and hook-and-bullet groups is that the development of energy resources on federal land must be carefully balanced against the amount of environmental damage from developing those resources, and that some areas, such as roadless and other high-quality wildlife habitats targeted by the Bush administration, should simply be off-limits. Energy proponents, of course, make exactly opposite claims.

The Atlantic Rim and other energy conflicts demonstrate how "politics makes strange bedfellows." Environmentalists dislike the land-disturbing and pollution effects of energy development, ranchers do not like seeing their private surface lands being trampled to develop subsurface federal energy resources (for example, coalbed-methane), and the hook-and-bullet crowd (such as the Theodore Roosevelt Conservation Partnership) wants to protect wildlife habitat. Because they include some Republican Party supporters, these unusual coalitions have had some success in fighting specific energy proposals. An important case was the Rocky Mountain Front in Montana, in which the Bush administration decided in 2004 to delay oil drilling permits, giving Congress time to pass legislation in 2006 completely banning new oil and gas development in the area. But the Rocky Mountain Front was an easy case because it contained very small amounts of energy resources and thus could easily be used as an election-year symbol to mollify critics.

Healthy Forests: Fire, Plans, and Roads

The concept of healthy forests was the central metaphor of forest management during the Bush administration, and it revolved around three core issues: fire, forest planning, and roads. The idea of ecosystem health is a central and heavily debated concept in ecology.[27] While there is widespread agreement that the U.S. Forest Service's policy of fire suppression has increased the frequency and intensity of fires, conflict has swirled around identifying the forestry practices that can be used to prevent fires that burn at an intensity and size outside the historic range of variability. Similar debates exist concerning the role of logging in preventing other natural processes exacerbated by fire suppression, such as disease and insect infestations. Complicating the situation, climate change has been increasingly identified as a primary source of forest health problems, especially in the western United States. National attention has focused on the role of fire at least since the great Yellowstone fires of 1988, and the encroaching human development on public lands in the "wildland-urban interface" has created daunting challenges for firefighters and land managers alike. Some spectacular fire seasons in Southern California and other western states during 2000 and 2002 were focusing events that put fire management high on the political agenda.

The main administrative response to these issues was Bush's Healthy Forests Initiative. The initiative claimed to promote forest health by removing bureaucratic barriers to forestry projects designed to reduce fire risks or harvest damaged trees (so-called salvage logging). The initiative developed a series of NEPA categorical exclusions (that is, for which NEPA analysis was not required) for hazardous fuel reduction projects, post-fire rehabilitation, harvesting of live trees on less than fifty acres, salvage logging of dead or dying trees, and tree harvesting to control insects.[28] Another strategy was to revise the Forest Service appeals process so that "emergency" and categorically excluded projects would be more difficult to appeal.

In addition to these administrative changes, the Healthy Forests Initiative formed the basis for the 2003 Healthy Forests Restoration Act. The act contained a variety of provisions, the most important of which were that it further defined the scope of fire hazard and fuel reduction treatments, removed more barriers to implementing those projects, and authorized millions of dollars in funding for other forest health issues. The legislative strategies of the act generally complemented the administrative changes to NEPA and the U.S. Forest Service appeals process.

Although not as clearly tied to fire management, two other important administrative changes were designed to increase the discretion of local national forests and reduce environmental restrictions on forest management. First, the National Forest Planning Rule of 2004 exempted individual national forest plans from NEPA analysis, removed the "viability regulation" that was previously used to protect biodiversity from timber harvesting and other resource extraction activities, and declared that forest plan provisions that have traditionally governed resource decisions would now be treated as "discretionary" rather than binding.

Second, the Bush administration completely rewrote the so-called Roadless Rule that was finalized at the end of the Clinton administration. The Clinton Roadless Rule, with some exceptions, banned any new road construction in existing roadless areas in the National Forest System to prevent habitat fragmentation and conserve scarce agency resources.[29] Bush replaced this system-wide ban with a petition process whereby individual states could decide which roadless areas they wanted to protect. Western states like Idaho petitioned to protect substantially fewer roadless acres than what the Clinton rule would have covered. Environmental groups successfully sued and struck down the Bush State Petitions Rule for an inadequate NEPA analysis, and the courts reinstated the Clinton rule. The Bush administration responded by encouraging states to circumvent the Roadless Rule by proceeding with state-level decisions through traditional rulemaking procedures under the federal Administrative Procedure Act of 1946.

Environmental groups have responded to these changes with lawsuits and appeals of individual forest projects. Timber industry groups and some U.S. Forest Service officials claim that this strategy has created "analysis paralysis." They argue that appeals and litigation have unnecessarily delayed forest health projects to the extent that fire and disease risk are increased, and economic returns from salvage logging vanish due to the decomposition of dead and damaged trees. For example, the Government Accountability Office (GAO) analyzed 818 fuel reduction projects covering 4.8 million acres in 2001–2002.[30] Among the analyzed decisions, 53 percent could not be appealed because of categorical exclusions, 58 percent of the eligible decisions were in fact appealed, and 25 total cases were litigated. At the same time, 73 percent of the appealed decisions proceeded unchanged, and 79 percent were processed within the prescribed ninety days. Overall only a relatively small percentage of cases were litigated or created the major delays portrayed by critics. But the significance of the numbers is still disputed—some environmental groups claimed the GAO report showed their strategies caused no delays, while some timber interests held it up as proof of their position.

Anadromous Fish and Western Watersheds

As mentioned earlier, water policy in the United States is generally more complex than land management because watersheds face a variety of environmental issues, provide multiple ecosystem services, and involve government and nongovernmental actors from every level of the federal system. However, one issue in the western United States perhaps generates the most conflict: anadromous fish.

Anadromous fish is the biological term for species like salmon and steelhead trout that are born in freshwater rivers, migrate to the ocean to spend some years of their lives foraging and growing, and return again to spawn in their natal streams. Anadromous fish have faced serious declines in population levels in the past two decades; many subpopulations (or "runs") are now listed as threatened or endangered species. These fish provide direct economic benefits to recreational and commercial fishing industries and are powerful cultural symbols to Native Americans and other western communities. The viability of anadromous fish populations depends on many factors: appropriate harvest levels, open ocean conditions that provide enough food, clean and cold water in spawning streams, the ability to navigate any obstructions, and high-quality riparian habitat. Anadromous fish are a nexus for policy conflict due to their connections with many water issues.

The administrative strategy is most apparent in the decisions of federal agencies like the Bureau of Reclamation (BuRec) and Army Corp of Engineers, which manage the operations of the federal dams and irrigation systems. The water supply decisions of these agencies must be made in conjunction with the USFWS and the National Marine Fisheries Service (NMFS), which are responsible for administering the ESA. Of particular importance is the requirement under Section 7 of the act that federal agencies must consult with the NMFS or the USFWS to issue "biological opinions" (BiOps) regarding the operation of federal dams and irrigation projects. These BiOps determine whether or not any operations will jeopardize endangered or threatened species, or destroy or adversely modify their designated critical habitat. If jeopardy is likely or adverse modification will occur, BiOps require the action agency to offer "reasonable and prudent" alternatives to the proposed action. BiOps are also required when the Federal Energy Regulatory Commission grants licenses for hydropower operations on private dams.

The Klamath River is emblematic of the conflict surrounding anadromous fish and BiOps.[31] Running from Oregon to the northern California coast, the Klamath River is heavily utilized for irrigation and hydropower, while also providing some of the most essential fish habitat along the Pacific coast. The river is divided into the relatively flat Upper Basin in Oregon, which contains 220,000 acres of irrigated farmland, and the more steeply graded Lower Basin in California. The fishery is used by recreational anglers, a coastal commercial fleet, and three local Native American tribes (Yurok, Hoopa, and Karuk). The energy company PacifiCorp operates five hydroelectric dams on the river; the largest of these is Iron Gate Dam, which is a significant fish passage barrier. At the center of the conflict are irrigation water diversions by the Klamath Reclamation Project, which reduce the flows available in the Lower Basin for migrating fish like the endangered Coho salmon and also decrease water levels in Upper Basin lakes containing the endangered Lost River and shortnose sucker fish.

In 2001 a major drought in the Klamath Basin forced BuRec to stop irrigation to comply with the minimum lake level and flow requirements contained in the BiOps governing the Klamath Project's annual operations. Klamath farmers reacted with outrage; they conducted political protests, formed a "bucket brigade" to move water to fields, and repeatedly forced open the irrigation headgates (where the water is diverted) until federal law enforcement stepped in.

It is at this point that the administrative strategy appears to have intervened in the Klamath conflict. At the very least, the Bush administration clearly communicated to lower-level officials in BuRec and the Department of the Interior that farmers should be favored over fish.[32] Under pressure from the administration, the Department of the Interior requested a peer-reviewed study by the nonpartisan National Research Council on the ecology of the Klamath River. The study came to the controversial conclusion that there was not enough scientific evidence to support increasing Upper Klamath lake levels or Klamath main-stem minimum flows above those seen in the previous ten years, thereby providing BuRec a scientific justification for a 2002 annual operating plan that renewed irrigation. In an act of political theater, the secretaries of the Interior and Agriculture presided over a ceremony reopening the canals. Subsequently, both NFMS and USFWS produced BiOps for Coho and sucker fish that substantially weakened the restrictions on irrigation withdrawals. Vice President Cheney was accused of personally pressuring BuRec to reopen the canals in 2002,[33] and NMFS scientists later claimed that Department of the Interior political appointees edited out portions of the draft BiOps that were critical of BuRec.

The reduced flows appeared to have a dire ecological consequence. In September 2002, one of the largest fish-kills in U.S. history occurred when approximately 34,000 fall-run Chinook salmon died in the Lower Klamath. While the proximate cause of the fish-kill was gill-rot disease exacerbated by overcrowding and high water temperatures, the California Department of Fish and Game pointed to low flows as the underlying issue.[34] At the same time, environmental and fishing groups were litigating the 2002 BiOp for not adequately analyzing the effects of subsequent years of low flows, and the courts rejected the 2002 BiOp and ordered NMFS and USFWS to write a new BiOp, a draft of which was released in June 2008.[35] The draft indicates that the Klamath Project operations are likely to jeopardize and adversely modified the habitat of the threatened coho salmon; the final draft and BuRec's response is still pending at the time of this writing. In the meantime, the Klamath is being operated according to court-ordered minimum flow standards set in the 2002 BiOp.

The Klamath illustrates how the Bush administration, BuRec, and water management interests pressured NMFS to define "jeopardy" or "reasonable and prudent" alternatives in ways that would limit the impact of the ESA on hydropower and irrigation operations. Environmental groups responded with litigation focused on whether or not the BiOps were consistent with the plain language and legislative intent of the act. Similar litigation strategies were pursued in many other western watersheds, such as the Sacramento–San Joaquin Delta in California and the Columbia River. In most cases, NMFS and other action agencies have been forced to rewrite BiOps while the courts take a direct hand in water management. For example, a federal judge ordered a series of dam spills in the Columbia River Basin to facilitate salmon migration, while another court ordered the cessation of water exports from the delta to southern California.[36] Despite these legal victories, the water management decisions of the past few years, combined with poor conditions in the open ocean, have left many salmon populations in such bad shape that the 2008 commercial and recreational salmon fishing seasons were completely closed for California and Oregon.

Endangered Species: Controversy, Consultation, and Climate Change

Passed in 1973, the ESA is the country's central law dedicated to preserving biological diversity, and it is widely regarded as one of the most powerful environmental statutes. In contrast to the previous cases, the Bush administration did not pursue any sweeping changes to the ESA regulatory structure until well into its second term, instead letting Congress take the lead. After the 2004 elections, Republican Party leaders quickly announced that "reform" of the ESA would be among their top priorities of the 109th Congress—as indeed it had been since the Republicans were swept to power in the 1994 midterm elections during Clinton's first term.[37] These efforts culminated with the House's narrow passage of a bill authored by House Resources Committee chairman Richard Pombo, R-Calif., on September 29, 2005, which, among other things, eliminated the act's critical habitat provisions as well as its requirement that agency decisions implementing the act be based on the best available science. However, Senate Wildlife Subcommittee chairman Lincoln Chaffee, R-R.I., prevented the bill from coming to a vote, because he favored a more moderate approach and was concerned that House leaders would be able to force the Senate to accept their bill in a conference committee between the two chambers.[38] Months later, Pombo was defeated in his reelection bid and Democrats regained the majority in both the House and the Senate, effectively killing any chance for significant legislative changes to the ESA before the end of Bush's second term.

The failure of the legislative reform strategy made the ESA a prime target for administrative proposals. During the first seven years of Bush's presidency, the USFWS proposed relatively few regulatory changes to the act but did pass new rules allowing federal agencies to "self-consult" on the potential effects of pesticides and fire reduction efforts on listed species, rather than seeking the opinion of expert wildlife agencies, in other words, to decide on their own whether their actions would harm listed species. (The pesticide rule was successfully challenged by environmental groups in litigation; a similar challenge to the fire rule is still pending.) In addition, the Bush administration reduced budgets and staffing for the USFWS and NMFS, the agencies primarily charged with ensuring the act's implementation.[39] Most notably, however, the USFWS simply stopped implementing some provisions of the act, placing far fewer species than any other administration onto the list of threatened and endangered species, setting a record by going more than two years without listing a single species, and finally acting only when compelled by court order.[40]

The latter half of Bush's second term, after Democrats regained majorities in Congress, saw more aggressive efforts to put the administration's stamp on the ESA regulatory framework. For example, the USFWS moved in the final year of the Bush administration to exempt climate change from ESA requirements and, specifically, the effect of greenhouse gas emissions on listed species. This policy first surfaced in conjunction with the agency's May 15, 2008, landmark decision listing the polar bear as threatened under the ESA in recognition of the fact that the bear's polar ice habitat is melting as a result of global warming. The USFWS, however, on the same day issued a director's memorandum, as well as a separate "special rule" specific to the polar bear under the ESA asserting that there is no causal connection between greenhouse gas emissions and effects on listed species, thus exempting any "incidental taking" of polar bears caused by activities undertaken anywhere in the United States outside of Alaska.[41] In essence, the USFWS listed the polar bear because of the threat posed by global warming while simultaneously exempting greenhouse gas emitters from the application of the ESA, a contradictory stance that was immediately challenged by environmentalists in court. Notably, despite these exemptions, numerous industry groups as well as the state of Alaska, at the direction of Governor Sarah Palin, have also sued to have the listing invalidated.[42]

Finally, in the eleventh hour of Bush's presidency, the USFWS pushed through a fundamental overhaul of ESA regulations. Among other provisions, the rule allowed all federal agencies to self-consult, curtailed the scope of actions subject to consultation, and broadly exempted greenhouse gas emissions from consultation requirements.[43] With little time to spare, the administration greatly expedited the rulemaking process, offering a highly truncated NEPA comment period of only ten days, and ordering a team of fifteen Department of the Interior officials to review more than 200,000 public comments on the proposal (most of them negative) in only thirty-two hours.[44] Notably, the USFWS's rewrite of ESA regulatory requirements was one of many examples of last-minute rulemaking by the Bush administration on a variety of politically sensitive environmental issues, including mountaintop removal coal mining, drinking water standards, and power plant pollution.[45] This type of "midnight rulemaking," by no means limited to the Bush administration, is a common tactic by lame-duck administrations that have been unable to gain sufficient political support to make the desired changes during the heart of their terms.[46] The new ESA rules, by far the most fundamental and far-reaching changes made since the USFWS and NMFS jointly promulgated regulations in 1986, are a prime example of this tactic, highlighting the Bush administration's reliance on the administrative presidency until its last days.

Collaborative Ecosystem Management and the Promise of Cooperation

Many observers have lamented the ubiquitous conflict over natural resources as a costly way to make public policy. The costs in terms of time and money spent on litigation and appeals are clearly very high. In addition, many of the underlying resource dilemmas remain unresolved as disputants continue to battle in administrative, legislative, and judicial arenas. These costs have led many researchers and practitioners to the idea of collaborative ecosystem management as a way to reduce conflict and encourage cooperation among stakeholders.

Collaborative management has many aliases, including adaptive management, watershed management, grassroots ecosystem management, and civic environmentalism. Regardless of nuanced differences among the labels, the hallmark of these policy processes is a search for mutually beneficial solutions to policy conflicts. Such win-win solutions are thought to emerge from encouraging broad participation from local stakeholders, emphasizing voluntary actions, seeking consensus decisions, and building trust-based policy networks. In addition, collaborative ecosystem management seeks to develop a better scientific understanding of how ecological processes affect resource outcomes across artificial jurisdictional and political boundaries.

Collaborative management is an institutional strategy for solving resource dilemmas. Like other public land and water management policies, collaborative management involves a particular set of institutional rules that influence how policy decisions are made, which in turn shape the rules governing resource use in a particular ecosystem. Proponents often compare the bottom-up and decentralized strategy of collaborative management to traditional resource management institutions that have achieved sustainable outcomes in some international cases. Elinor Ostrom argues these successful institutions have certain design principles, such as clearly defined resource boundaries, information about resource variability, monitoring and sanctioning mechanisms, local conflict resolution forums, and rules adapted to local circumstances.[47] The success of a particular ecosystem management program may be related to how well it reflects these principles.

Examples of Collaborative Management

The idea of collaborative management has spread like wildfire throughout natural resource management, and examples can be found in most resource management agencies in the United States, as well as throughout the world.[48] While it is difficult to say exactly when collaborative management was born, one of the earliest examples is the Chesapeake Bay Program, which began in 1983 as an informal agreement among the federal government, the District of Columbia, and the states of Maryland, Virginia, and Pennsylvania to work together to solve bay-wide problems. Since then, the program has evolved to include more formal agreements, supportive state and federal legislation, changes in agency regulations, and large amounts of local, state, and federal funding. One of the central goals of the program is to reduce nutrient inputs (phosphorous and nitrogen) from agricultural and urban runoff. The current price tag for restoring the Chesapeake Bay is $19 billion dollars, with about three-quarters of the funding coming from state governments.

Another important example from water management is CALFED, which began in 1994 with the signing of the Bay-Delta Accord, whereby California and the federal government agreed to resolve a conflict over water quality standards for salinity in the delta.[49] The CALFED program was administratively established in 1995, a comprehensive management plan was finalized in 2000, and a new state agency called the California Bay-Delta authority was created in 2003 to oversee plan implementation. The total price tag for restoring the delta is estimated at $8.5 billion. From 2000 to 2007, CALFED spent approximately $3.2 billion dollars, with about 45 percent going to water supply reliability projects and 33 percent to ecosystem restoration; 81 percent of the funds came from state sources.[50]

Two of the most important examples from federal land management are the Quincy Library Group and the Northwest Forest Plan. The Quincy Library Group formed in 1992 when environmental, timber, and local government stakeholders started meeting on neutral ground in the library in Quincy, California, with the goal of resolving the "timber wars" in the Plumas, Lassen, and Tahoe National Forests.[51] In 1993 the group released a "Community Stability Proposal" that built on some previous forest plans and proposed to increase logging for forest health purposes while preserving habitat for the California spotted owl and other sensitive environmental areas. Subsequently the Herger Feinstein Quincy Library Group Forest Recovery Act of 1999 legislatively mandated the U.S. Forest Service to update the management plans for the involved forests to reflect the group's proposal. The Quincy Library Group has been called the "poster child" for collaborative management, but many environmentalists have accused it of being a surrender to logging interests.

At around the same time, the Northwest Forest Plan was being developed on a much larger scale to deal with the conflicts between logging and threatened species like the northern spotted owl and marbled murrelet. Logging in the Pacific Northwest had always been particularly lucrative because of the large, old-growth trees in many areas. But both the ESA and the National Forest Management Act require the Forest Service to protect the viability of threatened species like the northern spotted owl that are particularly dependent on old-growth habitat for breeding. In the early 1990s, a series of lawsuits virtually halted logging on Pacific Northwest forests to protect the spotted owl. President Clinton responded to this crisis in 1993 by convening the collaborative Forest Ecosystem Management Assessment Team (FEMAT) to review forest management in the region. Some critics claimed that, consisting largely of scientists, FEMAT was too top-down and expert-driven, although it still required interagency cooperation.

The recommendations of FEMAT were eventually approved as the Northwest Forest Plan in 1994. The Northwest Forest Plan relies on four basic components: a system of land allocations that sets aside 78 percent of the forests for some type of old-growth reserve, an aquatic conservation strategy that restricts logging in riparian areas, a "survey and manage" requirement for population counts of hundreds of species, and an adaptive management program.[52] The Northwest Forest Plan is the earliest and largest example of an ecosystem management plan on public lands, and it established a model that was exported to other projects such as the Sierra Nevada Framework that updated management of many Sierra Nevada forests.[53]

The large-scale programs mentioned here are not the only ones; other programs concern the Everglades, the Great Lakes, the Gulf of Mexico, the Mississippi River, and the Columbia River. Furthermore, literally thousands of ecosystem management projects are occurring at the much smaller scale of local watersheds.[54] One of the more important policy questions in this area is whether these types of programs can succeed at the scale of major ecosystems like the California Bay-Delta, or whether they are viable only at the level of smaller watersheds, where cooperation may be easier to achieve among smaller networks of policy actors.

The Administrative Presidency and Collaborative Management

The ebb and flow of collaborative management has been affected heavily by administrative presidency strategies, because the involvement of federal agencies provides an opportunity to exercise political control. The Clinton administration was instrumental in bringing collaborative management to the forefront of conservation policy; it was directly involved with the creation of the Northwest Forest Plan, the Sierra Nevada Framework, and the Everglades Program, among others. Secretary of the Interior Bruce Babbitt was a champion of collaborative management and spent a lot of time spearheading specific projects such as reforming rangeland management.[55] The Clinton administration also made a variety of administrative changes to better integrate ecosystem management into the standard operating procedures of natural resource management agencies.[56]

In line with Bush's other policies, his administration used the administrative presidency in attempts to undermine Clinton-era ecosystem management programs. In response to several lawsuits from the timber industry, Bush used the sweetheart settlement strategy to weaken the survey-and-manage and aquatic conservation strategies of the Northwest Forest Plan. However, the courts set aside these changes in response to environmental group litigation, leaving the Northwest Forest Plan mostly intact.[57] In 2004 the Bush administration revised the Sierra Nevada Framework to increase logging levels and allowable tree diameters, and to make the framework consistent with the Quincy Library Group's plan. The group's initial plan called for more logging than allowed under the Clinton-era Sierra Nevada Framework. In general, federal funding for ecosystem management programs like the Chesapeake Bay Program, the Comprehensive Everglades Restoration Plan, and CALFED has fallen substantially short of what was promised. While funding shortfalls are also attributable to an unsympathetic Republican Congress and diversion of money for other priorities like the Iraq War, the Bush administration certainly did not fight hard to keep federal money flowing to these projects.

The Coexistence of Cooperation and Conflict

An underappreciated fact is that collaborative management often coexists with conflict. In cases like that of the Quincy Library Group, collaboration was catalyzed by a stalemate in which disputants become weary of ongoing legal battles without a clear winner. In other instances, collaboration is stimulated by some type of regulatory process or a court order. For example, in the remand of the 2004 Columbia River BiOps, the court ordered the disputants to engage in a collaborative process to develop an agreement on dam operations. The resulting Columbia Basin Fish Accords are basically a peace treaty that supports the most recent BiOps released in 2008.[58] In the Klamath, collaborative negotiations are currently ongoing under the rubric of Federal Energy Regulatory Commission relicensing of the PacifiCorp dams, including discussions of dam removal to comply with ESA requirements.[59]

The trend toward collaborative management continued to increase even while Bush administrative changes were evoking conflict. To some extent, the collaborative management concept is reflected in the Bush administration's four C's: communication, consultation, and cooperation, all in the service of conservation.[60] But most environmentalists view the four C's as greenwashing that uses the language of collaboration to obscure the administrative rollback of environmental laws. However, collaboration is really thriving at the local and state levels, with more new watershed groups and partnerships being formed all the time. This level of activity suggests that there are important roles for bottom-up, collaborative institutions, given that the boundary-spanning nature of ecosystems will always challenge more centralized policy institutions.

Effectiveness: Collaborative Management at a Crossroads

Given these issues and the relative youth of collaborative management, its effectiveness is a subject of considerable debate. Critics suggest collaborative management is symbolic policy that preserves the status quo by deflecting attention away from underlying problems. Consensus may produce lowest-common-denominator decisions rather than good decisions. Collaborative planning also may create unnecessary layers of decision making and cause cooperation to decrease in other existing planning processes. From a constitutional perspective, legal scholars worry that collaborative policy may abdicate federal authority to local groups.[61]

Research focused on collaborative management has provided no conclusive evidence on its effectiveness.[62] The record of large-scale ecosystem management programs is mixed at best. Perhaps most telling is that the key resource dilemmas targeted by the programs have not been solved. Populations of salmon and delta smelt (another threatened species) are at historically low levels in the California Bay-Delta. Although there were surprisingly high returns of Coho salmon to the Columbia River in fall 2008, the spring-run Chinook populations remained low. Water quality goals in the Chesapeake are not expected to be met on time, and water quality standards in Everglades National Park continue to be violated. In the Pacific Northwest, there has been a substantial decrease in the harvest of old-growth timber, but populations of northern spotted owls are not increasing; at least they have not disappeared.

These environmental problems are often accompanied by institutional collapse. CALFED provides the most spectacular example: the executive director and lead scientist resigned in 2004,[63] several independent reports criticized CALFED's governance structure, legislative oversight accused CALFED of spending money without results, stakeholders moved water management decisions outside the CALFED process (for example, using environmental litigation), the CALFED Bay-Delta Authority voted to disband itself in 2003, and the environmental analysis of the CALFED plan was rejected by California lower courts (although it was upheld on appeal).[64] Upon close examination, most large-scale ecosystem management programs exhibit similar signs of trouble, although it may be that success is possible only in the long term—but how long?

The record may be more hopeful for the thousands of smaller-scale partnerships. Authors like Edward Weber argue that smaller, local partnerships like the Henry's Fork Watershed Council in Idaho strengthen accountability to stakeholders at the local, community, state, and national levels.[65] In addition, stakeholders in these partnerships reported increased levels of trust and greater consideration of other stakeholders in their watersheds. A recent government report examining seven other case studies, including the widely acclaimed Blackfoot Challenge (Montana), also found that local partnerships improve relationships and cooperation among stakeholders.[66] But neither Weber nor the GAO closely examines environmental outcomes, which remain the largest uncertainty about the effectiveness of collaborative management. As the research on collaborative management continues to develop, the most likely conclusion is that collaborative management is successful in some situations but not in others; there are no panaceas in environmental policy.[67]

Conclusion: The Future of Natural Resource Management

What does the future hold? The administrative strategies of newly elected President Barack Obama will likely move away from those of the Bush administration and shift toward more pro-environmental policies. Environmental groups were quick to predict a more friendly administration under Obama, with hopes of rolling back some of Bush's rule changes (especially the late ones) and more pro-environmental political appointees.[68] Obama has promised increased funding for national parks, more emphasis on green energy with restrictions on oil and gas development on public lands, increased funding for wildfire management without cutting into other forest service programs, support for the Roadless Rule, and cooperation with

Congress to pass more wilderness legislation. Obama's overall approach to governing natural resources resembles that of the Clinton administration in some respects; in fact, many of Obama's transition advisors and appointees to natural resource positions were previously in the Clinton administration (for example, Deputy Interior Secretary David Hayes). Obama's appointment of Ken Salazar as secretary of the interior follows the classic pattern of interior west appointees, and Salazar's agricultural background signals a willingness to build political bridges among environmental, hook-and-bullet, and agricultural stewardship interests. However, the Obama administration will likely slow down the pace of economic development of public lands, as evidenced by the February 2009 withdrawal from energy leasing of 77 parcels of BLM land near Arches and Canyonlands National Parks in Utah. These facts demonstrate that administrative control of natural resource policies is not a partisan issue—it is only the direction in which the changes go that depend on political ideology.

The spread of collaborative management also shows no sign of slowing down, despite enduring questions about its effectiveness. Obama favors a "consensus" approach that will likely reinvigorate existing collaborative programs, and probably catalyze the creation of new ones. The promised benefits of the approach are attractive to stakeholders who are tired of conflict. It may be too early to condemn the effectiveness of collaborative management because it takes time for ecosystems to change, and the current methods of policy research need more development. Even if collaborative management has serious problems, it may be better than the alternative of doing nothing about ecosystem-scale problems. Alternative approaches to environmental policy, such as regulations and market mechanisms (for example, pollution trading), have solved some important problems but left many conflicts unresolved. Proponents of collaborative ecosystem management argue that local partnerships are the biggest hope for solving some of these complex issues. Critics argue that a stronger regulatory approach will be necessary if the underlying natural resource dilemmas continue to linger. Regardless of the debate, the mix of policy tools that evolves over time will continue to be a product of political negotiations among Congress, the president, the courts, interest groups, and other policy stakeholders.

Suggested Web Sites

Center for Biological Diversity (www.biologicaldiversity.org) One of the most active environmental groups in the country working on biodiversity issues; offers a lot of detailed information about ongoing policy conflicts, including links to relevant government documents.

Defenders of Wildlife (www.defenders.org) Organization dedicated to the preservation of all wild animals and native plants in their natural community; provides action alerts and information.

Greenwire (www.eenews.net/gw) The best Internet news service on environmental issues, including many direct links to key decision documents.

High Country News (www.hcn.org) A biweekly newspaper that reports on the West's natural resources, public lands, and changing communities; offers more in-depth articles than are found in Greenwire.

U.S. Department of the Interior (www.doi.gov) Gateway to information about many of the conflicts discussed in this chapter.

Notes

1. Bureau of Land Management, "Roan Plateau Record of Decision Facts and Figures," 2007, www.blm.gov/rmp/co/roanplateau/documents/Facts_and_Figures.pdf.
2. Noelle Straub, "Controversial Roan Plateau Lease Sales Yield a Record $114M," *Landletter,* August 21, 2008, www.eenews.net/Landletter/2008/08/21/12/.
3. Terry Moe and Scott Wilson, "Presidents and the Politics of Bureaucratic Structure," *Law and Contemporary Problems* 57 (1994): 1–44; Robert F. Durant, *The Administrative Presidency Revisited* (New York: SUNY Press, 1992); Richard W. Waterman, *Presidential Influence and the Administrative State* (Knoxville: University of Tennessee Press, 1989).
4. Natural Resources Defense Council, *Rewriting the Rules 3d Annual Edition: The Bush Administration's Assault on the Environment* (Washington, D.C.: NRDC, 2004).
5. For excellent overviews of Bush administration politics, see Holly Doremus, "Science Plays Defense: Natural Resources Management in the Bush Administration," *Ecology Law Quarterly* 32 (2005): 248; David H. Getches, "The Legacy of the Bush II Administration in Natural Resources: A Work in Progress," *Ecology Law Quarterly* 32 (2005); John Leshy, "Natural Resources Policy in the Bush (II) Administration: An Outsider's Somewhat Jaundiced Assessment," *Duke Environmental Law and Policy* 347 (2004); Robert B. Keiter, "Breaking Faith with Nature: The Bush Administration and Public Land Policy," *Journal of Land, Resources, and Environmental Law* 27 (2007).
6. Judith A. Layzer, *Natural Experiments: Ecosystem-Based Management and the Environment* (Cambridge: MIT Press, 2008).
7. Garrett Hardin, "The Tragedy of the Commons," *Science* 162 (1968): 1243–1248. One of the most famous passages defines the problem (p. 1244): "Therein is the tragedy. Each man is locked into a system that compels him to increase his herd without limit—in a world that is limited. Ruin is the destination toward which all men rush, each pursuing his own best interest in a society that believes in the freedom of the commons. Freedom in a commons brings ruin to all."
8. Elinor Ostrom and Edella Schlager, "The Formation of Property Rights," in *The Rights to Nature,* ed. S. S. Hanna, C. Folke, and K.-G. Maler (Washington, D.C.: Island Press, 1996).
9. George Cameron Coggins, Charles F. Wilkinson, and John D. Leshy, *Federal Public Land and Resources Law* (New York: Foundation Press, 2002).
10. Jonathon Thomson, "As Interior Turns: An Eight-Year Soap Opera in Which Federal Officials Screwed the Environment, the Taxpayers, and Each Other," *High Country News,* December 22, 2008.
11. Union of Concerned Scientists, "Scientific Integrity in Policy Making: Further Investigation of the Bush Administration's Misuse of Science"; "Statement: Restoring Scientific Integrity in Policymaking," www.ucsusa.org.
12. U.S Department of the Interior, Office of Inspector General, "Report of Investigation: Julie MacDonald, Deputy Assistant Secretary of Fish, Wildlife, and Parks," 2005.

13. U.S. Department of the Interior, Office of Inspector General, "Report of Investigation: The Endangered Species Act and the Conflict between Science and Policy," December 15, 2008.

14. Union of Concerned Scientists, "U.S. Fish & Wildlife Service Survey Summary," www .ucsusa.org/scientific_integrity/interference/us-fish-wildlife-service-survey.html.

15. David Malakoff, "Science Politics: White House Rebuts Charges It Has Politicized Science," *Science* 304 (5668): 184–185.

16. Ray Ring, "Freaky Fridays with the Bush Administration," *High Country News,* November 10, 2003.

17. Ray Ring, "Tipping the Scales," *High Country News,* February 16, 2004.

18. Michael Blumm, "The Bush Administration's Sweetheart Settlement Policy: A Trojan Horse Strategy for Advancing Commodity Production on Public Lands," *Environmental Law Reporter* 34 (2004): 10397–10420.

19. Gary Bryner, "The National Energy Policy: Assessing Energy Policy Choices," *University of Colorado Law Review* 73 (2002).

20. Executive Order 13212—Actions to Expedite Energy-Related Projects, *Federal Register* 66, 99 (May 22, 2001); see also Executive Order 13211—Actions Concerning Regulatory Actions That Significantly Affect Energy Supply, Distribution, or Use, *Federal Register* 66, 99 (May 22, 2001).

21. U.S. Government Accountability Office, "Oil and Gas Development: Increased Permitting Activity Has Lessened BLM's Ability to Meet Its Environmental Protection Responsibilities," GAO-05-418, June 2005.

22. April Reese, "The Leasing Protest Game," *High Country News,* April 16, 2008.

23. Emily Steinmetz, "The Great Giveaway: Utah BLM Swings the Door Wide for ATVs and Energy Development," *High Country News,* October 13, 2008.

24. U.S. Government Accountability Office, "Oil and Gas Development."

25. April Reese, "Groups File Suit of Leases in Inventories Roadless Areas in Utah," *Land Letter,* May 4, 2004, www.eenews.net/Landletter/2006/05/04/6/.

26. Dan Berman, "Group Sues BLM over Wyoming Lease Plans," *Land Letter,* August 23, 2007, www.eenews.net/Landletter/2007/08/23/9/.

27. Sven Eric Jorgensen, Robert Costanza, and Fu-Liu Xu, *Handbook of Ecological Indicators for Assessment of Ecosystem Health* (Boca Raton, Fla.: Taylor & Francis, 2005).

28. Jacqueline Vaughn Switzer and Hanna Cortner, *George W. Bush's Healthy Forests: Reframing the Environmental Debate* (Boulder: University Press of Colorado, 2005).

29. The Forest Service maintains the world's largest road network, with maintenance needs already far in excess of available budgets.

30. U.S. Government Accountability Office, "Forest Service: Information on Appeals and Litigation Involving Fuels Reduction Activities," GAO-04-52, October 24, 2003.

31. Holly Doremus and Dan A. Tarlock, *Water War in the Klamath Basin* (Covelo, Calif.: Island Press, 2008).

32. Tom Hamburger, "Oregon Water Saga Illuminates Rove's Methods with Agencies," *Wall Street Journal,* July 30, 2003.

33. Jo Becker and Barton Gellman, "Leaving No Tracks," *Washington Post,* June 27, 2007.

34. California Department of Fish and Game, *September 2002 Klamath River Fish-Kill: Final Analysis of Contributing Factors and Impacts* (California Department of Fish and Game, Northern California-North Coast Region, 2004).

35. National Marine Fisheries Service, Southwest Region, "Biological Opinion: Operation of the Klamath Project," June 17, 2008, http://swr.nmfs.noaa.gov/pdf/ Klamath_Ops_Draft_Final_June_17.pdf.

36. Patrick Reis, "Judge Demands Urgent Changes to Protect Fish in Calif.'s Central Valley," *Land Letter,* July 24, 2008.

37. Allison Freeman, "Larger GOP Majorities in Congress Propel ESA Revamp," *Land Letter,* November 11, 2004.

38. Allison Freeman, "Chafee Says ESA Negotiators Want to Avoid 'Pombo-ized' Conference," *E & E Daily,* February 6, 2006.

39. Natalie M. Henry, "Administration Lops 5 Percent Off ESA Budget," *E & E Daily*, February 4, 2004.
40. Margot Roosevelt, "Endangered Species List Jeopardized, Critics Say," *Los Angeles Times*, July 5, 2007.
41. U.S. Fish and Wildlife Service, "Special Rule for the Polar Bear," 73 *Federal Register* 28306 (May 15, 2008).
42. Rick Steiner, "Sarah Palin's Record on Environment Is Abysmal," *Seattle Post-Intelligencer*, September 7, 2008.
43. Dina Cappiello, "Bush Seeks to Ease Endangered-Species Rules," *Seattle Post-Intelligencer*, August 12, 2008.
44. Dino Cappiello, "Inside Washington: Fast Readers Wanted," *Associated Press*, October 21, 2008; Dina Cappiello, "U.S. Claims Rule Changes Don't Threaten Wildlife," *Associated Press*, October 27, 2008.
45. Jeffrey Smith, "A Last Push to Deregulate," *Washington Post*, October 31, 2008.
46. Stephen Power, "Bush Administration Rushes Regulatory Changes Before Time Is Up," *Wall Street Journal*, October 25, 2008.
47. Elinor Ostrom, *Governing the Commons: The Evolution of Institutions for Collective Action* (New York: Cambridge University Press, 1990).
48. Jules Pretty, "Social Capital and the Collective Management of Resources," *Science* 302 (2003): 1912–1914.
49. CALFED Bay-Delta Program, *CALFED Bay-Delta Program Record of Decision, 2003*, http://calwater.ca.gov/content/Documents/ROD8-28-00.pdf.
50. CALFED Bay-Delta Program, *CALFED Bay-Delta Program: Program Performance Assessment, 2007*, http://calwater.ca.gov/PerformanceTracking/about_program_performance.html.
51. Pat and George Terhune, "Quincy Library Group Case Study" (presented at the Workshop for Engaging, Empowering and Negotiating Community: Strategies for Conservation and Development, West Virginia University, Oct. 8–10, 1998), www.qlg.org/pub/miscdoc/terhunecasestudy.htm.
52. Lauren Rule, "Enforcing Ecosystem Management under the Northwest Forest Plan: The Judicial Role," *Fordham Environmental Law Journal* 12 (fall 2000): 211.
53. Robert B. Keiter, "Breaking Faith with Nature: The Bush Administration and Public Land Policy," *Journal of Land, Resources, and Environmental Law* 27 (2007).
54. Mark Lubell, Mark Schneider, John T. Scholz, and Mihriye Mete, "Watershed Partnerships and the Emergence of Collective Action Institutions," *American Journal of Political Science* 46 (2002): 148.
55. U.S. Department of the Interior, *Rangeland Reform '94: Draft Environmental Impact Statement* (Washington D.C.: Department of the Interior, Bureau of Land Management, 1994).
56. Robert B. Keiter, *Keeping Faith with Nature: Ecosystems, Democracy, and America's Public Lands* (New Haven: Yale University Press, 2003).
57. Ibid., note 36.
58. Bonneville Power Administration, *Administrator's Record of Decision on Columbia Basin Fish Accords*, www.bpa.gov/corporate/pubs/RODS/2008/MOA_ROD.pdf.
59. Ibid., note 26.
60. John Tierney, "Trying for Balance at Interior," *New York Times*, June 9, 2003.
61. George C. Coggins, "Regulating Federal Natural Resources: A Summary Case against Devolved Evolution," *Ecology Law Quarterly* 25 (1998).
62. Tomas M. Koontz, and Craig W. Thomas, "What Do We Know and Need to Know about the Environmental Outcomes of Collaborative Management?" *Public Administration Review* 66 (2006): 111–121; Paul A. Sabatier, Will Focht, Mark Lubell, Zev Trachtenburg, Arnold Vedlitz, and Marty Matlock, *Swimming Upstream: Collaborative Approaches to Watershed Management* (Cambridge: MIT Press, 2005).
63. Don Thompson, "Delta Problems Lead to Questions about Agency Designed to Save It," *Associated Press*, October 23, 2005.

64. Matt Jenkins, "Trouble in the Delta," *High Country News,* February 6, 2005; Dave Owen, "Law, Environmental Dynamism, and Reliability: The Rise and Fall of CALFED," *Environmental Law* 37 (2007): 1145.

65. Edward P. Weber, *Bringing Society Back In: Grassroots Ecosystem Management, Accountability, and Sustainable Communities* (Cambridge: MIT Press, 2003).

66. U.S. Government Accountability Office, "Natural Resource Management: Opportunities Exist to Enhance Federal Participation in Collaborative Efforts to Reduce Conflicts and Improve Natural Resource Conditions," GAO-08-262, February 2008.

67. Elinor Ostrom, Marco A. Janssen, and John M. Anderies. "Going Beyond Panaceas," *Proceedings of the National Academy of Sciences* 104 (2007): 15176–15178.

68. Noelle Straub, "Public Lands: A New Direction under Obama," *Greenwire,* November 7, 2008, www.eenews.net/Greenwire/2008/11/07/1/.

9

Applying Market Principles to Environmental Policy
Sheila M. Olmstead

Each day you make decisions that require tradeoffs. Should you walk to work or drive? Walking takes more time; driving costs money for gasoline and parking. You might also consider the benefits of exercise if you walk, or the costs to the environment of the emissions if you drive. In considering this question, you need to determine how to allocate important scarce resources—your time and money—to achieve a particular goal.

Economics is the study of the allocation of scarce resources, and economists typically apply two simple concepts, efficiency and cost-effectiveness, for making decisions systematically. Let's take a concrete environmental policy example. The Snake River in the Pacific Northwest provides water for drinking, agricultural irrigation, transportation, industrial production, and hydroelectricity generation. It also supports rapidly dwindling populations of endangered salmon species. If there is not enough water to provide as much of each of these services as it would take to satisfy everyone, we must trade off one good thing for another.

Some scientific evidence indicates that removing hydroelectric dams on the upper Snake River may assist in the recovery of salmon populations. Salmon declines may also be caused by too little water in the river, which might be addressed by reducing agricultural or urban water withdrawals. Each of these measures could be implemented at some cost. Benefit-cost analysis would compare the benefits of each measure (the expected increase in salmon populations) to its costs. An *efficient* policy choice would maximize net benefits; we would choose the policy that offered the greatest difference between benefits and costs.

What if the Endangered Species Act requires that a specific level of salmon recovery be achieved? In this case, the benefits of salmon recovery may never be quantified. But economics can still play a role in choosing policies to achieve salmon recovery. Cost-effectiveness analysis would compare the costs of each potential policy intervention that could achieve the mandated salmon recovery goal. Decision makers would then choose the least-cost or *cost-effective* policy option.

This discussion is highly simplified. Explaining the causes of Snake River salmon decline and forecasting the impact of policy changes on salmon populations are complex scientific tasks, and different experts have different models that produce different results.[1] The tradeoffs can also be multidimensional. Removing dams may sound like a great environmental idea, but hydroelectric power is an important source of clean energy in the Pacific

Northwest. Would the dams' hydroelectricity be replaced by coal- or gas-fired power plants? What would be the impacts of the increased emissions of local and global air pollutants? In this chapter we discuss some simple economic tools for examining such tradeoffs. The basic intuition we develop functions well even in complex settings.

Economic Concepts and Environmental Policy

Economic Efficiency and Benefit-Cost
Analysis of Environmental Policy

Many countries regulate emissions of sulfur dioxide (SO_2), an air pollutant that can damage human health and also causes acid rain, which harms forest and aquatic ecosystems. In the United States, power plants are a major source of SO_2 emissions, regulated under the Clean Air Act (CAA). As evidence regarding the damages from acid rain in the northeastern United States accumulated in the 1980s, Congress considered updating the CAA so that it would cover many old power plants not regulated by the original legislation. This process culminated in the 1990 CAA Amendments, which set a new goal for SO_2 emissions reductions from older power plants. Assume that it is 1989, and you have been asked to tell the U.S. Congress how much SO_2 emissions should be reduced, from an economic perspective.

First, consider the costs of reducing SO_2 emissions. Economic costs are *opportunity costs*—what we must give up by abating each ton of emissions, rather than spending that money on other important things. Emissions abatement can be achieved by removing SO_2 emissions from power plant smokestacks using a "scrubber," which requires an up-front investment, as well as labor and materials for routine operation. Power plants can also change the fuels they use to generate electricity, switching from high-sulfur to more expensive low-sulfur coal, or from coal to natural gas. Spending this money on pollution control leaves less to spend to improve a plant's operations or increase output. These costs are passed on by the firm to its employees (in the form of reduced wages), stockholders (in terms of lower share prices), consumers (in the form of higher prices), and other stakeholders.

If required to reduce emissions, firms will accomplish the cheapest abatement first, and resort to more and more expensive options as the amount of required abatement increases. The cost of abating each ton of pollution tends to rise slowly at first, as we abate the first tons of SO_2 emissions, and then more quickly. This typical pattern of costs is represented by the lower, convex curve in Figure 9-1, labeled total costs ($C(Q)$).

The value of reducing emissions declines as we abate more and more tons of SO_2. At high levels of SO_2 emissions (low abatement), this pollutant causes acid rain as well as respiratory and cardiovascular ailments in populated areas. But as the air gets cleaner, low SO_2 concentrations cause fewer problems. Thus, while the total benefits of reducing SO_2 may always increase as we reduce emissions, the benefit of each additional ton of abatement will

Figure 9-1   Comparing the Total Benefits and Costs of Pollution
Abatement

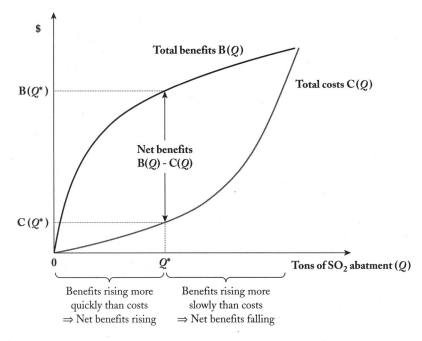

go down. This typical pattern of benefits is represented by the upper, concave curve in Figure 9-1, labeled total benefits, or *B(Q)*.[2]

Economic efficiency requires that we find the policy that will give us the greatest net benefits—the biggest difference between total benefits and total costs. In Figure 9-1, the efficient amount of SO_2 emissions abatement is marked as Q^*, where the vertical distance between the benefit and cost curves is biggest. Why would it be inefficient to abate more or less than Q^* tons of SO_2 emissions? To the right of Q^*, the total benefits of reducing pollution are still positive and still rising. But costs are rising faster than benefits. So for every dollar in benefit we gain by eliminating a ton of emissions, we incur greater costs. To the left of Q^*, the benefits of each ton of abatement are rising more quickly than costs, so if we move to the left, we will also reduce the policy's net benefits.

Note that we have emphasized the costs and benefits of reducing each individual ton of pollution. Where total benefits increase quickly, at low levels of abatement, the benefit of an additional ton is very high. Where the total benefits curve flattens out, the benefit of an additional ton is low. This concept of the decreasing "benefit of an additional ton" defines the economic concept of *marginal benefit*. On the cost side, where total costs are almost flat, at low levels of abatement, the cost of adding an additional ton is very low. As total costs get very steep, the cost of abating an additional ton is high. This concept of the increasing "cost of an additional ton" defines the concept of *marginal cost*. The efficient quantity of pollution abatement is the number of tons at which the marginal benefit of abating an additional ton is exactly equal to the marginal cost.[3]

What we have just done is a benefit-cost analysis of a potential SO_2 emissions reduction policy. If you had completed the analysis to advise Congress, the information amassed on benefits, costs, and the efficient quantity of pollution to abate would illuminate the tradeoffs involved in improving air quality. When Congress passed the CAA Amendments of 1990, it eventually required 10 million tons of SO_2 emissions abatement, roughly a 50 percent reduction in power plant emissions of this pollutant. Was this the efficient level of pollution control? Subsequent analysis (particularly of the human health benefits of avoided SO_2 emissions) suggests that the efficient amount of SO_2 abatement would have been higher than the 10-million-ton goal.[4] But economic efficiency is one of many criteria considered in the making of environmental policy, some others of which are detailed elsewhere in this book. An excellent summary of how economists see the role of benefit-cost analysis in public decision-making is offered by Nobel laureate Kenneth Arrow and coauthors:

> Although formal benefit-cost analysis should not be viewed as either necessary or sufficient for designing sensible public policy, it can provide an exceptionally useful framework for consistently organizing disparate information, and in this way, it can greatly improve the process and, hence, the outcome of policy analysis."[5]

There are many critiques of benefit-cost analysis.[6] A common critique is that basing environmental policy decisions on whether benefits outweigh costs ignores important political and ethical considerations. As is clear from the preceding quotation, most economists reject the idea that policy should be designed using strict benefit-cost tests. Even when citizens and their governments design policy based on concerns other than efficiency, however, collecting information about benefits and costs can be extremely useful. Some critics of benefit-cost analysis object to placing a dollar value on environmental goods and services, suggesting that these "priceless" resources are devalued when treated in monetary terms.[7] But benefit-cost analysis simply makes the tradeoffs represented by a policy choice explicit—it does not create the tradeoffs themselves. When environmental policy is made, we establish how much we are willing to spend to protect endangered species or avoid the human health impacts of pollution exposure. Whether we estimate the value of such things in advance and use these numbers to guide policy, or set policy first based on other criteria and then back out our implied values for such things, we have still made the same tradeoff. No economic argument can suggest whether explicit or implicit consideration of benefits and costs is *ethically* preferable. But the choice does not affect the outcome that a tradeoff has been made. Used as one of many inputs to the consideration of policy choices, benefit-cost analysis is a powerful and illuminating tool.

Figure 9-2   Marginal Costs of Protecting the California Condor

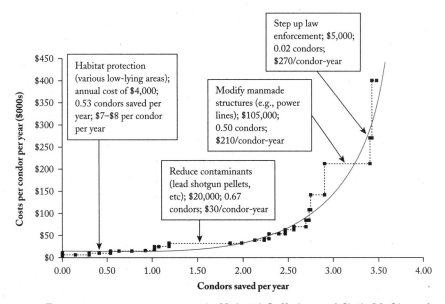

The Measurement of Environmental Benefits and Costs

Thus far, we have discussed benefits and costs abstractly. In an actual economic analysis, benefits and costs would be measured, so that the horizontal and vertical axes of Figure 9-1 would take on specific numerical units. Quantifying the costs of environmental policies can require rough approximations. For example, one study has estimated the costs of protecting California condors, an endangered species, following the near extinction of these enormous birds and their later reintroduction into the wild from a captive breeding program.[8] Figure 9-2 describes the costs of each potential step that policymakers might take to protect the condor population; when we graph the number of condors saved per year against the cost of each potential step taken to save them, we sketch out a marginal cost curve that is upward sloping like those we discussed for pollution abatement.

Economists measure the benefits of an environmental policy as the sum of individuals' willingness to pay for the changes it may induce. This notion is clearly anthropocentric—the changes induced by an environmental policy are economically beneficial only to the extent that human beings value them. This does not suggest improvements in ecosystem function or other "nonhuman" effects of a policy have no value. Many people value open space, endangered species preservation, and biodiversity and have shown through their memberships in environmental advocacy groups, votes in local referenda, and lobbying activities on global environmental issues that they are willing to sacrifice much for these causes. The economic value of an environmental amenity (like clean air or water, or open space) comprises the value that people experience from using it, and so-called nonuse value. Nonuse value captures the value people have for simply knowing that an endangered species (like the grizzly bear) or a pristine area (like the Arctic National Wildlife Refuge) exists, even if they never plan to see or use such resources. To carry out a benefit-cost analysis, however, it is not enough to know that people have some value for a policy's goal; we must measure that value to compare it to the policy's costs.

An in-depth discussion of environmental benefit estimation methods is beyond the scope of this chapter.[9] But we can sketch out the basic intuition behind the major approaches. Some benefits of environmental policies can be measured straightforwardly through their impacts on actual markets. For example, if we are considering a policy to reduce water pollution that may increase commercial fish populations, estimates of the increased market value of the total catch would be included in an estimate of the policy's total benefits.

For most environmental goods and services, however, measuring benefits is much trickier. The values that people have for using environmental amenities can often be measured indirectly through their behavior in markets. For example, many people spend money on wilderness vacations. While they are not purchasing wilderness, per se, when they do this, economists can estimate the recreational value of wilderness sites from travelers' expenditures. Travel-cost models are a class of statistical methods that economists use for this purpose.

Another method, the hedonic housing price model, is based on the idea that what people are willing to pay for a home reflects, in part, the environmental attributes of its neighborhood. Economists use statistical techniques to estimate what portion of a home's price is determined by environmental attributes, such as the surrounding air quality, controlling for other price determinants, like the home's physical characteristics, school district quality, and proximity to jobs and transportation. To estimate the value of human health impacts of an environmental policy, economists primarily use hedonic wage studies. These models estimate peoples' willingness to pay for small decreases in risks to life and health by examining the differences in wages for jobs with different levels of risk. As in the hedonic housing models, statistical methods must be used to control for the many other determinants of wages (for example, how skilled or educated a worker must be to take a particular job).

Travel-cost and hedonic models are *revealed preference* models—they estimate how people value a particular aspect of an environmental amenity from their actual behavior, revealed in markets. But if we were to stop with values expressed in markets, the benefits we could estimate for things like wilderness areas and species preservation would be incomplete. Nonuse value leaves no footprint in any market. Thus a *stated preference* approach must be used to quantify nonuse values. Economists design carefully structured surveys to ask people how much they are willing to pay for a specific improvement in environmental quality or a natural resource amenity, and they sum across individuals to assess a society's willingness to pay.

The Environmental Protection Agency's (EPA's) 1985 benefit-cost analysis of reducing the lead content of gasoline offers an example of what each side of such an analysis might include. The analysis quantified the main benefits from phasing out leaded gas: reduced human health damages from lead exposure (retardation of children's cognitive and physiological development and exacerbation of high blood pressure in adult males), reduction in other local air pollutants from vehicle emissions (since leaded gas destroyed catalytic converters, designed to reduce emissions), and lower costs of engine maintenance and related increases in fuel economy. The costs were primarily installation of new refinery equipment and production of alternative fuel additives. The study found that the lead phasedown policy had projected annual net benefits of $7 billion (in 1983 dollars), even though only a portion of benefits were actually quantified. The health benefits of the regulation that the EPA estimated included the avoided costs of medical care and of remedial education for affected children. Americans, if surveyed, would likely have had significant willingness to pay to avoid the lasting health and cognitive impacts of lead exposure, but these benefits were never quantified. Even with these gaps, acknowledged by the study's authors, this analysis helped to "sell" the regulation; a few years earlier, the EPA had decided upon a much weaker rule, citing potential costs to refineries.[10]

The fact that the EPA did not quantify some benefits of the U.S. lead phasedown brings us to an important point. In some cases existing estimation methods may be sufficient to evaluate the benefits of an environmental policy but are too complex and expensive to implement. In the lead case, this was immaterial. The benefits of the policy exceeded the costs by a large margin, even excluding those (presumably large) unquantified benefits, so the eventual policy decision was not affected by this choice. In other cases, when benefits are hard to quantify, it may matter for the ultimate policy outcome.

In some cases, economic tools simply prove insufficient to estimate the benefits (or avoided damages) from environmental policy. For example, climate science suggests that sudden, catastrophic events (like the reversal of thermohaline circulations, or sudden collapse of the Greenland or West Antarctic ice sheets) are possible outcomes of the current warming trend. The probabilities of such disastrous events may be very small. Combined with the fact that important climate change impacts may occur in the distant future, this makes estimating the benefits of current climate change policy a challenging and controversial task.[11] Some analysts have attempted, incorrectly, to estimate the benefits of avoiding the elimination of vital ecosystem services, such as pollination and nutrient cycling, using economic benefit estimation tools.[12] These tools measure our collective willingness to pay for small changes in the status quo. The elimination of Earth's vital ecosystem services would cause dramatic shifts in human and market activity of all kinds. While the benefit estimation techniques we have discussed are well suited to assessing the net effect of specific policies, like reducing air pollutant concentrations, or setting aside land to preserve open space, they are inadequate to the task of measuring the value of drastic changes in global ecosystems—efforts to use them for this purpose have resulted in, as one economist quipped, a "serious underestimate of infinity."[13] Estimation of the benefits from environmental policy is the subject of a great deal of economic research, and much progress has been made. But the limits of these tools remain a significant challenge to comprehensive benefit-cost analysis in some cases.

Cost-effective Environmental Policy

Economists' goal of maximizing net benefits is one of many competing goals in the policy process. Even when an environmental standard is inefficient (too stringent, or not stringent enough), economic analysis can still help to select the particular policy instruments used to achieve that goal. Earlier we defined the concept of cost-effectiveness as choosing the policy that can achieve a given environmental standard at least cost. Let's return to our SO_2 example to see how this works in practice.

Imagine that you are a policy analyst at the EPA, given the job of figuring out how U.S. power plants will meet the 10-million-ton reduction in SO_2 emissions required under the 1990 CAA Amendments. One important issue to consider is how much the policy will cost. All else equal, you would like to attain the new standard as cheaply as possible. We can reduce this problem to a simple case to demonstrate how an economist would answer this question. Assume that the entire 10-million-ton reduction will be achieved by two power plants, firms A and B. Each has a set of SO_2 abatement technologies, and the sequence of technologies for each firm and their associated costs form the marginal cost curves in Figure 9-3, labeled MC_A and MC_B. Notice that abatement increases from left to right for firm A, and from right to left for firm B. At any point along the horizontal axis, the sum of the two firms' emissions reductions will always equal 10 million tons, as the CAA Amendments require.

Let's begin with one simple solution that seems like a fair approach: divide the total required reduction in half and ask each firm to abate 5 million tons of SO_2. This allocation of pollution control is represented by the left-most dotted vertical line in Figure 9-3, and is often referred to as a "uniform pollution control standard," because the abatement requirement is uniform across firms. Is this the cheapest way to reduce pollution by 10 million tons? Suppose we require firm A to reduce one extra ton and require firm B to reduce one ton less? We would still achieve a 10-million-ton reduction, but that last ton would cost less than it did before. Firm B's cost curve lies above A's at the uniform standard, so when we shift responsibility for abating that ton from B to A, we reduce the total cost of achieving the new standard. How long can we move to the right along the horizontal axis and continue to lower total costs? Until the marginal costs of abatement for the two firms are exactly equal: where the two curves intersect, when firm A abates 6 million tons and B abates 4 million tons.

Figure 9-3   Cost-effective Pollution Abatement by Two Firms

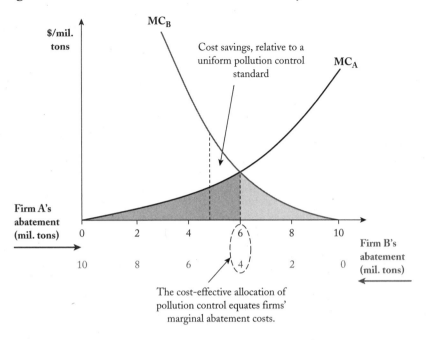

The cost savings from allocating abatement in this way, rather than using the uniform standard is equivalent to the difference in costs between firm A and firm B for the last million tons of abatement. On Figure 9-3, that is equal to the area between the two firms' marginal cost curves (the cost to firm B minus the cost to firm A), bounded by the dotted lines marking the uniform standard and the cost-effective allocation. Working in two dimensions, we cannot easily demonstrate how this works for more firms. But the rule of thumb for a cost-effective environmental policy instrument is the same for a large number of firms as it is in this simple example: a pollution control policy minimizes costs if the marginal abatement costs of all firms contributing to the aggregate abatement target are equal. The bigger the differences in abatement costs across regulated firms, the larger the potential cost savings.

You may have noticed that in order to identify the cost-effective pollution control allocation in this simple case, we needed a lot of information about each firm's abatement costs—we used their marginal cost curves to accomplish the task. As an EPA policy analyst, it is unlikely that you would have this information, and even less likely if we move from two power plants to the thousands eventually covered by the CAA Amendments of 1990. In a competitive market, the structure of firms' costs is proprietary information that they will not likely share with regulators. So how can a cost-effective pollution control policy be designed?

One class of environmental policy instruments, often called "market-based" or "incentive-based" approaches, do not require regulators to have specific information about individual firms' marginal abatement costs in order to attain a particular pollution control standard at least cost. In the case of the SO_2 emissions reduction required by the CAA Amendments of 1990, regulators chose one of these approaches, a system of tradable pollution permits, to achieve this goal.

A market for tradable pollution permits works quite simply. Return to the world of two firms, and assume that you have advised the EPA administrator to allocate responsibility for 5 million tons of SO_2 emissions abatement to each of the two firms. You add, however, the provision that the firms should be able to trade their allocations, so long as the aggregate reduction of 10 million tons is achieved. If we begin at the (5 million, 5 million) allocation in Figure 9-3, we can imagine the incentives for the two firms under this trading policy.

The last ton abated by firm B costs much more than the last ton abated by A if they each stick to their 5-million-ton abatement requirements. Firm B would be willing to pay A to increase its own abatement, so that B could abate fewer tons of SO_2. In fact, B would pay any price that lies below its own marginal abatement cost. Firm A would be willing to make such a deal, so long as B paid more than A's own marginal abatement cost. So the vertical distance between the two cost curves at (5 million, 5 million) represents the potential gain from trading for that last ton of abatement. The same is true of the next ton, and the next, all the way to the point at which B is abating 4 million tons and A is abating 6 million. Notice that the firms will trade permits until exactly the point at which the total costs of reducing 10 million tons of SO_2 are minimized.[14]

How much of a difference did this make in the SO_2 emissions abatement regulation we have been discussing? The U.S. SO_2 trading program has produced cost savings of about $1.8 billion annually, compared with the most likely alternative policy considered during deliberations over the 1990 CAA Amendments (which would have required each firm to install the same technology to reduce emissions).[15] In fact, the Environmental Defense Fund, an environmental advocacy organization, agreed to endorse and help write the legislation proposed by the George H. W. Bush administration to amend the CAA if the administration would increase the required emissions reduction (from 8 million tons, which it was proposing) to the eventual 10 million tons of SO_2, based on the potential cost savings of the tradable permit approach. In this case, the tradable permit policy was not only cost-effective, but it allowed political actors to take a step closer to the efficient level of abatement, with significant benefits for human and ecosystem health.[16]

Principles of Market-based Environmental Policy

You may have noticed that the notion that firms A and B are inherently doing something wrong when they produce SO_2 emissions along with electricity has been conspicuously lacking from our discussion. In economic terms, pollution is the result of a simple set of incentives facing firms and consumers that is "stacked against" environmental protection. The consumption and production decisions that result can be changed if we alter the relevant incentives. The social problem of pollution results from what economists call market failure. The three types of market failure most relevant to environmental policy are externalities, public goods, and the "tragedy of the commons."[17]

Let's consider externalities first. If you have driven a car, checked e-mail, or turned on a light today, you have contributed to the problem of global climate change. With near unanimity, the scientific community agrees that the accumulation of carbon dioxide (CO_2) and other heat-trapping gases in Earth's upper atmosphere has increased global mean surface temperatures by about 1 degree Fahrenheit since the start of the twentieth century, with consequences including sea level rise, regional changes in precipitation, increased frequency of extreme weather events, species migration and extinction, and spatial shifts in the prevalence of disease. Ask an economist, however, and he or she will suggest that the roots of the problem are not only in the complex dynamics of Earth's atmosphere, but also in the incentives facing individuals and firms when they choose to consume and produce energy. Each such decision imposes a small cost in terms of its contribution to future atmospheric carbon concentrations. However, the individuals making these decisions do not bear these costs. Your electricity bill does include the cost of producing electricity and moving it from the plant to your home, but (in most countries) it does not include the cost of the carbon emissions from electricity production. Carbon emissions are an *externality*— their costs are external to the transaction between the buyer and the seller of electricity. The market for energy is incomplete, since its price does not reflect the full cost of its provision.[18]

You also may have noticed that bringing nations together to negotiate a solution to the problem of global climate change seems to be difficult. Clean air and a stable global climate are *public goods*: everyone benefits from their provision, whether or not they have contributed, and we can all enjoy these goods without interfering with the ability of others to enjoy them. Other public goods include national defense, weather forecasting, and parks. If you have ever listened to public radio or watched public television without contributing money to these institutions, then you have been a free-rider. Free-riding is a rational response to the incentives created by a public good: many beneficiaries will pay nothing for its provision, and those who do pay will generally pay less than what, in their heart of hearts, they would be willing to pay. Markets for public goods are incomplete. Left to their own devices, markets will under-provide these valuable goods and services.

The third category of market failure most relevant to environmental policy is the tragedy of the commons.[19] A group of individuals sharing access to a common resource (a pasture for grazing cattle, a fishery, or a busy highway) will tend to overexploit it. The "tragedy" is that, if individuals could self-regulate and reduce their collective use of the resource, the productivity of the resource would increase, to everyone's benefit. But the actions of single individuals are not enough to make a difference. Individuals restricting their own use only bear the costs of this activity, with no benefits. The resulting spiral of overexploitation can destroy the resource entirely. A prominent example of the tragedy of the commons is the collapse of many deep-sea fisheries over the past few decades. But climate change is also an example of this type of market failure. The global upper atmosphere is a resource shared by everyone and owned by no one. The incentive for individual citizens to reduce carbon emissions (their exploitation of this resource) is small, thus the resource is overexploited.

When markets fail in these three ways and environmental damages result, government intervention may be required to fix the situation. Governments can correct externalities, provide public goods, and avert the tragedy of the commons through the assignment of property rights and the creation of markets for shared resources. From an economic perspective, the best way to do this is to use market principles to correct market failures.

Using Market Principles to Solve Environmental Problems

Like the global damages from carbon emissions, the local and regional damages from SO_2 emissions (for example, human health problems and acid rain) are external to power plants' production decisions and their consumers' decisions about how much energy to use. The tradable permit program described earlier is an excellent example of using market principles to correct market failures. The government distributed permits to power plants and allowed them to trade. Plants made these trades by deciding how to minimize the costs of producing power—for each ton of SO_2 that they produced before the regulation was passed, they now faced a choice. A plant could either continue to emit that ton, and use one of its permits, or it could spend money to abate that ton, freeing up a permit to sell to another power plant (and earning the permit price as a reward). The result is an active market for SO_2 emissions permits. In June 2008 alone, 250,000 tons of emissions were traded in this market, at an end-of-month price of $325 per ton.[20] By putting a price on pollution, the government has internalized its cost, represented by the price of a permit to emit one ton of SO_2, a cost that firms must now take into account when they decide how much electricity to produce.

Another way to use market principles to reduce pollution is to impose a tax. Rather than imposing a cap on the quantity of pollution, and allowing regulated firms to trade emissions permits to establish a market price for pollution, a tax imposes a specific price on pollution and allows firms to decide how much to pollute in response. A tax has an effect on firms' decisions that is essentially identical to the effect of the permit price created by a cap-and-trade policy; polluters decide, for each ton of emissions, whether to abate that ton (incurring the resulting abatement costs) or to pay the tax and continue to emit that ton.

Taxes on pollution may also be imposed indirectly. For example, many countries tax gasoline. In the United States, the revenues from most state gasoline taxes are used to maintain and expand transportation infrastructure; U.S. gas taxes are not explicit pollution control policies. However, economists have estimated the optimal U.S. gasoline tax, taking into account the most significant externalities: emissions of local pollutants (particulate matter and nitrous oxides), CO_2 emissions (which contribute to global climate change), traffic congestion, and the costs of accidents not borne by drivers.[21] In their estimation, the efficient tax would be $0.83/gallon. However, as the authors point out, most of these externalities depend on the number of miles driven, not the amount of gasoline consumed (only a proxy for miles driven); taxing miles driven, rather than gasoline, would be better from an economic perspective. This highlights the important fact that the choice of what to tax may be as important as the level of a tax. Taxes on air and water pollution (and inputs to polluting processes) are quite common, especially in Europe. China, Malaysia, Colombia, and many other countries have also experimented with this approach. Existing environmental taxes have tended to be lower than efficient levels.[22]

Some important differences exist between taxes and tradable permits. First, a cap-and-trade system pins down a total quantity of allowable pollution. The trade among firms that results establishes the permit price. Before any trading has taken place, we know exactly how much pollution the policy is going to allow, but we are uncertain how much it will cost society to achieve that goal.

In setting a tax, regulators pin down the price of pollution, creating some degree of certainty about how much a regulation may cost. As under the permit policy, firms make private choices about how much pollution to emit, comparing their abatement costs to the tax. But the total quantity of pollution that will result is uncertain. To be certain about how much pollution will result after the tax is imposed, regulators need to have good information about the cost of reducing pollution in the regulated industry. Both the total quantity of allowable pollution and the total cost of pollution reduction are important pieces of information to consider in designing environmental policy. Each of the two primary market-based approaches to internalizing the cost of pollution, taxes and permits, offers certainty over one, but not both, of these important variables.[23]

Taxes and tradable permits can also differ in their costs to regulated firms. Under a pollution tax, a firm must pay the tax for every ton of pollution it emits. Under a permit system, permits are typically given to firms for free, at least initially. So a permit system only requires firms to pay for pollution in excess of their permit allocations. For this reason, complying with a tax can be more expensive for firms than a permit system.[24] The political opposition that results may be one reason that there are few significant environmental taxes in the United States. Taxes may be preferable to tradable permits along many dimensions as a policy to address climate change, but serious discussion of a global carbon tax is lacking.[25]

If taxes and tradable permits are fundamentally equivalent pollution regulations from an economic perspective, what about those extra compliance costs? They are a transfer. Taxes create revenues for the government agency that collects them, whereas tradable permits distributed for free do not. The net impact of this difference between the two policies depends on how tax revenues are spent. From the standpoint of efficiency, the best thing to do with environmental tax revenues may be to use them to reduce other taxes in the economy that tend to distort consumers' and firms' decisions—taxes on income, sales, and capital gains, for example.[26] Society may benefit to a smaller degree if governments use tax revenues to provide additional goods and services.

Notice that as we have discussed the virtues of market-based approaches to environmental policy, all of the options we have mentioned require some role for government intervention, setting a tax, for example, or enforcing a cap on pollution. This is a critical point. Market-based approaches should not be conflated with voluntary (nonregulatory) environmental policies, which would not be expected to have a strong impact on environmental quality.

Market-based Environmental Policy Instruments in Practice

Using Markets to Reduce Air Pollution

Market-based approaches have reduced air pollutants other than SO_2. In the 1980s, the EPA implemented a lead-trading policy to enforce a regulation reducing the allowable lead content of gasoline by 90 percent. Earlier in this chapter, we discussed the benefit-cost analysis of this policy, which suggested that the benefits of eliminating lead in gasoline exceeded its costs. The policy the EPA chose to implement the lead phasedown had something to do with this; it lowered costs relative to a more prescriptive approach. Refiners producing gasoline with a lower lead content than was required earned credits that could be traded and banked. In each year of the program, more than 60 percent of the lead added to gasoline was associated with traded lead credits.[27] This policy successfully met its environmental goal, and the EPA estimated cost savings from the lead trading program of approximately $250 million per year until the phasedown was completed in 1987.[28]

The Kyoto Protocol, the 1997 international climate change treaty ratified by 184 countries and the European Union (EU) as of mid-February 2009, included emissions trading as a mechanism for achieving national emissions reduction targets. Among industrialized countries that took on emissions reduction targets under the Kyoto Protocol, the countries of the EU have opted to use an emissions trading system (ETS), established in 2005, to meet their emissions reduction targets. The protocol sets a cap on CO_2 emissions for the EU as a whole, allocated by the EU to member countries. Member countries then divide emissions allotments among the following industries: electric power generation; refineries; iron and steel; cement, glass, and ceramics; and pulp and paper.

Figure 9-4 European Union Carbon Dioxide Emissions Allowance Prices, 2005–2007

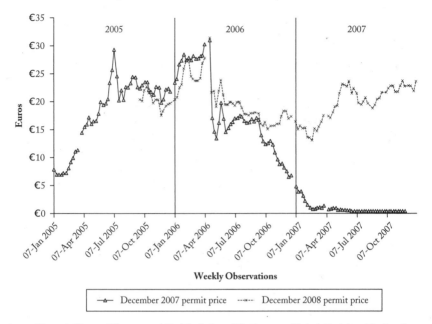

Source: From A. Denny Ellerman and Paul L. Joskow, *The European Union's Emissions Trading System in Perspective* (Washington, D.C.: Pew Center on Global Climate Change, 2008), 13, www.pewclimate .org. Reproduced with permission.

The EU ETS is the world's largest emissions trading system, covering almost 12,000 facilities in 27 countries in 2008, and accounting for nearly one-half of EU CO_2 emissions.[29] The Kyoto Protocol's emissions caps did not begin to bind until 2008, so the pilot phase of the EU ETS (2005–2007) was designed to set up the institutional and operating structures necessary for trading. The cap in the EU system in this pilot phase was a small reduction (a few percentage points) below expected emissions in the absence of the policy.

It is too early to estimate the cost savings from the ETS approach over more prescriptive approaches. However, early analyses of prices and abatement in the pilot phase offer some interesting lessons. Let's consider prices first. Figure 9-4 graphs the prices for emissions permits dated December 2007 (for the end of the pilot phase) and December 2008 (for the end of the first post-pilot year). Trading began in January 2005. Prices for December 2007 permits peaked around 30 Euros/ton in early April 2006, then fell dramatically, hovering around 17 Euros/ton through October 2006. Prices then began a steep decline, falling to zero by the end of 2007.

When European carbon emissions prices fell sharply in mid-2006, media coverage suggested that the market was not functioning well. Economists have a different opinion. When the EU ETS began, regulators had little information about facility-level emissions of CO_2. In addition, the required reduction in emissions in the pilot phase was actually quite small—well within the range of normal year-to-year fluctuations in emissions. So in the first fifteen months of the market's operation, regulated facilities could not be sure how valuable emissions permits would be. The EU released data on 2005 emissions and permits in April 2006, indicating that the total number of distributed emissions permits exceeded total emissions by a significant margin (this could have been due to abatement, changes in economic conditions or weather, or many other factors). This new information to the firms trading permits resulted in a surplus (supply was greater than demand). The steep April 2006 price decline is exactly what should have happened in a well-functioning market.

What about the fact that the price of permits for December 2007 emissions dropped to zero toward the end of 2007? Permits allocated in the pilot phase could not be carried over to the first official phase of trading, which began in January 2008. Thus, firms holding on to any excess permits on December 31, 2007, would find them worthless on January 1, 2008. The zero price reflects this simple fact. We can see from Figure 9-4 that the market was taking into account the value of future emissions permits. Prices for December 2008 permits also dropped in April 2006, given new information on how "binding" the emissions cap would really be, but that price drop was not as great as for 2007. By December 2007, when the price of the last pilot phase permits had dropped to zero, the price of 2008 carbon emissions allowances was between 23 and 24 Euros, or about \$34–\$35 per ton. The firms regulated under the EU ETS recognized that, going forward, emitting CO_2 would be costly.

Determining the impact of this new carbon market on emissions in the pilot phase is difficult, since it requires that we estimate what carbon emissions would have been in the absence of the ETS. There are some early estimates of the impact of the EU ETS on CO_2 emissions. Despite EU economic growth between 2005 and 2007, and increases in oil and gas prices (which would tend to increase demand for coal, increasing CO_2 emissions), some evidence indicates that CO_2 emissions were lower than expected during the pilot phase, perhaps by as much as 5 percent.[30] This is impressive, given the pilot phase's modest abatement goals and short duration. The cap on carbon emissions under the EU ETS is scheduled to drop in 2008–2012 and again, perhaps annually, from 2013 to 2020. The real test of this exciting new carbon trading system will be its effects beyond 2008, when EU nations must meet their Kyoto Protocol emissions targets.

The United States did not ratify the Kyoto Protocol, and it has not adopted a binding national greenhouse gas emissions reduction target. Nonetheless, support for action on climate change has led some states to enact policies to reduce greenhouse gas emissions. Though it is just starting, the largest market-based initiative is the Regional Greenhouse Gas Initiative (RGGI), an effort to develop a cap-and-trade program among nine northeastern states, initiated in 2003. In the 2008 U.S. presidential election, both candidates said they supported some form of cap-and-trade approach to limiting U.S. carbon emissions (see chapter 16). There are also two regional tradable permit markets for nitrogen oxides (NOx) in southern California and the northeastern and mid-Atlantic states, created primarily to reduce concentrations of ground-level ozone. The use of markets to reduce air pollution is a vibrant and growing area of environmental economics and policy.

Individual Tradable Quotas for Fishing

Thus far, we have talked about cap-and-trade policies as if they applied only to pollution problems. But a common application is to fisheries management, to avert the tragedy of the commons. The world's largest market for tradable individual fishing quotas (IFQs), created in 1986, is in New Zealand.[31] By 2004, it covered seventy different fish species, and the government of New Zealand had divided coastal waters into "species-regions," generating 275 separate markets that covered more than 85 percent of the commercial catch in the area extending 200 miles from New Zealand's coast.

A market for fishing quota works similarly to a market for pollution permits. The government establishes a total allowable catch (TAC), distributing shares to individual fishers. Fishers can trade their assigned quotas, which represent a percentage of the TAC for a particular species-region. Have the IFQ markets in New Zealand helped reduce overfishing and restore fish stocks? This question is much harder to answer than it was in the world of pollution control. Fish populations are hard to measure, and they depend critically on many things other than human fishing effort. But few, if any, species populations covered by New Zealand's extensive IFQ markets are worse off under the policy, and some show significant signs of recovery.[32] This stands in sharp contrast to the crashes of fish stocks in other parts of the world during this same time period.

In the United States, Pacific halibut and sablefish off the coast of Alaska, mid-Atlantic surf clams and ocean quahogs, South Atlantic wreckfish, and most recently red snapper in the Gulf of Mexico are all regulated using IFQ markets. Iceland manages stocks of twenty fish and shellfish species using IFQ markets, in a system established in 1990. In years to come, studies of these relatively new approaches will help policymakers assess the degree to which IFQ markets can help avert disastrous fishery collapses.

Waste Management Policies

Market-based approaches have also been used to manage solid waste. Some waste products have high recycling value. If you live in a community with curbside recycling, you may have seen low-income residents of the community picking aluminum cans out of recycling bins at the curb; they do this because it is much less costly to produce aluminum from scrap metal than from virgin ore, and as a result, those cans are quite valuable. But most household waste ends up as trash, disposed of legally in landfills or incinerators or illegally dumped. The marginal cost of public garbage collection and disposal for an American household has been estimated at \$1.03 per trash bag, but until recently, the marginal cost of disposal borne by households was approximately zero.[33]

An increasingly common waste management policy is the "pay-as-you-throw" system, a volume-based waste disposal charge often assessed as a requirement for the purchase of official garbage bags, stickers to attach to bags of specific volume, periodic disposal charges for official city trash cans of particular sizes, and (rarely) charges based on the measured weight of curbside trash. These systems function like an environmental tax, internalizing the costs of disposing of household waste. In 2003, more than four thousand U.S. communities had some form of pay-as-you-throw disposal.[34]

The most comprehensive study of a pay-as-you-throw policy was performed in Charlottesville, Virginia, which imposed a charge of 80 cents per trash bag.[35] This tax was estimated to have reduced the number of bags households threw out by about 37 percent. However, the effect was offset by two factors that have proven to be common problems with such programs. First, the reduction in the total weight of trash thrown away was much smaller (about a 14 percent reduction), since consumers compacted their trash in order to reduce the number of bags they used. Second, illegal disposal increased. As noted earlier in the discussion of the gasoline tax, Charlottesville's experience suggests that the decision of *what* to tax may be as (or more) important than how high the tax should be.

Habitat and Land Management Policies

Tradable development rights (TDRs) have been applied to solve problems as diverse as deforestation in the Brazilian Amazon and the development of former farmland in the Maryland suburbs of Washington, D.C.[36] Since the 1970s, TDRs have been implemented in thirty U.S. states, primarily to preserve farmland near urban areas. The program in Calvert County, Maryland, preserved an estimated 13,000 acres of farmland between 1978 and 2005. In Brazil, TDRs have been used to slow the conversion of ecologically valuable lands to agriculture since 1998; each parcel of private property that is developed must be offset by preserving a forested parcel elsewhere (within the same ecosystem and with land of greater or equal ecological value). Simulations of the Brazilian policy for the state of Minas Gerais suggest that TDRs lower the cost to landowners of protecting a unit of forested land. Landowners can develop the most profitable land and preserve less profitable land. But this highlights two of the chief problems with TDRs. First, how can land developers prove (and regulators ensure) that a preserved parcel is really additional—that it would not have remained in forest without the developer's efforts? Second, how can we measure the ecological equivalence of two land parcels? In the case of carbon emissions, each ton of emissions has essentially the same impact on our ultimate concern—atmospheric carbon concentrations—no matter where it is emitted. The same cannot be said of land preservation.

A related policy, wetlands mitigation banking, holds similar promise and faces similar challenges. Wetlands are classic public goods. They provide a rich set of ecosystem services, for which there are no markets, and from which everyone benefits, regardless of who pays for their preservation. Wetlands have been depleted rapidly in the United States and other parts of the world by conversion to agricultural and urban use. The externalities to wetlands conversion, such as increased flood risk, loss of habitat for birds, fish and mammals, and reduced groundwater recharge are taken into account only when governments intervene to require it.

Since the early 1990s, the United States has experimented with mitigation banking, a policy under which land developers compensate for any lost wetlands by preserving, expanding, or creating wetlands elsewhere.[37] Wetlands banks serve as central brokers, allowing developers to purchase credits, and fulfilling credits through the physical process of wetlands preservation, creation, and management. In 2005, there were 405 approved U.S. wetland banks in operation. We can think of mitigation banking as a market-based approach in two different ways. First, it is a tax on land development, internalizing some of the externalities of wetlands depletion. Second, given that the U.S. federal government has purported to enforce a "no net loss" policy with regard to the national stock of wetlands since 1989, we can think of mitigation banking as a cap-and-trade policy in which the cap on acres of wetlands lost is zero.

As in the case of TDRs, wetlands mitigation banking reduces the costs of preserving wetlands acreage but faces significant challenges. A wetland in a particular location provides a specific portfolio of biophysical services. For example, coastal wetlands support shellfish nurseries and may reduce damages from storm-related flooding. Inland wetlands may filter contaminants and provide islands of habitat for migratory bird species in overland flight. If development pressures in coastal cities create incentives for landowners to develop wetlands in these locations, and pay for wetlands creation inland, the net effect of these kinds of trades must be considered. This is a significant change from the simple ton-for-ton trading that occurs for some air pollutants.

This section offered a handful of examples of the many applications of market principles to environmental policy.[38] We emphasized the strong arguments in favor of taxes, tradable permits, and other market-based approaches, especially given that these policies can achieve environmental policy goals at less cost than more prescriptive approaches. But they are not appropriate solutions to all environmental problems. The issues we raised in our discussion of market-based land management policies arise in other contexts, as well. Market-based policies can be designed for situations in which the location of pollution emissions or natural resource amenities matters for the benefits of pollution control or resource management. But they are not workable in extreme cases. For example, the impacts of a toxic waste dump are highly localized. Economists would not advise setting a national limit on toxic waste disposal, and allowing firms to trade disposal permits, letting the waste end up where it may. Environmental problems at this end of the spectrum—the opposite end from a problem like carbon emissions, which can be reduced anywhere with essentially the same net effect—may be better addressed through prescriptive approaches.

Conclusions

Economics offers a powerful pair of tools—efficiency and cost-effectiveness—to consider environmental policy tradeoffs. Efficiency has to do with the setting of environmental policy goals: how much pollution should we reduce, or how many acres of wetlands should be preserved? An efficient pollution control policy equalizes the quantified benefits and costs of the last ton of pollution eliminated. The process used to determine whether an environmental policy is efficient is benefit-cost analysis. If a strict benefit-cost test were applied to the decision of how much SO_2 pollution to eliminate from power plant smokestacks in the 1990s, additional reductions would have been required. Benefit-cost analysis would also have suggested that lead be eliminated from U.S. gasoline sooner than it was. In other cases, applying the rule of efficiency may suggest that environmental standards should be weakened.

However, efficiency is not the only potential input to good environmental policy. The treatment of benefit-cost analysis in the major U.S. environmental statutes is a good indication of our ambivalence toward analyzing environmental tradeoffs in this systematic way; the statutes alternately "forbid, inhibit, tolerate, allow, invite, or require the use of economic analysis in environmental decision making."[39] For example, the CAA forbids the consideration of costs in setting the National Ambient Air Quality Standards, and the U.S. Safe Drinking Water Act requires benefit-cost analysis of all new drinking water contaminant standards. Environmental regulatory agencies are not economic agencies. While laying out the tradeoffs involved in setting environmental standards is critically important from an economic perspective, political, social, and ethical concerns may hold more influence than benefit-cost analysis.

Even when environmental standards are inefficient, however, policymakers can choose policies to achieve those standards at least cost. The billions of dollars saved by policies like SO_2 and CO_2 trading, paired with their proven environmental effectiveness, have made market-based approaches like tradable permits and taxes increasingly the policy instruments of choice for solving environmental problems. These innovative policy approaches are not appropriate for all situations. But if we understand the market incentives that create environmental problems, we can use market principles to solve them.

Suggested Web Sites

EPA National Center for Environmental Economics (yosemite.epa. gov/ee/epa/eed.nsf/webpages/homepage) Provides access to research reports, regulatory impact analyses, and other EPA publications.

OMB Office of Information and Regulatory Affairs (www.whitehouse .gov/OMB/inforeg) Provides a variety of information on the office's regulatory oversight mission, including pending regulations, the status of regulatory reviews, and prompt letters that encourage federal agencies to consider regulations that appear to have benefits greater than costs.

OMB Watch (www.ombwatch.org) Follows budgets and regulatory policies.

Resources for the Future Inc. (www.rff.org) Nonprofit research organization devoted to environmental and resource management issues.

Notes

1. For competing scientific opinions about Snake River salmon decline, see Charles C. Mann and Mark L. Plummer, "Can science rescue salmon?" *Science* 298 (2000): 716–719, with letters and responses. See also David L. Halsing and Michael R. Moore, "Cost-Effective Management Alternatives for Snake River Chinook Salmon: A Biological-Economic Synthesis," *Conservation Biology* 22, 2 (2000): 338–350.

2. In reality, each ton of emissions is not equivalent. SO_2 emissions in urban areas or those upwind of critical ecosystems may cause relatively greater harm. In addition, costs and benefits may not follow the smooth, continuous functions we depict in Figure 9-1. The simple curves help us to develop intuition that carries through even in more complex situations.

3. Since marginal benefits and costs represent the rate at which benefits and costs change when we add an additional ton of emissions reduction, they are also measured by the slope of the total benefit and cost curves; notice that net benefits are largest in Figure 9-1 (at Q^*) when the slopes of $B(Q)$ and $C(Q)$ are equal.

4. Dallas Burtraw, Alan J. Krupnick, Erin Mansur, David Austin, and Deirdre Farrell, "The Costs and Benefits of Reducing Air Pollutants Related to Acid Rain," *Contemporary Economic Policy* 16 (1998): 379–400.

5. Kenneth J. Arrow, Maureen L. Cropper, George C. Eads, Robert W. Hahn, Lester B. Lave, Roger G. Noll, Paul R. Portney, Milton Russell, Richard Schmalensee, V. Kerry Smith, and Robert N. Stavins, "Is There a Role for Benefit-Cost Analysis in Environmental, Health, and Safety Regulation?" *Science*, April 12, 1996, 221–222.

6. Stephen Kelman, "Cost-Benefit Analysis: An Ethical Critique," with replies, *AEI Journal on Government and Social Regulation* (January/February, 1981): 33–40.

7. Frank Ackerman and Lisa Heinzerling, *Priceless: On Knowing the Price of Everything and the Value of Nothing* (New York: New Press, 2004).

8. This discussion is based on Nathaniel O. Keohane, Benjamin Van Roy, and Richard J. Zeckhauser, "The Optimal Management of Environmental Quality with Stock and Flow Controls," AEI-Brookings Joint Center for Regulatory Studies Working Paper 05-09, June 2005.

9. See A. Myrick Freeman, III, *The Measurement of Environmental and Resource Values*, 2d ed. (Washington, D.C.: Resources for the Future, 2003).

10. Albert L. Nichols, "Lead in Gasoline," in Richard D. Morgenstern, ed., *Economic Analyses at EPA: Assessing Regulatory Impact* (Washington, D.C.: Resources for the Future, 1997), 49–86.

11. See Martin L. Weitzman, "A Review of the Stern Review on the Economics of Climate Change," *Journal of Economic Literature* 45, 3 (2007): 703–724.

12. Robert Costanza, Ralph d'Arge, Rudolf de Groot, Stephen Farber, Monica Grasso, Bruce Hannon, Karin Limburg, Shahid Naeem, Robert V. O'Neill, Jose Paruelo, Robert G. Raskin, Paul Sutton, and Marjan van den Belt, "The Value of the World's Ecosystem Services and Natural Capital," *Nature* 387 (1997): 253–260.

13. Michael Toman, "Why Not to Calculate the Value of the World's Ecosystem Services and Natural Capital," *Ecological Economics* 25 (1998): 57–60.
14. We emphasize the short-run cost-effectiveness of market-based approaches to environmental policy, a critical concept and one that is relatively easy to develop at an intuitive level. However, the greatest potential cost savings from these types of environmental policies may be achieved in the long run. Because they require firms to pay to pollute, market-based policies provide strong incentives for regulated firms to invest in technologies that reduce pollution abatement costs over time, either developing these technologies themselves or adopting cheaper pollution control technologies developed elsewhere.
15. Nathaniel O. Keohane, "Cost Savings from Allowance Trading in the 1990 Clean Air Act," in *Moving to Markets in Environmental Regulation: Lessons from Twenty Years of Experience*, ed. Charles E. Kolstad and Jody Freeman (New York: Oxford University Press, 2007).
16. The definitive overview of the SO_2 permit trading program is found in A. Denny Ellerman, Paul J. Joskow, Richard Schmalensee, Juan-Pablo Montero, and Elizabeth M. Bailey, *Markets for Clean Air: The U.S. Acid Rain Program* (New York: Cambridge University Press, 2000).
17. These concepts are described in much greater detail in Nathaniel O. Keohane and Sheila M. Olmstead, *Markets and the Environment* (Washington, D.C.: Island Press, 2007), chap. 5.
18. Pollution is a negative externality, but externalities can also be positive. For example, a child vaccinated against measles benefits because she is unlikely to contract that disease. But a vaccinated child also benefits her family, neighbors, and schoolmates, since she is less likely to expose them to disease.
19. Garrett Hardin, "The Tragedy of the Commons," *Science* 162 (1968): 1243–1248.
20. For current U.S. emissions market statistics, see new.evomarkets.com/index.php?page=Emissions_Markets.
21. Ian Parry and Kenneth Small, "Does Britain or the United States Have the Right Gasoline Tax?" *American Economic Review* 95 (2005): 1276–1289.
22. Robert N. Stavins, "Experience with Market-Based Environmental Policy Instruments," in *Handbook of Environmental Economics*, vol. I, Karl-Göran Mäler and Jeffrey Vincent, eds. (Amsterdam: Elsevier Science, 2003), 355–435.
23. This difference between the two approaches—taxes and permits—can cause one approach to be more efficient than the other when regulators are uncertain about abatement costs; see Martin L. Weitzman, "Prices v. Quantities," *Review of Economic Studies* 41 (1974): 477–491.
24. This distinction disappears if permits are auctioned rather than given away. But auctioned permit systems are rare. Even the biggest existing tradable permit systems, including the U.S. SO_2 trading program and the EU ETS, auction only a very small percentage of permits.
25. The EU tried to implement a carbon tax in the early 1990s but failed to achieve unanimous approval of its (then) fifteen member states; the ETS faced much less opposition. On the potential advantages of a carbon tax over permits, see William D. Nordhaus, "To Tax or Not to Tax: Alternative Approaches to Slowing Global Warming," *Review of Environmental Economics and Policy* 1, 1 (2007): 26–44.
26. This is actually more complicated, since environmental taxes may exacerbate the distortions introduced by other taxes. For a straightforward discussion of this and other comparisons between taxes and permits, see Lawrence H. Goulder and Ian W. H. Parry, "Instrument Choice in Environmental Policy," *Review of Environmental Economics and Policy* 2, 2 (2007): 152–174.
27. Robert W. Hahn and G. L. Hester, "Marketable Permits: Lessons for Theory and Practice," *Ecology Law Quarterly* 16 (1989): 361–406.
28. U.S. Environmental Protection Agency (EPA), Office of Policy Analysis, *Costs and Benefits of Reducing Lead in Gasoline, Final Regulatory Impact Analysis* (Washington, D.C.: EPA, 1985).

29. See A. Denny Ellerman and Barbara K. Buchner, "The European Union Emissions Trading Scheme: Origins, Allocation, and Early Results," *Review of Environmental Economics and Policy* 1, 1 (2007): 66–87; A. Denny Ellerman and Paul L. Joskow, *The European Union's Emissions Trading System in Perspective* (Washington, D.C.: Pew Center on Global Climate Change, 2008); Frank J. Convery and Luke Redmond, "Market and Price Developments in the European Union Emissions Trading Scheme," *Review of Environmental Economics and Policy* 1, 1 (2007): 88–111.

30. A. Denny Ellerman and Barbara K. Buchner, "Over-allocation or Abatement: A Preliminary Analysis of the EU ETS Based on the 2005-06 Emissions Data," *Environmental and Resource Economics* 41, 2 (2008): 267–287.

31. See Suzanne Iudicello, Michael Weber, and Robert Wieland, *Fish, Markets and Fishermen: The Economics of Overfishing* (Washington, D.C.: Island Press, 1999). For assessments of New Zealand's policy, see John H. Annala, "New Zealand's ITQ System: Have the First Eight Years Been a Success or a Failure?" *Reviews in Fish Biology and Fisheries* 6 (1996): 43–62; Richard G. Newell, James N. Sanchirico, and Suzi Kerr, "Fishing Quota Markets," *Journal of Environmental Economics and Management* 49, 3 (2005): 437–462.

32. See John H. Annala, *Report from the Fishery Assessment Plenary, May 1994: Stock Assessments and Yield Estimates,* MAF Fisheries Greta Point, Wellington, NZ, quoted in Annala, "New Zealand's ITQ System," 47.

33. See Robert Repetto, Roger C. Dower, Robin Jenkins, and Jacqueline Geoghegan, *Green Fees: How a Tax Shift Can Work for the Environment and the Economy* (Washington, D.C.: World Resources Institute, 1992).

34. Thomas Sterner, *Policy Instruments for Environmental and Natural Resource Management* (Washington, D.C.: Resources for the Future, 1992).

35. Don Fullerton and Thomas C. Kinnaman, "Household Responses to Pricing Garbage by the Bag," *American Economic Review* 86, 4 (1996): 971–984.

36. On Brazil, see Kenneth M. Chomitz, "Transferable Development Rights and Forest Protection: An Exploratory Analysis," *International Regional Science Review* 27, 3 (2004): 348–373. On Calvert County, Maryland, see Virginia McConnell, Margaret Walls, and Elizabeth Kopits, "Zoning, Transferable Development Rights and the Density of Development," *Journal of Urban Economics* 59 (2006): 440–457.

37. National Research Council, *Compensating for Wetland Losses under the Clean Water Act* (Washington, D.C.: National Academies Press, 2001); and David Salvesen, Lindell L. Marsh, and Douglas R. Porter, eds., *Mitigation Banking: Theory and Practice* (Washington, D.C.: Island Press, 1996).

38. For surveys of these approaches, see Stavins, "Experience with Market-Based Environmental Policy Instruments"; Sterner, *Policy Instruments for Environmental and Natural Resource Management*; and Theodore Panayotou, *Instruments of Change: Motivating and Financing Sustainable Development* (London: Earthscan Publications, 1998).

39. Richard D. Morgenstern, "Decision Making at EPA: Economics, Incentives and Efficiency," draft conference paper in *EPA at Thirty: Evaluating and Improving the Environmental Protection Agency* (Durham, N.C.: Duke University, 2000), 36–38.

10

Toward Sustainable Production
Finding Workable Strategies for Government and Industry
Daniel Press and Daniel A. Mazmanian

The greening of industry has emerged as an important topic among business, environmental, and government leaders only since the mid-1980s. At this stage, in what will require a profound transformation by the time it is complete, debate exists over which business and industry practices are most in need of change and how to bring such change about: Is policy intervention best applied at the stage of waste management, air and water pollution control, or energy usage? Can the most change be realized in production methods, product design, or the end products themselves? Will the strongest drive for change come at the stage of consumption and usage of products?

Equally unclear is the best position for society to adopt in order to promote the most comprehensive and cost-effective transformation.[1] Four broad approaches to this question illustrate the differences of opinion about how best to achieve industrial greening. The first approach involves government imposing on business and industry prescribed environmental protection technologies and methods of emissions reduction. A second, more flexible approach, would allow businesses to select their own most cost-effective strategies for reducing emissions, under the watchful eye of government. A third way is to use market-based incentives that provide bottom-line rewards for environmentally friendly business behavior, leaving change to the natural workings of the marketplace. The fourth approach is to rely largely on volunteerism, wherein businesses commit to environmental goals that match or exceed those required in exchange for relief from the prescribed technology and command-and-control regulations that would otherwise be imposed.

Since the mid-1990s, the range and extent of research on these approaches has expanded appreciably and heated debate has ensued about which approach or which mix of approaches to utilize. Some focus their attention mainly on the shortcomings of the nation's long-standing environmental policies—variously referred to as "command-and-control," "top-down," "deterrence-based" policies for air, water, land use, noise, and endangered species protection—and the need to appreciably loosen the strictures of these policies. Others focus on the growing importance of the corporate responsibility and quality management movements within and across industries—domestically and internationally—and how this shift is moving many businesses toward a greener path. All reformers want to know how best to accelerate their preferred strategy through various flexible governmental and voluntary policies, particularly in light of the unrelenting challenges to the environment posed by modern technological society, and ever-expanding global population, and the growing recognition of the serious challenges posed by climate change that will be with us for decades to come.

In assessing the contending positions and approaches, it is reasonable to assume that, all else being equal, business and industry owners, managers, and workers would prefer to live and work in a cleaner, more environmentally sustainable world. Yet seldom is all else equal. The market economy in which businesses operate has a long history of freely using natural resources and nature's goods, such as clean air, water, and soil as well as food and fodder, and shielding both producers and consumers from the environmental pollution and resource degradation associated with the extraction of these goods, their use in production, and their consumption. This is the very same market economy, after all, that nurtures consumer tastes and expectations, ultimately their demands, for ever more goods and services, resulting in the extraordinary material consumption of today's American lifestyle.[2]

Consequently, the greening of industry is neither a private business matter nor a minor marketplace imperfection so much as a serious "public" problem, in need of a public policy solution. Because significant costs can be associated with the transformation into a green economy, we do not expect businesses to automatically or enthusiastically assume these costs. Indeed, it is typically in a firm's best interest to minimize if not avoid the additional costs of transformation to the extent that such investments do not demonstrably improve its near-term market position. This is precisely why the first generation of environmental laws, starting in the 1970s in the United States, was compulsory for all business, creating the "command-and-control" regulatory regime of the first environmental epoch. As this chapter shows, a good deal of progress resulted but at great expense; arguably many unnecessary costs were incurred by business and government, costs that might be avoided under a different approach.

The Dilemma of Collective Action for Environmental Protection

How to bring about significant changes that are in the best interest of all sectors can be understood as one of a category of problems known as "collective action problems" or "collective action dilemmas."[3] These occur when individuals would be better off if they cooperate in pursuit of a common goal, but for one reason or another each chooses a less optimal course of action—one that typically satisfies some other highly important goal. The challenge to policymakers when facing collective action problems is to devise an approach that anticipates and counteracts the normal (in the language of game theory, the "rational") tendency of actors to forego the better *joint* gain for a nearer-term assured and secure, but lesser, *individual* gain.

The collective action dilemma in the case of the greening of industry has been portrayed by Matthew Potoski and Aseem Prakash as a two-dimensional

Figure 10-1 Green Industry as a Collective Action Dilemma

Government's choice	Firm's choice: **Evasion**	Firm's choice: **Self-policing**
Flexible regulation	**Cell A** Government as potential "sucker"	**Cell B** Win-win: superior outcomes for government and industry
Deterrence (through command-and-control)	**Cell C** Suboptimal for both government and business but a typical outcome	**Cell D** Green industry initiatives of the 1980s to today, with industry as potential "sucker"

Source: Based on Matthew Potoski and Aseem Prakash, "The Regulation Dilemma: Cooperation and Conflict in Environmental Governance," *Public Administration Review* 64 (March/April 2004): 137–148.

game-theoretic problem, which we have adapted in Figure 10-1. The vertical and horizontal labels show the options available to each player, and the four cells represent the payoff (or benefits) and risk (or costs) to each of the actors based on the combinations of each option. For example, should they decide to cooperate to maximize the gains to each (cell B)? Or should they not cooperate in order to avoid the possibility of being taken advantage of by the other or incurring some other cost (cell C), such as the loss of public confidence and trust on the part of government and market share and profitability on the part of business?

Although simplified, the game situation approximates closely the real world of the relations between business and government. Consequently, if left to its own devices, business would choose to have little or no governmental requirement placed on it to protect the environment. This would be only reasonable (rational) for a business trying to maximize its profits in a market economy. This option is represented by the "evasion" position on the horizontal dimension, on the "Firm's choice" axis. However, if compelled by law to provide environmental protection and safeguards, and possibly go even further to transform itself into a green company, business would prefer an approach that allowed for self-policing and regulatory flexibility. It would find this superior to being heavily regulated by a command-and-control government bureaucracy.

Government, in turn, has the choice of opting for a policy of "deterrence," which experience has shown to be workable based on the command-and-control regulatory approach taken to environmental protection since 1970. The downside, as experience has also shown, is that this approach has required the growth and support of a large government bureaucracy to carry out the oversight and regulation of businesses, the suppression of the creative energy on the part of firms that could be used to develop their own green business strategies, and ultimately the less than promised and far less than imaginable transformation of industry than could have occurred. Conversely, government could choose to be more flexible and lenient on industry, relying instead on a modest amount of monitoring combined with market forces, consumer demands, and new technology to ensure greater protection of the environment. There is risk in this approach for the government. It embraces the promise of an eventually large payoff, but as market forces and modest oversight combine to bring about the desired green transformation of business in the short term, some, if not most, businesses will not change their behavior or will do so insufficiently or slowly, absent stringent regulation. In the language of game theory, this raises the dual problems of "free-riding" (not paying one's share of the costs) or "shirking" (paying less than one's share of the costs).

This is the dilemma: As the logic of game theory suggests and a fair amount of experience affirms, under flexible regulatory systems that rely on market forces to bring about changed behavior, the market forces are insufficient and many businesses do not change or do so only minimally. When firms know that they are unlikely to be detected or penalized even when caught, they too often opt for evasion over committing the capital required to transform themselves. The result is that government (and thus the public) ends up being betrayed, realizing even less movement toward the green transformation than under a command-and-control approach: Government finds itself in the position of the "sucker," which is the worst possible outcome in a collective action game.

Armed with the insights of game theory, we find it logical that, left to its own resources and absent compulsion, business will choose evasion over greening. Government, in turn, will choose command-and-control over flexibility, not because it is optimal but to avoid the risk of ending up the sucker. Thus game theory tells us that most of the activity surrounding environmental protection can be expected to take place in the lower-left cell of Figure 10-1, cell C, the zone in which government regulates with a heavy hand to prevent business from evading environmental protection laws and regulations. This is precisely where the action took place throughout the first environmental epoch, which began in the 1970s.[4]

A second epoch began in the 1980s and continues today, characterized by recognition of the collective action dilemma and efforts to extricate government and business from its grasp. The challenge is how to combine flexible regulatory strategies with market forces to move the central theater of action out of the lower-left cell C to the upper-right cell B.

A number of pilot and experimental programs by government and business have been initiated and are reviewed in this chapter. The experience underscores how difficult it has been to dislodge the players from their long-standing positions. This should come as no surprise in light of the dilemma they face and the amount of time they have spent living and working under the command-and-control approach. The crux of the matter remains that, by and large, government is usually loath to relinquish its reliance on deterrence and most businesses can be expected to evade when circumstances allow.

Yet the need for society to find a win-win solution—a more optimal mix of flexibility and self-policing—continues and has motivated the continuing search for the needed policy breakthrough. A growing body of research on strategies that appear to work is guiding these efforts, at least on an experimental basis among self-motivated businesses.[5] Thus devising a new hybrid public policy approach seems feasible, at least in principle, within a game-theoretic framework. Of course, the direction of public policy is set by the politics of policymaking, not simply the logic of policy analysis, so this too will be considered in our final assessment.

What follows is an overview of the efforts made since 1970 to address the problems of environmental pollution and the degradation of our natural resources base by greening the practices of business and industry. This overview moves through the strict command-and-control environmental policy epoch, located schematically in cell C, and then turns to the market-oriented and flexible regulatory strategies that reflected a significant change in the understanding of the problem. In actuality, the debate and center of activity has moved only part way, with the innovative action taking place "under the shadow of regulation" (in cell D).

We examine several impressive examples of corporate self-regulation and voluntary green approaches of individual firms, often in conjunction with government, as illustrative of how change has occurred and how it can occur. These accomplishments need to be juxtaposed against the efforts by George W. Bush's administration to slow down, if not derail, the greening of America's economy. The chapter ends with an assessment of how we can best accomplish the much-needed green transformation of America's business and industry as we look to a future with ever increasing threats to our environment and natural resources at home and around the world, the need for revitalization of the nation's economy, and the desire to maintain the quality of life most Americans have come to expect and strive for.

The Accomplishments of Command-and-Control since 1970

Although the needed green transformation of the economy and society per se is actively being discussed and dominates the policy debate today, in large measure in response to concerns about climate change and energy pricing, command-and-control regulation remains the most widespread policy approach in practice. In a number of important respects, the approach has worked and continues to work to clean up the environment, in some instances quite admirably.[6] Moreover, evidence indicates that the nation's strict environmental regulations have spurred innovation in businesses, which ultimately provides them a source of competitive advantage in the market economy.[7] Also, one can point to the creation of jobs in the pollution control technology sector as a source of the economic growth and employment that has resulted from the traditional form of environmental regulation.[8]

Since the 1970s, government rules and regulations have spurred reductions throughout the nation in air, water, and soil contamination; these reductions are noted at numerous points throughout this book (see especially chapter 1). Nationwide air emissions trends from all industrial sources (including electricity-generating power plants) show that air emissions reached a peak in the early to mid-1970s, declined, and then plateaued from the mid-1980s onward.

Between 1990 and 2006, sulfur oxides emissions declined consistently (by as much as 40 percent), very likely as a consequence of the 1990 Clean Air Act's Acid Rain Program. Lead and volatile organic compounds also declined, by 3.5 percent and 27 percent, respectively. Other air pollutants exhibited more worrisome trends. Carbon monoxide from industrial processes fluctuated throughout the 1990s, probably as a function of economic conditions, but overall industry emitted about the same amount of carbon monoxide in 2006 as it did in 1990. Industrial nitrogen oxides decreased overall during the same time period, thanks to much cleaner fuel combustion, although emissions increased somewhat from noncombustion sources.[9] Official records for all environmental data are often unavailable for the same years (here we present ranges for the closest years); however, all of these figures should be viewed as rough approximations. Although the U.S. Environmental Protection Agency (EPA) officially reports impressive emissions reductions in its annual inventories, the agency admits, when pressed, that "estimates for the non-utility manufacturing sector are some of the most unreliable data we have in the national emission inventory."[10]

Water quality is even harder to assess reliably but has also improved somewhat, thanks largely to the thousands of municipal wastewater treatment plants built with financing from the federal government since 1970.[11] Today almost every American can expect drinkable water as a matter of course, with regular monitoring for quality and reasonably rapid responses to contamination threats. It is less clear, however, how industry's overall contribution to water quality protection has changed over the years, because such data are not routinely collected or centrally distributed.

Energy consumption also presents some progress. Manufacturing firms slowly reduced their annual primary energy consumption between the 1970s and early 1990s, going from a high of 24.7 quads (quadrillion British thermal units, or BTUs) in 1973 to 21.4 quads in 2005.[12] This roughly 16-percent overall (or total) decrease in primary energy consumption from 1973 to 2005 occurred while manufacturing output increased nearly 440 percent during the same time period.[13] At the same time, manufacturing industries reduced their energy intensity (the amount of energy it takes to manufacture a product) by 26.7 percent (usually measured in BTUs per dollar value of shipments and receipts) between 1980 and 1988.[14] Those reductions continued during the 1990s as the consumption per dollar value of shipments for those industries decreased 16 percent, from 5,500 BTUs in 1991 to 4,600 BTUs in 1998.[15] In one high energy sector, iron and steel, energy intensity decreased between 1998 and 2002, whether measured as the energy it took to produce a ton of steel or the energy it took to produce a dollar of value added.[16] This was probably a result of the industry's greater reliance on cleaner electric arc furnaces than the old basic oxygen furnaces, which consume enormous quantities of coal.

A great deal of money has been spent to accomplish these results, in terms of total dollars and as a percentage of the gross national product, and with them the costs borne by industry. This is reflected in the increasing level of expenditures by industry. In 1973, U.S. industries spent about $4.8 billion on pollution abatement, split almost equally between capital and operating costs. By 1994, American manufacturing was spending $10 billion on capital costs, but these costs dropped to just under $6 billion by 2005 (both in 2005 dollars). Operating costs dropped in the same decade, from $24.7 billion to $20.7 billion.[17] Chemical, coal, and petroleum companies spent the most in capital and operating costs, about $12 billion among them. Perhaps most significantly, today's operating costs represent steadily smaller proportions of industry's total economic output—this finding suggests either that new pollution abatement equipment can run more efficiently (and thus at less cost) or that industry is cutting corners.[18] Both explanations may be true.

Is the news about industrial pollution good, bad, or uncertain? Undeniably, the country's air would have been far worse if industry had not been installing abatement equipment since 1970. Moreover, it is remarkable that, thus far, air pollution seems to rise at a smaller rate than economic growth. The bad news is that, overall, industry is consuming as much or more energy and raw materials, which in turn creates serious pollution and resource degradation, and is burdening the nation's air, land, and water with larger pollutant loads each year. Thus, even if the rate of increase is small, the overall burden grows, which is not the right direction for protecting public and environmental health.

Regulatory Experiments in Industrial Greening

Command-and-control approaches have clearly resulted in better environmental practices in business and industry and a significant curbing of traditional patterns of environmental pollution, but they ultimately fall short of the fundamental transformation needed in business and industry. The best end-of-pipe pollution management has not sufficiently reduced the overall pollution load generated by an economy that is ever expanding to satisfy the needs of a global population projected to grow by 50 percent over the next fifty years.

Therefore, attention has begun to shift from pollution reduction to pollution prevention, and to do so by devising incentive-based, self-regulatory and voluntary policy approaches (see chapter 9). Building on the successes and limitations of command-and-control regulation, U.S. industry and government moved on a limited basis toward an industrial greening approach (see Figure 10-1, cell D). Characterized by industry self-policing and government deterrence, this approach has achieved some successes but is clearly suboptimal—from economic and environmental perspectives—to the relationship that could exist if the situation in cell B were the case (across-the-board cooperation by both business and industry).

A first phase in the movement toward greening has used market incentives, self-reporting, and environmental management systems to improve corporate environmental performance. More recently, bolder experiments in self-regulation have advanced industry closer to the cooperative zone.

Phase I: Market Incentives, Self-Reporting, and Environmental Management Systems

As indicated in chapter 9, incentive-based approaches to environmental policy—such as emissions taxes, tradable permit systems, and deposit-refund programs—can be both effective at preventing pollution and more economically efficient. The EPA and many states have experimented with a wide range of market incentives, mostly since the 1980s, many of which have demonstrated promising results.[19] Experimentation with these "efficiency-based regulatory reforms" characterizes the second epoch of the environmental movement.[20]

Two of the most well-known experiments with market incentives include the Acid Rain Program of the 1990 Clean Air Act and the tradable permits program in the Los Angeles basin, known as the Regional Clean Air Incentives Market (RECLAIM). By most accounts, the Acid Rain Program made good on economists' predictions: Emissions decreased, and industry spent less money overall.[21] The Los Angeles program has also worked reasonably well in reducing emissions overall and in keeping down pollution control costs. However, it has been faulted for failing to effectively address the serious pollution "hot spots" existing within the overall region.[22]

Another significant second-epoch regulatory experiment consisted of self-reporting, auditing, and disclosure requirements, beginning in 1986 with the Superfund Amendments and Reauthorization Act. This legislation created the Toxics Release Inventory (TRI), the first major federal environmental program that moved away from the traditional command-and-control approach (characterized by heavy fines, specified emissions levels, and mandatory pollution abatement technologies) toward a "softer, gentler" self-reporting and cooperative framework. The TRI requires companies that have ten or more employees, and that use significant amounts of any one of the hundreds of listed chemicals, to report their annual releases and transfers of these chemicals to the EPA, which then makes these data available to the public through an annual report, the TRI *Public Data Release.*

The TRI requires companies to report their activities but does not require that they change their behavior. To view such policies as "all study and no action," however, would be to miss their contribution to what David Morell calls "regulation by embarrassment."[23] Indeed, environmental groups such as Citizens for a Better Environment, INFORM, and Greenpeace have seized on TRI data to publicize particularly heavy polluters. Some organizations make TRI data easily available over the Internet, allowing communities to view local toxic releases in map form.[24] Moreover, many state environmental agencies are basing their rulemaking on the TRI reports for industries in their states. Some industries have called for an end to the TRI reporting process because of these new regulatory uses.

In 2006, U.S. industry generated over 2 million tons of toxic waste—or about 12 pounds per American—a little over a third of which was released to air, land, and water treated or untreated.[25] Making year-to-year comparisons in toxic releases is difficult, because the EPA has expanded the kinds of facilities required to report releases as well as added to the list of chemicals to report. But if we limit ourselves to the three hundred or so core chemicals from the original reporting industries, total on- and off-site releases decreased 75 percent from 1989 to 2006.[26]

Although the EPA and industry applaud declines in toxic releases with every new TRI report, critics of the program have raised serious doubts about the validity of TRI data. For example, the Environmental Integrity Project (EIP) challenged the TRI results in a 2004 report entitled "Who's Counting? The Systematic Underreporting of Toxic Air Emissions." The EIP compared TRI reports for refineries and chemical facilities in Texas with actual smokestack emissions, in some cases using infrared scanners aboard aerial surveys. The EIP and the Texas Commission on Environmental Quality found that, for ten of the most common hydrocarbons, the EPA's reports underestimated actual emissions by 25 percent to 440 percent, raising serious concerns about outdated or inaccurate estimation methods that never actually measure releases themselves.[27]

The TRI is the most widely known and used database of self-reported information, but it is not unique. Thousands of companies around the world implement corporate environmental reports (CERs) every year and submit annual documents similar to their financial reports. These include "management policies and systems; input/output inventor[ies] of environmental impacts; financial implications of environmental actions; relationships with stakeholders; and the [company's] sustainable development agenda."[28]

Despite the appealing logic of self-reporting and auditing, it is exceedingly difficult to tell what such information achieves. Firms may be reluctant to accurately disclose potential problems with their facilities, fearing that regulators or third-party organizations (such as environmental litigants) may seize on the data to impose fines, facility changes in equipment and operation, or both.[29] The relatively small amount of research done on self-reporting suggests that, at best, CER systems improve company data collection and internal management, while possibly rendering environmental issues more transparent to government and the public.[30] More critical research shows that self-audits overwhelmingly reveal inventory and reporting violations (for example, of hazardous materials) rather than the much more serious unlawful emissions releases that the EPA discovers during its standard enforcement procedures.[31]

The third innovation of industrial greening actually modifies company management philosophies and practices. To implement green strategies, firms have adopted environmental management systems that include corporate environmental pledges, internal training programs, environmental education programs, and the use of cradle-to-grave systems of management control such as full-cost accounting and total quality management.[32]

Given their interest in avoiding environmental protection costs, why do firms adopt environmental management systems? After all, they are costly—in terms of both money and staff time—and they open private firms to external scrutiny that may not be welcome. Potoski and Prakash report that annual third-party audits for ISO 14001 certification (an international environmental management system discussed later in this chapter) can cost a small firm from $25,000 to $100,000 and much, much more for larger firms.[33] Based on a survey of over two hundred U.S. manufacturing plants, Richard Florida and Derek Davison identify the three most important reasons given for adopting such systems: management "commitment to environmental improvement . . . corporate goals and objectives . . ., and business performance." Compliance with state and federal regulations and improved community relations were other frequently cited reasons.[34]

Firms that go green can also be rewarded by the financial markets. Some investment brokers offer socially responsible environmental investment portfolios, although they are only a small (but growing) part of the investments market. By the mid-1990s about forty mutual funds were managing $3 billion of green investments.[35] In 2008 the Social Investment Forum reported that socially responsible investment portfolios—those that select companies through a wide range of social screens, include shareholder advocacy, or invest in communities—had reached $2.71 trillion in assets, or a little over 11 percent of the total investment assets under U.S. management.[36]

Managers of green mutual funds are constantly updating their social ratings of industries worthy of investment. Indeed, a number of studies now suggest a strong correlation between profitability and greening, although researchers are quick to point out that just how a company's profits are tied to its investments in pollution prevention or abatement is not clear.[37]

Do environmental management systems make a difference? Because of the difficulty linking management changes to verifiable, objective environmental outcomes, the jury is still out on that question. Some researchers conclude that such systems are effective when they have strong support from top management, who in turn rely on the systems to greatly improve company environmental awareness and to better track the flow of raw materials, energy, labor, quality, and costs throughout the firm's operations.[38] And adopters of environmental management systems report that they recycle more, release fewer air, water, and waste emissions, and use less electricity than do nonadopters, but such findings are not based on third-party audits.[39]

Phase II: Self-Regulation

More recently, greening includes businesses and industries coming together in voluntary self-regulatory associations, at home and around the world. Some of these efforts are "invited" by regulators, whereas others are initiated and implemented by corporate leaders themselves or, in a few cases, by nongovernmental organizations. The primary attractions of self-regulating, voluntary associations are that they reduce the compliance costs that can come with the avoidance of command-and-control regulation, they signal a company's green intent to consumers and those up- and downstream in the production chain (green branding), and they help companies to establish greater rapport with regulators and policy makers.[40] From a public policy perspective, voluntary self-regulation also reduces the cost to government that comes with regulating many thousands of firms throughout the nation and it fills a void where, for whatever reason, regulations do not exist.

Nonetheless, critics raise several objections to self-regulation. It may be nothing more than "greenwashing" by firms wishing to improve their public image without fundamentally changing their production practices, although some companies address this charge by subjecting their environmental practices to third-party audits and then reporting the results using widely accepted indicators.[41] By its very nature—adopting changes internal to a firm—the exact effect of self-regulation may be exceedingly difficult to assess; regulators and the public, in effect, must trust that firms are honest when reporting on their voluntary activities. Also, cleaner manufacturing often requires management, labor, equipment, or process changes, usually up front, before potential savings can be realized. As a result, these initial costs of self-regulation can seriously discourage participation. Finally, it can be argued that voluntary environmental management may lead to lower productivity if new practices are cleaner but less efficient than old ones.[42]

Since the mid-1980s the EPA has launched more than fifty voluntary programs, emanating mostly from its office of air, followed by its toxics and pollution prevention office and its waste, water, policy, and research offices.[43] One of the earliest and best-known is the 33/50 toxics reduction program. The origins of 33/50 reach back to 1989, when the EPA had sufficient TRI data to rank the largest polluters and the chemicals they release. The ranking revealed that nine chemical and petroleum manufacturers were responsible for vast releases of toxics. Rather than call for further regulation of these companies, then–EPA administrator William Reilly convened meetings with the companies' senior management, environmental organizations, and agency staff. In 1991 he emerged with a pledge to lead the way in industrywide voluntary reductions.

The program was named for its goal of reducing releases of seventeen high-priority chemicals by 33 percent by 1992 and 50 percent by 1995. The seventeen chemicals were selected from the TRI list based on "their relative toxicity, volumes of use, and the potential for pollution prevention opportunities."[44] Significant decreases in the release levels for these chemicals were not the program's only objective. The EPA also wanted to promote flexibility by challenging corporations to reduce toxic emissions by whatever means they felt most appropriate. Participants were encouraged to adopt source reduction rather than end-of-pipe control methods. More than eight thousand companies were identified as potential program participants and invited to enroll in the program. According to the *1995 TRI Public Data Release*, roughly 1,300 companies signed up more than 6,000 facilities for the 33/50 Program.

The EPA reported that the cumulative reduction achieved by participants during the program's first five years (1988–1993) totaled 46 percent.[45] The 1996 TRI report indicated a 60-percent overall reduction in the releases and transfers of the seventeen chemicals between 1988 and 1996.[46]

In many ways, the 33/50 Program is a success story. Not only were the reduction goals achieved, but also an EPA-sponsored study revealed that source reduction accounted for 58 percent of the decrease in releases and transfers for the 33/50 chemicals.[47] In 1997 the program was recognized by the Innovations in American Government Award Program as one of the twenty-five best government innovations in the country. At the same time, caution is warranted. The Government Accountability Office (GAO, formerly the General Accounting Office) has pointed out that so-called paper reductions accounted for 400 million pounds—or 27 percent—of the reductions achieved between 1988 and 1991. In addition, many of the reductions in 33/50 Program chemicals cannot be attributed directly to the program because 26 percent of the 1988–1991 reductions were reported by nonparticipants, and 40 percent of the reductions occurred before the program was established.[48] Despite the criticism, the relative success of 33/50 prompted a flow of voluntary programs throughout the 1990s, funded in large part by the Clinton administration's Climate Action Plan, which started in 1994 with what became the Climate Leaders initiative—designed to induce firms to reduce the release of greenhouse gases.[49]

Performance Track is the most comprehensive of the EPA's voluntary program initiatives. Begun in 2000, it was designed to encourage companies to adopt management practices that would lead to emissions reductions beyond those legally required.[50] Participants have to commit to measurable improvements in environmental performance, implement an environmental management system, and demonstrate their compliance. The EPA may, in turn, grant regulatory flexibility or a reduction in other reporting requirements. According to a survey of program participants, the primary reason for participation was the resulting positive rapport with the EPA and public recognition accruing to those enrolled in the program for their environmental care and responsibility. Since the program's inception in 2000, membership has grown at 12 percent a year and by mid-2008 was approaching 550.[51]

Ultimately the EPA's pollution prevention programs are still relatively new and must be evaluated cautiously. Benefits have been forthcoming. However, Walter Rosenbaum points out that these programs are also part "fanfare and guesswork." For example, the problems with the self-reported industry data—on energy and material inputs and waste streams—make it very difficult to assess what is happening in a firm. Moreover, EPA evaluators have not performed life-cycle assessments to determine if greening is truly occurring, as opposed to problems being displaced to other media.[52] And a question always lingering in the background is how to reconcile a voluntary approach with the primarily regulatory strategy and organizational culture of U.S. environmental policy.

The EPA is not alone in its efforts to promote green management. In 1996 the International Organization for Standardization (ISO) released its ISO 14001 environmental management standards. A company registering for ISO

14001 certification must (1) develop an environmental management system, (2) demonstrate compliance with all local environmental laws, and (3) demonstrate a commitment to continuous improvement.[53] By December 2006 over 129,000 firms had been ISO 14001–certified worldwide, but the United States—with about 5,585 certified firms—lagged behind most other developed countries in the proportion of its companies that sought and obtained this voluntary certification.[54] Increasingly, large manufacturers require that their suppliers become ISO 14001 certified as well. Ford Motor Company led the way in the mid-1990s but was soon followed by all the major automakers.[55]

Potoski and Prakash analyzed ISO 14001–certified firms in the United States, asking whether their air emissions were significantly lower than those of noncertified firms, and indeed they were. Their explanation is that, on the spectrum of voluntary measures, ISO 14001 represents a "weak sword," because it requires only third-party audits. A "strong sword" system, like the EPA's Performance Track program, requires third-party monitoring, public disclosure of audit information, and sanctions by program sponsors.[56] It remains to be seen just how much more environmental performance strong-sword environmental management systems can spur over weak-sword programs.

Industry trade associations also lead voluntary self-regulation efforts by their member companies; the chemical industry provides one notable example. In response to extensive and highly negative media coverage, the Synthetic Organic Chemical Manufacturers Association (SOCMA) adopted its Responsible Care program in 1988. This sectorwide code of conduct is now required of all Chemical Manufacturers Association members and has been adopted in some form by chemical manufacturers in forty-six countries.[57] It consists of ten guiding principles and six management practice codes. The guiding principles emphasize responding to community concerns; ensuring safety in all phases of production, transportation, use, and disposal; developing safe chemicals and supporting research on health, safety, and environmental effects of products, processes, and wastes; and helping to create responsible laws and regulations. The management codes are designed to improve each facility's emergency response capabilities; pollution prevention efforts; and safety in production, sales, distribution, and final disposal.

The SOCMA recently renamed the program ChemStewards and added other management dimensions, such as worker health and safety. The Responsible Care/ChemStewards program has also spawned an extensive mutual assistance network within the chemical industry, a network that includes very senior management. Companies that are far along in their implementation of the codes are asked to help those companies having difficulty complying. Through its Partnership Program, the SOCMA actively pushes the envelope of Responsible Care beyond the chemical industry. Partners are industries and associations that are not SOCMA members but that make, use, formulate, distribute, transport, treat, or dispose of chemicals.[58]

Early assessments of the Responsible Care program revealed disappointing progress. In one study of sixteen medium- to large-sized firms, about half took the Responsible Care codes seriously—mostly by adopting environmental management systems and integrating environmental principles throughout the firms.[59] A study comparing the environmental performance of firms adopting Responsible Care with those that had not revealed essentially no difference, a discouraging result suggesting that management changes may not be resulting in measurable environmental improvements.[60] Other critics point to a large gap between improvements to which SOCMA members have committed themselves and what companies have actually achieved. Part of the problem is that some of the management codes lack clear performance indicators and company statistics are not yet independently validated by third-party observers.[61]

All critiques aside, the U.S. chemical industry certainly pollutes less for each gallon of product than it did in prior decades. Toxic releases, energy consumption, and air emissions data all show that the industry's total production has grown faster than its pollution levels.

Win-Win as a Business Proposition

Overall the national effort, under the Clean Air Act, to reduce the air pollution emitted by business and industry, particularly in major urban areas across the United States, has been reasonably successful. Significantly helping this effort has been a dramatic reduction since 1970 of emissions per automobile on the road today. Many of our most polluted waterways have been cleaned up over this time period as well.

Balanced against this record, little evidence indicates that the emissions reduction and cleanup was accomplished in the most cost-effective manner. Possibly more important in looking forward, more than three decades of experience did not result in any visible commitment by a majority of businesses in the United States to a comprehensive, green transition.

As a result, we cannot be sure to continue abating large-scale pollution, nor that the aggregate of emissions from American industry will remain below previous levels. That is, businesses have made little commitment to moving beyond the long-standing command-and-control regulatory approach to a life-cycle environmental analysis of their products. We are even less likely to see widespread closed-system toxics management in manufacturing or product use, or sustained attention to more global and growing problems such as greenhouse gas emissions, destruction of natural habitats, or depletion of ocean resources. Equally important, no national policy goals or mandated regulations exist in the United States to move industry in this direction.

An instructive lesson from the voluntary programs established since 1991 is that when businesses form an alliance within their sector, either voluntarily or under the pressure of government policy, significant reductions can be realized, as illustrated by the chemical industry. Yet this very example suggests that chemicals may be the proverbial exception to the rule, since the change in that industry was due to the extraordinary public pressure brought to bear in the early 1990s as a result of the few colossal environmental disasters experienced in the United States and abroad and the fact that the industry is fairly well concentrated. Thus cooperation was brought about among a relatively few number of actors. In effect, the conditions for moving into a win-win game position for both government and the chemical industry existed, in that flexible regulation and volunteerism could be achieved, and the action moved into cell B of Figure 10-1. Today, few other such examples can be found within major business and industrial sectors.

How might this situation be changed? After a thorough review of the pilots and experiments in flexible regulation, self-regulation, and voluntary approaches since the mid-1990s, Marc Eisner has woven together the best components from each into a promising synthesis.[62] His approach is designed to overcome the natural (that is, rational) reticence of business and industry, and move the greening agenda beyond cell D, into cell B. He focuses on bridging the gap between business and government, on "harnessing the market and industrial associations to achieve superior results by creating a system of government-supervised self-regulation."[63]

The central propositions of his policy synthesis are as follows:

- Market rewards should be the primary motivator (placing emphasis on the "carrot") while retaining in reserve the traditional regulatory "stick."
- Reliance should be placed on trade and business associations; these sectoral and quasigovernmental organizations can serve as the central implementers of greening policy (they are "quasi" in that they are nonprofit organizations, although they would be imbued with governing authority).
- Emphasis should be placed on disclosure and "sunshine" provisions over government-prescribed techniques of emissions reduction and on-site government inspection.
- Sectoral associations would serve as intermediary entities, both to implement policy and to assure the government that policy would be carried out as intended.

The proposal does not require significant new public laws or the creation of new government bureaucracy because they can be woven together from existing programs and authority.

The critical virtue of this approach is that, if adopted as the overall framework for greening, it would mitigate the government's fear of becoming a "sucker," as well as business' fear of an overbearing regulatory regime, on the one hand, and of other businesses evading their responsibilities to go green, on the other. In short, we have in Eisner's proposal a game-theoretic and pragmatically attractive approach to moving government and business into cell B. As we mentioned at the outset, policy is set by the politics of policymaking and not simply by the logic of policy analysis, as attractive as it may be, and to which we now turn.

Another instructive lesson comes from those who are reengineering to compete in the twenty-first century worldwide economy and doing so in ways that are beginning to anticipate when green production will be the norm, not the exception, in the economic marketplace. Box 10-1 illustrates how some firms are implementing this strategy.[64]

Box 10-1   Three Industries, Three Companies, One Industrial-Ecological Strategy

In an era of global trade dominated by Chinese manufacturing, it's easy to wonder how American manufacturers can remain in business, much less whether they will pursue greening strategies. On the one hand, companies in the global South enjoy access to large pools of low-wage workers and structure their manufacturing at very high outputs. On the other hand, many American facilities are old, employ a mature and higher paid workforce, face very high cultural and legal expectations of environmental and health considerations, and enjoy few protections from the United States' open trade-access policies. Combined, these factors reasonably suggest that the downward spiral in American manufacturing of the past several decades should end in complete collapse.

But there is a new and promising *industrial-ecological* manufacturing paradigm imaginable for mature industrial nations like the United States that takes advantage of very short supply and distribution chains. The idea is simple. Raw materials and energy have become so expensive that recycling often appears more attractive than making commodities (like steel, paper, aluminum, glass, and plastic containers) from virgin materials. In most heavy industries, recycled raw materials require far less energy than do new inputs to turn them back into usable products. The United States also produces enormous amounts of high-quality recyclables every year, some of which find their way to re-processors overseas.

Asian exporters put a high value on recyclables, too. They send full container ships to U.S. ports but have relatively little to fill them with for the return voyage, so scrap metals, paper, and plastics fit the bill nicely. While it may seem sensible to ship recyclables to any country willing or able to re-process them, the fuel demand for transporting, say, a load of scrap metal, from the American Midwest to an inland Chinese mill, *and back to the U.S.,* is enormous.

Increasingly, American firms find ways to capitalize on their local or regional advantages: very highly productive labor, sophisticated automation, a weak dollar (which makes U.S. exports possible), steady supplies of recyclables, and nearby markets for finished products. Three midwestern companies provide very good examples of how manufacturers can be green and competitive.

- **SSAB, Iowa, Inc., Davenport, Iowa** This relatively new (1996) steel mill on the banks of the Mississippi uses exclusively old steel from scrap yards, brokers, and pipe makers within a couple hours of the plant. SSAB bought 1.4 million tons of scrap steel in 2007 (for $250–$500 per ton, depending on the quality). Using an electric arc furnace, the plant's five hundred highly paid (but

(Continues)

Box 10-1   *(Continued)*

nonunion) employees produced about 1.2 million tons of high-strength steel plate and coil, worth nearly $1 billion. In recent years, SSAB's heavy plate steel became bulldozer buckets and other parts of heavy equipment manufactured in the many Caterpillar and John Deere facilities located nearby. Interestingly, 20 percent of SSAB's sales now go to makers of wind turbines, most of which also are manufactured and sold regionally.

- **Jupiter Aluminum Corporation, Hammond, Indiana** Nearly every American driver knows what their license plates look and feel like. Most people don't know that one company in the gritty, northern Indiana town of Hammond makes almost all of the aluminum used for license plates in the United States. Jupiter Aluminum produces the aluminum for license plates as well as gutters and downspouts entirely from recycled aluminum. Most recently, the company produced about 150 million tons of aluminum coil, drawing on 160 million tons of scrap that it purchases for about $1 per pound from scores of sellers in the Midwest. Jupiter's 268 employees shipped about $250 million worth of aluminum products in recent years, making their workforce tremendously productive (in terms of dollars of product per worker).

- **Corenso North America, Wisconsin Rapids, Wisconsin** Situated close to the banks of the Wisconsin River, Corenso produces the corrugated cardboard cores (tubes) on which many other companies wind their papers, sheet metals, fabrics, and ribbons. Employing about 170 union workers, Corenso uses exclusively scrap cardboard from the upper Midwest to make the cardboard strips the company then winds and glues into tubular cores. In recent years, Corenso bought over 45,000 tons of scrap cardboard for $100–$125 per ton, relying on three to five regional scrap brokers and distributors as well as cardboard drop-offs for local residents. Corenso turns that scrap into some 35,000 tons of coreboard valued at about $18 million.

Each of these facilities faces strong command-and-control regulations requiring them to keep air emissions and wastewater low. But they all went much further than this regulatory "floor." Under pressure by a very tough Iowa Department of Natural Resources, SSAB steel meets some of the most stringent particulate matter requirements faced by any steel mill anywhere in the world. Jupiter Aluminum installed an "oxy-fuel"-fired furnace, allowing it to burn natural gas in a pure oxygen environment, thereby eliminating all of its nitrogen oxide emissions. And Corenso's reliance on recycling means that the company can re-pulp scrap cardboard with no chemicals, thereby releasing almost no waste to the city sewage treatment plant or to the Wisconsin River.

Mixed Signals from Industry and Washington

Despite the good image nurtured by corporate public relations officers, many industry lobbyists still work assiduously at blocking or rolling back environmental mandates.[65] Industry political action committees are keeping up a steady stream of campaign contributions to anti-environmentalist legislators, just as they have done for years.[66] Indeed, the chemical industry's strong political lobbying to weaken existing environmental protection legislation and to prevent new legislation undermines the credibility of its own Responsible Care/ChemStewards program. The American Chemistry Council became concerned enough with its industry's poor reputation that it adopted third-party auditing as part of a newly reinvigorated Responsible Care initiative.[67]

For its part, George W. Bush's administration did little to move industry and the government toward win-win outcomes depicted in cell B; rather, the administration's general retreat from regulatory enforcement moved the country further into cell A (in which the federal government can end up being a "sucker").

From the start of the Bush administration, pro-enforcement advocates took a back seat while the EPA was instructed to drop air pollution lawsuits that were close to successful settlement, relax standards for mercury in air emissions and for arsenic in drinking water, and advance energy production goals over conservation and habitat protection.[68] The most significant retreat from command-and-control regulation came when the administration yielded to industry pressure on the subject of new source review. In place for decades, new source review required new, better pollution controls when industries upgraded or expanded their facilities. Led by electric power utilities burning coal in old plants, lobbyists argued that new source review would impose hundreds of millions of dollars in new, unnecessary costs—and could prevent much-needed expansion of the country's electric-power-generating capacity.[69] In the end, the revised regulations "said utilities would not have to add new pollution-control devices if upgrades and construction projects did not cost more than 20 percent of the plant's value—a loophole all sides said was huge."[70] From its first days in office, President Barack Obama's new administration signaled its intention to dramatically review and revise many rules, environmental ones foremost among them (see chapter 16).

Reaching beyond Win-Win

We assume that devising ways to improve protection of the environment will need to build on the several generations of existing law and public policy, and any thought of disregarding these and starting anew is unrealistic. For this reason, the synthetic approach conceived by Eisner, designed to harness the core self-interested impulses of business and government on behalf of protection of the natural environment, is appealing. To be successful, these policies require business to improve the production of material goods and services while reducing to a minimum the adverse impacts on the natural environment. Indeed, this is not only the win-win of game theory but also the "double bottom-line" aspiration of industrial ecology today. As a blueprint for a politically realistic, near-term policy goal, we believe Eisner provides an ambitious though realizable approach to environmental protection and the greening of industry.

Not even the best policy ideas succeed in the real world, of course. With this in mind, should the Eisner approach fail and it becomes necessary to look for more ambitious though over-the-horizon approaches, they do exist. We can suggest two options in particular to underscore the point. These are the "theory of economic dynamics of environmental law" articulated by David Driesen,[71] and steady-state, or "true cost economics," long advocated by Herman Daly.[72] In a recent treatise on law and the environment, Driesen argues that dramatic greening is unlikely until the priority given to efficiency and benefit-cost thinking in neoclassic microeconomic behavior is replaced by the goal of encouraging "dynamic technology change" and adaptation, in a world of growing natural resource scarcity.

A second and similarly ambitious and transformative approach consists of efforts to refocus attention at the macroeconomic level away from the exclusive attention on production of material goods and human services to balancing production with the costs to natural assets and the environment, a movement led by Daly and a small but growing number of "ecological economists" around the world.

In the effort to deal with climate change, many new policy ideas are being introduced that will address the range of environmental and resources issues raised throughout the first and second environmental epochs and that have been addressed piecemeal by the EPA and the federal policy it reflects. Today these issues are being tackled with new vigor and in a more comprehensive manner and, in many ways, not simply as public policy that government imposes on business and industry, but from myriad business concerns. These concerns motivate business and industry to think more in the longer term and strategically. On the one hand, both will anticipate enormous market opportunities at home and abroad. On the other hand, they will feel strong government pressure as the world begins to feel the unprecedented and challenging effects of climate change.

Market opportunities or challenges like the meltdown in the financial services sector in 2008 may shape industrial greening as much or more than new policy programs. The relatively low energy prices that American companies enjoyed throughout the 1990s and early 2000s have disappeared and are not likely to return soon. Moreover, President Obama's new administration will certainly be more receptive to adopting a national climate change strategy than was the Bush administration—indeed, two weeks into the new administration, Obama's new EPA administrator, Lisa Jackson, declared her intent to review California's Clean Air Act waiver request. If she grants the waiver, as expected, California would be allowed to regulate carbon dioxide emissions from automobiles, thereby forcing auto makers to build far more efficient vehicles much more quickly than federal rules require.

And for the first time in perhaps a generation, many large companies view green-tech as the next high-growth frontier for the United States.

Indeed, during his presidential campaign, President Obama repeatedly invoked the notion that five million new jobs could be created by the new, green economy. How rapidly and extensively green industry will grow may depend not only on energy and materials prices, but also on whether state and federal policymakers connect environmental policy to trade, development, labor, and tax policies.

Suggested Web Sites

Independent Analysis of Corporate Environmental and Social Performance

Corporate Social Responsibility Network (www.csrnetwork.com) A third-party "benchmarking" consulting group that offers corporate social and environmental responsibility auditing.

The Global Reporting Initiative (www.globalreporting.org) An independent nongovernmental organization charged with developing and disseminating globally applicable sustainability reporting guidelines.

Innovest Strategic Advisors Group (www.innovestgroup.com) A research and advisory firm specializing in analyzing companies' performance on environmental, social, and strategic governance issues.

The Pacific Sustainability Index (http://www.roberts.cmc.edu/PSI/whatthescoresmean.asp) Produced by the Roberts Environmental Center, the PSI relies on two different types of questionnaires, one general and one sector specific, to analyze the quality of sustainability reporting among some of the largest corporations in the world.

Six Sigma (www.isixsigma.com) Promoting in business the adoption, advancement, and integration of Six Sigma, a management and auditing methodology to identify errors or defects in manufacturing and service.

Business Sustainability Councils

World Business Council for Sustainable Development (www.wbcsd.ch) A global green industry clearinghouse.

World Resources Institute (http://povertyprofit.wri.org) Global environmental clearinghouse with programs tying industry to development.

Leading Business and Environment Journals

Business Strategy and the Environment (www3.interscience.wiley.com/cgi-bin/jhome/5329) Publishes scholarship on business responses to improving environmental performance.

Corporate Social Responsibility and Environmental Management (www3.interscience.wiley.com/cgi-bin/jhome/90513547) A journal specializing in research relating to the development of tools and techniques for improving corporate performance and accountability on social and environmental dimensions.

Environmental Quality Management (www3.interscience.wiley.com/cgi-bin/jhome/60500185) An applied and practice-oriented journal demonstrating how to improve environmental performance and exceed new voluntary standards such as ISO 14000.

The Green Business Letter (www.greenbizletter.com) A monthly newsletter providing information for businesses and universities wishing to integrate environmental thinking throughout their organizations in profitable ways.

U.S. Environmental Protection Agency Sites

Energy Star (www.energystar.gov) A good site for learning about energy efficiency programs and efficient equipment, lighting, and buildings.

National Environmental Performance Track (www.epa.gov/performance track) An EPA program inviting companies to join as members that receive recognition for achieving leading-edge environmental performance.

Partners for the Environment (www.epa.gov/epahome/hi-voluntary .htm) A clearinghouse for the EPA's voluntary pollution prevention and management programs.

Toxics Release Inventory (www.epa.gov/triexplorer) The nation's list of toxic chemical releases from manufacturing, power generation, and mining facilities.

Notes

1. Robert B. Gibson, ed., *Voluntary Initiatives: The New Politics of Corporate Greening* (Peterborough, Ontario: Broadview Press, 1999).
2. Thomas Princen, Michael Maniates, and Ken Conca, eds. *Confronting Consumption* (Cambridge: MIT Press, 2002).
3. Huib Pellikaan and Robert J. van der Veen, *Environmental Dilemmas and Policy Design* (New York: Cambridge University Press, 2002); Nives Dolak and Elinor Ostrom, eds., *The Commons in the New Millennium: Challenges and Adaptation* (Cambridge: MIT Press, 2003).
4. Daniel A. Mazmanian and Michael E. Kraft, "The Three Epochs of the Environmental Movement," in *Toward Sustainable Communities: Transition and Transformations in Environmental Policy,* 2d ed., ed. Daniel A. Mazmanian and Michael E. Kraft (Cambridge: MIT Press, 2009).
5. Daniel C. Esty and Andrew S. Winston, *Green to Gold: How Smart Companies Use Environmental Strategy to Innovate, Create Value, and Build Competitive Advantage* (New Haven, Connecticut: Yale University Press 2006); Matthew Potoski and Aseem Prakash, eds., *Voluntary Programs: A Club Framework* (Cambridge: MIT Press, forthcoming).
6. U.S. Environmental Protection Agency (EPA), *EPA FY 2009 President's Budget* (Washington, D.C.: EPA, February 2008), www.epa.gov/budget.
7. Michael E. Porter and Claas van der Linde, "Green and Competitive: Ending the Stalemate," *Harvard Business Review* 73 (September–October 1995): 120–134; Esty and Winston, *Green to Gold.*

8. Doris Fuchs and Daniel A. Mazmanian, "The Greening of Industry: Needs of the Field," *Business Strategy and Environment* 7 (1998): 193–203; Daniel Press, "Industry, Environmental Policy, and Environmental Outcomes," *Annual Review of Environment and Resources*, 32 (2007): 1.1–1.28.

9. U.S. EPA, Technology Transfer Network, Clearinghouse for Inventories & Emissions Factors, *National Air Pollutant Emissions Inventory, 1970–2006*, www.epa.gov/ttn/chief/trends, August 4, 2008.

10. Roy Huntley, Environmental Engineer, Emission Factor and Inventory Group, EPA, personal communication, August 26, 2004.

11. Cary Coglianese and Jennifer Nash, eds., *Regulating from the Inside: Can Environmental Management Systems Achieve Policy Goals?* (Washington D.C.: Resources for the Future, 2001).

12. U.S. Department of Energy (DOE), Energy Information Administration, *Annual Energy Review*, Energy Consumption by Sector (Washington, D.C.: 2008), www.eia.doe.gov/aer/consump.html.

13. U.S. Census Bureau, *Annual Survey of Manufactures, Statistics for Industry Groups and Industries, 1993 and 2005*, www.census.gov/mcd/asm-as1.html.

14. U.S. DOE, Energy Information Administration, *Annual Energy Review* (Washington, D.C.: DOE, 1991, 1997).

15. U.S. DOE, Energy Information Administration, data from 1998, 1994, and 1991 *Energy Consumption by Manufacturers* reports, www.eia.doe.gov/emeu/mecs/.

16. U.S. DOE, Energy Information Administration, manufacturing industry trend data 1998 and 2002, www.eia.doe.gov/emeu/efficiency/mecs_trend_9802/mecs_trend9802.html.

17. U.S. Department of Commerce, *Pollution Abatement Costs and Expenditures*, MA-200(80)-1 and MA-200(05) (Washington, D.C.: U.S. Department of Commerce, Bureau of the Census, 1980, 1985, 1993, 1994, 2005).

18. U.S. EPA, National Center for Environmental Economics. "Pollution Costs and Expenditures: 2005 Survey," http://yosemite.epa.gov/ee/epa/eed.nsf/webpages/pace2005.html#whyimportant.

19. Walter A. Rosenbaum, *Environmental Politics and Policy*, 6th ed. (Washington, D.C.: CQ Press, 2005), 163.

20. Mazmanian and Kraft, "The Three Epochs of the Environmental Movement."

21. U.S. EPA, *The EPA Acid Rain Program 2002 Progress Report* EPA-430-R-03-011, November 21, 2003, www.epa.gov/airmarkets/cmprpt/arp02/index.html.

22. Daniel A. Mazmanian, "Los Angeles's Clean Air Saga: Spanning Three Decades," in *Toward Sustainable Communities*, 2d ed. (Cambridge: MIT Press, 2009), chap. 4.

23. David Morell, STC Environmental, personal communication, 1995.

24. For an example, see the Right-to-Know Network (www.rtknet.org) or Environmental Defense's Web site (www.scorecard.org).

25. U.S. EPA, *2006 Toxics Release Inventory Public Data Release*, www.epa.gov/triexplorer, accessed September 16, 2008.

26. Ibid.

27. Environmental Integrity Project, "Who's Counting? The Systematic Underreporting of Toxic Air Emissions," June 22, 2004, www.environmentalintegrity.org/pub205.cfm.

28. David Annandale, Angus Morrison-Saunders, and George Bouma, "The Impact of Voluntary Environmental Protection Instruments on Company Environmental Performance," *Business Strategy and the Environment* 13 (2004): 1–12.

29. Alexander Pfaff and Chris William Sanchirico, "Big Field, Small Potatoes: An Empirical Assessment of EPA's Self-Audit Policy," *Journal of Policy Analysis and Management* 23 (summer 2004): 415–432.

30. Annandale et al., "The Impact of Voluntary Environmental Protection Instruments."

31. Pfaff and Sanchirico, "Big Field, Small Potatoes."

32. John T. Willig, ed., *Environmental TQM*, 2d ed. (New York: McGraw-Hill Executive Enterprises Publications, 1994); Coglianese and Nash, *Regulating from the Inside*;

Marc Allen Eisner, "Corporate Environmentalism, Regulatory Reform, and Industry Self-Regulation: Toward Genuine Regulatory Reinvention in the United States," *Governance: An International Journal of Policy, Administration, and Institutions,* 17 (April 2004): 145–167.

33. Aseem Prakash and Matthew Potoski, *The Voluntary Environmentalists: Green Clubs, ISO 14001, and Voluntary Environmental Regulations* (Cambridge, U.K.: Cambridge University Press, 2006), 92.

34. Richard Florida and Derek Davison, "Why Do Firms Adopt Advanced Environmental Practices (and Do They Make a Difference)?" in Coglianese and Nash, *Regulating from the Inside.*

35. Ricardo Sandoval, "How Green Are the Green Funds?" *Amicus Journal* 17 (spring 1995): 29–33. One widely respected eco-rating of Fortune 500 companies is provided by the Investor Responsibility Research Center in Washington, D.C., www.irrc.org.

36. Social Investment Forum, *2003 Report on Socially Responsible Investing Trends in the United States,* 2007, www.socialinvest.org/areas/research.

37. David Austin, "The Green and the Gold: How a Firm's Clean Quotient Affects Its Value," *Resources* 132 (summer 1998): 15–17.

38. Annandale et al., "The Impact of Voluntary Environmental Protection Instruments;" Bruce Smart, ed., *Beyond Compliance: A New Industry View of the Environment* (Washington, D.C.: World Resources Institute, 1992).

39. Florida and Davison, "Why Do Firms Adopt Advanced Environmental Practices?"

40. Potoski and Prakash, *Voluntary Programs.*

41. Jan Mazurek, "Third-Party Auditing of Environmental Management Systems," in Robert Durant, Daniel Fiorino, and Rosemary O'Leary, eds., *Environmental Governance Reconsidered* (Cambridge: MIT Press, 2004), chap. 13; Eisner, "Corporate Environmentalism."

42. Natalie Stoeckl, "The Private Costs and Benefits of Environmental Self-Regulation: Which Firms Have Most to Gain?" *Business Strategy and the Environment* 13 (2004): 135–155.

43. Daniel J. Fiorino, *The New Environmental Regulation* (Cambridge: MIT Press, 2006); Daniel J. Fiorino, "Green Clubs: A New Tool for Government," in Potoski and Prakash, *Voluntary Programs,* chap. 7.

44. U.S. EPA, *1995 Toxics Release Inventory Public Data Release,* EPA 745-R-97-005 (Washington, D.C.: EPA, April 1997).

45. U.S. EPA, *1993 Toxics Release Inventory Public Data Release,* EPA 745-R-95-010 (Washington, D.C.: EPA, 1995).

46. U.S. EPA, *1996 Toxics Release Inventory Public Data Release,* EPA 745-R-98-005 (Washington, D.C.: EPA, 1996).

47. U.S. EPA, *1995 Toxics Release Inventory Public Data Release.*

48. U.S. Government Accountability Office (GAO), *Toxic Substances: Status of EPA's Efforts to Reduce Toxic Releases* (Washington, D.C.: GAO, 1994).

49. Fiorino, *The New Environmental Regulation,* 135.

50. Cary Coglianese and Jennifer Nash, *Beyond Compliance: Business Decision Making and the US EPA's Performance Track Program* (Regulatory Policy Program, Kennedy School of Government, Harvard University, 2006).

51. Cary Coglianese and Jennifer Nash, "Government Clubs: Theory and Evidence from Environmental Programs," in Potoski and Prakash, *Voluntary Programs,* chap. 8.

52. Walter A. Rosenbaum, "Why Institutions Matter in Program Evaluation: The Case of EPA's Pollution Prevention Program," in *Environmental Program Evaluation: A Primer,* ed. Gerrit J. Knaap and Tschangho John Kim (Urbana: University of Illinois Press, 1998); Douglas J. Lober, "Pollution Prevention as Corporate Entrepreneurship," *Journal of Organizational Change Management* 11 (1998): 26–37.

53. Information on ISO 14001 is available at www.ecology.or.jp/isoworld/english/english.htm.

54. International Organization for Standardization (ISO), *Twelfth Cycle: The ISO Survey of ISO 9000 and ISO 14001 Certificates,* www.iso.org/iso/publications_and_e-products/management_standards_publications.htm#090504.
55. Eisner, "Corporate Environmentalism," 150.
56. Prakash and Potoski, *The Voluntary Environmentalists.*
57. Synthetic Organic Chemical Association (SOCMA), "Overview of Responsible Care," 2004, www.socma.com/responsiblecare/index.htm.
58. Lois R. Ember, "Responsible Care: Chemical Makers Still Counting on It to Improve Image," *Chemical and Engineering News,* May 29, 1995, 11.
59. J. Howard, J. Nash, and J. Ehrenfeld, "Standard or Smokescreen? Implementation of a Voluntary Environmental Code," *California Management Review* 42 (2000): 63–82.
60. A. King and M. Lenox, "Prospects for Industry Self-Regulation without Sanctions: A Study of Responsible Care in the Chemical Industry," *The Academy of Management Journal* 43 (2000): 698–716.
61. Ember, "Responsible Care," 13.
62. Eisner, "Corporate Environmentalism." See also Marc Allen Eisner, *Governing the Environment: The Transformation of Environmental Regulation* (Boulder: Lynne Rienner Publishers, 2007).
63. Eisner, "Corporate Environmentalism," 145.
64. For many more examples of innovative industrial greening, see Esty and Winston, *Green to Gold*; Aseem Prakash, *Greening the Firm: The Politics of Corporate Environmentalism* (Cambridge: Cambridge University Press, 2000); Roy Lewicki, Barbara Gray, and Michael Elliott, eds., *Making Sense of Intractable Environmental Conflicts: Concepts and Cases* (Washington, D.C.: Island Press, 2003); Andrew Hoffman, *Carbon Strategies: How Leading Companies Are Reducing Their Climate Change Footprint* (Ann Arbor: University of Michigan Press, 2007).
65. Marc S. Reisch, "Twenty Years after Bhopal: Smokescreen or True Reform? Has the Chemical Industry Changed Enough to Make Another Massive Accident Unlikely?" *Chemical and Engineering News,* June 7, 2004, 19–23.
66. Larry Makinson and Joshua Goldstein, *The Cash Constituents of Congress* (Washington, D.C.: Center for Responsive Politics, 1994).
67. Marc S. Reisch, "Track Us, Trust Us: American Chemistry Council Says Will Supply the Facts to Earn the Public's Trust," *Chemical and Engineering News,* June 7, 2004, 24–25.
68. Christopher Drew and Richard A. Oppel Jr., "How Industry Won the Battle of Pollution Control at E.P.A.," *New York Times,* March 6, 2004; Rosenbaum, *Environmental Politics and Policy*; Maurie J. Cohen, "George W. Bush and the Environmental Protection Agency: A Midterm Appraisal," *Society and Natural Resources* 17 (2004): 1–21.
69. Bruce Barcott, "Changing All the Rules," *New York Times,* April 4, 2004.
70. Drew and Oppel, "How Industry Won the Battle of Pollution Control."
71. David M. Driesen, *The Economic Dynamics of Environmental Law* (Cambridge: MIT Press, 2003).
72. Herman Daly, *Beyond Growth: The Economics of Sustainable Development* (Boston: Beacon Press, 1996). For a discussion of true cost economics, see Brendan Themes, "True Cost Economics: The Current Economic Model Has Failed Us," *Utne Reader,* August 26, 2004, www.utne.com/webwatch/2004_163/news/11366-1.html.

11

Sustainable Development and Urban Life in North America

Robert C. Paehlke

Because most Americans live in or near large cities, the physical environment most of us experience is urban or suburban in character. This chapter considers how cities can contribute to environmental sustainability, including how they are helping to reduce climate change. Sustainability, in its broadest sense, is about maintaining the capacity of nature to support human well-being over the long term. Avoiding or ameliorating climate change is one aspect of that well-being; having sufficient water, energy, and food to live comfortable lives is another.

Viewed the other way around, sustainability is about the efficiency with which we use resources by meeting human needs at the least cost to nature. Some European theorists call this relationship societal metabolism, analogous to the metabolism of the human body that guides the rate at which all living beings eat, drink, breathe, and excrete. The character of our economies and activities determines the "metabolic" rate of extractions from and returns to nature and, thereby, the number of humans that can survive comfortably for the long term within the earth's carrying capacity.

Since the late 1980s, especially after publication of the report of the World Commission on Environment and Development, the concept of sustainability has become increasingly central to environmental policy (see chapter 16).[1] Daniel Mazmanian and Michael Kraft see this emphasis on sustainability as a central aspect of environmental policy initiatives undertaken since that time.[2] Especially at the state and local levels, climate change concerns have driven environmental policy, but in almost every case the adopted policies also serve broader sustainability goals, as we discuss later in this chapter.

Whereas earlier periods were characterized by policy formulations that treated the pollution of air, water, and land separately, the pursuit of sustainability considers all material flows into and out of human economies in an integrated way. Recent policy has also witnessed a shift in the jurisdictional focus of environmental decisions away from national governments, in some cases to the global level through environmental treaties and, at the same time and especially, to state and local governments. This chapter considers how the quality and design of urban spaces, a key responsibility of state and local governments, strongly influences the sustainability of nature, as well as the sustainability of economic prosperity and our quality of life.

Defining and Measuring Sustainability

Sustainability can be defined either broadly or narrowly. Broadly, *environmental* sustainability is the capacity to continuously produce the necessities of a quality human existence within the bounds of a natural world of undiminished quality. Sustainability requires thinking about society in terms of a triple bottom line—economic prosperity, social well-being, and environmental quality.[3] In this view, economic prosperity is more a means than an end, and human well-being—rather than "mere" prosperity—is the central goal of society and public policy. At any given level of prosperity, individuals, communities, or nations experience widely varying levels of health, happiness, fairness, and education. Some minimum of prosperity is obviously necessary for comfortable survival, but beyond that, considerable variability is found in the quality of society—and the quality of life within each society—obtained for each increment of wealth. There is also considerable variability in the degree of prosperity that can be obtained from any given rate of energy and materials use.

In the simplest of examples, given that highly energy-efficient refrigerators can preserve food using only 10–20 percent of the energy of inefficient refrigerators, significantly more prosperity and well-being would be obtained per unit of energy were all refrigeration so efficient. The sum total of thousands upon thousands of such changes in product design and production techniques is called *eco-efficiency*. The hope regarding eco-efficiency is that adequate environmental protection can be achieved through such efficiency gains rather than through actions that might limit prosperity. As important as eco-efficiency are the differences in the efficiency with which prosperity results in well-being. For example, one community might invest its prosperity gains in health and education and thereby obtain greater societal well-being than a jurisdiction that spends its increments of wealth on junk food, military weapons, and "toys" for the rich. Thus a so-called double efficiency is built into the triple bottom line of sustainability theory. Societies can produce wealth from nature more, or less, efficiently and can produce well-being from prosperity more, or less, effectively.

These same kinds of initiatives to improve the efficiency of energy and materials use will also reduce greenhouse gas emissions. Recycling rather than mining raw ore uses less fossil energy and thus results in less climate change. Improved public transit has a similar effect, as does buying food or other bulk products produced nearby rather than shipped from a great distance. Improved sustainability and reduced emissions of greenhouse gases almost always move in tandem.

Eco-efficiency and Well-being

Using environmental indicators, analysts can estimate how efficiently wealth and well-being are generated in environmental terms. The good news is that industrial economies are probably becoming more efficient in terms of resource use per dollar of GDP (gross domestic product, the sum of all goods and services produced) per capita. The bad news is that human numbers and prosperity are probably advancing more rapidly than this type of efficiency is improving; thus we are slowly imposing upon nature more and more. The challenge of sustainability is to accelerate eco-efficiency and to find ways to get more health and happiness (or whatever else we take well-being to be) out of each increment of prosperity.

There are, of course, disagreements about the urgency of eco-efficiency improvements in particular cases. How important, some would argue, is the existence of some tropical insect or amphibian species? Are they more important than the continued export of tropical woods from a desperately poor country? Is the risk of climate change more important than the, sometimes assumed, right of each person to drive whenever and wherever he or she wishes? Despite the difficulty, with some effort we can get fairly wide agreement on how to measure environmental quality and thereby eco-efficiency (in terms of air and water quality, habitat protection, and the efficient use of scarce and essential resources). Such measures can then be used to compare community or national performances over time.

Whereas questions regarding environmental quality are challenging, the matter of getting more well-being from prosperity is almost always controversial. To begin with, well-being is frequently affected by the proportion of societal wealth that is expended collectively rather than by individuals, and by the overall pattern of wealth distribution. Little agreement exists politically about what expenditures produce greater well-being, or indeed what *is* well-being and what is not. Mercifully, although everyone's priorities are different, we do not have to agree on everything. I may listen to opera and you to hip-hop, but we can still agree that infant mortality is a priority, that less crime is good, and that improving literacy is important. It is not, then, an impossible task to collectively develop a definition of well-being that is independent of (though likely related to) prosperity and that will still make sense to most people, however much they might disagree about what constitutes overall quality of life.

Sustainability and Public Policy

Sustainability clearly has implications for virtually every aspect of public policy. In one analysis of these implications, John Robinson and Jon Tinker advocate two forms of "decoupling" as essential to moving toward sustainability.[4] One is the decoupling of economic output (as measured by GDP) from the increased use of energy and materials. The other is the partial decoupling of social well-being from GDP per capita (that is, improving quality of life faster than the rate at which wealth increases, getting more for our money).

The first decoupling might be advanced by increasing taxes on raw materials (and lowering taxes on income, for example) to encourage sustainable production innovations and altered consumer behavior. Environmentalists call such a strategy a tax-shift approach to environmental protection, or eco-taxation. Such policies have been widely used in Europe and are now being adopted in the form of carbon taxes in Canada. The second decoupling (of prosperity and well-being) might be advanced through improved health care or education, or even—arguably—through reductions in work time (freeing time for family and community life). Of course, well-being improvements can also result from increased prosperity, especially if that added prosperity includes more equitable economic distribution. From the perspective of sustainability analysis it is a mistake to think that the only way to improve well-being is through greater prosperity or to assume that the only way to enhance prosperity is to increase the use of energy and raw materials.

The contrasting perspective that takes prosperity as measured by GDP to be the overwhelmingly dominant goal of society and public policy might be called *economism*. In terms of sustainability analysis, economism consistently misdirects public policy by misconceiving fundamental objectives. There are three bottom lines, not one; economism, as a perspective, is unduly one-dimensional. The fact that greater prosperity *could be* channeled to environmental and social improvements is, in a sense, irrelevant; sustainability analysis measures performance within each of the three dimensions inde-pendently. Increased wealth may turn out to be better in terms of all three dimensions, but two other questions need to be answered first. Is well-being rising both absolutely and per unit of prosperity? And are we increasing materials and energy efficiency at least as fast as we are expanding GDP? Some environmentalists would argue that such a rate of improvement is insufficient for the achievement of sustainability, but all would agree that it is a necessary interim goal.[5]

In terms of concrete policies, one approach to triple-bottom-line thinking has focused on efforts to serve social policy and environmental policy objectives simultaneously. The city of Chicago, for example, has established a "Green Corps" of hard-to-employ ex-prisoners and trained them for environmentally positive jobs such as refurbishing old computers and detecting leaks in housing pressurization. Such "green jobs" policies are increasingly receiving broad-based support as a way to reindustrialize the Midwest and, as Van Jones puts it, to "solve our two biggest problems simultaneously."[6] The two biggest problems are economic failure and climate change.

Sustainability and the Economy

Achieving sustainability involves altering most aspects of both production and consumption. Increases in commodity prices make manufacturers more oriented to sustainability concerns because using less energy and materials reduces costs. Sustainability initiatives, however, can hurt some industries. For example, if consumers opt for more durable products or greater energy efficiency, some businesses could lose sales. Even though other businesses might gain, policies that advance sustainability carry much potential for political and policy conflict.

Within what might be called the political economy of sustainability decisions, the character and design of cities and urban transportation systems are especially important. Our choices of transportation mode and the amount that we travel daily are greatly affected by urban planning, housing prices, municipal tax rates, the location of employment opportunities, and even crime rates and patterns. Transportation decisions have a large influence on sustainability—automobiles require more energy, metal, concrete, and land per passenger-mile than do most other forms of transportation. It is not just a matter of creating good public transportation; it is a matter of designing cities where people consistently find it easier to walk or to take a streetcar than it is to drive. We choose to drive only in part because it is (sometimes) an enjoyable experience. We also drive because the distances we must go exclude walking and because low-density, suburban-style neighborhoods may all but preclude convenient and affordable public transit.

Sustainability in Cities

One of the best places to begin to understand the overall sustainability impacts of today's cities is with the pioneering work of Peter Newman and Jeffrey Kenworthy. Their study of thirty-six cities demonstrated that choice of transportation mode, transportation fuel use, and air quality are primarily a function of residential density and land use patterns.[7] That is, more compact cities and mixed-use zoning (putting residential and commercial development in proximity to one another) result in reduced automobile use and increased use of public transit, bicycling, and walking (Table 11-1). Low-density, suburban-style configurations, with segregated residential and commercial uses, subtly discourage the use of most means of mobility other than automobiles. In those settings, getting to work, school, or a store or visiting friends usually requires a car or makes people wish they had one.

Even a modest increase in overall residential density, however, changes that reality to one that can offer a real choice of transportation modes. As Table 11-1 illustrates, typical western North American cities, whose streetscapes and functional arrays were established after 1945, are dominated by automobile use, as is (not surprisingly) Detroit. Many large cities, especially in eastern North America (Chicago, New York, and Toronto, for example), are more compact and have viable public transit systems. Some cities (Portland, Oregon; San Francisco; and San Diego, for example) have succeeded in becoming exceptions to this pattern. European cities are typically very different. Their downtown streets were developed long before the automobile and are not easily altered (one does not tear down five-hundred-year-old cathedrals). Moreover, Europeans have consciously invested in high-quality, well-integrated public transit systems, partly because they faced high gasoline prices earlier than we did in North America. In Vienna, for example, the air, rail, subway, and light rail (streetcar) systems are seamlessly interconnected and almost always faster and cheaper than driving.

Thus moderate density levels (as in, for example, a mix of commercial development, low-rise apartments, townhouses, and single-family dwellings on

Table 11-1   Density and Transportation

City	Car Use (km per capita)	Population and Job Density	Transit Use (km per capita)
Houston	13,016	15	215
Phoenix	11,608	16	124
Detroit	11,239	21	171
Chicago	9,525	25	805
New York	8,317	30	1,334
Toronto	5,019	65	2,173
Munich	4,202	91	2,463
Paris	3,459	68	2,405
London	3,892	66	2,121

Source: Peter Newman and Jeffrey Kenworthy, *Sustainability and Cities: Overcoming Automobile Dependence* (Washington, D.C.: Island Press, 1999).

Note: All figures are for 1990; population and job density is a combined index.

relatively compact lots) encourage frequent transit service as well as more walking and bicycling. Many other aspects of sustainability also follow from these moderate density levels and mixed-use configurations. For example, farmland and wilderness nearer to urban and suburban residents are preserved, a possibility recognized by the American Farmland Trust and the U.S. Conference of Mayors in a joint list of "Ten Actions for Rural/Urban Leaders."[8]

In more compact cities fewer materials are needed per capita because existing infrastructure is more fully utilized—more people use each sidewalk, water pipe, or fiber-optic cable. Also, less energy is used because distances are shorter, transit delivers more passenger-miles per unit of energy, and multiple-family dwellings use less heating and cooling per person (because fewer walls are exterior walls and there is less roof per square foot of living space). In addition, compact mixed-use settings open the possibility for co-generation (using waste process heat for commercial and residential heating) or even technological innovations such as Toronto's massive new Deep Lake Water Cooling System, which uses water from Lake Ontario to cool much of the downtown, saving enough electricity to power 12,000 air-conditioned homes.[9] Some cities in Spain and Sweden have even eliminated garbage and recycling trucks in favor of vacuum tube systems hooked to a central processing facility.

It is now widely recognized that urban sprawl leads to greater greenhouse gas emissions. In the United States, hundreds of millions of tons of carbon dioxide are emitted by motor vehicles each year. Overall, 30 percent of greenhouse gases come from transportation, and this proportion is rising even though automobiles have become, on average, 1 percent more fuel efficient per year since 1970. In this same period, however, per-vehicle emissions from light trucks, sport-utility vehicles, and vans have risen 30 to 50 percent, and until recent gas price increases, the number of these vehicles was increasing as a proportion of all vehicles.[10] Moreover, again until very recently, average distances driven increased in large part because city plans favored distant low-density arrays. The overall result was a continuous increase in transportation-sector carbon emissions and a political reluctance on the part of the United States to join the Kyoto agreement on climate change.

Happily, this pattern finally appears to be changing, with the lead coming primarily from America's cities. As detailed later in this chapter, a majority of American cities have taken action on climate change, but so, too, recently has the state of California. In late 2008, Governor Arnold Schwarzenegger signed into law legislation that directs the California Air Resources Board to set regional targets for reducing greenhouse gas emissions, primarily by requiring more compact residential development with new housing located nearer to jobs. Those regions that comply with the creation of denser communities will thereafter get an increased share of state transportation funding.

Proponents of sustainable cities have long advocated an approach that goes even further: reduced automobile dependency. In *Winning Back the Cities*, Newman and Kenworthy suggest an interconnected three-part solution: light rail, urban villages, and traffic calming. Light rail is fuel efficient, clean, quiet, land efficient, and cost effective. It is used extensively in many cities, including Portland and Toronto, and throughout continental Europe. Urban villages are small-scale neighborhoods that "combine medium and high density housing with diverse commercial facilities, in car-free environments."[11] Arterial roads lead to parking at the edges of these transit-serviced urban arrays where internal access is limited to emergency and delivery vehicles. The village-scale neighborhoods are pedestrian friendly with small parks and outdoor cafés replacing most roadways. In other urban residential neighborhoods, traffic-calming measures restrain the speed of auto traffic and in effect guide through-traffic onto nearby arterial roads. The three initiatives together, especially with an added emphasis on pedestrian and bicycling corridors, make for vastly more livable (and sustainable) urban spaces.

This urban-oriented environmental vision is very different from the early days of environmentalism. In the late 1960s and early 1970s many environmentalists responded to urban pollution with ideas about getting "back to the land" and closer to nature. Today's approach is diametrically different—the emphasis is on reconfiguring settlement into more transit-friendly cities and on redesigning products and production processes. The notion that more and more people should live their everyday lives closer to nature may require more energy and materials and also runs the risk of "loving nature to death" through human overpopulation within scenic regions and once-wild spaces.

These proposals are in keeping with the new spirit of smart growth that is taking hold in many North American cities, sometimes as part of comprehensive state-level climate change initiatives.[12] In *Sustainability and Cities*, Newman and Kenworthy envision a sustainable city as one that is multicentered, with each node incorporating walking and bicycling access to work, shops, and local services. They describe a transition strategy in this way:

How can this future "Sustainable" City be achieved in stages? The stages are considered to be: (1) revitalizing the central and inner cities, (2) focusing development on transit-oriented locations that already exist and are underutilized, (3) discouraging urban sprawl by growth management strategies, and (4) extending transit systems, particularly rail systems, and building associated urban villages to provide a sub-center for all suburbs.[13]

Frequently used services are easily accessible by short walking or bicycling trips, and travel to other urban nodes by public transit is as convenient and affordable as by automobile. Cars remain for the uses to which they are best suited—for weekends in the country, for carpools, or for moving larger loads. In New York City, which has very high residential and commercial densities, significant automobile congestion and a well-developed transit system, Mayor Michael Bloomberg proposed to adopt a congestion pricing plan for automobile use similar to that used in London, England, to discourage cars from entering the city. The city also planned to convert its vast taxi fleet to hybrid vehicles but in late 2008 met a roadblock in federal court. In a narrow interpretation of the Clean Air Act, the court ruled, in support of taxi fleet owners, that vehicle emissions were primarily a matter of federal jurisdiction. The city may appeal or opt to work with the Obama administration to alter its rules.

Within sustainable cities, then, private automobiles become one transportation choice among many, rather than the only viable option. In European cities typically about 40 percent of trips to work are by public transit and 20 percent by walking or bicycling. In contrast, in Detroit, less than 1 percent of all trips are by public transit.[14] In many other North American cities, only poor, young, and elderly people regularly use public transit, though use has increased significantly in many cities, especially in the South and West. There are many reasons for this difference, not the least of which is habit—but the "driving" reason is sprawl syndrome. If cities are configured on the assumption that nearly everyone has a car, indeed everyone will need a car and will either use it for almost every purpose or experience considerable inconvenience. Moreover, when there are no separate pathways for bicycles used for transportation (rather than recreation), the risk of car-bicycle accidents is far higher. When too few people use transit, service is less frequent and systems lose money. Few who can afford to drive will opt for transit if service is infrequent or if residences, employment, and commerce are highly dispersed.

The Social Psychology of Urban Sprawl in America

Sprawl also has many less apparent causes, including for some the stresses of contemporary urban life and, for many, a search, perhaps not fully conscious, for an increased sense of community or a reconnection with nature. Advertising for automobiles and suburban housing plays on such desires. In ads, automobiles travel on winding, empty roads through stunning natural scenery or miraculously sit alone on mountaintops. Or they are used to get busy parents to soccer games or school plays—metaphors for family and community life. New suburban developments have bucolic names like Meadowbrook Estates. The quest for nature or community via a freeway is, of course, mostly an illusion. Most driving is on congested roads from one suburban parking lot to another, and many of the stresses of urban life result from automobile traffic itself. Sprawl begets traffic and air pollution that in turn encourages more people to desire an escape.

Driving becomes the most convenient way to travel if buildings and activities are arrayed in low-density patterns. Once a majority opts for single-family dwellings distant from nonresidential activities, heavy automobile use becomes a necessity. The resulting fossil fuel use accelerates climate change and is unsustainable in the long term. Yet our urban arrays—both buildings and infrastructure—are built to last for a century or more.[15] Indeed, given the environmental price paid to extract the materials to build cities, sustainability analysis indicates that most buildings and infrastructure *should* last for centuries. On all counts, urban sprawl is simply bad planning, planning with too short a time horizon. Unfortunately, other considerations affect the everyday decisions that produce this result.

Historically, inner cities in North America have had a higher concentration of social problems and related public costs, and many newer suburbs have avoided some of these costs through zoning and planning rules that exclude everyone without substantial income or wealth. This concentration of social problems has encouraged flight from inner cities, undermining the property tax base and exacerbating the deterioration of inner city infrastructure. This familiar tale has, however, been slowed or even reversed in many U.S. cities. Sprawling land use patterns are still with us, but cities like Chicago, Portland, and Pittsburgh are creating new residential housing downtown, and other cities such as New Orleans and even sprawl-famous Los Angeles are now adding popular streetcar systems that help to promote more compact development patterns.[16]

The recent fall in housing prices as well as resale challenges and foreclosures have often been most severe at a distance from city centers, shopping, and jobs.[17] This began when gasoline was at its peak price, but even with a decline in gas prices, many potential buyers of those homes remain wary of a return to higher prices when economic recovery takes hold. People wisely tend to think about the long term when they make housing decisions. The new Obama administration is committed to both economic recovery and climate change action. There are opportunities here to act on both simultaneously by encouraging further residential expansion in city centers and encouraging mixed-use restoration in failing suburbs.

Urban sprawl has deep historic roots as well as contemporary social and economic causes. One historic root cause lies in the response by urban planners to the ugly and unhealthy industrial cities of the late nineteenth and early twentieth centuries—the notion of a "garden city" far removed from industry and squalor. Planners of that era rendered people's dreams—separating family life from work in steel mills and slaughterhouses as soon as, and as far as, transportation options allowed. These patterns have continued, out of habit and owing to the ease of travel by automobile, even though many more people now work in more environmentally benign or even attractive workplaces.

Sprawl is also advanced by the comparatively low cost of land at the urban fringe. Moreover, many people choose to distance their residence from locally unwanted land uses including environmentally contaminated former industrial lands, from transportation and transmission corridors, and from rundown neighborhoods. These latter areas are often badly serviced commercially, and too often educational quality and infrastructure maintenance are low and crime and unemployment are high. All of these factors have contributed to the erosion of quality of life in some parts of the urban core and ultimately accelerate sprawl. Thus enhanced environmental sustainability requires social expenditures to improve the quality of life in inner cities. Fortunately some cities are beginning to reverse these patterns.

The quality of urban life is a subtle thing that depends on a widespread sense of trust and safety, but crime rates are often lower within the active streetscapes of neighborhoods with a mix of commercial and residential buildings. This is why the urban renewal attempts of the 1950s and 1960s failed so singularly despite good intentions and massive public expenditures.[18] Once a sense of safety was lost, urban streets were feared, and many people moved to protected buildings, other neighborhoods, or gated suburban communities. People were willing to drive many miles on a daily basis in order to reside within single-class, originally largely white, residential areas where there is rarely anyone on the street who is not in a vehicle. In a search for security and community we settled for the former and often lost much of the latter, save for select friends. Work and even shopping are now too frequently physically separated from residential areas, and a real sense of neighborhood and community is thereby undermined.

Public social life in America, as Robert Putnam has documented, is in decline.[19] One reason for this decline is the scarcity of spaces, settings, and opportunities in which people establish on a daily basis a sense of community. Whether in urban or suburban settings we typically no longer live near the people with whom we work. Nor do we often happen upon friends on downtown streets; rather, our business is conducted by driving to distant offices and malls. Moreover, in many suburban settings there are few drop-in community spaces. Civic life is minimal, in part because everyone works long hours and almost everyone commutes a considerable distance. That, combined with the pervasiveness of television, leaves less time for participatory citizen activities. The suburban setting chosen in the expectation of a greater sense of community is friendly enough but often less actively community oriented than the old urban neighborhoods of an earlier era.

From this perspective we can better understand the multidimensional potential of Newman and Kenworthy's urban villages. These intraurban islands can be both green (creating usable public space on lands that might have been used for roadways) and mixed use, with high potential for the natural evolution of a sense of community. Given proximity, more everyday activities can be conducted on foot. This approach, with transit availability and a high proportion of multiple-family dwellings (mixed with single-family options), will also result in reduced per-capita energy and materials use and greater environmental sustainability. Also contributing to sustainability is a new emphasis on the restoration, adaptation, and incorporation of existing buildings into the increasingly revitalized urban communities. Recent restoration and development efforts in parts of New York City's Harlem and much of downtown Oakland, California, serve as an inspiration in this regard. Finally, better land utilization within the urban core will free land at the city's periphery for agriculture, recreation, and habitat preservation; and urban community gardens, some on new green rooftops, can bring those realities right into the urban core.

Protecting Wilderness through Inner City Restoration

Sprawl threatens wilderness and habitat in at least five ways: (1) sprawl disperses what are called urban shadow functions (gravel pits and waste disposal sites, for example) into the countryside, (2) sprawl, as we have seen, encourages transportation options that are themselves more land intensive, (3) energy-inefficient transportation adds urgency to energy extraction activities within wilderness regions, (4) sprawl may contribute to a pattern of deteriorating urban cores and building everything anew at the periphery, thereby encouraging additional extraction of raw materials in wilderness areas, and (5) sprawl displaces near-urban agriculture often to lands of lesser quality, thereby requiring more land per unit of agricultural output.

Existing buildings and infrastructure are, in effect, embedded energy and previously lost wildlife habitat. Urban core restoration avoids imposing those costs a second time. In sum, social welfare, wilderness protection, and environmental sustainability are all linked to the restoration of America's inner cities. These things as well as architectural preservation, urban villages, and sprawl-fighting smart growth are all part of making cities more sustainable.

Urban villages emphasize quality mixed-use urban nodes where commercial and residential uses are close to one another, lessening the need for extensive transportation. Examples include the Pearl District in Portland, River Walk in San Antonio, and the Michigan Avenue area in Chicago. Effective mixed-use urban neighborhoods are what sustainable cities are all about. So, too, are imaginative policy initiatives; it is to these policies that we now turn.

Climate Change, Smart Growth, and Sustainability

Smart growth has gained considerable public attention as a concept. In part it was a response to the urban growth control measures of the 1960s and 1970s that, as Lamont Hempel notes, rarely succeeded because "the overall pattern has been to shift development to nearby communities."[20] The American Planning Association's Growing Smart guidelines specifically emphasize regional planning, the control of sprawl, environmental protection, and fiscal responsibility rather than growth at all costs. Smart growth does not oppose development so much as it seeks to create more sustainable communities. Sustainable community planning often uses highly participatory processes to create livable urban areas and restore local democracy, community, and civic life. Hempel, for example, sees sustainable communities and Putnam's sense of urgency regarding social capital as closely linked.[21]

Several cases demonstrating the historic roots of this linkage have been discussed by Alex Farrell and Maureen Hart.[22] Beginning in 1990, for example, citizens in the organization Sustainable Seattle systematically measured and reported their community's progress toward sustainability using a set of indicators chosen with extensive community involvement. Interestingly, many participatory sustainable community and smart growth initiatives have arisen following periods of local economic decline. In Pittsburgh, once characterized as a Rustbelt city, manufacturing fell from 50 percent of total employment to 11 percent between 1970 and 1990, and the city's population fell from 700,000 to 360,000 between 1950 and 1990. As Franklin Tugwell and colleagues put it, "Outside the former Soviet Union, few places on earth have undergone such profound economic change in times of peace. The result transformed the city. Prime riverfront lands became contaminated brownfields, often with rusted hulks of mills still present on-site."[23] The initial impetus for change in Pittsburgh came from an urgent need for a more sustainable economy; an emphasis on incorporating greener forms of development evolved through extensive public participation.

Transformations of this kind have increasingly been linked to climate change and to America's energy problems. In 2004 the Apollo Alliance (see list of Web sites) proposed revitalizing the American industrial economy by moving the United States to a commitment to join the global effort to reduce greenhouse gas emissions. By the 2008 presidential election campaign, there was wide support for national action on climate change and greater energy independence.

At the municipal government level, there have also been exciting initiatives on climate change, starting on the day that the Kyoto Protocol came into force in the 141 signatory nations that had ratified it to that point. Mayor Greg Nickels of Seattle challenged mayors elsewhere to join the effort to reduce global warming gases. Soon eight others from notably progressive cities—including San Francisco; Portland; Minneapolis; Burlington, Vermont; and Boulder, Colorado—had joined in writing to 400 others. The Conference of Mayors backed the effort unanimously. By 2006 it had the support of 250 cities and by late 2008, more than 900, with a total population of over 80 million.

Seattle's climate change efforts are handled by its Office of Sustainability and the Environment and include tree planting and urban reforestation, enhanced bicycling opportunities, green roofs on city buildings, improved walkability, technical assistance to builders, zoning changes downtown that discourage sprawl at the city's edges, shoreline and wetlands protection, reduced use of fossil fuels in city-owned vehicles, and additional increases in recycling and composting of waste.

Sustainability initiatives at the community level have also sometimes helped to advance aspirations for renewed democracy and civic life. The first steps in the U.S. Department of Energy's *Ten Steps to Sustainability* sought to involve communities in participatory local sustainability assessments.[24] The Sustainable Seattle initiative, one of the earliest of its kind, involved large numbers of citizens in the planning process. Sometimes it is even possible to achieve wide consensus, as in the case of the 1997 comprehensive regional conservation plan developed under the U.S. Endangered Species Act for a large region near San Diego.[25]

At the same time, *unsustainable* development tendencies continue within a pattern that might be called the big box syndrome. Many successful retailers have opted for a marketing strategy that emphasizes very large outlets at the periphery of urban regions, in low-cost locations likely to become the site of future urban sprawl, depending in the meantime on shoppers willing to take a long drive "in the country" (but near a freeway off-ramp). Urban locations are selected less often because land and labor costs are higher, as are property taxes. Taxes are lower because the municipal jurisdiction has few social problems or, for that matter, residents. This strategy helps to keep the price of goods low.

The net effect of these pressures, combined with extensive "exurban" residential developments (distant gated communities on golf courses, for example), is to remove land from agricultural use and to diminish wildlife habitat.[26] An Environmental Law Institute study of development in Virginia came to this conclusion: "Land use patterns in Virginia follow a national trend of rings of new residential developments around existing community centers. These new residential developments typically are bedroom communities from which residents must drive long distances to work, school, and other activities. This type of land use consumes farm land and open space, damaging Virginia's rural economy and natural heritage."[27] The overall result in many locations was, until the collapse of housing construction in 2008, a pattern whereby lands under development were expanding much more rapidly than was the population. As noted earlier, outer suburban and exurban areas have been among the hardest hit by the downturn.

From 1970 to 1990 the population of the Chicago metropolitan area expanded by 4 percent, but the area of developed land expanded by 46 percent. The population of the Los Angeles region expanded by 45 percent, whereas developed land expanded by 300 percent. This trend was accompanied by a sharp increase in vehicle-miles traveled, by 68 percent nationwide between 1980 and 1997.[28]

The clear alternative, one that is increasingly being adopted, is to guide a higher proportion of new development within existing urban configurations, more fully utilizing already urbanized spaces. A coordinated effort involving land use controls, incentives, and transit development is essential. Notable success stories in this regard include any number of European cities but also Portland, Chicago, Boston, Seattle, Toronto, and Vancouver, British Columbia.[29] In the 1970s Portland rejected the Mt. Hood freeway that would have eliminated three thousand homes through the downtown of the city. In its place the city built a light rail system in the face of much scoffing from traditional traffic experts and others. The initiative has been a stunning success, and within the downtown core a large fare-free zone has, in turn, spurred residential and commercial development. Boulder is notable for the extensive greenbelt surrounding the city and for encouraging residential development within its boundaries. Portland and Boulder initiated traffic-calming measures within residential areas, bicycle routes, and restraints on downtown parking. Boulder has also developed urban villages with restrictions on cars and a variety of transit-use incentive schemes.

Boston uses gas taxes to fund transit and has kept fares exceptionally low. It has also frozen the downtown parking supply. The result of these and other measures was a 34-percent increase in transit use (at a time when there was a 6-percent average increase in all U.S. cities); 22 percent of trips to work occurred via walking, cycling, or transit, well above the national average. Moreover, automobile use has declined by even more than transit use increases would explain because Boston reversed the trend of declining downtown residential population earlier than most, making the city core increasingly vital and attractive.

Other innovative initiatives to enhance sustainability undertaken by state, regional, and local jurisdictions include land trusts and transferable development rights to protect open spaces within an overall development plan. Advocates of urban sustainability have also advanced ideas such as location-efficient mortgages (which provide preferred rates to those living closer to public transit, where housing prices are typically higher) and land value taxation (which taxes land more heavily than buildings, thereby promoting somewhat more compact urban development and discouraging the speculative purchase of open land). Some progressive U.S. banks, such as ShoreBank, permit buyers of homes in transit-friendly locations to carry larger mortgages because their transportation costs are likely to be lower.[30]

Several municipal jurisdictions—such as Santa Monica, California; Austin, Texas; and Boulder—have undertaken green building initiatives that include, in some cases, tax advantages to builders for using green building materials. Many cities—including Chicago and Syracuse, New York—have provided financing or tax incentives to creative urban core preservation and restoration initiatives. And, within the private sector, the U.S. Green Building Council has developed LEED (Leadership in Energy and Environmental Design), a voluntary standard for the construction of high-performance, sustainable buildings that has resulted in numerous examples throughout the country.[31] Most of these green (LEED) buildings thus far are new, but some, including the 112-year-old Security Building in St. Louis, involve substantial (in this case, $14.5 million) renovations of historically important buildings.[32]

Increasing numbers of cities have now adopted LEED standards for new municipal buildings and some, including Los Angeles and Chicago, are looking to renovate all municipal buildings to a LEED standard. Toronto is considering a program that would reclad the exterior facades of all high-rise residential buildings in a comprehensive program that would reduce total greenhouse gas emissions in the city by several percentage points. Other cities are seeking to undertake or encourage the development of alternative sources of energy, including the extraction of methane from waste treatment plants and landfills. Austin Energy, an agency of the city of Austin, "represents the primary mechanism for the city to achieve its goals of reduced air emissions, and has invested in providing its energy from renewable sources, primarily from 165 large wind turbines (windmills) located in West Texas."[33]

Cities and states can also encourage green home construction with subsidies and policies that provide financial incentives for building green. In New York City, developer Les Bluestone interspersed seventy green homes (some triplexes) in vacant lots and around public housing towers. Energy-efficient boilers and appliances added $8,000 to the cost of each house, but some of that was refunded by the state of New York and a bank foundation that together promote reduced energy costs and other green features. Harlem developer Carleton Brown builds condominiums with cleaner indoor air and geothermal heating and cooling systems that save residents $1,000 per year through reduced energy use. The state of New Jersey offers builders up to $7,500 toward more efficient heating systems, triple-glazed windows, and other features.[34] Residents of Berkeley, California, can use city-approved solar contractors to install up to $20,000 worth of solar panels, with the city fronting the money as a loan that can be repaid through the resident's future property tax assessments. Energy efficiency improvements for homeowners are arranged similarly in the city of Cambridge, Massachusetts, and other jurisdictions. Austin has offered residents the option of buying electricity from renewable sources, and the owners of 55,000 homes in the city have accepted the offer.

On other sustainability fronts at the municipal level, Seattle was the first large U.S. city to achieve municipal waste reduction through the use of per-unit charges for municipal solid waste combined with no-cost pick up of recycling. Equally important, since the early 1990s, utilities in New England, New York state, and, following the power shortages of 2000–2001, California have achieved considerable success with promoting the more efficient use of electrical energy, in part through the imaginative use of regulated prices. California utilities, for example, gave customers who reduced consumption by 20 percent from the previous year a rebate on their utility bills. Since that program was started, further electricity shortfalls have been avoided and California's policies are now emulated widely.

Despite its wide reputation for domination by car-based transportation, California has one of the lowest greenhouse gas emissions per capita among states. Those low rates were achieved early and have held up despite continued rapid population and, until recently, economic growth. California has built on these achievements with the 2006 passage of the California Global Warming Solutions Act, which sets emissions reduction targets going forward to 2050 and includes a cap-and-trade program. It has also signed agreements to expand that program to other states, including Oregon, Washington, Arizona, and New Mexico (see chapter 2).

The Complex Politics of Sustainable Cities

Creating sustainable cities involves a complex array of conflicting political and economic interests. Nonetheless, considerable potential exists for easing environmental and social problems while simultaneously stimulating economic activity and local employment. Many U.S. cities, as we have seen, have undertaken significant sustainability and climate change initiatives at the same time that global-scale initiatives, such as the Kyoto Protocol, were viewed by national political leaders as a threat to the so-called American way of life. One underlying difference between these sharply contrasting policy views is the fact that cities are built to last for many decades and those that govern cities are forced to appreciate that reality. Others, including some national political leaders, were until recently able to pretend that climate change and energy supply limits did not exist.

Even urban planners often do not always appreciate that the demand for transportation energy can be driven upward by urban sprawl even when automobiles become, on average, more fuel efficient. As noted earlier, natural habitat is being consumed much more rapidly than the human population is growing. This lack of foresight has several causes. Planners do not often enough adopt a systems perspective—one that uses geographic information systems and other tools that incorporate the effects of sprawl on water quality and quantity, air quality, the protection of near-urban wildlife habitat and agricultural land, and numerous other sustainability variables. Moreover, developers, home buyers, and local officials make their decisions in terms of present, not possible future, energy supplies, traffic patterns, and access to nature. Homebuilders and buyers simply do not consider the economic and environmental implications of tens of thousands of developments similar to theirs.

Although some governments of inner cities are encouraging smart growth by promoting residential and commercial development downtown, jurisdictions at the urban periphery are still approving development patterns that have the opposite effect on the overall region. Arguably, then, sustainability may well require effective regional-scale urban governance. Both inside and outside local government, a wider appreciation of the notion of redefining progress is needed. For example, although having millions of people sitting in traffic jams in expensive new cars does add to the GDP, it is not necessarily evidence of economic health.[35] Triple bottom-line analysis and any prudent study of present trends and timelines make it clear that it is not too soon to undertake major urban redesign efforts. We must continue to look to those cities that have had notable successes to determine the elements of success that can be taken up elsewhere.

Elements of successful sustainability initiatives include (1) a participatory and inclusive urban planning process with a focus on sustainability, (2) improved public transit, (3) special attention to residential development and the affordability of housing within urban cores, (4) efforts to preserve existing historic buildings and architectural gems, and (5) diverse innovative policy initiatives that help to change habits (including transportation habits, investment habits, and the bureaucratic rules of the urban game). The first two elements were discussed earlier in this chapter, and their importance cannot be overestimated. In recent years the number of participatory sustainable city planning initiatives has been remarkable, and excellent Web sites that provide guidance for such initiatives are numerous.[36] The other three elements, however, warrant further attention.

As noted, many cities are expanding downtown residential opportunities. The effect of this mixed-use pattern is notable in terms of the overall quality of urban life and greater use of public transit. The famed urban analyst Jane Jacobs made clear how important mixed residential and commercial use is to the quality of urban life: neighborhoods and streets that are used both day and night, she argues, are more interesting, economically successful, and safer.[37] In terms of transportation, in Detroit—where the urban core is dominated by commercial uses and high quality residential opportunities are rare—public transit accounts for some 1 percent of motorized travel, whereas in the metropolitan Toronto area, which has a more balanced commercial-residential mix, public transit provides 24 percent.[38] Remarkably, given that they are both long-established cities, Detroit's residential density overall is about *half* that of Toronto.

Architectural preservation efforts are often at the heart of urban revitalization. This was true in Pittsburgh, where considerable emphasis has focused on rehabilitating existing housing stock and on improving residential energy efficiency.[39] Also especially notable in this regard are Savannah, Georgia, and Charleston, South Carolina—cities with an abundance of architectural history. Savannah's unique downtown streetscape design dating to the 1730s incorporates tree-lined boulevards and parks in the form of squares every two blocks, with residential neighborhoods predominating. Savannah miraculously survived the Civil War only to suffer the dual threats of decline and redevelopment a century later. Since the 1950s, however, preservation and restoration have taken hold and have transformed the residential and commercial core of the city, revitalizing it to the point where tourism emphasizing architecture and history is a leading local industry. Most residential buildings in the downtown are now restored to exacting historic specifications, and the overall effect is a highly livable and pedestrian-oriented city. This is equally true of nearby Charleston, which has the added benefit of an especially attractive seascape. In both cities the downtown commercial areas were doing well at least until the 2008 economic downturn, with new limited-scale hotels, inns, and condominiums being built and the entire region benefiting economically from the historically oriented urban restoration efforts.

Nevertheless, Pittsburgh, Savannah, and Charleston are not immune to sprawl within adjacent municipalities and countryside, but the restraint of sprawl begins with a viable urban core as an attractive residential alternative. The worst effects of existing sprawl can also be diminished through imaginative initiatives, both public and private. For example, one study showed that, in Los Angeles and Ottawa, Ontario, charging employees for parking (even when the same amount was added to employees' paychecks) significantly reduced single-passenger trips to work (by as much as 81 percent).[40] Generally, if driving is not subtly subsidized in these sorts of ways there is likely to be less of it, especially where public transit is improved. Most studies show the transit-driving playing field (in terms of public subsidies) to be tilted in favor of driving.[41] One particularly imaginative approach to this problem was implemented in Paris, France, where public transit is free on air pollution alert days.

In recent years great strides have been made in this regard in several American cities, most notably in Portland, where light rail lines and a streetcar have been added to stunning effect. The use of public transit in Portland is up 75 percent since 1990, and the city and Multnomah County are converting their vehicle fleets to hybrids and biodiesel-fueled vehicles. All of Portland's stop lights have been converted to super-efficient LED bulbs. These programs (and others) have allowed Portland's greenhouse gas emissions to remain relatively stable despite rapid population growth; per-capita emissions have declined by 12.5 percent since 1990. Arguably, Portland residents were Kyoto compliant during the period when the United States as a nation had declined to participate in global climate change efforts.[42]

Finally, rethinking cities and the pattern in which they are arrayed can sometimes be the result of accepting that the future will not be much like the past if that past was based on a small number of large industrial operations. Youngstown, Ohio, lost what was by far its largest employer in 1977 and struggled for decades with decline. Recently it has abandoned attracting a replacement industry and has encouraged the consolidation of residential housing and come to terms with an overall reduction in population. Instead of providing expensive municipal services to isolated households, the city is clearing some blocks of mostly abandoned dwellings by providing incentives to remaining residents to move elsewhere in the city. Some land is being converted to produce gardening and farmers' markets, and the city is hoping to use low taxes and property values to attract artists and small start-up, post-industrial firms.[43]

What is needed to advance sustainability at the level of the city varies enormously depending on circumstances. Higher levels of government need to set broad rules that provide incentives to all, but it is important to avoid limiting the range of initiatives that can be undertaken. Commonalities exist in reducing energy use and the distances that people need to travel, reducing waste, increasing the use of renewable energy, and diversifying economic opportunities, but each city will need to adapt broad principles to its own unique circumstances.

Conclusion

Some immediate steps can be taken to change everyday habits, short of reconfiguring settlement patterns. Making cities more transit, pedestrian, and bicycle friendly is an ongoing process that will take many years to see through. Building sustainable cities has both long- and short-term aspects, and the overall effort may ultimately require policy initiatives in political jurisdictions at all levels and technological innovations as well (such as increased use of telecommunications in the place of travel within everyday life).

In the end, however, sustainability is inevitably the result of thousands of collective and personal decisions. People acting politically at the local level can affect sustainability within the civic life of each community, just as each of us can do so in our choices about where to live and work and how to travel on a daily basis. Important changes do not require that we change the whole world all at once, but they do require that we learn to understand the complex connections between sustainability and our everyday habits and behaviors.

Suggested Web Sites

Alliance for Sustainable Colorado (www.sustainablecolorado.org) Collaboration between nonprofits, business, government, and universities seeking a more sustainable Colorado; housed in a LEED-standard building in Denver.

American Public Transportation Association (www.apta.com) Industry association that provides detailed up-to-date transit use statistics and other relevant information.

Apollo Alliance (www.apolloalliance.org) Coalition of environmental, labor, and political leaders working to reduce U.S. oil dependence and create millions of new jobs by investing in energy alternatives and energy efficiency.

Green for All (www.greenforall.org) Organization seeking to advance environmental protection and social justice simultaneously, by, for example, producing the extensive study *Green-Collar Jobs in America's Cities.*

Greenlining Institute (www.greenlining.org) California-based multi-ethnic public policy and advocacy organization focused on the full range of urban issues.

International Centre for Sustainable Cities (www.icsc.ca) Nonprofit organization based in Vancouver, British Columbia, that works with cities in several countries to solve problems related to growth.

Natural Step (www.naturalstep.org) Presents principles for achieving ecological and economic sustainability for corporations, entrepreneurs, and communities.

Obama's White House (www.whitehouse.gov/agenda/energy_and_environment) Presents a basic outline of where the Obama government hopes to go regarding energy and sustainability initiatives.

U.S. Green Building Council (www.usgbc.org) Provides extensive information on green building techniques and LEED standards.

Notes

1. World Commission on Environment and Development, *Our Common Future* (New York: Oxford, 1987).
2. Daniel A. Mazmanian and Michael E. Kraft, eds., *Toward Sustainable Communities: Transition and Transformations in Environmental Policy,* 2d ed. (Cambridge: MIT Press, 2009).

3. John Elkington, *Cannibals with Forks: The Triple Bottom Line of 21st Century Business* (Stony Creek, Conn.: New Society Publishers, 1998).

4. John Robinson and Jon Tinker, "Reconciling Ecological, Economic and Social Imperatives: A New Conceptual Framework," in *Surviving Globalism: The Social and Environmental Challenges*, ed. Ted Schrecker (London: Macmillan, 1997).

5. See, for example, discussion in Michael Carley and Philippe Spapens, *Sharing the World* (London: Earthscan, 1998); Ernst von Weizsäcker, Amory B. Lovins, and L. Hunter Lovins, *Factor Four: Doubling Wealth, Halving Resource Use* (London: Earthscan, 1998).

6. See Van Jones, *The Green Collar Economy: How One Solution Can Solve Our Two Biggest Problems* (New York: HarperOne, 2008). See also the Web site for Jones's Oakland-based organization, www.greenforall.org.

7. The study is detailed in Peter Newman and Jeffrey Kenworthy, *Sustainability and Cities: Overcoming Automobile Dependence* (Washington, D.C.: Island Press, 1999).

8. American Farmland Trust, "Ten Things Urban and Rural Leaders Can Do Together to Promote Smart Growth," April 2002, www.farmland.org/farm_city_forum/ten_things.htm. The American Farmland Trust Web site (www.farmland.org) also offers a discussion of farm-city forums.

9. For details on the Toronto project, see www.enwave.com.

10. James J. MacKenzie, "Driving the Road to Sustainable Transportation," in *Frontiers of Sustainability*, ed. Roger C. Dower et al. (Washington, D.C.: Island Press, 1997), 121–190.

11. Peter Newman and Jeffrey Kenworthy, *Winning Back the Cities* (Marrickville, New South Wales: Australian Consumers' Association, 1992).

12. New England Climate Change Coalition, "Coalition Welcomes Release of Climate Change Plan in Massachusetts," press release, May 6, 2004, www.newenglandclimate .org/massgovernmentrelease.htm. Since 2004, other states, especially California, have taken strong actions on climate change and have made an effort to encourage others to join in.

13. Newman and Kenworthy, *Sustainability and Cities*, 338.

14. Ibid., 213.

15. Colin J. Campbell and Jean Laherrére, "The End of Cheap Oil," *Scientific American* 278 (March 1998): 78–83.

16. Regarding Pittsburgh and many other sustainable city initiatives, see Kent E. Portney, *Taking Sustainable Cities Seriously: Economic Development, the Environment, and Quality of Life in American Cities* (Cambridge: MIT Press, 2003). Regarding the rapid growth of streetcar transit, see American Public Transportation Association, "Rail Organization Web Sites," www.apta.com/links/railorg.cfm#A1.

17. Peter S. Goodman, "Fuel Prices Shift Math for Life in Far Suburbs," www.nytimes.com, June 25, 2008. See also Damien Cave, "In Florida, Despair and Foreclosures," www.nytimes.com, February 8, 2009.

18. These particular renewal efforts were typically high-rise residential structures set apart from commercial development and available only to those with very low incomes. Thus they were segregated by both function and class, and often by race.

19. Robert D. Putnam, *Bowling Alone: The Collapse and Revival of American Community* (New York: Simon and Schuster, 2000).

20. Lamont C. Hempel, "Conceptual and Analytical Challenges in Building Sustainable Communities," in *Toward Sustainable Communities*, 2d ed., ed. Mazmanian and Kraft, 40.

21. Ibid., 42; see also the Web sites of the many cities involved and the City of Seattle's *Environmental Action Agenda 2006–2007*, www.seattle.gov/environment.

22. Alex Farrell and Maureen Hart, "What Does Sustainability Really Mean? The Search for Useful Indicators," *Environment* 40 (November 1998): 4–9, 26–31.

23. Franklin Tugwell, Andrew S. McElwaine, and Michele Kanche Fetting, "The Challenge of the Environmental City: A Pittsburgh Case Study," in *Toward Sustainable Communities*, 1st ed., ed. Mazmanian and Kraft (Cambridge: MIT Press, 1999), 197.

24. For details regarding such initiatives and regarding many aspects of sustainable cities, see Smart Communities Network, January 31, 2005, www.sustainable.doe.gov.
25. Michael E. Kraft and Daniel A. Mazmanian, "Conclusions: Toward Sustainable Communities," in *Toward Sustainable Communities*, 1st ed., ed. Mazmanian and Kraft, 298.
26. Golf courses almost always contribute to water problems if there is heavy pesticide and fertilizer use but can—if designed with ecological protection in mind—add to protected habitat compared with more intensive development alternatives.
27. Quoted from the Web site of the Environmental Law Institute of Washington, D.C. (www.eli.org), from materials available on May 13, 2001, and on file with the author.
28. Bennet Heart and Jennifer Biringer, "The Smart Growth-Climate Change Connection," retrieved January 31, 2005, from www.clf.org/transportation.
29. Newman and Kenworthy, *Sustainability and Cities*, chap. 4, provided data for this and the next paragraph.
30. See ShoreBank Web site (www.sbk.com).
31. See U.S. Green Building Council Web site (www.usgbc.org/leed).
32. Charlene Prost, "Rehab Brings 'Green' to Old Finance Hub," *St. Louis Post-Dispatch*, June 12, 2004, available from the U.S. Green Building Council, www.usgbc.org/news.
33. Kent E. Portney, "Sustainability in American Cities: A Comprehensive Look at What Cities Are Doing and Why," in Mazmanian and Kraft, *Toward Sustainable Communities*, 2d ed., 244.
34. Motoko Rich, "Green Gets Real with Affordable Housing and Affordable Rents," *New York Times*, May 6, 2004, www.nytimes.com.
35. See especially Clifford Cobb, Ted Halstead, and Jonathan Rowe, *The Genuine Progress Indicator* (San Francisco: Redefining Progress, 1995).
36. See, for example, Web sites such as www.cfpa.org (Center for Policy Alternatives), www.sprawlwatch.org, and www.lgc.org (Local Government Commission). For a discussion of the use of indicators in several U.S. sustainable city initiatives, see Portney, *Taking Sustainable Cities Seriously*, chap. 7.
37. Jane Jacobs, *The Death and Life of Great American Cities* (New York: Vintage, 1961).
38. Newman and Kenworthy, *Sustainability and Cities*, 213.
39. Tugwell et al., "The Challenge of the Environmental City," 187–215.
40. Richard W. Willson and Donald C. Shoup, "Parking Subsidies and Travel Choices: Assessing the Evidence," *Transportation: An International Journal Devoted to the Improvement of Transportation Planning and Practice* 17 (1990): 141–157.
41. See, for example, David Malin Roodman, *Paying the Piper: Subsidies, Politics, and the Environment* (Washington, D.C.: Worldwatch Institute, 1996).
42. See Michele M. Betsill and Barry G. Rabe, "Climate Change and Multilevel Governance: The Evolving State and Local Roles," in Mazmanian and Kraft, *Toward Sustainable Communities*, 2d ed.
43. See Les Christie, "The Incredible Shrinking City," www.cnnmoney.com, May 3, 2008.

12

Global Climate Change
Kyoto and Beyond
Henrik Selin and Stacy D. VanDeveer

Climate change issues and politics have become truly global as environmental impacts and environmental politics are visible worldwide. In the Arctic, indigenous peoples struggle to sustain their economic and cultural lives, polar bears fight to stay alive, and melting sea ice opens up new sea lanes for oil tankers and warships. In coastal areas and low-lying islands around the world—from Louisiana to Bangladesh and across the Caribbean and South Pacific—people worry about consequences of sea level rise and intensifying storm surges. Farmers in already dry areas from Texas to Tanzania are anxious about increasing droughts and water shortages. The list of such concerns is long—and it is growing. In response, people are engaging climate change issues in boardrooms, churches, schools, and public offices from city governments to the United Nations (UN), where UN Secretary-General Ban Ki-moon has declared climate change "the defining issue of our time."[1]

Global climate change governance is filled with irony and paradox. For example, while the U.S. federal government spends more money on funding climate change research than any other public authority in the world, it has been among the least receptive to scientific conclusions about the severity of climate change and the importance of taking political action. During the Kyoto Protocol negotiations, many of the policy ideas about how best to address climate change were proposed by the United States and opposed by the European Union (EU). Yet, in the decade following the adoption of the Kyoto Protocol in 1997, which included many specific policies for reducing greenhouse gas (GHG) emissions put forward by the United States, it was the EU and not the United States that enacted and refined these policies. Such EU efforts include the world's first and largest multilateral carbon dioxide (CO_2) emissions trading scheme.

Climate change politics and policymaking focus on both mitigation and adaptation issues. Mitigation efforts center on ways to reduce GHG emissions. Most anthropogenic (human-caused) GHG emissions come from the burning of fossil fuels and from deforestation and other land use changes. Mitigation policy focuses on switching to less carbon-intensive energy sources (including wind, solar, and hydro power); improving energy efficiency for vehicles, buildings, and appliances; and supporting the development of technologies that help reduce GHG emissions going into the atmosphere. Adaptation efforts seek to improve the ability of human societies (broadly) and local communities (more specifically) to adjust to the many challenges of a changing climate (for example, to alter agricultural practices in response to seasonal and precipitation changes, or to prepare urban areas located in coastal areas for rising sea levels).

This chapter explores climate change politics and policymaking across global, regional, national, and local governance levels. It argues that much more aggressive political action is necessary to meet the challenges posed by climate change causes and impacts, and it discusses issues critical for engendering more effective multilevel governance. The next section briefly discusses climate change science and the roles of the Intergovernmental Panel on Climate Change (IPCC). This is followed by an outline of the global legal framework on climate change that has developed in conjunction with the IPCC assessments, the 1992 UN Framework Convention on Climate Change (UNFCCC), and the 1997 Kyoto Protocol. Next, four important aspects of climate change politics are addressed: (1) EU leadership and policy responses, (2) U.S. federal and subnational climate change policymaking, (3) challenges facing developing countries, and (4) the proliferation in private sector engagement. The chapter ends with a few remarks about the future of climate change policy.

Climate Change Science, GHG Emissions, and the IPCC

Energy from the sun reaches Earth in the form of visible light, penetrating the atmosphere. Some of this energy is absorbed by clouds and Earth's atmosphere, while some is radiated back into space by clouds and Earth's surface in the form of long-wave infrared radiation. Naturally occurring gases in the lower atmosphere trap some of this outgoing infrared radiation in the form of heat, in what has been termed the greenhouse effect. GHGs have been present in the atmosphere for much of Earth's 4.5-billion-year history; without them, the planet would have average surface temperatures of approximately −20°C (0°Fahrenheit). The amount of solar energy that remains trapped in the atmosphere by GHGs has important long-term effects on the climate.

Current global climate changes are different from earlier alterations between warmer and cooler eras in that critical changes are driven by human behavior. Human activities influence both the amount of incoming energy absorbed by Earth's surface (through land use changes including deforestation) and the amount of energy trapped by GHGs (largely by releasing CO_2 into the atmosphere through the burning of fossil fuels). Since the beginning of the industrial revolution in the early nineteenth century, human activities have dramatically altered the composition of GHGs in the lower atmosphere by adding to the volume of naturally occurring gases (for example, CO_2 and methane) as well as by releasing human-made GHGs (for example, hydrofluorocarbons, or HFCs). Also, different GHGs trap varying amounts of energy, which means that small amounts of some GHGs (like methane or HFCs) can have relatively large warming effects.

There are enormous differences in national and per-capita GHG emissions (see Table 12-1). In 2007 a mere nineteen countries were responsible

Table 12-1   Top Five Estimated Emitters of Carbon Dioxide from
Fossil Fuel Use and Cement Production, 2007

Country/Region	Percent Share of Global Emissions	Metric Tons per Capita
China	24	5.1
United States	21	19.4
EU-15	12	8.6
India	8	1.8
Russia	6	11.8

Source: Netherlands Environmental Assessment Agency, "Global CO2 Emissions: Increase Continued in 2007," www.mnp.nl/en/publications/2008/GlobalCO2emissionsthrough2007.html.

for over 70 percent of global CO_2 emissions from fossil fuel use and cement production (two heavily carbon-intensive activities). China recently surpassed the United States as the world's largest CO_2 emitter, due to rapid industrialization based on fossil fuels, including substantial amounts of coal. However, in per-capita emissions, the United States still ranks much higher than China—19.4 metric tons vs. 5.1 metric tons. There are also significant differences in industrialized countries' per-capita emissions. For example, the fifteen EU member states (EU-15) that accepted a collective goal under the Kyoto Protocol (discussed later) have per-capita emissions that are less than half those of the United States. This demonstrates that countries' emissions levels are not simply a product of their relative wealth, but are shaped by a multitude of political, economic, geographic, cultural, and technical factors.

Researchers working across academic disciplines for over 150 years have contributed to our current—and still developing—understanding of the global climate system.[2] The British researcher John Tyndall, as early as 1859, formulated a theory of how CO_2 and other gases in the atmosphere keep Earth from freezing, arguing that Earth's temperature is maintained at a higher level with CO_2 than without CO_2. In 1869 the Swedish scientist Svante Arrhenius explored what could happen to the climate if atmospheric CO_2 concentrations increased, but he did not predict actual, significant changes. In 1938, however, the British engineer Guy Stewart Callendar proposed (to the Royal Meteorological Society) that human CO_2 emissions were changing the climate. Furthermore, Gilbert Plass, an American scientist, in 1956 calculated that adding CO_2 to the atmosphere would have significant heat-trapping effects.

Climate change science advanced when Charles David Keeling at the Mauna Loa Observatory in Hawaii began measuring CO_2 concentrations in open air in 1960. Before industrialization, atmospheric CO_2 concentrations were approximately 280 parts per million by volume (ppmv). Ice core data show that historical concentrations were relatively stable for at least several hundreds of thousands of years prior to the industrial revolution. Atmospheric CO_2 concentrations were approximately 385 ppmv in 2008 (far exceeding historical data), and they are growing at a rate of about 3 to 4 ppmv per year. While other GHGs besides CO_2 add to the warming trend, other kinds of emissions (mostly sulfate aerosols) have a cooling effect in that they repel incoming sunlight. This cooling effect roughly cancels out the warming effect of the GHGs in addition to CO_2, but this warming-cooling balance may change in the future.[3]

Until the 1980s, scientific work on global climate change was carried out across disciplines and research groups, with little effort or ability to bring it together in a systematic fashion. In fact, it was not until the IPCC was established in 1988 by the World Meteorological Organization and the UN Environment Programme that a concerted effort to expand research collaboration and synthesize scientific data existed. Through IPCC activities, thousands of climate change scientists and experts from most of the world's countries work together, tasked with assessing and summarizing the latest scientific, technical, and socioeconomic data on climate change and publishing the findings in periodic reports presented to international organizations and national governments around the world. In this respect, the IPCC was created to inform policymaking but not to formulate policy.

The IPCC has produced four sets of assessment reports, released in 1990, 1995, 2001, and 2007.[4] They address the scientific basis of climate change as well as socioeconomic issues related to reducing GHG emissions and adjusting to a changing climate. The first report stated that although much data indicated that human activity affected the variability of the climate system, the authors could not reach consensus. Signaling a higher degree of consensus, the 1995 report stated that the "balance of evidence" suggested "a discernable human influence on the climate." The report also noted that regional climatic changes were beginning to affect many physical and biological systems, and there were indications that social and economic systems were also affected. The 2001 report confirmed that global average surface temperatures had increased by 0.6°C over the past century, with a margin of error range of 0.2°C.

The 2007 IPCC report concluded, with at least 90 percent certainty, that most of the warming over the previous fifty years has been caused by GHG emissions attributable to a wide range of human activities. The report forecasted a 0.8–4.0°C rise in average surface temperatures by 2100 based on a range of GHG emissions scenarios. It projected that future changes could be expected to include changes in precipitation patterns and amounts, rising sea levels, and changes in the frequency and intensity of extreme weather events. If these projections are correct, the changes would have a significant impact on ecological systems and human societies around the world. The 2004 Arctic Impact Assessment report also noted that, over the past few decades, annual average temperatures had increased at almost twice the rate in the Arctic as in the rest of the world, documenting significant environmental changes across the region impacting wildlife and human societies.[5]

IPCC reports assessing a host of scientific and socioeconomic issues are intended to gather and present policy-relevant information for national policymakers. They are also widely reviewed and cited by people in international organizations, local governments, large and small firms, environmental advocacy groups, and many more. The reports include a set of different emissions scenarios (so-called SRES scenarios). Each scenario projects possible GHG emissions levels decades into the future, based on a different set of assumptions about future levels of economic growth and choices made by governments and citizens affecting the generation of GHG emissions. These scenarios are designed to help decision makers and planners think about how climate change may impact societies and the implications for projects such as the building of a new sewage treatment system in a coastal area affected by sea level rise or the design of new water policies in a drought-stricken region. Such scenarios make it clear that all countries face a host of adaptation challenges, even if these vary tremendously across societies. As such, all have at least some stake in international climate change politics.

International Law and Climate Change

Global climate change law and policy are shaped by a complex mix of changing scientific consensus and the material interests and values of state, nongovernmental, and private sector actors and are outlined in two major multilateral treaties: the 1992 UN Framework Convention on Climate Change and the 1997 Kyoto Protocol. The UNFCCC was negotiated between the publication of the first IPCC report and the 1992 UN Conference on Environment and Development in Rio de Janeiro, where it was adopted. It entered into force in 1994 and, by 2009, 191 countries and the EU had ratified the treaty. As a framework convention, the UNFCCC sets out a broad strategy for addressing climate change.

Like other framework conventions, the UNFCCC defines the issue at hand, sets up an administrative secretariat to oversee treaty activities, and lays out a legal and political framework under which states cooperate over time. The UNFCCC contains shared commitments by states to continue to research an environmental issue, to periodically report their findings and relevant domestic implementation activities, and to meet regularly to discuss common issues at Conferences of the Parties (COPs). Usually framework conventions do not include detailed commitments for mitigation or adaptation, leaving those issues to be addressed in subsequent protocols. Similar framework convention–protocol approaches have been applied to environmental issues such as protection of the stratospheric ozone layer, acid rain and related transboundary air pollution problems, and biodiversity loss.

The UNFCCC defines climate change as "a change of climate which is attributed directly or indirectly to human activity that alters the composition of the global atmosphere and which is in addition to natural climate variability observed over comparable time periods" (Article 1). Similarly, adverse effects of climate change are identified as "changes in the physical environment or biota resulting from climate change which have significant deleterious effects on the composition, resilience or productivity of natural and managed ecosystems or on the operation of socio-economic systems or on human health and welfare" (Article 1). To avoid adverse effects of climate change, the UNFCCC set the long-term objective of "stabilization of greenhouse gas concentrations in the atmosphere at a level that would prevent dangerous anthropogenic interference with the climate system" (Article 2).

The UNFCCC establishes that the world's countries have "common but differentiated responsibilities" in addressing climate change (Article 3). This principle refers to the notion that all countries share an obligation to act, but industrialized countries have a particular responsibility to take the lead in reducing GHG emissions because of their relative wealth and contribution to the problem through historical emissions. To this end, industrialized countries and countries with economies in transitions (that is, former communist countries) plus the European Economic Community (now the EU) are listed in Annex I. This Annex has been modified since the UNFCCC was adopted and currently lists forty countries and the EU.[6] The UNFCCC states (in Article 4) that Annex I countries should work to reduce their anthropogenic emissions to 1990 levels, but no deadline was set for this target. The UNFCCC did not assign non–Annex I countries (that is, developing countries) any GHG reduction commitments.

Responding to mounting scientific evidence about human-induced climate change, much of it presented in the second IPCC report, and to growing concern about negative economic and social effects of climate change among environmental advocates and policymakers, the UNFCCC parties negotiated the Kyoto Protocol between 1995 and 1997. The final stage of the protocol negotiations was contentious on a number of issues. In particular, U.S. and European negotiators differed on both the targets for emissions cuts that should be included in the agreement and the policy mechanisms that should be allowed or recommended for parties to reach their GHG reduction targets. Only as a result of last-minute compromises by a number of participants, brokered in part by an intervention by then–U.S. vice president Al Gore, did the parties agree on a final text.

The Kyoto Protocol regulates six GHGs: CO_2, methane, nitrous oxide, perfluorocarbons, HFCs, and sulfur hexafluoride. UNFCCC Annex I countries commit to collectively reduce their GHG emissions by 5 percent below 1990 levels by 2008–2012. Toward this goal, thirty-nine states on the UNFCCC Annex I list have individual targets. Some agreed to cut their emissions, while others merely consented to slow the growth in their emissions. For example, the EU-15 took on a collective target of an 8 percent reduction while the United States and Canada committed to cuts of 7 percent and 6 percent, respectively. In contrast, Iceland committed to limit its emissions at 10 percent above 1990 levels. Post-communist countries, such as Russia and those in Central and Eastern Europe, agreed to cuts from 1990 levels, but many of these cuts were achieved by the economic restructuring that followed the end of their communist political and economic systems.

The Kyoto Protocol outlines five ways that countries with reduction commitments may meet their targets. Countries may (1) develop national policies that lower domestic GHG emissions (the Kyoto Protocol does not restrict or mandate any particular domestic policy); (2) calculate benefits from domestic carbon sinks (for example, forests) that soak up more carbon than they emit, and count these toward national emissions reductions; (3) participate in transnational emissions trading schemes with other Annex I parties (that is, Annex I countries can create markets in which actors can buy and sell emissions permits); (4) develop joint implementation programs with other Annex I parties and get credit for lowering GHG emissions in those countries; and (5) design a partnership venture with a non–Annex I country through what is known as the Clean Development Mechanism (CDM) and get credit for lowering GHG emissions in the partner country.

The latter three options—international allowance trading, joint implementation programs, and the CDM—were intended to provide flexibility and reduce the costs of complying with the Kyoto commitments by allowing various actors to reduce emissions wherever (and however) it was most efficient, including in other countries. UNFCCC parties and observers hoped that these implementation mechanisms would help policymakers and private sector actors learn lessons about how best to reduce emissions over time in an affordable manner—in ways that would drive international investments between countries at various levels of economic development. The many rules, guidelines, and administrative procedures required to operate these mechanisms have been hammered out in negotiations between the parties since the adoption of the Kyoto Protocol. These rules and procedures are confirmed at annual UNFCCC COPs.

To enter into force, the Kyoto Protocol had to be ratified by fifty-five countries, including by Annex I countries responsible for 55 percent of that group's total GHG emissions. Although fifty-five countries quickly ratified the protocol, it took much longer to meet the 55 percent criterion. By the early 2000s, most Annex I countries had ratified, but either Russia or the United States needed to ratify to meet the 55 percent requirement. Eventually Russia ratified—under heavy pressure from EU officials, who made Russian ratification of the Kyoto Protocol an informal precondition for supporting Russia's membership application to the World Trade Organization. The treaty entered into force in 2005. Following Australia's ratification in 2008, the United States became the only major Annex I country that chose not to become a party. The Kyoto Protocol had been ratified by 184 countries and the EU as of mid-February 2009.

The Kyoto Protocol expires in 2012. Because this date is approaching and it takes years to negotiate and ratify treaties, UNFCCC parties formally began talking in 2007 about what the follow-up agreement to the Kyoto Protocol should include.[7] Debates about what should come after Kyoto are also commonplace among scholars, environmental advocacy groups, and private sector actors. At a UN-sponsored conference in Bali in December 2007, the UNFCCC parties launched a political process designed to negotiate a follow-up agreement to the Kyoto Protocol. A tentative location and date for adopting the next agreement was set for Copenhagen in December 2009, but political differences may cause delays. These negotiations include a host of major issues and challenges, including the following:

- Targets and timetables: What GHG reduction targets are both aggressive enough to make a real difference to atmospheric GHG concentrations, and politically, economically, and technically feasible?
- National commitments: Which countries can and should take on mandatory GHG emissions reduction commitments, and how should these commitments be formulated?
- Joint mitigation mechanisms: How should international collaboration through institutions like international permit trading, joint implementation programs, and the CDM be developed further?
- Forest issues: Should issues of deforestation and sustainable forest management be linked to climate change mitigation efforts and commitments under the new treaty? If so, how?
- Addressing adaptation: What should the treaty say about challenges associated with adapting to environmental and social impacts of climate change, and should it stipulate specific adaptation commitments?
- Financing and capacity building: How should international efforts support capacity building around the world, including financing and technology transfer to developing countries?
- Information and assessment: How should international cooperation generate and utilize data about environmental changes, the effects of specific policy measures, and calculations of economic costs and benefits?

EU Leadership and European Policy Responses

Since the 1990s the EU has emerged as a global leader in climate change policy.[8] Even as the EU has grown from fifteen members in the mid-1990s to twenty-seven members, EU institutions such as the European Commission (the administrative bureaucracy), the Council of Ministers (member state government officials), and the European Parliament (representatives elected by member state citizens) have collaborated with each other and with civil society and private sector actors to implement a set of pan-European climate change and energy-related policies and goals. The European Commission puts forward legislative proposals that are negotiated with and adopted or rejected by the Council of Ministers and the European Parliament. The population of EU-27 is almost 500 million, which means that roughly one in fourteen of the world's people live in the EU. Furthermore, twenty-five of the forty UNFCCC Annex I countries are currently EU members.[9]

EU officials and European political leaders in 2007 agreed that their actions in global political forums and in regional, collective climate change policymaking should be guided by the goal that global average surface temperatures should not rise above 2°C over preindustrial temperature levels.[10] This EU goal is related to the earlier commitment to "prevent dangerous anthropogenic interference with the climate system," as stated in the UNFCCC. Scientists linking atmospheric GHG levels with temperatures believe that this requires stabilizing atmospheric GHG concentrations below 550 ppmv (and preferably closer to 450 ppmv). To stay below 550 ppmv, global

GHG emissions could continue to increase at current rates only until around 2020. They would then need to be brought down much closer to preindustrial levels for global average surface temperature increases not to exceed 2°C.

The EU-15 collective Kyoto target (8 percent below 1990 GHG emission levels by 2012) was divided among member states in a so-called burden sharing agreement. In the 1990s the EU-15, assisted by the European Commission, devised differentiated reduction targets for each country based on the burden sharing concept.[11] Member states divided the joint Kyoto commitments amongst themselves (see Table 12-2). Under this agreement, several member states, including Denmark, Germany, Luxembourg, and the United Kingdom, took on relatively far-reaching commitments, while less wealthy member states such as Greece, Portugal, and Spain could increase their GHG emissions in the period up to 2012, as part of these countries' efforts to expand industrial production and accelerate economic growth.

A main EU policy instrument for meeting its Kyoto target is the union's Emissions Trading Scheme (ETS). Ironically, the EU was opposed to GHG emissions trading during the Kyoto negotiations—an issue championed by the United States, which drew on its domestic experience with emissions trading for sulfur dioxide and nitrogen oxide. The European Commission and several member states had attempted to enact an EU-wide carbon tax in the late 1990s. This effort failed when member states could not agree on a common tax. In the face of this policy failure and the need to meet its Kyoto target, the EU developed the ETS.[12] The first phase of the ETS operated between 2005 and 2007, while the second trading period operates from 2008 to 2012. A third period is set to begin in 2013.[13]

The EU ETS covers CO_2 emissions from over 11,500 major energy-intensive installations across all twenty-seven member states. Yet most installations are located in larger member states, with Germany having over 21.8 percent of all ETS allowances. The United Kingdom is second, with 11.8 percent of allowances.[14] During the first trading period, the ETS got off to a rough start. All allowances were distributed for free, and several member states allocated too many emissions permits, leading to a collapse of the price of emissions (see chapter 9). The European Commission and member state representatives have worked to reduce the allocation of permits in the second trading period, and to push member states to auction at least a portion of the allowances. In 2008 the EU also decided to require all airplane flights—both within the EU as well as international ones entering or leaving the EU—to participate in the EU ETS in the trading period that begins in 2013.

In addition to the ETS, the EU has expanded its energy-related policies over the past decade (on top of a general European policy commitment to energy efficiency that has outpaced that of the United States and many other states since the late 1970s). In 2007, EU political leaders adopted the following targets for 2020: a 20 percent reduction in energy consumption compared with projected trends; an increase to 20 percent in the share of total energy consumption from renewable sources; and an increase to 10 percent in the share of petrol and diesel consumption from biofuels. In 2008, as biofuel

Table 12-2   European Union (EU) Member States' Greenhouse Gas (GHG) Emissions Reduction Targets and National Changes in GHG Emissions, 1990–2006

EU-15 Member State	EU Burden-sharing Target	Percent Change in GHG Emissions, 1990–2006
Austria	−13	+15.1
Belgium	−7.5	−5.2
Denmark	−21	+2.1
Finland	0	+13.2
France	0	−3.9
Germany	−21	−18.2
Greece	+25	+27.3
Ireland	+13	+25.6
Italy	−6.5	+9.9
Luxembourg	−28	+1.0
Netherlands	−6	−2.0
Portugal	+27	+40.7
Spain	+15	+50.6
Sweden	+4	−8.7
United Kingdom	−12.5	−15.1
EU-15		−2.2
EU Member State (2004 and 2007 Enlargements)	**Kyoto Target**	
Bulgaria	−8	−38.9
Cyprus	None	+66.0
Czech Republic	−8	−23.7
Estonia	−8	−54.6
Hungary	−6	−20.0
Latvia	−8	−56.1
Lithuania	−8	−53.0
Malta	None	+45.0
Poland	−6	−11.7
Romania	−8	−36.7
Slovakia	−8	−33.6
Slovenia	−8	+10.8
EU-27		−7.7

Sources: European Environment Agency (EEA), *Annual European Community Greenhouse Gas Inventory 1990–2006*, Technical Report No. 6/2008 (Copenhagen: EEA, 2008); Miranda A. Schreurs, Henrik Selin, and Stacy D. VanDeveer, "Conflict and Cooperation in Transatlantic Climate Politics: Different Stories at Different Levels" in *Transatlantic Environmental and Energy Politics: Comparative and International Perspectives*, ed. M. A. Schreurs, H. Selin, and S. D. VanDeveer (Aldershot, U.K.: Ashgate, 2009).

mandates were blamed for some portion of global food price increases, European leaders backed off implementation of biofuel goals. These policy initiatives are intended to make European economies less carbon intensive, pursuing economic growth while reducing GHG emissions, thereby moving toward more sustainable development.

Some member states, however, struggle to meet their GHG reduction targets (see Table 12-2). By 2006 the EU-15 GHG emissions were 2.2 percent below 1990 levels.[15] It remains unclear if the EU-15 will reach its

Kyoto target of an 8 percent reduction by 2012. Many states that joined the EU after the Kyoto Protocol was concluded in 1997 have emissions well below their Kyoto targets. However, this is largely a result of reconstruction of old communist economies, rather than climate change policy. Since most of these states' emissions are on the rise, many observers doubt that they can achieve emissions reductions as they strive to promote future economic growth. Nevertheless, European leaders and environmental advocates often point out that the EU-15 have per-capita emissions less than half of those of the United States and, in contrast to the United States, Canada, and other industrial countries, EU emissions are in fact lower than they were in 1990.

With the global post-Kyoto negotiations in mind, in 2007 the EU-27 adopted a goal of 20 percent GHG reduction (below 1990 levels) by 2020. EU leaders have further stated that they will accept a 30 percent reduction goal (below 1990 levels) by 2020 if industrialized countries outside the EU also set such a goal. EU officials argue that global emissions must be cut by up to 50 percent by 2050 to avoid global average temperature increases exceeding 2°C. Accepting the principle of common but differentiated responsibilities, the European Commission states that this would require a 60 to 80 percent reduction in industrialized countries' emissions, allowing developing countries lower reduction commitments.[16] In addition, working with local authorities and domestic firms, several EU member states have set national, long-term GHG reduction goals beyond those mandated by the EU.

U.S. Federal and Subnational Climate Change Policy

In sharp contrast to the EU, the U.S. federal government refused ratification of the Kyoto Protocol. In July 1997, a few months before the Kyoto Protocol was adopted and signed by the Clinton administration (with substantial involvement by Vice President Al Gore), the Senate passed by 95–0 a Sense of the Senate resolution put forward by senators Robert Byrd, D-W.Va., and Chuck Hagel, R-Neb. The resolution opposed the draft treaty "because of the disparity of treatment between Annex I Parties and Developing Countries and the level of required emission reductions, could result in serious harm to the United States economy, including significant job loss, trade disadvantages, increased energy and consumer costs, or any combination thereof."[17] The Senate thereby rejected the principle of common but differentiated responsibilities—a principle it had accepted earlier in the decade when it ratified the UNFCCC.

Whereas European political leaders made climate change a priority, President George W. Bush's administration (2001–2009) opposed national, mandatory GHG reductions, despite having expressed support for CO_2 regulations during his 2000 presidential campaign.[18] U.S. federal policy under the Bush administration focused instead on voluntary programs and the support of scientific research and technological development under the Climate Change Science Program and the Climate Change Technology Program. Federal policy between 2001 and 2008 focused on "GHG intensity"

Table 12-3   U.S. States with the Lowest and Highest Changes in
Greenhouse Gas (GHG) Emissions, 1990–2003

Five Lowest GHG Emissions Trends (percent)	Five Highest GHG Emissions Trends (percent)
1. Delaware (–5)	1. Nevada (43)
2. Louisiana (–1)	2. Arizona (43)
3. Washington, D.C. (0)	3. New Hampshire (33)
4. Hawaii (0)	4. Colorado (33)
5. Connecticut (2)	5. Missouri (32)

Source: Barry G. Rabe, "States on Steroids: The Intergovernmental Odyssey of American Climate Policy," *Review of Policy Research* 25, 2 (2008): 105–128.

as measured by emissions divided by gross domestic product. Even though the U.S. economy's GHG intensity decreased during this period, national GHG emissions increased by 14.7 percent between 1990 and 2006.[19]

Looking below the federal level, however, significant differences are found in GHG emissions trends among U.S. states since 1990, ranging from a 5 percent decrease to a 43 percent increase (see Table 12-3).[20] These differences stem from a host of factors, including differential economic and population growth rates, differing energy and environmental policies, and substantial variance in the sources of energy used. U.S. states also have very different emissions profiles from major economic sectors such as energy production and transportation. U.S. state governments can also play significant roles in developing related energy and environmental policies to address climate change and other sustainable development issues (see chapter 2).

In part because of federal inaction, the most significant climate change policymaking in the United States since the early 2000s has occurred at state and municipal levels.[21] In the absence of federal leadership, and sometimes motivated by European examples, most U.S. states have taken initiatives beyond federal requirements and adopted numerical targets for short-term and long-term GHG reductions (see Table 12-4). By 2007, over half of all U.S. states had formulated individual climate change action plans and more have taken a host of actions, including establishing renewable portfolio standards requiring electricity providers to obtain a minimum percentage of their power from renewable sources, formulating ethanol mandates and incentives, setting CO_2 vehicle emissions standards based on a California initiative, adopting green building standards, and mandating the sale of more efficient appliances and electronic equipment.

Although many U.S. states are taking action, California has emerged as a leading force on policy development and GHG mitigation—sometimes ahead of EU policy goals.[22] In 2002 the California State Assembly and then-governor Gray Davis adopted the California Climate Bill, mandating that the California Air Resources Board establish a plan for achieving "maximal feasible reduction" of CO_2 emissions from vehicles, effective 2006. Carmakers are given until 2009 to meet these standards, but U.S. car manufacturers have

Table 12-4   U.S. Statewide Greenhouse Gas Reduction Targets
(as of 2008)

State	Goal
Arizona	2000 levels by 2020; 50% below 2000 levels by 2040
California	2000 levels by 2010; 1990 levels by 2020; 80% below 1990 levels by 2050
Colorado	20% below 2005 levels by 2020; 80% below 2005 levels by 2050
Connecticut	1990 levels by 2010; 10% below 1990 levels by 2020; 80% below 2001 levels by 2050
Florida	2000 levels by 2017; 1990 levels by 2025; 80% below 1990 levels by 2050
Hawaii	1990 levels by 2020
Illinois	1990 levels by 2020; 60% below 1990 levels by 2050
Maine	1990 levels by 2010; 10% below 1990 levels by 2020
Massachusetts	1990 levels by 2010; 10% below 1990 levels by 2020; 80% below 1990 levels by 2050
Minnesota	15% below 2005 levels by 2015; 30% below 2005 levels by 2025; 80% below 2005 levels by 2050
New Hampshire	1990 levels by 2010; 10% below 1990 levels by 2020
New Jersey	1990 levels by 2020; 80% below 2006 levels by 2050
New Mexico	2000 levels by 2012; 10% below 2000 levels by 2020; 75% below 2000 levels by 2050
New York	5% below 1990 levels by 2010; 10% below 1990 levels by 2020
Oregon	Stabilize by 2010; 10% below 1990 levels by 2020; 75% below 1990 levels by 2050
Rhode Island	1990 levels by 2010; 10% below 1990 levels by 2020
Utah	2005 levels by 2020
Vermont	1990 levels by 2010; 10% below 1990 levels by 2020
Washington	25% below 1990 levels by 2035; 50% below 1990 levels by 2050

Source: Pew Center on Global Climate Change, "U.S. States & Regions," www.pewclimate.org/states-regions.

challenged the standards in courts. California also established a renewable energy portfolio standard in 2002, mandating that 20 percent of its energy come from renewable resources by 2017. The target date was subsequently shifted to 2010 in the 2003 California Energy Action Plan. More recently, Governor Arnold Schwarzenegger announced a 33 percent renewable energy goal for electricity by 2020.

U.S. states are also enacting a multitude of collaborative standards and policies on GHGs.[23] In 2000 the Conference of New England Governors (Maine, New Hampshire, Vermont, Massachusetts, Rhode Island, and Connecticut) and Eastern Canadian Premiers (Nova Scotia, Newfoundland and Labrador, Prince Edward Island, New Brunswick, and Quebec) adopted a resolution recognizing climate change as a joint concern that affected their environments and economies. Based on this resolution, the governors and premiers in 2001 adopted a Climate Change Action Plan, under which states and provinces pledged to reduce their GHGs to 1990 levels by 2010 and 10 percent below 1990 levels by 2020. They also agreed to ultimately decrease emissions to levels that do not pose a threat to the climate, which according to an official estimate would require a 75 to 85 percent reduction from 2001 emission levels.

A second major multistate initiative in the Northeast is the Regional Greenhouse Gas Initiative (RGGI), proposed in 2003.[24] Beginning in 2009, it creates a cap-and-trade scheme for CO_2 emissions from major power plants in ten participating states: Maryland, Maine, Vermont, New Hampshire, Massachusetts, Rhode Island, Connecticut, New York, New Jersey, and Delaware. RGGI is designed to stabilize CO_2 emissions from the region's power sector between 2009 and 2015. Between 2015 and 2018, each state's annual CO_2 emissions budget is expected to decline by 2.5 percent per year, achieving a total 10 percent reduction by 2019. While the goals of both regional initiatives in the Northeast are relatively modest, they were more stringent than federal policy at the time of their adoption. Many state officials also framed the regional efforts in terms of influencing future federal policy and public and private sector views on climate change.

While the Northeast regional cooperation remains the most well developed to date, groups of states on the West Coast and in the Great Lakes region, respectively, have also begun discussions about climate change cooperation. Both regional efforts include discussions about establishing independent regional cap-and-trade systems or about linking up with other such systems. In 2007 the state-led initiative involving the largest group of states was announced: thirty-one states signed on as charter members of The Climate Registry. The Climate Registry does not mandate GHG reductions but is a collaborative effort to develop a common system for private and public entities to report GHG emissions, allowing officials to measure, verify, and publicly report emissions in a consistent manner. By 2008, forty states, three native tribes, and the District of Columbia were members (together with ten Canadian provinces and all six Mexican states along the U.S.-Mexican border).[25]

States also initiated legal action against federal authorities. Attorneys general from California, Connecticut, Illinois, Maine, Massachusetts, New Jersey, New Mexico, New York, Oregon, Rhode Island, Vermont, and Washington filed suit in federal court in February 2003, challenging a U.S. Environmental Protection Agency (EPA) decision during the Clinton administration not to classify CO_2 as a vehicle pollutant to be regulated under the Clean Air Act. Numerous state regulatory agencies, city officials, and environmental groups endorsed the suit. In April 2007 the U.S. Supreme Court ruled 5–4 that CO_2 can be classified as a pollutant under the Clean Air Act and that the EPA has the authority to regulate CO_2 emissions from vehicles. The ruling energized those in Congress and elsewhere who are pushing for the adoption of more aggressive national climate change policy as legal struggles continue.

Furthermore, U.S. municipalities are taking considerable action. By late 2008, more than 880 mayors from all fifty states, representing approximately 80 million Americans, had signed a declaration of meeting or exceeding the reductions negotiated in Kyoto for the United States. Over 260 North

American municipalities are members of the International Council for Local Environmental Initiatives and its Cities for Climate Protection program. Although many municipal climate change programs are modest, some have achieved impressive results.[26] American municipalities are also increasingly developing new GHG reduction and energy efficiency programs that rely in part on innovative private financing. In addition, a growing number of U.S. firms are seeking to reduce GHG emissions and are investing in low carbon technology.[27]

One 2007 estimate of CO_2 emissions reductions in U.S. states based on only three sets of policies—energy efficiency mandates, renewable portfolio standards, and impacts of the regional trading schemes under development in the Northeast and along the West Coast—suggests that such actions could cut 1.8 billion tons of CO_2 emissions by 2020.[28] Another estimate suggests that if seventeen of the states and 284 of the cities with explicit GHG reduction targets were to meet their goals by 2020, they would constitute almost 50 percent of the cuts needed for the United States to get back to 1990 emissions levels.[29] Yet many states, provinces, and municipalities are struggling to cut their GHG emissions, and many (perhaps most) are unlikely to meet their self-imposed and relatively modest short-term reduction targets. Nevertheless, important political and technical precedents for future climate change actions are being set all over North America, and the trend toward more ambitious public and private sector initiatives continues apace.

As the U.S. Supreme Court has established the ability to regulate CO_2 emissions under the Clean Air Act, President Barack Obama and the 111th Congress (2009–2011) face the challenge of expanding federal climate change policy to catch up with leading states, municipalities, and the federal courts. President Obama supported mandatory GHG controls and the creation of a national emissions trading system while in the Senate. Both houses of the U.S. Congress are also more favorably inclined to support climate policy measures than in previous years. President Obama—together with the Senate, which ratifies treaties by a two-thirds majority—will need to formulate domestic policy positions and international negotiating and policy positions on a follow-up treaty to the Kyoto Protocol. The world's attention is likely to focus on U.S. domestic policy developments and the country's climate-change-related foreign policies for many years to come.

Challenges Facing Developing Countries

As the international community struggles to address climate change under a post-Kyoto agreement and a multitude of associated programs and initiatives, many developing countries face myriad challenging mitigation and adaptation problems, alongside a multitude of other critical sustainable development issues (see chapter 13). The situation of relatively vulnerable developing countries gives rise to critical procedural and distributive social justice issues, from a global equity perspective.[30] Procedural justice refers to the ability to fully partake in collective decision-making processes focusing on mitigation and adaptation issues (including under the UNFCCC), whereas distributive justice concerns how climate change impacts or how mitigation policies affect societies and people differently.

For many developing countries, a set of important procedural justice issues relates to how international climate change policy is formulated and how these countries' domestic interests are represented and taken into account. Many governments—and particularly those of smaller developing countries—face multiple problems engaging actively in multilateral environmental negotiations and assessments.[31] These problems include having fewer human, economic, technical, and scientific resources (compared with leading industrialized countries) with which to prepare for international negotiations or implement resulting agreements. The significant capacity differences between wealthier industrialized countries and poorer developing countries risk skewing international assessments, debates, and decision making in favor of the perspectives and interests of more powerful countries.

The Kyoto Protocol exempted developing countries from mandatory GHG reductions based on the principle of common but differentiated responsibilities. This, however, may change in the next treaty. In particular, major, industrializing countries such as China, India, South Korea, Mexico, and Brazil are coming under increasing political pressure to accept some kind of GHG restrictions beyond 2012. While industrialized countries and countries with economies in transition may continue to set GHG reduction targets in national, annual, absolute terms under a subsequent treaty, some analysts and policymakers argue that the first developing countries taking action might be well served by a system based on per-capita income or per-capita emissions. Such a system might be more equitable and plausible for gradually expanding international participation and strengthening commitments over time.[32]

On distributive justice issues, the UNFCCC recognizes that some countries are "particularly vulnerable" to adverse effects of climate change (Preamble). Such countries include "low-lying and other small island countries, countries with low-lying coastal, arid and semi-arid areas or areas liable to floods, drought and desertification, and developing countries with fragile mountainous ecosystems." Many of the most harmful effects of a warming climate will take place in developing countries, which have historically contributed least to global GHG emissions. For example, countries in Southeast Asia with vast and densely populated low-lying coastal areas, including Bangladesh and India, will experience many of the first impacts of sea level rise and increased storm intensity. Changes in seasons and precipitation present a more acute threat to millions of poor, small-scale farmers in Africa and other tropical countries than they do to those in rich countries.

Developing countries typically have fewer resources to adapt to a changing climate than industrialized countries, which raises important concerns about both inter- and intragenerational equity in prioritizing the vulnerabilities of those who are most exposed.[33] For example, the Netherlands stands a better chance of managing sea level rise than does Bangladesh merely as a result of its greater wealth. Similarly, European and North American countries are likely better equipped (materially and institutionally) to adjust agricultural practices than are sub-Saharan African countries. Many similar issues can be extended to indigenous populations who are often among the most vulnerable in any society. For example, Arctic indigenous peoples are among the first to grapple with impacts of climate change resulting from activities with which they have had little to do.[34]

Simply put, adaption to ongoing and accelerating climate change requires the investment of additional resources. Annex II of the UNFCCC currently lists twenty-three countries and the EU as committed to providing "new and additional financial resources" to developing countries for addressing climate change issues (Article 4).[35] Helping particularly vulnerable countries and local communities that face significant challenges as a result of climate change should be a priority for the international community, but funding needs and requests have greatly outnumbered the amount of financial resources made available by UNFCCC Annex II countries and international organizations. As such, funding for adaptation is set to be a major issue under the UNFCCC and other international political and economic forums.

Policymaking and the Private Sector

Many industry organizations and individual firms led the opposition to climate change policy and GHG reductions in the 1990s, including during the Kyoto Protocol negotiations. Many of these were U.S. based. In addition, U.S. industrial interests have taken a multitude of political and legal steps to block the development of more ambitious federal and state climate change policy. Yet many firms have begun taking a more proactive stand on climate change and renewable energy issues. The World Economic Forum at its 2000 meeting recognized climate change as "the world's most pressing problem" as well as "the issue where business could most effectively adopt a leadership role."[36] Such changes within the private sector are driven by an acceptance of climate change as a serious societal and economic problem and by an interest in finding new business opportunities and markets.

Firms are central players on climate change issues in their roles as investors, polluters, innovators, experts, manufacturers, lobbyists, and employers.[37] In Europe, oil companies like BP and Shell accepted the need to control GHG emissions and began investing in low-carbon alternatives earlier than their U.S. counterparts. One study argues that this can be explained by societal factors, rather than corporate differences.[38] That is, compared with U.S. energy companies, European companies experienced more societal demands from the public and policymakers to take on climate change and fossil fuel issues, pushing these companies to act. Governmental supply of climate policies also has an impact on firms' responses to the climate issue; government pressure can push technological innovation and foster changes in corporate strategies to meet public demands and regulations.

If climate change policy expands and societies move toward low-carbon economies, there will be winners and losers in the private sector. Fossil fuel producers and other firms that are unwilling or unable to meet the carbon challenge will face increasing pressures. Yet any major market change creates business opportunities and market niches. A growing number of firms are helping to solve the climate crisis by investing in and developing clean technologies and services. Many industrialized and developing countries, for example, have experienced a boom in renewable energy production in the 2000s. Denmark, Germany, and Spain have long been investing in wind power. Denmark currently generates approximately 20 percent of its national electricity from wind turbines. Indian and Chinese firms are among the largest producers of renewable energy products and technologies.

Growing demand for clean technologies leads to expanding markets, allowing some firms to benefit from economies of scale as they produce and sell their products. That is, expanding markets help drive down per-unit production costs for cleaner technologies and consumer goods, which translates into cheaper goods for consumers who are seeking more climate-friendly alternatives. Recent private sector involvement in climate change also includes the creation of new markets for trading emissions permits, under both mandatory and voluntary schemes. Such markets have been established in a multitude of places, including London, Montreal, and Chicago. Trading data from these climate exchanges show that these carbon exchanges have experienced rapid year-on-year growth in the total amount of carbon traded and aggregate value of carbon traded.

However, European debates in 2007 and 2008 over regulations under the EU ETS and the formulation of climate and energy policy goals demonstrate that firms and governments sometimes remain hesitant to undertake aggressive action, fearing economic costs and loss of competitiveness. Similar debates occur in the United States and other industrialized and developing countries as firms and policymakers—sometimes in collaboration—attempt to shift mitigation costs to other countries. Firms also lead legal battles against regulations in California and other U.S. states. The debate about the reality of human-induced climate change is predominantly settled, but significant disagreements remain among private sector actors and across local, national, and international governance scales about allocation of costs and responsibilities for cutting GHG emissions and switching to low-carbon technology.

Where Do We Go from Here?

Climate change policy is developing across global, regional, national, and local governance scales. Both industrialized and developing countries face fundamental mitigation and adaptation challenges—the world's countries do not face the same challenges, but climate change affects all countries in many ways. While some opponents of climate change action believe that short-term mitigation costs are too high, a growing number of analysts and policymakers argue that early action is less costly for societies than is coping with severe climatic changes in the future (see also chapter 9).[39] The challenge of finding ways to significantly reduce GHG emissions while promoting sustainable development cannot be overstated (see chapters 13, 14, and 16). The Bali process seeks to conclude a third global treaty to follow the Kyoto Protocol. Even if these negotiations produce an agreement, climate change politics and policymaking within public and private sectors will continue for decades to come.

Effective climate change governance requires broad, but not universal, participation. To advance climate change policy action under the UNFCCC, major emitters such as the United States, the EU, China, and India must reach greater agreement on how to develop mitigation and adaptation policies beyond 2012—the global climate change agenda cannot be advanced sufficiently without the support of these key actors and other leading industrialized and developing countries. To achieve these goals, the Obama administration and the U.S. Congress will need more proactive engagement with other leading countries than occurred during the George W. Bush administration. During his tenure in the White House, Obama must show renewed U.S. leadership to address climate change, working closely with both domestic and foreign political leaders. Political and societal actions are required, but individuals' actions are needed, as well, to reduce their carbon footprints. If the challenges posed by climate change are to be met, we must all take responsibility for our impact on the global climate.

Suggested Web Sites

Climate Ark (www.climateark.org) A portal, search engine, and news feed covering climate change issues.

Dot Earth (http://dotearth.blogs.nytimes.com) Blog run by *New York Times* reporter Andrew C. Revkin; focuses on climate change science and policy issues.

European Union (http://ec.europa.eu/environment/climat/home_en .htm) Provides information about European perspectives and policy initiatives to address climate change.

Intergovernmental Panel on Climate Change (www.ipcc.ch) Panel of international experts conducting periodical assessments of scientific and socioeconomic information about climate change.

Pew Center on Global Climate Change (www.pewclimate.org) Offers information about international and U.S. climate change policymaking and private sector action.

Real Climate (www.realclimate.org) Provides commentaries on climate change science news by scientists working in different fields.

UN Framework Convention on Climate Change (http://unfccc.int) Web site operated by the UNFCCC Secretariat; contains information about meetings and other activities organized under the UNFCCC.

U.S. Environmental Protection Agency (www.epa.gov/climatechange) Provide information about climate change science, U.S. policy, and what people can do to lower their personal GHG emissions.

Notes

1. Ban Ki-moon, speech at Harvard University, October 21, 2008, www.hks. harvard.edu/news-events/news/articles/ban-ki-moon-forum-oct.
2. Spencer R. Weart, *The Discovery of Global Warming* (Cambridge: Harvard University Press, 2003).
3. For discussions about the latest developments in climate change science, see Real Climate (www.realclimate.org).
4. The IPCC reports and other data are available on the IPCC Web site (www.ipcc.ch).
5. Arctic Climate Impact Assessment, *Impacts of a Warming Arctic: Arctic Climate Impact Assessment* (Cambridge: Cambridge University Press, 2004).
6. The forty countries are Australia, Austria, Belarus, Belgium, Bulgaria, Canada, Croatia, Czech Republic, Denmark, Estonia, Finland, France, Germany, Greece, Hungary, Iceland, Ireland, Italy, Japan, Latvia, Lichtenstein, Lithuania, Luxembourg, Monaco, Netherlands, New Zealand, Norway, Poland, Portugal, Romania, Russian Federation, Slovakia, Slovenia, Spain, Sweden, Switzerland, Turkey, Ukraine, United Kingdom, and the United States.
7. Raymond Clemoncon, "The Bali Roadmap," *Journal of Environment and Development* 17, 1 (2008): 70–94; Joseph E. Aldy and Robert N. Stavins, "Climate Policy Architecture for the Post-Kyoto World," *Environment* 50, 3 (2008): 6–17; David G. Victor, "Toward Effective International Cooperation on Climate Change," *Global Environmental Politics* 6, 3 (2006): 90–103.
8. Miranda A. Schreurs, Henrik Selin, and Stacy D. VanDeveer, "Conflict and Cooperation in Transatlantic Climate Politics: Different Stories at Different Levels," in M. A. Schreurs, H. Selin, and S. D. VanDeveer, eds., *Transatlantic Environmental and Energy Politics: Comparative and International Perspectives* (Aldershot, U.K.: Ashgate, 2009).
9. The fifteen Annex I countries that are not EU members are Australia, Belarus, Canada, Croatia, Iceland, Japan, Lichtenstein, Monaco, New Zealand, Norway, Russia, Switzerland, Turkey, Ukraine, and the United States.
10. European Commission, *Limiting Global Climate Change to 2 Degrees Celsius: The Way Ahead for 2020 and Beyond* COM(2007) 2 Final (Brussels: European Commission, 2007); European Commission, *EU Action against Climate Change: Leading Global Action to 2020 and Beyond* (Brussels: European Commission, 2007).
11. Schreurs, Selin, and VanDeveer, "Conflict and Cooperation in Transatlantic Climate Politics."
12. Jon Birger Skjærseth and Jørgen Wettestad, *EU Emissions Trading: Initiating, Decision-Making and Implementation* (Aldershot, U.K.: Ashgate, 2008).
13. Ibid.
14. European Commission, *EU Action against Climate Change: EU Emissions Trading: An Open System Promoting Global Innovation* (Brussels: European Commission, 2007).
15. European Environment Agency (EEA), *Annual European Community Greenhouse Gas Inventory 1990–2006*, Technical Report No. 6/2008 (Copenhagen: EEA, 2008).
16. European Commission, *Limiting Global Climate Change to 2 Degrees Celsius.*
17. U.S. Senate, "Byrd-Hagel Resolution," www.nationalcenter.org/KyotoSenate.html.
18. Schreurs, Selin, and VanDeveer, "Conflict and Cooperation in Transatlantic Climate Politics."
19. Environmental Protections Agency (EPA), *Inventory of U.S. Greenhouse Gas Emissions and Sinks: 1990–2006* USEPA #430-R-08-005 (Washington, D.C.: EPA, 2008).
20. Barry G. Rabe, "States on Steroids: The Intergovernmental Odyssey of American Climate Policy," *Review of Policy Research* 25, 2 (2008): 105–128.
21. Henrik Selin and Stacy D. VanDeveer, "Political Science and Prediction: What's Next for US Climate Change Policy?" *Review of Policy Research* 24, 1 (2007): 1–27; Henrik Selin and Stacy D. VanDeveer, eds., *Changing Climates in North American Politics: Institutions, Policy Making and Multilevel Governance* (Cambridge: MIT Press, 2009).

22. Alexander E. Farrell and W. Michael Hanemann, "Field Notes on the Political Economy of California Climate Policy," in Selin and VanDeveer, eds., *Changing Climates in North American Politics*.

23. Henrik Selin and Stacy D. VanDeveer, "Climate Leadership in Northeast North America," in Selin and VanDeveer, eds., *Changing Climates in North American Politics*.

24. Selin and VanDeveer, "Climate Leadership in Northeast North America."

25. For more information, see www.theclimateregistry.org/.

26. Christopher Gore and Pamela Robinson, "Local Government Responses to Climate Change: Our Last, Best Hope?" in Selin and VanDeveer, eds., *Changing Climates in North American Politics*.

27. Charles A. Jones and David L. Levy, "Business Strategies and Climate Change," in Selin and VanDeveer, eds., *Changing Climates in North American Politics*.

28. John Byrne, Kristen Hughes, Wilson Rickerson, and Lado Kurdgelashvili, "American Policy Conflict in the Greenhouse: Divergent Trends in Federal, Regional, State and Local Green Energy and Climate Change Policy," *Energy Policy* 35, 9 (2007): 4555–4573.

29. Nicholas Lutsey and Daniel Sperling, "America's Bottom-Up Climate Change Mitigation Policy," *Energy Policy* 36, 2 (2008): 673–685.

30. W. Neil Adger, Jouni Paavola, and Saleemul Huq, "Toward Justice in Adaptation to Climate Change" in W. Neil Adger, Jouni Paavola, Saleemul Huq, and M. J. Mace, eds., *Fairness in Adaptation to Climate Change* (Cambridge: MIT Press, 2006).

31. Pamela S. Chasek, "NGOs and State Capacity in International Environmental Negotiations: The Experience of the Earth Negotiations Bulletin," *Review of European Community and International Environmental Law* 10, 2 (2001): 168–176; Ambuj Sagar and Stacy D. VanDeveer, "Capacity Development for the Environment: Broadening the Scope," *Global Environmental Politics* 5, 3 (2005): 14–22.

32. Aldy and Stavins, "Climate Policy Architecture for the Post-Kyoto World."

33. Adil Najam, Saleemul Huq, and Youba Sokona, "Climate Negotiations beyond Kyoto: Developing Countries Concerns and Interests," *Climate Policy* 3, 3 (2003): 221–231.

34. Arctic Climate Impact Assessment, *Impacts of a Warming Arctic*; Henrik Selin and Noelle Eckley Selin, "The Role of Indigenous Peoples in International Environmental Cooperation: Arctic Management of Toxic Substances," *Review of European Community and International Environmental Law* 17, 1 (2008): 72–83.

35. The twenty-three UNFCCC Annex II countries are Australia, Austria, Belgium, Canada, Denmark, Finland, France, Germany, Greece, Iceland, Ireland, Italy, Japan, Luxembourg, Netherlands, New Zealand, Norway, Portugal, Spain, Sweden, Switzerland, United Kingdom, and the United States.

36. "World Economic Forum: Climate Change Is Paramount," World Economic Forum Press Release, February 3, 2000, www.heatisonline.org/contentserver/objecthandlers/index.cfm?id=3461&method=full.

37. Jones and Levy, "Business Strategies and Climate Change."

38. Jon Birger Skjærseth and Tora Skodvin, "Climate Change and the Oil Industry: Common Problems, Different Strategies," *Global Environmental Politics* 1, 4 (2001): 43–64.

39. Nicholas Stern, *The Economics of Climate Change: The Stern Review* (Cambridge: Cambridge University Press, 2005).

13

Environment, Population, and
the Developing World

Richard J. Tobin

Environmental problems occasionally make life in the United States unpleasant, but most Americans tolerate this situation in exchange for the comforts associated with a developed economy. Most Europeans, Japanese, and Australians share similar lifestyles, so it is not surprising that they too typically take modern amenities for granted.

When lifestyles are viewed from a global perspective, however, much changes. Consider, for example, what life is like in much of the world. The U.S. gross national income (GNI) per capita was $45,850 per year, or almost $880 per week, in 2007. In contrast, weekly incomes are less than 5 percent of this amount in nearly fifty countries, even when adjusted for differences in prices and purchasing power. In several African countries, real per-capita incomes are about one-hundredth of those in the United States. Almost half of the world's population lives on less than two dollars a day. In south Asia and sub-Saharan Africa, more than 70 percent of the population is below this level.[1]

Low incomes are not the only problem facing many of the world's inhabitants. In some developing countries, women, often illiterate and with no formal education, marry as young as age thirteen. In some African countries, nearly half of all females are married before their twentieth birthday. In Niger and Bangladesh, more than a quarter of young women are married by the age of fifteen.[2] In many more countries, two-thirds or more are married by the age of eighteen—often to much older men with less education than their teenage brides. During their childbearing years, women in many developing countries will typically deliver as many as five or six babies, most without skilled birth attendants. This absence is not without consequences. The likelihood that a woman will die due to complications associated with pregnancy, childbirth, or an unsafe abortion is many times higher in poor countries than it is in Western Europe or the United States.

Many of the world's children are also at risk. Only seven of one thousand American children die before the age of five; in some Asian and African countries as many as 20 to 25 percent do. *Every week* about 190,000 children under age five die in developing countries from diseases that rarely kill Americans. Tetanus, measles, malaria, diarrhea, whooping cough, or acute respiratory infections cause most of these deaths, most of which can be easily and cheaply cured or prevented.[3]

Of the children from these poor countries who do survive their earliest years, millions will suffer brain damage because their pregnant mothers had no iodine in their diets; others will lose their sight and die because they lack vitamin A. Many will face a life of poverty, never to taste clean water, learn to read or write, visit a doctor, have access to even the cheapest medicines, or eat nutritious food regularly. To the extent that shelter is available, it is rudimentary, rarely with electricity or sanitary facilities. Many will use animal dung for cooking fuel. Hundreds of millions in the developing world will also become victims of floods, droughts, famine, desertification, land degradation, waterborne diseases, infestation of pests and rodents, and noxious levels of air pollution because their surroundings have been abused or poorly managed.

Many countries, especially in the Middle East and North Africa, suffer from shortages of water for agriculture, and the water that is available is often from nonrenewable sources. Most sewage in developing countries is discharged without any treatment, and pesticides and human wastes often contaminate well water. According to the Millennium Ecosystem Assessment, about half the urban population in Asia, Africa, and Latin America suffers from one or more diseases associated with inadequate water and sanitation.[4] The result is about 1.7 million deaths each year due to inadequate water, sanitation, and hygiene.

As children in developing countries grow older, many will find that their governments cannot provide the resources to ensure them a reasonable standard of living. Yet all around them are countries with living standards well beyond their comprehension. The average American uses about twenty-five times more electricity and consumes about 50 percent more calories per day—far in excess of minimum daily requirements—than does the typical Indian. An Indian mother might wonder why Americans consume a disproportionate share of the world's resources when she has malnourished children she cannot clothe or educate.

In short, life in much of Asia, Africa, and Latin America provides an array of problems different from those encountered in developed nations. Residents of poor countries must cope with widespread poverty, scarce opportunities for meaningful employment, and a lack of economic development. Yet both developed and developing nations often undergo environmental degradation. Those without property, for example, may be tempted to denude tropical forests for land to farm. Alternatively, pressures for development often force people to overexploit their natural and environmental resources.

These issues lead to the key question addressed in this chapter: Can the poorest countries, with the overwhelming majority of the world's population, improve their lot through sustainable development? According to the World Commission on Environment and Development, sustainable development meets the essential needs of the present generation for food, clothing, shelter, jobs, and health without "compromising the ability of future generations to meet their own needs."[5] Achieving this goal will require increased development without irreparable damage to the environment.

Whose responsibility is it to achieve sustainable development? One view is that richer nations have a moral obligation to assist less fortunate ones. If the former do not meet this obligation, not only will hundreds of millions of people in developing countries suffer, but the consequences will be felt in the developed countries as well. Others argue that poorer nations must accept responsibility for their own fate because outside efforts to help them only worsen the problem and lead to an unhealthy dependence. Advocates of this position insist that it is wrong to provide food to famine-stricken nations because they have exceeded their environment's carrying capacity.[6]

The richer nations, whichever position they take, cannot avoid affecting what happens in the developing world. It is thus useful to consider how events in rich nations influence the quest for sustainable development. At least two related factors affect this quest. The first is a country's population; the second is a country's capacity to support its population.

Population Growth: Cure or Culprit?

Population growth is one of the more contentious elements in the journey toward sustainable development. Depending on one's perspective, the world is either vastly overpopulated or capable of supporting as many as thirty times its current population (about 6.7 billion in mid-2008 and increasing at an annual rate of about 80 million per year).[7] Many of the developing nations are growing faster than the developed nations (Table 13-1), and more than 80 percent of the world's population lives outside the developed regions. If current growth rates continue, the proportion of those in developing countries will increase even more. Between 2000 and 2050 almost 99 percent of the world's population increase, estimated to be almost three billion people, will occur in the latter regions, exactly where the people and the environment can least afford such a surge. About two billion of the new inhabitants will live in countries that are not experiencing much, if any, economic growth.[8]

Africa is particularly prone to high rates of population growth, with some countries facing increases of 3 percent or more per year. This may not seem to be much until we realize that such rates will double the countries' populations in about twenty-four years. Fertility rates measure the number of children an average woman has during her lifetime. Fourteen of the seventeen countries with fertility rates at six or above are in Africa. By comparison, the birth rate in the United States was fourteen per thousand in 2007, and its fertility rate was 2.1.

Although many countries have altered their attitudes about population growth, many have also realized the immensity of the task. The theory of demographic transition suggests that societies go through three stages. In the first stage, in premodern societies, birth and death rates are high, and populations remain stable or increase at low rates. In the second stage, death rates decline and populations grow more rapidly because of vaccines, better health care, and more nutritious foods. As countries begin to reap the benefits of development, they enter the third stage. Infant mortality declines but so does the desire or need to have large families. Population growth slows considerably.

This model explains events in many developed countries. As standards of living increased, birth rates declined. The model's weakness is that it assumes

Table 13-1 Estimated Populations and Projected Growth Rates

Region or Country	Estimated Population (millions)			Rate of Annual Natural Increase	Number of Years to Double Population
	2008	2025	2050		
World total	6,705	8,000	9,352	1.2	60
More developed countries	1,227	1,269	1,294	0.2	360
United States[a]	305	356	438	0.6	120
Japan	128	119	95	0.0	—
Canada	33	38	42	0.3	240
Less developed regions	5,479	6,731	8,058	1.5	48
China	1,325	1,476	1,437	0.5	144
India	1,149	1,408	1,755	1.6	45
Sub-Saharan Africa	809	1,161	1,698	2.5	29
Brazil	195	229	260	1.3	55
Philippines	91	120	150	2.1	34
Nigeria	148	205	282	2.5	29
Mexico	108	124	132	1.6	45
Uganda	29	56	106	3.1	23
Yemen	22	35	56	3.2	23

Source: Population Reference Bureau, *2008 World Population Data Sheet* (Washington, D.C.: Population Reference Bureau, 2008), www.prb.org.

a. Although rates of natural increase in the United States are modest, immigration accounts for much of the projected increase in the U.S. population.

economic growth; in the absence of such growth, many nations are caught in a "demographic trap."[9] They get stuck in the second stage. This is the predicament of many countries today. In some African countries the situation is even worse. Their populations are growing faster than their economies, and living standards are declining. These declines create a cruel paradox. Larger populations produce increased demands for food, shelter, education, and health care; stagnant economies make it impossible to provide them.

The opportunity to lower death rates can also make it difficult to slow population growth. In nineteen African countries the average life expectancy at birth is less than fifty years (and forty years or less in several of these countries), compared with seventy-eight in the United States and eighty-two in Japan, as of 2007. If these Africans had access to the medicines, vitamins, and nutritious foods readily available elsewhere, then death rates would drop substantially. Life expectancies in these countries could be extended by twenty years or more.

There is some reason to expect death rates to decline. Despite the devastating impact of HIV/AIDS, especially in sub-Saharan Africa, development agencies have attempted to reduce infant mortality by immunizing children against potentially fatal illnesses and by providing inexpensive cures for diarrhea and other illnesses. These efforts have met with enormous success, and more progress is anticipated. Reduced mortality rates among children should also reduce fertility rates. Nonetheless, the change will be gradual, and millions of children will be born in the meantime. Most of the first-time mothers of the next twenty years have already been born.

The best-known and most controversial population programs are in India and China. India's family planning program started in the early 1950s as a low-key effort that achieved only modest success. The program changed from being voluntary to compulsory in the mid-1970s. The minimum age for marriage was increased, and India's states were encouraged to select their own methods to reduce growth.

Through a variety of approaches, India has been able to cut its fertility rate significantly, but cultural resistance may stifle further gains.[10] India currently adds about 18 million inhabitants each year. If such growth continues, India could become the world's most populous country by 2040.

Whether India does so depends on what happens in China. To reduce its growth rate, the Chinese government discourages early marriages. It also adopted a one-child-per-family policy in 1979, and the policy is applied in urban areas. The government gives one-child families monthly subsidies, educational benefits for their child, preferences for housing and health care, and higher pensions at retirement. Families that had previously agreed to have only one child but then had another are deprived of these benefits and penalized financially.

The most controversial elements of the policy involve the government's monitoring of women's menstrual cycles; instances of forced sterilizations and abortions, some occurring in the last trimester; and even female infanticide in rural areas.[11] Chinese officials admit that abortions have been forced on some unwilling women. These officials quickly add, however, that such practices represent aberrations, not accepted guidelines, and that they violate the government's policies.

China's initial efforts lowered annual rates of population growth considerably. Total fertility rates declined from 5.8 in 1970 to 1.6 in 2007. Despite this success, the one-child policy began to encounter extensive resistance and, in some areas, outright disregard. The government relaxed its restrictions and exempted certain families, particularly in rural areas. Perhaps because of China's success in lowering its birth rate, the Chinese have become less alarmed about limiting population growth. In the 1970s and 1980s, for example, China was concerned that its population growth was too high. By the mid 1990s, however, the government's view was that its growth rate was satisfactory. In addition, increasing incomes in urban areas allow many Chinese to pay the fines for having more than one child. In rural areas, restrictions on early marriages are often ignored.

For many years the U.S. government viewed rapidly growing populations as a threat to economic development. The United States backed its rhetoric with money; it was the largest donor to international population programs. The official U.S. position changed dramatically during the Reagan administration. Due to its opposition to abortion, the administration said the United States would no longer contribute to the UN Population Fund because it subsidized some of China's population programs. None of the fund's resources are used to provide abortions, but the U.S. ban on contributions nonetheless continued during George H. W. Bush's administration.

Within a day of taking office, President Bill Clinton announced his intention to alter these policies, to provide financial support to the fund, and to finance international population programs that rely on abortions. Just as Clinton had acted quickly, so too did George W. Bush. Within two days of becoming president in 2001, he reinstated Reagan's policy banning the use of federal funds by international organizations to support or advocate abortions. The cycle continued with President Barack Obama. Three days after he took office, he reversed the Bush rules and urged Congress to restore funding for the UN Population Fund. He also referred to the politicization of abortion as unfortunate, and he promised to seek a new dialogue involving all sides to work toward a common goal of reducing unintended pregnancies.[12]

Concerns about abortion are not the only reason many people have qualms about efforts to affect population increases. Their view is that large populations are a problem only when they are not used productively to enhance development. The solution to the lack of such development is not government intervention, they argue, but rather individual initiatives and the spread of capitalist, free-market economies. Advocates of this position also believe that larger populations can be advantageous because they enhance political power, contribute to economic development, encourage technological innovation, and stimulate agricultural production.[13] Other critics of population control programs also ask if it is appropriate for developed countries to impose their preferences on others.

Another much-debated issue involves the increased access to abortions, and who chooses to have them. The consequences of efforts to limit population growth are not always gender neutral. In parts of Asia, male children are highly prized as sources of future financial security, whereas females are viewed as liabilities. In years past, the sex of newborns was known only at birth, and in most countries newborn males slightly outnumber newborn females. With the advent of ultrasound, however, the sex of a fetus is easily ascertained months before a child is born. This knowledge can be the basis of a decision to abort female fetuses, notably in parts of India.[14] Other practices also seem to disadvantage females. In China, for example, the infant mortality rate is more than 30 percent higher for females than it is for males.

In sum, the appropriateness of different population sizes is debatable. There is no clear answer about whether growth by itself is good or bad. The important issue is a country's and the world's carrying capacity. Can it ensure a reasonable and sustainable standard of living? Can it do so in the future when the world's population will be substantially larger?

Providing Food and Fuel for Growing Populations

Sustainable development requires that environmental resources not be overtaxed so that they are available for future generations. When populations exceed sustainable yields of their forests, aquifers, and croplands, however, they are gradually destroyed.[15] The eventual result is an irreversible collapse of biological and environmental support systems. Is there any evidence that these systems are now being strained or will be in the near future?

The first place to look is in the area of food production. Nations can grow their own food, import it, or, as most nations do, rely on both options. The Earth is richly endowed with agricultural potential and production. Millions of acres of arable land remain to be cultivated in many developed countries, and farmers now produce enough food to satisfy the daily caloric and protein needs of a world population exceeding 12 billion, far more than are already alive.[16] These data suggest the ready availability of food as well as a potential for even higher levels of production. This good news must be balanced with the realization that hundreds of millions of people barely have enough food to survive.

As with economic development, the amount of food available in a country must increase at least as fast as the rate of population growth; otherwise, per-capita consumption will decline. If existing levels of caloric intake are already inadequate, then food production (and imports) must increase faster than population growth to meet minimum caloric needs. Assisted by the expanded use of irrigation, pesticides, and fertilizers, many developing countries, particularly in Asia, have dramatically increased their food production. Asia's three largest countries—China, India, and Indonesia—are no longer heavily dependent on imports.

Despite these and a few other notable successes, much of the developing world is in the midst of an agricultural crisis. Thirty-two African countries produced less food per capita in 2003 than they did in 1990. Between 1986–1995 and 1996–2005, per-capita food production decreased in twenty sub-Saharan countries. In another twenty-four countries in the same region, per-capita food production increased but at rates lower than the annual growth in population. The annual average increase in population growth was ten or more times higher in some countries than the annual average increase in food production.

The consequence was that average caloric consumption declined or imports of food had to increase dramatically (or both). With the international spike in food and fuel prices in 2007–2008, many countries found themselves without sufficient resources to import the food they needed to assure that even minimal levels of nutrition could be maintained (Table 13-2). In mid-2008, as an illustration, the Food and Agriculture Organization (FAO) identified thirty-four countries that were expected to lack the resources to respond to critical problems of food security.[17]

Agricultural production can be increased, but many countries suffer a shortage of land suitable for cultivation to support existing populations. Some countries have reached or exceeded the sustainable limits of production. Their populations are overexploiting the environment's carrying capacity and using their land beyond its capacity to sustain agricultural production. Farmers in India, Pakistan, Bangladesh, and West Africa may

Table 13-2   Changes in Agricultural Production and Daily Caloric Intake

Country	Index of Food Production per Capita (1999–2001 = 100) 2006	Daily Caloric Supply per Capita 1979–1981	1989–1991	2001–2003	Proportion of Population Undernourished (%) 2001–2003
United States	99	3,190	3,480	3,770	<2.5
Canada	103	2,930	3,030	3,180	<2.5
Bangladesh	106	1,980	2,070	2,160	32
Burundi	83	2,030	1,860	1,640	67
China	122	2,330	2,680	2,970	11
Cuba	58	2,880	2,880	2,610	11
Haiti	92	2,040	1,770	2,090	47
India	99	2,080	2,370	2,490	21
Kenya	110	2,250	2,020	2,040	38
Madagascar	97	2,370	2,110	2,040	36
Malawi	79	2,270	1,930	2,140	34
Sierra Leone	153	2,110	1,980	1,930	50
Zambia	96	2,220	1,960	1,930	47

Source: Food and Agriculture Organization, *The State of Food and Agriculture 2007* (Rome: FAO, 2007) and FAOSTAT, production index numbers, http://faostat.fao.org/site/601/DesktopDefault.aspx ?PageID=601.

already be farming virtually all the land suitable for agriculture, and the amount of arable land per capita is declining in many developing countries. The World Bank estimates that production has declined substantially in approximately one-sixth of the agricultural land in these countries. Likewise, the FAO estimates that nearly a quarter of the world's population depends on land whose productivity and ecosystem functions are declining.[18] If these trends continue, millions of acres of barren land will be added to the millions that are already beyond redemption.

Many developing countries rely on fish as their major source of protein. Unfortunately, the condition of many of the world's fisheries is perilous. About one-quarter of the most important marine fish stocks are depleted, overharvested, or recovering from overharvesting. Almost half are being exploited at or close to their maximum sustainable yield. Over four hundred oxygen-starved "dead zones" have been identified in the world's oceans and coastal areas. These zones, which can barely sustain marine life, have doubled in number every ten years since the 1960s. Many of these zones were once prime fishing grounds but have now collapsed.[19] So desperate are some subsistence fishers that they rely on cyanide or dynamite to catch the few fish that remain. Although production from aquaculture is increasing, many poor people cannot afford to purchase what they could formerly acquire without the need for cash.

It is important to appreciate as well that the nature of diets changes as nations urbanize. Irrespective of differences in prices and incomes, according to the International Food Policy Research Institute, "urban dwellers consume more wheat and less rice and demand more meat, milk products, and fish than their rural counterparts." This preference leads to increased requirements for grain to feed animals, the need for more space for forage, greater demands for water, and increased pollution from animal waste. Changes in the composition of diets can be anticipated in many countries. In fact, in virtually every low-income country, urbanization is increasing faster than overall population growth (in many instances, three to four times faster).

China provides an example. Although most Chinese live in rural areas, migration to urban areas has increased substantially over the past two decades. According to a survey of Chinese households in 2000, urban residents consumed about 40 percent more red meat and three times as much fish per capita as those in rural areas.[20]

Increased demand for meat has several environmental consequences. More grain must be produced to feed the livestock and poultry. In a typical year, as much as 35 to 40 percent of the world's grain production is used for animal feed, but the conversion from feed to meat is not a neat one. As many as ten pounds of grain are required to produce one pound of beef. Ruminant livestock need grazing land, which is already in short supply in many areas. Throughout the world, about twice as much land is devoted to animal grazing as is used for crops. If a land's carrying capacity is breached due to excessive exploitation, then the alternative is to use feedlot production, which requires even higher levels of grain and concentrates waste products in small areas.

Relying on Domestic Production

Imports offer a possible solution to deficiencies in domestic production, but here, too, many developing countries encounter problems. To finance imports, countries need foreign exchange, usually acquired through their own exports or from loans. Few developing countries have industrial products or professional services to export, so they must rely on minerals, natural resources (such as timber or petroleum), or cash crops (such as tea, sugar, coffee, cocoa, and rubber).

Prices for many of these commodities fluctuate widely. World prices for cocoa and cotton were about 50 percent lower in 2007 than they had been in 1980, even when adjusted for inflation.[21] To cope with declining prices for export crops, farmers often intensify production, which implies increased reliance on fertilizers and pesticides, or expand the area under cultivation to increase production. Unfortunately these seemingly rational reactions can depress prices as supply eventually outpaces demand. As the area used for export crops expands, production for domestic consumption may decline.

Opportunities exist to increase exports, but economic policies in the developed world can discourage expanded activity in developing countries. Every year farmers in Japan, Europe, and the United States receive billions of dollars in subsidies and other price-related supports from their governments. Government aid to farmers in a few developed countries, including

Japan, the United States, and those in the European Union, reached $258 billion in 2007. The U.S. share of this total was over $32 billion.[22]

The European Union provided over $134 billion for agricultural support for its farmers. In some years 40 percent or more of its annual budget is devoted to farm subsidies. So large are these supports, the president of the World Bank once noted, that the average European cow received a subsidy of about $2.50 per day, or more than the average daily income of about three billion people.[23] Japanese cows were even more privileged. They received a daily subsidy of about $7.50, or more than 1,800 times as much foreign assistance as Japan provided to sub-Saharan Africa each day.

Subsidies often lead to overproduction and surpluses, which discourage imports from developing countries, remove incentives to expand production, encourage the use of environmentally fragile land, and can increase prices to consumers in countries that provide the subsidies. Rice, sugar, cotton, wheat, and peanuts are easily and less expensively grown in many developing countries, but the U.S. government subsidizes its farmers to grow these crops or imposes tariffs on their importation.

Developing countries are increasingly irritated with trade and agricultural policies that they consider to be discriminatory. In response to a complaint from Brazil, the World Trade Organization (WTO) agreed in 2004 that European subsidies for sugar exports violated international trade rules. This decision followed another WTO decision in which it ruled that U.S. price supports for cotton resulted in excess production and exports as well as low international prices, thus causing "serious prejudice" to Brazil. African producers of cotton have also called for an end to government support for the production of cotton in developed countries, especially the United States, the world's largest exporter of cotton. Without access to export markets, developing countries are denied their best opportunity for development, which, historically, has provided the best cure for poverty and rapid population growth.

The Debt Conundrum

Developing countries could once depend on loans from private banks or foreign governments to help finance imports. Now, however, many low and middle income countries are burdened with considerable debts, which reached almost $3 trillion in 2006, 20 percent more than in 2000. A common measure of a nation's indebtedness is its debt service, which represents the total payments for interest and principal as a percentage of the country's exports of goods and services. These exports provide the foreign currencies that allow countries to repay their debts denominated in foreign currencies and to import foreign products, including food, medicines, petroleum, and machinery. When debt service increases, more export earnings are required to repay loans, and less money is available for development. Many developing nations, especially in Africa and Latin America, have encountered this problem.

The largest bilateral donors, including the United States, as well as the World Bank, the International Monetary Fund, the African Development

Fund, and the Inter-American Development Bank have agreed to cancel the debt of the world's most indebted countries, most of which are in Africa. In exchange for debt relief from the multilateral institutions, these so-called highly indebted poor countries (HIPC) are required to adopt reforms designed to encourage sustainable economic growth and to complete poverty reduction strategies that provide the poor with a better quality of life.

Initial reviews of the debt-relief initiative have been positive, but considerable uncertainty remains. Several of the HIPCs had not been repaying the debt they owed, and the debt relief has not eliminated the risk of future "debt distress" among many of the beneficiaries. In turn, the debt-relief initiative does not include commercial creditors, many of which have not been enthusiastic about forgiving their loans. Likewise, adopting reforms does not guarantee their implementation. As the World Bank noted, in the quest to meet the initiative's eligibility requirements, HIPCs have faced internal conflict, problems with governance, and difficulties in formulating their strategies for poverty reduction.[24]

The Destruction of Tropical Forests

The rain forests of Africa, South America, and Southeast Asia are treasure chests of incomparable biological diversity. These forests provide irreplaceable habitats for as much as 80 percent of the world's species of plants and animals, most of which remain to be discovered and described scientifically. Viable forests also stabilize soils, reduce the impact and incidence of floods, and regulate local climates, watersheds, and river systems.[25] In addition, increasing concern about global warming underscores the global importance of tropical forests. Through photosynthesis, trees and other plants remove carbon dioxide from the atmosphere and convert it into oxygen. More than one-quarter of the prescription drugs used in the United States have their origins in tropical plants.

At the beginning of the twentieth century, tropical forests covered approximately 10 percent of the Earth's surface, or about 5.8 million square miles. The deforestation of recent decades has diminished this area by about one-third. If current rates of deforestation continue unabated, only a few areas of forest will remain untouched. Humans will have destroyed a natural palliative for global warming and condemned half or more of all species to extinction.

Causes

Solutions to the problem of tropical deforestation depend on the root cause.[26] One view blames poverty and the pressures associated with growing populations and shifting cultivators. Landless peasants, so the argument goes, invade tropical forests and denude them for fuelwood, for grazing, or to grow crops with which to survive. Tropical soils are typically thin, relatively infertile, and lack sufficient nutrients, so frequent clearing of new areas is necessary. Such areas are ill suited for sustained agricultural production, as farmers in the Amazon know well.

Another explanation for deforestation places primary blame on commercial logging intended to satisfy demands for tropical hardwoods in developed countries. Whether strapped for foreign exchange, required to repay loans, or subjected to domestic pressure to develop their economies, governments in the developing world frequently regard tropical forests as sources of ready income. Exports of wood now produce billions of dollars in annual revenues for developing countries, and some countries impose few limits in their rush to the bank.

Recognizing the causes and consequences of deforestation is not enough to bring about a solution. Commercial logging can be highly profitable to those who own logging concessions, and few governments in developing countries are equipped to manage their forests properly. These governments often let logging companies harvest trees in designated areas under prescribed conditions. All too frequently, however, the conditions are inadequate or not well enforced, often due to rampant corruption.

An Alternative View of the Problem

As the pace of tropical deforestation has quickened, so have international pressures on developing countries to halt or mitigate it. In response, leaders of developing countries quickly emphasize how ironic it is that developed countries, whose increasing consumption creates the demand for tropical woods, are simultaneously calling for a reduction of logging and shifting cultivation in developing countries.

In addition, the developing countries point to Europe's destruction of its forests during the industrial revolution and the widespread cutting in the United States in the nineteenth century. Why then should developing countries be held to a different standard than the developed ones? Just as Europeans and Americans decided how and when to extract their resources, developing countries insist that they too should be permitted to determine their own patterns of consumption.

Will tropical forests survive? Solutions abound. What is lacking, however, is a consensus about which of these solutions will best meet the essential needs of the poor, the reasonable objectives of timber-exporting and -importing nations, and the inflexible imperatives of ecological stability.

Fortunately there is a growing realization that much can be done to stem the loss of tropical forests. For example, many countries have developed national forest programs that describe the status of their forests as well as strategies to preserve them for future generations. Unfortunately, implementation of these plans does not always parallel the good intentions associated with them. Likewise, rather than seeing forests solely as a source of wood or additional agricultural land, many countries are now examining the export potential of forest products other than wood. The expectation is that the sale of these products—such as cork, rattan, oils, resins, and medicinal plants—will provide economic incentives to maintain rather than destroy forests.

Other proposed options to maintain tropical forests include efforts to certify that timber exports are from sustainably managed and legally harvested forests. Importers and potential consumers would presumably avoid timber products without such certification. For such initiatives to be successful, however, exporters would have to accept the certification process and there would have to be widespread agreement about what sustainable management means. Such agreement is still absent. In addition, no country would want to subject itself to the potentially costly process of internationally accepted certification only to learn that its forestry exports do not meet the requirements for certification or that less-expensive timber is available from countries that do not participate in the certification program.

The International Tropical Timber Organization (ITTO) is one institution at the forefront of these certification efforts. Created in 1986, the ITTO encourages timber-exporting and -importing nations to collaborate to ensure the conservation and sustainable management of forests. Despite its good intentions, the ITTO has not achieved as much as its creators may have hoped, perhaps because it must rely on moral suasion and has no enforcement powers. In 2007, for example, about 8 percent of the world's forests were internationally certified, but nearly all of these were in Europe and North America. Less than 1 percent of Africa's and less than 2 percent of Asia's and Latin America's forests were certified in that year.

More than thirty national certification programs exist, but only four are in the developing world. Indonesia has one such program, but its forested area declined by almost 25 percent between 1990 and 2005. Other countries, without national certification programs, experienced even larger losses over the same period, including Honduras (38 percent), Nigeria (35 percent), and the Philippines (32 percent).[27]

Another approach to sustainable management would impose taxes on timber exports (or imports). The highest taxes would be imposed on logging that causes the greatest ecological damage; timber from sustainable operations would face the lowest taxes. Yet another option would increase reliance on community-based management of forest resources. Rather than allowing logging companies with no long-term interest in a forest to harvest trees, community-based management would place responsibility for decisions about logging (and other uses) with the people who live in or adjacent to forests. These people have the strongest incentives to manage forest resources wisely, particularly if they reap the long-term benefits of their management strategies.

Conflicting Signals from the Developed Nations

Improvements in the policies of many developing countries are surely necessary if sustainable development is to be achieved. As already noted, however, developed countries sometimes cause or contribute to environmental problems there.

Patterns of consumption provide an example. Although the United States and other developed nations can boast about their own comparatively low rates of population growth, developing nations reply that patterns of consumption, not population increases, are the real culprits. This view suggests that negative impacts on the environment are a function of a country's population growth, its consumption, and the technologies, such as automobiles, that enable this consumption.[28]

Applying this formula places major responsibility for environmental problems on rich nations, despite their relatively small numbers of global inhabitants. The inhabitants of these nations consume far more of the Earth's resources than their numbers justify. Consider that the richest one-quarter of the world's nations control about 75 percent of the world's income (and, according to the UN Development Programme, the richest 10 percent of Americans have a combined income greater than two billion of the world's poorest people). In addition, these nations consume a disproportionate share of all meat and fish and most of the world's energy, paper, chemicals, iron, and steel. These few nations similarly generate more than 90 percent of all hazardous and industrial wastes. The United States leads the world in per-capita production of trash and has one of the lowest rates of recycling among developed countries. Consider as well that these rich nations, most able to afford pollution control and conservation, bear the largest responsibility for global warming.[29]

In contrast, consumption patterns among the 20 percent of the world's population living in the lowest income countries account for less than 1.5 percent of the world's private consumption and only about 5 percent of the world's consumption of meat and fish. One estimate suggests that people in the developed world consume, on average, about thirty-two times as many resources as do people in developing countries.[30] Put in other terms, this means that the consumption of a single American is comparable to the consumption of thirty-two Kenyans.

Americans represent less than 5 percent of the Earth's inhabitants, yet they use about one-fifth of the world's energy. On a typical day in 2006, 300 million Americans consumed more petroleum than the 2.9 *billion* people who lived in China, India, Russia, Japan, and Brazil.[31] Of the petroleum that Americans did consume in that year, 60 percent was imported (compared with about 36 percent in 1975).

Much of this petroleum is used to fuel Americans' love for the automobile. Whereas Americans increased their numbers by about 30 percent between 1980 and 2006, the total number of registered motor vehicles in the United States grew by more than 55 percent over the same period. There are more motor vehicles than licensed drivers in the United States. An average American driver consumes about five times more gasoline each year than the typical European. Part of the explanation is that many European cars, often designed by U.S. manufacturers, are far more fuel efficient than are U.S. cars. Despite many Americans' belief that gasoline prices are too high, the price of gasoline in much of Western Europe is about two and one-half times higher than in the United States. Only in 2008 did the price of a gallon of gasoline in the United States briefly exceed the cost of the same amount of milk and many bottled waters—despite their inexhaustible supply.

Americans' extravagance with fossil fuels provides part of the explanation for U.S. production of about one-fifth of the emissions that contribute to global warming. The Intergovernmental Panel on Climate Change believes that a relatively safe level of carbon dioxide emissions is about 2.25 metric tons per person per year.[32] Each metric ton is about 2,205 pounds. With the exception of a few ministates, no country produces as much carbon dioxide per capita as does the United States. It produced 20.6 metric tons per capita compared with 9.8, 3.8, and 1.2 metric tons in Germany, China, and India, respectively, in 2004.[33] In other words, U.S. emissions per capita are about nine times higher than what sustainable levels of development would require. China's production of carbon dioxide has increased rapidly in recent years, but a notable portion of these increases is attributable to the production of goods destined for the United States.

Americans' patterns of food consumption are also of interest. As noted in Table 13-2, an average American consumes nearly 3,800 calories per day, among the highest levels in the world. Among young adults, about 25 percent of these calories are from sweetened beverages. Not surprisingly, almost two-thirds of American adults are either obese or overweight. According to the U.S. Centers for Disease Control and Prevention, no American state had a prevalence of adult obesity of more than 15 percent in 1990. By 2007, in contrast, all fifty states exceeded this percentage, and only one state, Colorado, had a prevalence of less than 20 percent.[34] Weight-related illnesses are responsible for the deaths of more Americans each year than are motor vehicle accidents.

Few nations waste as much food as does the United States. In the mid-1990s, the U.S. Department of Agriculture estimated that Americans wasted about 96 billion pounds of edible food each year—about one-quarter of all the food available to them. More recent estimates, based on research at the University of Arizona, suggest that as much as half of all food is wasted in the United States. The World Food Program believes that the U.S. food surplus is sufficient to "fill every empty stomach in Africa."[35]

Due to these kinds of inequalities in consumption, continued population growth in rich countries is a greater threat to the global environment than is such growth in the developing world. If relative consumption and levels of waste output remain unchanged, the 57 million extra inhabitants born in rich countries in the 1990s will pollute the globe more than the extra 900 million born elsewhere. Other experts suggest that if Americans want to maintain their present standard of living and levels of energy consumption, then their ideal population is about 50 million, far less than the mid-2008 U.S. population of about 304 million.[36] Given the existing U.S. population, the only viable alternative is to reduce consumption and to alter lifestyles.

Causes for Optimism?

There is cause for concern about the prospects for sustainable development among developing countries, but the situation is neither entirely bleak nor beyond hope. Smallpox, a killer of millions of people every year in the 1950s, has been eradicated (except in laboratories). Polio may soon be the next scourge to be eliminated. According to the United Nations, between

1990 and 2005 the proportion of children in developing countries under age five who were underweight declined by about 20 percent. Over the same period, infant mortality rates declined substantially and the proportion of births attended by skilled health staff increased by more than 25 percent. Deaths of children from measles—preventable through vaccines—declined by more than 60 percent during those same fifteen years.[37]

Further recognition of the global challenges associated with development came in 2000, when all members of the United Nations adopted eight Millennium Development Goals and agreed to achieve them by 2015. These goals seek to eradicate extreme poverty and hunger; achieve universal primary education; promote gender equity; reduce child mortality; improve maternal health; combat HIV/AIDs, malaria, and other diseases; ensure environmental sustainability; and develop a global partnership for development.

In another positive sign, in response to pressure from developing countries and through the auspices of the WTO, the United States and the European Union are discussing substantial reductions in agricultural subsidies. In 2005 the Group of Eight (G8) nations also pledged to double their development assistance by 2010. Half of the increase would go to Africa.

At the initiative of President George W. Bush, the United States committed $15 billion over five years, beginning in 2004, to fight HIV/AIDS, tuberculosis, and malaria in the developing world. The President's Emergency Program for AIDS Relief (PEPFAR) was deemed to be so successful and well received that Congress authorized the expenditure of an additional $48 billion in 2008 to continue the program for another five years. Private philanthropic support for development is also evident. The Bill and Melinda Gates Foundation donated $500 million to the Global Fund to Fight AIDS, Tuberculosis and Malaria in 2006. The William J. Clinton Foundation's HIV/AIDS Initiative has been similarly active and has successfully negotiated major reductions in the cost of antiretroviral drugs in many countries.

The international community is also demonstrating recognition of the Earth's ecological interconnectedness. The World Commission on Environment and Development was established in 1983 and charged with formulating long-term environmental strategies for achieving sustainable development. In *Our Common Future,* the commission emphasized that although environmental degradation is an issue of survival for developing nations, failure to address the degradation satisfactorily will guarantee unparalleled and undesirable global consequences from which no nation will escape.[38] The report's release in 1987 prompted increased international attention to environmental issues.

This attention manifested itself most noticeably in the UN Conference on Environment and Development in Rio de Janeiro, Brazil, in 1992 and a World Summit on Sustainable Development in Johannesburg, South Africa, in 2002. The 1992 conference led to the creation of the UN Commission on Sustainable Development, which meets annually to review progress in achieving sustainable development.

Delegates at the Rio conference also approved Agenda 21, a plan for enhancing global environmental quality. The price tag for the recommended actions is huge. Rich nations could provide the amount needed to meet the goals of Agenda 21 if they donated as little as 0.70 percent (*not* 7 percent, but seven-tenths of 1 percent) of their GNI to the developing world each year. Only Denmark, Luxembourg, the Netherlands, Norway, and Sweden exceeded this target in 2007. Belgium, Finland, and Ireland have pledged to move toward the recommended target. The United States typically provides more foreign aid than any other country, but this aid represented only 0.16 percent of the U.S. GNI in 2007. U.S. development assistance was thus well below the target level and tied for the lowest percentage among twenty-two developed countries. This situation has led some observers to label the United States as a "global Scrooge" based on its relative wealth but seeming unwillingness to share that wealth.

Of the U.S. aid that is provided, much is given to advance U.S. foreign policy objectives rather than to help the poorest countries and those most in need. In the mid-2000s, over one-third of U.S. development assistance went to Iraq and Afghanistan. Much U.S. foreign aid never leaves the United States. American firms are typically hired to implement U.S. foreign aid programs, and "Buy American" provisions often require recipients to purchase U.S. products, even when locally available items are less expensive.

Surveys of Americans' opinions about development assistance present an interesting, but mixed picture. About three-quarters of those surveyed in early 2008 agreed that cooperating with other countries on the environment, to control the spread of diseases, and to assist countries to develop clean water supplies is "very important." Despite such support, most Americans also believe that the United States is already doing more than its share to help less fortunate countries. Among adults surveyed in 2005 about U.S. foreign aid, nearly one in five believed that the United States gives 5 percent or more of its GNI to promote development, far higher than the actual level noted above. A large number of Americans also believe that U.S. foreign assistance should be reduced.[39]

In contrast to Americans' seeming reluctance to share their wealth, other nations have demonstrated an increased willingness to address globally shared environmental problems. The international community now operates a Global Environment Facility, a multibillion-dollar effort to finance environmental projects in developing countries. It distributes funds to address global warming, loss of biological diversity, pollution of international waters, and depletion of the ozone layer.

In addition, more than 190 countries have ratified the Convention on Biological Diversity (although not Iraq, Somalia, or the United States, the only major developed country not to have done so). The world community approved a Convention to Combat Desertification in 1996. The next year, representatives from more than 160 countries met in Kyoto, Japan, to discuss implementation of the 1992 UN Framework Convention on Climate Change. In an historic agreement, the Kyoto Protocol, most developed nations agreed to reduce emissions that contribute to global warming by an average of about 5 percent below 1990 levels in the five-year period from 2008 to 2012. Over 180 countries, excluding Kazakhstan and the United States, have ratified the protocol (see chapter 12).

Many developing nations recognize their obligations to protect their environments as well as the global commons. At the same time, however, these nations argue that success requires technical and financial assistance from their wealthy colleagues. However desirable sustainable development may be, poor nations cannot afford to address their environmental problems in the absence of cooperation from richer nations.

A further issue of growing importance is resentment in some poor countries toward the environmental sermons from developed countries. Global warming provides one of several examples. As China and India grow, they are under pressure from Europe and the United States to reduce the production of greenhouse gases. As some Indians and Chinese respond, however, why should they slow or alter their path to development to accommodate high standards of living elsewhere? Per-capita consumption of petroleum and emissions of carbon dioxide are far lower in India and China than in the United States. When India released its policy on climate change in 2008, Prime Minister Manmohan Singh observed that fairness dictates that everyone deserves equal per-capita emissions, regardless of where they live.[40] India is not willing, he noted, to accept a model of global development in which some countries continue to maintain high carbon emissions while the options available for developing countries are constrained.

Brazil has been subject to international criticism for deforestation of the Amazon. Brazil has had mixed success in halting illegal logging, but President Luiz Inácio Lula da Silva responded to complaints from Europeans by declaring that they should look at a map of Europe to see how much forested land remains there before telling Brazilians what they should do.[41] According to Lula da Silva, Europeans have 3 percent of their native flora remaining, compared with nearly 70 percent in Brazil.

U.S. officials upset Chinese and Indians with remarks indicating that their consumption of food is a primary cause of rapidly rising food prices. Speaking in April 2008, Secretary of State Condoleezza Rice commented that improved diets in India and China are one cause of skyrocketing prices for food. A few days later, President Bush identified a growing middle class in India, which is "demanding better food and nutrition," as a cause of higher prices. The reaction from India was understandably negative. "Why do Americans think they deserve to eat more than Indians?" asked one journalist. An Indian public official characterized the U.S. position as "Guys with gross obesity telling guys just emerging from emaciation to go on a major diet." This characterization may be indicative of a larger concern. The perception that Americans are global environmental culprits is widespread. When people in twenty-four countries were asked in 2008 which country is "hurting the world's environment the most," majorities or pluralities in thirteen countries cited the United States.[42]

Contentious debates and inflammatory rhetoric about blame and responsibility will not be productive. The economic, population, and environmental problems of the developing world dwarf those of the developed nations and are not amenable to quick resolution. Nonetheless, immediate action is imperative. Hundreds of millions of people are destroying their biological and environmental support systems at unprecedented rates to meet their daily needs for food, fuel, and fiber. The world will add several billion people in the next few decades, and all of them will have justifiable claims to be fed, clothed, educated, employed, and healthy. To accommodate these expectations, the world may need as much as 50 percent more energy in 2030 than it used in 2007. Most of the increase will come from fossil fuels, at least if governments continue their present energy policies.

Whether the environment can accommodate this unprecedented but predictable increase will depend not only on the poor who live in stagnant economies but also on a much smaller number of relatively rich overconsuming nations in the developed world. Unless developed nations are able to accommodate and support sustainable development everywhere, the future of billions of poor people will determine Americans' future as well.

As the authors of the Millennium Ecosystem Assessment concluded, the ability of the planet's ecosystems to sustain future generations is no longer assured.[43] Over the past fifty years the world has experienced unprecedented environmental change in response to ever-increasing demands for food, fuel, fiber, fresh water, and timber. Much of the environmental degradation that has occurred can be reversed, but as these authors warned, "the changes in policy and practice required are substantial and not currently underway."

If these experts are correct, unless the United States acts soon and in collaboration with other nations, Americans will increasingly suffer the adverse consequences of environmental damage caused by the billions of poor people we have chosen to neglect and perhaps even abandoned—just as these people will suffer from the environmental damage we inflict on them. In short, there are continuing questions about whether the current economic model that depends on growth and extravagant consumption among a few is ecologically sustainable and morally acceptable for everyone.[44]

Suggested Web Sites

Millennium Ecosystem Assessment (www.millenniumassessment.org) Provides an overview of the Millennium Ecosystem Assessment program, its history, and its findings, including slide presentations for the reports and press releases.

Population Reference Bureau (www.prb.org) A convenient source for current data on global population trends. Its annual World Population Data Sheet includes statistics for all of the world's nations on birth rates, growth rates, per-capita income, percentage undernourished, percentage in urban areas, and projected population size for 2025 and 2050.

UN Development Programme (www.undp.org) Provides links to activities and reports on economic development and the environment, including the Millennium Development Goals.

UN Division for Sustainable Development (www.un.org/esa/dsd) Provides useful links to reports of the World Commission on Environment and Development, Agenda 21, the Johannesburg Plan of Implementation, and other assessments of progress toward sustainable development.

UN Food and Agriculture Organization (www.fao.org) One of the largest UN organizations; focuses on agriculture, forestry, fisheries, and rural development. It works to alleviate poverty and hunger worldwide.

UN Population Fund (www.unfpa.org) Funds population assistance programs worldwide, particularly family planning and reproductive health, and issues reports on population growth and its effects.

World Bank (www.worldbank.org) One of the largest sources of economic development assistance to developing nations; also issues extensive reports on global economic conditions and poverty, including progress toward the Millennium Development Goals.

Notes

1. World Bank, World Development Indicators Database and *World Development Indicators 2007* (Washington, D.C.: World Bank, 2007), 63. Due to differences in the costs of goods and services from one country to another, GNI per capita does not provide comparable measures of economic well-being. To address this problem, economists have developed the concept of purchasing-power parity (PPP). PPP equalizes the prices of identical goods and services across all countries, with the United States as the base economy. For an amusing explanation of PPP, see the "Big Mac Index" of *The Economist,* at www.economist.com/markets/bigmac/, which compares the price of a McDonald's Big Mac hamburger in more than forty countries.

2. UNICEF, *Early Marriage: A Harmful Traditional Practice* (New York, 2005), www.unicef.org/publications/index_26024.html.

3. UN Development Programme (UNDP), *Human Development Report 2007/08* (New York: UNDP, 2007), 261–264, hdr.undp.org/en/; World Bank, *Global Monitoring Report 2008* (Washington, D.C.: World Bank, 2008), 2.

4. Millennium Ecosystem Assessment, *Ecosystems and Human Well-being: Current State and Trends,* vol. 1 (Washington, D.C.: Island Press, 2005), www.millenniumassessment.org/en/About.aspx.

5. World Commission on Environment and Development, *Our Common Future* (London: Oxford University Press, 1987), 8, 43.

6. John N. Wilford, "A Tough-Minded Ecologist Comes to Defense of Malthus," *New York Times,* June 30, 1987, C3.

7. U.S. Census Bureau, www.census.gov. See also Population Reference Bureau, "2008 World Population Data Sheet" (Washington, D.C.: Population Reference Bureau), www.prb.org/pdf08/08WPDS_Eng.pdf. For a discussion of the world's carrying capacity, see Jeroen C. J. M. Van Den Bergh and Piet Rietveld, "Reconsidering the Limits to World Population: Meta-analysis and Meta-prediction," *BioScience* 54 (March 2004): 195–204.

8. Commission on Growth and the Development, *The Growth Report: Strategies for Sustained Growth and Inclusive Development* (Washington, D.C.: World Bank, 2008), 19, www.growthcommission.org/index.php.

9. Lester R. Brown, "Analyzing the Demographic Trap," in *State of the World 1987,* ed. Lester R. Brown (New York: Norton, 1987), 20.

10. Population Reference Bureau, "India's Population Reality: Reconciling Change and Tradition," *Population Bulletin* 61 (September 2006), www.prb.org.

11. Joseph Kahn, "Harsh Birth Control Steps Fuel Violence in China," *New York Times,* May 22, 2007, A12; Jim Yardley, "China Sticking with One-Child Policy," *New York Times,* March 11, 2008.

12. Peter Baker, "Obama Reverses Rule on U.S. Abortion Aid," *New York Times,* January 23, 2009, A11.

13. For example, see Julian Simon, *The Ultimate Resource* (Princeton: Princeton University Press, 1981).

14. Population Reference Bureau, "India's Population Reality," 10; Therese Hesketh and Zhu Wei Xing, "Abnormal Sex Ratios in Human Populations: Causes and Consequences," *Proceedings of the National Academy of Sciences* 103 (2006): 13271–13275, www.pnas .org/content/103/36.toc.

15. Brown, *State of the World 1987*, 21.

16. Per Pinstrup-Anderson, former director of the International Food Policy Research Institute, believes the world can easily feed 12 billion people at the end of this century. See "Will the World Starve?" *The Economist*, June 10, 1995, 39.

17. FAO, *The State of Food and Agriculture 2007* (Rome: FAO, 2007) and "Crop Prospects and Food Situation: Countries in Crisis Requiring External Assistance," July 2008, www.fao.org/worldfoodsituation/wfs-home/en/.

18. World Bank, *World Development Indicators 2007*, 124; FAO, *Land Degradation Assessment in Drylands* (Rome: FAO, 2008).

19. FAO, *The State of World Fisheries and Aquaculture 2006* (Rome: FAO, 2007), 29, www.fao.org/corp/publications/en/; Robert J. Diaz and Rutger Rosenberg, "Spreading Dead Zones and Consequences for Marine Ecosystems," *Science* 321 (2008): 926–929.

20. Hsin-Hui Hsu, Wen S. Chern, and Fred Gale, "How Will Rising Income Affect the Structure of Food Demand," in Economic Research Service, *China's Food and Agriculture: Issues for the 21st Century* (Washington, D.C.: U.S. Department of Agriculture, 2002), 10–13, ers.usda.gov/publications/aib775.

21. World Bank, *World Development Indicators 2008* (Washington, D.C.: World Bank, 2008), 334.

22. Organization for Economic Co-operation and Development (OECD), *Agricultural Policies in OECD Countries: Monitoring and Evaluation 2007* (Paris: OECD, 2007).

23. Statement of James D. Wolfensohn, cited in David T. Cook, "Excerpts from a Monitor Breakfast on Poverty and Globalization," *Christian Science Monitor*, June 13, 2003.

24. World Bank, *World Development Indicators 2008*, 346; International Development Association and the International Monetary Fund, "Heavily Indebted Poor Countries (HIPC) Initiative and Multilateral Debt Relief Initiative (MDRI)—Status of Implementation," September 27, 2007.

25. National Academy of Sciences (NAS), *Population Growth and Economic Development: Policy Questions* (Washington, D.C.: NAS, 1986), 31.

26. For useful discussions of the causes of deforestation, see Helmut J. Geist and Eric Lambin, "Proximate Causes and Underlying Driving Forces of Tropical Deforestation," *BioScience* 52 (February 2002): 143–150; and Michael Williams, *Deforesting the Earth: From Prehistory to Global Crisis* (Chicago: University of Chicago Press, 2003).

27. International Tropical Timber Organization (ITTO), *Developing Forest Certification: Towards Increasing the Comparability and Acceptance of Forest Certification Systems Worldwide*, (Yokohama, Japan: ITTO, 2008), 26, www.itto.or.jp/live/Live_Server/ 4092/TS29.pdf.

28. Paul R. Ehrlich and John P. Holdren, "Impact of Population Growth," *Science* 171 (1971): 1212–1217.

29. UN Development Programme, *Human Development Report 2007/2008*, 2.

30. Jared Diamond, "What's Your Consumption Factor?" *New York Times*, January 2, 2008, A19.

31. U.S. Energy Information Administration, "Country Profiles," tonto.eia.doe.gov/country/ index.cfm?view=consumption.

32. Cited in Commission on Growth and the Development, *The Growth Report*, 85–86.

33. UN Development Programme, *Human Development Report 2007/2008*, 310–311. The figures on carbon dioxide emissions per capita differ from those in Table 12-1 because they reflect 2004 levels rather than 2007 levels.

34. Benjamin Caballero, "The Global Epidemic of Obesity: An Overview," *Epidemiological Reviews* 29 (2007): 2; Centers for Disease Control and Prevention, "Overweight and Obesity Trends among American Adults," www.cdc.gov/nccdphp/dnpa/ obesity/trend/index.htm.

35. Linda Scott Kantor, Kathryn Lipton, Alden Manchester, and Victor Oliveira, "Estimating and Addressing America's Food Losses," *Food Review* 20 (January–April 1997); FoodNavigator-USA, "US Wastes Half Its Food," November 26, 2004, foodnavigator-usa.com; World Food Program, "Hunger—Ten Odd Facts," www.wfp.org/english/?ModuleID=139&Key=1424&elemId=9.

36. Paul Harrison, *The Third Revolution: Environment, Population and a Sustainable World* (New York: I. B. Taurus, 1992), 256–257; David and Marcia Pimentel, "Land, Water and Energy Versus the Ideal U.S. Population," *NPG Forum* (January 2005), npg.org/forum_series/forum0205.html.

37. United Nations, *The Millennium Development Goals Report 2007* (New York: United Nations, 2007), www.un.org/millenniumgoals/.

38. World Commission on Environment and Development, *Our Common Future.*

39. "Confidence in U.S. Foreign Policy Index," *Public Agenda* 6 (spring 2008): 14 and 3 (fall 2006): 26, publicagenda.org; Gallup International, "Voice of the People 2005," www.americans-world.org/digest/overview/us_role/foot_note5.cfm.

40. Voice of America, "India Rejects Binding Commitment to Cut Greenhouse Gas Emissions," February 7, 2008, www.voanews.com.

41. "Welcome to Our Shrinking Jungle," *The Economist,* June 7, 2008, 49; "Brazilian President Rages at 'Meddlers' Criticizing Amazon Policies," June 5, 2008, www.terradaily.com.

42. Condoleezza Rice, "Remarks at the Peace Corps 2008 Worldwide Country Director Conference," April 28, 2008, www.state.gov/secretary/rm/2008/04/104120.htm; Heather Timmons, "Indians Find U.S. at Fault in Food Cost," *New York Times,* May 14, 2008, C1; "Melting Asia," *The Economist,* June 7, 2008, 30; Pew Global Attitudes Project, "Some Positive Signs for U.S. Image," June 12, 2008, 65, www.pewglobal.org.

43. Millennium Ecosystem Assessment, *Ecosystems and Human Well-being.*

44. UN Development Programme, *Human Development Report 2007/2008*, 15.

14

China
The Great Leap Backward?[1]
Elizabeth C. Economy

China's environmental problems are mounting. Water pollution and water scarcity are burdening the economy, rising levels of air pollution are endangering the health of millions of Chinese, and much of the country's land is rapidly turning into desert. China has become a world leader in air and water pollution and land degradation, as well as a top contributor to some of the world's most vexing global environmental problems, such as the illegal timber trade, marine pollution, and climate change. As China's pollution woes increase, so, too, do the risks to its economy, public health, social stability, and international reputation. As Pan Yue, a vice minister of China's Ministry of Environmental Protection (MEP)—formerly the State Environmental Protection Administration (SEPA)—warned in 2005, "The [economic] miracle will end soon because the environment can no longer keep pace."

During the run up to the 2008 Olympics, China's leaders ratcheted up their rhetoric by setting ambitious environmental targets, announcing greater levels of environmental investment, and exhorting business leaders and local officials to clean up their backyards. The rest of the world seems to have accepted that Beijing has charted a new course: as China declares itself open for environmentally friendly business, officials in the United States, the European Union, and Japan are asking not whether to invest but how much.

Unfortunately, much of this enthusiasm stems from the widespread but misguided belief that what Beijing says goes. The central government sets the country's agenda, but it does not control all aspects of its implementation. In fact, local officials rarely heed Beijing's environmental mandates, preferring to concentrate their energies and resources on further advancing economic growth. The truth is that turning the environmental situation in China around will require something far more difficult than setting targets and spending money; it will require revolutionary bottom-up political and economic reforms.

For one thing, China's leaders need to make it easy for local officials and factory owners to do the right thing when it comes to the environment by giving them the right incentives. At the same time, they must loosen the political restrictions they have placed on the courts, nongovernmental organizations (NGOs), and the media in order to enable these groups to become independent enforcers of environmental protection. The international community, for its part, must focus more on assisting reform and less on transferring cutting-edge technologies and developing demonstration projects. Doing so will mean diving into the trenches to work with local Chinese officials, factory owners, and environmental NGOs; enlisting international NGOs to help with education and enforcement policies; and persuading multinational corporations (MNCs) to use their economic leverage to ensure that their Chinese partners adopt the best environmental practices.

Without such a clear-eyed understanding not only of what China wants but also of what it needs, China will continue to have one of the world's worst environmental records, and the Chinese people and the rest of the world will pay the price.

Sins of Emission

China's rapid development, often touted as an economic miracle, has become an environmental disaster. Record growth necessarily requires the gargantuan consumption of resources, but in China energy use has been especially unclean and inefficient, with dire consequences for the country's air, land, and water.

The coal that has powered China's economic growth, for example, is also choking its people. Coal provides about 70 percent of China's energy needs: the country's coal demand reached 2.62 billion tons in 2007—more than the United States, Japan, and the United Kingdom combined. In 2000, China anticipated doubling its coal consumption by 2020; it surpassed this mark by 2007. Consumption in China is huge partly because it is inefficient: as one Chinese official told Der Spiegel in early 2006, "To produce goods worth $10,000 we need seven times the resources used by Japan, almost six times the resources used by the U.S. and—a particular source of embarrassment— almost three times the resources used by India."[2]

Meanwhile, this reliance on coal is devastating China's environment. The country is home to twenty of the world's thirty most polluted cities, and four of the worst off among them are in the coal-rich province of Shanxi, in northeastern China. As much as 90 percent of China's sulfur dioxide emissions and 50 percent of its particulate emissions are the result of coal use. Particulates are responsible for respiratory problems among the population, and acid rain, which is caused by sulfur dioxide emissions, falls on one-quarter of China's territory and on one-third of its agricultural land, diminishing agricultural output and eroding buildings.

Yet coal use may soon be the least of China's air-quality problems. The transportation boom poses a growing challenge to China's air quality. By the end of 2007, Chinese developers laid out more than 72,079 miles of new highways throughout the country. Some 20,133 new cars are hitting China's roads each day. By 2020, China is expected to have 130 million cars, and by 2050—or perhaps as early as 2040—it is expected to have even more cars than the United States. Beijing already pays a high price for this boom. In a 2006 survey, Chinese respondents rated Beijing the fifteenth most livable city in China, down from the fourth in 2005, with the drop due largely to increased traffic and pollution. Levels of airborne particulates are now six times higher in Beijing than in New York City.

China's grand-scale urbanization plans will aggravate matters. China's leaders plan to relocate 400 million people—equivalent to well over the entire population of the United States—to newly developed urban centers between 2000 and 2030. In the process, they will erect half of all the buildings expected to be constructed in the world during that period.[3] This is a troubling prospect considering that Chinese buildings are not energy efficient—in fact, they are roughly two and a half times less so than those in Germany. Furthermore, newly urbanized Chinese, who use air conditioners, televisions, and refrigerators, consume about three and a half times more energy than do their rural counterparts. And although China is one of the world's largest producers of solar cells, compact fluorescent lights, and energy-efficient windows, these are produced mostly for export. Unless more of these energy-saving goods stay at home, the building boom will result in skyrocketing energy consumption and pollution.

China's land has also suffered from unfettered development and environmental neglect. Centuries of deforestation, along with the overgrazing of grasslands and overcultivation of cropland, have left much of China's north and northwest seriously degraded. In the past half century, moreover, forests and farmland have had to make way for industry and sprawling cities, resulting in diminishing crop yields, a loss in biodiversity, and local climatic change. The Gobi Desert, which now engulfs much of western and northern China, is spreading by about 1,900 square miles annually; some reports say that despite Beijing's aggressive reforestation efforts, one-quarter of the entire country is now desert. China's State Forestry Administration estimates that desertification has hurt some 400 million Chinese, turning tens of millions of them into environmental refugees, in search of new homes and jobs. Meanwhile, much of China's arable soil is contaminated, raising concerns about food safety. As much as 10 percent of China's farmland is believed to be polluted,[4] and every year 12 million tons of grain are contaminated with heavy metals absorbed from the soil.

Water Hazard

And then there is the problem of access to clean water. Although China holds the fourth-largest freshwater resources in the world (after Brazil, Russia, and Canada), skyrocketing demand, overuse, inefficiencies, pollution, and unequal distribution have produced a situation in which two-thirds of China's approximately 660 cities have less water than they need and more than one-sixth of them suffer severe shortages. According to Ma Jun, a leading Chinese water expert, several cities near Beijing and Tianjin, in the northeastern region of the country, could run out of water in five to seven years.[5]

Growing demand is part of the problem, of course, but so is enormous waste. The agricultural sector lays claim to 66 percent of the water China consumes, mostly for irrigation, and manages to waste more than half of that. Chinese industries are highly inefficient: they generally use 10 to 20 percent more water than do their counterparts in developed countries. Urban China is an especially huge squanderer: it loses up to 20 percent of the water it consumes through leaky pipes—a problem that China's Ministry of Construction has pledged to address in the next two to three years. As urbanization proceeds and incomes rise, the Chinese, much like people in Europe and the United States, have become larger consumers of water: they take lengthy showers, use washing machines and dishwashers, and purchase second homes with lawns that need to be watered. Water consumption in Chinese cities jumped by 6.6 percent during 2004–2005. McKinsey & Company estimates that by 2025, China's growing urban population will increase urban water demands by an additional 70 to 100 percent.[6] China's plundering of its ground-water reserves, which has created massive underground tunnels, is causing a corollary problem: some of China's wealthiest cities are sinking—in the case of Shanghai and Tianjin, by more than six feet during the past decade and a half. In Beijing, subsidence has destroyed factories, buildings, and underground pipelines and is threatening the city's main international airport.

Pollution is also endangering China's water supplies. China's ground water, which provides 70 percent of the country's total drinking water, is under threat from a variety of sources, such as polluted surface water, hazardous waste sites, and pesticides and fertilizers.[7] According to one report by the government-run Xinhua News Agency, the aquifers in 90 percent of Chinese cities are polluted. More than 75 percent of the river water flowing through China's urban areas is considered unsuitable for drinking or fishing, and the Chinese government deems about 30 percent of the river water throughout the country to be unfit for use in agriculture or industry. As a result, nearly 700 million people drink water contaminated with animal and human waste.[8] The World Bank has found that the failure to provide fully two-thirds of the rural population with piped water is a leading cause of death among children under the age of five and is responsible for as much as 11 percent of the cases of gastrointestinal cancer in China.

One of the problems is that although China has plenty of laws and regulations designed to ensure clean water, factory owners and local officials do not enforce them. A 2005 survey of 509 cities revealed that only 23 percent of factories properly treated sewage before disposing of it. According to another report, today one-third of all industrial wastewater in China and two-thirds of household sewage are released untreated.[9] Recent Chinese studies of two of the country's most important sources of water—the Yangtze and Yellow Rivers—illustrate the growing challenge. The Yangtze River, which stretches all the way from the Tibetan Plateau to Shanghai, receives 40 percent of the country's sewage, 80 percent of it untreated.[10] In 2007 the Chinese government announced that it was delaying, in part because of pollution, the development of a $60 billion plan to divert the river in order to supply the water-starved cities of Beijing and Tianjin. The first of three South-to-North Water Transfer Project routes is now slated for completion in 2010. The Yellow River supplies water to more than 150 million people and 15 percent of China's agricultural land, but two-thirds of its water is considered unsafe to drink[11] and 10 percent of its water is classified as sewage.[12] In early 2007,

Chinese officials announced that over one-third of the fish species native to the Yellow River had become extinct due to damming or pollution.[13]

China's leaders are also increasingly concerned about how climate change may exacerbate their domestic environmental situation. In the spring of 2007, Beijing released its first national assessment report on climate change, predicting a 30 percent drop in precipitation in three of China's seven major river regions—around the Huai, Liao, and Hai Rivers—and a 37 percent decline in the country's wheat, rice, and corn yields in the second half of the century. It also predicted that the Yangtze and Yellow Rivers, which derive much of their water from glaciers in Tibet, would overflow as the glaciers melted and then dry up. And both Chinese and international scientists now warn that due to rising sea levels, Shanghai could be submerged by 2050.

Collateral Damage

China's environmental problems are already affecting the rest of the world. Japan and South Korea have long suffered from the acid rain produced by China's coal-fired power plants and from the eastbound dust storms that sweep across the Gobi Desert in the spring and dump toxic yellow dust on their land. Researchers in the United States are tracking dust, sulfur, soot, and trace metals as these travel across the Pacific from China. Scientists have also traced rising levels of mercury deposits on U.S. soil back to coal-fired power plants and cement factories in China. (When ingested in significant quantities, mercury can cause birth defects and developmental problems.) Reportedly, 25 to 40 percent of all mercury emissions in the world come from China.[14]

What China dumps into its waters also pollutes the rest of the world. According to the international NGO the World Wildlife Fund, China is now the largest polluter of the Pacific Ocean. Over a quarter of China's coastal waters are classified as Level 4, or unfit for direct human consumption.[15] As Liu Quangfeng, an adviser to the National People's Congress, put it, "Almost no river that flows into the Bo Hai [a sea along China's northern coast] is clean." China releases about 2.8 billion tons of contaminated water into the Bo Hai annually, and the content of heavy metal in the mud at the bottom of it is now 2,000 times as high as China's own official safety standard. The prawn catch has dropped by 90 percent over the past fifteen years. In 2006, in the heavily industrialized southeastern provinces of Guangdong and Fujian, almost 8.3 billion tons of sewage were discharged into the ocean without treatment, a 60 percent increase from 2001.[16] More than 80 percent of the East China Sea, one of the world's largest fisheries, is now rated unsuitable for fishing, up from 53 percent in 2000.[17]

Furthermore, China is already attracting international attention for its rapidly growing contribution to climate change. Several reports by the Netherlands Environmental Assessment Agency have confirmed that China has already surpassed the United States as the world's largest contributor of atmospheric carbon dioxide, a leading greenhouse gas. Unless China rethinks its use of various sources of energy and adopts cutting-edge environmentally friendly technologies, warned Fatih Birol, the chief economist of the International Energy Agency, in April 2006, in twenty-five years China will emit twice as much carbon dioxide as all the countries of the Organization for Economic Cooperation and Development combined.

China's close economic partners in the developing world face additional environmental burdens from China's economic activities. Chinese multinationals, which are exploiting natural resources in Africa, Latin America, and Southeast Asia in order to fuel China's continued economic rise, are devastating these regions' habitats in the process. China's hunger for timber has exploded over the past decade and a half, and particularly since 1998, when devastating floods led Beijing to crack down on domestic logging. China's timber imports more than tripled between 1993 and 2005. According to the World Wildlife Fund, China's demand for timber, paper, and pulp will likely increase by 33 percent between 2005 and 2010.[18]

China is already the largest importer of illegally logged timber in the world: an estimated 50 percent of its timber imports are reportedly illegal.[19] Illegal logging is especially damaging to the environment because it often targets rare old-growth forests, endangers biodiversity, and ignores sustainable forestry practices. In 2006 the government of Cambodia, for example, disregarded its own laws and awarded China's Wuzhishan LS Group a 99-year concession that was twenty times as large as the size permitted by Cambodian law. The company's practices, including the spraying of large amounts of herbicides, have prompted repeated protests by local Cambodians.[20] According to the international NGO Global Witness, Chinese companies have destroyed large parts of the forests along the Chinese-Myanmar border and are now moving deeper into Myanmar's forests in their search for timber.[21] In many instances, illicit logging activity takes place with the active support of corrupt local officials. Central government officials in Myanmar and Indonesia, countries where China's loggers are active, have protested such arrangements to Beijing, but relief has been limited. These activities, along with those of Chinese mining and energy companies, raise serious environmental concerns for many local populations in the developing world.

Spoiling the Party

In the view of China's leaders, however, damage to the environment itself is a secondary problem. Of greater concern to them are its indirect effects: the threat it poses to the continuation of the Chinese economic miracle and to public health, social stability, and the country's international reputation. Taken together, these challenges could undermine the authority of the Communist Party.

China's leaders are worried about the environment's impact on the economy. Several studies conducted both inside and outside China estimate that environmental degradation and pollution cost the Chinese economy between 8 percent and 12 percent of gross domestic product (GDP) annually. The Chinese media frequently publish the results of studies on the impact of pollution on agriculture, industrial output, or public health: water pollution costs of $35.8 billion one year, air pollution costs of $27.5 billion another, and on and on, with weather disasters ($26.5 billion), acid rain ($13.3 billion), desertification ($6 billion), or crop damage from soil pollution ($2.5 billion) adding to the tab. The city of Chongqing, which sits on the banks of the Yangtze River, estimates that dealing with the effects of water pollution on its agriculture and public health costs as much as 4.3 percent of the city's annual gross product. Shanxi Province has watched its coal resources fuel the rest of the country while it pays the price in withered trees, contaminated air and water, and land subsidence. Local authorities there estimate the costs of environmental degradation and pollution at 10.9 percent of the province's annual gross product and have called on Beijing to compensate the province for its "contribution and sacrifice."

The damage has been visible across China. Off the coast of Tianjin, China's Bohai Sea has become heavily contaminated by chemical discharge from surrounding factories and experienced more frequent red tides in recent years, crippling the region's fishing industry. China's largest freshwater lake, Poyang, fell to a record-low surface area during a drought in 2007 that left more than 760,000 people in Jiangxi to face water shortages, damaged 400,000 hectares of crops, and led to a loss of 37.4 million metric tons of grain.

China's Ministry of Health is also sounding the alarm with increasing urgency. In a survey of thirty cities and seventy-eight counties released in spring 2007, the ministry blamed worsening air and water pollution for dramatic increases in the incidence of cancer throughout the country: a 19 percent rise in urban areas and a 23 percent rise in rural areas since 2005.[22] One research institute affiliated with China's MEP has put the country's total number of premature deaths caused by respiratory diseases related to air pollution at 400,000 a year. But this may be a conservative estimate: according to a joint research project by the World Bank and the Chinese government released in spring 2007, the total number of such deaths is 750,000 a year. (Beijing is said not to have wanted to release the latter figure for fear of inciting social unrest.) Less well documented but potentially even more devastating is the health impact of China's polluted water. Today, fully 190 million Chinese are sick from drinking contaminated water. All along China's major rivers, villages report skyrocketing rates of diarrheal diseases, cancer, tumors, leukemia, and stunted growth. The widespread use of toxic additives in rearing livestock is also threatening food safety. In June 2008 the Ministry of Agriculture's chief veterinarian reported that 60 million people in twelve Chinese provinces are at risk of snail fever (or schistosomiasis), a parasitic disease that can cause liver and intestinal damage.

Social unrest over these issues is rising. In spring 2006, China's top environmental official, Zhou Shengxian, announced that there had been 51,000 pollution-related protests in 2005, which amounts to almost 1,000 protests each week. Citizen complaints about the environment, expressed on official hotlines and in letters to local officials, are increasing at a rate of 50 percent a year; in September 2007 the number reached one million. But few of them are resolved satisfactorily, and so people throughout the country are increasingly taking to the streets. For several months in 2006, for example, the residents of six neighboring villages in Gansu Province held repeated protests against zinc and iron smelters that they believed were poisoning them. Fully half of the four to five thousand villagers exhibited lead-related illnesses, ranging from vitamin D deficiency to neurological problems.

Many pollution-related marches are relatively small and peaceful. But when such demonstrations fail, the protesters sometimes resort to violence. On the evening of July 29, 2007, thousands of villagers besieged a brewery in Yuanshi in Sichuan Province for dumping untreated wastewater into the local water supplies. The paramilitary People's Armed Police reportedly dispatched hundreds of police to break up the protest; seven people were arrested and twenty were injured in the incident's aftermath. The Information Centre for Human Rights and Democracy, a group based in Hong Kong, described the incident as "violent and bloody." China's leaders have generally managed to prevent—if sometimes violently—discontent over environmental issues from spreading across provincial boundaries or morphing into calls for broader political reform.

But social unrest is also brewing among China's urban middle class. In January 2008, hundreds of people in Shanghai marched in protest against plans to extend the city's high-speed magnetic levitation ("maglev") train, concerned that the train's proximity would expose them to radiation. Even after the city government announced in March that the train project would not be one of its top priorities in 2008, some fifty suburban homeowners gathered in a second protest against the plan's potential negative impact on their health and property value. In May 2008, several hundred people in Chengdu marched peacefully to demonstrate against PetroChina's plans to construct an ethylene plant and oil refinery on the city's outskirts, which would cause serious air and water pollution.

In the face of such problems, China's leaders have recently injected a new urgency into their rhetoric concerning the need to protect the country's environment. On paper, this has translated into an aggressive strategy to increase investment in environmental protection, set ambitious targets for the reduction of pollution and energy intensity (the amount of energy used to produce a unit of GDP), and introduce new environmentally friendly technologies. In 2005, Beijing set out a number of impressive targets for its next five-year plan: by 2010, it wants 10 percent of the nation's power to come from renewable energy sources, energy intensity to have been reduced by 20 percent and key pollutants such as sulfur dioxide by 10 percent, water consumption to have decreased by 30 percent, and investment in environmental protection to have increased from 1.3 to 1.6 percent of GDP. Premier Wen Jiabao has issued a stern warning to local officials to shut down some of the plants in the most energy-intensive industries—power generation and aluminum, copper, steel, coke and coal, and cement production—and to slow the growth of other industries by denying them tax breaks and other production incentives.

These goals are laudable—even breathtaking in some respects—but history suggests that only limited optimism is warranted; achieving such targets has proved elusive in the past. In 2001 the Chinese government pledged to cut sulfur dioxide emissions by 10 percent between 2002 and 2005. Instead, emissions rose by 27 percent during this period. The most recently reported results are a mixed bag. On the one hand, between 2006 and 2007, both sulfur dioxide and chemical oxygen demand (COD) emissions dropped 4.66 percent and 3.14 percent, respectively. The share of renewables in China's total energy consumption also rose from 7.5 to 8 percent between 2005 and 2006.[23] On the other hand, in late 2007 Beijing lowered the target for investment in environmental protection from 1.6 percent of the GDP by 2010 to 1.35 percent. The percentage of coastal waters classified as Level 4 in 2007, moreover, increased by 1.1 percent from 2006. Perhaps worried that yet another target would fall by the wayside, Beijing in early 2007 revised its announced goal of reducing the country's water consumption by 30 percent by 2010 to just 20 percent.

Even the Olympics proved to be an almost insurmountable challenge. Since Beijing promised in 2001 to hold a "green Olympics" in 2008, Beijing's organizing committee pulled out all the stops. In preparation for the Olympics in August, Beijing was ringed with rows of newly planted trees, hybrid taxis and buses were roaming its streets (some of which were lined with solar-powered lamps), the most heavily polluting factories were pushed outside the city limits, and some Olympic venues showcased Beijing's introduction of energy-saving technologies. Yet in key respects, Beijing failed to deliver. City officials backtracked from their pledge to provide safe tap water to all of Beijing for the Olympics, providing it only for residents of the Olympic Village.[24] They undertook drastic stopgap measures for the duration of the games, such as banning half of the city's three million cars from the city's streets and halting production at many factories in Beijing, as well as in five neighboring provinces. Whatever progress city authorities had managed over the past six years—such as increasing the number of days per year that the city's air is deemed to be clean—was not enough to ensure that the air would be clean for the Olympic Games. On the night of the opening ceremonies, Beijing's sky was shrouded in haze; in the weeks to follow, the city's air quality fluctuated day by day. In some cases, the Olympics even got in the way of improvement. In late June 2008, a group of villagers outside of Beijing filed a lawsuit against the nearby chemical factory for polluting and causing a high number of cancer cases in the community. But the villagers were reportedly told that they would have to wait until the fall, after the Olympics were over, before their case could be settled. In the end, the inability of Beijing to fulfill its Olympics promises symbolized the intractability of China's environmental challenges and the limits of Beijing's approach to addressing them.

Little seems to have changed since. From late 2008 continuing into 2009, the global financial crisis rippled through China's economy and toppled its double-digit GDP growth. Beijing responded early on in November 2008 by introducing a 4 trillion yuan ($586 billion) stimulus plan, of which 350 billion yuan ($51.3 billion) was initially set aside for environmental protection projects. But the allocation shrank to 210 billion yuan when Beijing announced changes to the stimulus during the National People's Congress in March 2009—and details on how the funding will be administered remain unknown. The largest bulk of the stimulus package, moreover, was earmarked for infrastructure building and tax cuts for energy-intensive sectors like the steel and automobile industries, a total of 1.5 trillion yuan ($219.3 billion). This is likely to increase China's reliance on fossil fuels, such as coal and oil. More than 600,000 factories in China shut down by January 1, 2009, amid the global economic downturn; energy consumption and pollution levels took a brief dive as a result, but it is unlikely that this moment of lull will last. More than 35 million people in China were unemployed as of early 2009, and the figure is expected to exceed 50 million by the end of the year. Such domestic pressures mean Beijing will have to resuscitate its economy by reopening many of those factories, allowing polluting factories to continue to operate, or both. China's economic health will likely continue to take precedence over the health of its environment.

Problems with the Locals

Something has got to give. The costs of inaction to China's economy, public health, and international reputation are growing. And perhaps more important, social discontent is rising. The Chinese people have run out of patience with the government's inability or unwillingness to turn the environmental situation around. And the government is well aware of the increasing potential for environmental protest to ignite broader social unrest.

One event in May 2007 particularly alarmed China's leaders. For several days in the coastal city of Xiamen, after months of mounting opposition to the planned construction of a $1.4 billion petrochemical plant nearby, students and professors at Xiamen University, among others, are said to have sent out a million mobile-phone text messages calling on their fellow citizens to take to the streets on June 1. That day, and the following, protesters reportedly numbering between 7,000 and 20,000 marched peacefully through the city, some defying threats of expulsion from school or from the Communist Party. The protest was captured on video and uploaded to YouTube. One video featured a haunting voice-over that linked the Xiamen demonstration to an ongoing environmental crisis near Tai Hu, a lake some 400 miles away (a large bloom of blue-green algae caused by industrial wastewater and sewage dumped in the lake had contaminated the water supply of the city of Wuxi). It also referred to the Tiananmen Square protest of 1989. The Xiamen march, the narrator said, was perhaps "the first genuine parade since Tiananmen."

In response, city authorities stayed the construction of the plant and submitted the plan for environmental review by the central government. Less than a year later in Dongshan County (about 60 miles southwest of Xiamen), rumors spread that the chemical plant would be relocated there instead, only to spark another wave of protests. On the morning of February 28, 2008, demonstrators staged a peaceful sit-in to block traffic on the county's main road, reportedly attracting some 10,000 people to join in by nightfall. The protest lasted almost five days, erupting into violence against the police on the second day after a woman was allegedly slapped by a local official during a shouting match. After two days of continued arrests and injuries, the protests quieted down, and the plant's construction has been suspended indefinitely. In the immediate aftermath of the 2007 protests in Xiamen, local authorities also launched an all-out campaign to discredit the protesters and their videos. Still, more comments about the protest and calls not to forget Tiananmen appeared on various Web sites. Such messages, posted openly and accessible to all Chinese, represented the Chinese leadership's greatest fear, namely, that its failure to protect the environment may be linked to broad-based demands for political change.

Such public demonstrations are also evidence that China's environmental challenges cannot be met with only impressive targets and more investment. They must be tackled with a fundamental reform of how the country does business and protects the environment. So far, Beijing has structured its environmental protection efforts in much the same way that it has pursued economic growth: by granting local authorities and factory owners wide decision-making power and by actively courting the international community and Chinese NGOs for their expertise while carefully monitoring their activities.

Consider, for example, China's most important environmental authority, the Ministry of Environmental Protection, which has become a wellspring of China's most innovative environmental policies: it has promoted an environmental impact assessment law; a law requiring local officials to release information about environmental disasters, pollution statistics, and the names of known polluters to the public; an experiment to calculate the costs of environmental degradation and pollution to the country's GDP; and an all-out effort to halt over one hundred large-scale infrastructure projects that had proceeded without proper environmental impact assessments. But even after its promotion to cabinet level, MEP still operates with barely three hundred full-time professional staff in the capital and only a few hundred employees spread throughout the country. (By contrast, the U.S. Environmental Protection Agency has a staff of over five thousand in Washington, D.C., alone.) And authority for enforcing MEP's mandates rests overwhelmingly with local officials and the local environmental protection officials they oversee. In some cases, this has allowed for exciting experimentation. In the eastern province of Jiangsu, for instance, the World Bank and the Natural Resources Defense Council have launched the Greenwatch program, which grades 12,000 factories according to their compliance with standards for industrial wastewater treatment and discloses both the ratings and the reasons for them. More often, however, China's highly decentralized system has meant limited progress: only about 10 percent of China's more than 660 cities meet the standards required to receive the designation of National Model Environmental City from MEP. According to Wang Canfa, one of China's top environmental lawyers, barely 10 percent of China's environmental laws and regulations are actually enforced.[25]

One of the problems is that local officials have few incentives to place a priority on environmental protection. Even as Beijing touts the need to protect the environment—and introduces initiatives that tie energy and environmental conservation with fiscal incentives and official performance ratings—Premier Wen has called for quadrupling the Chinese economy by 2020. The price of water is rising in some cities, such as Beijing, but in many others it remains as low as 20 percent of the replacement cost. That ensures that factories and municipalities have little reason to invest in wastewater treatment or other water-conservation efforts. Fines for polluting are so low that factory managers often prefer to pay them rather than adopt costlier pollution-control technologies.

Local governments also turn a blind eye to serious pollution problems out of self-interest. Officials sometimes have a direct financial stake in factories or personal relationships with their owners. And the local environmental protection bureaus tasked with guarding against such corruption must report to the local governments, making them easy targets for political pressure. In recent years, the Chinese media have uncovered cases in which local officials have put pressure on the courts, the press, or even hospitals to prevent the wrongdoings of factories from coming to light. (In 2007, in the province of Zhejiang, officials reportedly promised factories with an output of $1.2 million or more that they would not be subjected to government inspections without the factories' prior approval.[26])

Moreover, local officials frequently divert environmental protection funds and spend them on unrelated or ancillary endeavors. The Chinese Academy for Environmental Planning, which reports to MEP, disclosed in 2007 that only half of the 1.3 percent of the country's annual GDP dedicated to environmental protection between 2001 and 2005 had found its way to legitimate projects. According to the study, about 60 percent of the environmental protection funds spent in urban areas during that period went into the creation of, among other things, parks, factory production lines, gas stations, and sewage-treatment plants rather than into waste- or wastewater-treatment facilities.

Many local officials also thwart efforts to hold them accountable for their failure to protect the environment. In 2005 MEP, then known as SEPA, launched the "Green GDP" campaign, a project designed to calculate the costs of environmental degradation and pollution to local economies and provide a basis for evaluating the performance of local officials both according to their economic stewardship and according to how well they protect the environment. Several provinces balked, however, worried that the numbers would reveal the extent of the damage suffered by the environment. SEPA's partner in the 2005 Green GDP campaign, the National Bureau of Statistics (NBS) of China, also undermined the effort by announcing that it did not possess the tools to do Green GDP accounting accurately and that in any case it did not believe officials should be evaluated on such a basis. After releasing a partial report in September 2006, the NBS has refused to release further findings to the public.

Another problem is that many Chinese companies see little direct value in ratcheting up their environmental protection efforts. The computer manufacturer Lenovo and the appliance manufacturer Haier have received high marks for taking creative environmental measures, and the solar energy company

Suntech has become a leading exporter of solar cells. But a recent poll found that only 18 percent of Chinese companies believed that they could thrive economically while doing the right thing environmentally.[27] Another poll of business executives found that an overwhelming proportion of them do not understand the benefits of responsible corporate behavior, such as environmental protection, or they consider the requirements too burdensome.

Not Good Enough

The limitations of the formal authorities tasked with environmental protection in China have led the country's leaders to seek assistance from others outside the bureaucracy. Over the past fifteen years or so, China's NGOs, the Chinese media, and the international community have become central actors in the country's bid to rescue its environment. But the Chinese government remains wary of them.

China's homegrown environmental activists and their allies in the media have become the most potent—and potentially explosive—force for environmental change in China. From four or five NGOs devoted primarily to environmental education and biodiversity protection in the mid-1990s, the Chinese environmental movement has grown to include thousands of NGOs, run primarily by dynamic Chinese in their thirties and forties. These groups now routinely expose polluting factories to the central government, sue for the rights of villagers poisoned by contaminated water or air, give seed money to small newer NGOs throughout the country, and go undercover to expose multinationals that ignore international environmental standards. They often protest via letters to the government, campaigns on the Internet, and editorials in Chinese newspapers. The media are an important ally in this fight: they shame polluters, uncover environmental abuse, and highlight environmental protection successes.

Beijing has come to tolerate NGOs and media outlets that play environmental watchdog at the local level, but it remains vigilant in making sure that certain limits are not crossed, and especially that the central government is not criticized directly. The penalties for misjudging these boundaries can be severe. Wu Lihong worked for sixteen years to address the pollution in Tai Hu (which recently spawned blue-green algae), gathering evidence that has forced almost two hundred factories to close. Although in 2005 Beijing honored Wu as one of the country's top environmentalists, he was beaten by local thugs several times during the course of his investigations, and in 2006 the government of the town of Yixing arrested him on dubious charges of blackmail. And Yu Xiaogang, the 2006 winner of the prestigious Goldman Environmental Prize, honoring grassroots environmentalists, was forbidden to travel abroad in retaliation for educating villagers about the potential downsides of a proposed dam relocation in Yunnan Province.

The Chinese government's openness to environmental cooperation with the international community is also fraught. Beijing has welcomed bilateral agreements for technology development or financial assistance for demonstration projects, but it is concerned about other endeavors. On the one hand, it lauds international environmental NGOs for their contributions to China's environmental protection efforts. On the other hand, it fears that some of them will become advocates for democratization.

The government also subjects MNCs to an uncertain operating environment. Many corporations have responded to the government's calls that they assume a leading role in the country's environmental protection efforts by deploying top-of-the-line environmental technologies, financing environmental education in Chinese schools, undertaking community-based efforts, and raising operating standards in their industries. Coca-Cola, for example, recently pledged to become a net-zero consumer of water, and provided hydrofluorocarbon-free insulation and refrigerants for coolers and vending machines at all Olympic venues. Sometimes, MNCs have been given awards or significant publicity. But in the past two years, Chinese officials (as well as local NGOs) have adopted a much tougher stance toward them, arguing at times that MNCs have turned China into the pollution capital of the world. On issues such as electronic waste, the detractors have a point. But China's attacks, with Internet postings accusing MNCs of practicing "eco-colonialism," have become unjustifiably broad. Such antiforeign sentiment spiked in late 2006, after the release of a pollution map listing more than three thousand factories that were violating water pollution standards. The thirty-three among them that supplied MNCs were immediately targeted in the media, while the other few thousand Chinese factories cited somehow escaped the frenzy. A few Chinese officials and activists privately acknowledge that domestic Chinese companies pollute far more than foreign companies, but it seems unlikely that the spotlight will move off MNCs in the near future. For now, it is simply more expedient to let international corporations bear the bulk of the blame.

From Red to Green

Why is China unable to get its environmental house in order? Its top officials want what the United States, Europe, and Japan have: thriving economies with manageable environmental problems. But they are unwilling to pay the political and economic price to get there. Beijing's message to local officials continues to be that economic growth cannot be sacrificed to environmental protection—the two objectives must go hand in hand.

This, however, works only sometimes. Greater energy efficiency can bring economic benefits, and investments to reduce pollution, such as in building wastewater-treatment plants, are expenses that can be balanced against the costs of losing crops to contaminated soil and having a sickly work force. Yet much of the time, charting a new environmental course comes with serious economic costs up front. Growth slows down in some industries or some regions. Some businesses are forced to close down. Developing pollution-treatment and pollution-prevention technologies requires serious investment. In fact, it is because they recognize these costs that local officials in China pursue their short-term economic interests first and for the most part ignore Beijing's directives to change their ways.

This is not an unusual problem. All countries suffer internal tugs of war over how to balance the short-term costs of improving environmental protection with the long-term costs of failing to do so. But China faces an additional burden. Its environmental problems stem as much from China's corrupt and undemocratic political system as from Beijing's continued focus on economic growth. Local officials and business leaders routinely—and with impunity—ignore environmental laws and regulations, abscond with environmental protection funds, and silence those who challenge them. Thus, improving the environment in China is not simply a matter of mandating pollution-control technologies; it is also a matter of reforming the country's political culture. Effective environmental protection requires transparent information, official accountability, and an independent legal system. But these features are the building blocks of a political system fundamentally different from that of China today, and so far there is little indication that China's leaders will risk the authority of the Communist Party on charting a new environmental course. Until the party is willing to open the door to such reform, it will not have the wherewithal to meet its ambitious environmental targets and lead a growing economy with manageable environmental problems.

Given this reality, the United States—and the rest of the world—will have to get much smarter about how to cooperate with China in order to assist its environmental protection efforts. Above all, the United States must devise a limited and coherent set of priorities. China's needs are vast, but its capacity is poor; therefore, launching one or two significant initiatives over the next five to ten years would do more good than a vast array of uncoordinated projects. These endeavors could focus on discrete issues, such as climate change or the illegal timber trade; institutional changes, such as strengthening the legal system in regard to China's environmental protection efforts; or broad reforms, such as promoting energy efficiency throughout the Chinese economy. The last Strategic Economic Dialogue between the United States and China led by the Treasury Department in June 2008 produced a ten-year framework for the two countries to address together energy security, climate change, and environmental issues. U.S. leadership will be key in this partnership. Although U.S. NGOs and U.S.-based MNCs are often at the forefront of environmental policy and technological innovation, the U.S. government itself has not been a world leader on key environmental concerns. Unless the United States improves its own policies and practices on, for example, climate change, the illegal timber trade, and energy efficiency, it will have little credibility or leverage to push China.

This may change with a new U.S. administration under President Barack Obama. The Obama administration includes a team of officials with strong environmental track records, and has established new positions in both the White House and the State Department to oversee climate and energy policy. The February 2009 U.S. economic stimulus package included a $62.2 billion fund to improve energy efficiency and another $20 billion in green tax incentives, with $7.5 billion allocated for renewable energy transmission. During the same month, Secretary of State Hillary Clinton visited Japan, Indonesia,

South Korea, and China with climate change at the top of her agenda, signaling a new desire in Washington to step up to the leadership plate. This is all a solid start, but just how far-reaching these changes will be remains to be seen.

China, for its part, will undoubtedly continue to place a priority on gaining easy access to financial and technological assistance. Granting this, however, would be the wrong way to go. Joint efforts between the United States and China, such as the recently announced project to capture methane from fifteen Chinese coal mines, are important, of course. But the systemic changes needed to set China on a new environmental trajectory necessitate a bottom-up overhaul. One way to start would be to promote energy efficiency in Chinese factories and buildings. Simply bringing these up to world standards would bring vast gains. While some companies are adopting energy-efficient technologies on their own, international and Chinese NGOs, Chinese environmental protection bureaus, and MNCs could audit and rate Chinese factories based on how well their manufacturing processes and building standards meet a set of energy-efficiency targets. Their scores (and the factors that determined them) could then be disclosed to the public via the Internet and the print media, and factories with subpar performances could be given the means to improve their practices.

A pilot program in Guangdong Province, which is run under the auspices of the U.S. consulate in Hong Kong, provides just such a mechanism. Factories that apply for energy audits can take out loans from participating banks to pay for efficiency upgrades, with the expectation that they will pay the loans back over time out of the savings they will realize from using fewer materials or conserving energy. Such programs should be encouraged and could be reinforced by requiring, for example, that the U.S.-based MNCs that work with the participating factories reward those that meet or exceed the standards and penalize those that do not (the MNCs could either expand or reduce their orders, for example). NGOs and the media in China could also publicize the names of the factories that refuse to cooperate. These initiatives would have the advantages of operating within the realities of China's environmental protection system, providing both incentives and disincentives to encourage factories to comply; strengthening the role of key actors such as NGOs, the media, and local environmental protection bureaus; and engaging new actors such as Chinese banks. It is likely that as with the Greenwatch program, factory owners and local officials not used to transparency would oppose such efforts, but if they were persuaded that full participation would bring more sales to MNCs and grow local economies, many of them would be more open to public disclosure.

Of course, much of the burden and the opportunity for China to revolutionize the way it reconciles environmental protection and economic development rests with the Chinese government itself. No amount of international assistance can transform China's domestic environment or its contribution to global environmental challenges. Real change will arise only from strong central leadership and the development of a system of incentives that make it easier for local officials and the Chinese people to embrace environmental protection. This will sometimes mean making tough economic choices.

Improvements to energy efficiency, of the type promoted by the program in Guangdong, are reforms of the low-hanging-fruit variety: they promise both economic gains and benefits to the environment. It will be more difficult to implement reforms that are economically costly (such as reforms that raise the costs of manufacturing in order to encourage conservation and recycling and those that impose higher fines against polluters), those likely to be unpopular (such as reforms that hike the price of water), or those that could undermine the Communist Party's authority (such as reforms that open up the media or give freer rein to civil society). But such measures are necessary. Their high up-front costs must be weighed against the long-term costs to economic growth, public health, and social stability in which the Chinese government's continued inaction would result. The government must ensure greater accountability among local officials by promoting greater grassroots oversight, greater transparency via the media or other outlets, and greater independence in the legal system.

China's leaders have shown themselves capable of bold reform in the past. Two and half decades ago, Deng Xiaoping and his supporters launched a set of ambitious reforms despite stiff political resistance and set the current economic miracle in motion. To continue on its extraordinary trajectory, China needs leaders with the vision to introduce a new set of economic and political initiatives that will transform the way the country does business. Without such measures, China will not return to global preeminence in the twenty-first century. Instead, it will suffer stagnation or regression—and all because leaders who recognized the challenge before them were unwilling to do what was necessary to surmount it.

General References

Elizabeth C. Economy, *The River Runs Black: The Environmental Challenge to China's Future* (Ithaca, N.Y.: Cornell University Press, 2004). Examines China's environmental crisis and its socioeconomic implications as China becomes a major global player. The book underscores the link between China's environmental agenda and its fundamental political challenges, and highlights the role of the country's burgeoning grassroots environmental movement.

Peter Ho and Richard Edmonds, eds., *China's Embedded Activism: Opportunities and Constraints of a Social Movement* (New York: Routledge, 2007). Argues that China's semiauthoritarian limitations on the freedom of association and speech, coupled with increased social spaces for civic action, has created a milieu in which activism occurs in an embedded fashion. The book includes case studies about environmental civic organizations in China.

Jun Ma, *China's Water Crisis* (Hong Kong: Pacific Century, 2003). Provides a comprehensive analysis of China's acute water issues. It chronicles China's history of floods, water scarcity, and pollution problems in all seven of China's major drainage basins, and proposes solutions for future sustainable management.

Steven Van Holde, "Consuming China: Social, Political, and Environmental Consequences of China's Consumer Revolution," paper presented at the annual meeting of the ISA's 49th annual convention at the Hilton San Francisco, March 26, 2008, available at www.allacademic.com/meta/ p253792_index.html. Explores how China's state-guided consumerism has helped to promote economic growth and protect the Communist Party's hold on power while simultaneously spawning unequalled environmental devastation. The paper focuses on the political economy of consumerism in the auto, housing, and tourist industries.

Suggested Web Sites

Center for Legal Assistance to Pollution Victims (www.clapv.org/new/ en) A group of Chinese lawyers and environmentalists who provide free legal service to pollution victims.

China Dialogue (www.chinadialogue.net) Online resource that provides news coverage and analysis on environmental issues, both in and outside China.

China Environment Forum at the Woodrow Wilson International Center for Scholars (www.wilsoncenter.org/index.cfm?topic_id=1421& fuseaction=topics.home) Academic resource and discussion forum for U.S. and Chinese energy and environment scholars, businesses, policymakers, and civil society. Publishes the China Environment Series and environmental health research briefs.

Greenpeace in China (www.greenpeace.org/china/en) Covers the international environmental group's campaigns in China.

Institute of Public and Environmental Affairs (www.ipe.org.cn/ english/index.jsp) Educational resource on China's environment, founded by Ma Jun; features a water and air pollution map of China.

Natural Resource Defense Council (www.nrdc.org) Environmental advocacy group that runs clean energy and legal training projects in China.

New York Times **Choking on Growth series** (www.nytimes.com/ interactive/2007/08/26/world/asia/choking_on_growth.html) Special report series covering a wide range of China's environmental crises.

Probe International (www.probeinternational.org) Environmental group that follows closely China's dam projects and broader water-related issues.

World Wildlife Fund (www.wwfchina.org/english) Online resource for the international group's conservation and environmental education projects in China.

Notes

1. This chapter appeared originally as an article in *Foreign Affairs* 86, 5 (September/ October, 2007), copyright (2007) by the Council on Foreign Relations, Inc. The article has been updated and revised for this volume and is reprinted with permission.
2. "Fearing Social Unrest, China Tries to Rein in Unbridled Capitalism," *Der Speigel*, January 18, 2006.
3. Michael Totten, "China's New Energy Paradigm," Conservation International briefing paper, April 22, 2007, www.biodiversityscience.org/xp/frontlines/2007/04220702.xml.
4. "Soil Survey to Monitor Pollution," *China Daily*, April 9, 2007.

5. Daniel Griffiths, "Drought Worsens China Water Woes," *BBC News*, May 31, 2006.
6. Janamitra Devan, Stefano Negri, and Jonathan R. Woetzel, "Meeting the Challenges of China's Growing Cities," *The McKinsey Quarterly*, No. 3 (July 2008).
7. "Health Expert Blames Pollution for China's Cancer Rise," *Reuters*, May 16, 2007.
8. "Toxic Rivers and Thirsty Cities," China Environment Forum, Woodrow Wilson International Center for Scholars, May 2007, www.wilsoncenter.org/index.cfm?fuseaction=topics.item&news_id=224022&topic_id=1421.
9. Ibid.
10. "Pollution Turning China's Yangtze River 'Cancerous,' " *Agence-France Presse*, May 31, 2006, www.cosmosmagazine.com/news/302/pollution-turning-chinas-yangtze-river-cancerous.
11. Brian Handwerk, "A Third of Fish Species in China Extinct, Officials Say," *National Geographic News*, January 19, 2007, http://news.nationalgeographic.com/news/2007/01/070119-fish-china.html.
12. "Water Flow in China's Yellow River Hits Record Low," *Reuters*, November 8, 2006, www.planetark.org/dailynewsstory.cfm/newsid/38868/story.htm.
13. Ibid.
14. Juli S. Kim, "Transboundary Air Pollution—Will China Choke on Its Success?" China Environment Health Project Research Brief, China Environment Forum, Woodrow Wilson International Center for Scholars, February 2, 2007, www.wilsoncenter.org/index.cfm?topic_id=1421&fuseaction=topics.item&news_id=218780.
15. "Pollution Emissions on Wane in Cleaner China," *Xinhua News Agency*, June 5, 2008.
16. "Guangdong Coast Choked by Record Levels of Sewage," *Xinhua News Agency*, May 17, 2007, http://english.mep.gov.cn/News_service/media_news/200712/t20071217_114792.htm.
17. "One of the World's Top Fisheries Dying," *Xinhua News Agency*, August 17, 2006.
18. Dennis Chong, "Russia: Industry Plunders Forests," *Standard*, March 27, 2005, www.ecoearth.info/shared/reader/welcome.aspx?linkid=40297&keybold=campaigns%20NGO%20business.
19. "A Choice for China: Ending the Destruction of Burma's Northern Frontier Forests," Global Witness briefing document (October 2005), 24.
20. Yin Soeum, "Cambodia Feels China's Hard Edge," *Asia Times*, December 8, 2006, www.atimes.com/atimes/Southeast_Asia/HL08Ae01.html.
21. EIA/Telepak, "Stemming the Tide: Halting the Regional Trade in Stolen Timber in Asia," November 2005, 1, www.eia-international.org/files/reports114-1.pdf.
22. "Health Expert Blames Pollution for China's Cancer Rise," *Reuters*, May 16, 2007.
23. "Renewable Energy Accounts for 8% of Total Consumed Energy Last Year," *People's Daily Online*, September 20, 2007, http://english.people.com.cn/90001/90778/90857/90860/6267454.html.
24. Stephen Wade, "Olympic Adventure: Water Drinking," *Associated Press*, May 9, 2007, www.usatoday.com/sports/olympics/2007-05-09-3179851128_x.htm?loc=interstitialskip.
25. "China Improves Enforcement of Environmental Laws," *XinhuaNet*, October 9, 2005, http://en.chinacourt.org/public/detail.php?id=3957.
26. "Gov't Protection of Polluting Factories Causes Concern," *Xinhua News Agency*, November 28, 2006, www.china.org.cn/english/government/190419.htm.
27. Peng Lei, Baijin Long, and Dennis Pamlin, "Chinese Companies in the 21st Century," World Wildlife Fund Trade and Investment Programme, April 2005, http://assets.panda.org/downloads/chinese_companies_in_the_21st_century_bl.pdf.

15

Environmental Security

Richard A. Matthew

The 2008 U.S. presidential election was unique in many ways, not least of which was the attention given by both major candidates to strategic threats posed by energy and environmental problems. Much of the debate focused on "energy security," especially the danger of energy dependence. For example, Sen. John McCain, R-Ariz., told a Washington state audience in May 2008 that coming up with new forms of clean energy is "a national security issue when we're dependent on more than $400 billion a year in imported oil from countries that don't like us very much . . . some of that money is helping terrorist organizations."[1] But related environmental issues such as climate change were also frequently discussed in a national security context. Then-senator Barack Obama, D-Ill., stated that climate change "will lead to devastating weather patterns, terrible storms, drought, and famine. That means people competing for food and water in the next fifty years in the very places that have known horrific violence in the last fifty: Africa, the Middle East, and South Asia. . . . This is not just an economic issue or an environmental concern—this is a national security crisis."[2]

Many scholars foresee even wider consequences of global environmental change for the international community. Numerous assessments support the claim that, at some point during the 1980s or early 1990s, the production and consumption activities of humankind overshot the carrying capacity of the planet.[3] According to this sobering literature, we continue spiraling farther and farther away from an equilibrium point, and perhaps closer and closer to a global catastrophe. While this latter scenario is a worst-case one based on educated guesses and speculation, it has some solid empirical roots. Throughout much of the world, evidence continues to mount that the trajectories of land conversion, climate change, biodiversity loss, ecosystem destruction, water scarcity, energy demand, and the unsustainable use of many other natural resources are all growing steeper.[4]

However one imagines the future, the Obama administration will inherit the environmental security legacy of its predecessors and will have to decide whether to supplement, amplify, redirect, or terminate the various parts of this legacy. It will have to act in a world in which many of its foreign partners, such as the United Kingdom, and a sizable portion of its domestic populace see a planet in crisis and believe that crafting more effective and aggressive environmental policies should be a national priority. Grounded in reports by influential expert groups such as the Intergovernmental Panel on Climate Change, this growing community is concerned that the time horizon for action is shrinking while the scale and urgency of the challenges are growing.[5] If this fear is correct, and the empirical evidence is compelling in this regard, then an administration that fails to act quickly and decisively may be an administration that fails the nation and the world.

So what is currently in place in Washington, D.C., under the rubric of environmental security? How was it put in place—and why? And, most important, is there a solid platform—in place or within reach—on which the Obama administration can build? Or should it start this process anew, or perhaps direct its efforts elsewhere?

Following a brief review of the concept of environmental security, this chapter describes the main initiatives of Bill Clinton's and George W. Bush's administrations. It then presents the environmental security challenges facing the Obama administration and sketches out some policies and positions worth considering in 2009 and beyond.

The Concept of Environmental Security

The term *environmental security* evokes remarkably different images in different parts of the American environmental community. For some, the only compelling way to interpret the term is as a call to protect the environment from wasteful and destructive human behavior. Others, however, regard it as a subset of the concept of human security, valuable insofar as it draws our attention to the heightened vulnerability some people have to droughts, floods, landslides, and other environmental threats.

Still others are sharply critical of the term, deploring it as a risky tactic to leverage the attention-grabbing word *security* into a policy realm that has often been underfunded and marginalized. This tactic is risky, the argument goes, because it facilitates viewing environmental problems through the dark glasses of national defense, which tends to reveal a zero-sum world in which gains for one mean losses for another. In such a world, coercion is required to achieve and preserve that security. This is not the approach most environmentalists regard as viable or ethical.

However, for some environmentalists the term also and importantly refers to the ways in which the U.S. government has sought to integrate the environment into national security and foreign policy, especially since the end of the Cold War. This chapter is about this very specific meaning of the term. This is not to deny the value of other ways of using the term or of the rich and often spirited debate that has taken place for some two decades among proponents of different perspectives. Rather, it is to suggest that there is an interesting and perhaps hopeful story to be told about the explicit and elaborate attempt by the Clinton administration to integrate the environment into defense and foreign policy in the 1990s, the energetic rollback of much of this effort that took place during George W. Bush's first term, and the recent—albeit cautious—recovery of environmental security during the last two or three years of Bush's presidency.

With all due respect for the nuances that characterize much academic writing on this subject, I try to provide a context for the term that is brief and simple. Environmental security is not, in general, the site of detailed interrogations of the word *environment*. *Environment* tends to be used in this realm to mean natural resources and ecosystems—or ecosystem services—in the common sense of these terms.[6]

The word *security* is far more elusive. From about the time of World War I, when security studies emerged as a specialized area of research and education, until the Cold War began to wind down in the 1980s, the predominant referent for security was the state. The challenge assumed by most scholars and policymakers was to figure out what states needed to do to survive and flourish in an anarchic world in which countries often went to war with each other. Ideas that were discussed widely—and that often informed defense and foreign policy—included creating international institutions like the United Nations and beefing up international law, promoting democracy, encouraging free trade, forming strategic military alliances, challenging fascist and communist ideologies, and deterring threats with large conventional forces and robust nuclear arsenals.

As the Cold War came to an end, two distinct but related alternatives to this predominant view emerged. One approach sought to shift attention from states to people. The most influential argument for this change can be found in the UN Development Programme's 1994 *Human Development Report*:

> The concept of security has for too long been interpreted narrowly: as security of territory from external aggression. . . . It has been related more to nation-states than to people. . . . Forgotten were the legitimate concerns of ordinary people who sought security in their daily lives. . . . With the dark shadows of the cold war receding, one can now see that many conflicts are within nations rather than between nations. . . . In the final analysis, human security is a child who did not die, a disease that did not spread, a job that was not cut, an ethnic tension that did not explode in violence. . . . Human security is not a concern with weapons—it is a concern with human life and dignity.[7]

In a parallel discourse, others argued for broadening the concept of national security to include a richer understanding of threat, vulnerability, and the elements of power. These thinkers often built on Richard Ullman's seminal 1983 article "Redefining Security," in which he sought to expand the concept of security to include nonmilitary threats to a state's range of policy options or the quality of life of its citizens.[8] This perspective was central to the influential report prepared by the U.S. Commission on National Security/21st Century, also called the Hart-Rudman Commission Report.[9]

Among the several forces that motivated both expanding the definition of national security and promoting the concept of human security was the growing concern that some forms of environmental change—such as ozone depletion and global warming—threatened the lives and welfare of people on an unprecedented scale that deserved the highest level of government attention and resources.[10] In direct response to this concern, the environment formally became an element of U.S. defense policy in 1991, when it was first included in the *National Security Strategy of the United States* by President George H. W. Bush.[11]

The argument that environmental change threatens human security is fairly easy to make because the threshold for human security can easily be imagined as being quite low. A more controversial question has to do with whether it is really accurate and useful to link environmental change to national security. Obviously, if environmental change is understood as an existential threat to humankind, as something that could destroy the ecology of the planet as we know it, then it qualifies as a national security issue. But three less speculative arguments are generally made to justify the linkage:[12]

Argument 1: Linking the Environment to Violent Conflict

In the aftermath of World War II, Fairfield Osborn, recalling the work two centuries earlier of Thomas Malthus, wrote: "When will it be openly recognized that one of the principal causes of the aggressive attitudes of individual nations and of much of the present discord among groups of nations is traceable to diminishing productive lands and to increasing population pressures?"[13] Discussed throughout the 1960s and 1970s, updated versions of the "scarcity-conflict thesis," developed by scholars such as Paul R. Ehrlich, Donella Meadows, and Thomas Homer-Dixon, have been influential in both academic and policy circles around the world.[14]

Homer-Dixon, a Canadian political scientist, initiated considerable debate and policy activity with his study of the social effects of scarcities of water, fish, cropland, and pasture. He briefed Vice President Al Gore and many other senior Washington officials on numerous occasions in the 1990s, and his work therefore deserves a brief summary here. According to Homer-Dixon, resource scarcity may arise from a real decrease in the supply of a resource (for example, the depletion of a fishery due to overfishing or global warming); an increase in demand due to population growth or changes in production or consumption practices; or institutional factors (for example, the privatization of resources in a manner that benefits a few at the expense of the many). Based on a series of case studies carried out in the 1990s, he concluded that under certain social conditions violent civil conflict can be triggered or amplified by resource scarcity. He also argued that the explanatory weight of resource scarcity in violent civil conflict would likely increase over time as resource scarcities became more widespread and acute, especially throughout Africa and parts of Asia (see Box 15-1). Homer-Dixon's core insight has received some empirical support through a number of quantitative studies.[15]

A complementary—or alternative—analysis known as the "resource curse" focuses on the ways in which certain high value natural resources such as gold and diamonds may contribute to violent conflict, especially where there is a weak or corrupt regime and other sources of social tension.[16] For example, when Charles Taylor's Revolutionary United Front (RUF) invaded Sierra Leone in 1991, one of his goals was to gain control over diamond fields lying within 100 miles of the Liberian border. The armed conflict in

Box 15-1   Thomas Homer-Dixon's Key Findings

1. Under certain circumstances, scarcities of renewable resources such as cropland, fresh water, and forests produce civil violence and instability. However, the role of this "environmental scarcity" is often obscure. Environmental scarcity acts mainly by generating intermediate social effects, such as poverty and migrations, which analysts often interpret as the immediate causes of the conflict.

2. Environmental scarcity is caused by the degradation and depletion of renewable resources, the increased demand for these resources, their unequal distribution, or some combination of the three. These sources of scarcity often interact and reinforce one another.

3. Environmental scarcity often encourages powerful groups to capture valuable environmental resources and prompts marginal groups to migrate to ecologically sensitive areas. These two processes—called resource capture and ecological marginalization—in turn reinforce environmental scarcity and raise the potential for social instability.

4. Societies can adapt to environmental scarcity either by using their indigenous environmental resources more efficiently or by decoupling from their dependence on these resources. In either case, the capacity to adapt depends on the supply of social and technical "ingenuity" available in the society.

5. If social and economic adaptation is unsuccessful, environmental scarcity constrains economic development and contributes to migrations.

6. In the absence of adaptation, environmental scarcity sharpens existing distinctions among social groups.

7. In the absence of adaptation, environmental scarcity weakens states.

8. The intermediate social effects of environmental scarcity—including constrained economic productivity, population movements, social segmentation, and weakening of states—can cause ethnic conflicts, insurgencies, and coups d'état.

9. Environmental scarcity rarely contributes directly to interstate conflict.

10. Conflicts generated in part by environmental scarcity can have significant indirect effects on the international community.

Source: Adapted from Project Description at www.library.utoronto.ca/pcs/eps/descrip.htm.

Angola between the Movimento Popular de Libertação de Angola (MPLA) and the União Nacional para a Independência Total de Angola (UNITA) was funded by—and often fought over—control of the diamonds in the north of the country. In Cambodia, the Khmer Rouge supported itself in the 1990s by exploiting timber and rubies in the areas under its control. These cases are illustrative of a much larger set of violent conflicts in which control over lucrative resources has been a fundamental source of financial support— and often personal gain—for both rebel and government combatants.

Since the publication of the 2007 IPCC reports, there has been a flurry of activity exploring the possibility that climate change may intensify linkages between the environment and conflict as it amplifies competition for dwindling resources like water and fuelwood, forces people to migrate, or throws governments into disarray by overwhelming them with natural disasters.[17] For example, according to the German Advisory Council on Global Change report *World in Transition: Climate Change as a Security Risk*, "Climate change will overstretch many societies' adaptive capacities within the coming decades," creating conditions highly conducive to violent conflict.[18]

This concern is echoed in the CNA Corporation's 2007 report on *National Security and the Threat of Climate Change*, prepared by a group of retired generals and admirals known as the Military Advisory Board. This distinguished group contends that "climate change acts as a threat multiplier for instability in some of the most volatile regions of the world" and predicts that "projected climate change will add to tensions even in stable regions of the world."[19]

Not everyone agrees that the linkages between natural resources or climate change and conflict are clear, significant, or growing in importance.[20] In particular, from Julian Simon to Bjorn Lomborg, the so-called cornucopian thinkers have identified numerous ways in which technological innovations tend to disarm concerns about the negative social effects of scarcity and other environmental stresses.[21] For example, according to these scholars, scarcity often encourages the development of technologies that allow humans to discover new reserves (a process that could ultimately lead to deep sea and deep space extraction), reduce losses during the extraction and production phases, develop substitutes (such as plastic piping that can be used instead of copper piping for many applications), overcome shortages through world trade, and recycle waste byproducts and used goods.[22]

Argument 2: The Environmental Effects of War and Other Military Activities

Research on the effects of military activities—including weapons development, training, and war fighting—on the environment is far less controversial and tends to be undertaken by practitioners carrying out assessments as opposed to scholars working in ivory towers.[23] This work generally demonstrates that the environmental impacts of military activities can be dramatic. Examples include enormous quantities of fossil fuels used in highly inefficient ways; land and water systems poisoned with toxic releases; solid and liquid waste dumped directly into oceans from bases and naval vessels; trees razed to deprive enemies of cover; extensive systems of roads and trenches constructed with purely military objectives in mind and no regard for ecosystem integrity; defoliants like Agent Orange deployed to demoralize people and damage economies; soldiers billeted in areas—including protected areas—where they quickly draw down local resources; landmines and unexploded ordnance left behind that contaminate the terrain for decades; and so on. Indeed, the U.S. Army's Rocky Mountain Arsenal in Colorado may be the most degraded piece of land in the country. And the possibility of violent conflict involving weapons of mass destruction has fueled many apocalyptic films and novels imagining the environment a nuclear war might leave behind.

War can take many unexpected tolls on the environment as well. Violent conflict can slow or halt environmental monitoring and research, damage the science community and hence its ability to contribute to policy-making and governance, and absorb the budgets and undermine the work of environmental agencies. Moreover, war can displace people into fragile ecosystems and protected areas, where in their struggle to survive they may cause extensive environmental damage. Even the early days after a war can be hard on the environment, as returnees and survivors are liable to exploit whatever natural capital is readily available to quickly meet basic needs, generate employment and restart the economy, without adequate consideration of long-term effects. Ironically, in some cases when military activity and its legacy displace people from ecosystems and disrupt and slow down economies, the rate at which natural resources are depleted may be reduced, providing some ecological benefits.

Argument 3: Linking the Environment to Peace and Security

A third argument is worth outlining briefly because it has informed a fair amount of activity in Washington. The basic idea, promoted by Al Gore when he was vice president, is that the environment can be integrated into the defense arena in some positive ways. In particular, military technology and expertise—such as surveillance assets—may be useful for environmental monitoring, data collection, and assessment. The environment might also be a safe issue for bringing militaries into communication, building trust and understanding as they cooperate on a shared problem such as nuclear waste disposal. And, finally, if the environment starts wars, supports wars, or is damaged by wars, then it probably needs to be included in peace-making and peace-building activities as well.[24]

In summary, at least three ways of linking the environment to national security have been influential over the past two decades. Variants of these three arguments circulated freely in Washington in the 1990s and inspired the Clinton administration to create a number of new positions, programs, and mandates.

Environmental Security in the Clinton Years[25]

When Bill Clinton and Al Gore took office in January 1993, several conditions were in place that encouraged a higher profile for the environment in defense and foreign policy. First, there was a foundation on which to build that stretched back to the 1960s—the dawn of the contemporary environmental movement that was framed by the work of people like Rachel Carson, Paul R. Ehrlich, and Garrett Hardin.[26] For example, the 1960 Sikes Act required the Department of Defense (DOD), which today manages some 27 million acres of land, to consider developing plans for wildlife management, conservation, and rehabilitation.

Policy activity accelerated in the following decade as events like the first Earth Day (1970) and the Stockholm Conference (1972) raised awareness and concern nationwide. Although most of this activity took place in the domestic policy arena, several small moves were made in the security realm. For example, DOD Directive 5100.50, "Protection and Enhancement of Environmental Quality," was issued in 1973. And DOD activities—specifically the use of defoliants in Southeast Asia during the Vietnam War—can be linked to two important international agreements: the Additional Protocol I to the 1949 Geneva Convention on the Protection of Victims of International Armed Conflicts (1977) and the Convention on the Prohibition of Military or Any Other Hostile Use of Environmental Modification Techniques (1977).

In 1984 Congress established the Defense Environmental Restoration Account to fund the cleanup of contaminated military sites. In general, the focus of these and other activities was on protecting troops, disposing of waste, and cleaning up hazardous materials, and many analysts have argued that they posed only the weakest of constraints on what the DOD actually did. But they did constitute a regulatory universe on which the Clinton administration could build.

A second force pushing in this direction was the enormous growth in public concern that began with the 1987 release of the World Commission on Environment and Development report, *Our Common Future*, and culminated with the Rio Summit on Environment and Development in 1992.[27] The output from Rio—including the Rio Declaration, *Agenda 21*, the Framework Convention on Climate Change, and the Convention on Biological Diversity—was truly remarkable, setting in motion a carefully conceived and inclusive process for environmental rescue and sustainable development on a global scale. Both Clinton and Gore recognized the impact of Rio on the post–Cold War world and promised that the administration would assume a leadership position on the international front.

A third force, mentioned earlier, was the end of the Cold War. By the time Clinton and Gore assumed office, few people were arguing that the Soviet Union might recover and reemerge as America's principal threat. The 1990s became an era of rethinking security—of introducing human security, broadening the concept of national security, and exploring the salience of a range of potential threats and vulnerabilities including those related to environmental change. Moreover, the Cold War had cost the United States and the Soviet Union several trillion dollars in defense spending—was there now a peace dividend that could be applied to other pressing issues like the environment?

Fourth, a rich strand of neo-Malthusian scholarship developed by Jared Diamond, Peter Gleick, Norman Myers, Thomas Homer-Dixon, and others, and popularized through the work of journalists such as Robert Kaplan, caught the attention of the new administration because it seemed to offer a reasonable explanation for what was happening in hot spots like Somalia and Haiti.[28] The key insight from this literature, albeit an insight stripped of the nuance and qualification evident in most of the academic writing, was readily grasped and shared: resource scarcity and population growth had created highly volatile situations that could push millions of people across borders in search of new livelihoods, implode into civil violence, or sink an entire people into misery and despair. Faced with any of these outcomes, the actions of the United States would be of great importance to the world. It had to be prepared for this.

Against this background, Clinton and Gore began to broaden significantly the integration of environment and national security. They wanted to encourage analysts to think about environmental threats and develop early warning systems; they wanted to green military activities and clean up bases; and they wanted to pursue peace through environmental cooperation.

These goals were part of a broader initiative to restructure national security and foreign policy after the Cold War. As Robert Durant argued, "Downsizing, realigning, and defunding the U.S. military were on many minds as the post-Cold War era dawned."[29] It was virtually inevitable that, following Ronald Reagan's defense build-up in the late 1980s, the Clinton administration would move quickly to reduce the defense budget and figure out what sort of restructuring was now needed. The restructuring effort envisioned necessarily involved many parts of the government. Defense policy, for example, is implemented by the DOD but it is crafted at its most general level by the president in consultation with the National Security Council (which is composed of the National Security Advisor, the vice president, and members from the DOD and the Department of State), together with inputs from the intelligence community and Congress. This consultation process generates the president's annual National Security Strategy, which the commands must then carry out.

Clinton and Gore believed that U.S. security required both a new national security strategy and a reorganization of the DOD. Eileen Claussen, formerly head of atmospheric programs at the Environmental Protection Agency (EPA), was appointed special assistant to the president for global environmental affairs at the National Security Council. Working with Secretary of Defense Les Aspin (and, a year later, with Secretary of Defense William Perry), they immediately created four new offices, including that of the Undersecretary of Defense for Acquisition and Technology (USDAT), which was first headed by John Deutch.

USDAT in turn housed the newly created Office of the Deputy Under-secretary of Defense for Environmental Security (DUSDES), headed by Sherri Wasserman Goodman. The mandate of this office included the familiar issues of environmental planning, base cleanup, compliance with regulations, pollution prevention, education and training, technology development, military-to-military programs, and resource conservation measures. But Undersecretary Goodman and her principal assistant, Gary Vest, proved innovative and aggressive in widening the activities of their office to encompass more fully the problem of environmental threats to national security. In the latter half of the 1990s, both individuals were prominent around the world in a wide range of venues. As a result, a more comprehensive concept of environmental security (that is, something beyond cleanup, compliance, and conservation) gained attention, legitimacy, and substance at home and abroad.

The Goodman-Vest years began with an attempt to green the DOD that immediately triggered a counter-offensive from war-fighting professionals already worried about what post–Cold War budget cuts could do to military readiness. Durant described the fairly aggressive program envisioned by Goodman and Vest in 1993 "to align corporate structures, processes, and procedures better with greening strategies by enhancing civilian ENR [environmental and natural resources] control, by redressing inadequate management systems critical to greening, and by creating parallel decision structures to ensure a role for greening proponents in readiness and weapons system decisions."[30] Military professionals turned to Deutch and to the House and Senate Armed Services Committees to point out how such a program might constrain the commands—which are the power centers of the entire defense system—and began offering other ways of greening the military and streamlining management systems that effectively diluted the power of Goodman's office.[31] This is not to deny that important institutional reforms and progress on a number of environmental fronts were achieved, including the development of a small but committed cadre of insiders who understood that environmental security captured something truly important to the country. For its proponents, environmental security was a concept that connoted critical linkages that had to be made, acknowledged, and acted on.[32]

The concept gained supporters, but the concrete results of this ambitious reorganization were mixed. One important area in which little seems to have been achieved was base cleanup. The EPA is responsible for identifying contaminated sites—both private and public—and singling out the top priorities for immediate redress. The manner in which military sites were assessed in the 1980s, which involves grouping contaminated spots on a single base, led to the military's having the largest presence on the National Priorities List of contaminated sites. During the Clinton years, the explicit goal was to tackle this list by accelerating the pace of base cleanup, especially for those facilities that were being closed and handed over for civilian use. But pitched battles within the DOD and between the White House and Congress over the assessment process and over where the funds for cleanup should come from, as well as concerns about how Goodman's office—which controlled a multibillion-dollar budget for cleanup—was expending funds, made progress difficult. Durant concluded that during the Clinton era, "base clean-ups did accelerate appreciably but with downward adjustments in protective standards for public health, safety, and the environment."[33]

Another area with mixed results has to do with the more than 27 million acres managed by the DOD. According to the Sikes Act (1960), the military is expected to develop a plan for wildlife management, rehabilitation, and conservation. Another of Goodman's goals was to amend this act to give it more teeth, bringing civilian experts from other agencies into the process of developing Integrated Natural Resource Management Plans. The end result was an amendment that encouraged and facilitated but did not require the cooperation sought by Goodman and Vest. In terms of several other goals sought by DUSDES—such as pollution prevention and energy conservation—precise data have proved difficult to obtain, although Kent Butts reported considerable progress, citing, for example, a 50-percent reduction in toxic waste during this period.[34]

In 1996 Secretary of Defense Perry presented the doctrine of "preventative defense," which gave considerable support to the goal of using environmental security to expand military-to-military contact programs and hence to promote security through cooperation. One of the ugly legacies of the Cold War was a large amount of radioactive waste, significant quantities of which had been dumped by the Soviets into the Barents and Kara Seas in the Arctic Ocean. Gore became a strong advocate of working with the Russians and others to assist in the decommissioning of nuclear submarines and the safe disposal of nuclear materials. He worked with his Russian counterpart to establish the Gore-Chernomyrdin Commission in 1993; supported the creation of the Arctic Military Environment Cooperation program; and promoted environmental security in the context of NATO's Committee on the Challenges of Modern Society. Under Gore's aegis, the DOD cooperated with Sweden to develop guidelines for environmental standards for military training and operations. The Australia-Canada-U.S. trilateral commission is another example of an attempt to address environmental problems cooperatively. This expansion of military-to-military contact has provided the DOD with an enduring and valuable tool for building confidence, learning about other militaries, professionalizing other militaries, involving civilian experts, and thinking through security challenges in environmentally stressed areas of Africa and elsewhere.

Another important environmental security measure shaped by Gore involved building a bridge between intelligence assets and archives and civilian experts who might be able to use these to advance environmental goals. In response to Gore's efforts, the CIA permitted civilian scientists to examine archived material that might be useful in assessing environmental degradation. The Medea Group, set up by the National Intelligence Council (NIC) in 1992, determined that archived satellite imagery was of great scientific value. The NIC began exploring ways to make the CIA's data-gathering and -analysis capabilities available to environmental consumers, including foreign and nongovernmental organizations. In 1997 the Director of Central Intelligence Environmental Center was created partly for this purpose.

In a similar vein, Gore established the State Failure Task Force to study why some states appeared more vulnerable to institutional breakdown, civil war, and other serious problems that could necessitate humanitarian responses, provide a smokescreen for corruption, create safe havens for terrorists and criminals, and generate various negative externalities. When the first task force report did not identify the environment as a major factor in state failure, Gore requested that a second study focused on this dimension be carried out.[35]

In addition to seeking to green the conventional military and intelligence communities, and to investigate and prepare for environmentally related conflicts and breakdowns, the Clinton administration also promoted environmental security through the Department of State. For the environmental community, the milestone moment came at Stanford University in April 1996 when Secretary of State Warren Christopher announced that "the environment has a profound impact on our national interests in two ways: First, environmental forces transcend borders and oceans to threaten directly the health, prosperity and jobs of American citizens. Second, addressing natural resource issues is frequently critical to achieving political and economic stability, and to pursuing our strategic goals around the world." Christopher argued that "environmental initiatives can be important, low-cost, high-impact tools in promoting our national security interests."[36]

He also promised that DOS would henceforth produce an annual environmental diplomacy report to assess global environmental trends and identify American priorities; establish Environmental Opportunity Hubs at twelve strategically located U.S. embassies to coordinate and support efforts to assess and address regional environmental issues around the world; organize an international conference on treaty compliance and enforcement by 2000; and promote private-public partnerships as well as bilateral and multilateral initiatives to identify and then direct environmental problems into the societal settings that have the resources and will to solve them. Although the environmental diplomacy reports ceased after the first year, and the conference on treaty compliance was never held, the regional environmental hubs continue to function quite well in different regions of the world, and private-public partnerships along with bilateral and multilateral initiatives continue to be important elements of U.S. foreign policy, albeit widely regarded as underutilized in recent years.

Environmental Security in the Bush Years

However analysts choose to assess the security policy of the Bush administration, the term *environmental security* is not likely to figure prominently alongside terms such as *the axis of evil, the revolution in military affairs, preemptive war,* and *the global war on terrorism.* The administration's security policy will more likely be associated with debates over torture and surveillance; events such as the September 11 terrorist attacks, the demise of the nuclear test ban, arms control negotiations with North Korea, and the wars in Afghanistan and Iraq; and the creation of ambitious new institutions such as the Department of Homeland Security. The environment has been excluded from the lion's share of this activity and also from the massive increases in defense spending that took place from 2001 to 2007.

In the concluding chapter of his authoritative study *The Greening of the U.S. Military,* Robert Durant argued that the Bush administration immediately took steps to dismantle much of the environmental security architecture of its predecessor and generally reduced environmental constraints on the security community. DUSDES and the independent Deputy Undersecretary Office for Industrial Affairs and Installations were combined under the new name Deputy Undersecretary of Defense for Installations and Environment (DUSDIE). As Durant wrote, "not only did the reorganization signal the demise of environmental security as a central component of national defense policy, it also failed to put a fence around ENR [environmental and natural resource] funds, thus leaving them susceptible to budget raids for core military responsibilities on installations."[37]

The early sentiment of the Bush-Cheney regime was clearly anti-environmental, and from his inauguration speech on, Bush emphasized his desire to rebuild a military that had been neglected by his predecessor. When the Republicans gained control of Congress after the first midterm elections, the Senate and House Armed Forces Committees worked with the Pentagon to try to gain a wide range of exemptions from compliance with environmental regulations, and to ensure that defense dollars were not expended on environmental goals. Among the revisions they sought were the following:

> Exempting the military from the Clean Air Act (CAA) for five years; exempting munitions, explosives, and other equipment from classifications as pollutants or "dredge or fill material" under the Clean Water Act; excluding munitions and other DoD equipment from classification as solid wastes under the RCRA; allowing the president to declare any military action exempt from the Coastal Zone Management Act; and exempting the military from the Marine Mammal Protection Act (MMPA) and the Migratory Bird Treaty Act.[38]

Although these sought-after changes were generally denied or diluted, the DOD found many other ways to reduce the burdens of compliance and cleanup, and to slow down or halt much of the Clinton-era greening process. A few Clinton-Gore measures were left standing such as the Arctic Military Environmental Cooperation Program and the regional environmental hubs, but nothing was strengthened and much was cut or left to whither over time.

The Bush-Cheney administration expressed no interest whatsoever in the linkages between the environment and conflict or state failure, or in using intelligence assets in support of environmental programs, and the terrorist attacks of September 11, 2001, provided it with an alternative security focus that would shape most White House activity for the next seven years. The 2002 *National Security Strategy*, focused largely on the threat of terrorism, made no mention of environmental security. The administration did not just shift gears on defense; it changed direction. Indeed, for six years it defied science and refused to take any action at all on issues such as mitigating and adapting to climate change, even as the rest of the world increased activity dramatically on this front.

Hurricane Katrina, however, did force the environment into the White House worldview, and the following year, in 2006, the *National Security Strategy of the United States* included the following paragraphs:[39]

> Environmental destruction, whether caused by human behavior or cataclysmic mega-disasters such as floods, hurricanes, earthquakes, or tsunamis. Problems of this scope may overwhelm the capacity of local authorities to respond, and may even overtax national militaries, requiring a larger international response.
>
> These challenges are not traditional national security concerns, such as the conflict of arms or ideologies. But if left unaddressed they can threaten national security.[40]

Bush finally recognized in 2007 that climate change science might have a place in policymaking, acknowledging at last that the consensus-based assessment of human-induced climate change prepared by thousands of the world's top scientists could no longer be dismissed out of hand. By then, however, dissatisfaction with his administration was so high and widespread—unprecedented, according to many polls—that the introduction of significant new policy initiatives—or the resurrection of old ones—was simply not possible.

Within the DOD, however, the acknowledgment of climate change created an opening for a new discussion about environmental security. For example, a retreat organized by the Triangle Institute for Security Studies at Duke University in 2007 brought together many of the military and academic proponents of environmental security who had been prominent during the Clinton-Gore years to discuss links between climate change and security. The new Africa Command, which became operational in 2007, was also shaped in some important measure by environmental security thinking, although it is too early to assess the performance of this novel command.[41]

Looking Ahead

As I write this chapter, Barack Obama has been elected the next president and analysts around the world are offering advice on what the agenda should be for his first year in office. By all accounts, addressing the current economic crisis and resolving the wars in Iraq and Afghanistan are immediate priorities. But most commentators also see the environment as an issue that cannot be neglected. Should environmental security be part of the new

Table 15-1 Examples of Environmental Security Concerns

Security Issue	Environmental Issue		
	Natural Resources	Ecosystem Services	Climate Change
Conflict or Humanitarian Disaster	Conflict over fresh water scarcity or control of diamonds	Humanitarian disaster due to sudden breakdown of tropical forest ecosystem	Disastrous mass migration due to severe fires, flooding, or drought
Impact of Military Activities	Radioactive contamination of water sources	Disruption of fragile Arctic ecosystem	High carbon emissions due to inefficient fossil fuel use
Conflict Resolution, Peace Making, and Peace Building	Mechanisms for fair use of natural resources included in peace treaties	Rehabilitation of forests destroyed during periods of violent conflict	Integration of climate change adaptation into peace building

administration's approach to addressing environmental challenges? As noted earlier, some environmentalists are very uncomfortable with this concept, and they were, perhaps, pleased that it was largely rejected by the Bush administration.[42] But although one might agree that thinking of environmental challenges as particularly well suited to being resolved through the skills and mindset of the security community would be a dangerous move, the experience of the past two decades at least raises questions about how serious this risk really is. It needs to be weighed against the potential value of greening the military and encouraging it to prepare for disasters, conflicts and crises that might be tied closely to natural resource scarcity, ecosystem collapse, or other forms of environmental change. The sorts of environmental security issues that the Obama administration faces can be presented schematically by summarizing elements of the preceding sections (see Table 15-1).

Current research suggests strongly that many of these issues are and will continue to be most acute in certain regions of the world, notably those tropical areas of Africa and Asia that also suffer from poverty, weak government, poor infrastructure, ethnic identity and material conflicts, and other factors that increase vulnerability to things like flooding and drought. For example, the German Advisory Council on Global Change identified a number of "conflict constellations" related to climate change. One of these is water scarcity in areas that "lack the political and institutional framework necessary for the adaptation of water and crisis management systems. This could overstretch existing conflict resolution mechanisms, ultimately leading to destabilization and violence." Another is climate-induced "regional food crises . . . [that] further undermine the economic performance of weak and unstable states, thereby encouraging or exacerbating destabilization, the collapse of social systems, and violent conflicts."[43] The council also worries that severe weather events and floods could undermine crisis management systems and trigger migration and other social problems.

Box 15-2   Emerging Crises

As climate change refashions ecosystems around the world, many analysts are attempting to assess the potential for old problems to intensify and new zones of conflict and suffering to emerge. Key areas of concern include the following:

- The socioeconomic impacts of massive water shortages in India and Pakistan as snow- and ice-fed river systems—the region's major source of fresh water—disappear over the next three decades.
- A deepening of food insecurity throughout sub-Saharan Africa and South Asia as monsoon patterns change and desertification expands.
- The potential for rivalry in the Arctic Ocean as massive ice melt creates access to vast gas and mineral resources in a fragile environment that many conservationists would like to protect.
- More hurricanes in the Caribbean and tropical cyclones in the Indian Ocean, causing massive flooding in low-lying regions such as Bangladesh.
- Migration of devastating tropical diseases such as malaria into regions previously protected by moderate temperatures.
- Higher levels of population displacement in Africa and Asia as people struggle to contend with food, water, and energy shortages.

Of course, fires, floods, and droughts can occur anywhere; militaries can leave their ecological footprints anywhere; and the need for some form of conflict resolution is perennial and universal. Although the costs of environmental change may be disproportionately borne by vulnerable people in the developing world, the costs experienced at home—as Hurricane Katrina made very clear—can also mount very quickly.

These issues are complex and synergistic (see Box 15-2). Thus, for example, climate change may cause the collapse of an ecosystem, forcing people to migrate into a neighboring area of water scarcity, leading to conflict with local inhabitants. Once such a destructive chain of interactions has crossed a certain threshold, it may be very expensive and difficult or even impossible to stop. A better approach is to work on reducing threats and vulnerabilities through environmentally sound management, conservation, mitigation, and adaptation strategies.

Can the United States do this? If it fails to invest in building the capacity to respond to environmental challenges, and the projections of many researchers prove correct that environmental stresses are intensifying, then one can imagine the twenty-first century as the age of global catastrophe. Although Bjorn Lomborg and other skeptics could be correct, and global environmental challenges

Table 15-2   Environmental Security Scenarios[a]

		Environment-related Challenges	
		Diffuse, low intensity	Acute, high intensity
U.S. Capacity to Prevent, Mitigate and Adapt	Weak	1. Chronic pain, persistent turbulence	2. Converging crises, global catastrophe
	Strong	3. One planet, many worlds	4. Cosmopolitan leadership, global governance

a. Table and accompanying text adapted from Richard A. Matthew, "Challenges for Human and International Security: Resource Scarcity," *Coping with Crisis, Working Paper Series* (New York: International Peace Institute, 2008).

might prove far less acute and urgent over the next few decades than the majority of analysts predict, the costs of acting on this assumption would be unbearable if it is wrong. Given that we have to act with some uncertainty about the future of environmental change and its social impacts, we need to ask the following question: fifty or a hundred years from now, would we prefer to have bequeathed a world in which we have made some progress on social issues but that is in the throes of a global environmental catastrophe that societies simply cannot survive, or a world in which we have a well-managed environment but have perhaps spent more in this sector than in retrospect was needed? Table 15-2 presents four different scenarios that could be played out over the next several decades. Given that the future is an uncertain place, the prudent course of action may well be to work toward scenario 4.

1. **Chronic pain, persistent turbulence.** In this scenario, the challenges related to resource scarcity and environmental change become a "permanent" feature of world affairs. Considerable human capital is expended to responding to a growing stream of virulent disease outbreaks, lethal heat waves, severe weather disasters, and the like. Technological innovations, human ingenuity, and, at times, good luck provide intermittent relief.

2. **Converging crises, global catastrophe.** Here a series of crises converge, interact, and dramatically alter the condition of humankind. For example, climate change generates long and intense droughts that destroy the world's food system, causing mass migrations across borders and into new ecological spaces, which triggers a virulent and highly contagious new zoonotic disease. Wars break out, and in desperation several countries use nuclear weapons.

3. **One planet, many worlds.** In this scenario the challenges related to resource scarcity and environmental change become a "permanent" feature of world affairs, but some countries and regions are able to mitigate and adapt while others are not. Dismayed by the spiraling costs of humanitarian assistance, the areas of the world that are managing reasonably well coordinate their policies to contain areas of great upheaval and misery. In this scenario, the wealthy countries discover that for the foreseeable future they can solve

most challenges they face, and they decide that the actual cost of extending ingenuity and capacity to the poorer parts of the world is considerably greater than the costs of containment strategies. The wall between rich and poor becomes increasingly impermeable.

4. Cosmopolitan leadership, global governance. In the fourth scenario, the challenges related to resource scarcity and environmental change prove highly synergistic with other security challenges, some of which are perennial (infectious disease, poverty, and crime) and some of which are relatively new (age-related chronic illness, car accidents). However, over the years the United States participates in creating rich transnational governance networks connecting it to the European Union; middle powers such as Canada, Australia, and Japan; and newly emerging economies like Brazil, China, and India. Through this experience, a truly international leadership emerges dedicated to addressing the challenges of resource scarcity and other forms of global change. Setting norms, redistributing wealth, sharing knowledge, and providing transparent and objective sites for dispute resolution and program design, this leadership begins to implement fair but forceful policies that begin to have a positive impact on world affairs. In this scenario, the wealthy countries discover that for the foreseeable future they can solve most challenges they face, and they decide that they also can and must, for moral and prudential reasons, support the actual cost of extending ingenuity and capacity to the poorer parts of the world. This cost is bearable in part because the developing world has considerable ingenuity of its own and, once given adequate infrastructure, quickly develops indigenous capacity to address local and regional problems.

Challenges for the Obama Administration

In the environmental arena, the U.S. government is often trapped in that uncomfortable policy space defined, on the one hand, by the constant pressure to focus on actions that have quick and concrete results and, on the other hand, by an understanding that many environmental challenges may require commitments measured in decades and made with others in order to have truly positive and enduring effects. Moreover, in both government and business, senior decision makers are likely to be risk averse, indebted to the status quo, and most comfortable with innovations that yield incremental reforms.

In this context, perhaps the single most important step for the Obama administration to take is to invest in preparing American youth to take on these challenges, especially by supporting them with education that will give them the knowledge and leadership skills they will need to succeed. In particular, this education should have a strong science component, encourage a high level of global proficiency, and stress the importance of actions that are both empirically and ethically grounded but that also appreciate the need for innovation, creativity, and experimentation.

Education that prepares the next generation is the most important policy the Obama administration could adopt, but much more than this needs to be done. At the very least, and with regard to the security community, programs should be resurrected, strengthened, or put in place to promote sustainable resource management, ecosystem protection, and the reduction of carbon emissions; to better prepare the military for the growing role it is playing in responding to environmental and humanitarian disasters; and to assist with adaptation to environmental change. Specific measures might include the following:

- Participating in and supporting international research and dialogue on the linkages among natural resources, ecosystems, and climate change; and human, national, and international security.
- Expanding the commitment to greening military activities and base cleanup. For example, considering its share of the gross domestic product, the DOD alone is probably responsible for 1 to 3 percent of global carbon emissions; therefore, if the department could improve efficiency and adopt greener technologies, it would have a positive impact on mitigating climate change.
- Supporting the United Nations effort to integrate the environment into peace-building activities.
- Developing a more cost-effective approach to providing disaster and humanitarian assistance. Today, only the DOD has the skills and human resources to deploy quickly to a major disaster at home or abroad, but this is a costly service. The military is obliged to maintain war-fighting readiness, even as it rescues flood victims or delivers food. It has tremendous experience that the country would be ill advised to lose, but soldiers cannot be both first responders and warriors all the time.
- Taking advantage of the opportunities that disasters and breakdowns provide to rebuild greener and more resilient infrastructure and systems. For example, many people are wisely calling for the government to use the opportunity provided by the current recession to build a greener economy.

The agenda for the Obama administration will be a full one, and the president will face great pressure to create jobs, reduce home foreclosures, ease credit, bring home troops, and reform health care. But every job, home, soldier, and hospital depends on a reliable supply of water, air, and energy; and the costs of mismanaging these precious resources cannot be projected into the future or displaced across class lines and political borders forever. The concept of environmental security does not please everyone, and it cannot do all the hard work that needs to be done to save our planet's environment. But clear and important goals can be pursued by linking the environment to security, and it may be wiser to learn from and build on past experiments than to ignore them.

Suggested Web Sites

Center for Unconventional Security Affairs (www.cusa.uci.edu) A research and education program at the University of California–Irvine that studies the environmental dimensions of human security, violent conflict, and peace building.

Environmental Change and Security Program (ECSP) (www.wilson center.org/index.cfm?fuseaction=topics.home&topic_id=1413) A program that brings together academics and policymakers working on population, environmental change, and security issues.

Global Environmental Change and Human Security (www.gechs.org) A global research program that focuses on the links between global environmental change and human security.

Institute for Environmental Security (www.envirosecurity.org) Think-tank located in The Hague; raises awareness about the environmental dimensions of conflict and peace.

International Peace Research Institute, Oslo (www.prio.no) Conducts research and maintains excellent databases on violent conflict.

The Project on Environmental Scarcities, State Capacity, and Civil Violence (www.library.utoronto.ca/pcs/state.htm) Web site for one of Thomas Homer-Dixon's research projects.

U.S. Department of Defense (www.DOD.gov) Includes extensive information about the department's environmental activities and policies.

Notes

1. "McCain: Clean Energy a 'National Security Issue'," http://cnn.com/2008/POLITICS/05/13/mccain.environment/index.html.
2. "Remarks of Senator Barack Obama: A New Strategy for a New World," Washington D.C., July 15, 2008, www.barackobama.com/2008/07/15/remarks_of_senator_barack_obam_96.php.
3. See, for example, Mathis Wackernagel et al., "Tracing the Ecological Overshoot of the Human Economy," *Proceedings of the National Academy of Sciences* 99 (2002), www.pnas.org/cgi/reprint/99/14/9266; James Gustav Speth, *The Bridge at the End of the World; Capitalism, the Environment, and Crossing from Crisis to Sustainability* (New Haven: Yale University Press, 2008); Lester Brown, *Plan B 3.0: Mobilizing to Save Civilization*, 3d ed. (New York: Norton, 2008).
4. See, for example, UN Development Programme, *Global Environmental Outlook 3* (London: Earthscan, 2002).
5. Intergovernmental Panel on Climate Change, *Working Group II Report: Climate Change Impacts, Adaptation, and Vulnerability*, 2007, www.ipcc.ch.
6. Ecosystem services include hydrological, nutrient, and other biogeochemical cycles; sinks that capture carbon and other elements; genetic diversity; the conditions for natural evolution; and a range of other functions or amenities such as filtering water and neutralizing waste.
7. UN Development Programme, *Human Development Report* (Oxford: Oxford University Press, 1994), 22.
8. Richard Ullman, "Redefining Security," *International Security* 8, 1 (1983): 129–153.
9. *U.S. Commission on National Security/21st Century* at www.au.af.mil/au/awc/awcgate/nssg/.
10. Daniel Deudney and Richard Matthew, *Contested Grounds: Security and Conflict in the New Environmental Politics* (Albany: State University of New York Press, 1999); Steve Lonergan, *Global Environmental Change and Human Security Science Plan*, International Human Dimensions Programme on Global Environmental Change (IHDP) Report 11 (Bonn: IHDP, 1999); Norman Myers, *Ultimate Security: The Environmental Basis of Political Stability* (New York: Norton, 1993).

11. National Security Council, *The National Security Strategy of the United States,* August 1991, www.fas.org/man/docs/918015-nss.htm.
12. Variants of the following discussion of three arguments linking the environment to national security appear in a number of my writings on this topic, such as Richard A. Matthew, "Challenges for Human and International Security: Resource Scarcity," *Coping with Crisis, Working Paper Series* (New York: International Peace Institute, 2008).
13. Fairfield Osborn, *Our Plundered Planet* (New York: Grosset & Dunlap, 1948), 200–201.
14. For discussions on the 1960s and 1970s, see H. Barnett and C. Morse, *Scarcity and Growth: The Economics of Natural Resource Availability* (Baltimore: Johns Hopkins University Press, 1963) and V. K. Smith, *Scarcity and Growth Reconsidered* (Baltimore: Johns Hopkins University Press, 1979). For updated versions of the scarcity-conflict thesis, see Paul R. Ehrlich, *The Population Bomb* (New York: Ballantine, 1968), Donella Meadows and Dennis Meadows, *The Limits to Growth: A Report for the Club of Rome's Project on the Predicament of Mankind* (New York: Universe Books, 1972), and Thomas Homer-Dixon, *Environment, Scarcity and Violence* (Princeton: Princeton University Press, 1999). For a popular account of this position, see Robert Kaplan, "The Coming Anarchy: How Scarcity, Crime, Overpopulation, Tribalism, and Disease Are Rapidly Destroying the Social Fabric of Our Planet," 1994, http://theatlantic.com/politics/foreign/anarchy.htm.
15. See, for example, Wenche Hauge and Tanja Ellingsen, "Beyond Environmental Scarcity: Causal Pathways to Conflict," *Journal of Peace Research* 35, 3 (1998): 299–317.
16. See, for example, Ian Bannon and Paul Collier, *Natural Resources and Violent Conflict Options and Actions* (Washington, D.C.: World Bank, 2003); Paul Collier, "Economic Causes of Civil Conflict and Their Implications for Policy," World Bank Group, 2000, www.worldbank.org/research/conflict/papers/civilconflict.pdf; and Paul Collier, "Doing Well Out of War: An Economic Perspective," in Mats Berdal and David Malone, eds., *Greed and Grievance: Economic Agendas in Civil Wars* (Boulder, Colo.: Lynne Rienner, 2000), 91–111.
17. Earlier work exists on this linkage in both academic and popular literatures, including Bob Reiss, *The Coming Storm: Extreme Weather and Our Terrifying Future* (New York: Hyperion, 2002); and Jeffrey Sachs, "Climate Change and War," 2005, www.tompaine.com/print/climate_change_and_war.php.
18. German Advisory Council on Global Change, *World in Transition: Climate Change as a Security Risk* (London: Earthscan, 2008), 1.
19. CNA Corporation, *National Security and the Threat of Climate Change,* 2007, http://securityandclimate.cna.org/report, 6, 7.
20. For discussion, see Jon Barnet and Neil Adger, "Climate Change, Human Security and Violent Conflict," *Political Geography* 26 (2007): 639–655.
21. Bjorn Lomborg, *The Skeptical Environmentalist: Measuring the Real State of the World* (Cambridge: Cambridge University Press, 2001); Julian Simon, *The Ultimate Resource 2* (Princeton: Princeton University Press, 1998).
22. For a counterargument, see Thomas Homer-Dixon, *The Ingenuity Gap* (New York: Knopf, 2000).
23. Richard A. Matthew, Mark Halle, and Jason Switzer, *Conserving the Peace: Resources, Livelihoods, and Security* (Geneva: International Institute for Sustainable Development, 2002).
24. See, for example, Ken Conca and Geoff Dabelko, *Environmental Peacemaking* (Washington, D.C.: Woodrow Wilson Press, 2002); Matthew, Halle, and Switzer, *Conserving the Peace.*
25. Portions of this section are based on Richard A. Matthew, "The Environment as a National Security Issue," *Journal of Policy History* 12, 1 (2000): 101–122; Matthew, "In Defense of Environment and Security Research," *Environmental Change and Security Project Report* 8 (summer 2002): 109–124.
26. Rachel Carson, *Silent Spring* (New York: Houghton Mifflin, 1962); Ehrlich, *The Population Bomb*; Garrett Hardin, "Tragedy of the Commons," *Science* 162 (1968), 1243–1248.

27. See, for example, Edward O. Wilson, *Diversity of Life* (Cambridge: Harvard University Press, 1992).

28. Jared Diamond, "Ecological Collapse of Past Civilizations," *Proceedings of the American Philosophical Society* 138 (1994): 363–370; Diamond, *Collapse: How Societies Choose to Fail or Succeed* (New York: Viking, 2004); Peter Gleick, "The Implications of Global Climate Changes for International Security," *Climate Change* 15 (1989): 303–325; Gleick, "Water and Conflict: Fresh Water Resources and International Security," *International Security* 18 (1993): 79–112; Myers, *Ultimate Security;* Homer-Dixon, *Environment, Scarcity and Violence;* Homer-Dixon, *The Ingenuity Gap;* Homer-Dixon, *The Upside of Down: Catastrophe, Creativity and the Renewal of Civilization* (New York: Island Press, 2006); Kaplan, "The Coming Anarchy."

29. Robert F. Durant, *The Greening of the U.S. Military: Environmental Policy, National Security, and Organizational Change* (Washington, D.C.: Georgetown University Press, 2007), 29.

30. Ibid., 69.

31. Ibid., 73.

32. See, for example, Kent Hughes Butts, *Environmental Security: What Is DoD's Role?* Occasional Paper (Carlisle Barracks: Strategic Studies Institute, Army War College, 1993); Kent Hughes Butts, "Why the Military Is Good for the Environment," in Jyrki Kakonen, ed., *Green Security or Militarized Environment* (New York: Brookfield, 1994); Butts, "National Security, the Environment, and DOD," *Environmental Change and Security Project Report* 2 (1996): 22–27.

33. Durant, *The Greening of the U.S. Military,* 101.

34. Butts, "Why the Military Is Good for the Environment"; Butts, "National Security, the Environment, and DOD."

35. For discussion, see Daniel Lambach and Tobias Debiel, *State Failure Revisited I: Globalization of Security and Neighborhood Effects,* INEF Report 87 (2007); Lambach and Debiel, *State Failure Revisited II: Actors of Violence and Alternative Forms of Governance,* INEF Report 89 (2007).

36. Warren Christopher, *In the Stream of History: Shaping Foreign Policy for a New Era* (Stanford: Stanford University Press, 1998).

37. Durant, *The Greening of the U.S. Military,* 228.

38. Durant, *The Greening of the U.S. Military,* 229.

39. Geoff Dabelko, "Environment Back in National Security," 2006, http://gristmill.grist.org/story/2006/3/21/231714/520.

40. National Security Council, *National Security Strategy,* March 2006, www.whitehouse.gov/nsc/nss/2006/index.html.

41. In 2007, the author participated in the Triangle Institute retreat on climate change and security and in meetings about environmental security set up by Africa Command.

42. But equally unhappy, no doubt, that the environment was rejected everywhere else as well.

43. German Advisory Council on Global Change, *World in Transition: Climate Change as a Security Risk,* 2, 3.

16

Conclusion
Toward Sustainable Development?
Norman J. Vig and Michael E. Kraft

What is required of us now is a new era of responsibility.

President Barack Obama,
Inaugural Address, January 20, 2009

The twenty-first century opened with a bang. The terrorist attacks on New York and Washington, D.C., on September 11, 2001, symbolized a new form of conflict in the world—one not between nation-states or international alliances, but between dispersed nongovernmental organizations (NGOs) and their perceived ideological enemies. The United States was suddenly challenged by forces that were only dimly understood but that seemed capable of inflicting enormous physical and political damage, even on the world's sole remaining superpower.

"The world has changed" was a common refrain after 9/11. But the planet we inhabit was changing in many other respects, as well. Global trends such as accelerated climate change; loss of biological diversity; and chemical contamination of air, water, and soils are altering the life support systems on which we all depend. Indeed, there is mounting evidence that our way of life is unsustainable in myriad ways.[1] These new global challenges are beginning to reshape the way in which we think about environmental problems at all levels.

One of the most significant trends of the past decade has been the rapid economic ascent of much of the nonwestern world. What Fareed Zakaria calls the "rise of the rest" is perhaps the single most important environmental development of our time.[2] Although poverty, human suffering, and rapid population growth remain overwhelming realities in many countries, especially in Africa and South Asia (see chapter 13), the unprecedented global economic boom of the past two decades has raised hundreds of millions of people out of poverty and dispersed wealth more widely than at any time in the modern world. The experience of China (chapter 14) is most striking, but other large countries such as Brazil, India, Indonesia, Mexico, Russia, South Africa, South Korea, Turkey, and some of the oil-based states of the Middle East have also undergone rapid development.

Much of the world's population has benefited greatly from this economic growth. But there are less benign consequences, as well. According to Zakaria,

"The most acute problem of plenty is the impact of global growth on natural resources and the environment. It is not an exaggeration to say that the world is running out of clean air, potable water, agricultural produce, and many vital commodities."[3] World population is still rising rapidly and will reach 8 billion by about 2025 and 9.4 billion by 2050. As billions of people also raise their living standards, they will require far more resources, placing enormous strain on food production, land use, water supplies, and energy production. As in the case of China, pollution of all kinds is likely to increase substantially in coming years.

At the same time, the world political order is rapidly being reshaped as the United States and other western powers are losing their capacity to write and enforce the rules of the global economic and political system. Power is being dispersed and shared with the newly wealthy nations that are no longer willing to accept dictates from the West. In fact, global economic growth has intensified national identities while simultaneously diffusing universal business, professional, and technical standards that undermine national political control. Economic development shifts power away from national governments to a host of other actors, including business corporations, trade associations, financial centers, local and regional governments, ethnic groups, NGOs, and other nonstate groups of all kinds. These power shifts may undermine the capacity of governments to impose effective controls on environmental degradation at the national level, while at the same time further compounding the difficulties of reaching international agreements on global issues such as climate change.[4] At a minimum, they suggest the need to rethink the means by which environmental policies are designed and implemented, a matter we return to later in this chapter.

These pressures are already influencing the global environmental agenda. One indicator is the emergence of global warming or climate change as the dominant environmental issue of the decade (chapter 12). Influenced in part by the rapid increase in greenhouse gas (GHG) emissions from large developing countries such as China and India, in part by the Bush administration's refusal to confront the problem, and in part by new scientific evidence of accelerating impacts on global ecosystems, public opinion in the United States (and indeed throughout the world) appeared to shift toward supporting actions to address climate change, at least temporarily (chapter 3).[5]

The Fourth Assessment Report of the UN Intergovernmental Panel on Climate Change (IPCC), issued in February 2007, concluded that evidence of global warming is "unequivocal" and that human activity is "very likely" (with 90 percent certainty) the main driver of temperature changes since 1950.[6] Subsequent reports detailed the potentially disastrous consequences of current trends and the need for urgent actions to mitigate or adapt to them.[7] Other scientific studies suggested that climate change may be progressing even more quickly than the IPCC predicted—as indicated by such phenomena as accelerating melting of glaciers and Arctic ice packs—and that gases other than carbon dioxide may be playing a larger role than previously thought.[8]

Another indicator of changing perceptions is the growing linkage between energy and environmental issues and national security concerns (chapter 15).

Although fears about energy "dependence" have been around since the 1970s, the Iraq war and spiking oil prices brought this issue to the fore in the 2008 presidential election campaign. As Richard A. Matthew points out in chapter 15, the concept of environmental security has many meanings but is becoming much broader than simply worries about oil supplies from the Middle East. Issues such as climate change, water scarcities, and natural disasters began to be incorporated into strategic defense thinking in the 1990s but were downplayed by the Bush administration. However, these challenges are likely to have a growing effect on national and international policies in the future.

The severe financial crisis and economic recession that struck the United States and global markets in 2008–2009 will have other unforeseen effects on environmental policies. On the one hand, a worldwide slowdown in economic production and consumption would reduce strains on global resources (as indicated, for example, by the steep decline in oil prices in late 2008) and mitigate pollution growth. On the other hand, it is likely to divert attention from environmental problems and international efforts to address them as nations and groups scramble to protect their economic interests.

In the following section we discuss the concept of sustainable development to help put these broader trends and challenges in context. This is followed by a more detailed discussion of major energy and environmental issues facing the Obama administration in the coming years. In the next section we briefly consider several ideas for reforming environmental policy in the United States to improve its effectiveness. Finally, we return to the broader question of sustainability.

Sustainable Development

Although it has earlier roots, the concept of sustainable development first gained wide recognition in the 1987 report of the World Commission on Environment and Development, *Our Common Future*, which defined it as "development that meets the needs of the present without compromising the ability of future generations to meet their own needs."[9] This concept attempted to reconcile the twin imperatives of economic growth (especially in the less-developed world) and preservation of the Earth's environment. As such, it broke with earlier concepts such as Malthusian scarcity, "tragedy of the commons," and "limits to growth" that were popular in the 1960s and 1970s.[10] In effect, sustainable development theory argued that continuous growth is possible if it is done in the right way—that is, without exhausting critical resources or destabilizing the ecosystems on which human life depends. It also asserted a moral obligation toward future (unborn) generations and toward those in greatest social need at present (distributive justice).[11]

Sustainable development was largely pushed by the developing countries. They did not want to limit their own economic growth in order to satisfy the environmental concerns of the developed countries, especially since the latter were consuming most of the world's resources and were largely responsible for existing environmental pollution. If they were to follow a different path, developing nations demanded massive economic and technical assistance from the industrialized world. These principles were spelled out at the UN Conference on Sustainable Development in Rio de Janeiro in 1992 and were incorporated into several international environmental treaties such as the Framework Convention on Climate Change and the Convention on Biological Diversity. Although the assistance promised to the developing countries largely failed to materialize in the 1990s, sustainable development remains a guiding principle of the United Nations, the European Union, and international lending agencies such as the World Bank.[12] It influenced the drafting of the UN Millennium Development Goals and has been adopted as an objective by numerous national and city governments, business corporations, private foundations, religious bodies, universities and colleges, and other NGOs throughout the world. Indeed, it is the most universally shared general environmental principle of our time.

However, as Richard J. Tobin makes clear in chapter 13, sustainable development remains an elusive goal in much of the world, especially in the fifty or so poorest countries. Many of these nations are overexploiting their agricultural land, water supplies, timber resources, fisheries, and other essential ecological services. Even so, the per-capita consumption levels in these areas are miniscule compared to those of developed nations. As Tobin writes, "consumption patterns among the 20 percent of the world's population living in the lowest income countries account for less than 1.5 percent of the world's private consumption. . . . One estimate suggests that people in the developed world consume, on average, about thirty-two times as many resources as do people in developing countries." Yet almost 99 percent of the world's population increase between 2000 and 2050 is expected to occur in the developing countries. Tobin argues that unless developed countries greatly reduce their consumption and provide far more assistance to poorer countries, sustainable development will not be possible.

In chapter 14 Elizabeth C. Economy paints a very grim picture of China: "China's rapid development, often touted as an economic miracle, has become an environmental disaster." By almost every measure other than on a per-capita basis, China has become the world's largest polluter. Much of the problem lies in the central government's inability to enforce environmental laws at the local level, where officials almost always opt for maximizing economic growth. The country's heavy reliance on coal (70 percent of its commercial energy production is from coal) is especially troubling for the rest of the world. China is already the largest source of carbon dioxide emissions, and by one estimate in twenty-five years the country could emit twice as much carbon dioxide as all other currently industrialized nations combined. Although U.S. and multinational assistance can help to encourage adoption of more efficient technologies, Economy argues that no amount of foreign aid can reverse the situation. Unless China itself undergoes a new "bottom-up" reform and restructuring, the Chinese people and the rest of the world will pay an enormous price.

It is unlikely that developing countries will agree to significant reforms unless the United States and other wealthy nations begin to take sustainable development seriously. So far there has been talk but little action, even in the

European Union where sustainable development has been institutionalized as a fundamental treaty obligation.[13] In the United States, President Bill Clinton established a President's Council on Sustainable Development in 1993. It met for six years and issued several reports, but neither other federal agencies nor Congress paid much attention to it. The Bush administration was hostile to the entire concept, and it largely disappeared from the Washington vocabulary during 2001–2008. With a few exceptions, U.S. development assistance remained pitifully low, while the administration failed to take any serious action on global warming.[14] President Bush also issued an executive order banning all U.S. aid to international agencies that advocate family planning on grounds that it might encourage abortions. (President Barack Obama reversed this policy during his first week in office.)[15]

However, the picture seems brighter if we look beyond the federal government. As Robert C. Paehlke points out in chapter 11, many states and cities, as well as other community organizations, have adopted sustainable development goals and are increasingly motivated by sustainability considerations in their planning processes.[16] Many cities and counties have drafted innovative plans for reconfiguring housing, business centers, and transportation under the rubric of "smart growth." Along with their state counterparts, they have also committed to a wide range of renewable energy and climate change goals (chapters 2, 11, and 12). At the same time, as Daniel Press and Daniel A. Mazmanian point out in chapter 10, many businesses and industries are moving toward "green" production processes and products. There are many motivations for this movement, including perceived opportunities for growth and profits in environmentally friendly technologies, goods, and services. Indeed, the idea of a sustainable economy is catching on rapidly as a legitimate social goal in the United States, in part because business attitudes are changing and in part because the public demands greater accountability from the private sector.[17]

Sustainable development potentially involves all human interactions with the natural environment, at all levels, over an indefinite time frame. It is thus an extremely broad and malleable concept that can mean almost anything. It now appears that its greatest current utility is in motivating and legitimizing plans, projects, and investments at the local and corporate levels, in wealthier societies as well as in the rapidly developing new world. It will be critical for the United States, as well as the emerging economic powers such as China and India, to integrate sustainability much more fully into their national and international economic policies in the future. The current global economic recession will provide both challenges and opportunities in this regard.

Major Policy Issues

As President Obama took office on January 20, 2009, he faced a host of critical issues around the world and at home. Among them were urgent matters of energy and environmental policy that had been neglected for years. During his campaign he had laid out the most challenging environmental agenda in history, and by his inauguration he had assembled an impressive cabinet and staff to undertake it. This section briefly reviews some of the major issues he faced in his first term.

Energy and Climate Change

No issue received more attention during the 2008 presidential campaign than the need for new energy policies to reduce our vulnerability to supply shocks and to address climate change. Indeed, GOP candidate John McCain, R-Ariz., stressed many of the same themes as Obama, though Obama's proposals generally went farther.[18] They covered five major areas: (1) the need for accelerated research and development (R&D) on alternative sources of energy, including advanced biofuels; (2) the need to invest far more in existing renewable energy technologies, such as wind generation and solar panels, and to modernize the national electricity grid; (3) the need to accelerate energy efficiency and conservation programs, especially through higher mileage standards for cars and crash programs to improve the energy efficiency of buildings; (4) the need to create a national cap-and-trade program to control GHG emissions; and (5) the need to reengage in international climate change negotiations and to restore U.S. leadership in this area.

Although the United States spends more on energy-related R&D than any other country, until recently relatively little of it has been devoted to renewable energy compared with the amounts spent on other sources such as nuclear power, "clean coal," oil production, and fossil fuel refinements. The Bush administration did increase funding for energy efficiency and renewable energy to $1.7 billion in 2008 from about $1 billion in 2000.[19] Nevertheless, according to Department of Energy projections, the contribution of renewable energy to national U.S. energy supplies would only increase from 6 percent in 2007 to 7 percent in 2030, while coal would increase from 23 percent to 26 percent over the same period.[20] President Obama called for a drastic change in this scenario. He promised to double renewable energy production in three years, with a goal of producing 25 percent of the nation's electricity from renewable sources by 2025. He also advocated raising fuel-economy standards for cars by 4 percent a year; production of at least one million plug-in electric vehicles by 2015; and creation of a low-carbon standard for transportation fuels to reduce their carbon content by 10 percent by 2020. Building standards would also be raised drastically to improve energy efficiency, and most federal buildings would be retrofit to reduce energy consumption.[21] All of this would require large-scale investment beyond R&D. Obama pledged to spend $150 billion over ten years on green energy projects and to introduce a variety of tax incentives to encourage the new technologies. Many of these measures were incorporated into the $787 billion economic stimulus package passed in February 2009.

The need for a national system to control GHG emissions has been debated in Congress for years. In the 110th Congress (2007–2009), at least ten major proposals for a market-based cap-and-trade program were introduced (chapter 9).[22] The most prominent of these, the Lieberman-Warner Climate Security Act of 2008, had bipartisan sponsorship but failed to win enough support to bring it to a vote (see chapter 5). This bill would have distributed tradable allowances primarily on the basis of current emissions and provided generous offsets that companies could claim to meet their obligations; and it would have gradually lowered the overall emissions cap to about 70 percent below 2005 levels by 2050. President Obama advocates a considerably tougher approach that requires emissions credits to be auctioned (that is, paid for) and that would aim to reduce national emissions to 1990 levels by 2020 and to 80 percent below 1990 levels by 2050. These reductions are of the magnitude that most scientists have said will be necessary to limit the buildup of carbon dioxide in the atmosphere to 550 parts per million, the maximum level for keeping global warming from reaching calamitous levels (see chapter 12). Other scientists now say that even this level is far too high.

President Obama has appointed Carol Browner to serve as White House coordinator of energy and climate policy—a new position. It remains to be seen whether she will have the stature to pull cabinet officers and other advisers together in support of a climate plan.[23] At least some of the president's economic advisers have argued for postponing action on such controversial matters until the condition of the economy improves. It will also be extremely difficult to reach a consensus on a bill in Congress, even within the Democratic majority. Part of the reason is that states have very different economic interests based on their current fuel supplies and potential costs of controls.[24] As Barry G. Rabe points out in chapter 2, states' receptivity to carbon controls and their experience with cap-and-trade policies also vary greatly.[25] The problems that the European Union has encountered in launching its Emissions Trading Scheme (discussed in chapter 9) are also instructive. All of this means that the details of any such program will be extremely important and that many political compromises will likely have to be made.

Even without a cap-and-trade program in place, the Environmental Protection Agency (EPA) has been authorized by the U.S. Supreme Court to regulate GHG emissions under the Clean Air Act (chapter 6), and it has indicated that it intends to do so.[26] The first step is to make a determination based on the latest scientific evidence as to whether carbon dioxide is a pollutant that endangers public health. That finding is likely to lead to an extensive rulemaking process to establish emissions limits. If enacted by Congress, a cap-and-trade system could then be implemented to achieve the desired goals.

The president has pledged to restore American leadership in global climate negotiations by reengaging in talks under the UN Framework Convention on Climate Change (UNFCCC). He has also promised to create a new Global Energy Forum involving the world's largest energy-consuming nations—the G8 developed countries, plus Brazil, China, India, Mexico, and South Africa. The UNFCCC negotiations to establish a treaty to supplant the Kyoto Protocol after 2012 have been difficult without the participation of the largest GHG emitters (chapter 12). At its last major conference of the parties in Bali, Indonesia, in December 2007, an action plan was adopted for completion of an agreement at Copenhagen in December 2009.[27] Secretary of State Hillary Clinton is likely to play a critical role in these negotiations, but whether the United States is willing to commit to new international treaty obligations will depend on many factors, including the state of the economy and whether agreement can be reached on a climate change policy at home. It is unlikely that Congress will agree to mandatory GHG limits unless China also agrees to do so, and vice versa. Hence the Obama administration will make climate change a centerpiece of the United States' relations with China.[28]

Air and Water Pollution

President Obama has promised to "restore the integrity" of the EPA. At her confirmation hearings, the new EPA administrator, Lisa P. Jackson, declared, "If I am confirmed, political appointees will not compromise the integrity of E.P.A.'s technical experts to advance particular regulatory outcomes."[29] The influence of scientists at the EPA and throughout the government is likely to be strengthened (see chapters 4 and 7). But the agency will face a number of difficult decisions over pollution controls that have been postponed or embroiled in controversy during the Bush administration. One concerns whether to grant California and thirteen other states a waiver to set carbon dioxide emission standards for vehicles for the first time under the Clean Air Act (discussed in chapter 7). President Obama ordered the EPA to reconsider this issue during the first week of his presidency.[30] Others will involve decisions on whether to tighten rules on pollution from sources such as power plants, oil refineries, mining operations, and agricultural feedlots. In particular, the EPA will need to remedy the Bush administration's failure to establish viable standards for mercury emissions from coal-fired power plants (see chapter 7).

However, some progress was made during the Bush presidency. Long-term trends toward improved air quality continued for the most part after 2000 (see chapter 1 for details). Emissions of fine particles ($PM_{2.5}$), for which national standards were initiated during the Clinton administration, declined by more than half during 2000–2007.[31] New regulations on diesel engine emissions, covering trucks and buses, off-road vehicles and equipment, ships, and locomotives, and for small engines such as lawnmowers and outboard motors, were adopted or implemented. Ambient air quality standards for ozone, particulates, and lead were also tightened toward the end of the Bush presidency. These standards were less stringent than recommended by environmental groups and EPA scientists and advisers; nevertheless, they represented significant improvements.[32] Still, as noted in chapter 1, more than half of all Americans live in counties that do not meet at least one of the National Ambient Air Quality Standards (in most cases for ozone or fine particles).[33] Long-term exposure to these pollutants and to other hazardous chemicals in the air is a major cause of respiratory diseases such as asthma, bronchitis, and chronic obstructive pulmonary disease (COPD), as well as of heart disease, neurological disorders, and cancer.[34]

Less progress has been made in controlling water pollution. Based on the spotty national statistics we have, nearly half of all surveyed river and stream miles and almost 60 percent of lakes, ponds, and reservoirs continue to be impaired (see chapter 1). The Bush administration saw some backsliding in this area, especially in regard to mining and energy production. For example, rules finalized at the end of 2008 allow mountaintop coal mining operations to dump more of their wastes in streams and valleys.[35] Most of the other pollution of rivers and lakes also comes from nonpoint (indirect) sources such as farm fields, feedlots, golf courses, and urban streets. State and local governments play a dominant role in land use decisions, making enforcement of runoff controls difficult. The EPA requires states to establish specific daily pollution limits for polluted waters (Total Maximum Daily Loads, or TMDL) to encourage them to take stronger action. President Obama has promised a variety of actions to address these problems, including restoration of funding for the Clean Water State Revolving Fund, which has been cut substantially since 2000. This fund supports local projects for wastewater treatment, nonpoint source pollution control, and watershed and estuary management.[36] Obama has also pledged to tighten regulations on concentrated animal-feeding operations and on drinking water protection, two other areas in which the Bush administration relaxed the rules.

Another problem is that the Supreme Court has muddied the waters (literally) with a ruling in June 2006 that has been interpreted to exclude many smaller and seasonal wetlands and streams from coverage as "navigable waters" under the Clean Water Act.[37] As a result, the EPA "dropped or delayed more than 400 cases involving suspected violations of the law."[38] A new law pending in Congress, the Clean Water Restoration Act, would reinstate the broad definition of navigable waters that prevailed in the courts before 2006. It will be interesting to see if this becomes a priority of the Obama administration.

Hazardous, Toxic, and Nuclear Wastes

Another set of knotty EPA issues concerns storage and disposal of especially hazardous or toxic wastes. The Comprehensive Environmental Response, Compensation, and Liability (Superfund) Act of 1980 required responsible parties to clean up the most serious toxic waste dumps in the country. Since then more than 2,000 areas have been designated as federal or state Superfund sites on the National Priorities List, and more than 1,000 have been cleaned up (1,255 remained on the list at the end of 2008). However, the cleanup process has slowed down as funds have been cut by Congress. During the Bush administration, work was completed on only half as many sites as during the Clinton administration.[39] On the other hand, legislation was passed to accelerate the restoration of brownfields—areas not as seriously contaminated that can be rendered suitable for industrial, commercial, and other restricted uses. Hundreds of such projects have received grants from the EPA, but it is estimated that there are at least 450,000 more contaminated sites in the nation. President Obama has promised to increase funding for the cleanup programs.

Under the Emergency Planning and Community Right-to-Know Act of 1986, companies with more than ten employees are required to report on their inventories, use, storage, and disposal of hundreds of toxic chemicals.

These reports are published in the EPA's Toxics Release Inventory, perhaps the government's most effective environmental information disclosure program. Many companies have been shamed into reducing their discharges of toxic materials, and others have reduced their use of hazardous chemicals voluntarily (see chapter 10). The Bush administration relied heavily on volunteer programs and attempted to reduce reporting requirements.[40] However, the EPA has assessed the potential health effects of only a small percentage of more than eighty thousand chemicals used in commerce since the 1970s. Many of these chemicals are now ubiquitous; for example, one study found that blood from the umbilical cords of ten babies born in U.S. hospitals in 2004 contained almost three hundred industrial compounds, pollutants, pesticides, and other chemicals.[41] These substances have been found in the blood and breast milk of people living in some of the most remote areas of the world. Industrial and agricultural development is now circulating pollutants throughout the global troposphere; pollution from Beijing now affects Los Angeles (see chapter 14).

Nuclear wastes present special problems since they remain radioactive for tens of thousands of years. Although President Bush approved the long-awaited nuclear waste repository at Yucca Mountain, Nevada, in 2002, it remains to be seen whether this facility will ever be operational (President Obama has opposed the site); the Nuclear Regulatory Commission is currently considering a proposal to license it. In the meantime, spent fuel continues to accumulate in cooling ponds and dry cask storage containers at some one hundred nuclear power plants throughout the U.S. These present threats of terrorist attacks or diversion of nuclear materials, as well as of potential site contamination. Nevertheless, nuclear energy provides 70 percent of the electricity not produced by fossil fuels in the United States, and the need for alternatives to carbon fuels has revived interest in nuclear power. President Obama has not ruled out a new generation of "safe" nuclear plants as part of the future energy infrastructure, if better storage and proliferation safeguards can be developed. It will be interesting to see how this debate evolves.

Endangered Species and Biological Diversity

Loss of biodiversity ranks with climate change as the greatest long-term threat to the global environment. Scientists believe that the current rate of extinction is 1,000 to 10,000 times the normal rate, and amounts to the sixth great extinction in geological history.[42] The World Wildlife Fund reported in 2004 that, on average, populations of land, freshwater, and marine species declined 40 percent between 1970 and 2000.[43] In 2008 the International Union for Conservation of Nature concluded that at least a quarter of the world's mammal species are headed for extinction in the near future.[44] Natural systems that support the greatest diversity of species—such as rainforests, wetlands, and coastal estuaries—are threatened by human development throughout the world. These issues are addressed in part by the international Convention on Biological Diversity, which the United States has not yet ratified.

We are just beginning to inventory and understand the full richness of biological diversity in the United States.[45] Over 200,000 native species are currently known to exist, more than 10 percent of all documented species on Earth. Of nearly 21,000 species assessed recently, one-third are considered at risk. The Endangered Species Act (ESA) has protected a relatively small share of these species, with 572 animals and 746 plants listed as endangered or threatened as of January 2009.[46] Only 60 new species were listed during the Bush administration by July 2008, compared with 522 during the Clinton administration and 231 during the single-term presidency of Bush's father.[47] The Bush administration weakened implementation of the ESA by refusing to list new species until ordered to by a court; by delisting species such as the gray wolf that are still considered threatened; by cutting funds for critical habitat restoration; by exempting military and homeland security activities from the law; and by failing to defend the law against property-rights litigation.[48]

After failing in efforts to amend the ESA during 2003–2006, the Interior Department issued new rules in August 2008 that would fundamentally change the way the law works (see chapter 8). These regulations would allow federal agencies such as the Army Corps of Engineers and the Federal Highway Administration to make decisions on their own as to whether their proposed construction projects would adversely affect endangered species, without consultation by wildlife experts at the U.S. Fish and Wildlife Service or the National Marine Fisheries Service, as had been required since the law was written. They would also exempt GHG emissions from consideration of species protection.[49] It was anticipated that the Obama administration or Congress would reverse these and other last-minute rules of the Bush presidency.[50]

The attempt to rewrite the ESA was only one of many actions taken by the Bush administration that affected biological diversity. As Mark Lubell and Brian Segee show in chapter 8, systematic efforts were made to alter the rules on forest management and to open access to resources on public lands. Attempts to bypass the Roadless Area Rule of the Clinton administration allowed greater habitat fragmentation and opened more areas to logging and mining. Forest management plans announced late in the administration released millions of acres for logging in the Tongass National Forest in Alaska and in old-growth forests in Oregon.[51] The Bush administration gave less support to collaborative ecosystem management than its predecessor. President Obama is expected to restore emphasis on ecosystem management and building consensus among stakeholders and scientists, perhaps along the lines of the Clinton administration's habitat conservation plans in the 1990s.

Drill Here, Drill Now, Drill Everywhere

This mantra, popularized in the waning months of the 2008 election campaign of John McCain and his running mate, Alaska governor Sarah Palin, became a flashpoint between the candidates and the parties. The Republicans sought to take advantage of record oil and gasoline prices by calling for opening public lands and virtually all offshore areas along the East

and West coasts to oil and gas exploration. President Bush rescinded an executive order of his father, George H. W. Bush, that banned oil and gas drilling
on the Outer Continental Shelf.[52] Barack Obama and most Democrats
argued, on the other hand, that the nation could not produce its way out of
the energy crisis, and placed far more emphasis on development of alternative energy sources.[53] Toward the end of the campaign, Obama and other
Democrats indicated some flexibility on offshore drilling if it was part of a
comprehensive energy package, and the House of Representatives voted to
end the ban on offshore drilling.[54] Whether the Obama administration will
allow this to occur remains to be seen. The possibility of drilling in the Arctic
National Wildlife Refuge remains another sore point. Although Congress
has resisted efforts to open the refuge to oil and gas exploration (see chapter
5), many Republicans, including Governor Palin, continue to push for it.[55]

President Obama and his interior secretary, Ken Salazar, will face many
difficult decisions about these and other proposed oil-, gas-, and coal-
producing sites such as the Roan Plateau in Colorado (see chapter 8). As if
to make the point, on Election Day the Interior Department announced a
huge sale of oil and gas leases on public lands in Utah near Arches National
Park and Dinosaur National Monument.[56] Although this sale was later can-
celed by Secretary Salazar, it symbolized the massive expansion of energy
exploration promoted by the Bush administration.[57] Given concerns about
energy security (chapter 15), the pressures for increased domestic production
will continue. How the new administration balances these needs with protection of public lands and investments in new energy technologies will be
one of the greatest challenges of the Obama presidency. It will also be necessary to clean up the corruption that developed in parts of the Interior
Department, especially in the Minerals Management Service, which over-
sees oil and gas leases and collection of royalties.[58]

The Need for Reform

Restoring professional integrity to the Department of the Interior and the
EPA is only part of the job. There is a deeper need to reconsider the methods
by which environmental regulation and natural resource management have
been conducted over the past several decades. Most of the environmental laws
enacted in the 1970s and 1980s established command-and-control regulation.
They set federal standards for each pollutant and each type of facility that were
to be legally enforced against industry, with stiff fines and other penalties for
noncompliance. These standards required uniform pollution control technologies and cleanup procedures. For the most part, they were aimed at controlling
pollution after the fact—for example, by requiring filters on smokestacks or catalytic converters on automobiles—rather than changing industrial processes or
technologies to eliminate generation of pollutants in the first place (pollution
prevention). The implementation of regulations created an adversarial relationship between government and regulated parties, which often led to protracted
litigation in the courts (see chapter 6). In natural resource management, an

older set of principles such as "multiple use" and "sustained yield" guidelines governed the forestry and land use agencies, but these were open to local interpretation and political interference that frequently produced controversies such as those discussed in chapter 8.

Although the traditional regulatory system has brought considerable progress in reducing pollution and preserving resources (see chapters 1 and 10), policy scholars have increasingly called for reforms. Basically they have argued that although legal coercion was necessary to eliminate the worst sources of pollution and to establish essential health and environmental safeguards, we have now moved to a new generation of environmental problems for which the old methods are often ineffective or even counterproductive. They have called for much greater flexibility in the means allowed to achieve pollution goals and for greater incentives for voluntary cooperation and performance that goes beyond minimum legal requirements. In short, they advocate a more results-based approach to environmental governance that relies more heavily on collaborative decision making and continuous social learning to achieve common goals. These newer approaches would not replace traditional regulation but would supplement it in areas in which win-win solutions are possible.[59]

Carol Browner was a strong advocate of these ideas when she was EPA administrator in the Clinton administration, and she will likely continue to push for them as energy and climate change "czar" in the Obama White House. Such efforts would also appear to be congruent with President Obama's statements on the need for smarter government and greater collaboration and transparency in decision making.

Smart Regulation

Smart regulation refers to a set of design principles for regulatory reform that emphasize use of a broader range of policy instruments that are more flexible, less interventionist, and more results oriented.[60] A substantial literature now exists on the adoption and success of new environmental policy instruments throughout the world.[61] In the United States, such changes began in the 1970s but were accelerated in the 1990s. The Clean Air Act of 1990 was the first major legislation to establish a cap-and-trade program to reduce air pollution (sulfur and nitrogen oxides that cause acid rain). The success of this program (emissions levels fell faster than anticipated, and at less cost), together with anti-regulatory pressures after the Republicans gained control of Congress in 1994, led to broader efforts by the Clinton administration to "reinvent" government.

The EPA adopted some fifty new programs during 1994–2000 to experiment with alternative methods. These programs included the Common Sense Initiative that involved extensive dialogue between government, industry, and other stakeholder representatives to set voluntary pollution control targets in six key sectors (iron and steel, petroleum refining, computers and electronics, metal finishing, printing, and auto manufacturing); Project XL, which involved negotiated agreements with specific firms that were willing to go beyond compliance with legal requirements in exchange for regulatory flexibility in meeting their goals; and the National Environmental Performance Track for recognizing and rewarding companies and communities that consistently perform better than required by law.[62] Overall, these programs had mixed success, but they were valuable learning experiments both for government and for the private institutions that participated.[63]

The new programs also encouraged a burst of voluntary actions within industry to improve environmental management (see chapter 10). These self-regulatory efforts had many impressive results, particularly in reducing the use and release of toxic chemicals. The reporting requirements of the Toxics Release Inventory, together with EPA programs for rewarding companies that go beyond legal compliance, led to greater transparency and accountability as companies sought to prove their green credentials. They also encouraged companies to seek various forms of environmental certification that would reassure their customers and shareholders. The Securities and Exchange Commission now requires all publicly listed companies to include information on their discharges of materials and other environmental liabilities in their annual reports. Although some of this is "greenwashing," environmental performance is becoming a more important consideration for those making financial investments.[64]

Economic Instruments

Programs such as cap-and-trade systems make direct use of economic market forces to encourage behavioral changes that benefit the environment (see chapter 9). Instead of imposing regulatory mandates to install particular types of equipment and to meet specific emissions limits, market-based systems attach a price to pollution and leave it up to private sector actors to decide how best to reduce their costs. This can be accomplished through cap-and-trade systems that set overall emissions caps and allow participants to buy and sell pollution credits or allowances at the going market rate. As the cap goes down, the price of allowances will rise and companies will be forced to adapt by reducing their need for them. Alternatively, a system of taxes or fees can be imposed that arbitrarily sets the price of pollution units at a level that will force emitters to adopt new equipment or processes in order to avoid paying the levies. The difficulty with this approach is in knowing how high to set the tax; if it is too low, it will not produce the overall results desired.

In theory, either of these approaches can result in a cost effective (least cost) path to achieve the desired outcomes. European countries have made extensive use of environmental taxes to drive behavioral change, and the European Union has implemented a cap-and-trade system that is reducing carbon dioxide emissions (see chapter 9). In the United States it has been more difficult to impose taxes, although state and local governments make wide use of tax incentives, fees, and other charges (chapter 2). Most political leaders, including President Obama, now support a cap-and-trade system to control GHG emissions, as discussed earlier.

However, many economists and environmentalists also favor targeted tax increases, for example, on gasoline or on gas-guzzling vehicles. Some conservatives have also argued that revenue-neutral tax swaps would be preferable to mandatory emissions limits under a cap-and-trade scheme—that is, pollution or GHG taxes would be offset by tax cuts on "goods," such as income and payroll taxes.[65] Others have called for elimination of tax subsidies to dirty industries (such as oil and coal companies) or for conditioning of tax breaks and subsidies on commitments to energy or environmental goals (for example, in auto manufacturing). The American Recovery and Reinvestment Act passed in February 2009 contained tax incentives and loan guarantees intended to leverage up to $100 billion in private sector investments in clean energy.

Collaborative Management

One of the problems with traditional regulation is that each environmental medium (air, water, soil) and each type of problem (air emissions, water discharges, toxic waste) is dealt with separately, under different laws, and by different agency bureaus (see chapter 1 and appendix 1). Critics have long called for a more integrated approach that focuses more holistically on the health of natural systems that are subject to multiple stresses and whose boundaries do not coincide with single legal jurisdictions (for example, large watersheds and forest complexes). This concern led to the adoption of what came to be known as ecosystem management in the U.S. Forest Service and some of the Interior Department bureaus starting in the 1980s (see chapter 8). The ecosystem approach was greatly expanded in the 1990s during the Clinton administration to better address both large restoration projects (such as the Florida Everglades and Northwest Forest plans) and smaller watersheds and ecosystems that need to be protected to preserve unique amenities or endangered species. Hundreds of individual habitat conservation plans were negotiated during the Clinton administration.[66]

All of these initiatives, as well as many of the new EPA programs discussed earlier, also differed in that they relied heavily on collaborative decision making, rather than on traditional "top-down" processes under single-agency authorities. This collaboration spanned federal, state, and local boundaries as well as cutting across different statutory and agency jurisdictions. Although initiated by a lead government agency, multiple public and private stakeholders, including citizen groups, were brought together for the first time to try to reach consensus on plans for future management of an ecosystem or resource base. For example, habitat conservation plans would attempt to define which types of development might be permitted and which parts or areas of an ecosystem would need to be protected. They would usually provide for careful scientific monitoring of the system to allow management adjustments as necessary (adaptive management). Restoration plans, such as those for the Chesapeake Bay, the Florida Everglades, and the Great Lakes, would contain broader recommendations for pollution control and land management across several states and multiple local jurisdictions.

As Lubell and Segee point out in chapter 8, these efforts at public-private collaboration have a mixed record of success to date. In some cases planning processes have broken down or have ended in stalemate, but in many others they have helped to build networks of trust and to diffuse conflict. The Bush administration gave lip service to collaboration and cooperation but preferred to control resource decision making through traditional agency processes that allowed political appointees to determine outcomes. Nevertheless, voluntary collaboration is gaining as an alternative to the conflict and litigation that has characterized resource management in the past. President Obama has placed great emphasis on cooperation and transparency as means to overcome traditional lobbyist and special-interest-driven policymaking. Thus we will likely see renewed efforts to involve citizens and public interest groups more fully at all levels of environmental policymaking and management.

Is Sustainability Possible?

This is the fundamental *question of responsibility* that we face in the coming years. A decade may be the time limit we have, for example, to develop a global system to halt the rising level of GHG emissions at a level that can then be ratcheted downward over the next several decades. Some scientists now argue that even the targets recommended by international bodies such as the IPCC are much too high, and that the world will need to go carbon neutral, or even "carbon negative," by 2050 if we are to prevent a planetary catastrophe.[67] Jeffrey Sachs, a development economist who directs the Earth Institute at Columbia University, has argued that without a fundamentally new set of energy technologies on a global scale we cannot possibly achieve sustainable economic growth. He and others have called for a "moonshot" commitment to new technological development rather than relying on control technologies likely to emerge from a cap-and-trade system.[68] Former vice president and Nobel Prize–winner Al Gore has called for converting the entire U.S. electricity grid to carbon-free fuels in ten years.[69] President Obama's goal of producing 25 percent of our nation's electricity from renewable sources by 2025 is a step in the right direction but obviously falls well short of this goal.

In chapter 15 Matthew argues persuasively that these challenges must now become an integral part of our national security planning and strategies, as well. Emerging crises such as massive fresh water shortages, food shortages, and damage from tropical storms and sea level rises now have the potential to create millions of environmental refugees and generate new conflicts over resources. He lays out four possible global scenarios that could result, including possibilities for chronic turbulence or converging crises leading to global warfare. However, he also sees the potential for new forms of international collaboration and governance to avoid the worst of these outcomes. In the future the United States will have to play a much more active and responsible role on the international stage to achieve this goal.

One thing is certain, and that is that governments at all levels, every part of the private sector, and citizens from all walks of life will have to pay far more attention to sustainability imperatives in the future. This will require much greater integration of environmental considerations into all spheres of policymaking. It will also demand greater awareness and sacrifice on the part of all of us. Present levels of consumption and waste in the United States and other wealthy countries cannot be maintained if the rest of the world is to continue to grow and prosper. In the current economic downturn it will be especially difficult to focus people's attention on broader issues of this kind.[70] Nevertheless, we will be forced to deal with our impacts on the planet, whether we want to or not.

Notes

1. The landmark *Millennium Ecosystem Assessment*, issued March 30, 2005, concluded that "approximately 60 percent of the ecosystem services that support life on Earth . . . are being degraded or used unsustainably." The assessment was conducted by some 1,300 experts from 95 countries. See www.maweb.org for details.
2. Fareed Zakaria, *The Post-American World* (New York: Norton, 2008).
3. Ibid., 30.
4. Ibid., 37–38.
5. See Andrew C. Revkin, "As China Goes, So Goes Global Warming," *New York Times*, December 16, 2007; and "International Polls Find Robust Global Support for Increased Efforts to Address Climate Change," PIPA poll, December 5, 2007. For these and other recent polls, see www.worldpublicopinion.org/pipa/articles/btenvironmentra.
6. Elisabeth Rosenthal and Andrew C. Revkin, "Panel Sees Centuries of Warming Due to Humans," *New York Times*, February 2, 2007; Revkin, "Science Panel Says Global Warming Is 'Unequivocal'," *New York Times*, February 3, 2007.
7. The panel issued four reports during 2007. See also Andrew C. Revkin, "U.N. Study Shows Likely Impact of Global Warming," *New York Times*, April 4, 2007; James Kanter and Andrew C. Revkin, "Scientists Detail Climate Changes, Poles to Tropics," *New York Times*, April 7, 2007; Elisabeth Rosenthal, "U.N. Report Describes Risks of Inaction on Climate Change," *New York Times*, November 17, 2007; Rosenthal, "Climate Panel Says Immediate Changes are Necessary," *New York Times*, November 18, 2007; and Revkin, "U.N. Warns of Climate-Related Setbacks," *New York Times*, November 28, 2007. The reports are available at www.ipcc.ch/.
8. Andrew C. Revkin, "Arctic Melt Unnerves the Experts," Science Times, *New York Times*, October 2, 2007; Revkin, "U.S. Report Foresees Effects of Climate Shift," *New York Times*, May 28, 2008; Juliet Eilperin, "Faster Climate Change Feared," *Washington Post*, December 28, 2008; Richard Morgan, "Beyond Carbon: Scientists Worry about Nitrogen's Effects," *New York Times*, September 2, 2008. See also Worldwatch Institute, *State of the World 2009: Into a Warming World* (New York: Norton, 2009).
9. World Commission on Environment and Development, *Our Common Future* (Oxford: Oxford University Press, 1987), 43. For a review of the origins of the idea of sustainability and its many meanings, see Lamont C. Hempel, "Conceptual and Analytical Challenges in Building Sustainable Communities," in Daniel A. Mazmanian and Michael E. Kraft, eds., *Toward Sustainable Communities: Transition and Transformations in Environmental Policy*, 2d ed. (Cambridge: MIT Press, 2009).
10. See, for example, Paul R. Ehrlich, *The Population Bomb* (New York: Ballantine Books, 1968); Garrett Hardin, "The Tragedy of the Commons," *Science*, December 13, 1968, 1243–1248; and Donella H. Meadows et al., *The Limits to Growth: A Report for the Club of Rome's Project on the Predicament of Mankind*, 2d ed. (New York: Universe Books, 1974).
11. Keekok Lee, Alan Holland, and Desmond McNeill, *Global Sustainable Development in the 21st Century* (Edinburgh: Edinburgh University Press, 2000).
12. See Adil Najam, "The View from the South: Developing Countries in Global Environmental Politics," in Regina S. Axelrod, David Leonard Downie, and Norman J.

Vig, eds., *The Global Environment: Institutions, Law, and Policy,* 2d ed. (Washington, D.C.: CQ Press, 2005), 225–243.

13. Susan Baker and John McCormick, "Sustainable Development: Comparative Understandings and Responses," in Norman J. Vig and Michael G. Faure, eds., *Green Giants? Environmental Policies of the United States and the European Union* (Cambridge: MIT Press, 2004), 277–302.

14. The United States has ranked at or near the bottom of OECD countries in per-capita overseas development assistance, and relatively little of this has been allocated to environmental priorities; see Paul G. Harris, "International Development Assistance and Burden Sharing," in Vig and Faure, *Green Giants?* 253–276.

15. Peter Baker, "Obama Reverses Rule on U.S. Abortion Aid," *New York Times,* January 24, 2009.

16. See also Mazmanian and Kraft, *Toward Sustainable Communities.*

17. See, for example, Worldwatch Institute, *2008 State of the World: Innovations for a Sustainable Economy* (New York: Norton, 2008).

18. For a comparison, see Andrew C. Revkin, "On Global Warming, McCain and Obama Agree: Urgent Action Is Needed," *New York Times,* October 19, 2008.

19. John M. Broder, Andrew C. Revkin, Felicity Barringer, and Cornelia Dean, "Environmental Views, Past and Present," *New York Times,* February 7, 2009.

20. Clifford Krauss, "Energy Research on a Shoestring," *New York Times,* January 25, 2007.

21. These promises and many more were published on the Obama-Biden campaign Web page at barackobama.com.

22. These ten bills are summarized and compared by the Pew Center on Global Climate Change at www.pewclimate.org/docUploads/Chart-and-Graph-120108.pdf.

23. See Margaret Kriz, "Carol Browner: Power Player," *National Journal,* January 31, 2009.

24. Felicity Barringer, "States' Battles over Energy Grow Fiercer with U.S. in a Policy Gridlock," *New York Times,* March 20, 2008.

25. For details, see Barry G. Rabe and Christopher P. Borick, "The Climate of Opinion: State Views on Climate Change and Policy Options," Brookings Institution, *Issues in Governance Studies,* No. 19, September 2008; and Rabe, "The Complexities of Carbon Cap-and-Trade Policies: Early Lessons from the States," Brookings Institution, Governance Studies Paper, October 2008 (both available at www.brookings.edu).

26. John M. Broder, "E.P.A. Expected to Regulate Carbon Dioxide and Other Heat-Trapping Gases," *New York Times,* February 19, 2009.

27. Thomas Fuller and Elisabeth Rosenthal, "At Divided Climate Talks, Consensus That U.S. Is at Fault," *New York Times,* December 14, 2007; Fuller and Andrew C. Revkin, "Climate Plan Looks Beyond Bush's Tenure," *New York Times,* December 16, 2007; Mark Landler, "Clinton Paints China Policy with a New Green Hue," *New York Times,* February 22, 2009; Elisabeth Rosenthal, "Obama's Backing Increases Hopes for Climate Pact," *New York Times,* March 1, 2009.

28. Edward Wong and Andrew C. Revkin, "Experts in U.S. and China See a Chance for Cooperation against Climate Change," *New York Times,* February 5, 2009. See also James Russell, "Carbon Emissions on the Rise," *World Watch,* January/February 2009, 28.

29. John M. Broder, "E.P.A. Pick Vows to Put Science First," *New York Times,* January 15, 2009. See also Juliet Eilperin, "EPA, Interior Dept. Chiefs Will Be Busy Erasing Bush's Mark," *Washington Post,* November 28, 2008.

30. John M. Broder and Peter Baker, "Obama's Order Likely to Tighten Auto Standards," *New York Times,* January 26, 2009.

31. See Broder et al., "Environmental Views, Past, and Present," for a review of the Bush record.

32. See, for example, Matthew L. Wald, "Environmental Agency Tightens Smog Standard," *New York Times,* March 13, 2008; David Stout, "In Revising Clean Air Rules, E.P.A. Draws Praise and Criticism in Same Week," *New York Times,* March 15, 2008; and H. Josef Hebert, "Groups Sue Government over New Smog Rules," May 27, 2008, washingtonpost.com.

33. See the air quality trend data at www.epa.gov/airtrends/sixpoll.html.

34. See, for example, American Lung Association, "Highlights of Recent Research on Particulate Air Pollution: Effects of Long-Term Exposure," at www.lungusa.org.

35. John M. Broder, "Rule to Expand Mountaintop Coal Mining," *New York Times*, August 23, 2007; Robert Pear and Felicity Barringer, "Coal Mining Debris Rule Is Approved," *New York Times*, December 3, 2008.

36. Obama's economic stimulus plan as passed by the House of Representatives contained funding for 1,300 wastewater treatment projects, 380 drinking water projects, and 1,000 rural water and sewer system projects. Philip Rucker, "Obama Details Recovery Plan," *Washington Post*, January 25, 2009.

37. *Rapano v. United States*, June 19, 2006. In the 5–4 decision, Justice Anthony Kennedy attempted to find middle ground between conservatives and liberals on the court by ruling that waters could be protected under the Clean Water Act only if a "significant nexus" could be proven to a navigable body of water downstream. This had made it very difficult to determine which wetlands are covered.

38. Editorial, "Clearer Rules, Cleaner Waters," *New York Times*, August 18, 2008.

39. These and other data can be found on the EPA Web site, www.epa.gov/superfund/sites.

40. For example, under the proposed rules only companies using more than 5,000 (rather than 500) pounds of the most hazardous chemicals would be required to make detailed reports on discharges. Firms would also need to report every two years instead of annually. Tom Meersman, "EPA Tries to Ease Chemical Disclosure Rules," Minneapolis *Star Tribune*, January 16, 2006.

41. Tom Meersman, "Numerous Man-made Chemicals Are in Blood of Newborns, Research Finds," Minneapolis *Star Tribune*, July 14, 2005. See also John Wargo, *Our Children's Toxic Legacy* (New Haven: Yale University Press, 1996).

42. See, for example, Niles Eldredge, "The Sixth Extinction," www.actionbioscience.org/newfrontiers/eldredge2.html.

43. World Wildlife Fund for Nature, *Living Planet Report 2004*, October 2004, www.panda.org/downloads/general/lpr2004.pdf.

44. James Kanter, "One in 4 Mammals Threatened with Extinction, Group Finds," *New York Times*, October 7, 2008; Verlyn Klinkenborg, "Watching the Numbers and Charting the Losses—of Species," *New York Times*, October 15, 2008.

45. B. A. Stein, L. S. Kutner, and J. S. Adams, eds., *Precious Heritage: The Status of Biodiversity in the United States* (Oxford: Oxford University Press, 2000). See also Stein, "A Fragile Cornucopia: Assessing the Status of U.S. Biodiversity," *Environment* (September 2001): 10–22.

46. The daily list of endangered and threatened species can be found at http://ecos.fws .gov/tess_public/TESSBoxcore.

47. Jerry Adler, "The Race for Survival," *Newsweek*, June 9, 2008, 44. This article gives an excellent overview of ESA history and issues.

48. Michael Grunwald, "Bush Seeks to Curb Endangered Species Suits," *Washington Post*, April 12, 2001; Jenifer 8. Lee, "Money Gone, U.S. Suspends Designations of Habitats," *New York Times*, May 29, 2003.

49. Juliet Eilperin, "Endangered Species Act Changes Give Agencies More Say," *Washington Post*, August 12, 2008; Felicity Barringer, "Rule Eases a Mandate Under a Law on Wildlife," *New York Times*, December 12, 2008.

50. Ceci Connolly and R. Jeffrey Smith, "Obama Positioned to Quickly Reverse Bush Actions," *Washington Post*, November 9, 2008.

51. Christopher Lee, "New Forest Plan Opens Up Millions of Acres to Logging," Minneapolis *Star Tribune*, January 26, 2008; Felicity Barringer, "Move to Increase Logging on Oregon Land," *New York Times*, January 1, 2009.

52. Dan Eggen and Steven Mufson, "Bush Rescinds Father's Offshore Oil Ban," *Washington Post*, July 15, 2008.

53. See, for example, Michael Powell and Michael Cooper, "Obama Assails Remarks by McCain on Drilling," *New York Times*, June 25, 2008. The Obama campaign also

pointed to the fact that oil and gas companies already had leases on 68 million acres on which they were not drilling. See also Felicity Barringer, "With High Gasoline Prices in Mind, How Much Oil Is There on Public Lands?" *New York Times*, August 3, 2008.

54. Carl Hulse, "Democrats Reluctantly Embrace Offshore Drilling, but Link Bill to Clean Energy," *New York Times*, September 12, 2008. Although the energy bill failed, the House of Representatives passed a spending bill on September 24, 2008, that ended the ban on offshore drilling.

55. Sarah Palin, "The Case for Drilling in ANWR," Minneapolis *Star Tribune*, February 1, 2009.

56. Felicity Barringer, "U.S. to Open Public Land for Drilling," *New York Times*, November 8, 2008.

57. Leslie Kaufman, "Interior Secretary Cancels Drilling Leases on Public Lands in Utah," *New York Times*, February 5, 2009.

58. The department reached a nadir in September 2008, when the inspector general revealed that some employees of the Minerals Management Service had taken lavish gifts from energy lobbyists and engaged in drug and sex parties with oil company employees. Charlie Savage, "Sex, Drug Use and Graft Cited in Interior Department," *New York Times*, September 10, 2008.

59. Robert F. Durant, Daniel J. Fiorino, and Rosemary O'Leary, eds., *Environmental Governance Reconsidered* (Cambridge: MIT Press, 2004); Fiorino, *The New Environmental Regulation* (Cambridge: MIT Press, 2006); Marc Allen Eisner, *Governing the Environment: The Transformation of Environmental Regulation* (Boulder, Colo.: Lynne Rienner, 2007); and Mazmanian and Kraft, *Toward Sustainable Communities*.

60. For a summary comparison of old and new forms of regulation, see Fiorino, *New Environmental Regulation*, 196–197.

61. See, for example, Neil Gunningham and Peter Grabowsky, *Smart Regulation: Designing Environmental Policy* (Oxford, U.K.: Clarendon Press, 1998); Winston Harrington, Richard D. Morgenstern, and Thomas Sterner, eds., *Choosing Environmental Policy: Comparing Instruments and Outcomes in the United States and Europe* (Washington, D.C.: Resources for the Future, 2004); Theo de Bruijn and Vicky Norberg-Bohm, *Industrial Transformation: Environmental Policy Innovation in the United States and Europe* (Cambridge: MIT Press, 2005); and Andrew Jordan, R. K. W. Wurzel, and Anthony R. Zito, eds., *'New' Instruments of Environmental Governance? National Experience and Prospects* (London: Frank Cass, 2003).

62. These are analyzed by Fiorino in chapter 5 of *New Environmental Regulation*. Cf. Eisner, *Governing the Environment*, for a critique.

63. Alfred A. Marcus, Donald A. Geffen, and Ken Sexton, *Reinventing Environmental Regulation: Lessons from Project XL* (Washington, D.C.: Resources for the Future, 2002).

64. Matthew J. Kiernan, *Investing in a Sustainable World* (New York: Amacom, 2009).

65. See, for example, Bob Inglis and Arthur B. Laffer, "An Emissions Plan Conservatives Could Warm To," *New York Times*, December 28, 2008. Such revenue-neutral tax changes have been used in Germany and elsewhere.

66. On the history and success of ecosystem management, see Hanna J. Cortner and Margaret A. Moote, *The Politics of Ecosystem Management* (Washington, D.C.: Island Press, 1999); and Judith J. Layzer, *Natural Experiments: Ecosystem-Based Management and the Environment* (Cambridge: MIT Press, 2008).

67. Deborah Zabarenko, "Halt All Carbon Emissions by 2050: Worldwatch," uk.reuters.com, January 14, 2009. See Worldwatch Institute, *State of the World 2009*.

68. Andrew C. Revkin, "A Shift in the Debate over Global Warming," *New York Times*, Week in Review, April 6, 2008.

69. John M. Broder, "Gore Calls for Energy Shift to Avoid a Global Crisis," *New York Times*, July 18, 2008.

70. See Andrew C. Revkin, "Environment Issues Slide in Poll of Public Concerns," *New York Times*, January 23, 2009. In this survey, global warming had fallen to thirtieth place as a public concern.

Appendix 1 Major Federal Laws on the Environment, 1969–2008

Legislation	Implementing Agency	Key Provisions
		Nixon Administration
National Environmental Policy Act of 1969, PL 91-190	All federal agencies	Declared a national policy to "encourage productive and enjoyable harmony between man and his environment"; required environmental impact statements; created Council on Environmental Quality.
Resources Recovery Act of 1970, PL 91-512	Health, Education, and Welfare Department (later Environmental Protection Agency)	Set up a program of demonstration and construction grants for innovative solid waste management systems; provided state and local agencies with technical and financial assistance in developing resource recovery and waste disposal systems.
Clean Air Act Amendments of 1970, PL 91-604	Environmental Protection Agency (EPA)	Required administrator to set national primary and secondary air quality standards and certain emissions limits; required states to develop implementation plans by specific dates; required reductions in automobile emissions.
Federal Water Pollution Control Act (Clean Water Act) Amendments of 1972, PL 92-500	EPA	Set national water quality goals; established pollutant discharge permit system; increased federal grants to states to construct waste treatment plants.
Federal Environmental Pesticides Control Act of 1972 (amended the Federal Insecticide, Fungicide, and Rodenticide Act [FIFRA] of 1947), PL 92-516	EPA	Required registration of all pesticides in U.S. commerce; allowed administrator to cancel or suspend registration under specified circumstances.
Marine Protection Act of 1972, PL 92-532	EPA	Regulated dumping of waste materials into the oceans and coastal waters.

(Continued on next page)

Appendix 1 Major Federal Laws on the Environment, 1969–2008 (*Continued*)

Legislation	Implementing Agency	Key Provisions
Nixon Administration (Continued)		
Coastal Zone Management Act of 1972, PL 92-583	Office of Coastal Zone Management, Commerce Department	Authorized federal grants to the states to develop coastal zone management plans under federal guidelines.
Endangered Species Act of 1973, PL 93-205	Fish and Wildlife Service, Interior Department	Broadened federal authority to protect all "threatened" as well as "endangered" species; authorized grant program to assist state programs; required coordination among all federal agencies.
Ford Administration		
Safe Drinking Water Act of 1974, PL 93-523	EPA	Authorized federal government to set standards to safeguard the quality of public drinking water supplies and to regulate state programs for protecting underground water sources.
Toxic Substances Control Act of 1976, PL 94-469	EPA	Authorized premarket testing of chemical substances; allowed the EPA to ban or regulate the manufacture, sale, or use of any chemical presenting an "unreasonable risk of injury to health or environment"; prohibited most uses of PCBs.
Federal Land Policy and Management Act of 1976, PL 94-579	Bureau of Land Management, Interior Department	Gave Bureau of Land Management authority to manage public lands for long-term benefits; officially ended policy of conveying public lands into private ownership.
Resource Conservation and Recovery Act of 1976, PL 94-580	EPA	Required the EPA to set regulations for hazardous waste treatment, storage, transportation, and disposal; provided assistance for state hazardous waste programs under federal guidelines.
National Forest Management Act of 1976, PL 94-588	U.S. Forest Service, Agriculture Department	Gave statutory permanence to national forest lands and set new standards for their management; restricted timber harvesting to protect soil and watersheds; limited clear-cutting.

Act	Agency	Description
Surface Mining Control and Reclamation Act of 1977, PL 95-87	Interior Department	Established environmental controls over strip mining; limited mining on farmland, alluvial valleys, and slopes; required restoration of land to original contours.
Clean Air Act Amendments of 1977, PL 95-95	EPA	Amended and extended Clean Air Act; postponed deadlines for compliance with auto emissions and air quality standards; set new standards for "prevention of significant deterioration" in clean air areas.
Clean Water Act Amendments of 1977, PL 95-217	EPA	Extended deadlines for industry and cities to meet treatment standards; set national standards for industrial pretreatment of wastes; increased funding for sewage treatment construction grants and gave states flexibility in determining spending priorities.
Public Utility Regulatory Policies Act of 1978, PL 95-617	Energy Department, states	Provided for Energy Department and Federal Energy Regulatory Commission regulation of electric and natural gas utilities and crude oil transportation systems in order to promote energy conservation and efficiency; allowed small cogeneration and renewable energy projects to sell power to utilities.
Alaska National Interest Lands Conservation Act of 1980, PL 96-487	Interior Department, Agriculture Department	Protected 102 million acres of Alaskan land as national wilderness, wildlife refuges, and parks.
Comprehensive Environmental Response, Compensation, and Liability Act of 1980 (CERCLA), PL 96-510	EPA	Authorized federal government to respond to hazardous waste emergencies and to clean up chemical dump sites; created $1.6 billion "Superfund"; established liability for cleanup costs.

Act	Agency	Description
Nuclear Waste Policy Act of 1982, PL 97-425; Nuclear Waste Policy Amendments Act of 1987, PL 100-203	Energy Department	Established a national plan for the permanent disposal of high-level nuclear waste; authorized the Energy Department to site, obtain a license for, construct, and operate geologic repositories for spent fuel from commercial nuclear power plants. Amendments in 1987 specified Yucca Mountain, Nevada, as the sole national site to be studied.

(Continued on next page)

Appendix 1 Major Federal Laws on the Environment, 1969–2008 *(Continued)*

Legislation	Implementing Agency	Key Provisions
	Reagan Administration (Continued)	
Resource Conservation and Recovery Act Amendments of 1984, PL 98-616	EPA	Revised and strengthened EPA procedures for regulating hazardous waste facilities; authorized grants to states for solid and hazardous waste management; prohibited land disposal of certain hazardous liquid wastes; required states to consider recycling in comprehensive solid waste plans.
Food Security Act of 1985 (also called the farm bill), PL 99-198. Renewed in 1990, 1996, 2002, and 2008.	Agriculture Department	Limited federal program benefits for producers of commodities on highly erodible land or converted wetlands; established a conservation reserve program; authorized Agriculture Department technical assistance for subsurface water quality preservation; revised and extended the Soil and Water Conservation Act (1977) programs through the year 2008. The 1996 renewal of the farm bill authorized $56 billion over seven years for a variety of farm and forestry programs. These include an Environmental Quality Incentives Program to provide assistance and incentive payments to farmers, especially those facing serious threats to soil, water, grazing lands, wetlands, and wildlife habitat. Spending was increased substantially in 2002.
Safe Drinking Water Act of 1986, PL 99-339	EPA	Reauthorized the Safe Drinking Water Act of 1974 and revised EPA safe drinking water programs, including grants to states for drinking water standards enforcement and groundwater protection programs; accelerated EPA schedule for setting standards for maximum contaminant levels of eighty-three toxic pollutants.
Superfund Amendments and Reauthorization Act of 1986 (SARA), PL 99-499	EPA	Provided $8.5 billion through 1991 to clean up the nation's most dangerous abandoned chemical waste dumps; set strict standards and timetables for cleaning up such sites; required that industry provide local communities with information on hazardous chemicals used or emitted.
Clean Water Act Amendments of 1987, PL 100-4	EPA	Amended the Federal Water Pollution Control Act of 1972; extended and revised EPA water pollution control programs, including grants to states for construction of wastewater treatment facilities and implementation of mandated nonpoint-source pollution management plans; expanded EPA enforcement authority; established a national estuary program.

Act	Agency	Description
Global Climate Protection Act of 1987, PL 100-204	State Department	Authorized the State Department to develop an approach to the problems of global climate change; created an intergovernmental task force to develop U.S. strategy for dealing with the threat posed by global warming.
Ocean Dumping Act of 1988, PL 100-688	EPA	Amended the Marine Protection, Research, and Sanctuaries Act of 1972 to end all ocean disposal of sewage sludge and industrial waste by December 31, 1991; revised EPA regulation of ocean dumping by establishing dumping fees, permit requirements, and civil penalties for violations.

George H. W. Bush Administration

Act	Agency	Description
Oil Pollution Act of 1990, PL 101-380	Transportation Department, Commerce Department	Sharply increased liability limits for oil spill cleanup costs and damages; required double hulls on oil tankers and barges by 2015; required federal government to direct cleanups of major spills; required increased contingency planning and preparedness for spills; preserved states' rights to adopt more stringent liability laws and to create state oil spill compensation funds.
Pollution Prevention Act of 1990, PL 101-508	EPA	Established Office of Pollution Prevention in the EPA to coordinate agency efforts at source reduction; created voluntary program to improve lighting efficiency; stated waste minimization was to be primary means of hazardous waste management; mandated source reduction and recycling report to accompany annual toxics release inventory under SARA in order to promote voluntary industry reduction of hazardous waste.
Clean Air Act Amendments of 1990, PL 101-549	EPA	Amended the Clean Air Act of 1970 by setting new requirements and deadlines of three to twenty years for major urban areas to meet federal clean air standards; imposed new, stricter emissions standards for motor vehicles and mandated cleaner fuels; required reduction in emission of sulfur dioxide and nitrogen oxides by power plants to limit acid deposition and created a market system of emissions allowances; required regulation to set emissions limits for all major sources of toxic or hazardous air pollutants and listed 189 chemicals to be regulated; prohibited the use of CFCs by the year 2000 and set phase-out of other ozone-depleting chemicals.

(Continued on next page)

Appendix 1 Major Federal Laws on the Environment, 1969–2008 *(Continued)*

Legislation	Implementing Agency	Key Provisions
George H. W. Bush Administration (Continued)		
Intermodal Surface Transportation Efficiency Act of 1991 (ISTEA, also called the highway bill), PL 102-240	Transportation Department	Authorized $151 billion over six years for transportation, including $31 billion for mass transit; required statewide and metropolitan long-term transportation planning; authorized states and communities to use transportation funds for public transit that reduces air pollution and energy use consistent with Clean Air Act of 1990; required community planners to analyze land use and energy implications of transportation projects they review.
Energy Policy Act of 1992, PL 102-486	Energy Department	Comprehensive energy act designed to reduce U.S. dependency on imported oil. Mandated restructuring of the electric utility industry to promote competition; encouraged energy conservation and efficiency; promoted renewable energy and alternative fuels for cars; eased licensing requirements for nuclear power plants; authorized extensive energy research and development.
The Omnibus Water Act of 1992, PL 102-575	Interior Department	Authorized completion of major water projects in the West; revised the Central Valley Project in California to allow transfer of water rights to urban areas and to encourage conservation through a tiered pricing system that allocates water more flexibly and efficiency; mandated extensive wildlife and environmental protection, mitigation, and restoration programs.
Clinton Administration		
Food Quality Protection Act of 1996, PL 104-170	EPA	A major revision of FIFRA that adopted a new approach to regulating pesticides used on food, fiber, and other crops by requiring EPA to consider the diversity of ways in which people are exposed to such chemicals. Created a uniform "reasonable risk" health standard for both raw and processed foods that replaced the requirements of the 1958 Delaney Clause of the Food, Drug, and Cosmetic Act that barred the sale of processed food containing even trace amounts of chemicals found to cause cancer; required the EPA to take extra steps to protect children by establishing an additional tenfold margin of safety in setting acceptable risk standards.

Act	Agency	Description
Safe Drinking Water Act Amendments of 1996, PL 104-182	EPA	Granted local water systems greater flexibility to focus on the most serious public health risks; authorized $7.6 billion through 2003 for state-administered loan and grant funds to help localities with the cost of compliance; created a "right-to-know" provision requiring large water systems to provide their customers with annual reports on the safety of local water supplies, including information on contaminants found in drinking water and their health effects. Small water systems are eligible for waivers from costly regulations.
Transportation Equity Act for the 21st Century (also called ISTEA II or TEA 21), PL 105-178	Transportation Department	Authorized a six-year, $218 billion program that increased by 40 percent spending to improve the nation's highways and mass transit systems; provided $41 billion for mass transit programs, with over $29 billion coming from the Highway Trust Fund; provided $592 million for research and development on new highway technologies, including transportation-related environmental issues; provided $148 million for a scenic byways program and $270 million for building and maintaining trails; continued support for improvement of bicycle paths.

George W. Bush Administration

Act	Agency	Description
The Small Business Liability Relief and Brownfields Revitalization Act of 2002, PL 107-118	EPA	Amended CERCLA (Superfund) to provide liability protection for prospective purchasers of brownfields and small business owners who contributed to waste sites; authorized increased funding for state and local programs that assess and clean up such abandoned or underused industrial or commercial sites.
The Healthy Forests Restoration Act of 2003, PL 108-148	Agriculture Department, Interior Department	Intended to reduce the risks of forest fires on federal lands by authorizing the cutting of timber in selected areas managed by the Forest Service and the Bureau of Land Management. Sought to protect communities, watersheds, and certain other lands from the effects of catastrophic wildfires. Directed the Secretary of Agriculture and the Secretary of the Interior to plan and conduct hazardous fuel reduction programs on federal lands within their jurisdictions.
The Energy Policy Act of 2005, PL 109-58	Energy Department	Intended to increase the supply of energy resources and improve the efficiency of energy use through provision of tax incentives and loan guarantees for various kinds of energy production, particularly oil, natural gas, and nuclear

(Continued on next page)

Appendix 1 Major Federal Laws on the Environment, 1969–2008 (*Continued*)

Legislation	Implementing Agency	Key Provisions
	George W. Bush Administration (Continued)	
The Energy Policy Act of 2005, PL 109-58 (*Continued*)	Energy Department	power. Also called for expanded energy research and development, expedited building for new energy facilities, improved energy efficiency standards for federal office buildings, and modernization of the nation's electricity grid.
Energy Independence and Security Act of 2007, PL 110-140	Energy Department, Transportation Department	Set a national automobile fuel-economy standard of 35 miles per gallon by 2020, the first significant change in the Corporate Average Fuel Economy standards since 1975. Also sought to increase the supply of alternative fuel sources by setting a renewable fuel standard that requires fuel producers to use at least 36 billion gallons of biofuels by 2022; 21 billion gallons of that amount are to come from sources other than corn-based ethanol. Included provisions to improve energy efficiency in lighting and appliances and for federal agency efficiency and renewable energy use.
	Obama Administration	
The American Recovery and Reinvestment Act of 2009 PL 111-5	Energy Department, Transportation Department, Treasury Department	Although not a stand-alone environmental or energy policy, the economic stimulus bill contained about $80 billion in spending, tax incentives, and loan guarantees to promote energy efficiency, renewable energy sources, fuel-efficient cars, mass transit, and clean coal, including $3.4 billion for research on capturing and storing carbon dioxide from coal-fired power plants, $2 billon for research on advanced car batteries, $17 billion in grants and loans to modernize the nation's electric grid and increase its capacity to transmit power from renewable sources, and nearly $18 billion for mass transit, Amtrak, and high-speed rail.

| Omnibus Public Lands Management Act of 2009, PL 111-11 | Interior Department, Agriculture Department | Consolidated 164 separate public lands measures that protect two million acres of wilderness in nine states; establish new national trails, national parks, and a new national monument; provide legal status for the 26 million acre National Landscape Conservation System that contains areas of archaeological and cultural significance; and protect 1,100 miles of 86 new wild and scenic rivers in eight states. Together the measures constitute the most significant expansion of federal land conservation programs in 15 years. |

Note: We include the economic stimulus measure of February 2009 and the Omnibus Public Lands Management Act of March 2009 in this appendix because of their breadth and importance. Congress approved and the president signed both acts as this edition was being completed. We cannot include other acts that may be approved later in 2009, and for that reason we have left the formal coverage of the appendix as 1969 through 2008. As always, for an update on legislative developments, consult *CQ Weekly* or other professional news sources, or Congressional Quarterly's annual *Almanac*, which summarizes key legislation enacted by Congress and describes the major issues and leading policy actors.

Appendix 2   Budgets of Selected Environmental and Natural Resource Agencies, 1980–2008 (in billions of nominal and constant dollars)

Agency	1980	1990	2000	2008 est.
Environmental Protection Agency (EPA) Operating Budget[a]	1.269 3.196	1.901 3.290	2.48 3.227	3.229 3.229
Interior Department Total Budget	4.674 11.775	6.681 11.562	8.394 10.923	11.033 11.033
Selected Agencies				
Bureau of Land Management	0.919 2.315	1.226 2.122	1.616 2.103	1.815 1.815
Fish and Wildlife Service	0.435 1.097	1.133 1.961	1.498 1.949	1.367 1.367
National Park Service	0.531 1.338	1.275 2.206	2.071 2.695	2.421 2.421
Forest Service	2.250 5.667	3.473 6.011	3.728 4.851	4.488 4.488

Source: Office of Management and Budget, *Budget of the United States Government,* fiscal years 1982, 1992, 2002, 2009 (Washington, D.C.: U.S. Government Printing Office, 1981, 1991, 2001, 2008).

Note: The upper figure for each agency represents budget authority in nominal dollars, that is, the real amount for the year in which the budget was authorized. The lower figure represents budget authority in constant 2008 dollars to permit comparisons over time. These adjustments use the implicit price deflator for federal nondefense expenditures as calculated by the Bureau of Economic Analysis, Department of Commerce.

a. The EPA operating budget, which supplies funds for most of the agency's research, regulation, and enforcement programs, is the most meaningful figure. The other two major elements of the total EPA budget historically have been Superfund allocations and sewage treatment construction or water infrastructure grants (both of which are now consolidated into the category of state and tribal assistance grants). We exclude both of these categories to calculate the EPA's operating budget. The EPA and the White House define the agency's operating budget differently. They do not exclude all of these amounts and thus arrive at a somewhat higher figure. The president's proposed fiscal 2009 budget reported an EPA operating budget of $4.2 billion for 2008. The total EPA budget for fiscal 2008 was $7.426 billion, of which $1.26 billion was allocated for Superfund and $2.93 billion for the assistance grants.

For consistency, all figures in the table are taken from the president's proposed budget for the respective years and all represent final budget authority except for 2008, where the amounts listed are estimates. Final 2008 budget figures should be close to these amounts. President Obama proposed a significant increase in the EPA's budget for fiscal 2010, reversing budget decreases during the Bush presidency.

Appendix 3   Employees in Selected Federal Agencies and Departments, 1980, 1990, 2000, and 2008

Agency/Department	Personnel[a]			
	1980	1990	2000	2008
Environmental Protection Agency	12,891	16,513	17,416	17,309
Bureau of Land Management	9,655	8,753	9,328	7,951
Fish and Wildlife Service	7,672	7,124	7,011	8,515
National Park Service	13,934	17,781	18,418	20,739
Office of Surface Mining	1,014	1,145	622	528
Forest Service	40,606	40,991	33,426	33,180
Army Corps of Engineers (civil functions)	32,757	28,272	22,624	21,007
U.S. Geological Survey	14,416	10,451	9,417	8,308
Natural Resources Conservation Service (formerly Soil Conservation Service)	15,856	15,482	9,628	12,275

Source: U.S. Senate Committee on Governmental Affairs, "Organization of Federal Executive Departments and Agencies," January 1, 1980, and January 1, 1990; and Office of Management and Budget, *Budget of the United States Government,* fiscal years 1982, 1992, 2002, and 2009 (Washington, D.C.: U.S. Government Printing Office, 1981, 1991, 2001, and 2008).

a. Personnel totals represent full-time equivalent employment, reflecting both permanent and temporary employees. Data for 2000 are based on the fiscal 2002 proposed budget submitted to Congress by the Bush administration in early 2001, and data for 2008 are taken from the administration's proposed fiscal 2009 budget submitted to Congress in early 2008. Because of organizational changes within departments and agencies, the data presented here are not necessarily an accurate record of agency personnel growth or decline over time. The information is presented chiefly to provide an indicator of approximate agency size during different time periods.

Appendix 4   Federal Spending on Natural Resources and the
Environment, Selected Fiscal Years, 1980–2008
(in billions of nominal and constant dollars)

Budget Item	1980	1990	2000	2008 est.
Water resources	4.085	4.332	4.803	6.682
	10.291	7.497	6.250	6.682
Conservation and land	1.572	4.362	6.604	9.811
management	3.960	7.549	8.593	9.811
Recreational resources	1.373	1.816	2.737	3.382
	3.459	3.143	3.561	3.382
Pollution control and abatement	4.672	5.559	7.490	7.663
	11.770	9.620	9.746	7.663
Other natural resources	1.395	2.077	3.397	5.507
	3.514	3.594	4.420	5.507
Total	13.097	18.146	25.031	33.045
	32.996	31.402	32.571	33.045

Source: Office of Management and Budget, *Historical Tables, Budget of the United States Government Fiscal Year 2009* (Washington, D.C.: U.S. Government Printing Office, 2008).

Note: The upper figure for each budget category represents budget authority in nominal dollars, that is, the real budget for the given year. Figures for 1980 are provided to indicate pre–Reagan administration spending bases. The lower figure for each category represents budget authority in constant 2008 dollars. These adjustments are made using the implicit price deflator for federal nondefense spending as calculated by the Bureau of Economic Analysis, Department of Commerce. The natural resources and environment function in the federal budget reported in this table does not include environmental cleanup programs within the Departments of Defense and Energy, which are substantial.

Author Citations Index

Note: These names appear in the chapter endnotes (indicated by *n* and *nn* and followed by the note number[s]).

Subject Index

Note: Boxes, figures, tables, and note(s) are indicated by *b*, *f*, *t*, and *n* (*nn*), respectively.